P9-CPY-947

Also by Geoffrey C. Ward

Treasures of the World: The Maharajahs

*Before the Trumpet: Young Franklin Roosevelt,
    1882–1905*

*A First-Class Temperament: The Emergence of
    Franklin Roosevelt*

The Civil War: An Illustrated History
    (with Ken Burns and Ric Burns)

*American Originals: The Private Worlds of
    Some Singular Men and Women*

*Tiger-Wallahs: Encounters with the Men
    Who Tried to Save the Greatest of the Cats*
    (with Diane Raines Ward)

Baseball: An Illustrated History
    (with Ken Burns)

*Constant Companion: The Unknown Story
    of the Intimate Friendship Between
    Franklin Roosevelt and Margaret Suckley*

The West: An Illustrated History

The Year of the Tiger

*Not for Ourselves Alone: The Story of
    Elizabeth Cady Stanton and Susan B. Anthony*
    (with Ken Burns)

Also by Ken Burns

The Civil War: An Illustrated History
    (with Geoffrey C. Ward and Ric Burns)

Baseball: An Illustrated History
    (with Geoffrey C. Ward)

The Shakers: Hands to Work, Hearts to God
    (with Amy S. Burns)

Lewis & Clark
    (with Dayton Duncan)

*Not for Ourselves Alone: The Story of
    Elizabeth Cady Stanton and Susan B. Anthony*
    (with Geoffrey C. Ward)

(Cooty)

Reminiscing

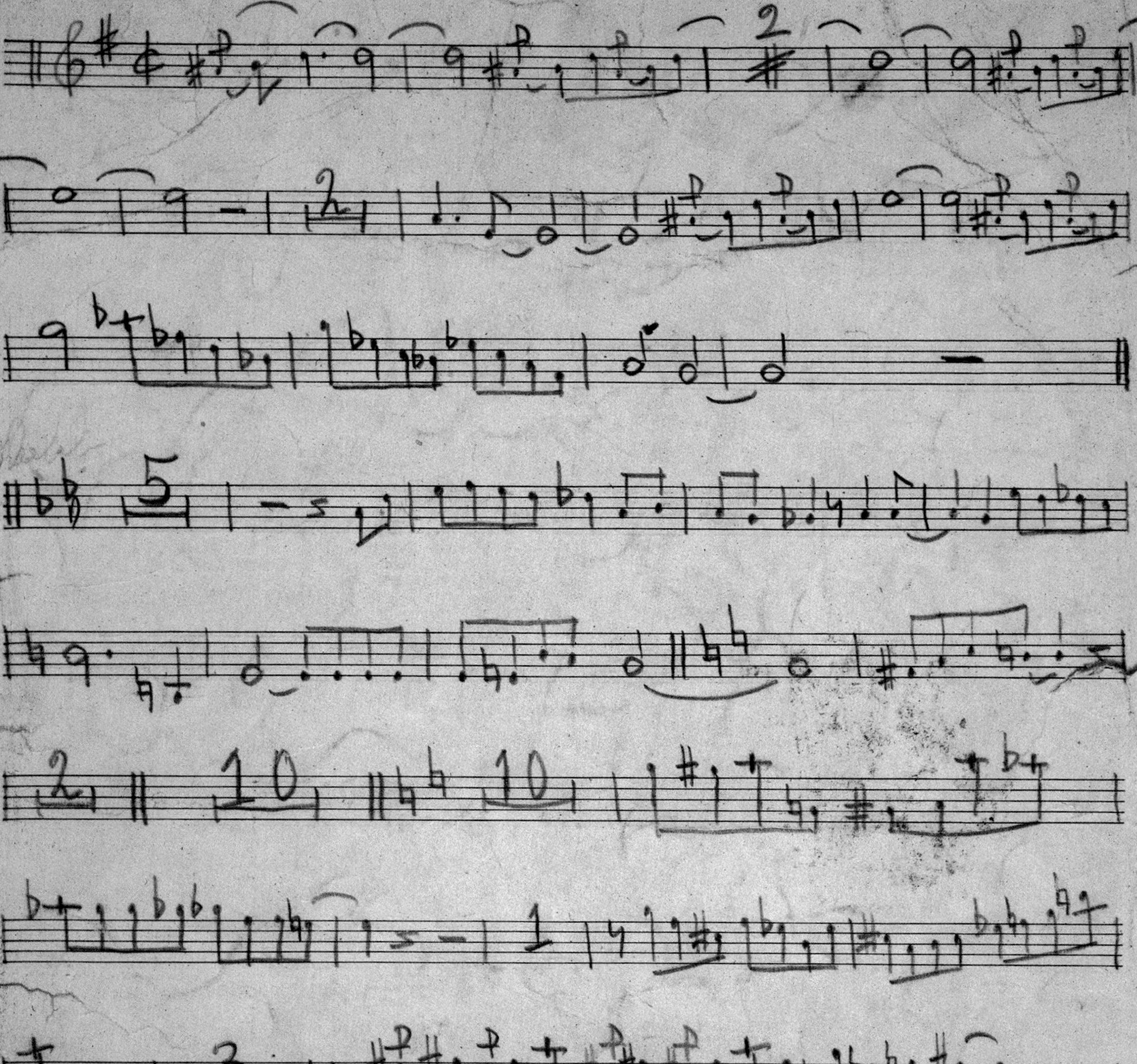

No. 3. 10 Staves (Medium)

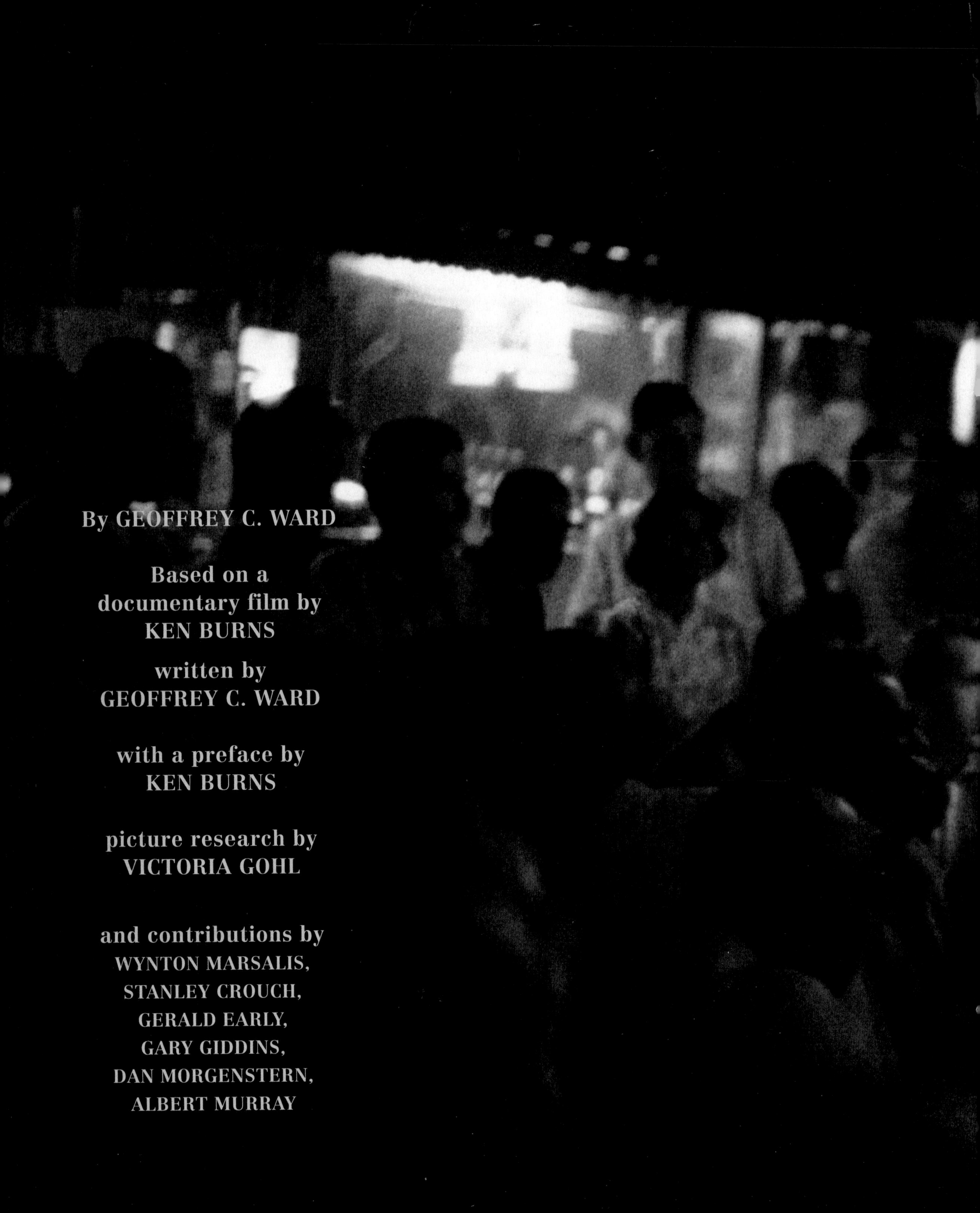

By GEOFFREY C. WARD

Based on a
documentary film by
KEN BURNS

written by
GEOFFREY C. WARD

with a preface by
KEN BURNS

picture research by
VICTORIA GOHL

and contributions by
WYNTON MARSALIS,
STANLEY CROUCH,
GERALD EARLY,
GARY GIDDINS,
DAN MORGENSTERN,
ALBERT MURRAY

JAZZ

A HISTORY OF
AMERICA'S MUSIC

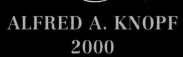

ALFRED A. KNOPF
2000

This Is a Borzoi Book
Published by Alfred A. Knopf

Copyright © 2000 by The Jazz Film Project, Inc.
"The Presence Is Always the Point," copyright © 2000
by Stanley Crouch. "White Noise and White Knights:
Some Thoughts on Race, Jazz, and the White Jazz
Musician," copyright © 2000 by Gerald Early.
"Extreme Jazz: The Avant-Garde," copyright © 2000
by Gary Giddins. "Reminiscing in Tempo," copyright
© 2000 by Dan Morgenstern

All rights reserved under International and Pan-
American Copyright Conventions. Published in the
United States by Alfred A. Knopf, a division of Random
House, Inc., New York, and simultaneously in Canada
by Random House of Canada Limited, Toronto.
Distributed by Random House, Inc., New York.

Portions of this work were originally published in
Vanity Fair.

www.aaknopf.com

Knopf, Borzoi Books, and the colophon are registered
trademarks of Random House, Inc.

Owing to a limitation of space, all acknowledgments
for permission to reprint previously published
material can be found on pages 487–8.

Library of Congress Cataloging-in-Publication Data
Ward, Geoffrey C.
        Jazz: a history of America's music / by Geoffrey
    C. Ward ; based on a documentary film by Ken
    Burns written by Geoffrey C. Ward ; with a preface
    by Ken Burns.
            p.   cm.
        Includes bibliographical references and
        indexes.
        ISBN 0-679-44551-X
        1. Jazz—History and criticism. 2. Jazz—
    Pictorial works. I. Burns, Ken

ML3506.W37 2000
781.65'09—dc21

                        00-022604

Manufactured in the United States of America

Published November 9, 2000
Reprinted Once
Third Printing, December 2000

CONTENTS

Front and back endpapers:
Fifty-second Street

Preceding pages:
Cootie Williams's trumpet part from Duke Ellington's
    "Reminiscing in Tempo," written in the composer's
    hand, 1935
Manhattan jazz club interior, about 1960
The Ornette Coleman Quartet, 1959: Coleman,
    Don Cherry, Billy Higgins (partially obscured),
    Charlie Haden

Following pages:
Louis Armstrong
Apollo Theater marquee, Harlem, about 1934
Frank Trumbauer
Billie Holiday
Duke Ellington
The hands of Art Tatum
Charlie Parker
Miles Davis
Dave Brubeck (foreground) and Paul Desmond
Benny Goodman
Dancers at Harlem's Savoy Ballroom, moving to a ballad
    played by the Lucky Millinder Orchestra, 1942

OUR ART

*Put it this way. Jazz is a good barometer of freedom. . . .
In its beginnings, the United States of America spawned
certain ideals of freedom and independence through
which, eventually, jazz was evolved, and the music is so
free that many people say it is the only unhampered,
unhindered expression of complete freedom yet produced
in this country.*

—Duke Ellington

In a filmed interview for a documentary history of our national pastime I made several years ago, the writer and essayist Gerald Early said that "when they study our civilization two thousand years from now, there will only be three things that Americans will be known for: the Constitution, baseball and jazz music. They're the three most beautiful things Americans have ever created." Early's words tend to put a smile on the face of the listener, as if he meant them as a joke, a passing comment of little import, but I think he was deadly serious—and absolutely correct. And I realized that my colleagues and I have worked almost unceasingly for nearly seventeen years to honor that truth. Having grappled with constitutional issues in our series on the Civil War (the Constitution's greatest test) and many other films, and having explored our national pastime and its exquisite lessons in our baseball series, we have over the past several years struggled to understand the utterly American art form of jazz, first in a ten-part documentary history for national public television that will be broadcast in January 2001, and now in this companion volume.

What each of the three projects daily reminded us was that the genius of America is improvisation; that our unique experiment is a profound intersection of freedom and creativity, for better and for worse, in nearly every gesture and breath. The Constitution is the greatest improvisational document ever created. Written on four pieces of parchment at the end of the eighteenth century, it is still able to adjudicate the thorniest problems of the fledgling twenty-first. It set us on our improvisatory course, emphasizing that we are a nation in the process of becoming, always striving to create a more perfect union, always, as the Declaration of Independence mysteriously put it, in *pursuit* of happiness. More than anything, it

has helped to ensure our future by making us Americans unusually curious, unsatisfied, experimenting.

In baseball, we have a simple children's stick-and-ball game that offers, in the totality of its experience, not just games won and lost, careers rising and falling, but a unique sense of time, memory, family, and home that has meant something for nearly every generation of this republic. A three-hundred hitter means the same thing to my daughters as it does to me, as it did to my father and my grandfather and my great-grandfather. There's almost nothing else in American life that you can say that about.

And then there is jazz—"our art," the trumpeter Wynton Marsalis calls it—the only art form created by Americans, an enduring and indelible expression of our genius and promise, "a painless way," Marsalis told us, "of understanding ourselves." In an earlier film, the writer Shelby Foote said that the Civil War defined us; it was, in his words, "the crossroads of our being." We searched for a sense of what we had become after that war, and found in baseball a complex and revealing mirror of who we were that went far beyond the box score. In *Jazz,* we complete our trilogy on American life, finding in the music's lines and phrases and riffs not only a meditation on American creativity, but a joyous and sublime celebration of its redemptive future possibilities—at both a collective and an intensely personal and psychological level.

For those of us engaged in trying to understand it for film and book, the history of jazz turns out to be much more than a study of this extraordinary American music. Jazz has been a prism through which so much of American history can be seen—a curious and unusually objective witness to the twentieth century. And so *Jazz* necessarily becomes a story about race and race relations and prejudice, about minstrelsy and Jim Crow, lynchings and civil rights. Instead of suggesting that black history is an inconsequential, politically correct addendum to the American narrative, relegated in the national dialogue to February, the coldest and shortest month, our study of jazz offers the explosive hypothesis that those who have had the peculiar experience of being unfree in a free land might actually be at the center of our history. African-Americans in general, and black jazz musicians in particular, carry a complicated message to the rest of us, a reminder of our great promise and our great failing; and the music they

created and then generously shared with the rest of the world processes the contradictions many of us would rather ignore. Embodied in the music, in its riveting personalities and soaring artistic achievement, is our oft-neglected conscience, a message of hope and transcendence, of affirmation in the face of adversity, unequaled in the unfolding drama we call American history. Jazz seemed to us a template of change in an ever-changing world and yet a repository of carefully conserved verities as old as the American promise of freedom. In clubs and on the concert stage, jazz has kept the American message alive.

But jazz is much more. It is the story of two world wars and a devastating depression, the sound track that helped Americans get through the worst of times. Jazz is about sex, the way men and women talk to each other and conduct the complicated rituals of courtship—a sophisticated and elegant mating call that has all but disappeared from popular music in recent times. It is about drugs and the terrible cost of addiction and the high price of creativity. It is about the growth and explosion of radio and the soul of great American cities—New Orleans, where the music was born, and Chicago, Kansas City, and New York, where it grew up. It is about immigration and assimilation and feeling dispossessed—and the music that came to the rescue. It is about movement and dance and showing your behind. It's about entertainment, the frequently dismissed but sacred communion between artist and audience. It's about solitude and loneliness and the nearly unbearable burden of consciousness. It's about suffering and celebration— it's greatly about celebration—and tapping your feet.

And jazz is the story of the dozens of extraordinary human beings we who have worked on book and film have come to know like family members; protean geniuses—black and white, male and female, addicts and orphans, prostitutes and pimps, sons of privilege and of despair—who, much like the political figures charged with inventing this country, took enormous risks, shouldered unimaginable responsibility, and are able to do what the rest of us can only dream of: create art on the spot.

It has taken us nearly six years to plan, research, write, shoot, edit, and finish this film and this book. We involved the talents of a half-dozen producers and co-producers, nearly two dozen scholars, more than a score of editors and their assistants, and innumerable technicians. We filmed nearly a hundred interviews—from musicians and family members and unabashed fans to writers, critics, and historians—and lost to the merciless passage of time dozens of friends dedicated to jazz. We searched through hundreds of archives and listened to thousands of pieces of music—music that changed our lives—to make this documentary. It represents, we believe, the most comprehensive treatment of jazz ever committed to film. And yet much has had to be left out, dozens of worthy musicians, stories, and moments, so as to honor our aim of making a compelling narrative for a general audience. The true story of jazz, which can never be fully told, is the story of a million nights when, against all odds, men and women of all colors and often astonishing gifts came together and made great art, in each instance recalling centuries of human suffering, cruelty, negotiation, search, and finally joy. It was our decision to follow several remarkable and emblematic stories and try to tell them well, rather than to attempt to be encyclopedic and tell none well. We beg the indulgence of those inside jazz who bridle at these omissions and hope that those new to the music will continue to explore the infinitely rich landscape of "our art."

There are other dangers in the path we have chosen. The very strength of the documentary, it must be said, is also its great weakness. The form is dialectically preoccupied, imprisoned by the need to accentuate opposites, point out good and bad, reveal saints and sinners, expose fraud and exalt heroism, without much recourse to mitigating wisdom and reconciliation. Jazz asked more of us. It is about reconciliation.

Jazz is about peeling away the layers of artifice to get at what is. Jazz looks at a situation and says, "This is." It might be ugly, it might be shameful, it might be beautiful, it might be revelatory, but all those things are true and part of the American experience. Jazz has afforded us the opportunity to explore the sense of our national character and soul at its most profound center. Involved in that is a certain amount of risk and challenge, of tension and attention, a certain presence that suggests how we might become as a people.

Each new project holds out the promise of nearly daily surprise and delight as we seek to discover and then share with a broad national audience the mysteries of whatever subject we're exploring. In the Civil War series, one could not be unaffected by the life and example of Abraham Lincoln, just as the story of Jackie Robinson in *Baseball* stood out in proud and heroic relief. But I was hardly prepared for my response to jazz—and to that "family member" who changed me in ways words will never be able to describe.

When I began the project, I had perhaps two jazz records in my fairly large music collection. Today, I can't find all the others. I listen to jazz all the time—old and new, straight-ahead and avant-garde and fusion, swing and bop and cool. I play it day and night, in the car, as I go to bed, as I write now, its sophisticated rhythms and elegant lines simply medicine for me. But there is one musician whose work I listen to more than any other. The biggest surprise and delight has been getting to know the power, force, and genius of Louis Armstrong.

Even the most cursory study will reveal his centrality to the music we now call jazz. I knew from the outset that Armstrong was important to the history, but he had mostly seemed to me a guy with a smile and a handkerchief, a singer of popular songs like "Hello, Dolly!" and "It's a Wonderful World." I had no inkling of the truth, borne out in interview after interview, record after record: Louis Armstrong is quite simply the most important person in American music. He is to twentieth-century music (I did not say jazz) what Einstein is to physics, Freud is to psychiatry, and the Wright Brothers are to travel. First, Armstrong transformed instrumental playing, liberating jazz, cutting it loose from nearly all constraints, essentially inventing what we call swinging; then he brought an equally great revolution to singing. And he did it all with a heart and a humanity so spiritually encompassing that my own contemplation of mortality is now tempered by the hope that I will get to hear him playing with Gabriel someday (and, as he would say, blowing Gabriel out of the clouds). To make this discovery was startling—and exhilarating.

Each time we did an interview for the film—whether it was with musicians who played with Armstrong years ago or with those struggling today to come to terms with his legacy; whether with critics, writers, historians, friends, hangers-on, or managers—each would in the end shake his head and say that Louis Armstrong was a "gift from God" or "an angel." Near the end of the editing process, I was on the road and happened upon a woman who, for lack of a better word, is a psychic, a medium familiar with things not of this world. When

I told her of the interviews and how each person had called Armstrong an angel, she closed her eyes and smiled and said softly, "Biggest wings I've ever seen."

But maybe Wynton Marsalis, a great trumpet player in his own right, said it best when I asked him about Louis. Having already insisted that Armstrong was chosen by God "to bring the feeling and message and the identity of jazz to everybody," he added a final reflection:

> Louis Armstrong's overwhelming message is one of love. When you hear his music, it's of joy. . . . He was just not going to be defeated by the forces of life. And these forces visit all of us. . . . My great-great-grandmother used to say that "life has a board for every behind" and it's a board just fit to yours, so maybe your board is not going to work on someone else's behind. And when it's your turn . . . that paddle is going to be put on your booty and it's going to hurt as bad as it can hurt. And Louis Armstrong is there to tell you after you get that paddling, "It's all right, son."

Ken Burns
Walpole, New Hampshire

ic celebrates life—human life. The range of it. The absurdity ...rance of it. The greatness of it. The intelligence of it. The sex... ...ndity of it. And it deals with it in all of its . . . it deals with i...

—WYNTON

It's the ultimate in rugged individualism. It's going out there on that stage and saying: It doesn't matter how anybody else did it. This is the way I'm going to do it.
—GARY GIDDINS

When you see a jazz musician playing, you're looking at a pioneer, you're looking at an explorer, you're looking at an experimenter, you're looking at a scientist, you're looking at all those things because it's the creative process incarnate!
—ALBERT MURRAY

It is America's music—born out of a million American negotiations: between having and not having; between happy and sad, country and city; between black and white and men and women; between the Old Africa and the Old Europe—which could only have happened in an entirely New World.

It is an improvisational art, making itself up as it goes along—just like the country that gave it birth.

It rewards individual expression but demands selfless collaboration.

It is forever changing but nearly always rooted in the blues.

It has a rich tradition and its own rules, but it is brand-new every night.

It is about just making a living and taking terrible risks, losing everything and finding love, making things simple and dressing to the nines.

It has enjoyed huge popularity and survived hard times, but it has always reflected Americans—all Americans—at their best.

"Jazz," the drummer Art Blakey liked to say, "washes away the dust of everyday life."

Above all, it swings.

GUMBO

In September of 1931, brightly colored posters began appearing on walls all over Austin, Texas. They portrayed a beaming young black man hold- ing a golden trumpet and were startling for that place and time in their neutral candor; there was nothing clownish or exaggerated about them; they contained not a trace of the crude minstrelsy with which black Americans were then universally por- trayed. "Louis Armstrong, King of the Trumpet, and His Orchestra," the posters said, were to play four dances at the downtown Hotel Driskill begin- ning on the evening of October 12.

Among those who paid seventy-five cents to get in that night was a freshman at the University of Texas named Charlie Black. The posters had drawn him in. He knew little about jazz music, had never even heard of Armstrong. He just knew there

The Original Superior Orchestra, about 1908. Bunk Johnson is the cornetist; Peter Bocage plays the violin; the clarinetist is Louis "Big Eye" Nelson. This group specialized in variations on ragtime intended for more polite listeners, but John- son and Bocage also played in the Eagle Band, which played the blues and catered to a far rougher crowd.

were likely to be lots of girls to dance with. Everyone on the dance floor was white; only Armstrong, his musicians, and the waiters were African-American.

Then, Black remembered, Armstrong began to play,

> mostly with his eyes closed, letting flow from that inner space of music things that had never before existed. . . . Steamwhistle power, lyric grace, alternated at will, even blended.
>
> He was the first genius I had ever seen. . . . It is impossible to overstate the significance of a sixteen-year-old southern boy's seeing genius, for the first time, in a black. We literally never saw a black, then, in any but a servant's capacity. There were of course black professionals and intellectuals in Austin, as one later learned, but they kept to themselves, out back of town, no doubt shunning humiliation. I liked most of the blacks I knew—I loved a few of them—like Old Buck Green, born and raised a slave, who still plays the harmonica through my mouth, having taught me when he was seventy-five and I was ten. Some were honored and venerated, in that paradoxical white southern way—Buck Green again comes to mind. But genius—fine control over total power, all height and depth, forever and ever? It had simply never entered my mind . . . that I would see this for the first time in a black man. You don't get over that. . . . The lies reel, and contradict one another, and simper in silliness and fade into shadow. But the seen truth remains.

Standing next to Black was a boy from Austin High School. "We listened together for a long time," Black remembered. "Then he turned to me, shook his head as if clearing it—as I'm sure he was—of an unacceptable though vague thought, and pronounced the judgment of the time and place: 'After all, he's nothing but a goddamn nigger!'" The boy moved away. But nothing was ever the same for Black again. "Louis opened my eyes wide and put to me a choice. Blacks, the saying went, were 'all right in their place.' [But] what was the 'place' of such a man, and of the people from which he sprung?"

Charlie Black went on to become Professor Charles L. Black Jr., a distinguished teacher of constitutional law. In 1954 he would help provide the answer to the question Louis Armstrong's music had first posed for him: he volunteered for the team of lawyers, black and white, who finally persuaded the U.S. Supreme Court in the case of *Brown v. Board of Education of Topeka* that segregating schoolchildren on the basis of race was unconstitutional, that "separate but equal" no longer could be tolerated under American law.

Genius is ultimately untraceable. No amount of historical or psychological sleuthing can ever fully explain the emergence of artists like Bach or Picasso or Louis Armstrong, who appear as if from nowhere and through the power of their own individual imaginations transform an art. The origins of the kind of music Armstrong played remain elusive, too. Jazz music belongs to all Americans, has come to be seen by the rest of the world as the symbol of all that is best about us, but it was created by people routinely denied the most basic benefits of being American. It grew up in a thousand places but it could only have been born in New Orleans, Louis Armstrong's hometown.

In the early morning hours of January 12, 1819, the brig *Clio* anchored off the levee at New Orleans at the end of a three-week voyage from New York. Among her passengers was the architect Benjamin Henry Latrobe, the father of the Greek Revival style in America, fresh from rebuilding the U.S. Capitol in Washington. He was a worldly, well-traveled man—born in England, he had lived and worked in France, Germany, and Italy—and he was eager for his first glimpse of the South's biggest city and most important port. But when dawn finally came, Latrobe wrote, "so thick a fog enveloped the city that the ear alone could ascertain its existence" and he heard "a sound more strange than any that is heard anywhere else in the world. . . . It is a more incessant, loud, rapid, and various gabble of tongues of all tones than was ever heard at Babel."

The sun eventually warmed away the fog and Latrobe and his fellow passengers could go ashore to discover for themselves the source of this strange cacophony. An open-air market stretched along the levee, Latrobe wrote, "as far as the eye could reach to the West, and to the Market house to the East," two rows of clamoring shopkeepers advertising everything from bananas to tin buckets, fresh fish to rare books:

> some having stalls or tables with a Tilt or awning of canvas . . . but the majority having their wares on the ground . . . on a piece of canvas or a parcel of Palmetto leaves. The articles to be sold were not more various than the Sellers. White men and women, and of all hues of brown, and of all Classes of faces, from round

The old French Market as it looked about 1895. Although this photograph was made seventy-six years after Benjamin Henry Latrobe first saw it, its interior still echoed with many of the disparate voices that so astonished him.

The corner of St. Peter and Royal Streets in the heart of the French Quarter, photographed in 1884. These colonial-style buildings were built in the 1840s, four decades after New Orleans came under American control, and their wonderfully ornate ironwork was added later still. Architecture like this was clear evidence that the citizens of New Orleans still seemed determined to keep their city a place apart.

Yankees, to grisly and lean Spaniards, black Negroes and negresses, filthy Indians half naked, Mulattoes, curly and straight-haired, Quateroons of all shades, long-haired and frizzled, the women dressed in the most flaring yellow and scarlet gowns, the men capped and hatted. . . . I cannot suppose that my eye took in less than 500 sellers and buyers, all of whom appeared to strain their voices, to exceed each other in loudness.

From this unprecedented blend of voices from everywhere on earth would eventually come America's most distinctive music.

"Everything has an *odd* look," Latrobe wrote of New Orleans at the end of his first day in the city; it was "impossible not to stare at a sight wholly new, even to one who has traveled much in Europe and America."

In fact, New Orleans *was* a sight wholly new, the most cosmopolitan city in the country, perhaps the world. Established by France in 1718, in the midst of a mosquito-infested swamp ninety miles north of the Mississippi's mouth, it was briefly ruled by Spain, reclaimed by France, visited by ships from everywhere, then more or less peacefully invaded by American flatboatmen whom the city's French-speaking citizens derided as "Kaintucks," and finally sold to the United States as part of the Louisiana Purchase in 1803.

"There are in fact three societies here," Latrobe noted a few days after he had settled into his hotel overlooking the old French drilling ground that would soon be known as Jackson Square: "1. The French, 2. The American, and 3. The mixed." Latrobe had only begun dimly to understand the city's infinite stratifications. The French themselves were divided. Some were descendants of the city's early settlers; others were refugees from Canada and the French Revolution, from the Napoleonic wars or from the slave rebellions that had only recently overthrown French rule in

When Currier & Ives published this lithographed bird's-eye view in 1885, New Orleans was still the busiest port in the South. The broad thoroughfare (on the opposite page) that runs diagonally from the riverfront to the distant shore of Lake Pontchartrain is Canal Street. It marked the dividing line between "Downtown" (farthest from the observer), the oldest, most fashionable part of the city, where many Creoles of Color made their homes, and "Uptown," or the "American Quarter," occupied by newer arrivals including black immigrants from the countryside.

Daguerreotypes of Creoles of Color, believed to have been made about 1865. The identities of the sitters are unknown but their elegant attire hints at the level of prosperity some nonwhites were able to reach in cosmopolitan New Orleans.

Haiti and Santo Domingo. But all sought to retain their language and Roman Catholic customs, and all proudly differentiated themselves from the Protestant American newcomers now flooding into the town, whose culture, Latrobe noted, seemed antithetical to theirs. The Americans' "business is to make money," he wrote. "They are in an eternal bustle. Their limbs, their heads and their hearts, move to that sole object."

Nor did the city's complexities end there. The "Crescent City"—so called because it was built along a bend in the river—was also home to Choctaw and Natchez Indians. It would soon witness an influx of people from the Balkans: Dalmatians, Serbs, Montenegrins, Greeks, Albanians. Spanish-speaking Filipinos came and stayed, too, alongside Chinese and Malays. After 1850, large numbers of German and Irish and Sicilian immigrants would be added to the mix. By 1860, 40 percent of the people of New Orleans were foreign-born.

New Orleans was a center of the southern slave trade, as well. It would eventually boast two dozen slave auction houses and, several times a year, the spacious ballrooms of its two grandest hotels doubled as showrooms for human merchandise. But it was also home to the most prosperous community of free people of color in the South. Many were the descendants of French colonists and their African- and Native-American wives and mistresses. They called themselves "Creoles of Color" and spoke French or a distinctive patois that white Americans called "nigger French." A wealthy few sent their children to Paris to school.

Creoles controlled cigarmaking and bricklaying, carpentry and shoemaking in the city. Many lived south of Canal Street in the original, most fashionable section, called "Downtown," and were at best ambivalent about the black servants and slaves and menial workers who crowded together in the "American quarter," called "Uptown."

"See, people down here are very prejudiced," the Creole violinist Paul Dominguez explained. "And your color makes all the difference. . . . [W]e Downtown people, we try to be intelligent. Everybody learn a trade. We try to bar jail. Uptown, across Canal, yonder, they used to jail. There's a vast difference in this town. Uptown folk are all ruffians, cut up in the face, and live on the river. All cotton—be longshoremen, screwmen. And me, I ain't never been on the river a *day in my life*"

Some years after Latrobe's arrival a visitor named James R. Creecy captured something of the city's heterogeneous character in doggerel:

> Have you ever been in New Orleans?
>   If not, you'd better go.
> It's a nation of a queer place; day and
>   night a show!
> Frenchmen, Spaniards, West Indians,
>   Creoles, Mustees,
> Yankees, Kentuckians, Tennesseeans,
>   lawyers and trustees,
> Clergymen, priests, friars, nuns,
>   women of all stains;
> Negroes in purple and fine linen, and
>   slaves in rags and chains.
> Ships, arks, steamboats, robbers,
>   pirates, alligators,
> Assassins, gamblers, drunkards and
>   cotton speculators;
> Sailors, soldiers, pretty girls, and ugly
>   fortune-tellers;
> Pimps, imps, shrimps, and all sorts of
>   dirty fellows;
> White men with black wives, *et vice-
>   versa,* too.
> A progeny of all colors—an infernal
>   motley crew.

Each element in this progeny of all colors, this infernal motley crew, would bring a unique brand of music to the New Orleans mix and in so doing prepare the ground for jazz.

AURORA BOREALIS

"A bunch of us kids, playing, would suddenly hear sounds," the New Orleans guitarist Danny Barker remembered. "It was like a phenomenon, like the *Aurora Borealis*. The sounds of men playing would be so clear, but we wouldn't be sure where they were coming from. So we'd start running—'It's this way!' 'It's that way!'—and,

New Orleans sugar mill workers of every kind and color line up together to get their weekly pay in this turn-of-the-century photograph by Georges François Mugnier.

sometimes, after running for a while, you'd find you'd be nowhere near that music. But that music could come on any time like that. The city was full of the sounds of music."

Barker was remembering his own early-twentieth-century New Orleans boyhood, but the muddy streets of his hometown had always been alive with music. Long before Latrobe's visit, dancing had been central to the lives of New Orleans citizens: "In the winter," said an early French visitor, "they dance to keep warm, and in the summer they dance to keep cool." And the city's Latin-Catholic tradition, which held that there was nothing sinful about dancing, that Sundays were for celebration as well as worship, proved stubbornly resistant to efforts by Protestant American newcomers to change New Orleans ways. When a band of clergymen called upon the city at least to

limit the dancing season in 1831, the New Orleans *Bee* denounced them as "men who were ordered by God to preach to the world that the dance is a Satanic invention . . . that the Creator gave us the instinct of pleasure only so that we might procure the glory of resisting it." In any case, they had no impact on New Orleans. Ten years later, more than eighty public ballrooms were flourishing in the city, which had become, one visitor wrote, "one vast waltzing and gallopading hall."

Creole musicians—sometimes whole orchestras, more often a string trio or quartet—supplied most of the music for the city's dancers, both white and Creole: waltzes, polkas, schottisches, quadrilles, and sensual, syncopated contredanses, including habaneras, filled with Spanish rhythms carried to New Orleans from Haiti and Cuba.

They played for the celebrated—or notorious—"quadroon balls," too, at which white men sought out Creole women to be their mistresses. Nonwhite males were officially barred, though, since men and women alike often wore masks, it was sometimes hard to tell just who was asking whom to dance. As Danny Barker remarked, in New Orleans there has always been "a whole lot of integrating going on."

Well before the Civil War, the city also exhibited what the New Orleans *Picayune* called "a real mania for horn and trumpet playing," and dance musicians often doubled in the marching bands that seemed always to be playing somewhere in town—entertaining picnickers in the parks or along the southern shore of Lake Pontchartrain, waging what one observer called "a windy war" by blaring different airs from

The sensation Thomas Dartmouth "Daddy" Rice set off when he first performed "Jump Jim Crow" at the American Theater on New York's Bowery on November 25, 1833—an event important enough to be commemorated in this painting by an unidentified artist—would resonate for decades. Minstrel shows brought a lively if distorted form of African-American song and dance to white Americans who couldn't seem to get enough of it. The 1867 collection of so-called Negro melodies (below) was just one of thousands of attempts to cash in on the craze Daddy Rice began.

the decks of steamboats anchored side by side, escorting mourners to and from the cemetery "preceded, followed and hemmed in on every side by a . . . collection of all colors, sexes and conditions."

The New Orleans funeral parade—accompanied by a slow and stately hymn on the way to the graveyard, a stirring lighthearted anthem on the way back—was remarked upon by nearly every early visitor to the city in part because there were so many of them. New Orleans's incessant gaiety could not disguise the fact that the city—surrounded by swamps, subject to annual flooding, lacking in the most basic sanitation—was a breeding ground for disease. Yellow fever scythed its way through the population twenty-three times between 1817 and 1860. Thousands died. Cholera and malaria killed thousands more; as late as 1880, nearly half the nonwhite babies born in New Orleans did not live to see their

first birthday and the average life expectancy of a black citizen was just thirty-six (the average white citizen lived only a decade longer).

Music provided New Orleans with solace, then, as well as high spirits. Theaters featured the bizarre mongrel music of the minstrel show—so-called plantation melodies, often derived from authentic black songs and spirituals but turned into formal compositions by white and black songwriters, performed by whites blacked-up as blacks (and often in later years by blacks blacked-up as whites *playing* blacks). For almost a century, the minstrel show would be the most popular form of entertainment in America, a ritualized blend of lively music, knockabout comedy, sophisticated elegance, the reinforcement of ugly and persistent stereotypes—and simultaneous unabashed enthusiasm for the music and dance of the country's most

despised minority. The first big minstrel hit was written down and performed by a white man in blackface named Thomas Dartmouth "Daddy" Rice—who said *he'd* first heard it being sung by a black stable hand cleaning out a horse's stall. Rice named the tune after the stable hand—Jim Crow—and performed it several times in New Orleans to great applause.

At least once, the Crescent City put its own characteristic spin on minstrelsy. When the well-known blackface entertainer Mick Saunders came to town in 1840 to offer his version of two stock minstrel characters, the sharpster and the shuffling simpleton, he found himself sharing the stage with a real black street vendor, remembered only as "Old Corn Meal," who performed songs he'd been singing on the city streets for years—"My Long Tail Blue," "Old Rosin the Bow," and a series of variations on "The Star-Spangled Banner" that brought down the house.

By 1850, the city supported two symphony orchestras, one white and one Creole, as well as three opera houses, each offering separate tiers of seats for whites, Creoles, and slaves—who were officially supposed to bring with them notes signed by their masters granting permission to

Minstrel star Lew Dockstader—the big man wearing a top hat at center stage—leads his fifty-man company in *The Possum Hunt Club*, a timely 1910 show in which Dockstader played a waiter chosen to accompany former President Theodore Roosevelt to Africa. Al Jolson was among the graduates of Dockstader's well-known company.

attend before they were issued tickets. Visitors from the North were sometimes startled to hear among the cries of street vendors the sound of slaves singing arias; New Orleanians thought nothing of it.

Slaves made their own kind of music, as well. Out for a Sunday afternoon stroll along St. Peter Street not long after he arrived in the city, Benjamin Latrobe heard what he remembered as a "most extraordinary noise, which I supposed to proceed from . . . horses tramping on a wooden floor." Hurrying up the street, he discovered that "it proceeded from a crowd of five or six

hundred persons, assembled in . . . a public square. . . . All those who were engaged in the business seemed to be blacks."

He had happened upon Congo Square, a grassy plain on the northwestern edge of the city where the city fathers permitted slaves to dance and sing for a few hours on Sundays. The dancers, Latrobe noted, were formed into two circular groups "in the midst of which were . . . two women dancing. They held each a coarse handkerchief . . . & set to each other in a miserably dull & slow figure, hardly moving their feet or bodies."

The music consisted of two drums and a stringed instrument . . . [one of which was] a cylindrical drum, about one foot in diameter. . . . They made an incredible noise. The most curious instrument, however, was a stringed instrument, which no doubt was imported from Africa. On the top of the finger board was the rude figure of a man in a sitting posture, and two pegs behind him to which the strings were fastened. The body was a calabash. It was played upon by a very little old man, apparently eighty or ninety years old. . . . A Man sang an uncouth song to the dancing which I suppose was in some African language for it was not French, and the Women screamed a detestable burthen on one single note. The allowed amusements of Sundays, have, it seems, perpetuated here those of Africa among its inhabitants.

To Latrobe and the other curious whites who turned out to see and hear them over the years, the slave dances at Congo Square and the music that accompanied them, filled with complex polyrhythms, seemed to provide an authentic glimpse of Africa. And some of those who danced there in the early years really had been brought from West Africa in chains. To these people, for whom music and dancing had always been an integral part of everyday life, Congo Square must have offered a precious opportunity to recover at least a little of what they had lost when they were taken from their homes.

But adversity demanded improvisation. To survive in America, slaves needed to be able to incorporate everything they saw and heard around them, had to find ways to make it all their own. At the time of Latrobe's visit in 1819, the importation of slaves from overseas had been illegal for more than a decade; within a few years of it, most of those who continued to gather in Congo Square had no firsthand memories of Africa at all. They were immigrants or the children of immigrants from the West Indies, their music already heavily alloyed with the infectious Latin-tinged pulse of the Caribbean, their religion a blend of Catholicism and West African spirit worship they called *vodoun*—"voodoo" to the whites who both feared and were fascinated by it.

Others had filtered into the city from the interior of the South, where the music of their ancestors had long since merged with that of their masters. European instruments—fiddles and fifes, Jew's harps, triangles, and tambourines—now appeared alongside drums and rattles and banjos, while the musicians played French and Spanish melodies and dances—along with wholly American songs like "Old Virginia Never Tire" and "Hey Jim Along Josey"— to which the dancers performed jigs and fandangos and Virginia reels that would have mystified their African forebears.

Nor was Congo Square the slaves' only dancing place. Despite a battery of ordinances meant to keep them quiescent and confined at home, New Orleans slaves drank and danced nightly in so many illicit taverns, the editor of the *Bee* complained in 1833, that "Not a street, nor a corner can be passed without encountering [them]. The noise and disturbance is very disagreeable to the neighbors, though it may be profitable to the proprietor."

The New Orleans good-time tradition, the city's near-universal fondness for music and dancing, combined with the surprisingly porous nature of its racial walls, made every kind of music available to every resident. All of them would find their way into jazz.

When Confederate guns opened up on Fort Sumter in Charleston harbor in the early morning hours of April 12, 1861, beginning the Civil War, it was General Pierre Gustave Toutant Beauregard, a favorite son of New Orleans, who gave the first order to fire. His state—and his native city—had already been out of the Union for more than two months. But New Orleans would not be part of the Confederacy for long. Just over a year later, on April 24, 1862, a Union fleet steamed up the river and forced the city's surrender. Federal occupation seemed to signal a new birth of freedom for the thousands of runaway slaves who soon crowded into the city from the southern interior.

"We wish," said the black-owned New Orleans *Tribune* shortly after the war ended, "to be respected and treated as men—not as Africans or Negroes, or colored people, but as Americans and American citizens." Under Reconstruction and in the face of sporadic and sometimes violent

THE FUTURE MUSIC OF THIS COUNTRY

In 1892, the Czech composer Antonín Dvořák arrived in America to become director of the brand-new National Conservatory of Music of America in New York. He was already celebrated for the skill with which he incorporated themes based upon the native songs and dances of his native Bohemia into his symphonic music, and it was the hope of the conservatory's wealthy founder, Mrs. Jeanette Thurber, that he would be able to show young would-be American composers how to do the same thing in the United States. It was a hope Dvořák fully shared: "I did not come to America to interpret Wagner for the public," he said not long after his arrival. "I came to discover what young Americans had in them and to help them express it." He traveled as far west as Iowa during his three years in the United States and grew to admire the chants and rhythms of Native American music, but it was African-American music that moved him most. "I am now satisfied that the future music of this country must be founded upon what are called the negro melodies," he said. "In the negro melodies of America I discovered all that is needed for a great and noble school of music. They are pathetic, tender, passionate, melancholy, solemn, religious, bold, merry. gay, or what you will."

Dvořák's own best-known American-inspired work, Symphony no. 9 in E Minor *(From the New World)* may or may not have drawn upon Negro spirituals—scholars still differ—but it was otherwise indistinguishable from the work of other European composers working in the Romantic idiom. Nonetheless, Dvořák's emphasis on the importance of native forms had a lasting, if indirect, effect on American music. Both Aaron Copland and George Gershwin would study with former students of Dvořák. So, informally, would Duke Ellington, who would demonstrate to the world a whole new way to incorporate the facts of American life into a "serious and original . . . great and noble" wholly American kind of music.

white resistance, real progress would be made toward that goal: public facilities and public schools were integrated, at least on paper, and some black and Creole students peaceably attended classes alongside whites. Citizens of color sued for—and won—the right to sit wherever they liked at the French Opera House. Backed by federal bayonets, they also forced the city to end the system of separate streetcars. Black and white baseball teams played one another, black and white longshoremen went out on strike together, and each year elderly white and black veterans of the 1815 Battle of New Orleans dined amicably together on its anniversary. In 1874, the editor of another newspaper saw evidence of New Orleans's "catholicity of spirit" in the fact that "in our midst the civil and public rights of the colored race [are] more fully realized than has been the case in any other southern city."

It was all too good to last. Three years later, in 1877, the last federal troops were withdrawn from the former Confederacy as white rule and strict segregation were again brutally being reimposed upon the whole region. But for a time, at least, cosmopolitan New Orleans would escape the worst of it.

Meanwhile, the city's rich musical heritage grew steadily richer. Brass bands captivated the whole country after the Civil War— virtually every small town in America boasted at least one—and the New Orleans "mania" for them that had been noted before the war seems only to have intensified afterwards. Citizens of every color and nationality continued to march to German bands, French bands, Irish bands, Italian bands (that highlighted a lyrical, ornamented clarinet style born in Sicily), and the regimental bands of the occupying forces, both black and white. When Patrick Sarsfield Gilmore, the master cornetist and bandleader, who was as celebrated as John Philip Sousa in his day, presented a Grand National Concert at Lafayette Square, five hundred New Orleans brass players turned out to play with him. Every summer during

Scott Joplin's 1899 "Maple Leaf Rag," the biggest hit of the ragtime era, and "Fashion Rag," one of the thousands of tunes published in the hope of matching its spectacular success

the 1880s, a summer resort called West End, on Lake Pontchartrain just north of the city, played host to bands from all over the country with concerts day and night at which were played every kind of music from plantation ditties to operatic overtures, waltzes to so-called "coon songs."

Big-time black bands came to town, too, often as part of minstrel companies, among them the "Louisiana Slave Troupe and Brass Band," "Smallwood's Great Contraband Minstrels Brass Band," and Billy Kersand's minstrel band that marched at the head of the Mardi Gras Finale one year with such precision that its leader's standard offer of one thousand dollars to any group that could beat them in "drilling or parading" found no takers.

Black and Creole fraternal and social organizations, as well as the musicians themselves, organized bands. When a memorial parade for the assassinated Republican President James Garfield moved slowly through the city in 1881, several black outfits played dirges alongside white ones. Some musicians—like those in the Eclipse Band, outfitted and trained on for-

mer governor Henry Clay Warmouth's Magnolia plantation in Plaquemine Parish— prided themselves on their ability to read as well as play and were openly scornful of the untutored players who dared compete with them: "fakers," they called them, "ear-men," "routiners," who relied on guesswork and momentary inspiration, not written notes.

By the mid-1890s, three new kinds of music had begun to filter into the city—three strains without which there would have been no jazz.

The first was ragtime, the formal outgrowth of the decades-old African-American improvisational practice of "ragging" tunes—syncopating and rearranging them to provide livelier, more danceable versions. Created by black musicians in the cities of the Midwest, who had found a way to recreate something like the percussive sound of the banjo on the piano, ragtime drew upon everything that had gone before—spirituals and minstrel tunes, European folk melodies, operatic arias and military marches—all filled with broken

The Mathews and Lockport Brass Band, 1904. The name painted on the drum refers not to the musicians—their identities have long since been lost—but to the two small neighboring towns southwest of New Orleans from which they came. At Mardi Gras time, rural brass bands like theirs often made their way to the big city, adding their rough-hewn sound to the joyous celebration.

During the 1890s, African-Americans streamed into New Orleans as never before, taking jobs on the busy waterfront and bringing with them both the blues and the music of the black Baptist church (below).

chords and set to fresh rhythms. Spread first by itinerant pianists, and then by the sale of sheet music, ragtime caught the fancy of young dancers all over the country who loved it all the more because—since it encouraged young men and women to dance close together as couples rather than in groups—their parents did not. "Ragtime is syncopation gone mad," the editor of *Etude* magazine would write, "and its victims, in my opinion, can be treated successfully only like the dog with rabies, with

THE STUFF THE PEOPLE WANTED

"Each one of my blues is based on some old Negro song of the South," William Christopher Handy wrote in his autobiography. "Something that sticks in my mind, that I hum to myself when I'm not thinking about it. Some old song that is a part of the memories of my childhood and of my race. I can tell you the exact song I used as a basis for any one of my blues." Handy was from Alabama, the son and grandson of Baptist ministers who took a grim view of the kind of secular music he helped spread around the world. He taught music at A & M College in Huntsville and played cornet in a traveling minstrel troupe. In 1902, while leading his own orchestra for white dancers in Cleveland, Mississippi, he learned a lesson about music he would never forget.

"Someone sent up an odd request. Would we play some of 'our native music'? This baffled me. The men in the group could not 'fake' and 'sell' it like minstrel men. They were all musicians who bowed strictly to the authority of printed notes."

The audience then asked Handy's band to take a break and allow a "local" outfit to play a few tunes of their own.

> We eased out gracefully as the newcomers entered. They were led by a long-legged chocolate boy, and their band consisted of just three pieces, a battered guitar, a mandolin, and a worn-out bass. . . . They struck up one of those over-and-over strains that seem to have no very clear beginning and certainly no ending at all. The strumming attained a disturbing monotony, but on and on it went, a kind of stuff that has long been associated with cane rows and levee camps. It was not really annoying or unpleasant, but I commenced to wonder if anybody besides small-town rounders and their running mates could go for it.
>
> The answer was not long in coming. A rain of silver dollars began to fall around the outlandish, stomping feet. The dancers went wild. Dollars, quarters, halves— the shower grew heavier and continued so long I strained my neck to get a better look. There before the boys lay more money than my nine musicians were being paid for the entire engagement. Then I saw the beauty of primitive music. They had the stuff the people wanted. It touched the spot. Their music wanted polishing, but it contained the essence. . . . That night, a composer was born, an *American* composer.

Handy began writing down the blues he heard. In 1909, living and working now in Memphis, he orchestrated a tune being sung there about the monumentally corrupt Boss Ed Crump, then running for mayor. The lyrics were not especially flattering to the candidate:

> Mr. Crump doan allow no easy riders here.
> We doan care what Mr. Crump don't
>   allow;
> We gonna Barrel-house anyhow.
> Mr. Crump can go and catch some air.

But Crump didn't seem to mind. He liked the tune and so did the black and white voters who came out to his rallies to hear Handy's band play it. In 1912, Handy published it with brand-new lyrics as "The Memphis Blues." It was not the first blues ever published—it was delayed just long enough for two other songwriters to get there first—but it launched Handy on the career that earned him the title "Father of the Blues," helped make the blues into an industry, and whetted the public's appetite for jazz.

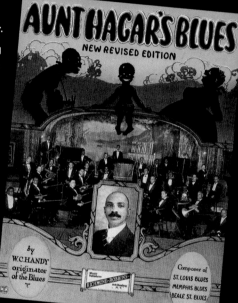

W. C. Handy's "Aunt Hagar's Blues," a musical portrait of a churchly woman who, despite the stern admonitions of her preacher, finds the blues impossible to resist

a dose of lead. Whether it is simply a passing phase of our decadent art culture or an infectious disease which has come to stay, like leprosy, time alone can tell."

Despite that kind of criticism—and in part perhaps because of it—ragtime had come to stay; jaunty, propulsive, irresistible, it would be America's best-loved music for a quarter of a century. Nowhere was ragtime more popular or more ubiquitous than in New Orleans; by the turn of the century, Crescent City musicians, in dance halls as well as street parades, were routinely giving every kind of music the ragtime treatment.

Meanwhile, a steady stream of black refugees from the Mississippi Delta was pouring into the city, people for whom even hard labor on the levee promised a better life than any they could hope to have back home, chopping cotton or cutting cane. They brought with them as part of their baggage two interrelated forms essential to the development of jazz—the sacred music of the Baptist church and that music's profane twin, the blues.

No one knows where or when the blues were born: "Ain't no first blues," the New Orleans clarinetist Louis "Big Eye" Nelson remembered: "The blues always been." Blues lyrics could be about anything— empty pockets, a mean boss, the devil himself—but most were about the relationship between men and women and each performer was expected to tell a story and to make the listener feel better, not worse:

> I'm goin' to lay my head on some
>   lonesome railroad track,
> I'm goin' to lay my head on some
>   lonesome railroad track—
> and when the train come along, I'll
>   snatch my damn head back.

The earliest blues singers—wandering guitarists who played for pennies along the southern roads—followed no strict musical form. But as first New Orleans musicians and then others around the country began to try to play the blues on their instruments and songwriters started to see commercial possibilities in them, an agreed-upon form was developed: stripped to the essentials, blues came to be built on just three chords most often arranged in twelve-bar sequences that somehow allowed for an infinite number of variations and were capable of expressing an infinite number of emotions.

The blues were good-time music, which was why, to many churchgoers, they were anathema, the work of the devil, forbidden to the saved. But musically, the blues and the hymns black Baptists sang and played in church had always been virtually interchangeable—filled with identical bent notes, moans, and cries. And in the 1890s, the distinction would blur still further as the new Holiness churches that had begun to spring up in the black neighborhoods of big cities all over the country started employing tambourines, drums, pianos, cornets, even trombones in order to make their noise still more joyful to the Lord. "Those Baptist rhythms were similar to the jazz rhythms," said the New Orleans banjoist Johnny St. Cyr, "and the singing was very much on the blues side." "You heard the pastors in the Baptist churches," echoed the drummer Paul Barbarin, "they were singing rhythm. More so than a jazz band."

"In the [church]," the New Orleans clarinet master Sidney Bechet would remember, "the people clapped their hands—that was their rhythm. In the blues it was further down; they didn't need the clapping but they remembered it. . . . And both of them, the spirituals and the blues, they was a prayer. One was praying to God and the other was praying to what's human. It's like one was saying, 'Oh God, let me go,' and the other was saying, 'Oh, Mister, let me be.' "

Jazz music would eventually embody both kinds of invocation, the sacred and the secular, and New Orleans musicians would be the first to deepen the infinitely expressive sound of the blues by bringing it to their horns, the first to echo the collective "moan" of the congregation, the first to reproduce the call-and-response patterns of the religious exhorter and his transported flock.

SEPARATE BUT EQUAL

In the spring of 1885, the New England novelist and critic Charles Dudley Warner had visited the International Cotton Exposition at New Orleans and been astonished by what he saw: "white and colored people mingled freely" at the fairgrounds, he wrote home in wonder, "talking and looking at what was of common interest," still seeming to associate "in unconscious equality of privileges."

But by the 1890s, Jim Crow laws that strictly segregated the rest of the South had begun to delimit life in New Orleans as well. "There are differences between the colored man and the white man which neither education nor law can abrogate," said the New Orleans *Picayune*. "To sit by a negro's side at a hotel table or a concert hall [is], in the opinion of the white people, to ignore the truth." New statutes now barred blacks entirely from theaters where they had once at least been permitted a separate section of their own. "Negroes were not allowed in the places where [classical music] was played," the drummer Baby Dodds remembered, "so I heard it by standing on the outside . . . in the hallway of the Tulane theater. . . . One side was an opera house and the other was this theater and we'd stand in between to hear the music."

In 1890, a bill requiring that blacks and whites occupy different cars on trains traveling within the state easily passed the legislature despite the protest of sixteen black and Creole legislators that the bill was "unconstitutional, unamerican, unjust." Two years later, a New Orleans Creole named Homer Adolph Plessy set out to test the new law by boarding an excursion train and insisting on sitting in the "whites only" car. He was, he said, of "seven-eighths Caucasian and one-eighth African blood . . . [and] the admixture of colored blood is not discernible." He was arrested anyway (the police had been tipped off), tried and con-

victed, and in 1896, in the case of *Plessy v. Ferguson,* the Supreme Court of the United States upheld his conviction. "Separate but equal facilities," it said, were constitutional. That decision would govern life in the American South—and in New Orleans—for nearly sixty years.

Black children were removed from the public schools—though, New Orleans being New Orleans, a considerable number who were especially light-skinned continued to attend them undetected. Black and white boxers and bicycle racers and ball teams were now forbidden to compete against one another. The Louisiana legislature rewrote the state constitution to bar all would-be voters whose grandfathers had been slaves. Ninety-five percent of the city's black men had been entitled to vote in 1897; just 1 percent would be welcome at the polls in 1901. Seating on city streetcars was once again strictly segregated, despite an exasperated warning from the president of the transportation company that "the greatest ethnologist the world has ever seen would be at a loss to classify streetcar passengers in this city."

Overnight, the rarefied world of the Creoles of Color was turned upside down. A little white blood had formerly carried with it certain privileges in New Orleans. Now, a single drop of black blood—any "traceable amount," according to state statute—was enough to rank a person as a second-class citizen.

Creole musicians were especially dislocated by the changes all around them. John Robichaux had been perhaps the city's favorite Creole musician, a well-schooled violinist with a waxed moustache whose elegantly dressed "society"—or "sit-down" —orchestra played sweet dance music for white patrons at two of the most prestigious venues in the city, the Grunewald Hotel and Antoine's Restaurant. "He had the rich people's jobs all sewed up," the bassist George "Pops" Foster remembered. But now, even Robichaux often found himself displaced by white musicians, forced to join a separate

The three-boy band shown here worked New Orleans streetcars for tourists' tips in 1910. Cornetist Albert "Abbie" Brunies, center, grew up to become a professional musician, working with both Papa Jack Laine's and Johnny Fischer's brass bands. His younger brother, George, right, became far better known. He would one day play trombone with the New Orleans Rhythm Kings, perhaps the most musically gifted of the white bands that headed north after 1917. Much later, on advice from a numerologist, he would drop the "e" from both halves of his name and call himself "Georg Brunis."

musician's union and for the first time compete on an equal footing with blacks.

"You know what happened to us [Creole] musicians," Paul Dominguez said.

We were all educated in music and knew our instruments—[but now] we had to change. See us Downtown people, we didn't think so much of this rough Uptown [music] until we couldn't make a living otherwise. . . .

Say, for instance, I was working with the Olympia Band, working one or two nights a week for two dollars and a half a night. The [gambling den called The] 25's here in [the vice district] pay you a dollar and a quarter and tips, but you working seven nights. Naturally, wouldn't I quit the Olympia and go to this tonk? Wouldn't I? . . . Well . . . that's how they make a fiddler out of a violinist . . . a fiddler is *not* a violinist, but a violinist can be a fiddler. If I wanted to make a living, I had to be rowdy like the other group. I had to jazz it or rag it or any other damn thing. . . . [Buddy] Bolden caused all that.

THE *FEELING* OF THE MAN

In the summer of 1898, the Crescent City shared fully in the fevered patriotism that gripped the country as it went to war with Spain. "New Orleans was very enthusiastic," noted Colonel Leonard Wood, commander of the Rough Riders, as he passed through town on the way to the front, "Streets full of people and best of all the American flag in the hands of all. The cost of this war is amply repaid by seeing the old flag as one sees it today in the South. We are indeed once more a united country."

The city's brass bands vied with one another to see which could provide the most impressive send-off from the levee as American troops boarded troopships for Tampa,

New Orleans bands were expected to be able to play for any and all occasions. The Peerless Orchestra was no exception. When its men played at the opening of Dixie Park (above) they would likely have worn marching uniforms (opposite, top); when called upon to play indoors for the dance sponsored by the black social club called Ten Well-Known Gentlemen (below), they adopted more elegant attire.

The only known photograph of Buddy Bolden and his orchestra, made in 1905. Standing, left to right, William Warner, Willie Cornish, Buddy Bolden, and James Johnson; seated are Frank Lewis and Jefferson Mumford.

the jumping-off point for the assault on Cuba. When it came time to bid farewell to the men of the all-black tenth cavalry, the best-loved black band in town did the honors, and its leader, the cornetist Buddy Bolden, played "Home, Sweet Home" with such tenderness and conviction that some of the men jumped overboard and swam for shore—or so old New Orleans musicians liked to remember.

Like a good many of the stories that would swirl around Buddy Bolden, it clearly never happened. Army officers were rarely impressed by homesickness or sentimental

music, no matter how beautifully played; and any soldier, black or white, who had tried to desert by jumping ship would have been recaptured immediately—or shot in the water. But the fact that Bolden's contemporaries found the legend wholly plausible is vivid evidence of the special power his playing must have had.

If the memories of those who heard him are to be trusted, he seems from the first to have been solidly in the American brass band tradition of master cornetists but also somehow different from other New Orleans musicians—louder, bolder, more innovative.

People sought him out not just to hear his band but to hear *him* and what he personally could do with the tunes he played. Marching bands had long since begun to "rag" their music, adding syncopation and embellishments to familiar strains as they moved through the city streets. But Buddy Bolden may have been the *very* first—and was certainly one of the first—to bring that sound inside the dance hall and blend it with the blues.

He remains something of a mystery. Tales tell of a big, flamboyant man who liked to wear his collar open on parade days so that the adoring women who carried his hat and coat could admire his broad chest and red flannel undershirt, but in the single battered photograph that survives he seems sure of himself but otherwise unprepossessing and of normal size. He was never recorded, so that no one now can be sure just how his music sounded. And madness would cut short his career before jazz—the distinctive blend of blues and church music, ragtime and military marches, and all the other elements of the New Orleans mix he helped to pioneer—was known much beyond the confines of his city.

It took the jazz historian Donald M. Marquis more than a decade to hunt down even a handful of indisputable facts about his life. Charles Joseph Bolden was born in New Orleans in 1877, the year Reconstruction ended. The grandson of a slave and the son of a drayman who died when the boy was only seven, Bolden grew up and lived for most of his life on First Street, in an integrated workingman's neighborhood where every kind of music was his for the hearing. Most of the neighbors were Irish and German immigrants: the white jazz clarinetist Larry Shields was born just two doors up the street. Brass bands, both black and white, paraded often through the neighborhood.

Bolden is thought to have attended the Fisk School for Boys, where the rudiments of music were part of the curriculum, and he is known regularly to have worshipped at the St. John Baptist Church, celebrated for the special fervor with which its congregation sang spirituals and jubilees. The trombonist Kid Ory alleged that Bolden also often attended a Holiness church at Jackson and Franklin "but not for religion, he went there to get ideas on music. He'd hear those songs and he would change them a little. In those . . . churches they sometimes had drums and a piano while the people sang and clapped their hands. Sometimes they'd have guests and invite a trumpet player or a trombone player to come over

and play with them. . . . That's where Buddy got it from and that's how it all started." In any case, Bolden's listeners would later routinely compare the response Baptist preachers elicited from the faithful to the shouts of approval that greeted his playing on the bandstand.

He mastered the plasterer's trade—few New Orleans musicians expected to support themselves as musicians in those days—but about 1894 he also took cornet lessons from a neighbor who happened to be keeping company with his widowed mother. Soon, he was playing with a string band for dancing, then leading his own brass band and billing himself as "Professor" Bolden. He and his men performed everything demanding New Orleans audiences could want—waltzes, mazurkas, schottisches, polkas, rags, spirituals, blues. And they performed them all over town: in street parades and at tea dances, at picnic grounds and balloon ascensions, and for black dancers at Masonic Hall, Globe Hall, Jackson Hall, Perseverance Hall, and Union Sons Hall—better known to the patrons who savored its ripe humid atmosphere as Funky Butt Hall.

His more decorous appearances ended with a honeyed version of "Home, Sweet Home" to signal to the dancers that it was time to leave. But around midnight, at places where more was expected of him, he would roar into a signature tune called "Don't Go Away Nobody" and the crowd knew it was in for slow-dancing till sunup. "[O]n those old . . . low-down blues," a fellow musician recalled, "that boy could make the women jump out the window. . . . [H]e had a moan in his cornet that just went through you, just like you were in church or something."

Bolden was an entertainer as well as a musician. His best-known number was variously known as "Funky Butt" and "Buddy Bolden's Blues," with changeable lyrics made up for the occasion. Most were simply raunchy but one version ridiculed a local judge named J. J. Fogarty, who seemed to have it in for members of Bolden's band. "The police put you in jail if they heard you singing that song," one musician remembered, and once, when Bolden launched into it during a street parade, "the people started singing, [and] policemen began whipping heads."

By the time this photograph was taken during the 1930s, Funky Butt Hall, right, where Buddy Bolden often played the blues till dawn, had been transformed into the Greater St. Matthews Baptist Church.

At first, Creole musicians were openly scornful of Bolden and what they called his "ratty" music. Pops Foster recalled that Bolden "played very good for the style of stuff he was doing. He played nothing but the blues and all that stink music, and he played it loud." The cornetist Peter Bocage was only slightly more generous: "He had a good tone, but . . . [h]e played everything in B-flat. He played a lot of blues, slow drag. . . . Blues was their standby."

But the raw power of his music—and its obvious impact on the crowds that turned out to hear him—began to win the grudging respect of some Creoles. The clarinetist George Baquet remembered first hearing Bolden and his band at an after-midnight dance at Odd Fellow's Hall.

Nobody took their hats off. It was plenty rough. You paid fifteen cents and walked in. The band, six of them, was sitting on a low stand. They had their hats on and were resting, pretty sleepy. All of a sudden, Buddy stomps, knocks on the floor with his trumpet to give the beat and they all sit up straight. They played "Make Me a Pallet." Everybody rose and yelled out, "Oh, Mr. Bolden, play it for us, Buddy, play it!" I'd never heard anything like that before. I'd played "legitimate" stuff. But this, it was something that pulled me in. They got me up on the stand and I played with them. After that I didn't play legitimate so much.

John Robichaux was Bolden's greatest rival. On weekend afternoons he and his well-turned-out Creole orchestra presided over the music pavilion in the center of Lincoln Park. Bolden reigned supreme just across Short Street in Johnson Park, and nothing pleased him more than to point his cornet at Robichaux's listeners and blow something so loud, so hot, that they could not resist rushing over to hear what else he had in store for them. He was, he said, "calling my children home."

Soon, younger Creole musicians, too, were answering his call, seeking a way to incorporate into their own playing his driving beat, his affinity for the blues, his eagerness to improvise. Bolden and his men "made their own music and they played it their own way, you understand?" Peter Bocage said. "So that's the way jazz started—just through the *feeling* of the man . . . his improvisations."

There was, as yet, no name for the music Buddy Bolden and other New Orleans musicians—black, Creole, and white—began to play at the dawn of the new century, and some older musicians would call what they played "ragtime" to the end of their lives. But the eventual result would be a brand-new form—"not spirituals or the blues or ragtime" or any of the other kinds of music heard in the streets of New Orleans, one musician remembered, "but everything all at once, each one putting something over on the other." Like the city that gave it birth, like the country that would soon embrace it, this new music would always be more than the sum of its parts.

HELLISH DREAMS

On the evening of Monday, July 23, 1900, three New Orleans policemen spotted two black men sitting on the back steps of a white family's house near the corner of Dryade and Washington Streets. They asked the men what they were doing there.

One gave his name as Robert Charles. He had come to New Orleans from Mississippi six years earlier, after a shootout with a white railroad employee who had dared try to take from him a gun Charles claimed was his. He had become convinced that there was no future for blacks in America, and between odd jobs he handed out pamphlets on the street, calling for wholesale emigration to Africa.

Charles told the policemen he was waiting for a friend. An officer ordered him to

move on and when Charles refused, swung his nightstick, then drew his revolver. Charles pulled his own pistol. The policeman fell, wounded. Charles was hit, too, but made it to his rooming house and picked up a rifle. When the police came after him, he shot and killed two of them before getting away again. The news spread across the city. The following evening hundreds of angry whites gathered at the city's monument to Robert E. Lee. The crowd's self-appointed leader was the mayor of nearby Kenner. "The only way you can teach these niggers a lesson and put them in their place," he shouted, "is to go out and lynch a few of them."

At about that time, Big Eye Nelson remembered, Buddy Bolden was getting ready to play with a string band at The 25's, at the corner of Iberville and Franklin in the black section of the red-light district. Nelson was playing bass that evening and had just slipped his instrument out of its case when a woman ran in off the street and urged the musicians to "knock off"—a white mob was on its way.

Bolden paid no attention: "We never had nothing like that in New Orleans yet," one of his men told her, "and it won't happen tonight." The band began to play. Then, suddenly, the street outside was filled with the sound of running, shouting men. There were shots, curses, screams.

"Me, I was sitting at the inside end of the bandstand playing bass," Nelson recalled. "All them boys flung themselves on me in getting away from the door and out toward the back. The bass was bust to kindling. . . . We made it out the window . . . and into the alley but, man, that alley was already loaded with folks." Nelson, Bolden, and their companions eventually found sanctuary in a friend's house, but the cornetist's gold watch was left behind, hanging on the wall above the bandstand, and when the three-day riot finally ended, the body of Big Eye Nelson's father was found among the dead.

For four days after that, no one could find Robert Charles. Then, a black informer told

The most miserable feeling a youngster in New Orleans can experience is to be in the classroom studying when he hears a brass band approaching, swinging like crazy past the school and then fading off into the distance. You will witness a lot of sad expressions in that room. Now, if it happens to be lunch-hour recess—12 to 1— when the bell rings at 1 p.m. a lot of seats will be vacant. . . . The music would excite and move you to such an extent that when you would realize it, you had second-lined maybe ten or twenty blocks from school.

—DANNY BARKER

Papa Jack Laine, seated, and his Reliance Marching Band in 1910. Laine was an entrepreneur as well as a musician. He paid two thousand dollars for a languishing tent show that year, grandly renamed it Laine's Greater Majestic Minstrels, and set it up near the streetcar barns at Canal and White Streets, expecting big profits. Instead, a summer hurricane blew away the tent and most of his savings. Laine was a mentor to scores of white musicians: six years after this photograph was taken, clarinetist Alcide "Yellow" Nuñez, second from left, would be working in Chicago with a group called Stein's Band from Dixie, the precursor of the Original Dixieland Jazz Band.

the police he was hiding in a house on Saratoga Street. Hundreds of armed whites joined the police who surrounded it. In the gun battle that followed Charles managed to kill five more attackers and wound another twenty before they finally killed him, then poured so many bullets into his corpse that he became unrecognizable—inspiring the false story that he had somehow escaped.

Whites blamed all the trouble on outside agitators from the North. "Under the dark, seething mass of humanity that surrounds us . . . all appears peaceful and delightful," the New Orleans *Daily State* warned its readers, "we know not, it seems what hellish dreams are arising underneath. . . . We are . . . under the regime of the free negro in the midst of a dangerous element of servile uprising, not for any real cause, but

from the native race hatred of the negro, inflamed continually by our Northern philanthropists."

Robert Charles became a folk hero to a good many black people in New Orleans. Someone wrote a song about him, too; but even years later, it was thought unwise to sing it in the presence of whites.

Race relations in the city never recovered —even when it came to music. For years, black and white bands had played for picnickers along the shores of Lake Pontchartrain, the drummer Paul Barbarin recalled:

On Mondays at Lucian's Pavilion there was always an attraction. You would find a picnic plus the Imperial, the Superior or the Olympia Band. Imag-

Will Marion Cook and song sheets for three of his hits

Ragtime, born in the black neighborhoods of the middle west, had already swept New York City by 1898, and the African-American cakewalk was the dance of choice among young people of all races. To men like the classically trained composer Will Marion Cook, a former student of Antonin Dvořák's, and the poet Paul Laurence Dunbar the time seemed ripe to mount an all-black show on Broadway. *Clorindy, or the Origin of the Cakewalk* was the result. An hour-long series of skits filled with so many crude minstrel-style gags that Cook's mother wept with embarrassment when she first heard them, *Clorindy* nonetheless brought twenty-six African-American performers onstage to dazzle Manhattan theater audiences.

Opening night at the Casino Roof Garden was a triumph, Cook remembered: "My chorus sang like Russians, dancing meanwhile like Negroes and cakewalking like angels! When the last note sounded, the audience stood and cheered for at least ten minutes. . . . It was pandemonium but pandemonium was never dearer to my heart. . . . I was so delirious that I drank a glass of water, thought it wine and got gloriously drunk. Negroes were at last on Broadway, and there to stay. . . . Nothing could stop us, and nothing did for a decade."

Other successful shows followed for Will Marion Cook —including *In Dahomey* and *Bandana Land*—and he vowed someday to write one that opened with at least ten minutes of serious music "worthy of his talents" before returning to the light-hearted material white audiences had come to expect from black entertainers. Other black songwriters, including Bob Cole and the Johnson brothers, James Weldon and J. Rosamond, managed to get their work produced on Broadway, as well.

But by 1910, white theatergoers had lost interest in the novelty of seeing black productions. Black casts would not reappear on Broadway until the 1920s, their return brought about in part by the power and popularity of still another African-American creation just being born when Cook and Dunbar put on their first show—jazz music.

ine the summer sunshine, the blue lake, the camps white, green, yellow, every color of paint. The white summer dresses, many colored parasols. The gold lettering on the brewery trucks, the harness shining . . . About five or six bands playing five or six different tunes, and not over 100 yards apart. Laughing men rolling a half keg of beer along the boardwalk to a camp. Hot dogs, oysters, crawfish, green crabs and fat lake trout. Everybody eating, singing and making music. This was a friendly place and a friendly time. Maybe two camps away there would be a white band. Don't think we didn't have many great white jazzmen in those days. We had 'em. And they played great. But there was honest, musical rivalry.

After the Robert Charles riot, that honest rivalry would sometimes turn poisonous. At the turn of the century the best-known leader of a white marching band was Papa Jack Laine, a drummer, blacksmith, and sometime boxer who began organizing his Reliance Brass Bands while still in grade school and kept at it for more than forty years; by 1910 he controlled enough musicians to send ten different outfits into the streets on a single day. Two generations of white New Orleans musicians got their start through him: "I picked them boys up playing . . . when they were in knee-pants," he liked to say.

Laine would contend all his life that nonwhites had had nothing whatsoever to do with the music he and his men played; the only reason they ever learned how to syncopate, he claimed, was from listening to him. But two of the musicians he most often hired were actually light-skinned Creoles: clarinetist Achille Baquet and the trombone player Dave Perkins, who routinely stood on the rear platform of New Orleans streetcars rather than have to choose between sitting at the front with whites or in the back with blacks. (They were both "niggers,"

Laine admitted many years later, but "they played so good we couldn't tell what color they was.")

The pointless argument over ownership of America's music started early and, sadly, has never really stopped.

JELLY ROLL

"It is evidently known, beyond contradiction, that New Orleans is the cradle of jazz," Jelly Roll Morton would write in 1938, "and I, myself, happened to be [its] creator in the year 1902." Morton had been only twelve years old in 1902, his kind of music had long been out of fashion when he made his pronouncement, and to many of those who remembered Morton at all it then seemed just the latest in a lifelong series of outrageous boasts. "He claimed he invented a lot of things he didn't," Pops Foster said. "If you'd listen to him talk long enough, he'd claim he invented the piano or anything else that came to his mind."

Jazz had no single creator, of course; it began as a gumbo stirred and seasoned by hundreds of hands. But Morton's claim had more heft than it seemed to have at the time he made it. "He could back up everything he *said,*" his friend the clarinetist Omer Simeon once said, "with what he could *do.*" Morton was in fact among the first to play jazz, its first theorist and composer and master of form, the first to write it down, and by doing so, among the first to help spread New Orleans music across the country. From the beginning he seems to have wanted, both in his elegant piano playing and in the tunes he began composing about 1905, to produce music that incorporated both blues and ragtime but was clearly different from either one.

The blues were full of passion but too simple, he said; besides, most blues musicians were mere "one-tune piano players." Ragtime players, on the other hand, were too prone to speeding things up, while the principle underlying the music they played

Jelly Roll Morton was just twenty when this portrait was made but already a three-year veteran of the road. "He never stopped running," a friend said, "couldn't seem to rest one place more than a few days."

was just "a certain kind of syncopation, and only certain tunes can be played in that idea."

"Jazz music," on the other hand, he said, is "a *style,* not compositions. Any kind of music may be played in jazz, if one has the knowledge." No one had more style—or more knowledge—than Jelly Roll Morton. "No jazz piano player," he said, "can ever really play jazz unless they try to get the imitation of a band," and, true to that belief, he sought to reproduce something like the polyphony of the New Orleans marching bands at the keyboard: his left hand repro-

Louise Monette, the mother of Jelly Roll Morton

duced the bass line, sometimes interspersed with figures reminiscent of tailgate trombone, while his right hand mirrored the instrumental lead of the cornet and clarinet. He brought to everything he played—ragtime and blues, French and Italian operatic airs, Spanish popular songs and dances—a new, smoother kind of syncopation. Each tune was transformed under his long, supple fingers and to the rhythm of his loudly tapping foot into something altogether new. "You could go by a house where Jelly Roll was playing," the bass player Bill Johnson recalled, "and you'd know it was him because nobody . . . did play just like him."

He was born Ferdinand Joseph Lamothe in New Orleans on October 20, 1890—he eventually changed his last name to Morton for "business reasons," he once explained, "because I didn't want to be called 'Frenchy' "—and he embodied within himself all the racial contradictions of his hometown. He would one day claim that his ancestors "were in the city of New Orleans long before the Louisiana Purchase and all my folks came directly from the shores . . . of France," and he rarely missed an opportunity to contrast his own light skin

and slender features with those of blacks, many of whom, he liked to say, had "lips like bumpers on a boxcar." In fact, the members of his family were relative newcomers to the city, and he was not French at all but the illegitimate son of a Creole mother and father who traced their ancestry back to the island of Haiti.

Nor did his Creole airs keep him from eagerly immersing himself early in the mostly black world of the blues that were everywhere around him. As he himself said about his city, "We had all nations in New Orleans, but with the music we could creep in close to other people," and he never forgot the first blues he heard, played and sung by a neighbor woman named Mamie Desdoumes. She had just three fingers on her right hand, Morton remembered, and only knew one tune, which she played on the piano "all day long after she would first get up in the morning":

> I stood on the corner, my feet was
> dripping wet,
> I asked every man I met . . .
> Can't give me a dollar, give me a lousy
> dime,
> Just to feed that hungry man of mine.

Morton would one day make blues like that his own.

His father's wayward ways soon drove his mother to leave him and move in with another man. "We always had some kind of musical instrument in the house," Morton recalled, "including guitar, drums, piano, trombone, . . . harmonica, and jew's harp. We had lots of 'em and everybody played for their pleasure." At the age of seven, he was already good enough at guitar to play for dances in a string trio. A few years later, he was singing in a quartet that specialized in performing spirituals at wakes in exchange for "plenty ham sandwiches, cheese sandwiches, mustard slathered all over the bread." From the first he loved the sound of the piano best, but feared that his friends would call him a "sissy" if he tried it. Then, he was taken to the French Opera

House where, he told an interviewer, "I happened to notice a pianist . . . that didn't wear long hair. That was the first time I decided that the instrument was good for a gentleman same as it was a lady."

When Morton was fourteen, his mother died and he and his two sisters moved in with relatives. The following year—wearing long pants stolen from an uncle's closet to fool the policemen who had orders to chase away youngsters in short ones—he began venturing into Storyville, the wide-open, eighteen-square-block vice district. Named after Joseph Story, the upright alderman who had proposed setting the area aside in 1897 in a futile effort to bring a measure of order to his raucous city, it was a place unlike any other in America, a magnet to men from every state and every stratum of society, all intent on pleasure. Some two thousand prostitutes plied their trade in its 230 brothels, their special talents and racial background—"white," "colored," or "octoroon"—were catalogued annually in an official *Blue Book* sold for a quarter on street corners. No one knows how many more women worked the wooden one-room cribs that lined the nearby streets and alleyways. All the customers were white—or at least able to pass for white—but an unofficial "black Storyville" took up the better part of several more blocks beginning just across Canal Street.

In later years, the legend would grow that Storyville—called "the District" by most musicians—was the birthplace of jazz. It wasn't. Few bands ever played in its crowded bars and brothels, largely because management didn't believe dancers could be counted upon to buy drinks. But parlor pianists were in great demand. They didn't take up much space; helped pull men in off the street; provided music for the "naked dances" and sexual circuses featured at some houses; and created a mood that helped persuade customers to empty their pockets.

One Saturday evening, Morton heard that a Storyville madame was looking for

Tom Anderson's Annex at the corner of Basin and Iberville Streets was the most lavish establishment in Storyville. One hundred electric bulbs in the ceiling of the bar cast a blinding light. The gleaming bar itself was half a block long and manned by a dozen bartenders. There were "Private Rooms for the Fair Sex" upstairs, and Anderson's was one of the few places in the District big enough to employ a full-size dance band. Every single building on the block was a brothel, all of them conveniently located right across Basin Street from the terminus of the Southern Railroad that hauled hundreds of potential customers into town at all hours of the day and night.

a new piano player. By then, he said, he was already one of the best "junior pianists" in the city and easily got the job. To mollify the great-grandmother with whom he and his sisters were then living he explained that he wouldn't be coming home at night any more because he was working the late shift at a barrel factory.

Most whorehouses guaranteed their piano players just a dollar a night; a few went as high as five but, Morton recalled, "very often men would come into the houses and hand you a twenty or . . . a fifty-dollar note. . . . Wine flowed much more than water." Morton claimed that—for him at least—any night he made less than a hundred dollars was "a bad night."

"The piano players waited for their tricks just like the girls did," Pops Foster explained.

If a trick was good for the girls, it was good for the piano player too. Most of the guys who went in the whorehouses were half stewed and the drunker they were, the more money they'd tip. The customer picked out the girl and piano player he wanted, and they'd go off to a room. The customer and the girl would drink and make love while the piano player played some slow blues.

After hours, Morton haunted the back room of a place called The Frenchman's where, he said, "everything in the line of hilarity" was available and all the piano players in the District hung out. "We had Spanish [pianists]," he remembered, "we had colored, we had white, we had Frenchmen, we had Americans. We had 'em from all

parts of the world. New Orleans was the stompin' grounds for all the greatest pianists in the country."

Even Morton never claimed to be the District's best piano player; that honor went to the "man of a thousand songs," a ragtime specialist named Tony Jackson, composer of the perennial favorite "Pretty Baby." But, Pops Foster remembered, "Jelly was the best *entertaining* piano player by himself. He knew all the dirty songs and . . . [w]hen a customer would come in the door, Jelly would make up a dirty rhyme on your name and play it to his piano playing." Many years later, Morton would record for the Library of Congress some of the spectacularly gamey tunes he wrote during his Storyville days. They constitute the most vivid possible proof that when it comes to sex and sin, the citizens of the new millennium know nothing their forefathers hadn't already worked out for themselves.

Morton also began to compose more respectable tunes as well as play them, including "The Wolverines" (renamed "Wolverine Blues" by his music publisher, to his fury); "Milneburg Joys," a paean to a Lake Pontchartrain picnic grove; and "Jelly Roll Blues," a paean to himself:

In New Orleans, Louisiana town,
There's the finest boy for miles around
Lord, Mister Jelly Roll, your affection he has stole. . . .
He's so tall and chancey,
He's the lady's fancy.
Everybody know him,
Certainly do adore him.

When you see him strolling, everybody opens up,
He's red hot stuff,
Friends, you can't get enough.
Play it soft—don't abuse.
Play them Jelly Roll Blues.

Morton's best-known early piece was "King Porter Stomp." Named for his friend, the Florida-born pianist Porter King, he kept it in his arsenal as his secret weapon in contests with other piano players; and in a simplified version it would one day be recorded by more than thirty bands and provide Benny Goodman with one of his biggest hits.

Morton's skill and showmanship eventually landed him jobs with the District's highest-paying "land-ladies"—Hilma Burt, Josie Arlington, Gypsy Schaefer, Lulu White "the Octoroon Queen," Antonia Gonzales, who billed herself as "the only Singer of Opera and Female Cornetist in the Tenderloin," and "Countess" Willie V. Piazza, who once shot and killed a customer who had mistreated one of her girls and then was found blameless by twelve sympathetic New Orleans jurors.

Morton was soon doing well, so well that he could afford a finely tailored suit, a gleaming pair of the fashionable shoes called St. Louis flats, and a Stetson hat. "Those days," he remembered, "I thought I would die unless I had a hat with the emblem in it of the name of Stetson." His high-toned clothes proved his downfall. On her way back from church one Sunday morning, his great-grandmother spotted him coming home from work. How could he afford to look so sharp? she asked, and in an uncharacteristic burst of candor, he told her. She threw him out of the house. "A musician is nothing but a bum and a scalawag," she told him. "I don't want you around your sisters, I reckon you better move."

He continued to send money home for the rest of his life, but from the age of seventeen he was on his own, sometimes working in New Orleans but most often on the road: Biloxi, Jacksonville, Gulfport, Memphis, Chicago, Selma, Houston, Oklahoma City, St. Louis, Indianapolis, Philadelphia, Detroit—and in 1917 all the way west to Los Angeles.

Music was always his "first line of business," he said, but when gigs proved hard to find, he had other ways of making a living. He sometimes blacked-up and performed as one half of a vaudeville duo with a comic named Sammy Russell, and it was during one of their early ad-lib routines, he said, that he gave himself his celebrated nickname.

Sam said to me, "You don't know who you talkin' to." I told him I didn't care and we had a little argument. I finally asked him who was he, and he stated to me he was "Sweet Papa Cream Puff, right outa the bakery shop." That seemed to produce a great big laugh. While I was standin' there muggin', . . . a thought came to me that I better say somethin' about the bakery shop, [so I said] I was "Sweet Papa Jelly Roll, with stove pipes in my hips—and all the women in town was dyin' to turn my damper down."

Between engagements, Morton also gambled at cards, pimped, hustled pool, and peddled door-to-door a sticky elixir made up of salt and Coca-Cola that he claimed would cure tuberculosis. Showmanship was always central to his style. The pianist James P. Johnson remembered seeing him work in California:

He would take his overcoat off. It had a special lining that would catch everybody's eye, so he would turn it inside out and, instead of folding it, he would lay it lengthwise along the top of the upright piano. He would do this very slowly, very carefully and very solemnly as if the coat was worth a fortune and had to be handled very tenderly. Then he'd take a big silk handkerchief, shake it out to show it off properly, and dust off the stool. He'd sit down then, hit his special chord—every tickler had his special trademark chord, like a signal—and he'd be gone! The first rag he'd always play was always a spirited one to astound the audience.

Everywhere Jelly Roll Morton went, New Orleans music went, too, even though he often found himself forced to play with musicians who knew little or nothing about it. "When it was a New Orleans man, that wasn't so much trouble," he remembered, "because those boys knew a lot of my breaks, but in traveling from place to place I found other musicians had to be taught. So . . . I began writing down this peculiar form of mathematics and harmonics that was strange to all the world."

In the process of "writing down" New Orleans polyphony in order that uninitiated musicians could play it, Morton also broke the music down as no one ever had before and few have done since. One by one, he set forth its basic elements:

How to play *breaks*—brief solos played while the band unexpectedly falls silent, meant to add excitement: "A break . . . is like a musical surprise," Morton said.

The "Mirror Ballroom" of Hilma Burt's whorehouse, located next door to Anderson's Annex. Jelly Roll Morton played piano here for the women and their customers but since he was only twelve years old in 1902 when this photograph is said to have been taken, the man at the piano is most likely one of his predecessors.

"Without breaks and without clean breaks and without beautiful ideas in breaks, you . . . haven't got a jazz band and you can't play jazz. Even if a tune hasn't got a break in it, it's always necessary to arrange some kind of a spot to make a break."

How to add *riffs*—unison phrases repeated at regular intervals, meant both to spur on a soloist and to reassure listeners that the band is still working together: "Now the riff is what we call a foundation," he said, "like something that you walk on."

How to mix in what he called the "Spanish tinge"—the languorous bass rhythm of the tango and the earlier Spanish and Caribbean dances New Orleans had always

loved—without which Morton believed jazz lacked the proper "seasoning." "You leave the left hand just the same [i.e., playing a tango rhythm]. The difference comes in the right hand—in the syncopation which gives it an entirely different color that really changes from red to blue."

How to set the proper tempo—"A lot of people have the wrong conception of jazz," he said. "Jazz music is to be played sweet. Soft, plenty rhythm."

When you have your plenty rhythm with your plenty swing, it becomes beautiful. . . . You can't make crescendos and diminuendos when one

is playing triple forte. You've got to be able to come down in order to go up. If a glass of water is full you can't fill it any more, but if you have half a glass you have an opportunity to put more water in it, and jazz music is based on the same principles.

Despite Morton's efforts, New Orleans music would remain "strange to all the world" for another decade. The Victrola had been introduced in 1901, but no one had yet thought to record New Orleans musicians or the new music they were creating. Jazz was moving across the country, one musician at a time.

A SKY FULL
OF NEW MOONS

Late one April afternoon in 1907, not long after Jelly Roll Morton started composing his own music, a band led by the eighteen-year-old Creole cornetist Freddie Keppard was scheduled to play for a lawn party at the home of Mr. and Mrs. Omar Bechet at 414 Girod Street in New Orleans. Their son Leonard, a promising student of dentistry, was turning twenty-one. There was to be music and dancing on the lawn and plenty of Creole food.

The clarinetist, George Baquet, was late for the engagement and, since the guests had begun to arrive, Keppard and the rest of the band set up in the kitchen and started to play as best they could without him. Then, from somewhere inside the house, a clarinet joined in. "Who the hell is that?" Keppard asked, and went looking for the source of the sound. Eventually, he found the Bechets' youngest son, Sidney, perched in his brother's dentist chair in a darkened room and playing as loudly as he could. The sturdy, round-faced boy was just nine years old and entirely self-taught.

Keppard asked him to come out into the kitchen. "I'll never forget that feeling I had," Bechet remembered, "playing with those men. . . . They were masters. . . . They really gave me the feeling of being discontented until I'd be able to work regular with them. Oh, it was grand!" George Baquet eventually turned up—he'd been playing in a parade. He took out his clarinet, Bechet recalled, "and he ran his hand over my head and . . . just laughed. And he kept me there all evening, playing right along beside of him. That night, I guess I was the richest kid in New Orleans. You couldn't have bought me for a sky full of new moons."

Baquet offered to give the prodigy lessons in exchange for pouches of Bull Durham chewing tobacco. Other clarinetists tried to help him, too. Classically trained Luis "Papa" Tio sought to persuade

Sidney Bechet, already on the road at nineteen. He had, he said, a lifelong "need to be moving."

The Eagle Band which, the bassist George "Pops" Foster said, "played hot all the time." As with a good many New Orleans outfits, its personnel often changed. In this 1916 version, Frankie Dusen is the trombonist and leader and Louis "Big Eye" Nelson plays the clarinet. The cornetist was Buddy Petit who, Danny Barker recalled, played with such power that during parades admirers "would be ten deep around [him] as he walked along."

him to avoid the raw new kind of music now being heard in the streets of his city. "No! No! No!" he told the boy. "We do not like to bark like a dog or meow like a cat!" But Bechet preferred the big "ratty" sound of Big Eye Nelson to Tio's "legitimate" tone: "Some musicians played . . . prettily," he said, "but I like the playing that makes me want to dance." From the first he was too impatient to take instruction from anyone for long. Nor could anyone make him study theory. "He wouldn't learn notes," Nelson remembered, "but he was my best scholar."

The boy's parents had hoped music would be a hobby not a profession—as it was in many Creole families, as it had been with all four of his older brothers. They sug-

gested he become a bricklayer or perhaps a hairdresser, instead of a musician. "We didn't want to jeopardize our family by mixing with the rough element," Leonard Bechet remembered. "We worried a lot about Sidney when he'd be out playing."

The boy didn't care. All he wanted to do was play—and hang around the musicians decades older than he whom he already considered his peers. Still wearing short pants, Bechet was soon sitting in with some of the best bands in New Orleans. At fourteen, he joined forces with another Creole prodigy, cornetist Buddy Petit, and formed a seven-piece band called the Young Olympians, marching in parades, performing at picnics, and cutting a wide swath

among the girls who came out to see them. "We could never keep our hands on that Sidney," Big Eye Nelson once admitted. "Regular little devil running off down the alley after them little women."

The Bechets did everything they could to dissuade their boy from pursuing music. They got a municipal magistrate to order him to stay in school—he paid no attention—and when they locked up his clarinet he either borrowed someone else's or talked whoever had hired him for the evening into putting up enough money to get one out of pawn.

At fifteen or so, he signed on with the hardest-driving outfit in town, the Eagle Band, led by the cornetist Willie "Bunk"

Johnson. Creole musicians, Bechet said, were "damn fine . . . some of the best for ragtime; but when it came to the blues you couldn't beat Bunk or the Eagle Orchestra." This was a "gut-bucket band," Bechet remembered, "a low-down band" and virtually unbeatable in a street contest. When a downtown Creole band strayed across Canal Street into uptown territory, one Creole musician remembered, the only thing to do was "get out of that neighborhood if you see the Eagle Band coming."

Bechet loved it, loved playing at rough joints including Funky Butt Hall, where Buddy Bolden had once held sway, and also loved the worldly ways of its leader, whose heroic drinking and constant womanizing Bechet eagerly learned to emulate. He soon left home to devote himself full-time to music and the musician's peripatetic life, finding quarters where he could—"Tonight he might be here," a friend remembered, "and tomorrow night there"—and playing three and four engagements a day, so many that he sometimes fell asleep on the streetcars that took him from one to the next.

Later, members of Bechet's family would be philosophical about the life he had chosen to lead. "A person has to go through all that rough stuff like Sidney went through to play music like him," Leonard Bechet once told an interviewer. "You have to play with all varieties of people. You have to play real *hard* when you play for Negroes. You got to *go* some to avoid their criticism. . . . If you do, you get that drive. Bolden had it. Bunk Johnson had it."

Sidney Bechet had it, too, and he expressed it with such passion and volume that it sometimes seemed about to tear his instrument apart. "He was always fiery," said Peter Bocage. "It's his makeup. He don't sit still one minute. There's always something he's got to be doing. And when he plays he's the same way. He's fired up all the time."

Bechet quickly earned two reputations. As a difficult personality—"powerful mean," he once admitted, and unwilling to work in any band in which anyone was paid a penny more than he was; and as a clarinet player unlike any other, in New Orleans or anywhere else, who saw music as something like perpetual combat in which he was determined always to come out on top. New Orleans brass band music was an ensemble art, but the cornetist had generally been the first among equals. It was he who played the lead, stating the theme around which the clarinet was expected to weave obbligato embellishments. But second best was never enough for Sidney Bechet. He tried playing lead cornet himself for a time—and was said by those who heard him to have been as loud and forceful as anyone in town. But even on clarinet he performed with such power that he routinely overshadowed cornetists accustomed to the hero's role. "When Sidney was playing . . . around 1914 to 1916," his fellow clarinetist Albert Nicholas said, "he outplayed them all."

Soon, being the most admired clarinetist in his hometown didn't satisfy him, either. "There was so many fine musicianers around New Orleans then, so much a man could learn from," he remembered. "But I was getting restless. I'd been hearing so much about up North, about this place and that place. I was having an itch to go." An enterprising young New Orleans pianist and songwriter named Clarence Williams gave him his first chance to see the wider world. Williams thought big. By traveling from town to town with a quartet that performed comedy acts as well as playing his music, he was sure he could boost the sales of his song sheets at the five-and-dime stores that peddled them. Things didn't work out that way. He had neglected to ensure enough bookings to keep his little troupe in business. "We'd heard all about how the North was freer, and we were wanting to go real bad," Bechet said. "But my God, where do we end up but in Texas. . . . We played dances, shows and one-night stands. . . . For a while there it was nothing but one dime store after another." The quartet

Edward "Kid" Ory, playing trombone, second from left, and his Woodland Band, 1905. Ory grew up on the Woodland Plantation in La Place, Louisiana, less than thirty miles from New Orleans. As a boy, he fashioned homemade instruments from cigar boxes and fishing line for a band of playmates. At thirteen, he organized fish fries and played at baseball games to raise money for factory-made instruments. His Creole family, like Jelly Roll Morton's and Sidney Bechet's, initially took a dim view of his becoming a musician but he paid no attention: "I couldn't see anything but music. . . . The girls was worrying me. . . . I was sure if I learned music, I can get a girl, you know."

eventually fell apart. Bechet joined a carnival, which got him only as far as a little redneck town near Beaumont where black strangers were warned to move on by nightfall and black citizens were forbidden to leave their homes after dark. There, after playing a dance in someone's house, Bechet somehow found himself walking along the railroad tracks after midnight with what he called "an interfering white man . . . who won't stay with his own and won't let you be." Words were exchanged. Bechet felled the man with a piece of wood, then jumped a freight to Galveston, where one of his brothers was living. There, he befriended a Mexican guitarist, with whom he was picked up late one night for being drunk and disorderly. Bechet escaped being brutalized in jail only because his captors wore themselves out beating and kicking his companion senseless. Then, he sat listening in the darkness as his fellow prisoners sang a blues:

> Tied in a hundred feet of chain,
> Every link of the chain was initial to
>   his name
> Warden come early that morning for
>   him to be hung
> On account of something he hadn't
>   done.

"Oh my God, that was a blues," Bechet remembered. "The way they sang it there, it was something you would send down to earth if it had been given to you to be God. What you'd send to your son in trouble if he was on earth and you was in Heaven."

Bechet's brother bailed him out the next morning and he made his way back to New Orleans as fast as he could. But as soon as he got the chance, Sidney Bechet would be on his way again. He would remain restless and dissatisfied all his life. No musician in the whole history of jazz had a more powerful personality, and none would be able to express it more powerfully on his horn. But that same personality would trip him up again and again. "Somehow, there's just no need to go looking for trouble," he wrote.

"The way it is, trouble comes looking for you." Over the coming years, it would come often looking for Sidney Bechet.

BETTER THAN THE REST

By 1906, Buddy Bolden was the best-known black musician in New Orleans, hailed as *King* Bolden by the children who gathered in front of his home on First Street each morning, just to hear him practice. "He blew his horn so loud," one of them recalled, "he'd blow everyone out of the house." But there were other, younger claimants to his crown, most notably young Freddie Keppard whose ability to play loud may even have exceeded Bolden's. Bolden had always been a heavy drinker: "[He] drank all the whiskey he could find or anybody else could find," Jelly Roll Morton remembered. Soon, he started to develop headaches, began to talk to himself, quarreled with the members of his band, seemed increasingly agitated and frightened of everything. His mother did what she could to calm his fears but nothing seemed to help.

On March 2 of that year, his name appeared in the newspapers for the first and only time in his life.

Thinking that he was being drugged by his mother, Charles Bolden, a negro, living at 2302 First street, jumped out of bed yesterday afternoon while in a state of dementia and struck her over the head with a water pitcher. Bolden, who is a musician, has been sick for some time. His mother was by his bedside yesterday afternoon giving what succor she could when suddenly his mind was carried away with the belief that she was administering some deadly drug to him. Grabbing the water pitcher, he broke it over his mother's head, inflicting a scalp wound, which was pronounced not serious.

He spent a day or two in detention and seemed all right again after his release. But he soon proved so quarrelsome, so unreliable, so suspicious, one musician remembered, that his band fell apart and "all his good friends left him." Challenged to a contest at Globe Hall with a mostly Creole band led by cornetist Manuel Perez and his old friend Big Eye Nelson, he failed to turn up at the appointed time. On Labor Day, he set out to play in the big annual parade, just as he had for years. But somewhere along the line of march he abruptly walked away from the other musicians and went home. He would never play his horn in public again.

On March 13, 1907, a little over a year after his first arrest, his mother again had to call the police. She was afraid her son would hurt her—or himself. In April, he was locked up in the State Insane Asylum at Jackson. He was just twenty-nine years old and would never leave the institution. One of the doctors in charge later described his condition:

Accessible and answers fairly well. Paranoid delusions, also grandiose. Auditory hallucinations and visual. Talks to self. Much reaction. Picks things off wall. Tears his clothes. Insight and judgment lacking. . . . [L]ooks deteriorated, but memory is good. Has a string of talk that is incoherent. Hears the voices of people that bothered him before he came here. . . . DIAGNOSIS: *Dementia praecox,* paranoid type.

No longer able to recognize his own mother when she came to visit, too disturbed even to play in the Colored Patient's Band, Bolden would live on for twenty-five years, oblivious to what happened to the music he had been among the first to play. Sometimes, though, the chaplain remembered, he would ask to borrow a cornet and blow a chorus or two—enough so that "you could tell he was better than the rest."

A lull on Canal Street during the 1910 Mardi Gras Procession, still remembered in New Orleans because, for the first time in the history of the annual revels, it snowed that day. The musicians in the foreground belong to Papa Jack Laine's Reliance Marching Band.

THE GIFT

*One day in late 1912, before Sidney Bechet had
left his parents' home to fend for himself, Bunk
Johnson had turned up at the Bechets's door, asking for him. He'd heard a boys' quartet singing
for pennies on a street corner in black Storyville,
Johnson said: Sidney had to come and hear "how
they sing and harmonize." Bechet agreed to go with
him. The boys were "real good," he remembered,
so good he asked them to come home with him for
dinner. He wanted his family to hear them sing.*

*The bright-eyed eleven-year-old who sang tenor
said he would love to come—the prospect of a good
Creole meal was very pleasing—but the soles of
his shoes were so full of holes that it would be
painful for him to walk all the way across town to
get there. Bechet, only fifteen himself but already
earning a grown-up's wages, grandly tossed the*

The Original Tuxedo Jazz Band played for white picnickers—and every other kind of audience in New Orleans. Oscar
"Papa" Celestin, the cornetist, and trombonist William "Bébé" Ridgley shared its leadership until 1925, when Celestin
formed his own Tuxedo Jazz Orchestra that specialized in playing for dances. He was a mentor to a host of fine musicians, including Louis Armstrong, who recalled the Tuxedo Band as "the hottest in town."

boy a fifty-cent piece to get his shoes resoled, then hurried home again to tell his mother there'd be guests for dinner.

The eleven-year-old pocketed the coin. Neither he nor his friends ever bothered to turn up at the Bechets. "I remember running around with a lot of bad boys," the boy wrote many years later, "which did a lot of crazy things." He was known by the pimps and prostitutes who were his closest neighbors as "Little Louis," but his full name was Louis Armstrong, and the story of his rise is as astonishing, as American—and ultimately as inexplicable—as Abraham Lincoln's.

"My whole life has been happiness," he wrote toward the end of it. "Through all the misfortunes . . . I did not plan anything. Life was there for me, and I accepted it." Raised mostly on the turbulent streets of black Storyville, and surrounded from birth by enough vice and violence to fill a sociologist's file cabinet, he took part in some of it, observed all of it, made no easy judgments about any of it, and managed miraculously to incorporate it all into his art—the good and the bad, the ugly as well as the beautiful. In the process, his unrivaled genius, his "gift," he called it, helped turn jazz into a soloist's art—influenced every singer, every instrumentalist, every *artist,* who

came after him. For more than five decades, he would make everyone who heard him feel that no matter how bad things got, everything was bound to turn out all right, after all.

He was born on August 4, 1901—not, as he himself always believed, on July 4, 1900—at 723 Jane Alley in a section of New Orleans so violent it was called "The Battlefield." His father, William Armstrong, who stoked boilers at a turpentine factory when he could find work, abandoned his children early and only rarely saw them afterward. "We had no father," Armstrong remembered.

His mother—Mary Albert, known as Mayann—was just fifteen, a refugee from the sugarcane fields. She sometimes worked as a prostitute to support herself and left her son in her own mother's charge for the first five years of his life. But after she took him back again and moved him and his younger sister Beatrice (later known as Mama Lucy) into her single rented room at Liberty and Perdido Streets in the heart of black Storyville, she regularly took her children to church every Sunday and taught them independence and self-respect. "[S]he held her head up at all

times," Armstrong recalled. "She never envied no one, or anything they have. I guess I inherited that . . . from Mayann."

That would remain Armstrong's attitude all his life: "I say, never worry what the other fella have, as long as you're having a nice time in your way," he would tell an interviewer when his was one of the most famous faces on earth. "Things ain't never going to get that bad where I can't enjoy a good meal at least once a day and if I have to take a bath in that tin tub again, I'm *still* gonna wash my ass."

As a small boy he was left pretty much on his own to tumble through the muddy streets, dodging wagons and horses, playing and squabbling with other boys, chasing after the music that would become his life. Brass bands often blared their way through the neighborhood, and Funky Butt Hall was just a few steps from his mother's room. There, on Saturday nights, the musicians played on the sidewalk out front for half an hour or so to help draw a crowd for the dance that began inside at sundown. Louis would stand alongside the other children then, listening and dancing, and after the musicians and the grown-up dancers had filed inside—"It was a real rough place," Armstrong remembered. "You'd have to take your razor with you, 'cause you might have to scratch somebody before you leave"—he peered through the cracks in the hall's weathered wall and watched all that went on inside: the blues-drenched music, the sweating dancers who "got down to the floor and wiggled" when they weren't clinging closely to one another in the sensual slow drag, and the fights that sometimes sent everybody spilling out into the street again.

> All of 'em was huggin' their chick you know with their hat on their arm. That's the only time they take their hat off, and they put it on their arm and dance with the chick. . . . they ain't gonna drop it. And nobody better touch it, cause there'll be the

Louis Armstrong was born in this battered house at the corner of Jane Alley and Perdido Street in 1901. The photograph was taken sixty-two years later, shortly before the heedless city tore the building down.

Nineteen-year-old Louis Armstrong, his mother Mayann, and his sister Beatrice pose for a New Orleans photographer in 1920.

The Morris Karnofsky family that treated the young Louis Armstrong with unexpected kindness, photographed in 1917

damndest fight you ever had in your life . . . if you touch that Stetson. They'd wait till the dance is over and the guy would walk up and say, "Did you touch my hat, partner?" and he'd say, "Yeah." "Wop!" he'd hit him right in the chops. And the battle royal's on.

The heroes of his neighborhood were pimps and gamblers. "I was brought up around them people," he said. "They lived happily and they didn't have a whole lot of money, but they . . . always had a little pad and a clean shirt on, collar and tie and that blue suit'd been pressed so much it looked like a mirror, but it's sharp just the same." Armstrong sometimes speculated on what he might have become if he hadn't resolved early on to be a musician: a small-time gambler, he finally decided, who wouldn't "steal too much."

Mayann sent her boy to the Fisk School for Boys on Franklin Street, the same school Buddy Bolden had attended twenty years earlier, but before and after school, start-

ing at the age of seven and continuing for four years, he worked for a Russian Jewish immigrant named Morris Karnofsky, who collected rags and bones and old bottles and delivered coal to the prostitutes of Storyville. Louis rode in the wagon, blowing a long tin horn to let clients know the Karnofskys were coming. He especially enjoyed carrying buckets of coal into the cribs, he recalled, because he could hear music from the nearby honky-tonks and also get "my little peek" at the women waiting for customers in their underwear.

He liked the Karnofskys, too. "Every night we would come in late . . . from buying old rags and bones," he remembered. "When they would have their supper they would fix a plate for me, saying, 'You've worked—might as well eat here with us . . . by the time you get home it will be way too late for your supper.' " After dinner, as Mrs. Karnofsky sang lullabies to her infant son and the family joined in, "so soft and sweet," Louis would be given a part to sing, too. In a world in which most of

the whites he encountered were at best contemptuous, the hospitality of the Karnofskys was a revelation. "They were always warm and kind to me, which was very noticeable to me—just a kid who could use a little word of kindness, . . . just starting out in the world." Because of that kindness, Louis Armstrong would always retain a special affection for Jews—they had "wonderful souls," he said; all his life he would wear a Star of David, and when he finally settled down he saw to it that his breadbox was perpetually stocked with matzohs.

At about the age of ten and "after blowing my tin horn so long," Armstrong wrote, "I wondered how I would do blowing a real horn." When he spotted a battered cornet in a pawnshop window he asked his employer if he would advance him five dollars to buy it. He did, and Armstrong paid him back from his earnings at fifty cents a week.

The little cornet was real dirty and had turned real black. Morris (one of the Karnofsky boys) cleaned [it] with some brass polish and poured some oil all through it. . . . He requested me to play a tune on it. Although I could not play a good tune, Morris applauded me just the same which made me feel very good. As a young boy coming up, the people whom I worked for were very much concerned about my future in music. They could see that I had music in my soul. They really wanted me to be something in life. And music was it. Appreciating my every effort.

When Armstrong was eleven, and despite the kindness of the Karnofskys, he left his job, dropped out of school in the middle of the third grade, and began to drift into trouble. "You must realize it was very shaky . . . during my days growing up in New Orleans," he wrote. "You had to fight and do a lot of ungodly things to keep from being trampled on," enough ungodly things evi-

The Colored Waif's Home Brass Band, 1913. Twelve-year-old Louis Armstrong sits proudly just behind the band's manager, Peter Davis. After Davis allowed him to join the band, Armstrong recalled, "I was in seventh heaven. My ambition had been realized."

dently so that his name became familiar to the police of the Third Ward.

Music still fascinated him, though, and he soon organized the street-corner quartet that had so impressed Sidney Bechet, singing and dancing for tips while keeping a sharp eye out for truant officers and policemen. "A drunk [would] come along and maybe give us a dollar," Armstrong said. "The grown folks were working for a dollar a day." In the early hours of New Year's Day, 1913, at the corner of Rampart and Perdido, his sharp eye failed him. Years later, he offered his own version of what happened. Earlier that winter he had noticed that the latest in the long series of "stepfathers" who moved in with Mayann over the years owned a .38 revolver, which he kept in a trunk beneath her bed. On New Year's Eve—when Louis and the members of his quartet planned to stay out late, hoping for especially big tips from cheer-ful revelers—it struck Louis as a fine idea to spirit the weapon out of the house so that at the stroke of midnight he could pull it out of his shirt and make his own contri-bution to the spectacular din with which the city customarily hailed the coming of the New Year:

Everybody shot their pistols, shotguns, firecrackers, roman candles. . . . And we went up Rampart Street singing

Johnny Fischer's Marching Band swings into action along North Rampart Street in New Orleans, about 1910. The two small boys hurrying to keep up at the right are the first sign of the cheering, dancing second line that will soon engulf the musicians as they move through the streets. "For the least significant occasion, there would be some music," the guitarist Danny Barker remembered. "That's why so many kids in New Orleans took up music. They heard it all the time."

"My Brazilian Beauty," that was our theme . . . "My Brazilian beauty, down on the Amazon, that's where my love has gone, gone, gone. . . ." And just then a little old cat across the street pulls out a pistol . . . a kid's pistol [and fires]. The cats in my quarter said, "Get him Dipper," and I said, "OK"— "Voom! Voom! Voom!" Aww, it was fun. And then all of a sudden two arms hugged me, and I looked up and there was a big tall detective. Boy, I thought the world was coming to an end . . . and I cried, "Oh Mister, . . . let me alone, just take the pistol."

The policeman took the pistol—and the boy. He spent a cold, frightened night in jail and the next morning, because the juvenile judge considered him "an old offender," he found himself sentenced to an indeterminate term in the Colored Waif's Home.

It seemed a grim place, at least at first, run along strict military lines: runaways received more than one hundred lashes, administered while the other boys held the fugitive down. For the first two weeks, Louis was so anxious and homesick he barely ate. But even in the Waif's Home, New Orleans music was inescapable, Armstrong remembered, and as he lay in his dormitory bed on Saturday nights the sounds of Freddie Keppard's cornet sometimes drifted in through the open window from one nearby lawn party or another. "Them cats was playing so fine," he recalled. "Just relaxed music."

He wanted to play that relaxed music, too. The pride of the school was its uni-formed marching band, which raised funds by playing engagements all around the city. (One reason for the band's popularity was that, unlike the members of grown-up bands, its musicians were so happy to be out on the streets again even if only for an afternoon that they never complained when asked to march long distances; a veteran remembered once walking twenty-five miles in the blazing sun.)

Armstrong desperately wanted to join, but the music director, Peter Davis, barred him for weeks, convinced that no boy from the "Battlefield" could ever amount to any-thing. "I had a bad stamp," Armstrong recalled. "I was a bad boy running around with bad kids in a bad neighborhood." He did everything he could think of to persuade Davis to take a chance on him, tapping out rhythms with a pair of chair rungs, breaking into "comedy dances" whenever the band began to play.

Finally, the director relented, allowing Armstrong first to try the tambourine, then the alto horn and bugle, finally the cornet. He swiftly mastered all the best-loved marching tunes—"Home, Sweet Home," "Maryland, My Maryland," and "Ole Miss" —and soon developed what an older musician called a "good solid tone" remarkable for one so young. In June, Davis took him aside to tell him he was now the leader of the band. "I jumped straight in the air," Armstrong remembered, "and ran to the mess room to tell the boys the good news."

Soon, the drummer Zutty Singleton remembered, Armstrong's reputation began to build beyond the Waif's Home.

> Some of the fellows that were sent there would come back and say how fine this Louis Armstrong was playing. Then I saw Louis playing in a band at a picnic. He was marching along with the band, so we got up real close to him to see if he was actually playing those notes. We didn't believe he could learn to play in that short time. I can still remember he was playing "Maryland, My Maryland." And he sure was swingin' out that melody.

When Armstrong led the band through his old neighborhood for the first time that summer, he remembered, "all the whores, gamblers, thieves and beggars were waiting for the band because they knew that Mayann's son would be in it." But, he said, "they had never dreamed that I would be playing the cornet, blowing it as good as I could. They ran to wake up Mama . . . so she could see me go by." The onlookers—Armstrong called them "the *sporting* crowd"—were so proud to see that "Little Louis," someone from their neighborhood, was doing so well, he remembered, that they filled his hat and those of the other boys with enough nickels and dimes and

Freddie Keppard—known as "King" Keppard to his fans—in the uniform of his own Olympia Orchestra, photographed before circumstances forced his exit from New Orleans. In addition to being a gifted and powerful cornet player, an admiring Sidney Bechet remembered, Keppard "was a hell of a go-round man."

quarters to buy uniforms and brand-new instruments for the band.

As Armstrong played and practiced within the walls of the Waif's Home, times outside were getting hard. Ships now shunned New Orleans in favor of ports further east, Biloxi and Miami. There were fewer and fewer jobs for musicians, black or white.

Then, in the early morning hours of Easter Sunday, 1913, the proprietors of the Tuxedo dance hall and the rival 102 Ranch just across Franklin Street in Storyville got into a shootout that left both of them dead and several hapless witnesses wounded. The city closed all the dance halls for several months. Some musicians abandoned music altogether.

New Orleans music on the move: Papa Jack Laine's Reliance Marching Band, left, provides the music for the smartly turned-out members of the West End fire department at the 1912 Firemen's Parade in Biloxi, Mississippi. The West End district of New Orleans was adjacent to a resort of that name on the south shore of Lake Pontchartrain celebrated for weekend band concerts. They would be immortalized sixteen years later in Louis Armstrong's recording of King Oliver's "West End Blues."

By the summer of 1914, Freddie Keppard and George Baquet—who had been playing at the Tuxedo when the shooting began—had made it all the way to Los Angeles. There, with five other New Orleans refugees, they formed the Original Creole Orchestra and were happy to get a night's work playing between boxing matches at Doyle's Arena. The fight crowd's reaction to their music that night was decidedly mixed. A local sportswriter declared it a "disgusting exhibition. . . . While waiting for [the fighters] someone connected with the management had an unhappy inspiration to allow a company of negroes, perpetrating a vile imitation of music, to enter the ring and insult the audience by very obviously begging for coins."

But George Baquet remembered that when they broke into a New Orleans version of a Broadway tune called "In Far-off Mandalay" from ringside and Keppard stepped up onto a bench to blow his cornet, using his derby as a mute, the whole crowd began to sway in time with the music. The band was made to climb into the ring and perform another number; a fighter named Battling Brant, waiting for his introduction, was so excited by their playing he broke into a dance; and afterwards a representative of the vaudeville impresario Alec Pantages who had happened to be in the crowd offered the group a contract. He didn't care what kind of an act they put on, he said, as long as he had that music.

Keppard and the Original Creole Orchestra would tour vaudeville theaters for the next four years. Traveling from Winnipeg to Brooklyn, Boston to Salt Lake City, they put on the kind of show white audiences then expected from black entertainers, corked-up, cracking jokes, dressed as countrified field hands. But everywhere they went, they, like Jelly Roll Morton, played the big-city music of New Orleans.

By the time Freddie Keppard and his band began touring in vaudeville in the summer of 1914, thirteen-year-old Louis Armstrong was back on the street. His good behavior and startling musicianship had something to do with it. But so had the intervention of two white strangers. For a poor, wayward black boy to get a second chance in that place and time, influential whites had to be persuaded to take an interest in him. Powerless to do anything to free her boy on her own, his mother had asked the family whose washing she did to vouch for him, while his absentee father persuaded the man who ran the turpentine plant in which he sometimes worked to intercede with the judge on Louis's behalf.

It was a lesson Louis Armstrong never forgot. Much later in his life, when people asked him to explain his stubborn loyalty to his white manager Joe Glaser, whose crude ways at one time or another alienated a good many of the people with whom he came in contact, Armstrong liked to recall advice given to him by a black bouncer back in Storyville: "Always keep a white man behind you that'll put his hand on your shoulder and say, 'That's *my* nigger.' " To some, that smacked of subservience; to Armstrong, it was simple realism. The bouncer's clear-eyed counsel had only served to reaffirm what life in New Orleans had taught him. In a world run by whites, a black man, no matter how gifted he might be, would always need protection to get ahead.

Armstrong was still scuffling to support his mother and sister. Over the next few years he would work at any number of jobs to put food on the table: he sold newspapers—and sometimes fought white boys who considered such sales their exclusive territory; he unloaded banana boats and downed so many bananas on the sly that in later years he could not abide even the smell of one; he bought up broken lumps of coal for resale at a nickel a bucket; he rifled through barrels of food discarded by produce houses, looking for unspoiled fruit and vegetables to sell to restaurants—even dipped his face in flour, entered an amateur con-

TO PUT A WEEPING IN THEIR HEARTS

The Square Deal Boys gather a steadily growing crowd as they make their way down Dumaine Street toward a funeral home, 1946.

More than three decades after Louis Armstrong marched in his first funeral parades, New Orleans musicians still followed the same time-honored form. They played a mournful hymn on the way to the cemetery, the drummer Baby Dodds recalled, "to put a weeping in their hearts." They had no duties during the actual burial and on hot afternoons, as the minister spoke at the graveside, some of the men would scatter for refreshments. It was up to the drummer, Dodds remembered, to get them back in line when the time came.

> When they put the body in the ground and say, "ashes to ashes"—well, that's the drummer's cue right there.... And the snare drummer alone goes out into the middle of the street and he'd start to roll and he rolled loud. . . . And you could see guys jumpin' over graves and comin' out of people's houses and out of bar rooms and, oh, just flyin'. And it just gave me so much pleasure to see those guys that had overstayed themselves & come out runnin'. Some of them with a sandwich in their hand or a jelly roll stickin' out where they're tryin' to chew fast and get it down. Some guys with some whiskey in their hands. And some guys kiss their woman and say, "I'll see you, so long, goodbye" and the door slam, BAM! See 'em runnin' down the steps, some guys with no [uniform] cap, that had left their cap, had to go back & get it. . . .

Then, reunited, the men would march away from the cemetery playing something joyous, like "Oh, Didn't He Ramble," in celebration of the departed's entry into heaven.

test at the Iroquois Theater, and took his prize money home to his mother.

And all the while, he looked for opportunities to play the music that now meant everything to him. "I remember once when Louis came out to Lincoln Park in New Orleans to listen to the Kid Ory Band," the cornetist Mutt Carey said. "I was playing trumpet with the Kid then and I let Louis sit in on my chair. Now, at that time, I was the 'Blues King' of New Orleans, and when Louis played that day he played more blues than I ever heard in my life. It never did strike my mind that blues could be interpreted so many different ways."

It was Armstrong's soulful blues playing that got him his first real jobs, working in three-piece bands, first at a honky-tonk owned by a Frenchman named Henry Ponce, and then at the Sicilian Henry Matranga's, both in black Storyville. Every night there was rough, Armstrong recalled, but Saturday night was special. The streets were crowded with men in overalls, in from the sawmills and levees and cane and cotton fields, with a week's pay in their pockets and looking for a good time. Some carried .45's; most carried knives or razors. The sporting crowd that profited from their

visits was rough and often violent, too— "a notorious group," Armstrong remembered—that included Cheeky Black, Funky Stella and Cross-Eyed Louise, Long Head Willie Logan, Roughhouse Camel, Cocaine Buddy, Mary Meat Market, and Black Benny Williams, a six-foot-six sometime parade drummer who acted as the boy's protector for a time. Armstrong now had neighborhood nicknames of his own, among them "Hammock Face," "Rhythm Jaws," "Dippermouth," and "Satchelmouth."

Each of the tonks in which he played had three rooms, Armstrong remembered: a bar, a room given over to a card game called cotch, and another "for dancing—doing that slow drag, close together, humping up one shoulder—maybe throw a little wiggle into it." Pine benches lined the walls. Armstrong and his companions played from a bandstand so small they could not turn around. "Drinks were cheap—and strong. Used to get beer in tin lard buckets and it was *cold*— liked to see that sweat on the outside."

The men were expected to play all night. After four in the morning, Armstrong remembered, the whores, powdered with pink chalk they had scented with fifteen-cent perfume, would begin to trickle in,

"big stockings full of dollars—and give us a tip to pay the blues. . . . [T]hey was attractive and very encouraging to look at." They were also not to be trifled with. He once watched as a celebrated prostitute named Mary Jack the Bear and a younger rival remembered only as Deborah battled one another in the middle of Gravier Street, slashing each other with knives until the faces of both women were masks of blood.

Early one Sunday morning, Armstrong himself came close to a violent end. As he and Henry Ponce lounged in the doorway of Ponce's tonk talking about the blues he'd just finished playing, several men appeared across the street, all of them employees of Ponce's archrival, a Sicilian club owner named Joe Segretta. Suddenly, one of them pulled a pistol and opened fire. Bullets whistled past Armstrong's head. Ponce drew his gun and fired back. His attackers ran and Ponce ran after them, firing as he went. When the smoke cleared, three of his would-be assassins lay writhing in the street. As friends rushed to Armstrong's side, asking if he'd been hit, he fainted. "I continued to work in tonks" after that, he wrote, but "I was always on the alert."

———————

Armstrong's growing reputation as a musician did nothing to shield him from the indignities of daily life for black citizens of New Orleans. One evening he was having a beer with friends in Henry Matranga's place, he remembered, "when Captain Jackson, the meanest guy on the police force," burst in with several other officers. Someone had just been robbed on Rampart Street, he said, so everybody in the tonk was going to jail. Protesting their innocence, Armstrong and the others were marched to the Parish Prison, just a couple of blocks away.

There, he found himself surrounded by convicted criminals with names like Dirty Dog and Steel Arm Johnny who were awaiting transfer to state prison. Sore Dick, the black "captain of the yard," made him sweep the prison yard with a broom over and over again. "All newcomers, I later found out, had to sweep out the yard whether it needed it or not. That is the way they get you in the groove before you start serving a term." Armstrong spent several days behind bars fearing the worst before Henry Matranga's lawyers arranged for his release. "It was part of a system that always worked in those days," he said. "Nevertheless, I'll never forget that experience as a stay-a-whiler with those long-termers."

He never forgot what happened the next day, either. It happened to be Mardi Gras, and members of the Zulu Social Aid and Pleasure Club, the oldest black krewe in the city, were marching through the Uptown streets in blackface just as they did every year. The club had been formed by men from Armstrong's own neighborhood in 1909 to parody the white krewes that otherwise dominated the festivities. It was made up, he wrote, of "coal-cart drivers, bar tenders, waiters, hustlers, etc. But they loved each other . . . and put their best foot forward." They were the boisterous escorts of a mule-drawn float that carried the gaudy King of the Zulus, also in blackface, who was meant to be a grotesque caricature of "Rex," Carnival's white king. The

Joe "King" Oliver, about 1905

King's costume varied every year—a woman's evening gown instead of Rex's flowing robes, a hambone in place of a jeweled scepter—but it was "the dream of every boy in the neighborhood," Armstrong said, to be chosen King and he had been especially proud as a small boy when one of his several stepfathers had been picked for the honor.

White onlookers thought the marchers hilarious. Some members of the city's black establishment already thought them a grotesque embarrassment. But to Armstrong and his friends and neighbors from the poorest part of town, parading in blackface provided a rare sanctioned opportunity to lampoon white stereotyping and parody white society all at the same time. Best of all from Armstrong's point of view this particular year, a local character named Garfield Carter—known in black Storyville as "Papa Gar"—dared to parade alongside the Zulu King's float disguised as the notorious Captain Jackson himself, strutting along in open blackfaced mockery of the man who had put Armstrong and so many of his friends in jail. At the sight of him, Armstrong remembered, the crowds

in black Storyville went wild with laughter: "It's a funny thing," he wrote, "how life can be such a drag one minute and a solid sender the next."

Armstrong was still working in tonks when he came to the attention of the man who would become his mentor, Joe "King" Oliver—"the top cornet in New Orleans, the first big musician in my life and still . . . the best I ever met." Oliver was then playing with the trombonist Kid Ory at Pete Lala's in Storyville and when it closed at midnight it became his habit to come and listen to the youthful Armstrong.

"I loved Joe Oliver," Armstrong said., "He did more for young musicians . . . than anyone I know of." That was not his reputation. He was "rough as pig-iron," Ory said. Short and barrel-chested, he weighed well over two hundred pounds and because he had lost the sight in one eye and, inside or out, always wore a derby hat cocked at an angle to hide it, he was known as "ol' Cocky"— but few dared use his nickname in his presence. He kept a brick near him on the bandstand to bang on the floor if his men didn't heed the stomping foot with which he started and stopped each number, and to keep would-be rivals from seeing just what he was doing on the bandstand he sometimes covered his fingers with a handkerchief. A musician who played with him a few years later remembered that rehearsals were sometimes accompanied by a certain tension.

> The King would walk in with the music on his arm and his gun in the bosom of his coat. He would throw everything down on the table and look around to see if everybody was there. Then he would pick up his gun and ask, "Is everybody here?" Everybody reported yes, we were there, then he would put his gun back on the table, and the rehearsal would go on.

According to the pianist Richard M. Jones, who claimed to have been an eyewitness,

Oliver had been appearing at a cabaret called the Abadie at Marais and Bienville, when he snatched the crown as the city's finest cornetist from Buddy Bolden's heir, Freddie Keppard. For days, Oliver had been irritated that Keppard was drawing big crowds to another club just down the street. Finally, he could stand it no longer. "Get in B-flat," the pianist remembered being told. "He didn't even mention a tune." Then, Oliver stalked outside, "lifted his horn to his lips and blew the most beautiful stuff I have ever heard. People started pouring out of the other spots along the street to see who was blowing all that horn. Before long our place was full and Joe came in, smiling, and said, 'Now, that ——— won't bother me no more.' "

To ballyhoo their upcoming appearances, Oliver and Kid Ory and their band often performed from the back of a mule-drawn furniture wagon as it moved through the streets. Louis Armstrong described the contests that frequently followed:

> The wagon would pull up in the neighborhood and start playing. They was always catchy tunes. . . . People came out the doors from all over the neighborhood. . . . Now Kid Ory and Joe Oliver's band liable to be playing for one dance, and here come the Imperial Band, playing for another dance, so they'd pull up together, and that's where that bucking contest used to come. . . . They chained the wheels to these furniture wagons so they couldn't move. Just stay there and blow, and the crowd would applaud. . . . Different tunes, trying to outplay each other. King Oliver and Ory used to cut them all. And after they'd pull off, Ory used to play a little thing . . . on the trombone, people would just roll [on the ground laughing], 'cause, they know what he's sayin,' you know . . . "Kiss my fucking ass."

But in the end, it was neither Joe Oliver's volume nor his competitiveness that pulled in the crowds; it was his craft. Oliver was a master of mood. He could play roughly enough to suit the whores and pimps of Storyville and sweetly enough to please white dancers at Tulane University. And he was a showman, besides; the finest manipulator of mutes in the business, he employed a whole arsenal of objects—water glasses, buckets, kazoos that fit into the bell of his horn—anything to make his cornet growl or groan, crow like a rooster or cry like a baby. "Joe could make his horn sound like a holy roller meeting," Mutt Carey said. "God, what that man could do with his horn!"

Armstrong looked for opportunities just to be close to his idol. "He was the nearest thing to Buddy Bolden to me," he said. "When he went into a bar to yackety with the guys—he didn't drink—or when he'd be parading and not blowing, I'd hold his horn so all he had to do was wipe his brow and walk." Armstrong ran errands for Oliver's wife, too—and got to eat delicious meals of red beans and rice in return—and whenever he could he asked Oliver for tips on how to improve his playing.

The younger man already had begun to develop the astonishing facility that would one day dazzle the musical world and he loved to play what he called "figurations"—ornate improvisations on the chord changes, he remembered, "just like a clarinet player." Sidney Bechet himself had once been astonished to hear Armstrong race effortlessly through a clarinet solo on "High Society" made famous by Alphonse Picou. Virtuosic displays like that left Joe Oliver cold. With him, melody always came first. "Play some lead on that horn, boy," he told Armstrong over and over again. "Play the lead so people can know what you're doing."

The older man admired the boy's big warm tone, liked his eagerness and willingness to learn, began to let him substitute for him in the band he led with Kid Ory,

and one day passed on to him a battered cornet. Armstrong was overwhelmed: "I prized that horn and guarded it with my life," he recalled. "I blew on it for a long, long time before I was fortunate to get another one."

BLESSED

During the summer of 1914—the same summer thirteen-year-old Louis Armstrong was released from the Colored Waif's Home in New Orleans—a fifteen-year-old boy from Washington, D.C., on vacation with his mother in the resort town of Asbury Park, New Jersey, took a temporary job washing dishes at the Plaza Hotel. He hated the hot steamy work "with a perfect hatred," he would admit many years later, but while he was at it the headwaiter talked him into going to hear a Philadelphia ragtime pianist named Harvey Brooks during his off-hours. It changed his life. "I cannot tell you what that music did to me," he would one day tell an interviewer. "It was different from the average piano selection. The individuality of the man showed itself in the composition as he played it. I said right then, 'That's how I would like to play a piano, so without being told, everybody would know I was playing.' "

Everything Edward Kennedy Ellington would do during his long career as pianist, bandleader, composer, and arranger would be built upon that conception. No one remotely familiar with his touch on the piano or the sound of the orchestra he led for fifty years could ever mistake it for anyone else's. And at the same time, he would find ways to encompass within his astonishing outpouring of music everything he saw and heard around him, would manage to make it representative not only of what he himself called "Negro feeling put to rhythm and tune," but of the rhythm and feeling of his whole country. "At its best," his friend the novelist and critic Albert Murray wrote, "an Ellington performance

Daisy Ellington, Duke Ellington's mother

Edward Kennedy Ellington himself, already regal at the age of four

J. E. Ellington and the son who admired him, photographed sometime during the 1920s

sounds as if it knows the truth about all the other music in the world and is looking for something better. Not even the Constitution represents a more intrinsically American statement and achievement than that."

Ellington would remain a major figure in American music for more than half a century, yet almost no one claimed to have known him well. His younger sister, Ruth, remembered that "there was just veil after veil after veil." His private feelings were kept private, expressed only through his music. He is largely missing from his own autobiography, *Music Is My Mistress,* a compilation of shrewd but benign jottings about people he'd known, places he'd been. Reading it, one would think he'd never had to struggle, never made an enemy or suffered a slight. The Ellington papers deposited at the Smithsonian Institution document his methods of composition but offer precious few clues to the personality of the man who moved the pen. Offstage as well as on, he seems almost always to have

been the Duke, glittering but opaque, his languid, courtly manner part put-on and part put off, designed both to delight the public he professed to love madly—and to keep it at a proper, respectful distance.

Ellington's snug, cosseted boyhood could not have been more different from Louis Armstrong's. He was born in the home of his maternal grandparents on Twentieth Street in northwest Washington on April 22, 1899, and spent his earliest years in a big comfortable house on Ward's Place, just a few blocks from the White House.

The nation's capital then had the largest black population of any city in the United States—nearly one hundred thousand souls—and as the cornetist Rex Stewart, who would one day become one of Ellington's brightest stars, remembered, Northwest Washington was the home of "the lighter complexioned people with better-type jobs, such as schoolteachers, . . . clerks, or in government service."

Ellington's father, James Edward Ellington—known as "J.E." to outsiders and "Uncle Ed" to his own children because being called "father" made him feel old—was a man of modest means but lofty aspirations, a "Chesterfieldian gentleman," according to his daughter, Ruth, "who wore gloves and spats." A former coachman and chauffeur, he was butler to a prominent Washington physician, sometimes served as a caterer at the White House, and eventually became a blueprint maker at the Washington Navy Yard. But his son remembered that "he raised his family as if he were a millionaire" and was given to gallant flattery of the sort for which Ellington himself would one day be celebrated. When it snowed, he liked to say, "the millions of beautiful snowflakes" were a tribute to the beauty of his wife, Daisy.

She was the daughter of a police captain and so devoutly religious, her daughter remembered, that she wore no lipstick "because she thought that a woman should not be attracting another man." She had lost one child in infancy and so focused special attention on the son who seemed to represent the second chance for which she'd prayed. Nothing was too good for him: "I was pampered and spoiled rotten, by all the women in the family," Ellington remembered; "my feet were not allowed to touch the ground until the age of six." His mother took him to church twice each Sunday, once to the Nineteenth Street Baptist Church to which her family had always gone, and again to the John Wesley African Methodist Church favored by her husband; she saw to it that not one but *two* doctors were in attendance when her boy fell ill with pneumonia; played light classics on the piano for him so beautifully that he sometimes wept; and made certain when he was old enough to reach the piano keys himself that he faithfully practiced following each lesson with the neighborhood teacher, Marietta Clinkscales.

"As though I were some very, very special child," Ellington wrote, "my mother would say, 'Edward, you are blessed!' " But being blessed was not enough. He must allow nothing to stop him, she said. Unpleasant facts and potential barriers were simply to be ignored. In *his* life there were to be "no boxes"; he "could do anything anyone else could do." In part because she believed that, he would believe it, too, and his mother would always remain the most important person in the world to him.

His mother's enthusiasm for her boy was evidently contagious. "Everything Edward did was wonderful," his sister remembered. "Everybody in the whole family, aunts, uncles, cousins—everybody adored Edward. So whatever he did was marvelous, whatever he played was wonderful." One of his cousins remembered that she and her sister had been expected to curtsy to the bright-eyed little boy whom an admiring schoolmate would soon nickname "Duke."

Ellington's own memories of his boyhood were understandably idyllic: eating grapes

The Nineteenth Street Baptist Church, one of the two churches to which Daisy Ellington took her son each Sunday; and (opposite page) the Gayety Burlesque, where the boy began his secular schooling at the age of twelve

from the arbor in his grandmother's shady backyard; dining on steak and terrapin brought home for the family from one or another of the elegant affairs his father catered; playing baseball with neighborhood boys on Sixteenth Street while President Theodore Roosevelt, out for his afternoon ride, watched from horseback.

The Ellington children, Ruth Ellington recalled, were raised in a household "full of love, where people [did] not talk of hostile incidents. . . . I guess that was their way of protecting us." As the years went by, that determined reticence must sometimes have been hard to maintain. In Washington as elsewhere, the federal government had long since beaten a dispiriting retreat from Reconstruction. Black Washingtonians had once played a real part in the running of their city; now, they were largely powerless and Jim Crow laws and southern custom had combined to segregate housing and public facilities.

Still, the poet Paul Laurence Dunbar wrote in 1900 that Washington had "a higher standard of culture among people of color than obtains in any other city." It was the home of Howard University. There were independent black churches, schools, theaters, orchestras, choral societies, a conservatory of music. A tightly knit group of some sixty families reigned over Washington's colored world, the descendants of free blacks and mostly of "doe-nut or gingercake color," according to the black-owned Washington *Bee*. Just below them were businessmen, professionals, and government workers like the J. E. Ellingtons. At the bottom of the ladder were those whom the *Bee* called the "masses," mostly darkskinned descendants of slaves who lived largely out of sight in the fetid alleys behind some of the city's most elegant dwellings. "I don't know how many castes of Negroes there were in the city at that time," Duke Ellington remembered, "but I do know that

if you decided to mix carelessly with another you would be told that one just did not do that sort of thing. It might be wonderful for somebody, but not for me and my cousins."

Ellington's reticence about his private life started early. He remained close to his mother but determined also to be his own man, which meant learning early how to keep some things from her. Like Jelly Roll Morton before him, he was unwilling to bend to his family's strictures and soon got to know other worlds, out from under his mother's watchful eye. At twelve, he and his friends began slipping into the Gayety Burlesque Theater, where—when he could tear his eyes away from the "rather gorgeous girls"—he got his first taste of the show-business glamour of which he would one day be a master; "I am a man of the theater," he liked to say. Soon, he was also a regular at Frank Holliday's pool room next to the Howard Theater at Seventh and T Streets, a meeting place for men from every segment of the city's black population: gamblers and pool hustlers as well as college graduates and Pullman porters with colorful stories of all the places they had been. "You would hear them say," Ellington recalled, " 'I just left Chicago, or last night I was in Cleveland.' " There was always something worth hearing being said in that poolroom, where it "always sounded as if the prime authorities on every subject had been assembled. . . . Baseball, football, basketball, boxing, wrestling, racing, medicine, law, politics, everything was discussed with authority." It was the beginning of a lifetime of careful listening by Ellington. And it was at Holliday's pool hall, he remembered, that he saw for the first time how "all levels could and should mix."

In 1913, some black Washingtonians had thought they saw encouraging signs of political change. On March 4, Woodrow Wilson, the former Democratic governor of New Jersey, was sworn in as President of the United States. During the presidential campaign he had declared it his "warmest wish to see justice done to the colored people in every matter, and not mere grudging justice, but justice executed with liberality and cordial good feeling." No Democratic presidential candidate had ever seemed so sympathetic to African-American aspirations, and many of the city's black citizens attended the ceremony at the Capitol to hear what the future might hold for them.

Among them had been Jane Thompson Stewart of Georgetown and her five-year-old son, Rex. It was a bitterly cold day, he recalled, and his mother decided to get some coffee from an outdoor vendor. But when she courteously asked him for two cups he looked right through her. She tried again, only to be ignored again, Rex Stewart remembered.

> At last Mother said, "I want two cups of coffee," in a loud voice which seemed to shock the attendant into answering, "How's that auntie?" It was the first time I had seen my mother angry. She seemed to start swelling up like a giant, as she replied, "I'm not your auntie and I am not here to be insulted. This is a very cold day and I demand a hot beverage for my son and myself, in the name of common decency."

The vendor told her he wasn't selling "nigger coffee" and if he had been he still wouldn't sell it to her because he didn't like "smart niggers." A white stranger intervened and intimidated the man into pouring two nickel cups of coffee. The vendor demanded a dollar, and when the boy and his mother finished their coffies, contemptuously smashed the cups they'd used.

It might as well have been an omen. The new President had had no intention of honoring his pledge. Within three months he issued an executive order that imposed Jim Crow on the federal government itself. Restrooms in all federal buildings were segregated. Black clerks were separated from white colleagues alongside whom they'd worked for years. The whole city fell in line: The National Theater hired a black doorman because the managers thought he would be best able to detect light-skinned would-be ticket-buyers trying to pass for white. At the dedication of the Lincoln Memorial armed Marines would make sure black invitees—including the president of Tuskegee Institute, one of the speakers—did not stray from their separate roped-off seats across a dirt road from the Great Emancipator.

Black Washingtonians redoubled their efforts at building self-reliance. Community newspapers exhorted their readers to forget the differences that had divided them; patronize black businesses and boycott white ones that discriminated against them; support black charities and take pride in black achievements. Meanwhile, the assistant superintendent of the Colored Schools urged that the children in his charge be "taught about the great men of our race" so that they might "escape being overwhelmed by white prestige and avoid impairment of colored initiative." Ellington was in eighth grade at William Lloyd Garrison Junior High when the Wilson administration began, and remembered all his life the lessons its principal, Miss Boston, had sought to inculcate in all her students:

> When we went out into the world, we would have the grave responsibility of being practically always on stage, for every time they would see a Negro they would go into a reappraisal of the race. She taught us that proper speech and good manners were our first obligations, because as representatives of the Negro race we were to command respect for our people. This being an all-colored school, Negro history was crammed into the curriculum, so that we would know our people all the way back. They had pride there, the greatest race pride.

After returning from his dishwashing sojourn in Asbury Park in 1914, Ellington entered Samuel H. Armstrong Technical High School. He was now determined to become a piano player—in part, he liked to say, because he had noticed that girls were attracted to piano players and he was attracted to girls. In fact, it was because of the instant excitement he had felt at hearing Harvey Brooks play, the conviction that music would be his way to express himself.

An able but alcoholic pianist named Lester Dishman gave him lessons for a time, in exchange for the boy's help in navigating from one engagement to the next. Soon, Rex Stewart remembered, Ellington was playing piano for teenage dances at True Reformers Hall on U Street for seventy-five cents a night, "and fixing that famous hypnotic grin on the nearest pretty girl." And he had begun to work up his own tunes, including "Soda Fountain Rag" and "What You Gonna Do When the Bed Breaks Down?" which he remembered as "a pretty good 'hug-and-rubbin' crawl." Its title alone must have appalled his mother, but it made him very popular among his classmates.

THE ORIGINATORS OF JAZZ

On May 13, 1915, a five-piece white group from New Orleans arrived in Chicago for a six-week engagement at a basement restaurant at Randolph and Clark called Lamb's Café. They billed themselves as "Brown's Band from Dixieland," after their trombonist, Tom Brown, a veteran of Papa Jack Laine's marching bands. The kind of music they played was already growing familiar in black neighborhoods of the city, but most white Chicagoans had never heard anything like it, and at first they were anything but enthusiastic. The cashier covered her ears whenever the men began to play, and a string orchestra quit rather than perform on the same bandstand with anyone making such crude noises.

Vaudeville dancer and comedian Joe Frisco, arms outstretched, poses for a publicity photograph on a Chicago street during the summer of 1915. Behind him, fresh from New Orleans and not at all sure how their music will go over in the Windy City, are the five members of Brown's Band from Dixieland, including trombonist Tom Brown (over Frisco's left shoulder) and clarinetist Larry Shields.

"[O]ur debut was pitiful," the cornetist Ray Lopez later admitted. "Those Yankees wouldn't listen or dance. They just walked out on us. We took turns talking to the customers. 'Folks, this is New Orleans music. Hot music. People down South dance. You've got to dance. Come on and try. Have fun!' For six nights we pleaded. No dice." Then, a touring vaudeville company reserved the café for a party and word got out that they had had a good time; after that, Lopez remembered, their music "caught on like magic"—until the restaurant closed for renovations. Brown's Band from Dixieland broke up soon afterward, and most of its members went back home to New Orleans.

Meanwhile, out on the road, Freddie Keppard's playing was winning him an enthusiastic following at least among those musicians who managed to hear him. "He hit the highest and the lowest notes on a trumpet that anybody outside of Gabriel ever did," his friend and fellow Creole Jelly Roll Morton remembered. "[He] had all degrees of power, great imagination and more tone than anybody." It was said he played so loudly that people who sat in the front rows sometimes asked to move back when he began to blow, and the saxophonist Garvin Bushell remembered that when Keppard played in a cabaret he "could make the glasses on the bar move—they'd bet on that." But for all his artistry and power, Keppard was also suspicious and self-protective, so fearful other cornetists would copy his fingering that, like Joe Oliver, he was said sometimes to use a handkerchief to hide his right hand when he played.

In December of 1915, Keppard and his Original Creole Orchestra were playing a New York theater when a spokesman for the Victor Talking Machine company is said to have offered to record them. But first, he explained, they would have to hold a tryout to see if the firm's primitive recording device could pick up the sound of the band's bass player. Keppard turned Victor down. His clarinetist George Baquet said it was

The barnstorming Creole Orchestra with Freddie Keppard and George Bacquet advertises its wares in Los Angeles, 1914.

because Keppard had felt insulted at being asked to audition without pay; others remembered him saying, "Nothing doing, boys. We won't put our stuff on records for everybody to steal"; still others heard he'd asked for as much money as was paid to the operatic tenor Enrico Caruso, the best-selling recording artist in the world, and was turned down flat. Keppard's friend Sidney Bechet declared there was only one real reason for his reluctance to record: "Freddie just didn't care to, that's all." In any case, he passed up the opportunity to become the first jazz musician to make a recording.

Tom Brown's success at Lamb's Café had inspired other Chicago club owners to look for more white bands from "Dixie." One of them was a hastily put-together quintet from New Orleans led by the drummer Johnny Stein that included the pianist Henry Ragas and three more veterans of Papa Jack Laine's marching bands—clarinetist Alcide "Yellow" Nuñez, trombonist Eddie "Daddy" Edwards, and cornetist Dominick James "Nick" LaRocca.

In April of 1916, their band was booked into a cheap cabaret called the New Schiller Café, on Thirty-first Street, which was fortunate enough to be visited one Saturday night by a phalanx of some sixty determined women from the Anti-Saloon League, intent on exposing the evils of alcohol. With them came a reporter from the Chicago *Herald*. The story that appeared the next day under the headline "Sixty Women Rip Mask off Vice" turned out to be a publicist's dream.

A line of taxicabs radiated from the Schiller to the east, west, north and south. In front of the doors a crowd of people fought for admission. A perspiring doorman held them back. "Can't come in," he shouted. "We're crowded to capacity." . . . [Once inside] it was impossible for anyone to be heard. The shriek of women's drunken laughter rivaled the blatant scream of the imported New Orleans

Jass Band, which never seemed to stop playing. Men and women sat, arms about each other, singing, shouting, making the night hideous, while their unfortunate brethren and sisters fought in vain to join them.

The newspaper reporter may have hoped readers would be horrified by the vice he and the crusaders had uncovered, but a good many were simply intrigued, wanted to see and hear for themselves what all the fuss was about. Crowds at the café doubled overnight. "The impact we had on the people of Chicago was terrific," LaRocca remembered. "Women stood up on the dance floor, doing wild dances. They had to pull them off. . . . The more they would carry on, the better we could play. . . . The crowd would start yelling, 'Give us some more jass.' I can still see these women who would try and put on a show . . . raise their dresses above their knees and carry on, men shrieking and everybody having a good time."

LaRocca had never been one of New Orleans's best-known cornetists—he had been hired for the Chicago job mostly because he had happened to be able to come up with the $125 needed to pay the group's railfare north from New Orleans—but he burned with ambition, was determined not to return to New Orleans a failure. Raised in the tough "Irish Channel" section of New Orleans, he was the son of a shoemaker from Sicily, and therefore a member of one of his polyglot hometown's most disdained minorities. The city's celebrated spirit of tolerance had never extended to Italian-Americans. There were thought to be some eighteen thousand of them living in New Orleans by the turn of the century, and in the minds of a good many of their fellow citizens they were all tarred with the Mafia brush. Warfare between rival Italian gangs had led to a police crackdown in 1890, the year after LaRocca's birth, and when someone shotgunned the police chief to death on Basin

Street the following year, nineteen Sicilians were indicted for the crime. Nine were tried. When six were found not guilty and the jury could not agree on a verdict for the other three, a mob of indignant whites and blacks stormed into the Orleans Parish Prison and butchered all nine of the accused, plus two others who had not yet come to trial. The mayor commended the mob for its swift work: "The Italians had taken the law into their own hands," he said, "and we had no choice but to do the same."

No one was ever indicted for the lynching but its memory remained raw for decades. As LaRocca was growing up, he and other Italian-Americans in New Orleans were routinely taunted with cries of "Who Killa da Chief?" As a Sicilian, he always felt himself something of an outsider in his own hometown—"a poor dago boy from the wrong side of the track," he said—a fact which may help account both for his enormous drive to succeed and for his unwillingness to acknowledge that African-Americans—members of the only minority he felt that he himself could look down upon—could have had anything whatsoever to do with creating the music he would later claim to have come up with all on his own.

Had LaRocca's father had his way, he would never have been a jazz musician at all. The old man had himself once played the cornet for dancers in his off-hours, but he believed professional musicians were "bums," and insisted that his son study to become a doctor so that he could demonstrate to the world that Italians were as good as anyone else. When Nick proudly performed his first tune for his parents at about the age of nine, his father waited until the boy was finished awkwardly fingering the valves on his own old cornet, then tore the horn from his son's hands and smashed it with an ax. When the boy stubbornly bought himself another cornet and began practicing it in secret in the outhouse, his father crushed that one, too.

Then, his father died. LaRocca immediately abandoned all thought of a medical career. He worked as a stagehand at the French opera house, learned electrical contracting work, and played music whenever he could, just for "eats" at first and then for pay. Never able to read music, he was an aggressive but unconventional player; like his idol, Ray Lopez, he held his horn in his right hand and fingered the valves with his left.

By the time he got to Chicago to join Johnny Stein at the New Schiller Café, in 1916, he had worked in at least fifteen New Orleans bands. Stein's group, too, broke up after the café's management refused them a raise and the trombonist punched the drummer in the nose. LaRocca then talked three of the men—Edwards, Ragas, and Nuñez—into joining him in a new cooperative group called the Original Dixieland Jass Band. They added a drummer, Tony Sbarbaro, and eventually replaced Nuñez with clarinetist Larry Shields, who had been born in a shotgun house just two doors up the street from Buddy Bolden's family home.

The ODJB spent the next six months at a gangster hangout called the Casino Gardens that billed itself as "The Theatrical Profession's Most Popular Rendezvous." The

vaudeville star Al Jolson heard them there and would later claim that he was largely responsible for getting them the New York engagement that would finally make all of LaRocca's dreams come true—in the Paradise Ballroom, part of the new Reisenweber Restaurant complex on Columbus Circle.

They opened there on January 17, 1917. At first, Manhattan dancers fled the dance floor when the band began to play, just as Chicagoans had initially fled from Tom Brown's outfit. LaRocca remembered drunken patrons shouting, "Tell those farmers to go home!" But after the master of ceremonies carefully explained, "This music's meant for dancing," a few venturesome couples tried it. More joined them. "This 'jaz' thing sounds like . . . musicians trying to draw business into a sideshow," *Variety* reported. "It's what would be called 'stewed music' for you have to be that way to like it." But its impact on dancers was undeniable.

[O]ne thing is certain. . . . the melodies as played by the Jazz organization at Reisenweber's are quite conducive to making the dancers on

the floor loosen up and go to the limit in their stepping. Gingery, swinging music is what the dancers want. . . . Late in the morning, the jazzers go to work and the dancers hit the floor, to remain there till they topple over. . . . If the dancers see someone they know at the tables, it's common to hear, "Oh, Boy!" as they roll their eyes while floating past. And the "Oh, Boy!" expression probably describes the Jazz Band better than anything else could.

Reisenweber's ran newspaper advertisements hailing jazz as "An Overnight Furore —the Fad of the Hour," and put up a neon sign: THE ORIGINAL DIXIELAND JAZZ BAND—THE CREATORS OF JAZZ. (The spelling had been hastily changed from "Jass," LaRocca remembered, because small boys had been spotted scurrying along nearby streets scratching the letter "J" off their posters.)

Within a week of the opening at Reisenweber's, Columbia Records decided to try and record the music that was making such a stir. On January 30, 1917, the ODJB assembled in a tiny studio and nervously

The same air of cheerful anarchy that put off the first New Yorkers who heard the Original Dixieland Jazz Band in 1917 had become a selling point by the time this cartoon was drawn for the Victor Talking Machine Company three years later.

the spring of 1914, the dance team of Vernon and Irene Castle embarked on what they called their "Whirlwind Tour" of the United States—thirty cities in twenty-eight days. Vernon Castle was an English entertainer whose real name was Vernon Blyth; his wife was a doctor's daughter from Westchester County. They were so slender, one reporter noted, that "standing side by side [they] are about as wide as one rather slim human being." But they were elegant dancers, refined and reassuring to parents worried about the morals of their children.

Ragtime had spawned a host of provocative dances, all of them born in African-American dance halls but eagerly embraced by young dancers of all races. The New York *Herald* spoke for a good many older white people in deploring ragtime as "symbolic of the primitive morality and perceptible moral limitations of the Negro type." Some black Americans were worried, as well, but for different reasons. "The Negro Race is dancing itself to death," warned the Reverend Adam Clayton Powell Sr., pastor of Harlem's Abyssinian Baptist Church. "Our people are too frivolous because they feed on too much trash. You can see the effects of the Tango, the Chicago, the Turkey Trot, the Texas Tommy and ragtime music not only in their conversations but in the movement of their bodies about the home."

"We were clean-cut," Irene Castle remembered, "we were married, and when we danced there was nothing suggestive about it. We made dancing look like the fun it was and so gradually we became a middle ground both sides could accept." The couple grew so popular that when Irene Castle bobbed her hair, 250,000 American women were said to have followed suit.

The Castles danced beautifully but they owed a great deal to the blend of rhythmic drive and musical polish provided by the ten-piece black orchestra that traveled with them everywhere—and to its remarkable conductor, James Reese Europe. Born in Alabama and raised in Washington where he studied violin and piano, he had acted as musical director for all-black revues on Broadway and saw it as his duty to reveal to the world "the musical proficiency of the African race." The New York local of the American Federation of Musicians barred blacks, and so, in 1910, Europe

Vernon and Irene Castle offer lessons in suitably decorous dancing to the readers of *The Ladies Home Journal*, December 1914.

MR. AND MRS. VERNON CASTLE'S
III: THE CASTLE FOX TROT
DESCRIBED BY MR. CASTLE

NEW DANCES FOR THIS WINTER
WITH PHOTOGRAPHS OF EACH STEP
ESPECIALLY POSED BY MR. AND MRS. CASTLE
PHOTOGRAPHS COPYRIGHT BY IRA L. HILL'S STUDIO

NUMBER ONE
In Taking the Slow Steps the Stride Should be as Long as Possible

NUMBER TWO
This is the Second Slow Step at the Beginning of the Dance

NUMBER THREE
I Walk a Little to the Side Instead of Directly Facing You

NUMBER FOUR
By Stopping Suddenly You Will Find You Unconsciously Fall Into Half a "Grapevine" Step

NUMBER FIVE
This Step is Very Much Like the First, With the Addition of a Very Pretty Little Back Kick

NUMBER SIX
In This Picture My Wife is Just About to Draw the Left Foot Up to the Right Foot

NUMBER SEVEN
This is Exactly the Same Step on the Other Side

NUMBER EIGHT
This Picture Was Taken Just After We Had Made the Turn

Page 24

(Page 25)

helped establish a rival organization, the Clef Club, to defend their interests and act as a clearinghouse for jobs. Two years later, he organized and led a pioneering concert of African-American music at Carnegie Hall. His 105-piece Clef Club Symphony Orchestra performed ragtime, spirituals, plantation songs, choral works, show tunes—and instrumental numbers featuring ten grand pianos all playing at once. It was a triumph. "The Negroes," said the New York *Evening-Journal,* "have given us the only music of our own that is American—national, original and real."

Europe tried always to present black music with dignity, though even he sometimes had to cater to the curious expectations of white audiences. [The] Europe gang were absolute reading sharks," remembered his pianist, Eubie Blake. "They could read a moving snake and if a fly lit on that paper he got played . . . but the people wanted to believe that Negroes couldn't learn to read music but had a natural talent for it. So we never played with no music. . . .

I'd get all the latest Broadway music from the publisher, and we'd learn the tunes and rehearse 'em until we had 'em all down pat. Never made no mistakes. . . . All the high-tone, big-time folks would say, 'Isn't it wonderful how these untrained, primitive musicians can pick up all the latest songs instantly without being able to read music?' "

"During breath-catching intermissions" on the Castle tour, W. C. Handy wrote, "Jim would sit at the piano and play slowly the 'Memphis Blues.' He did this so often that the Castles became intrigued by its rhythm, and Jim asked why they didn't originate a slow dance adaptable to it." The result was the fox-trot, the Castles' longest-lasting legacy and the basis for scores of dances and thousands of songs over the coming years.

Europe's was the first black orchestra ever to record, and the smaller bands he supplied for New York society dances were so popular that one white bandleader complained to a newspaper that it "will not be long before the poor white musician will be obliged to blacken his face to make a livelihood or starve." Europe was unrepentant. There was now a new kind of Negro musician at work, he said, who combined "serious study" with "a natural talent" and who was contributing to American music "whatever distinctive quality it possesses." When the New York local of the musician's union became the first in the country to integrate its ranks, Europe signed right up but he was still not satisfied. Black performers were doing better now, he told a reporter, but black composers were still paid far less than their white counterparts. That, too, would change, he said: "Some day it will be different and justice will prevail."

Europe's "Castle House Rag" was named for a short-lived institution organized by Manhattan society matrons so that young people could dance safely to his orchestra without being exposed to what they called "discredited elements."

James Reese Europe and roughly two-thirds of the Clef Club Symphony Orchestra he led at the Manhattan Casino in Harlem in 1911. His "Monster Melange and Dancefest" included new music by black composers, a minstrel show, and orchestral versions of Negro spirituals.

played two tunes—"Indiana" and "Darktown Strutters' Ball." Things did not go well. The songs were new to the musicians and they'd had little more than an hour to rehearse; the band's sheer volume overwhelmed the primitive recording machinery—a big funnel-shaped sheet-metal horn into which everyone had to play, connected to a crude stylus that cut grooves in a wax disc. The result sounded so like chaos to Columbia executives that they paid the musicians their fee of $250 and shelved the records.

For most Americans, jazz remained a secret. That month, Duke Ellington was still a high school senior in Washington, ostensibly studying to become a commercial artist, actually shirking his studies—he earned only mediocre marks and got a "D" for "Deficient" in the only formal music class in which he ever enrolled—in order to spend as much time as he could around the ragtime pianists who had become his heroes. They "sounded so good to me," Ellington remembered. "And they *looked* so good! Particularly when they flashed their left hands." Many of them treated the youngster with extraordinary kindness, and Oliver "Doc" Perry, one of the city's best-known bandleaders, thought enough of him to become his "piano parent," Ellington recalled, teaching him "to read notes, not spell 'em out."

His idols included both local men and visiting stars, classically trained pianists and those who'd worked out their styles all on their own:

Each would take his turn and display his own devices. Doc Perry and Louis [Brown] were the Conservatory Boys but they also had profound respect for the cats who played by ear, and in spite of the fact that their techniques were as foreign to each other as Chinese, they lauded them, praised them and there was the most wonderful exchange. Everybody seemed to get

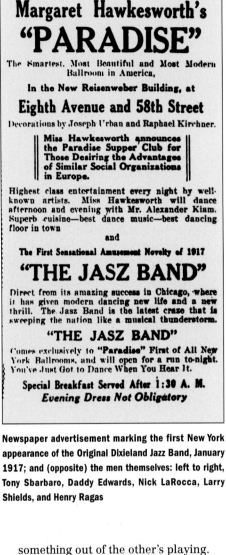

Newspaper advertisement marking the first New York appearance of the Original Dixieland Jazz Band, January 1917; and (opposite) the men themselves: left to right, Tony Sbarbaro, Daddy Edwards, Nick LaRocca, Larry Shields, and Henry Ragas

something out of the other's playing. There was a fusion of the two right where I was standing, leaning over the piano with both my ears twenty feet high. . . . It was a wonderful, healthy climate for everybody.

The mature Ellington's music—performed by a band made up of men whose styles and personalities under anyone else's leadership would have seemed fated to clash or cancel one another out—would foster precisely that kind of healthy climate, would

be based on just that kind of quintessentially American exchange.

The boy's schoolwork continued to suffer, but he was good enough at painting to win a scholarship to the Pratt Institute in New York from the National Association for the Advancement of Colored People. Then,

in February—with just four months to go till graduation, and to his mother's horror—Ellington gave up his scholarship and dropped out of school. (He may have abandoned art but he would remain faithful to color all his life: from "Mood Indigo" and "Magenta Haze" to "Blue Rose" and "Blue Cellophane," it would suffuse his music.) For better or worse, he had decided to become a full-time musician. Ragtime, popular songs, light classics, and the blues—Ellington hoped to master them all. But of jazz—the music that had been born in New Orleans, the music that had begun to draw big crowds in Chicago and New York, the music he would one day make his own—it was unlikely that he had yet heard a single note.

Within just a few weeks, that would change at last—for him and for the whole country.

THE
JAZZ AGE

On February 26, 1917, President Woodrow Wilson appeared before a joint session of Congress to ask for the power to arm American merchant ships against unrestricted attacks by German submarines in the Atlantic. Wilson had struggled hard to keep the country out of the European war that had now been raging for nearly three years—his new policy was still called "armed neutrality"—and much of the country remained opposed to taking sides. But it looked more and more likely now that German belligerence would draw America into the conflict anyway.

That same day, the members of the Original Dixieland Jazz Band tried again to record their version of New Orleans music. They were at the New York studios of the Victor Talking Machine Company this time, and they were going to play

Bennie Krueger's Brunswick Orchestra and the singer Dorothy Jardon garner some publicity for their appearance at Brooklyn's Brighton Beach Pavilion in the summer of 1922. The bandleader is at the left, playing C-melody saxophone. "Jazz maniacs were being born," remembered the songwriter Hoagy Carmichael, "and I was one of them."

two tunes they played often—"Dixieland Jass Band One-Step" and "Livery Stable Blues." The Victor engineer worked hard to balance the instruments properly. The emphasis was on comedy: Nick LaRocca made his cornet whinny like a horse; Larry Shields crowed like a rooster with his clarinet; Daddy Edwards made his trombone moo. No one improvised; every note had been carefully worked out in advance.

But the music was hotter and livelier than anything that had ever been recorded before—the engineer had insisted the men play especially fast to fit the whole tune on a record—and most Americans still had never heard anything remotely like it. Released on March 7, the record cut that day would sell more than a million copies at seventy-five cents each—more than any single record by Caruso or John Phillip Sousa had ever sold—and before long the ODJB was back in the studio recording more tunes: "At the Jazz Band Ball," "Fidgety Feet," "Sensation Rag," "Tiger Rag," "Clarinet Marmalade Blues."

"One moment jazz was unknown, obscure—a low noise in a low dive," the bandleader Paul Whiteman remembered (with some help from his silent writing partner Mary Margaret McBride). "The next it had become a serious pastime of a hundred million people, the diversion of princes and millionaires. . . . The time was ripe. . . . The war spirit was on the loose. The whole tempo of the country was speeded up. Wheels turned like mad. Every factory was manned by night shifts. Americans . . . lived harder, faster than ever before. They could not go without some new outlet. Work was not enough and America had not yet found out how to play. . . . Meanwhile was brewing in New Orleans a restorative for the national nerve complaint . . . [t]he great American noise, jazz."

The ODJB's version of that noise was rowdy, irreverent, assertive, and utterly American. "An Englishman entered a place as if he were its master," the New York

Times critic Olin Downes wrote, "whereas an American entered as if he didn't care who in blazes the master might be. Something like that [is] in this music." Young people loved it, and Victor couldn't believe its luck—though it wasn't entirely sure just what it was its engineers had recorded. Jazz was "organized disorganization," the Victor advertising copywriters said.

> Spell it Jass, Jaz, or Jazz—nothing can spoil a Jass band. A Jass Band is the newest thing in cabarets, adding greatly to the hilarity thereof. You never know what it's going to do next, but you can always tell what those who hear it are going to do—they're going to "shake a leg."
>
> The Jass Band is the very latest thing in the development of music. It has sufficient power and penetration to inject new life into a mummy, and will keep ordinary human dancers on their feet till breakfast time.

LaRocca and his men cheerfully played along with the publicity department, pretending everything they did had been made up on the spot, declaring themselves "musi-

The record that started it all, "Livery Stable Blues," by the Original Dixieland "Jass" Band

cal anarchists," allowing Daddy Edwards to claim, "None of us know music," when he himself read it perfectly well.

Back in New Orleans, musicians were swept up in the excitement engendered by the Original Dixieland Jazz Band's success. Dance-band violinists all over town lost their jobs because the ODJB did not happen to have one; Kid Ory fired one of the members of the sextet in which he and Joe Oliver played just to match its five-man line-up; and Oliver himself soon joined an exodus of musicians, both black and white, hurrying north to Chicago, where club owners were now frantically looking for people to bring Crescent City music to their clientele.

Louis Armstrong listened to the ODJB's records along with the rest of the country. He had somehow managed to save up enough money to buy a wind-up Victrola—on which he had been listening to operatic arias by Caruso and the Irish tenor John McCormack, whose "beautiful phrasing" he especially admired—when the first jazz sides appeared. "We thought they were great," he remembered. "Everybody was blowing a whole lot of jazz in New Orleans but [the Original Dixieland Jazz Band's] the one that put it over." He liked the sound of Nick LaRocca's cornet well enough, but he loved Larry Shields's clarinet solo on "Clarinet Marmalade" and was soon intimidating other cornetists by the ease with which he could reproduce it flawlessly on his horn.

Sidney Bechet, on the other hand, was scornful of the ODJB and its claim to have written tunes like "Livery Stable Blues." "Those were all numbers they had learned from playing opposite us back in New Orleans," he said later. "All these Dixieland musicians could do was play what they learned from us, and after that there wasn't anything more for them to do." But the jazz mania sparked by the ODJB provided fresh opportunities even for Bechet. In July, a vaudeville impresario turned up in New Orleans and persuaded him and four other

JASS, JASZ, JAZZ

"Jazz," wrote the bandleader Paul Whiteman in 1926, was originally a "slang phrase of the underworld with a meaning unmentionable in polite society. . . . It reached the drawing room finally on the strength of its terse expressive virility. On the way up, it was variously a verb and a noun, generally denoting speed or quick action of some kind. It appears now to be firmly established as a member of that long list of American words in good social standing." The New Orleans music spreading fast across the country had first been called "ratty music," "gut-bucket music," "hot music." But now, people began to call it "jass," "jasz," and "jazz," though no one has ever been entirely sure why. As early as 1906, a San Francisco sportswriter was using the word to denote pep and enthusiasm on the baseball field, and there were those who thought it might have originally come from a West African word for speeding things up. But most authorities believe that the term, like the music, came from New Orleans—from the jasmine perfume allegedly favored by the city's prostitutes, or from "jezebel," a common nineteenth-century term for a prostitute, or as a synonym for sexual intercourse in Storyville, where some brothels were said to have been called "jays'n houses." "The original meaning of jazz was procreation," says the trumpet player Wynton Marsalis, "you can't get deeper or more profound than that unless you're contemplating the Creator."

The Original Dixieland Jass Band changed the spelling of its name soon after the RCA Victor catalogue at right was published in March 1917, but five years later, the singer Sarah Martin (below) was still calling her group the "Jass Fools."

New Victor Records Jass Band and other Dance Selections

The Original Dixieland Jass Band

SPELL it Jass, Jas, Jaz or Jazz—nothing can spoil a Jass band. Some say the Jass band originated in Chicago, Chicago says it comes from San Francisco—San Francisco being away off across the continent. Anyway, a Jass band is the newest thing in the cabarets, adding greatly to the hilarity thereof.

They say the first instrument of the first Jass band was an empty lard can, by humming into which, sounds were produced resembling those of a saxophone with the croup. Since then the Jass band has grown in size and ferocity, and only musicians to join her touring stock company, playing the band's biggest hits: "They are all red hot," the Indianapolis *Freeman* said about Bechet and his companions, "and the tremendous crowds howl and rave to hear them play the 'Livery Stable Blues.' "

THE HELLFIGHTERS

America had entered the Great War on April 6, 1917—just thirty-one days after the release of the ODJB's first record—and on New Year's Day of the following year, the two thousand men of the Fifteenth New York Regiment landed at Brest on the coast of Brittany. The French soldiers and sailors and civilians who turned out to greet them had never seen or heard anything like these Americans. The officers were white, as had been all of the American combat soldiers who had trooped ashore in France since the previous June. But these enlisted men were all black. So were all the members of the big regimental band, and as it swung into its distinctive version of the "Marseillaise," the onlookers on shore were still more puzzled. These Americans played with such spirit and rhythmic drive that it took the French eight or ten bars to recognize their own national anthem. Then, one of the musicians in the band remembered, "there came over their faces an astonished look" followed instantly by "alert snap-to-it attention and [a] salute by every French soldier or sailor present."

Marching at the head of the band was its director, Lieutenant James Reese Europe, who had been the most eagerly sought-after society dance bandleader in New York before America entered the war, the man who, as musical director for the dancers Vernon and Irene Castle, had introduced the country to the fox-trot. He had joined up two years earlier, he told a friend, not out of any special sense of patriotism or because he was especially fond of martial music, but because he thought a National Guard unit for Harlem would "bring

Lieutenant James Reese Europe in France, 1918

together all classes of men who stand for something in the community" and he would have felt remiss if he were not a part of it.

The regiment had first been sent south for training, to Spartanburg, South Carolina, over the strenuous objections of the city's mayor. "I was sorry to learn that the Fifteenth Regiment has been ordered here," he told the press, "for, with their northern ideas about race equality, they will probably expect to be treated like white men. I can say right here that they will not be treated as anything except negroes. . . . This thing is like waving a red flag in the face of a bull, something that can't be done without trouble."

On the first Saturday after the regiment's arrival, Europe's band played a concert in downtown Spartanburg. A big muttering crowd of local whites gathered, Major Arthur W. Little remembered, and

> the talk which some of us overheard through that crowd during the early stages of the concert was by no means reassuring. . . . But there must be something in the time-honored line about music and its charms; for, gradually, . . . the noises of the crowd grew less and less, until finally, in that great public square of converging city streets, silence reigned. Lieutenant Europe conducted, as was his custom, with but a few seconds between numbers, and the program appeared to be short. When the final piece had been played and the forty or fifty bandsmen had filed out of the stand in perfect order with the "Hep— Hep—Hep—" of the sergeants as the only sound from their ranks, the flower of Spartanburg's citizenry looked at each other foolishly, and one could be heard to say: —"Is that all?" while another would say: — "When do they play again?"

The next day, members of the Spartanburg chamber of commerce came calling upon Major Little. Would the band be available to play for dancing the following Saturday at the country club?

Europe's music may have mollified some white citizens of Spartanburg, but others continued to be angered by the presence of black troops. In the interest of keeping the peace, the men pledged to follow Jim Crow practice whenever they went into town and to do their best to look the other way when insulted. But white troops from other New York units training nearby had made no such promises. They berated shop owners who wouldn't serve their fellow soldiers, whatever their color, and when a black doughboy was assaulted for failing to leave the sidewalk fast enough to suit several

Members of Europe's Hellfighter's Band

James Europe and his men outside a Paris hospital, serenading wounded troops. "When they played the 'Memphis Blues,'" wrote the Kentucky-born war correspondent Irvin S. Cobb, "the men did not march, the music poured in at their ears and ran down to their heels, and instead of marching they literally danced their way along. I think surely this must be the best regimental band in our army. Certainly it is the best one I have heard in Europe during this war."

lounging whites, white New Yorkers beat his attackers to the ground. Then, when the proprietor of a downtown hotel knocked a black private down for having failed to doff his hat before buying a newspaper in the lobby, officers had to restrain angry white troops from burning the place down. Finally, it had been thought best to have the

regiment's training completed in France, where, their commander assured his men, there was "no color line."

Not long after the Europe band came ashore in France, Army brass saw that its brand of martial ragtime would be good for morale, providing "the feel of home" for bored or battered doughboys, while win-

ning new friends among the French. The songwriter Noble Sissle, who served as the band's vocalist, remembered its first appearance before French civilians, a Lincoln's Birthday concert at the Nantes opera house. The men played French marches, "The Stars and Stripes Forever," plantation melodies, and ragtime pieces, which the French had never heard before. Then came "the fireworks," Sissle wrote, W. C. Handy's "Memphis Blues": it began with a "soul-rousing crash" of cymbals by the drummers, their shoulders shaking in time, then "both director and musicians seemed to forget their surroundings. . . . Cornet and clarinet players began to manipulate notes in that typical rhythm which no artist has ever put down on paper. The audience could stand it no longer, the 'jazz germ' hit them and it seemed to find the vital spot, loosening all muscles and causing what is known in American as an 'eagle rocking it.' "

The music Europe's men played was still orchestrated ragtime meant for marching, not jazz, and no one was allowed to improvise. But it was filled with jazz elements —breaks, riffs, trombone smears, and rhythmic excitement no other marching band could come close to matching. "Everywhere we gave a concert it was a riot," Europe told a reporter, "but the supreme moment came in the Tuileries Gardens when we gave a concert in conjunction with the greatest bands in the world—the British Grenadier's Band, the Band of the *Garde Republicain* and the Royal Italian Band. My band, of course, could not compare with any of these, yet the crowd, and it was such a crowd as I never saw anywhere else in the world, deserted them for us. We played to 50,000 people, at least, and had we wished it, we might be playing yet."

The British and French and Italian bandmasters were impressed, too, and asked to examine the instruments Europe's men had used; they couldn't believe that such sounds could be made through ordinary horns. It was not the instruments his men played, Europe patiently explained, but the

The Hellfighters Band leads the 369th Infantry up Fifth Avenue past the New York Public Library, February 17, 1919.

way they played them that made the difference. "We play the music as it is written," but play it in a syncopated manner that is "a racial musical characteristic. I have to call a daily rehearsal of my band to prevent the musicians from adding to their music more than I wish them to. Whenever possible they all embroider their parts in order to produce new, peculiar sounds. Some of these effects are excellent and some are not, and I have to be continually on the lookout to cut out the results of the musicians' originality."

On the night of April 20, 1918, Europe became the first African-American officer to face combat during the war, accompanying a French night patrol across no-man's-land under heavy enemy fire. Six weeks later, he survived a German poison gas attack that left his lungs too weak for further fighting but failed to dim his creativity. Lying on a hospital cot he wrote a new song, "On Patrol in No Man's Land," then arranged it for the regimental band with special effects—sirens and alarm bells, artillery explosions, and rattling bursts of machine-gun fire, all to be produced by the band's two drummers.

Meanwhile, the men of the Fifteenth New York—its name now changed to the 369th Infantry Regiment, U.S. Army—endured 191 unbroken days of combat, won 171 decorations for bravery, more than any other American unit, and took special pride in the name the French gave them—the Hellfighters. After the fighting was finally over, they came home to New York on February 17, 1919, to a victory parade up Fifth Avenue to Harlem. Thousands of New Yorkers, white as well as black, poured into the streets to cheer them. "Never in the history of Father Knickerbocker," one newspaperman wrote, "has such a rousing royal welcome been given returning heroes. . . . Not for many a day is it likely that thousands of white and colored citizens will participate in such a tumultuous and enthusiastic demonstration."

"Lieutenant Jim Europe's 369th Infantry ('Hellfighters') Band" started a triumphant tour almost as soon as it got home from the front, drawing big, cheering crowds in Brooklyn, Albany, Buffalo, Cleveland, Toledo, Pittsburgh, St. Louis, and Chicago—where the editors of the *Defender* drew lessons from the success of what they called this " 'hot-stuff' musical organization."

The most prejudiced enemy of our Race could not sit through an evening with Europe without coming away with a changed viewpoint. For he is compelled in spite of himself to see us in a new light. It is a well-known fact that the white people view us largely from the standpoint of the cook, porter, and waiter, and his limited opportunities are responsible for much of the distorted opinion held concerning us. Europe and his band are worth more to our Race than a thousand speeches from so-called Race orators and uplifters. Mere windjamming has never given any race material help. It may be entertaining in a way to recite to audiences of our own people in a flamboyant style the doings of the Race, but the spellbinder's efforts, being confined almost exclusively to audiences of our own people, is of as much help in

properly presenting our cause to those whom we desire most to reach as a man trying to lift himself by pulling at his own bootstraps. Experience has shown that most of our spellbinders are in it for what there is in it. The good they do us is nil.

Jim Europe was just thirty-nine that spring, and he had big plans: a National Negro Symphony Orchestra, a new musical on Broadway, new ways in which jazz elements might be fused with other forms to express what he called "the soul of the Negro." "We won *France* by playing music which was ours and not a pale imitation of others," he told an interviewer, "and if we are to develop in America we must develop along our own lines."

In Boston on the morning of May 9, Europe and his men were to receive still another honor. After they played on the steps of the Massachusetts State House, Governor Calvin Coolidge was to present them with a wreath to lay at the base of the Memorial to the Fifty-fourth Massachusetts Volunteers, the first black regiment to fight in the Civil War. But during intermission at a concert the evening before the ceremony was to take place, as Europe sat in his dressing room at Mechanic's Hall, he was confronted by one of his two drummers, a high-strung man named Herbert Wright. The men exchanged words. Wright accused his boss of treating him unfairly, then without warning plunged a pen knife into Europe's neck. The wound did not seem serious at first and as Europe left for the hospital, he told his men to finish the concert. He would meet them for the capitol ceremony in the morning. But that night, Jim Europe bled to death.

New York City gave him a public funeral, the first ever granted to a black citizen. Thousands of mourners, black and white, turned out to see the procession pass from Harlem, down the West Side to St. Mark's Episcopal Church. "Before Jim Europe came to New York," a black

mourner told a reporter for the New York *Tribune,* "the colored man knew nothing but Negro dances and porter's work. All that has been changed. Jim Europe was the living open sesame to the colored. . . . He took them from their porter's places and raised them to positions of importance as real musicians."

An editorial writer for the New York *Times* saw more clearly than most what Europe's loss meant, not merely to the African-American community but to American music as a whole.

To those who think that contemporary ragtime, however imperfect, is a stage in the evolution of a different sort of music which may eventually possess considerable merit will regret the untimely death of a man who ranked as one of the greatest ragtime conductors, perhaps the greatest, we have had. Ragtime may be negro music, but it is American negro music, more alive than much other American music; and Europe was one of the Americans who was contributing most to its development.

THE HIGHWAY THE WHOLE WORLD WILL SWING ALONG

A few days after Jim Europe and his men returned from Europe, the Original Dixieland Jazz Band had set sail for England. Despite the war, the words "jazz" and "jazzy" were already commonplace in London, though few Britons knew anything about the music itself other than that it was loud, peppy, up-to-date, and had something to do with black Americans. When Nick LaRocca and his men landed in England, the London *Daily News* felt the need to reassure its readers that they were "all white—as white as they can possibly be."

America's music establishes its first beachhead overseas. (Right) the drummer Tony Sbarbaro examines a poster that advertises the Original Dixeland's appearance at London's Palladium in the spring of 1919 and proclaims him and his fellow New Orleanians "the Creators of Jazz." (Above) the ODJB onstage at the Palais de Danse at Hammersmith, its southern roots proudly proclaimed on the men's hats. Two of the original members of the band were gone, replaced by New Orleans trombonist Emile Christian and pianist Billy Jones, an Englishman.

So many American doughboys cheered the ODJB so loudly during their first appearance on a variety bill at the Hippodrome Theater that the British headliner whom they had outshone demanded they be fired. The band reopened at the Palladium five nights later—billed as "the last word of a gee whiz world"—and sold it out, did almost as well in Glasgow, played for royalty at Buckingham Palace, and, on the evening of June 28, the day the Versailles Treaty formally ending the war was finally signed in France, performed for glittering celebrants at a victory ball at the fashionable Savoy Restaurant. A teddy bear atop Tony Sbarbaro's drum flew a tiny American flag that night, and when the men struck up the "Star-Spangled Banner" before the dancing began, members of the U.S. Marine band crowded around to see just how so few men had managed to make so much noise.

When Americans had first gone off to war, a Tin Pan Alley songwriter had rushed out a timely tune called "We're Going to Celebrate the End of the War in Ragtime." But when the troops marched home they would find their country undergoing the most rapid change in its history, and jazz, not ragtime, would set the pace.

The cheers that greeted Jim Europe and his "Hellfighters" had not echoed long. Inflation raged all across the country in 1919. There were some thirty-six hundred strikes that year; in Boston, even the police walked off their jobs. Exaggerated fears of "Reds" and "Radicals" would lead to the arrest by the federal government of more than six thousand persons, most of them innocent of any crime. Congress turned its back on the world, refusing to join the League of Nations, and it would soon limit immigration to exclude newcomers who were not of "Nordic" or "Teutonic" stock.

A resurgent Ku Klux Klan—four million strong by 1924—was only the most public manifestation of the xenophobia that gripped much of the country. The aspirations of every minority came under attack, but black Americans were the most frequent targets. More than seventy were killed by white mobs during the last nine months of 1919—ten of them returning American soldiers, still in uniform—and there were race riots in northern cities. Thirty-eight people were killed in Chicago in a week-long battle that ended only with the arrival of National Guardsmen.

In response to the continuing violence, a new spirit of assertiveness and self-reliance began to grow in black neighborhoods. "The *Old* Negro goes," said the Harlem *Crusader*. "His abject crawling and pleading have availed the Cause nothing." "The NEW NEGRO," echoed the Kansas City *Call*, "does not fear the face of day. The time for cringing is over." The NAACP launched a nationwide crusade against lynching. W. E. B. DuBois, the editor of its journal, *The Crisis*, set forth its fighting credo:

We return from the slavery of uniform which the world's madness demanded [of] us to don the freedom of civil garb. We stand again to look America squarely in the face . . . : This country of ours, despite all its better souls have done and dreamed, is yet a shameful land.

It lynches. . . . It disfranchises its own citizens. . . . It encourages ignorance. . . . It steals from us. . . . It insults us. . . .

We return from fighting. We return fighting.

Make way for Democracy! We saved it in France, and by the Great Jehovah, we will save it in the U.S.A. Or know the reason why.

Everywhere, African-Americans redoubled their efforts to build their own institutions—banks, businesses, baseball teams—while men like Alain Locke and James Weldon Johnson began to prophesy that a "race genius" was bound to come along soon, someone who could take black folk music—spirituals, blues, ragtime—and transform it into something altogether new, altogether American. Somehow, they failed to see that

jazz would be that music; that point would first have to be made overseas, by someone who had never set foot in the United States.

On the Fourth of July, 1919, just five days after the ODJB's triumph at the Savoy ball in London, the Southern Syncopated Orchestra, a troupe of some forty black musicians and singers, opened a five-month run at the Royal Philharmonic Hall. Their musical director, Will Marion Cook, was a proud, irascible man. A product of the same middle-class Washington world from which Duke Ellington came, he had studied violin at Oberlin College, in Berlin, and with Antonín Dvořák during the Czech composer's brief sojourn in New York, only to abandon the concert stage at thirty because he had come to see that there was no future on it for a black artist. According to Ellington, who knew him well, the catalyst had been a patronizing review that called him "the world's greatest Negro violinist." Cook called upon the critic, smashed his violin across his desk, saying, "I am the greatest violinist in the *world!*" then stormed out, vowing never to play in public again. He had turned his attention first to bringing the most authentically African-American

music the traffic would bear to turn-of-the-century Broadway, writing the score for the poet Paul Lawrence Dunbar's revue *Clorindy, or the Origin of the Cakewalk,* as well as three hit shows for the comedy team of Bert Williams and George Walker—*In Dahomey, In Abyssinia,* and *Bandana Land.*

Cook continued to believe it his mission to "place the musical art of the Negro—truly American, distinctive, characteristic, sublime—in the sphere it properly belongs . . . for in the democracy of art, the prejudices of race must disappear." The "musical art of the Negro," according to Cook's definition, included everything "from the old spirituals to the standard works of the modern Negro composers"—everything, that is, except jazz. He had deplored Jim Europe's brassier arrangements for being "undignified," loathed the Original Dixieland Jazz Band and its white imitators, whose crude novelty music he saw as just the latest manifestation of the old minstrelsy he detested, and insisted that all of his musicians play his orchestrations precisely as written—with a single exception. Twenty-one-year-old Sidney Bechet, whom Cook had found playing in Chicago, was allowed to improvise his own solo just

Sidney Bechet, at far right, and the Jazz Kings, the group he often played for in and around London after the Southern Syncopated Orchestra fell apart, 1921

Mug shots of Sidney Bechet made by the London police, 1922

before the finale each night on a tune called "Characteristic Blues." It brought down the house. "I don't know which took the more exercise, the audience or the performers," wrote the reviewer for the London *Daily Herald.* "As the music grew raggier and raggier they swayed and we swayed . . . they snapped their fingers and clapped their hands, as we clapped more, and were all quite excited."

The Swiss conductor Ernest Ansermet came several times to hear Bechet that summer and later wrote about him and his music in a prophetic article for the *Revue Romande.*

There is in the Southern Syncopated Orchestra an extraordinary clarinet virtuoso who is, so it seems, the first of his race to have composed perfectly formed blues on the clarinet. I've heard two of them which he had elaborated at great length, then played to his companions so that they could make up an accompaniment. Extremely difficult, they are equally admirable for their richness of invention, force of accent, and daring novelty and the unexpected. . . .

I wish to set down the name of this artist of genius; as for myself, I shall never forget it, it is Sidney Bechet. When one has tried so hard so often in the past to discover one of the figures to whom we owe the advent of an art . . . what a moving thing it is to meet this very black, fat boy with white teeth and that narrow forehead, who is very glad one likes what he does, but who can say nothing of his art, save that he follows his "own way," and then one thinks that his "own way" is perhaps the highway the whole world will swing along tomorrow.

Sidney Bechet would follow his own way all his life. He was a "good friend and a fine fellow," a fellow member of the orchestra remembered, "but he just couldn't trust himself. He was so impetuous. . . . when the time came nothing on earth would stop him

from doing what he wanted to do." One evening, as Cook's wife, the soprano Abbie Mitchell, began her big number, an aria from *Madame Butterfly,* Bechet jumped up from his chair in the orchestra, strode into her spotlight and began blowing a complex, keening obbligato. Cook, who detested onstage surprises of any kind, wanted to fire Bechet on the spot until his wife told him how much she'd liked it.

After the Southern Syncopated Orchestra split up, Bechet would stay on in London, playing with a shifting cast of former band members who called themselves the Jazz Kings. It was the kind of outfit he liked—there was no cornet or trumpet player to compete with him for the lead— and they were eventually booked to follow the Original Dixieland Jazz Band into the vast Palais de Danse at Hammersmith, sometimes performing for five thousand dancers an evening. When the Palais closed at midnight, Bechet moved on to play until dawn at a small club called Rector's where, a regular remembered, he liked to sit down in the middle of the dance floor, "legs crossed, tailor-fashion, and proceed to give us solos, . . . usually starting off with the Prologue from *Pagliacci.*"

Bechet was often playing a new instrument now—the soprano saxophone, preferring it to the clarinet, he said, because it was so loud. No brass player would ever again be able to drown him out. Musicians derided it as "Sidney's fish horn" at first, and made fun of the distinctive tremolo with which he played it, but that same huge impassioned sound would soon overwhelm nearly everyone who tried to play alongside him. It was unlike anything anyone had ever heard before and has never been duplicated since.

Bechet's private life remained as turbulent as his music. He drank too much, lost jobs for failing to turn up on time and didn't seem to care. He gambled, too, once betting and losing his horn to a fellow musician who charitably gave it back because without it Bechet couldn't earn a living. And he pursued—and was pursued by—British women. He was "as attractive as a panther," the smitten shipping-company heiress Nancy Cunard remembered, "and rather like one—young with a beautiful, light-brown skin, rippling blue-black hair. He had innate courtesy and beautiful clothes." Then, in a murky incident never fully explained, he was arrested, accused of assaulting a London prostitute. It was just "a silly man-woman kind of dispute," Bechet claimed, but he was found guilty and sentenced to two weeks in Brixton Prison, followed by deportation. "Oh, I can be mean," Bechet admitted many years later. "I know that. But not to the music. That's the thing you gotta trust. You gotta mean it, and you got to treat it gentle."

FAST FINGERS

Louis Armstrong had been sad to see Joe Oliver head north for Chicago in 1918, but he was thrilled when he was asked to take his mentor's place as lead cornetist at Pete Lala's cabaret in the band Oliver and Kid Ory had led. He did his best to master its repertoire, even wrote a tune of his own which Clarence Williams bought from him for fifty dollars. (As "I Wish I Could Shimmy Like My Sister Kate," it would eventually become a big hit up north.) He competed in bucking contests, too, facing off against other cornetists, including Sam Morgan, Chris Kelly, Ernest "Punch" Miller, and Buddy Petit.

But his chief rival was Henry "Kid" Rena, a Creole fellow graduate of the Colored Waif's Home band, who shared his delight in high notes and elaborate embellishment. "Kid Rena and I used to have some awful battles," Armstrong remembered. "Rena could all but whistle through that cornet of his, but then my chops were pretty strong, too." Sidney Bechet had earlier defied New Orleans tradition by trying to capture the lead from the cornet. Now, Armstrong and Rena sought somehow both to retain the lead and to take over the clarinet's embellishing role as well. Armstrong continued to play clarinetlike "figurations . . . fast fingers and everything," and when he marched in Oscar "Papa" Celestin's elite Tuxedo Brass Band, the best—and most handsomely uniformed—marching outfit in town, he sometimes mystified his fellow musicians. "I didn't never understand Louis Armstrong," the trombonist Sunny Henry admitted, "because that son-of-a-gun he . . . didn't care what you played. . . . He would play an obbligato all the time; be off [the melody], you understand; he wouldn't never once play straight with you. But everything he put in there, by Ned, it worked."

Soon, Armstrong remembered, "I was beginning to get very popular around that good old town of mine." His responsibilities were increasing along with his reputation. At eighteen, he married a hot-tempered prostitute named Daisy Parker, who ate up his earnings and variously attacked him with a razor, a bread knife, and bricks, which, he remembered, she could hurl as fast and as accurately as Satchel Paige would later throw a baseball. And when a cousin gave birth to a baby named Clarence and then died, and then the infant suffered brain damage, he took on his care, as well.

Out-of-town musicians offered him work from time to time, but he still had little thought of moving away from his home-town. "I used to see so many kids leave," Armstrong said, "and then you look around and they have to hobo their way back home. Wasn't nobody going to get me to leave New Orleans but Papa Joe [Oliver]."

He had to wait four years before Papa Joe finally sent him the telegram he was waiting for, but he put the time to good use. He spent three summers playing for dancers aboard steamboats owned by four brothers named Streckfus, whose fleet of floating ballrooms plowed up and down the Mississippi—from New Orleans all the way north to St. Paul, Minnesota, and back again. The bandleader and pianist, Fate

Fate Marable's band aboard the S.S. *Sidney*, 1919. Young Louis Armstrong is second from left; the bassist is George "Pops" Foster; Baby Dodds sits behind the drums. The big dance floor was filled most evenings with white dancers from small river towns, many of whom had never before encountered black musicians. "We had to listen to plenty of nasty remarks," Armstrong recalled. "We were used to that kind of jive, and we would just keep on swinging as though nothing had happened. Before the evening was over they *loved* us. We couldn't turn [around] for them singing our praises and begging us to hurry back."

*There was a saying in New Orleans. When some musician
would get a job on the riverboats with Fate Marable,
they'd say, "Well, you're going to the conservatory."*

—ZUTTY SINGLETON

Marable, who doubled on calliope, was a disciplinarian who insisted that his young cornetist learn to read music as well as play it. The nine men in his band were expected to play waltzes, light classics, and the latest songs, while a cashier with sharp ears for music tallied up the wrong notes played each evening and dunned errant musicians accordingly. A man who failed to live up to Marable's rules was literally given the ax; when he got to work the next day he would find a hatchet on his chair signaling that he was through. But Armstrong got paid fifty dollars a week plus a five-dollar bonus, more money than he had ever seen, and he got to play alongside some of the best young musicians in New Orleans including Pops Foster, the clarinetist Johnny Dodds and his drummer brother, Warren, known as "Baby."

According to Baby Dodds, the band had included white musicians until they began grumbling about working for a colored man—even one so light-skinned and red-haired as Fate Marable—and the Streckfus brothers were trying their all-black outfit only as an experiment. "They'd advertise before we got there that we were colored," Dodds said, "so people wouldn't be disappointed," and he remembered once docking at Hannibal, Missouri, where whites had filed aboard, then just stared, refusing to dance. "They saw Negro roustabouts but had never seen a Negro with a tie and collar on, a white shirt, playing music. They just didn't know what to make of it." But they listened and the next time they docked at Hannibal, Dodds said, "My God, you couldn't get them off the boat. . . . They were the dancingest people I ever found."

At St. Louis, there were Monday-evening cruises for black dancers only. Pops Foster remembered that the musicians called Monday "Getaway Night" because "they could get away with anything." They drank, smoked, got to talk to the customers and to put on a livelier show. Baby Dodds drew special attention to himself by shimmying while playing drums: "The colored people

had never seen anything like that," he said. "Used to have a bunch around me packed five or six deep; and Louis Armstrong would have a bunch five or six deep. It was a wonderful thing, and we were the two sensational men on the boat, Louis and I."

When their boat tied up at Davenport, Iowa, in the summer of 1920, a seventeen-year-old high school student named Leon "Bix" Beiderbecke heard Armstrong play—and never forgot it. Neither did a young trombonist from Texas named Jack Teagarden, who happened to be standing on the New Orleans levee one moonlit evening when he heard the distant sound of a cornet from somewhere across the water. He couldn't see anything at first except the vague form of an excursion boat gliding toward him through the mist. But the sound, growing louder as the boat neared shore, was unlike anything he had ever heard before. It was Louis Armstrong, he remembered, "descending from the sky like a god."

On July 4, 1919, Louis Armstrong, Johnny Dodds, and Pops Foster went ashore together at St. Louis and stopped in a bar owned by a man named Boots to buy themselves a half pint of whiskey each. They planned to celebrate that night—Armstrong believed he had been born on Independence Day and that he was turning nineteen—but they also had heard that Prohibition was soon to begin, Foster remembered, and wanted to have something to tide them over until sanity returned. It would not return for thirteen years. The Fifteenth Amendment went into effect on January 20, 1920. Intended to close down the corner saloon traditionally frequented only by men, it spawned tens of thousands of speakeasies and roadhouses instead, to which both men and women flocked. Alcohol never went away; it just went underground. Prohibition encouraged organized crime, corrupted American politics. But for jazz music —which had started out in the saloons as well as the streets of New Orleans—and for

jazz musicians, it would prove a godsend. Theirs would become the music of choice in cabarets and speakeasies and roadhouses, would provide the accompaniment for the period F. Scott Fitzgerald would soon call the Jazz Age.

I'D GO TO HELL TO HEAR A GOOD BAND

By the time the Original Dixieland Jazz Band got back to New York in July of 1920, they found the city filled with noisy imitators: the Louisiana Five, Georgia Five, Alabama Five, St. Louis Five, Domino Five, Original Indiana Five, the Frisco Jass Band, and the Original New Orleans Jazz Band, which featured four authentic New Orleans musicians but was actually the creation of a Brooklyn-born ragtime piano player named Jimmy Durante. "In some of those bands in those days the cornet player played the melody," Durante remembered, "in some others the clarinet played the melody. In our band, *nobody* played the melody."

For most of these groups melody—and music—were less important than noise and novelty. The message they seemed to want to convey, Ralph Berton, the younger brother of the drummer Vic Berton, remembered was, "Let's all get loaded and see how nutty we can sound." The Louisiana Five's biggest hit was "Yelping Hound Blues," on which Tom Brown's one-time clarinetist Yellow Nuñez imitated a dog baying at the moon. One of the most popular jazz groups in town, Earl Fuller's Famous Jazz Band at Rector's restaurant, played almost entirely for laughs: as its leader played piano, drummer John Lucas banged away at what was advertised as "64 square feet" of bells, cymbals, woodblocks, and "pieces of . . . apparatus [that] are electrically worked," the trombonist used his foot to manipulate his slide, and Ted Lewis juggled a top hat with one hand while playing clarinet with the wobbliest comic tone he could muster.

Nut jazz. The Frisco Syncopators (top) and a clownish outfit led by the dummer Albert "Doc" Wrixon (bottom) who sometimes worked aboard the same Streckfus boats on which Louis Armstrong had played.

The ODJB continued to do well for a time, even attempting a somewhat smoother style that included a saxophone. But nothing Nick LaRocca or his publicists could think of could restore the band's preeminence, not even an elaborately staged appearance at the Bronx Zoo, where their music allegedly inspired a polar bear to shimmy with pleasure but drove a female hippopotamus to take cover underwater. Too much drinking and too many one-nighters eventually wore its members down; one by one they would leave the road until Nick LaRocca himself suffered a nervous breakdown in 1925, abandoned music, and returned to the construction business in New Orleans as if he'd never left it.

Later on, as the first jazz histories were published, filled with praise for Creole and black musicians from New Orleans like Sidney Bechet, Joe Oliver, and Louis Armstrong, LaRocca would react violently, convinced conspirators were out to strip him of the credit for creating jazz that he was sure belonged to him alone. Like his mentor, Papa Jack Laine, LaRocca would always insist that his music—and *all* jazz music—had nothing at all to do with black people. "Our music is strictly white man's music. We patterned our earlier efforts after military marches, which we heard in park concerts in our youth. Many writers have attributed this rhythm that we introduced as something coming from the African jungles and crediting the Negro race with it. My contention is that the Negroes learned to play this rhythm and music from the whites. . . . The Negro did not play any kind of music equal to white men at any time."

The postwar decade would one day be caricatured as "the Roaring Twenties," and it was a time of unprecedented prosperity—the nation's total wealth nearly doubled between 1920 and 1929, manufactures rose by 60 percent, for the first time most people lived in urban areas—and in homes lit by electricity. They made more money than

Vassar's Scale Steppers at the Lincoln Gardens on Chicago's South Side, 1921. Violinist Milton Vassar, second from left, was the leader; Tommy Ladnier from New Orleans, kneeling, played trumpet. The following year, this same bandstand would be occupied by King Oliver and Louis Armstrong.

they ever had before and, spurred on by the giant new advertising industry, spent it faster, too—on washing machines and refrigerators and vacuum cleaners, twelve million radios, thirty million automobiles, and untold millions of tickets to the movies, that ushered them into a new, fast-living world of luxury and glamour their grandparents could never have imagined. Meanwhile, at the polls and in the workplace as

well as on the dance floor, women had begun to assert a new independence.

For many of the millions of people for whom the twenties never roared at all, fearful of such rapid change and nostalgic for the small-town America of the turn of the century, jazz music came to seem not merely an annoyance but a threat, one more cause of loosening morals and frightening dislocation. Ragtime had been bad

enough, with its insinuating rhythms and daring couple-dancing, but the jumpy, raucous version of New Orleans polyphony projected by the ODJB and many of its imitators seemed much worse. "As I understand it," said Professor Henry Van Dyck of Princeton University, "it is not music at all. It is merely an irritation of the nerves of hearing, a sensual teasing of the strings of physical passion. Its fault lies not in syncopation, for that is a legitimate device when sparingly used. But 'jazz' is an unmitigated cacophony, a combination of disagreeable sounds in complicated discords, a willful ugliness and a deliberate vulgarity." The editor of *Musical Courier* reported on a poll of academically trained musicians: most found "the 'ad libbing' or 'jazzing' of a piece . . . thoroughly objectionable," he said, "and several of them advanced the opinion that this Bolshevistic smashing of the rules and tenets of decorous music" spelled disaster for American music.

For some, jazz simply became synonymous with noise. Thomas Edison, whose invention of the phonograph had made its sudden rapid spread possible, claimed that he played jazz records backwards because "they sound better that way." When the *New York Times* reported that the citizens of one Siberian village had driven hungry polar bears from its streets by banging pots and pans, the headline read "Jazz Frightens Bears," and when a celebrated British conductor collapsed with a fatal heart attack while visiting Coney Island, the same paper blamed the jazz bands now loudly competing with one another along the boardwalk for his demise.

Jazz—and the dancing it inspired—was also said to be having a catastrophic impact on the national character. "Moral disaster is coming to hundreds of young American girls," reported the New York *American,* "through the pathological, nerve-irritating, sex-exciting music of jazz orchestras." In just two years in Chicago alone, the Illinois Vigilance Association reported in 1923, the downfall of one thousand girls could be traced directly to the pernicious influence of jazz music. In Cincinnati, the Salvation Army obtained a court injunction to stop construction of a theater next to a home for expectant mothers on the grounds that "the enforced proximity of a theater and jazz palace" would implant dangerous "jazz emotions" in helpless infants. A social worker reported on the "unwholesome excitement" she now encountered even at small-town dances in the Midwest. "Boy-and-girl couples leave the hall in a state of dangerous disturbance. Any worker who has gone into the night to gather the facts of activities outside the dance hall is appalled . . . by the blatant disregard of even the elementary rules of civilization. . . . We must expect a few casualties in social intercourse, but the modern dance is producing little short of holocaust."

Beyond its disturbing sounds, its fast pace, and its supposed impact on morals, jazz was also condemned because of its origins. Many white older Americans were appalled to see their children dancing to music that was believed to have emerged from what the music critic of the New York *Herald Tribune* called "the Negro brothels of the South." "Jazz," said the editor of *Etude,* "is often associated with vile surroundings, filthy words, unmentionable dances." It was originally "the accompaniment of the voodoo dancer," declared Mrs. Max Obendorfer, national music chairman of the General Federation of Women's Clubs, "stimulating the half-crazed barbarian to the vilest deeds. . . . [It] has also been employed by other barbaric people to stimulate brutality and sensuality." (Blacks were not the sole sources of the jazz contagion. The critic Carl Engel also worried about the effects on Anglo-Saxon youth of what he called "Semitic purveyors of Broadway melodies," while Henry Ford's *Dearborn Independent* blamed what it called "the abandoned sensuousness of sliding notes" on sinister Jews.)

There was nothing new in these attitudes. Twenty years earlier, many whites had deplored ragtime in part because it was based on black songs and dances, just as their descendants would one day denounce rock 'n' roll because of its links to the African-American blues tradition. But something altogether new really was happening here and there across the country. A few white youths—living in small towns and comfortable suburbs as well as big-city slums—started to see more than mere novelty and excitement in this new primarily black music, began actually to hear their own feelings mirrored in the playing of African-Americans, and to look for ways they might participate in it themselves. In a country in which by law and custom blacks and whites were forbidden to compete on anything like an equal basis in any arena—even boxing: the heavyweight title was then off-limits to black challengers—these young men were willing to brave a brand new world created by black Americans and in which black musicians remained the most admired figures.

Nothing quite like it had ever happened before in America.

In late 1921, eight white musicians who called themselves the New Orleans Rhythm Kings had begun what would turn into a seventeen-month run at a little cellar cabaret called the Friar's Inn, at 343 South Wabash on Chicago's Near North Side. The club advertised itself as the "Land of Bohemia Where Good Fellows Get Together." It "smelled just right," one visitor remembered, "funky, run-down, sinister and dusty" and the good fellows who sometimes got together there included the gangster Dion O'Banion, nicknamed "the Florist" because he provided the flowers for gangland funerals (and sometimes the corpses, as well), and young Al Capone, who would soon order O'Banion murdered and then take over his post as boss of the North Side.

The most celebrated members of the New Orleans Rhythm Kings—cornetist Paul Mares, trombonist George Brunies, and clarinetist Leon Roppolo—were all really from New Orleans. Mares, who had put the band together, was becomingly modest about its attainments. "We had only two tempos, slow drag and the two-four one-step," he recalled. "We did our best to copy the colored music we'd heard at home. We did the best we could, but naturally we couldn't play real colored style."

For whatever reason, the Rhythm Kings sounded very different from the Original

The New Orleans Rhythm Kings at the Friar's Inn in 1922. George Brunies plays trombone, Paul Mares is on cornet, Leon Ropollo plays clarinet.

Dixieland Jazz Band and its host of white imitators—less ragtimey and agitated, more relaxed and flowing. They had relatively little interest in comedy, and in part because the Friar's Inn was a small place with a low ceiling, they had also learned to modulate their sound. Mares stayed carefully in the middle range of his cornet and modeled his blues-based style after King Oliver's, while Brunies was solidly in the New Orleans tailgate trombone tradition. But Leon Ropollo's lyrical clarinet had its own unmistakable sound, suffused with an eerie melancholy even on the most apparently cheerful tunes. (Like Buddy Bolden, Ropollo would eventually go mad and be confined to a Louisiana asylum.) Ralph Berton summed up the band's impact on young white jazz enthusiasts in Chicago. "They played not in the zany, tongue-in-cheek spirit of the white bands . . . but *seriously*—mean and low

down, pretty or funky, driving or lyrical, but always *for real.* As we said in those days— there was no higher praise—*they played like niggers.*"

Most of the New Orleans Rhythm Kings themselves were under twenty-one and therefore forbidden to drink on the Friar's Inn bandstand, and underage fans were barred from the club altogether, one remembered, "so the only way we could hear them was to go down and stand in the doorway and listen. It was great when someone opened the door and we could hear it louder."

But some exceptions were evidently made and in the spring of 1922, one of the Friar's Inn's frequent patrons was a jug-eared nineteen-year-old prep school boy from Iowa named Leon Bix Beiderbecke. "Bix would come in and quietly sit and have

dinner," the Rhythm Kings' banjo player, Lou Black, remembered. "Our rhythm section played for the dinner crowd, starting at 6 p.m., and the full band came on about 10 p.m. Bix would stay to hear the music. Our headwaiter . . . didn't think a high school student should be in the club so late. He often made a menacing move towards Bix to throw him out. When he tried, the whole band would stand up and say, 'If he goes, so do we.' This was a great band, make no mistake about it. When we got to cooking, Jemima, our hat-check girl, would come out and start dancing right in front of her counter."

Beiderbecke wasn't interested in dancing. He had with him a battered cornet in a paper bag and lived for the moments when his heroes allowed him to sit in. His favorite tune was "Angry," Paul Mares remembered. "It sometimes seemed like that was the only tune he knew."

For Beiderbecke, just being there was an act of rebellion. His parents had sent him to the highly disciplined Lake Forest Academy in the Chicago suburb of Lake Forest the previous September precisely to keep his mind off jazz, yet night after night since his arrival he had been leaving his dormitory room, with or without permission from the headmaster, and traveling thirty-five miles into the city to seek out the music that already seemed to be all that mattered to him. Twice, he had been officially censured by the school and there had been talk of expelling him if he did not mend his ways. He paid no attention. It was as if he could not help himself.

Bix Beiderbecke was a shy, deeply self-doubting product of the Iowa corn country, who never learned more than the rudiments of written music and rarely spoke unless someone spoke to him first. His favorite phrase was "What the hell?" He was never a virtuoso in the sense in which that term applied to Louis Armstrong or Sidney Bechet; he can be heard on some 250 recordings but never won any serious

Bismarck and Agatha Beiderbecke of Davenport, Iowa, and their children in 1904. Bix sits on his father's lap, flanked by his brother Charles and sister Mary Louise.

derisively called "the Number One jazz saint," and to inflate his genuine gifts until he came somehow to seem a white counterpart to Louis Armstrong. None of this was fair to him or to his music.

For Armstrong's mother and the people among whom they lived in black Storyville, jazz music had been a step up, a way out for "Little Louis"; for Bix Beiderbecke's parents and their neighbors in Davenport, Iowa, his decision to become a jazz musician would come to seem like a plunge into the netherworld. He was born at 1934 Grand Avenue in Davenport, Iowa, on March 10, 1903. His father, Bismarck Beiderbecke, was a well-to-do coal-and-lumber merchant named after the Iron Chancellor of his family's native Germany. His mother, Agatha, was a steamboat captain's daughter. Both loved music—he had performed in his father's choral group; she was a gifted amateur pianist and played organ in the Presbyterian church—and they encouraged their younger son's early interest in the piano. He could play a one-fingered version of one of his mother's favorites, "Oh, Mr. Dooley," before he was three, and at seven was the subject of an admiring article in the Davenport *Daily Democrat* that began, "Little Bickie Beiderbecke plays any selection he hears!"

"He was a dreamy little fellow," his kindergarten teacher remembered, "and was happy finding his own niche rather than joining the larger group." Bix would always be dreamy, always remain a little apart from everyone else. At ten, his older brother, Charles, remembered, "he stopped coming home for supper," hurrying down to the riverfront instead, and slipping aboard one or another of the excursion boats to play the calliope. "Mother understood how distracted he was by his music. . . . I can remember having supper without Bix and hearing tunes played as only he could play them. . . . It was reassuring to know where he was." The plots of the silent films Bix and his friends paid a nickel to see on Saturday afternoons didn't interest him

celebrity outside the circle of his fellow musicians; and he drank himself to death before he was twenty-nine. But the understated eloquence of his solos and the silvery brilliance of his tone—"every note went through you like a shaft of light," a friend remembered, "making you feel all clear and clean and open"—would bring a kind of quiet lyricism to jazz and provide a whole generation of young white musicians with the proof they badly needed that they, too, might make a lasting contribution to this new American music.

"Bix was a mystery to us," one of his most ardent disciples remembered. "We knew him, admired him, thought he was a great guy. But in a way we didn't know him at all. He wasn't really *like* us." And, because he seemed unknowable even by those with whom he shared the bandstand, and because he died so soon, some romantic writers—who understood him even less well than his friends had—sought posthumously to transform him into a kind of selfless martyr to his art, to make him what the British saxophonist and writer Benny Green

The S.S. *Capitol*, the Streckfus steamboat on which both
Louis Armstrong and Bix Beiderbecke played during their
early years

much, but the minute the lights went on again, a friend remembered, he'd rush home to see if he could duplicate the melodies the accompanist had played during the action. He would always remain interested in the piano, struggling to work out fresh harmonies whenever he could get to a keyboard. But perhaps because his ear had been so accurate as a boy he never fully mastered music theory, a failing that would only add to the lack of self-confidence that seemed always to plague him.

In January of 1919, his brother returned from the army with a wind-up Victrola and an armful of records, including the Original Dixieland Jazz Band's frantic version of "Tiger Rag." Bix was fifteen—and transfixed. He listened to it over and over again, his brother remembered, "his head almost in the bell," then borrowed a neighbor's cornet and began to teach himself to play it, slowing down the turntable to hear each separate note, transposing it for the piano, then trying to reproduce it on his horn. "At first it was hard on the rest of us, his playing consisted of short blasting notes, until he got a mute. The mute was a godsend and we were able to go on with our lives."

Beiderbecke never had any formal instruction on his instrument, but two other young cornetists, both from New Orleans, deeply influenced him. The first was Louis Armstrong, just two years older than he, whom he heard playing aboard a Streckfus boat that spent a month based at Davenport in the late spring of 1920. "Bix would come aboard," Armstrong recalled, "listen, then go home and practice what he heard. He was never satisfied." The following winter, Beiderbecke heard a youthful white musician named Emmet Hardy, who played accompaniment for a shimmy dancer at a downtown Davenport theater with such beauty and drive that after Hardy's early death Beiderbecke would write his mother that her son had been "the greatest musician I have ever heard."

Bix couldn't get into the local musician's union because he couldn't read music well enough, but he found plenty of nonunion pickup jobs with small-time bands in and around his hometown: Billy Greer's Melody Jazz Band, Buckley's Novelty Orchestra, the Ralph Miedke Society Orchestra, the Ten Capitol Harmony Syncopaters, and the grandly named Plantation Jazz Orchestra with which he sailed for a time aboard the Streckfus steamer *Majestic* in the summer of 1921. That July, he heard Louis Armstrong again when his boat and the *St. Paul* both docked at the little town of Louisiana, Missouri; Armstrong and the Fate Marable band were "the talk of the River," Bix wrote home.

By the age of eighteen, Bix was good enough to play alongside older musicians—and to join them behind the bandstand between sets to sip corn whiskey and bootleg gin. At nineteen, he was arrested for what the Davenport police blotter called a "lewd and lascivious act with a child"—apparently just a fellow teenager, a girl from down the street. The case never reached court but the scandal must have been humiliating to him and to his family.

Bix's parents were appalled. Classical music was one thing. Jazz—and the sordid life it seemed to encourage—was quite another. It represented everything they detested, constituted a serious threat to the peace and stability of life in respectable communities like theirs. They had always wanted their boy to go on to Princeton, and in the autumn of 1921, evidently hoping to force him to focus on his studies and wean him away from jazz and the bad habits they believed went with it, they packed him off to Lake Forest.

It didn't work. Within a week of his arrival at school in September, he was writing home to tell his brother that he had already managed to make it to the South Side and talk his way into three different black clubs on Thirty-fifth Street in eager search of what he called "real jazz niggers." "Don't think I'm getting hard Burnie," he wrote, "but I'd go to hell to hear a good band."

Bix Beiderbecke as a student at Lake Forest Academy. "If you don't mind," he wrote home soon after reaching the school, "please send me all those Dixieland Jazz records I ordered. My room-mate has a victrola."

Bix Beiderbecke was a musician before he was anything else, eager to hear and learn from the best, whatever their color. At Thanksgiving, he slipped into the Hotel Sherman to hear Louis Panico, the cornetist with Isham Jones's white dance band. Panico was a mute specialist and an admirer of Joe Oliver, celebrated for his comedy effects and skilled enough to publish a book on cornet technique called *The Novelty Cornetist*. "When I told him I lived on the old Mississippi & played on the *Capitol*," Bix proudly reported home, "he told me he would show me how to laugh [on his horn] which he doesn't often do."

Bix helped organize a band on campus and almost immediately got in trouble with the headmaster for performing indecorously at a school dance. He had also already begun to develop the spare cornet style for which he would one day be remembered. When a schoolmate who prided himself on playing saxophone with a lot of flash accused him of being too restrained—"a note miser"—Beiderbecke shot back, "The trouble with you is you play so many notes, but they mean so little." From the beginning, Bix wanted every note to mean as much as possible.

He began regularly leaving the campus to play at downtown Chicago hotels. Once, when he appeared at an exclusive girls' school, the headmistress took the bandleader aside to complain: "That *nice boy* of yours is exciting my girls!" she said. "Make him stop." In May of 1922 alone, he slipped out of his room at different times to play in Gary, Indiana, at the Edgewater Beach Hotel, and at Northwestern University, and also found time to hear the New Orleans Rhythm Kings at the Friar's Inn as well as Joe Oliver, now appearing at a South Side café called the Lincoln Gardens. His grades understandably went from bad to worse.

Then, in the early morning hours of May 20, he was caught on the fire escape, trying to climb back into his dormitory room. The faculty voted to expel him the next day. His disappointed father came to take him home, but the boy somehow talked him into letting him spend the rest of the year seeing if he couldn't earn a living as a musician. He worked excursion boats and dance bands in Michigan and Wisconsin, then returned to Chicago and joined a youthful septet, the Royal Harmonists of Indiana, for an engagement in Syracuse, New York.

Its banjo player was Eddie Condon, an Indiana saloon-keeper's son who was just seventeen but already a fast talker—his nickname was "Slick." Beiderbecke didn't impress him much at their first meeting. Bix was wearing a battered cap and a threadbare green overcoat, Condon remembered, and "had a round face and eyes that had no desire to focus on what was in

front of him." They boarded the train for Syracuse and went to sleep. The next morning, bored by the flat Ohio landscape sliding past the window, Condon began idly to play his banjo. The saxophone player unpacked his horn. "Finally," Condon recalled, "Beiderbecke took out a silver cornet . . . put it to his lips and blew a phrase. The sound came out like a girl saying yes. . . . 'All right,' Beiderbecke said, '*Panama*.' At last I was playing music; so far as I was concerned it could go on forever. We disrupted the train. People crowded in from the other coaches; they stood in the aisles and on the seats. We couldn't wait to get to Syracuse; I hoped I would be stuck forever with Beiderbecke."

HYPNOSIS AT FIRST HEARING

Louis Armstrong had also been traveling that summer. On July 8, 1922, he boarded a train at New Orleans, bound for Chicago. He was twenty-one years old and finally going to join his idol, King Oliver. He had been making $1.50 an evening in New Orleans; in Chicago he could look forward to $52.50 a week, plus roughly the same amount in tips from enthralled customers. "There was plenty of work [in Chicago]," Armstrong remembered, "lots of *Dough* flying around, all kinds of beautiful women at your service. A musician in Chicago in the early twenties [was] treated and respected just like—some kind of a god."

He carried only his cornet case and an old valise that held his patched, threadbare tuxedo. His mother, Mayann, had packed him a trout sandwich to eat aboard the train and made sure he was wearing long underwear; she had heard that where he was going it was cold even in midsummer.

In setting out for Chicago, Armstrong was joining what came to be called the "Great Migration," a northern exodus that since 1917 had sent more than a million African-Americans northward—and

Above, the Chicago *Defender* advertises just some of the entertainment available to black residents of the city's South Side on June 17, 1922. King Oliver is already starring at the Lincoln Gardens and about to send for Louis Armstrong to come north and join him. (Opposite) Armstrong and Oliver in Chicago, 1922. Oliver, said the younger man, was "always my inspiration and my idol. No trumpet player ever had the fire that Oliver had. Man, he really could *punch* a number."

that would propel a million more to follow before the end of the 1920s. As Alain Locke explained in the introduction to his 1925 compendium of black art and literature called *The New Negro,* there was no single reason for this exodus.

The tide of Negro migration, northward and cityward, is not to be fully explained as a blind flood started by the demands of war industry coupled with the shutting off of foreign immigration, or by the pressure of poor crops coupled with increased social terrorism in certain sections of the South and Southwest. Neither labor demand, the boll weevil, nor the Ku Klux Klan is a basic factor, however contributory any or all of them may have been. The wash and rush of this human tide on the beach line of the northern city centers is to be explained primarily in terms of a new vision of opportunity, of social and economic freedom, of a spirit to seize, even in the face of an extortionate and heavy toll, a chance for the improvement of conditions. With each successive wave of it, the movement toward the larger and the more democratic chance—in the Negro's case a deliberate flight not only from countryside to city, but from medieval America to modern.

Most immigrants from the deep South ended up at the end of the Illinois Central line, in Chicago. It was considered "the safest place near New Orleans," Danny Barker recalled. "All other places between those two points were looked upon as just visiting points. . . . I recall relatives returning to New Orleans telling humorous tales of looking out the windows of the train at such places as Memphis, Bowling Green, Kankakee, Natchez. They would say, 'I just can't figure how colored folks can live in them places that close to Chicago and not *go* there.' " Well over one hundred thousand black Americans now called Chicago

Michigan Avenue in downtown Chicago, 1924.
The city's tallest buildings and most fashionable
neighborhoods were a long way from the crowded
South Side where most black refugees from Jim
Crow settled. But they kept coming anyway. In
Chicago, one explained, colored people were not
"required to say, 'yes, ma'am' or 'yes, sir' to white
people whether you desired to or not." "You
can go anywhere you want," another said, and
"don't have to look up to the white man, get off
the street for him, and go to the buzzard roost
[segregated balcony] at shows."

home, most of them clustered together on the South Side, and not even the vicious race riots that had gripped the city during the summer of 1919 could shake their belief that life in the North was preferable to returning to the Jim Crow South. The "Stroll"—the black bright-light district that shifted slowly down South State Street during the decade as more and more migrants poured into South Side tenements—was "the Bohemia of the Colored Folks," according to the black-owned Chicago *Whip,* a "Mecca for Pleasure," celebrated in black communities all over the country. There were clubs that limited their clientele to blacks only, and others, called black-and-tans, that welcomed patrons of both races. Shops and restaurants never closed their doors. "Excitement from noon to noon," the poet Langston Hughes recalled. "Midnight was like day. The street was full of workers and gamblers, prostitutes and pimps, church folk and sinners." And the police largely looked the other way, under orders from Big Bill Thompson, the red-faced, spectacularly corrupt Democratic mayor of the city who took a dim view of Prohibition—"I'm as wet as the middle of the Atlantic Ocean," he said—and, as he moved from club to club with his entourage, liked to bellow: "Get a horn and blow loud for Chicago. Let the jazz band play! Let's show 'em, we're all live ones!"

Louis Armstrong had never been so far from home before, and when he stepped down at Chicago's Twelfth Street Station and Joe Oliver was not there to meet him, he asked himself if he had made a mistake leaving New Orleans.

> I saw a million people, but not Mister Joe, and I didn't give a damn who else was there. I never seen a city that big. All those tall buildings, I thought they were universities. I said, no, this is the wrong city. I was just fixing to go back home—standing there in my box-back suit, padded shoulders,

King Oliver's Creole Jazz Band, 1923. Left to right, Baby Dodds, trombonist Honoré Dutrey, Joe Oliver, bassist Bill Johnson, Louis Armstrong, clarinetist Johnny Dodds, and pianist Lil Hardin

> wide-legged pants—when a redcap Joe left word with came up to me.

The redcap put him in a taxi and sent him along to the Lincoln Gardens Café, an enormous and ornate dance hall at Thirty-first and Cottage Grove, just a few blocks from the Stroll, in the heart of the South Side. When he got there and heard the music drifting out through the door, Armstrong remembered, he said to himself, "No, I ain't supposed to be in *this* band, they're too good." But then Oliver spotted him: "You little fool," he said. "Come on in here."

Once Armstrong was inside, everything seemed familiar. The sound of Oliver's foot could be heard stomping off the tempo just as it had back in New Orleans; the musicians were free to shed their coats if things got too hot; and a bucket of water with a dipper and a big block of ice floating in it occupied a corner of the bandstand in case

anybody got thirsty. Oliver invited him to play. "That was heaven," Armstrong wrote. "Papa Joe was so elated that he played half an hour overtime. I was so happy I did not know what to do. I had hit the big time. I was up North with the Greats. I was playing with my idol, The King, Joe Oliver. All of my boyhood dreams had come true at last. . . . I was home."

Joe Oliver's Creole Jazz Band would remain Armstrong's home for the next two years. It was an all-round orchestra and sounded good at any speed. "We played so soft," said the drummer, Baby Dodds, "that you could . . . hear the people's feet dancing. The music was so soothing and then when we put a little jump into it, the patrons just had to dance." And its members were all expected to be showmen: Oliver was a master of what Northerners called "New Orleans hokum"—comedy vocal effects built around his profusion of mutes. Baby Dodds shimmied at the drums. The bassist Bill Johnson sometimes played while lying down. Louis Armstrong danced, too, he remembered, and slid and fell "like I was going to hurt myself."

But it was the music that he and Oliver played together that now began to draw big crowds to the Lincoln Gardens. Oliver and Armstrong perfected a style of playing duet breaks by which Armstrong seemed instinctively to know just what his boss was about to play and was always ready with the perfect complement to it. Different every night, but in perfect harmony, their breaks mystified the musicians who began crowding around the bandstand to hear them. It was not magic, of course, but craft. "While the rest of the band was playing," Armstrong explained, "Oliver'd lean over to me and move the valves on his cornet in the notes he would play in the next break. . . . Whatever Mister Joe played I just tried to make it sound as pretty as I could. I never blew my horn over Joe Oliver at no time unless he said, 'Take it!' "

Among those who regularly turned out to hear Oliver and Armstrong at the Lincoln Gardens was a band of eager white high school boys, some of them in knee pants. "Night after night we made the trip" to the South Side, one remembered, and neither the fact that the club was "by and for Negroes," nor the presence of the 350-pound bouncer who razzed them genially every evening about coming to the South Side for their "music lessons," could keep them away.

They were a rough-hewn bunch, rebellious and headstrong. Some were streetwise products of the city slums; others came from comfortable suburban homes or were refugees from the rural heartland, captivated by what one musician called "the bursting feeling of life in the city." But all of them felt alienated from the worlds in which they had been brought up, and each came to see jazz both as an outlet for emotions they otherwise could not express and

Members of the Austin High Gang. Left to right, would-be clarinetist Frank Teschemacher; cornetist Jimmy McPartland and his guitar- and banjo-playing brother, Richard; tenor saxophonist Lawrence "Bud" Freeman and his brother, Arny, who became an actor instead of a musician. "For my money," Bud Freeman remembered, "Chicago was the greatest place for a young jazz musician to be born."

as a symbol of personal defiance, what one of them would call "a collectively improvised nose-thumbing at all pillars of all communities, [a] syncopated Bronx cheer for the righteous squares everywhere."

Among the first were a handful of high school students who got together in the autumn of 1922 in a manicured West Side neighborhood called Austin and therefore became known to jazz history as the Austin High Gang—though none of them was ever actually graduated from that school. They included fifteen-year-old Jimmy McPartland, already a veteran street fighter from the roughest part of the Near West Side, who thought he might like to play cornet; his guitarist brother, Richard; a shy, bespectacled violin student named Frank Teschemacher, who would soon shift his allegiance to jazz clarinet; and Bud Freeman, another product of a tough part of town and already interested in the saxophone. They would soon be joined by Dave

Tough, a reticent bookish would-be drummer from the prosperous suburb of Oak Park. All of them felt themselves to be outsiders; at fifteen, both Tough and Jimmy McPartland were already drinking hard.

Their journey into jazz had begun with white bands. "Every day after school," McPartland remembered, "we used to go to a little place called the Spoon and Straw. It was just an ice cream parlor. But they had a Victrola there, and we used to sit around listening to records. One day we put on some new records by the New Orleans Rhythm Kings. Boy, when we heard that, I'll tell you, we were out of our minds. Everybody flipped. It was wonderful. We stayed there from about three in the afternoon until eight at night, just listening to those records . . . and we decided we would get a band and try to play like these guys."

Just as Bix Beiderbecke had done a few years earlier, they doggedly learned their first tunes from records: "We'd have to tune our instruments up to the record machine, to the pitch, and go ahead with a few notes. Then stop!" McPartland said. "A few more bars of the record, each guy would pick out his notes and boom! . . . Each guy'd pick his notes, so we got the right harmonies and everything. We developed ourselves. Because you were allowed to copy anything from the record of the ensembles, but you had to play your own solo. Each guy had to play his own solo his own way, not the way the guy did it on the record. . . . We just said, 'That's not fair, you can't copy a guy's music.' "

They began hanging around the door of the Friar's Inn to hear their heroes in person, formed a group of their own called the Blue Friars in homage to them, and started getting pickup jobs around town. Then, after playing a fraternity party at the University of Chicago, on the South Side, a college student took several of them along with him to hear Oliver and Armstrong at the Lincoln Gardens. "After that," Bud Freeman remembered, "we never went back to the New Orleans Rhythm Kings because

THE EMPRESS OF THE BLUES

In the spring of 1927, the train carrying the blues singer Bessie Smith and her band was halted outside a southern Ohio town. Floodwaters covered the track. The troupe had to be ferried to the theater in which they were to perform by rowboat. When the audience called upon Smith to sing a blues about the flood she said she was sorry she didn't know any, but as soon as she got home she wrote one out. She was first and foremost a spectacular entertainer, but her public—overwhelmingly black, mostly poor—also looked to her to say what they could not. "When I was a little girl," the gospel singer Mahalia Jackson remembered, "I felt she was having troubles like me. That's why it was such a comfort for the people of the South to hear her. She expressed something they couldn't put into words."

Bessie Smith was not the first woman to record the blues. Mamie Smith beat her to it in 1920—and sold seventy-five thousand copies for Okeh records in one week in Harlem alone. And there were other singers with big followings, including Ma Rainey, the "Mother of the Blues"; Ida Cox, "Queen of the Blues"; Clara Smith, "The World's Champion Moaner"; Chippie Hill; Sippie Wallace; and Alberta Hunter. But almost from the moment she recorded "Down-Hearted Blues" for Columbia in 1923, Bessie Smith was the unchallenged "Empress of the Blues," celebrated both for her majestic voice and for the utter lack of sentimentality or self-pity in her songs.

Born in Chattanooga in 1894, she began singing for pennies on streetcorners at nine and, while still a child, traveled the South in a tent show with Ma Rainey. Then she moved up to become a star on the black vaudeville circuit officially known as the "Theater Owners Booking Association," or T.O.B.A.—but remembered by black performers as "Tough on Black Asses." "She was new," the trumpet player Adolphus "Doc" Cheatham remembered, "and people had begun to listen to the blues. Some liked it and some didn't. Some people—the schoolteachers—came to hear Bessie Smith, but they didn't want to be seen in there. So they would hide their faces."

The records Bessie Smith and her rivals made were a sensation in black communities all over the country. Newsboys sold blues records. So did door-to-door salesmen. Pullman porters carried copies south to peddle at whistlestops. The Chicago *Defender* urged "lovers of music everywhere and those who desire to help in any advance of the Race" to buy the work of black singers and musicians. Soon, Okeh, Paramount, Vocalion, and Columbia had all developed specialty labels meant for black audiences—race records—just as they had already created special ethnic catalogues for other minorites. And W. C. Handy's song-publishing partner, Harry Pace, had established the first black-owned recording company, Black Swan, with the slogan, "The Only Genuine Colored Records—Others Are Only Passing for Colored." Soon, race records were selling more than 5 million copies a year.

Bessie Smith lived the life she sang about in her songs. Her first agents, the songwriter Clarence Williams and Frank Walker, supervisor of race records for Columbia, did her out of her royalties. In 1923, she married Jack Gee, a nightwatchman who liked to pretend he'd once been a policeman but proved more interested in collecting her earnings than in making her happy. The two fought—with words and fists—for six tumultuous years, during which she also took a host of lovers, both men and women. Once, she chased her husband down the railroad track, firing a revolver. Drinking only made her meaner. If she didn't like the way things were going onstage she was known to tear the curtains down around her. She could not abide rivals and sometimes refused to appear on the bill with other singers if they were more slender or lighter-skinned than she. "She would tell *anybody* to kiss her ass," a niece remembered. "Nobody messed with Bessie, black or white, it didn't make any difference."

One hot July night in 1927, she and her troupe were performing under canvas in Concord, North Carolina. A member of the band stepped out to have a smoke and spotted half a dozen hooded men who were about to collapse the tent on Smith and her audience. He urged her to flee. Smith wouldn't hear of it. Instead, she ran toward the Klansmen, shaking her fist and cursing. "I'll get the whole damn tent out here," she shouted. "You just pick up them sheets and run." The Klansmen, faced with the prospect of a confrontation with scores of her angry fans, took off instead. Smith returned to the bandstand, told her band they were "nothin' but a bunch of sissies," and began again to sing.

(Above) Bessie Smith in repose and (below) in action on a Philadelphia stage, billed as "the Greatest and Highest Salaried Race Star in the World"

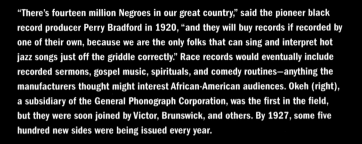

"There's fourteen million Negroes in our great country," said the pioneer black record producer Perry Bradford in 1920, "and they will buy records if recorded by one of their own, because we are the only folks that can sing and interpret hot jazz songs just off the griddle correctly." Race records would eventually include recorded sermons, gospel music, spirituals, and comedy routines—anything the manufacturers thought might interest African-American audiences. Okeh (right), a subsidiary of the General Phonograph Corporation, was the first in the field, but they were soon joined by Victor, Brunswick, and others. By 1927, some five hundred new sides were being issued every year.

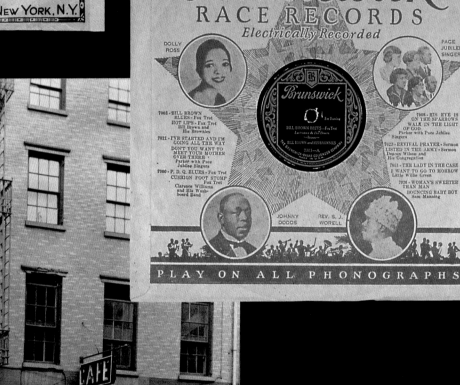

Jack and Irving Mills, whose first offices were at Forty-seventh Street and Eighth Avenue (left), built their music-publishing business on vaudeville tunes—"Mr. Gallagher and Mr. Shean" was their first big hit—but when the blues excitement broke in 1920 they began buying up blues songs as fast as they could find them. Before long, Irving Mills would have some of New York's most gifted African-American songwriters working for him, and then he would form a fateful partnership with the young Duke Ellington.

OKεh
TRUETONE

RACE RECORDS

VICTOR

Brings Back the Old-Time Melodies

How the dear old Southern melodies sung and played upon the Victor bring back old-time thrill! Exquisitely blended voices, fine instrumentation and faultless is bring out the rich harmony and sentiment of these cherished songs in full perfection. You never truly known their heart touching beauty and power till you have heard them on the Victor.

Here are a few out of hundreds—

By the Swanee River   Pryor's Band   10 in.   1997. My Old Kentucky Home   10 in.
Carry Me Back to Old Virginny   10 in.   Haydn Quartet with Orchestra
   Haydn Quartet with Orchestra   4040. My Old Kentucky Home   7 & 10 in.
Dixie   Pryor's Band   10 in.   Miss Morgan with Orchestra
Dixie   Harlan and Stanley with Orch.   10 in.   2808. Old Folks at Home   7 & 10 in.
Dixie   Emma Eames   12 in.   Miss Morgan with Orchestra
Dreaming on the Ohio Haydn Quartet 7 & 10 in.   95033. Old Folks at Home   12 in.
In the Evening by the Moonlight   10 in.   Adelina Patti
   Haydn Quartet with Orchestra   94005. Old Folks at Home   10 in.
I's Gwine Back to Dixie   10 in.   Nellie Melba
   Haydn Quartet with Orchestra   2736. Old Black Joe   7 & 10 in.
Little Alabama Coon   10 in.   Rogers with Orchestra
Massa's in the Cold, Cold Ground   8 & 10 in.   4514. Sounds from Dixie   10 in.
   Haydn Quartet   Pryor's Band
                                       125. The Cornfield Medley Haydn Quartet 7 & 10 in.
                                       4515. Turkey in de Straw   7 & 10 in.
                                              Golden with Orchestra
                                       4103. Whistling Coon   10 in.
                                              Kernell with Orchestra

Ask any Victor Dealer to play them for you.
Or write us for complete catalogue.

Victor Talking Machine Co.
Camden N J

FILL IN, CUT OUT AND MAIL TODAY

when we heard . . . King Oliver . . . we knew that we were hearing the real thing for the first time. . . . *We had to hear that music as one had to eat."*

Other young white musicians who had also rejected the commercial dance music—by turns sentimental and frenetic—that still meant jazz to their family and friends in favor of the more exciting sounds of the South Side soon found themselves following Armstrong and Oliver all over town, just as the Austin High Gang did.

Eddie Condon first heard them play for a private fraternity party at a North Side Club called the Chez Paree. It was "hypnosis at first hearing," he remembered. "The two wove around each other, like suspicious women talking about the same man." Soon he, too, was a regular at the Lincoln Gardens.

In the cubicle outside where we paid admission, the sound was loud: it came like a muscle flexing regularly, four to the bar. As the door opened the [cornets], King and Louis, one or both, soared above everything else. The whole joint was rocking. Tables, chairs, walls, people, moved with the rhythm. It was dark, smoky, gin-smelling. People in the balcony leaned over and their drinks spilled on the customers below. There was a false ceiling made of chicken wire covered with phony maple leaves, the real roof was twenty-five feet up. A round, glass bowl hung from the middle of the chicken wire; when the blues were played it turned slowly and a baby spotlight worked over it. There was a floor show and a master of ceremonies named King Jones. He would stand in front of Oliver and shout, "Oh! One more chorus, King!" Oliver and Louis would roll on and on, piling up choruses, with the rhythm section building the beat until the whole thing got inside your head and blew your

brains out. There was a place near the band reserved for musicians who came to listen and to learn; we sat there, stiff with education, joy and a licorice-tasting gin purchased from the waiters for two dollars a pint. You could bring your own but it didn't matter much; in the end the effect was the same—the band playing . . . and everything and everybody moving, sliding, tapping out the rhythm, inhaling the smoke, swallowing the gin.

Bud Freeman learned more than music from his visits to the South Side. The dancing fascinated him, too: "I never saw people enjoy it so much," he wrote. "Their bodies seemed to be glued together, as though they were trying to go through each other. . . . They did not have the money to go to a club or dance hall more than once a week, but they had a wonderful freedom of spirit when they felt this music. I didn't know a white man with money who had that spirit."

"In those days," Freeman continued, "we were brainwashed into believing that blacks were inferior to us, . . . to look down on any race that wasn't white. . . . Now here were these black people who were allowed no privileges. They were not allowed to come into our shops and cinemas, but we whites were allowed to go out to their community, where they treated us beautifully. I found their way of life equally as important as their music. It was not just their music that moved me but the whole picture of an oppressed people who appeared to be much happier than we whites who had everything. It was on the strength of this that I developed a love for them and became a jazz musician."

On April 5, 1923, King Oliver, Louis Armstrong, and the rest of the Creole Jazz Band took the train from Chicago to Richmond, Indiana, home of the Gennett Record Company. It was not especially friendly territory for jazz—or for black Americans. Gennett was best known for far less venturesome recording—the National Marimba Orchestra, William Jennings Bryan reciting the Twenty-third Psalm, and a singer of sacred songs named Homer Rodeheaver—and the company did a brisk local business, as well, turning out anti-Catholic, anti-Jewish, and anti-black anthems for the Ku Klux Klan, which then largely ran the state of Indiana.

Gennett had recorded just one well-known jazz group—the New Orleans Rhythm Kings. Now they were going to make their first recording of a New Orleans black ensemble. It wasn't easy. The recording studio was a made-over barn; trains pulling in and out of the nearby railroad yards interrupted the sessions; and Armstrong's sound proved so overpowering the sound engineer ordered him to stand well back from the recording horn to keep him from drowning out Joe Oliver.

The nine sides they cut that day and the next were a pale reflection of what Bix Beiderbecke and the Austin High Gang and their friends had heard live at the Lincoln Gardens. There was no time for the "piling up choruses" that so moved Eddie Condon; Oliver sounded more restrained than contemporary accounts suggest he was when on the bandstand (perhaps because, like his old rival Freddie Keppard, he was apprehensive about putting his best material on records for anyone to steal); Baby Dodds was limited to playing woodblocks and the snare because the bass drum could not yet be recorded; and Armstrong was sometimes hard to hear.

But the records still capture the joy and excitement, the rich polyphony and rocking but relaxed tempo that characterized the best New Orleans music. The two-cornet breaks that so excited Chicagoans still have the power to astonish. And on a tune called "Chimes Blues," Armstrong takes his first short recorded solo; it may or may not have been planned out in advance with Oliver's help, but it is played with utter self-assurance, and is already suffused with the overwhelming warmth

Louis and Lil Hardin Armstrong's wedding portrait, 1924. "When Lil and I got married," Armstrong remembered, "we made the rounds of the nightclubs. And everybody threw rice on us as we were getting in and out of the cabs."

that would make his sound instantly recognizable throughout his life.

The Gennett catalogue featured the Creole Jazz Band recordings as "Snappy Dance Hits . . . by Exclusive Gennett Colored Artists," and by summer, Oliver and Armstrong were in demand all over town. Allotted twenty minutes to play for a music trades convention at a fashionable North Side hotel, they were not allowed offstage for better than two hours. The delegates cheered especially loudly, according to the industry journal *Talking Machine*, for "the little frog-mouthed boy who played cornet."

Almost in spite of himself, Louis Armstrong was beginning to outshine his mentor, a fact not lost on the Creole Jazz Band's pianist, Lil Hardin. She was unlike any woman Armstrong had ever met. Born in Memphis, and raised by a mother who believed the blues "worthless, immoral music, played by worthless, immoral loafers," she studied classical piano and attended Fisk University intending to become a music teacher—until she discovered that there was much better money to be made playing piano, first as a song

plugger, demonstrating new tunes in a music store to promote the sale of sheet music, then with jazz bands. She liked playing with King Oliver, though she did not find him an easy man to work for. Once, when she tried adding a little piano obbligato to the mix, he stopped her cold. He already *had* a clarinetist, he said.

When Armstrong first joined the band, she admitted to one interviewer, she had not thought much of him.

> All along I'd been hearing from all the musicians about "Little Louis". . . what a good trumpet player he was gonna be. . . . So when he brought Little Louis . . . to meet me, Little Louis was 226 pounds. So I said, " 'Little Louis,' how come you call him 'Little Louis,' big as he is?" . . . I wasn't impressed at all. . . . I didn't like the way he was dressed, I didn't like the way he talked. . . . Well you know, girls wore garters . . . on their stockings, so when I'd sit down to play I would roll my stocking down so the garter [was] below my knee. . . . And first thing Louis spied was my knee, and he was looking and I said, "This guy's got ideas he'd better not put in words."

She had heard nothing special in Armstrong's playing either because, she said, he was so careful always to follow Oliver's lead, and so she had been genuinely startled when she heard her boss say in an unguarded moment that while his protégé could now play better than he could, "as long as I keep him with me, he won't be able to get ahead of me. I'll still be the 'King.' " It was their first recording date at the Gennett studio that had made her see things differently. "They put Louis about fifteen feet away over in the corner. . . . And Louis was . . . looking all sad, you know. He thought it was bad for him to have to be separated from the band. . . . I looked at him and smiled to reassure him that he was alright, . . . and then I said to myself, 'Now, if they have to put him that far away in order to hear Joe, he's *gotta* be better.' Then I was convinced."

Hardin was ambitious, articulate, and, like Armstrong, unhappily married. Despite her initial impression of him and the differences in their backgrounds, she fell in love and determined to marry him—and to make him a star in his own right. Armstrong was astonished: "[W]ho was I," he asked later, to think that "a big high-powered chick like Lil" could be interested in him. "I just couldn't conceive the idea." Neither could the other men in the band, some of whom complained about a "country son of a bitch" like him courting such a sophisticated woman. "The musicians, as soon as they found out we were dating," Hardin recalled, "they all quit speaking to us almost. They didn't like it because they knew I was going to start something. I thought the best thing to do was to get him away from Joe."

It would not be easy.

THE BEST IN THE WORLD

That same spring, Jelly Roll Morton turned up in Chicago. He had always promoted himself as the creator of jazz, but for several years, as the music's popularity spread, he had been living on the West Coast. There, according to the red-haired singer Ada "Bricktop" Smith, he hadn't been able to "decide whether to be a pimp or a piano player. I told him to be both." He seems to have followed that advice, performing at the Cadillac Café on Central Avenue in Los Angeles, where, according to him, "we didn't have anything but movie stars . . . as long as I stayed there," and making a point between sets of dropping in on other piano players, announcing, "Whenever you see *me* walk in, get up off that piano," and then taking over the keyboard. But he also profited handsomely from what he called "The Pacific Coast Line," a group of prostitutes who brought him their pay. He ran a seedy

hotel and gambling den in Los Angeles, as well; was falsely accused of murder by a jealous woman; operated a San Francisco night club; and lost all his money playing cards in Seattle.

Then, he received a telegram from the Chicago-based Melrose Publishing Company offering what Morton remembered as three thousand dollars for the rights to the tune the New Orleans Rhythm Kings and

Jelly Roll Morton, 1924. "No piano player could touch him," his music publisher Lester Melrose remembered. "Jelly led the way on the piano, the best at the time we ever heard, and we heard them all."

"Wolverine Blues," Jelly Roll Morton's first genuine hit

others had made popular, "Wolverine Blues." Morton took the money, then headed for Chicago. With Joe Oliver and Louis Armstrong and other New Orleans musicians like Freddie Keppard and the clarinetist Jimmy Noone doing well all over town, and with youthful white musicians whom he believed mere imitators doing even better, he was determined to get in on the action.

One day that May, Lester Melrose, the younger of the Melrose brothers, recalled, "A fellow walked into our store with a big red bandanna around his neck and a ten-gallon cowboy hat on his head and hollered, 'Listen everybody, I'm Jelly Roll Morton from New Orleans, the originator of jazz!' He talked for an hour without stopping about how good he was and then he sat down at the piano and proved he was every bit as good as he claimed and better."

"How you like that one?" he asked after racing through a new number.

"That's a good one," said one of the brothers.

"*Good*, hell," Morton answered, "That's *perfect*."

The Melrose brothers agreed to publish more of his songs and helped get him a recording contract with Gennett, mostly for piano solos—"King Porter Stomp," "The Pearls," "Kansas City Stomps" (named not for the midwestern city but for a Tijuana bar Morton had visited on his travels). He also played on six sides with the New Orleans Rhythm Kings and thus became the first black musician known ever to have recorded with white ones. (Just finding him a place to stay overnight in Richmond, Indiana, was a challenge. "We thought it best to say that he was Cuban," the trombonist George Brunies remembered, "so that's what we did.")

When the Pennsylvania-born pianist Earl Hines arrived in Chicago in 1923, he remembered, Morton was "the most popular underworld pianist around. [He] was a fair-complected man and sort of handsome. Nowadays you'd say he was overdressed, but he was the kind of fellow who carried his pearl-handled pistols with him and had plenty of money in his pocket at all times. If anybody tried to put him in a corner . . . he'd say things like, 'I've got more suits than you've got handkerchiefs!,' or, 'I've been further around the world than you've been around a teacup!' He had written any number of tunes and everybody thought a lot of him."

Despite the popularity of his music it was hard for Morton to get or hold jobs playing in person. "He'd talk himself [into] a job," Pops Foster said, "but he'd just keep talking to the guy who was going to hire him and before he'd get to play, he'd talk himself right out. The guy would fire Jelly just so he wouldn't have to listen to him talk." There was more to it than that. Most Chicago clubs were run by whites—many of them were linked with the mob—upon whom Morton's innate swagger, his Creole hauteur, and his refusal ever to accept anything but fair treatment grated hard. Instead of trying to negotiate when a club owner offered him a salary he thought unworthy of his talent, Morton felt compelled to tell

him off: "You bring [the white bandleader] Paul Whiteman out here and pay any price he wants because he has the name of 'King of Jazz.' But you happen to be talking to the real king of jazz. I invented it and I brought it here." The club owner showed him the door. "Jelly Roll was not a good old-time Southern darkey like Joe Oliver," Lester Melrose once explained; he would always refuse to toe anyone else's mark.

LET YOUR INNER SELF BREAK THROUGH

In late January of 1923, Duke Ellington had paid his way into the segregated balcony of the Howard Theater in Washington to see a traveling vaudeville revue called *How Come*. It was little more than a series of sketches, but the title role—a Chinese laundryman who implausibly happened also to be a master of the soprano saxophone—was played by Sidney Bechet, back home again after his time in a British prison. Toward the end of the performance, Bechet stepped forward to play a blues-drenched solo that Ellington never forgot. First there was the sheer beauty of his sound—"all wood," he said—and then it was "*au naturel*," he remembered, "all soul, all from the inside." Bechet seemed to be "*calling somebody*" whatever he played. "It was my first encounter with the New Orleans idiom. I had never heard anything like it. It was a completely new sound and conception to me." When the time came, Ellington would make that sound and conception central elements in his own extraordinary music.

Still just twenty-four, Ellington had already made himself one of the most successful dance bandleaders in town. The Duke's Serenaders played all over the city and its suburbs, but Washington had come to seem too small and sedate for him. He longed for what he called "the whirl of New York." He had married Edna Thompson, a neighbor's daughter and high school classmate, four years earlier and had a son named Mercer, but just a few weeks after hearing Sidney Bechet, Ellington left them behind and headed north to join two young friends, the drummer Sonny Greer and a one-time schoolmate named Otto Hardwick, who played alto saxophone.

"Harlem, in our minds," Ellington remembered, had "the world's most glamorous atmosphere. We *had* to go there." New York was now home to more African-Americans than any other northern city, and most lived uptown, in Harlem. "It is a mecca for the sightseer, the pleasure-seeker, the curious, the adventurous, the enterprising, the ambitious, and the talented of the entire Negro world," wrote the poet James Weldon Johnson, "for the lure of it has reached down to every isle of the Carib Sea and penetrated even into Africa." The NAACP had its headquarters in Harlem; so did the Urban League and Marcus Garvey's Universal Negro Improvement Association. It was the home of a host of black poets and writers and artists, too, all eagerly examining what it meant to be black and American, part of what would come to be called the Harlem Renaissance. It would also be Duke Ellington's home for much of his life.

Harlem offered black musicians plenty of theater and nightclub and dance-hall jobs—and Broadway and the record companies were only a subway ride away. But some residents found jazz an embarrassment, vulgar, low-life music, unworthy of a race now committed to uplifting itself. "You usually weren't allowed to play blues and boogie-woogie in the average Negro middle-class home," the saxophonist Garvin Bushell remembered. "That music supposedly suggested a low element." The alto saxophonist and arranger Benny Carter agreed: "I had the feeling they sort of looked down on jazz as my folks did," he recalled. "It wasn't quite the music they would have liked to hear."

Duke Ellington wanted to hear it, and he wanted to play it, too. He and his friends worked first for Wilbur Sweatman, a vaudeville performer best known for being able to perform "The Rosary" on three clarinets at once, but when Sweatman's band left town to go on tour, they stayed behind, scuffling for work, sometimes hustling pool to feed themselves.

They also hung around Ellington's heroes, the masters of what some called "eastern ragtime"—Harlem stride piano. They called themselves "ticklers," but the nicknames they awarded one another— "the Bear," "the Beetle," "the Beast," "the Brute"—were warlike, befitting the perennial piano wars they waged among themselves. They were an elite corps, as colorful

The stride master. James P. Johnson outside his New York home, sometime during the 1920s

as they were competitive, and they had made something altogether new out of ragtime. "It was '*orchestral* piano,'" one of them remembered, "full, round, big, widespread chords . . . moving against the right hand. The other boys from the South and West . . . played in smaller dimensions. . . . We wouldn't dare do that because [our] public was used to better playing." "The tempo was the lope," Ellington said.

James P. Johnson was the elder statesman. A big man who chewed a big cigar, he was a composer and conductor as well as a pianist—his piano rolls had helped inspire Ellington to become a musician. Johnson was shy and soft-spoken most of the time, but he loved combat with other piano players so much, one of them remembered, that his wife would have to come to Harlem from Queens and "go from street to street until she heard the piano, . . . recognize his style and then go up to the apartment to get him out of there and take him home."

Johnson's good friend and greatest rival was William Henry Joseph Bonaparte Bertholoff Smith—Willie "the Lion"—who sometimes said he had earned his nick-

Young Duke Ellington's advertisement in the Washington, D.C., telephone directory, 1919

IRRESISTIBLE JASS
FURNISHED TO OUR SELECT PATRONS
The Duke's Serenaders
COLORED SYNCOPATERS
E. K. ELLINGTON, Mgr.
2728 SHERMAN AVE. N. W. Phone Columbia 7842

The block-long Renaissance Ballroom and Casino at 138th Street and Seventh Avenue, just one of the Harlem venues where the young Duke Ellington hoped to play one day. "It is impossible to enter New York," Ellington wrote, "without feeling that something wonderful is about to happen."

Willie the Lion Smith. His advice to young pianists like Duke Ellington was simple: "Get around, be on the scene, play it clean, be seen, be keen, and be over eighteen."

name for bravery in battle during World War I, and at other times claimed he'd been named "the Lion of Judea" because of his devotion to Judaism. No one enjoyed piano combat more or fared better at it than the man Ellington always called "the Lion." "Sometimes we got carving battles going that would last for four or five hours," Smith remembered.

> We would embroider the melodies with our own original ideas and try to develop patterns that had more originality than those played before us. Sometimes it was just a question of who could think up the most patterns within a given tune. It was pure improvisation. You had to have your own individual style and be able to play in all the keys. In those days we could all copy each other's shouts by learning them by ear. Sometimes, in order to keep the others from picking up too much of my stuff, I'd perform in the hard keys, B major and E major.

The Lion took a shine to Ellington and his friends, steered them toward pickup jobs, and took them along to rent parties—all-night dances, held in crowded apartments, where the cost of admission helped hold off the landlord—at which Smith, Johnson, and their rivals did genial battle. "They would crowd a hundred or more people into a seven-room railroad flat," the Lion recalled, "and the walls would bulge—some of the parties spread to the halls and all over the building." He and Johnson customarily fought to a draw, Ellington remembered. "It was never to the blood. With those two giants it was always a *sporting* event. Neither cut the other. They had too much respect for that."

Ellington himself eventually backed off from the piano battles, he said. "I needed to write myself some music I could *play.*"

In September of 1923, Ellington, Greer, and Hardwick found themselves downtown playing in a five-piece band at a cellar club called the Kentucky Club, on Forty-ninth Street, just off Times Square. Their leader was a banjo player, sometime saxophonist, and small-time impresario named Elmer Snowden. His band was called the Washington Black Sox—a reference to the Chicago baseball team that had thrown the 1919 World Series—and it was playing what Ellington remembered as sweet, unobtrusive "under-conversation music" that featured the "fragile and genteel" trumpet of another young friend from Washington, a sometime student at Howard University named Arthur Whetsel.

Then, Snowden signed up a remarkable young cornetist whose influence on Ellington—and through him on the whole history of jazz music—would be immense. James "Bubber" Miley had been born in South Carolina but brought up in New York and he was already skilled at producing muted novelty sounds when he visited Chicago on tour, went to see King Oliver and—like the members of the Austin High Gang—had his whole conception of the music changed forever.

The Washingtonians at the Hollywood Club just off Times Square, 1924. Left to right, Sonny Greer, Charlie Irvis, Bubber Miley, Elmer Snowden, Otto Hardwick, and Duke Ellington, who would soon take over as leader. "The Hollywood Club was a good place for us to be," Ellington wrote, "because it stayed open all night."

Garvin Bushell happened to be with him when it happened. "Bubber and I sat there with our mouths open," he remembered. "The trumpets . . . in the East had a better 'legitimate' quality, but the sound of Oliver touched you more. It was less cultivated but more expressive of how the people felt. He played things that hit you inside."

Back in New York, Miley made it his business to master the art of hitting people inside, too, and eventually brought to the Black Sox orchestra a repertoire of muted churchly moans and cries more startling even than King Oliver's. Miley "used to growl all night long," Ellington said, "playing gut-bucket on his horn. It was then that our music acquired new colors and characteristics." Miley's sound also brought the men their first serious notice. "This colored band . . . includes a trumpet player who never need doff his chapeau to any cornetist in the business," wrote Abel Green of the New York *Clipper.* "He exacts the eeriest sort of modulations and 'singing' notes heard. . . . The boys look neat in dress suits and labor hard, but not in vain at their music. They disclose painstaking rehearsal, playing without music."

"That was when we decided to forget all about the sweet music," Ellington said. In fact, he never forgot about anything. Nothing would ever be alien to the music he was about to begin composing; it would always represent the most delicate possible balance between sweet and hot. He was in charge now. The men in the band had chosen him to be their leader after they found Elmer Snowden helping himself to more than his share of their pay. "There was some sort of magnetism to [Ellington] you wouldn't understand," Sonny Greer explained to an interviewer many years later. "In my whole life, I've never seen another man like him. When he walks into a strange room, the whole place lights up."

Ellington changed the band's name to the Washingtonians and started writing songs and making the rounds of music publishers on Broadway, sometimes selling hastily written-out blues for fifteen dollars outright and yearning for something more. He eventually sought out Will Marion Cook, white-haired now and called "Dad" by young songwriters who hoped to match his record of success. Cook remained as touchy as ever, but was willing to offer counsel to a suitably deferential newcomer from his native Washington like the young Ellington. One summer day, as they rode home together through Central Park in a taxi with an open top, Cook urged Ellington to get formal training at a conservatory.

"Dad, I don't want to go to the conservatory," Ellington answered, "because they're not teaching what I want to learn."

In that case, Cook told him, "First . . . find the logical way, and when you find it, avoid it, and let your inner self break through and guide you. Don't try to be anybody else but yourself."

Duke Ellington would follow that advice all his life.

THE KING OF JAZZ

On the snowy afternoon of February 12, 1924, jazz, which had been born in the streets and the dance halls of New Orleans, and nurtured in big-city saloons and speakeasies and vaudeville theaters, found itself for the first time on the concert stage. It was a distinctive kind of jazz, to be sure —so-called *symphonic* jazz—and it was to be presented at Manhattan's exalted

Paul Whiteman. "He trembles, wobbles, quivers," wrote the *New York Times* critic, "a piece of jazz jelly, conducting his orchestra with the back of the trousers of the right leg, and the face of a mandarin the while."

Aeolian Hall by the best-known dance bandleader in America.

Paul Whiteman was a formally trained musician from Colorado who had first heard jazz being played by New Orleans musicians in San Francisco in 1915. "We first met— Jazz and I—at a dance hall dive on the Barbary Coast," he remembered. "It screeched and bellowed at me from a trick platform in the middle of a smoke-hazed, beer-fumed room." Everything had seemed to go wrong for him that day, he remembered: he was bored with his job playing viola with the San Francisco Symphony, he had been soaked with rain going to and from a dismal rehearsal, had cracked his shaving mirror, even overcooked his breakfast eggs. A

friend had had to drag him to the club. All of that was forgotten the moment the musicians began to play. "My whole body began to sit up and take notice. It was like coming out of blackness into bright lights. My blues faded when treated to the Georgia blues that some trombonist was wailing about. My head was dizzy, but my feet seemed to understand that tune. I wanted to whoop. I wanted to dance. I wanted to sing. I did them all. Raucous? Yes. Crude— undoubtedly. Unmusical—as sure as you live! But rhythmic, catching as the small pox, and spirit-lifting."

Three years later, he abandoned his symphonic career and joined a dance band—only to be fired two days later for being unable to improvise on the spot. "You can't *jazz*," his boss said, when asked for an explanation, "that's all." Humiliated but still drawn to the music, Whiteman determined to find a way to orchestrate jazz, to retain its rhythm and color and harmony while rendering it as precise and predictable as symphonic music. His father— superintendent of music for the Denver public schools—was scornful of jazz and deeply disappointed by his son's decision to abandon classical music, which may account in part for Whiteman's self-appointed mission to "remove the stigma of barbaric strains and jungle cacophony," and "make a lady of jazz."

In any case, with arrangements by the pianist Ferde Grofé—who would eventually go on to compose semiclassical pieces like the "Grand Canyon Suite"—Whiteman turned his orchestra into what he called "an efficient arrangement. Every member knows exactly what he is to play every minute of the time. Even the smears are indicated in the music." He brought his men east to Atlantic City in 1918, made a recording of "Whispering" in 1920, which would sell more than 2.5 million copies, played for the *Ziegfeld Follies,* and eventually settled into a long successful run playing for wealthy dancers at the Palais Royal nightclub on Broadway. Other orchestra leaders had experimented with arranged jazz, including Paul Specht, Vincent Lopez, and Art Hickman—whose California dance band may have been the first to use a whole section of saxophones. But none could match either the smooth polish of Whiteman's music or the tireless energy with which he promoted it. A big man—he stood well over six feet tall, sometimes weighed more than three hundred pounds, and bore a startling resemblance to the corpulent movie comic Oliver Hardy—Whiteman was a master of public relations, willing to go along with almost any publicity stunt so long as it drew attention to his band.

The Aeolian Hall concert was his idea, meant to lend artistic legitimacy to his music—and to head off the challenge of Vincent Lopez, who had announced plans for a Manhattan concert of his own. To ensure that serious attention would be paid, Whiteman let it be known that he had sent complimentary tickets to the most eminent figures in music whether or not they actually were able to attend—Igor Stravinsky, Leopold Stokowski, Sergei Rachmaninoff, John McCormack, Amelita Galli-Curci, as well as every music critic in the Northeast. "Mr. Whiteman," the program promised, "intends to point out the tremendous strides which have been made in popular music from the day of discordant popular music which sprang into existence about ten years ago, to the melodious music of today, which—for no good reason—is still called Jazz."

To show how far Whiteman thought American music had come, the program opened with a raucous five-man lampoon of "Livery Stable Blues," the recording by the Original Dixieland Jass Band that had started the national mania for the music seven years earlier. (Whiteman was said to have been momentarily unnerved by the unexpected enthusiasm with which the audience received what was meant to be a burlesque.) Everything that followed over the next four hours was elegant and orchestral, without a hint of improvisation. White-

PAUL WHITEMAN
AND HIS
Palais Royal Orchestra
WILL OFFER
An Experiment in Modern Music
Zez Confrey
and
George Gershwin
New Typically American Compositions by Victor Herbert, George Gershwin and Zez Confrey will be played for the first time.
AEOLIAN CONCERT HALL
Tuesday, Feb. 12th (LINCOLN'S BIRTHDAY) at 3 P.M.
Tickets now on Sale, 55c. to $2.20
Victor Records   Chickering Pianos   Buescher Instruments

Poster for Paul Whiteman's concert at New York's Aeolian Hall, 1924

man's twenty-three men—including eight violinists—performed syncopated versions of light classics and old favorites such as "A Pretty Girl Is Like a Melody," "To a Wild Rose," and "Song of the Volga Boatmen." The climax was a brand-new specially commissioned work by George Gershwin, an immigrants' son, who, like Duke Ellington, had spent hours listening to the masters of Harlem stride. Gershwin's piece, "Rhapsody in Blue," was something new—a classical piece suffused with jazz feeling—and would become one of the best-loved compositions in all of American music.

The New York *Herald* called the concert "an uproarious success." The orchestra was made to play five encores. Whiteman, said *Variety,* "had proven conclusively that the dance orchestra or the band or the jazz craze, or any of the other names it has been identified with, will never die. It is part of

American culture and an absolute necessity." And though his men had actually played precious little jazz that afternoon, Whiteman was now billed everywhere as "The King of Jazz."

Later, some would accuse him of diluting jazz, and he himself evidently shared something of their concern. "The demoniac energy, the fantastic riot of accents and the humorous moods have all had to be toned down," he once said. "I hope in toning it down we shall not, as some critics have predicted, take the life out of our music." Others charged him with misappropriating the music of African-Americans. He himself was always unpretentious about his achievements—"I know as much about *real* jazz," he would confide to one interviewer, "as F. Scott Fitzgerald knew about the Jazz Age"—and he was perfectly clear about the artistic debt he owed to black musicians, as the very first paragraph of his autobiography makes clear: "Jazz came to America three hundred years ago in chains. The psalm-singing Dutch traders, sailing a man of war across the ocean, described their cargo as 'fourteen black African slaves for sale in His Majesty's Colonies'. . . . [P]riceless freight destined three centuries later to set a whole nation dancing. . . . Jazz . . . was to be their gift to . . . posterity." He regularly gave work to black arrangers, too, and in 1923, a year before his Aeolian Hall concert, he had stunned his own managers by offering jobs in his orchestra to two members of Armand Piron's black New Orleans ensemble at the Roseland Ballroom. They didn't accept, one of them explained many years later, only because they were tired of New York and wanted to "get home."

Black musicians may have resented the celebrity and riches Whiteman had gained playing music they had pioneered, but few seem to have harbored personal grudges against him. No one could deny the quality of his musicianship, and if his efforts to "elevate" jazz sometimes seemed naïve and even patronizing in retrospect, those same efforts also redounded to the benefit of all jazz musicians of whatever color. "Paul Whiteman was known as the King of Jazz," wrote Duke Ellington, who admired Whiteman's lofty ambitions for his music, his eye for first-rate musicians, and the managerial skill with which he built and ran his band, "and no one as yet has come near carrying that title with more certainty and dignity. . . . I used to hear Whiteman records taking the snobbishness out of . . . music and opening the doors."

THE ONE THING

Not even the reassuring sounds of Paul Whiteman and his genteel competitors could win over people like Bix Beiderbecke's parents. They still detested jazz in all its forms, still hoped their son could be persuaded to abandon the music—and the musician's life—that had brought an abrupt end to his education and destroyed their dream of having him go on to college and a career in business. In February of 1923, he had dutifully returned to Davenport and gone to work for his father, weighing coal, collecting payment from customers, standing in line at the bank to deposit checks. It was tedious and demeaning work but he kept at it for five months, living for the evenings when he could get out of the house and sit in with local bands.

By July, he could stand it no more and left for Chicago. During the days he played aboard a Lake Michigan excursion boat in a band that included an often-seasick fourteen-year-old clarinetist named Benny Goodman, and he spent as many evenings as he could at the Lincoln Gardens listening to Oliver and Armstrong. Sometimes, a friend recalled, he was even allowed to sit in for a chorus or two and was rewarded with "friendly nods of approval" from the band. It was from listening to Armstrong, Beiderbecke's friend Esten Spurrier said, that Bix learned how to construct a coherent solo. He called it "the correlated chorus, play two measures, then two related,

and you had four measures upon which you played another four measures related to the first four, and so on, *ad infinitum,* to the end of the chorus."

In the autumn, Bix found himself in Ohio, part of a brand-new septet at the Stockton Club, a seedy roadhouse just outside the town of Hamilton. It was run by gangsters—illegal gambling went on upstairs—and at first the group had little more than enthusiasm to recommend it. They played Jelly Roll Morton's "Wolverine Blues" so often that when someone suggested they call themselves the "Wolverines," the name stuck. The engagement came to an abrupt end on New Year's Eve when two rival groups of small-time hoodlums turned up for the festivities. The manager tried to segregate them, seating the boys from Cincinnati and their girlfriends on one side of the dance floor and those from Hamilton on the other. But as the band played and bootleg liquor flowed, words led to punches, and the air was soon filled with bottles and furniture. Stories differ as to what happened next. One musician recalled playing "Chinatown, My Chinatown" for what seemed like an hour while the gangs battled back and forth, but another remembered that he and the rest of the band had all hidden behind chairs and tables for fear of injuring their lips or fingers. The Stockton Club was padlocked the next day in any case—too many citizens had turned up in bandages for the authorities to ignore its illegal existence any longer—and the Wolverines were out of a job.

They moved on to Cincinnati, where they played in a dingy third-floor ballroom called Doyle's Dancing Academy. Older dancers stayed away—the Wolverines had no sweet arrangements or slow dances to please them—but young working girls and high school students and a scattering of local musicians crowded the floor for the hot numbers. Students on nearby campuses liked them, too. And in February, buoyed by these first tentative signs of success, the Wolverines hired the same Gennett studio

at which King Oliver and Louis Armstrong had first recorded almost a year earlier, and cut four sides.

It was Beiderbecke, just twenty-one, who set the Wolverines apart—now soaring above his friends, now spurring them on to greater effort. Ralph Berton remembered the impact on him of first hearing Beiderbecke on record:

> It was tantalizing; somehow simultaneously excitingly hot and quietly cool and detached; a controlled ardor, a passion veiled in reticence. It had a chaste *understatement* never heard before in jazz, flowing yet so naturally from an open horn, staying modestly and casually within the middle register. The *attack* was like nothing I'd heard on any brass instrument in classical music or jazz—each note not as though blown, but struck.

Then, Bix got a letter from a friend, a laconic would-be songwriter named Hoagy Carmichael, who was leading a dance band at Indiana University while studying law. If the group could get to Indianapolis on its own, Carmichael suggested, he might be able to arrange a full season of weekend dances for them on and around the campus. It sounded good to the Wolverines, but the manager of Doyle's Dance Academy refused to let them go. They had signed a contract that still had weeks to run, and as insurance against their skipping out on him, he locked their instruments in his ballroom. The next night, Bix and his friends somehow slipped into the building and, using a length of clothesline, carefully lowered from the third-floor window into a waiting car their tuba, string bass, and brightly painted bass drum, then set out for Indianapolis.

There, they were a sensation. They cut more records, performed for nearly all the university's fraternities and sororities, and played dances all over Indiana and Michigan. The leader of a band that had the bad luck to precede them on one bandstand recalled their impact.

Jazz is the product of a restless age:
an age in which the fever of war is only
now beginning to abate its fury; when
men and women, after their efforts in
the great struggle, are still too much
disturbed to be content with a tranquil
existence; when freaks and stunts and
sensations are the order—or disorder—
of the day; when painters delight in por-
traying that which is not, and sculptors
in twisting the human limbs into strange,
fantastic shapes; when America is turning
out her merchandise [at] an unprece-
dented speed and motor cars are racing
along the roads; when aeroplanes are
beating successive records and ladies are
in so great a hurry that they wear short
skirts which enable them to move fast
and cut off their hair to save a few pre-
cious moments of the day; when the
extremes of Bolshevism and Fascismo
are pursuing their own ways simul-
taneously, and the whole world is rushing
helter-skelter in unknown directions.

Amid this seething, bubbling turmoil,
jazz hurried along its course riding
exultantly on the eddying stream. Never-
theless, the end of civilization is not yet,
and jazz will either be trained and turned
to artistic uses or else vanish utterly
from our midst as a living force. But even
if it disappears altogether it will not have
existed in vain. For its record will remain
as an interesting human document—
the spirit of the age written in the music
of the people.

—R. W. S. MENDL, 1926

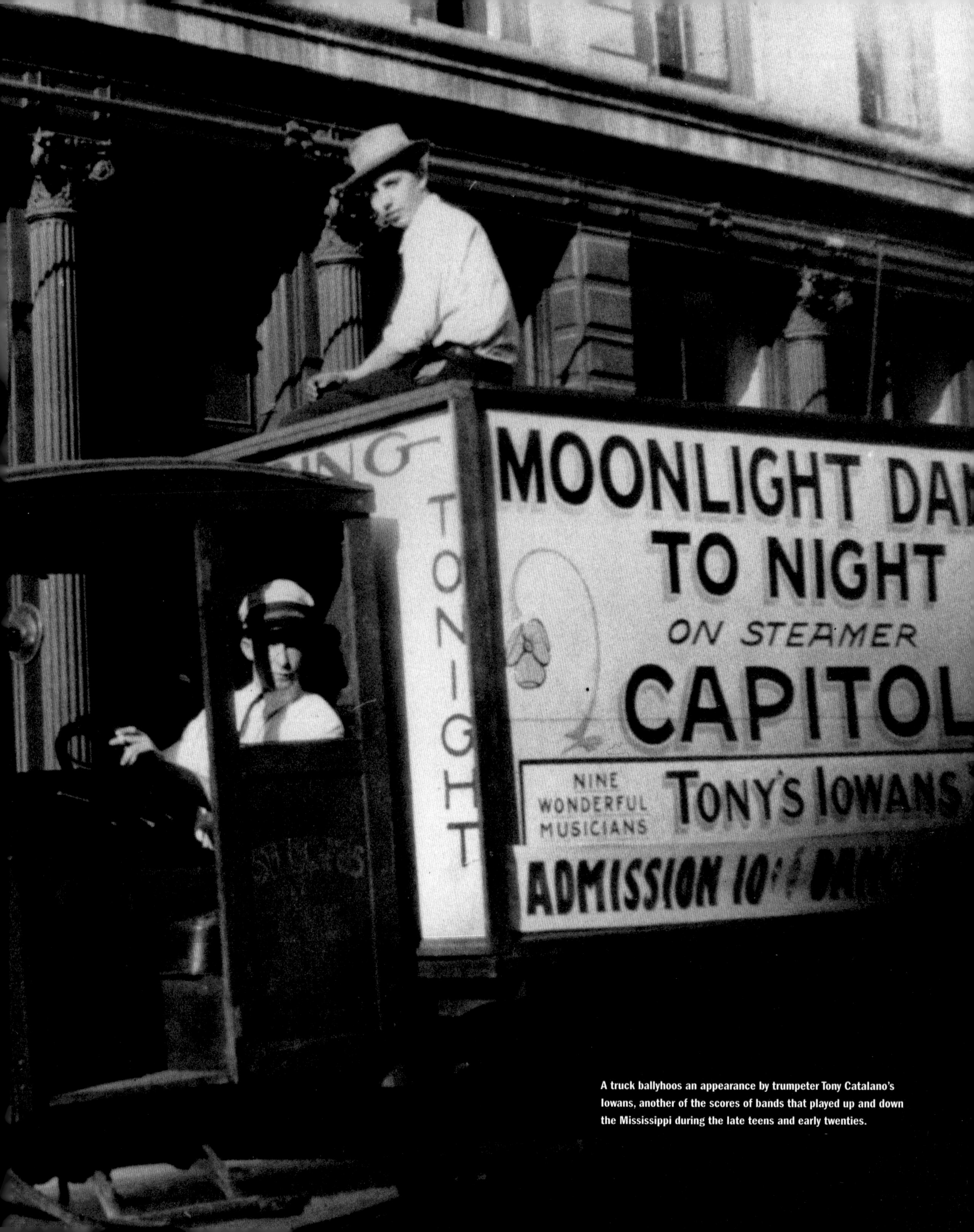

MOONLIGHT DAN
TO NIGHT
ON STEAMER
CAPITOL
NINE
WONDERFUL
MUSICIANS
TONY'S IOWANS
ADMISSION 10

A truck ballyhoos an appearance by trumpeter Tony Catalano's
Iowans, another of the scores of bands that played up and down
the Mississippi during the late teens and early twenties.

THE BIG
EASTER EVENT

WOLVERINE DIAMOND
DANCE
—MUSIC—
BY THE FAMOUS WOLVERINE JAZZ BAND
TWO DIAMOND RINGS GIVEN AWAY ABSOLUTELY FREE
UNDER PERSONAL DIRECTION OF BILLY CONNORS AND BERNARD HINES
TUESDAY NITE, APRIL 22nd, 1924
DANCING
8.30 - 12
CIVIC HALL
Admission 88c
Dance 75c 10c
MARION
INDIANA
KNOWN BY HER PRODUCTS

We played a set or two kind of soft and sweet. Our band's turn ended with a few polite hand-claps. Then the Wolverines started! Bix and the boys crushed into their tune, and the place was kind of stunned. Then the place started to rock. . . . The kids forgot about poise and delicacy and were jiving like at a football rally. Soon, the dancers gathered around Bix, Jimmy [Hartwell] and George [Johnson], listening with their ears practically in their horns. . . . Following every hot lick . . . laughing at every hot break and roaring into king-size appreciation at every hot chorus. This was a spectacle.

Everywhere, people warmed to Beiderbecke's sound but Bix himself remained stubbornly elusive. Even the stories his friends told and retold about him don't reveal much. He always had a jug of corn whiskey nearby and cared little for food, fueling himself with chili and oyster crackers (and if the restaurant kitchen ran out of chili, making do with more crackers spattered with catsup). He washed less often than some of his friends liked, rarely bothered to clean his horn because he said it sounded "hard" when he did, followed the fortunes of his favorite baseball player, Rogers Hornsby of the St. Louis Cardinals, disliked Mozart and Beethoven, and enjoyed both the absurdity of surrealist

The Wolverines on tour, 1924. The promise of jewelry as well as hot music was meant to pull crowds into the Madison, Indiana, Easter dance advertised above. In Indianapolis a few weeks later, the band found itself dwarfed by the spectacular art nouveau backdrop at the Palace Theater. Bix Beiderbecke is second from the right.

The Wolverines in the Gennett recording studio in Richmond, Indiana, February 18, 1924. Left to right, Min Leibrook (tuba), Jimmy Hartwell (clarinet), George Johnson (tenor saxophone), Bob Gillette (banjo), Vic Moore (drums), Dick Voynow (piano), Bix Beiderbecke (cornet), Al Gandee (trombone)

poetry and P. G. Wodehouse's whimsical fiction about the British upper classes.

Mostly, he kept to himself. He "had an air of cynicism and boredom about most things, just sitting around, lazy-like with his legs crossed and his body drooping," wrote the Chicago-born clarinetist Milton "Mezz" Mezzrow, who first got to know him that summer, "but it wasn't an act with him. . . . His shying away from things showed that what got most people worked up left him completely cold. . . . Music was the one thing that really brought him to life. Not

even whiskey could do it, and he gave it every chance." Mezzrow identified with black musicians so deeply that he rarely even listened to anyone else. But Bix, he said, was different. "Despite the whiskey fumes that blew out of his battered cornet, I had never heard a tone like he got before or since. He played mostly open horn, every note full, big, rich and round, standing out like a pearl, . . . with a powerful drive that few white musicians had in those days. . . . Powerful and energetic, every note packing a solid punch, with his head always in

full control over his heart." Playing with him, Mezzrow remembered, had been "like slipping into a suit made to order for you by a fine tailor, silk-lined all through."

In late summer the Wolverines got the kind of offer they'd been waiting for: a thirty-day New York City engagement at the Cinderella Ballroom, on Broadway. They left Indiana on Labor Day in two ancient touring cars. It would take them three days to get there but they were finally headed for the Big Time.

HERE COMES TROUBLE ITSELF

Twenty-five-year-old Sidney Bechet was already a legend among musicians when he finally got back to New York after three years abroad, both for the power and passion of his playing and for the combative personality that threatened always to plunge him into difficulty. But he still had not been heard on records.

Then, on June 30, 1923, almost three months after Oliver and Armstrong made their first recordings, Bechet finally got to cut two sides—"Wild Cat Blues" and "Kansas City Blues"—with Clarence Williams's Blue Five. From the opening note, he is fully in charge. As he wails and weaves and roars his extravagant way through the tunes, the cornetist sensibly retreats to a subordinate role. No previous jazz record had ever given so much time to a soloist; and no soloist on records had come anywhere near matching the emotional power of his playing. He went on to record with a whole series of blues singers, some good, some bad, but all immeasurably bolstered by his presence—though his sheer volume sometimes got him in trouble. "When it got to my chorus," he remembered, "the needle would jump. I couldn't play the way I wanted to. The engineers would almost go crazy when they saw me coming into the studios. They'd say, 'Here comes trouble itself.'"

Bechet's sound was a revelation to young musicians. In Boston, Harry Carney and Johnny Hodges, both future stars of the Duke Ellington orchestra, wore out Bechet's first records. If it hadn't been for him, Hodges would remember, "I'd probably just be playing for a hobby." In Bechet's hometown of New Orleans, the clarinetist Barney Bigard, another future Ellingtonian, recalled "every time you would pass someone's house that had the . . . windows open they would be playing [Sidney] on their Victrola."

Bechet delighted in the sensation he was causing and kept a sharp eye out for competition. When the Missouri-born tenor saxophonist Coleman Hawkins was overheard to say that New Orleans musicians couldn't play, Bechet hurried down to the Band Box club to challenge him. The two men battled all night, and when at six the following morning Hawkins finally packed up his horn and fled the stand, Bechet was said to have followed him up the street, still playing.

But Bechet's explosive personality, his inherent inability ever to take orders from anybody, continued to undercut him. He got a job with James P. Johnson only to find that "Johnson wanted to make . . . orchestrational Jazz, and I was playing New Orleans, playing foundations in the numbers, but ad-libbing and giving my improvisation to it. . . . If you know in advance every note you're going to play and just the way you're going to play there's no need to have feelings." Johnson told him ⁴ stick to the arrangements. Bechet wouldn't, and Johnson let him go.

Then, in 1924, he took a summer job playing dances in New England with Duke Ellington, who was himself temporarily without a bandstand; the gangsters who owned the Hollywood Inn had deliberately set the club on fire in April in order to collect insurance money rather than settle for the lean profits they would have made during the hot summer months.

Bechet "fitted our band like a glove," Ellington remembered, and Ellington loved the competitive spirit Bechet brought to the group. He was "like a gladiator," Ellington said. "He'd go out and blow and the next guy to follow him had to beat what he did." His main challenger was Bubber Miley. "They would growl at each other something awful, Bechet would go out and play ten choruses and Bubber would play ten choruses, and while one was playing the other was back there taking nips!"

Over the years, Ellington would earn a well-deserved reputation for putting up with unreasonable behavior by his musicians—provided they could play. But Ellington was only twenty-five years old in 1924, and older and more experienced men than he had found Bechet impossible to control. Bechet insisted on bringing to work a massive German shepherd named Goola; he somehow convinced himself that Bubber Miley and trombonist Charlie Irvis, another master of the muted growl, were conspiring against him; and he once ran up a two-hundred-dollar "transportation" bill by hiring a New York taxi to take him to a dance date outside Boston, then paying for a night in the local whorehouse for the cabbie so that he wouldn't have to look for a ride back to the city again the next day.

Finally, after Bechet arrived three days late for an engagement and claimed it wasn't his fault—his taxi driver had gotten lost, he said—Ellington sadly let him go. "Bechet was always a rover," he said, "who wanted to see over the other side of the hill." But Ellington remained determined to find men who would bring more of the New Orleans sound that Bechet epitomized into his own music.

READY FOR THE NEW DAY

During the first two weeks of October of 1924, a prescient jazz enthusiast visiting the West Side of Manhattan could, within one evening and without walking more than four blocks, have seen and heard three of the music's best-remembered figures at the dawn of their careers, could have witnessed the first stirrings of the transformation that would turn what had mostly been a novelty music into an art.

Duke Ellington and his Washingtonians were now back in residence at their cellar club at Forty-ninth Street and Broadway. It had been renamed the Hollywood Club and refurbished by its owners after the convenient seasonal fire—there would be a second blaze the following January, this one

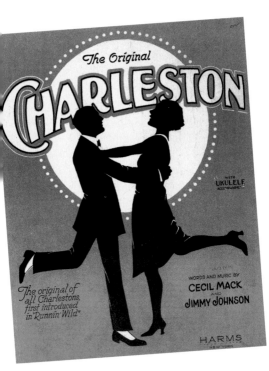

The Original CHARLESTON

WITH UKULELE ACCOMPANIMENT

The original of all Charlestons, first introduced in "Runnin' Wild"

WORDS AND MUSIC BY
CECIL MACK
AND
JIMMY JOHNSON

HARMS
NEW YORK

Despite the publisher's claim that this version was the original, the Charleston was an African-American dance long before it was published, in 1923. "Jimmy Johnson" was the pianist and composer James P. Johnson, and the song was the hit of his Broadway show, *Runnin' Wild*.

Jazz, which took its name from music—Negro music—has spread itself revealingly over the American temperament and become the expression medium for it, a sign and symbol of the American pace, of its moving spirit. . . . What an immense, even if unconscious, irony the Negroes have devised! They, who of all Americans are . . . least considered and most denied, have forged the key to the interpretation of the American spirit.

—CHARLES S. JOHNSON,
Opportunity, 1925

signaled by a helpful hint from the manager to Sonny Greer that it might be wise for him to take his drums home after work—but it remained an unprepossessing spot: Greer had standing orders to step up the volume of his playing whenever the rats that sometimes scuttled among the tables began to squeak. The band still had just six pieces, and Ellington was mostly arranging other people's tunes rather than writing his own. But the fresh colors and textures he had already begun to develop in his arrangements and the startling growls of Bubber Miley and Charlie Irvis were drawing so much attention that the club had begun to advertise itself as the place "Where the Professional Musician Makes His Rendezvous." Paul Whiteman was a frequent early-morning visitor after finishing up at the Palais Royal around the corner, Ellington remembered, and he usually left a fifty-dollar tip.

Just a block down Broadway at Forty-eighth Street, Bix Beiderbecke and the Wolverines—their name changed to "The Personality Kids" for their New York debut—were playing at the Cinderella Ballroom. Word of their consistently hot music had preceded them—it was then still rare for any white band to play serious jazz and nothing but jazz, especially in New York—and on opening night in September at least fifty musicians had climbed the stairs to the second-floor ballroom, eager to hear the Wolverines in person. Paul Whiteman and Beiderbecke's first hero, Nick LaRocca, were there, and so was a young jazz fan from Yale, Richardson Turner. "No one was dancing," he recalled. "The Wolverines were playing. It's impossible to put into words the electrical thrill that bunch produced. . . . Bix played in an unorthodox way. He shook the horn with all his fingers up and played leaning over at the floor at about a 45 degree angle. . . . They took about ten 'last' choruses—standing up around the drums—playing at the drummer. It was fantastic!"

Abel Green, now working for *Variety*, agreed, pronouncing the Wolverine Orchestra "a torrid unit." "Their sense of rhythm and tempo is ultra for this type of dance music and their unquestionable favor with the dance fan speaks for itself." But in the end, the Wolverines would prove altogether too ultra for the Cinderella Ballroom. The frantic dance called the Charleston had caught on with young New Yorkers, and the Wolverines were the ideal band to spur them on, but, as their saxophone player George Johnson remembered, "Those who did not dance it, and some of those who did, found a crowded floor a disadvantage, objecting to the danger to life and limb in the shape of flying feet. . . . [Soon,] the Charleston dancers came to the Cinderella and the rest of the dancers who liked less violence went elsewhere."

Bix, as always, seemed unconcerned, turning up to play each evening, drinking and fooling with the piano through the day. "In the morning," a musician who roomed with him in New York remembered, "Bix would sit on the edge of the bed, swing his legs a few times. Then he would reach for a barrel-shaped glass that he had in his suitcase. He'd pour four healthy ounces of gin, drink it 'as is,' and say that he had drunk his daily 'orange juice.' He'd splash some water on his face, comb his hair, and was ready for the new day."

The Wolverines' contract was not renewed, and in October, Bix would accept an offer to bring his bright sound to one of the Detroit-based orchestras run by one of Paul Whiteman's chief rivals, Jean Goldkette. Before he left, he sent to Chicago for seventeen-year-old Jimmy McPartland to replace him. "I like you, kid," Bix told his young admirer. "You sound like me. But you don't copy me." To a young admirer like McPartland, still searching for a way to bring something of his own to the music, there could have been no higher praise.

Many of the dancers who found the floor at the Cinderella too crowded hurried back

Fletcher Henderson, back row, second from right, was graduated with his class from Atlanta University, 1920, intending to pursue a career in science. Instead, within a few years he found himself producing records with titles like "Shake It and Break It."

down the stairs and up Broadway to the Roseland Ballroom, on Fifty-first Street. It was the biggest and most opulent dance hall in New York, with two orchestras alternating every evening. At one end of the vast dance floor was Sam Lanin's white orchestra; at the other was the most admired black band in the city, led by Fletcher Henderson. And sitting in its brass section was a brand-new cornetist, Louis Armstrong.

It had taken Lil Hardin more than a year to get Armstrong to marry her and then to leave Joe Oliver. He owed "Mr. Joe" everything, he said, and he wasn't sure he could make it on his own. But his bride persisted: "I don't want to be married to a second trumpet-player," she told him. "I want you to play first!" He finally, reluctantly, left the Creole Jazz Band in June of 1924, only to be turned down flat by Sammy Stewart, leader of Chicago's most elegant black dance band. "I wasn't 'dicty' enough," Armstrong remembered, "regardless of how

good I played, I wasn't up to his society." He took a job at the Dreamland Café instead, backing a journeyman singer named Ollie Powers. Then, he got a telegram from Fletcher Henderson offering him fifty-five dollars a week to come to New York.

Even though he was no longer in Joe Oliver's band, he could not bring himself to say yes until the older man gave him permission to go: "When I explained to the King that it was my one big chance to New York, where the people *really do things,* he dug me (I knew he would) and released me."

Fletcher Henderson was one of the biggest names in dance music, though he had never planned to be a musician at all. Born in Cuthbert, Georgia, the son of a piano teacher and the principal of an industrial training school, he was an Atlanta University graduate and had initially come north to New York to pursue an advanced degree in chemistry at Colum-

bia, His savings had run out before he could get started, and to support himself, he took a job as a song-plugger with W. C. Handy, then joined the Black Swan record company as an accompanist. He preferred the label's more genteel offerings—spirituals, popular songs, and excerpts from operas—to jazz or blues and was uncomfortable when asked to accompany Ethel Waters on tour. "[H]e wasn't sure it would be dignified enough for him, a college student . . . to be the piano player for a girl who sang blues in a cellar," she remembered. "Before he would go . . . Fletcher had his whole family come up from Georgia to look me over and see if it would be all right," and to get him to play the kind of "damn-it-to-hell" bass line she insisted upon, she made him listen again and again to piano rolls by James P. Johnson.

In 1923, Henderson found himself leading a band of his own at the Club Alabam, on Forty-fourth Street, just off Broadway. (The men elected him their leader because of his good looks and elegant manners.) The band already included at least three musicians who would become important jazz soloists—Coleman Hawkins, cornetist Joe Smith, and trombonist Big Charlie Green —and Henderson was sometimes billed as "the Colored King of Jazz." But, like the or-

THE MOTHER OF US ALL

"God," Ethel Waters wrote, "made me tough, headstrong and resilient." She was born in 1896 in the red-light district of Chester, Pennsylvania, the unwanted outcome of a rape. Her mother was only twelve. Her grandmother tried to raise her right, but by the age of ten, she was the leader of a gang of children, who stole food to survive and acted as lookouts for the pimps and prostitutes in their neighborhood.

She began her career as a shimmy dancer and singer. "I sure knew how to roll and quiver," she remembered, and soon found herself appearing in black theaters and tent shows for ten dollars a week, billed as "Sweet Mama Stringbean." Some of her records were in the bawdiest blues tradition—"Organ Grinder Blues," "Do What You Did Last Night," "Handyman." But unlike Bessie Smith and the other blues stars of her time she had a light, clear voice, specialized in sly insinuation, and did not indulge in what she called "unladylike shouts and growls."

In 1925, her manager insisted she try what he called "white time"—the all-white vaudeville circuit—and brought her new, Tin Pan Alley songs to perform, including "My Man" and "He's Funny That Way." She was certain she would fail. "I thought white people wouldn't understand my type of work," she recalled, "and I wasn't going to change it." But white people loved it. One New York critic hailed her as "the greatest artist of her race and generation." She became the first black woman to headline at the Palace Theater in New York, starred at

the Plantation and Cotton Clubs, and went to Hollywood in 1929 to appear in a film in which she introduced her best-remembered song, "Am I Blue." For a time the best-paid woman in show business, black or white, Ethel Waters demonstrated that black performers were not necessarily limited to the blues, that they could successfully perform every kind of material and appeal to every kind of audience. Lena Horne once paid her the highest possible compliment: Ethel Waters, she said, was "the Mother of us all."

Ethel Waters as the star of her first Broadway show, the 1927 revue *Africana*. "It was a good, fast show," she remembered, "and gave the theater-going ofays of Broadway their first long look at me."

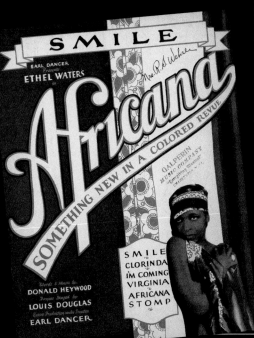

ganization led by Paul Whiteman, his was not primarily a jazz band at all; it was a popular dance orchestra specializing in cheerful light music with only a judicious jazz seasoning, still very much in the East Coast tradition best described by Garvin Bushell. New Yorkers "played foxtrot rhythm and still adhered to the two-beat rhythmic feel . . . nearer the ragtime style and . . . less blues. There wasn't an eastern performer who could really play the blues. . . . We didn't put that quarter tone pitch in the music the way the Southerners did. Up North we leaned to the ragtime conception—a lot of notes." Henderson's arrangements were written by the young alto saxophonist Don Redman and consciously patterned at first after those of the Whiteman band, syncopated but stiff, filled with brief staccato solos and call-and-response figures scored for the reed and brass sections. The result was "soft, sweet and perfect," said a writer for the Chicago *Defender,* "not the sloppy New Orleans hokum, but peppy blue syncopation in dance rhythm, . . . not at all like the average Negro orchestra, but in a class with the good white orchestras such as Paul Whiteman."

Praise like that had helped win Henderson his invitation to play at Roseland in the summer of 1924. Then, just days after the engagement began, Joe Smith abruptly left for a better-paying job in a Broadway pit band. Recordings by Joe Oliver and other New Orleans masters had begun to sell well in the city, and the black band from New Orleans that Henderson was replacing at Roseland, led by the violinist Armand J. Piron, had been popular with its clientele. And so, casting around for a replacement, Henderson resolved to find someone who could bring some Crescent City fire to his band. While on the road with Ethel Waters in 1921 he had heard Louis Armstrong in New Orleans, had even offered him a job which Armstrong had turned down. "Knowing the way that horn sounded," he said, "I had to try to get him for my band. . . . Truthfully, I didn't expect him to accept the

Times Square in the midtwenties. The Roseland Ballroom, home base for Fletcher Henderson's orchestra for many years, is at the left.

offer and I was very surprised when he came to New York and joined us."

Armstrong's arrival in New York on September 30 had not been auspicious, Don Redman remembered: "[The drummer] Kaiser Marshall had a car and brought us downtown to meet Louis. He was big and fat, and wore high top shoes with hooks in them, and long underwear down to his socks. When I got a load of that, I said to myself, Who in the hell is this guy? It *can't* be Louis Armstrong." And his arrival at the first rehearsal with the band was no more promising. The Henderson men prided themselves on always looking sharp—"English walking suits that cost a hundred-ten dollars," Marshall remembered, "seven-dollar spats and eighteen-dollar shoes." Armstrong turned up wearing the kind of big thick-soled footwear policemen wore, "and came walking across the floor, clump-clump-clump, and grinned and said hello to the boys."

No one was impressed. "The band was . . . inclined to be a little bit reserved toward the new arrival," Henderson said, "and there seemed to be a little tension in the air." Armstrong had learned to read in Fate Marable's band but still preferred to play mostly by ear, and the first sheet music Henderson handed him—"a medley of beautiful Irish waltzes"—seemed especially intimidating to the newcomer. He was "perplexed by the trumpet part I gave him," Henderson said, "marked with a *diminuendo* down to *pp* [*pianissimo*—very soft]. The band followed these notations and was playing very softly, while Louis still played . . . at full volume. I asked him about that *pp,* and Louis broke us all up by replying, 'Oh, I thought that meant pound plenty.' There was no tension after that."

Armstrong still felt out of place among Henderson's musicians, he said, until at a rehearsal a few days later, Charlie Green and the tuba player got into a shoving match. "Oh, I'm gonna *like* this band," he said. It liked him, too, and so did the

dancers at Roseland, once he got over his initial nervousness. His section-mate Howard Scott remembered his debut: "He was scared at first. He said, 'How am I doing, Scottie?' I said, 'Listen, just close your eyes and play what you feel. . . . Just let it go, Louis. Be yourself. . . . Forget about all the people.' So he did. People stopped dancing to come around and listen to him . . . and we were told that there were some people passing by [in the street] that stopped, listening to him. He was so loud. The next night you couldn't get into the place."

"You got to remember that all along I was just a young kid coming up," Armstrong later explained. "I couldn't read music like a lot of them cats, but I never was embarrassed in music with bands 'cause I'd state my case. I'd say, 'Now I can *blow*—and you give me elbow room, you going to have a nice time. But don't put me to no tests.'"

Because Armstrong's innovations would soon be so universal, not only in jazz but throughout all of American popular music, and because he was given so little solo space on the records he began making that fall with Fletcher Henderson, it is hard now to hear him freshly, as the dancers at Roseland and scores of awestruck New York musicians did in 1924. The Henderson sides feature the kind of jaunty choruses, carefully arranged breaks, and stiff agitated solos that were being played by men in half a dozen other bands. Then, suddenly, Louis Armstrong bursts forth, as if from another universe, boldly pointing the way to the future. He is simultaneously hotter than anyone else and more relaxed, pushing or retarding the beat whenever it suits his purposes, sustaining end-of-phrase tones instead of biting them off as the New Yorkers did, soaring above the sometimes plodding ensemble, always unmistakably himself and always related to the blues, no matter the tune or tempo.

Armstrong's presence transformed the Henderson orchestra. At his suggestion, the

clarinetist Buster Bailey, another veteran of the King Oliver band, was added to deepen the orchestra's down-home flavor. Don Redman began to work on a new kind of arrangement—less self-consciously "symphonic," simultaneously more supple and more driving—in which the sections played figures intended to sound like improvisations. Coleman Hawkins remembered a night at Roseland when the crowd wouldn't let Armstrong stop after soloing on a pseudo-Oriental novelty called "Shanghai Shuffle." "I think they made him play ten choruses. After that . . . a dancer lifted Armstrong onto his shoulders. Fletcher Henderson kept beating out the rhythm on the piano and I stood silent, feeling almost bashful, asking myself if I would ever be able to attain a small part of Armstrong's greatness." Until that moment, Hawkins had been best known as a master of comedy effects on his instrument—clucking and slap-tonguing in the vaudeville tradition—but afterward he devoted himself to finding a way to incorporate Armstrong's ideas into his own playing, and in the process transformed the role of the tenor saxophone in jazz.

Whenever they could get away from the Hollywood Club, Duke Ellington and his men came to Roseland to hear Armstrong, too. "There weren't the words coined for describing that kick," Ellington remembered. "Everybody on the street was talking about the guy." And, like Hawkins, Ellington himself would soon be searching for ways to adapt Armstrong's ideas to his own music.

Armstrong dazzled the musicians of New York, but he was also broadening his own horizons by listening closely to the dance bands of Sam Lanin and Vincent Lopez that sometimes appeared opposite the Henderson Orchestra. Each boasted an able lead cornetist who played in ways with which Armstrong was still largely unfamiliar. When he heard Vic D'Ippolito playing for Lanin, Armstrong recalled, "I commenced

The Fletcher Henderson Orchestra, 1924. Left to right, Howard Scott (trumpet), Coleman Hawkins (tenor saxophone), Louis Armstrong (cornet), Charlie Dixon (banjo), Fletcher Henderson (piano and leader), Kaiser Marshall (drums), Buster Bailey (clarinet and saxophones), Elmer Chambers (trumpet), Charlie Green (trombone), Bob Escudero (tuba), and Don Redman (arranger and alto saxophonist). "For years," the writer Wilder Hobson recalled, "virtually every musician in New York . . . listened to Fletcher Henderson."

to notice how valuable a first chair man is. Vic had tone and he had punch." B. A. Rolfe, who played with Lopez, was still more impressive: a European-born cornetist—he had toured the Continent as "The Boy Trumpet Wonder"—he was fond of acrobatic effects, a master of his instrument's upper register. After hearing Rolfe win applause night after night during a week-long engagement in Pittsburgh for soaring through "Shadowland" an octave higher than it was written, Armstrong resolved to "go after that high range."

Soon, he would be unmatchable. In that time, cornetists and trumpet players rarely played higher than high C. Armstrong would come to routinely finish up his choruses on F, and he did so with a big, robust tone very different from the thin, almost falsetto one that even Rolfe required to reach such dizzying heights. Other trumpet players would eventually play higher than Armstrong had, but no one has ever gone so high with such a consistent blend of power and warmth.

The cornetist Rex Stewart, then playing with a long-forgotten band called Leon Abbey's Bluesicians, remembered going with two other brass players to hear Armstrong play with the Henderson band one evening at the Savoy Ballroom in Harlem. "We decided that the only proper way to enjoy Armstrong was to help the mood along with liquid refreshments. So we all filled Coca-Cola bottles with our favorite refreshments. I chose gin, which was a mistake. . . . Every time he'd end on a soaring F, I tossed a Coke bottle, and you couldn't

Alberta Hunter, 1923. "Louis Armstrong played with all the love he had," she remembered. "Everybody loved him."

even hear the crash over the applause. But the bouncers didn't understand." Stewart's enthusiasm for Louis Armstrong got him barred from the Savoy for several years.

Within days of Armstrong's arrival in New York, his New Orleans acquaintance Clarence Williams had begun clamoring to get him into the recording studio. During the next fourteen months he would accompany fifteen different blues and novelty singers, including Ma Rainey, Alberta Hunter, Clara Smith, and the formidable Empress of the Blues herself, Bessie Smith, whom he remembered as a "very quiet woman—didn't bother nobody. But God, don't mess with her." On records like "Cold in Hand Blues," his spare, poignant phrasing perfectly complimented Smith's magisterial voice and sometimes added a fresh countermelody all his own. He was not always happy about the singers with whom he found himself working, he said later, but "Everything I did with her I *like*." Smith was less generous. Armstrong played too loudly, she said, by which she meant that he some-

times dared compete with her voice for the listener's attention; she preferred Joe Smith, who was careful always to keep discreetly in the background.

Armstrong also found himself sometimes recording with Sidney Bechet, a fact which did not always please his fellow New Orleanian. From the moment Bechet started making records, he had been the star of every instrumental session on which he had played; even when asked to accompany vocalists his presence often left a more lasting impression than did their singing. Then, Armstrong came to town. Bechet had been present, playing as a guest with the pit band at the Lafayette Theater, when the younger man made his Harlem debut, playing several choruses of "Whatcha-Call-'Em Blues" onstage with the Henderson Orchestra. Bechet heard the crowd cheer the newcomer; worse, he found that his fellow musicians couldn't seem to stop talking about him.

He and Armstrong were always cordial enough with one another, but had never

really been friends. The old New Orleans antipathy between Creoles and blacks may have had something to do with it. So might the fact that at their first meeting, eleven-year-old Armstrong had made off with the older boy's half dollar. But beyond all that, each saw the other as his only real rival. Something of their competitiveness can be heard on two recordings of a tune called "Cake-Walking Babies" they made that winter. The first version was cut three days before Christmas for Gennet, and from the opening chorus it seems almost like an ambush. Bechet hurls himself to the forefront, as if determined to demonstrate once and for all that all the fuss being made about Armstrong is misguided, that he remains unrivaled as the hottest soloist in jazz. Armstrong, his cornet muted and his efforts further hampered by poorly balanced recording that pushes him into the background, does his best to hold on to the lead and has no trouble keeping up with Bechet's headlong rush, but there is no question as to who is in charge.

Gertrude "Ma" Rainey and her Georgia Minstrels in Chicago in 1925. Her piano player, Thomas A. Dorsey, then celebrated for his risqué tunes, would soon leave all that behind, and become the father of modern gospel music. "I'm not ashamed of my blues," he said later. "A beat is a beat."

Less than three weeks later, the two men faced off again, this time in the studios of the Okeh Record Company. If Armstrong had been caught off-stride by Bechet's ferocity the first time they'd tackled this tune, he was more than ready for him now. The record remains mostly an ensemble piece, but each man plays a furious solo and each takes a swooping break so dramatic it still takes the listener's breath away. The contest seems more or less a draw up to that point. Then, Armstrong suddenly launches into a series of ripping, tearing, rhythmically complicated runs that no other musician of the day, not even Sidney Bechet, could match.

Many years later, Armstrong's greater celebrity still rankled with Bechet. Bud Freeman once made the mistake of praising him too extravagantly in Bechet's presence. "Well, I don't know, man," Bechet responded. "I might have some things I want to say myself."

"The band gained a lot from Louis and he gained a lot from us," Fletcher Henderson recalled. "[H]e *really* learned to read in my band, and to read in just about every key. [And] he made the men really swing-conscious with that New Orleans style of his." Before Armstrong's arrival, most New York bands were still playing "oompah and ricky-tick," the trumpeter Max Kaminsky remembered, "breaking up the rhythm into choppy syncopation." Armstrong changed all that, moving the music away from the two-beat feel made famous by the Original Dixieland Jazz Band toward the flowing, evenly distributed 4/4 that would one day become the pulsing heart of big band swing. It was only the first of his many gifts to American music.

"Above all," Kaminsky wrote, "above . . . the electrifying tone, the magnificence of his ideas and the rightness of his harmonic sense, his superb technique, his power and ease, his hotness and intensity, his complete mastery of his horn—above all this he had the swing. No one knew what

Louis Armstrong in New York, 1925

swing was till Louis came along. It's more than just the beat, it's conceiving the phrases in the very feeling of the beat, molding and building them so that they're an integral, indivisible part of the tempo.

The others had the idea of it, but Louis could do it; he was the heir of all that had gone before and the father of all that was to come."

FREEDOM OF EXPRESSION
WITH A GROOVE

An Interview with
WYNTON MARSALIS

Wynton Marsalis is the best-known jazz musician in America. Trumpet player, composer, educator, and artistic director of Jazz at Lincoln Center, he was born October 18, 1961, in New Orleans. His father, Ellis, is a jazz pianist and teacher. His mother, Dolores Ferdinand Ellis, is a home economics major and the mother of six sons, four of whom are musicians. Marsalis acted as Senior Creative advisor for the Jazz film project, and Ken Burns spoke with him on camera several times over the course of the five years it took to complete it. The following interview was culled from those conversations.

What is jazz?

Jazz music is freedom of expression with a groove. Jazz music is down-home and it's sophisticated. The feeling of jazz is like the feeling you get going into your favorite grandmother's house. You know there's all kind of things in there that you might not recognize, but it's accumulated wisdom. The whole feeling of the house is warm. And it's a familiar place. You've been there before, and then when you sit down to that table to eat—well, everything is laid out for you.

Jazz objectifies America. It's an art form that can give us a painless way of understanding ourselves. That's really the best thing about art, really. You can learn about yourself and you can have a good time doing it. That's what jazz music does for you.

What is the special genius of jazz?

The real power and innovation of jazz is that a group of people can come together and create art—improvised art—and can negotiate their agendas with each other. And that negotiation *is* the art. Like, you'll hear all the time that Bach improvised, and he did improvise. But he wasn't going to go to the second viola and say, "Okay, let's play 'Ein' feste Burg.' " They were not going to do that. Whereas in jazz, I could go to Milwaukee tomorrow and walk into a bar at 2:30 in the morning. There'll be three musicians playing there and I'll say, "What you want to play man? Let's play some blues." Well, all four of us are going to start playing and everybody will just start comping and playing and listening. You never know what they're going to do. So, that's our art. The four of us can now have a dialogue. We can have a conversation. We can speak to each other in the language of music. And that is art. That is our art.

That spirit of improvisation seems utterly American as well.

The whole conception of improvisation is a part of all of American life. And if you were a slave, you had to learn how to improvise. You came on the land, you couldn't speak the language. You had all kind of foods you weren't used to eating. You had another whole system to deal with. If you couldn't improvise, you were going to be in a world of trouble. You were not going to be able to survive.

You have said that jazz is the distillation of the American spirit, and the clearest way you know of discovering who we are. What do you mean?

In American life you have all these different agendas. You have conflict all the time and we're attempting to achieve harmony through conflict. It seems strange to say that, but it's like an argument that you have with the intent to work something out, not an argument that you have with the intent to argue. And that's what jazz music is. You have eight musicians and they're all standing on the bandstand and each one has his own personality and his own agenda. There's written music but then you leave that score and are left to make intelligent decisions. Decisions that have soul. Decisions that allow your personality to breathe and to speak, but decisions that allow for other people's personalities to breathe, too. Invariably they're going to play something that you would not play. So, you have to learn when to say a little something, when to get out of the way. But you're always negotiating: Who are you going to go with? You going to go with the piano? Do you know where the drums are? And so you have that question of the integrity, the intent, the will to play together. That's what jazz music is. So you have yourself, your individual expression—and then you have to figure out how to fit in with everybody else. And that's exactly like democracy.

Jazz music explains to you what it means to be American. Which is that it's a process. And democracy is a process. It's not always going to go your way. Sometimes you have to play that riff and listen to what somebody else is playing. Jazz believes in freedom of expression. But it also believes in people communicating with each other. A lot of times things might not work out. But there's always another time: "So, okay, we messed that up. Let's play another tune." It's like Charlie Parker told a musician once, "Well, what do *you* want to play? 'Cause we can play a lot of tunes. No sense in playing something that's going to leave you out."

Does it strike you as ironic that America's greatest music should have been created by America's most maligned minority?

white people. So you have that basic three-caste system, none of whom like the other one or trust the other one. But they all know each other because they see each other every day. They live around each other, they eat the same food, they speak essentially the same language. They listen to the same music. They have a common experience. Then, the Creole people are forced at a certain point to integrate with the dark-skinned people. Well, they didn't want to do that but they had to compete with them for jobs. Well, now you start to get jazz. Because then it's, "Okay, now how am I going to deal with what *they're* doing?"

What's the role of the blues in that potent mix?

The blues, they feel good. The blues is many things—a philosophy and a form, a musical form of bars and measures, a whole body of melodies and themes. It's a harmonic system. It's a system of call and response. It's a bunch of moans and groans and shouts and cries. Dissonance and consonance. Blues is many things. And it can interface with music all over the world.

Blues is like the folk themes and little nuggets and kernels that are developed through the art of jazz into jazz music. You have to have that blues. Blues is like the roux in a gumbo. Now you might have a soup, and it might be killin', but if you don't have that roux, you cannot have no gumbo. People ask me if jazz always has the blues in it. I say, if it sounds good it does.

The history of jazz is filled with extraordinary personalities, towering geniuses. What is it that puts Louis Armstrong in a category all his own?

When you talk about Louis Armstrong, well, you're talking about the deepest human feeling, and the highest level of musical sophistication in the same man. That's a rare occurrence in the history of music. He was chosen to bring the feeling and the message and the identity of jazz to everybody. He brought it to all the musicians. He brought it all over the world. He's the embodiment of jazz music. He's deeply down-home and soulful with tremendous compassion, but he has plenty of fire and is built like a bull and would knock you out if he had to. And he knows about the low life. He knows about poverty. He knows about prostitution. He's also regal at the same time. He has a spiritual presence. He's always trying to make situations better. That's how his playing is. He could play the trumpet better than anybody. He could play higher with more dexterity than anyone else. And the thing that made him so great as a musician is that he heard what everybody was playing. And not only did he hear what they were playing, he heard what they were *trying* to play. And all of that he played.

Louis Armstrong invented a new style of playing. He created

Well, it's not ironic if you know mythology. God gives the message, not man. And the message comes from where you least expect it. That's how it always is in myth. The person who you keep out and you push down and you kick—Cinderella—that's the one with the moral authority, with the gift. That's as old as night and day, as old as dust.

Jazz music was created by people who wanted to be American people. It comes from the consciousness of those who are outside of something but in the middle of it. People like Buddy Bolden, like Louis Armstrong, these are people who were American in the realest sense. They'd been denied access to a recognition as Americans but that doesn't alter the fact that they *were* American. They had access to all of the information that other Americans had access to. And they came together in New Orleans and synthesized many different ways of living and approaches to experience and that became jazz music. And they were forced to negotiate their agendas. They didn't do it because they wanted to do it; they were forced to do it through segregation. First you have the Creoles, who are segregated from the darker-skinned Negroes, so they don't like each other at all. Then you have the

the coherent solo, fused the sound of the blues with the American popular song, extended the range of the trumpet. Louis Armstrong created the melodic and rhythmic vocabulary that all the big bands wrote music out of. And all the musicians imitated him. It's hard for us really to think today of just how popular he was. Everybody on every instrument tried to play like him—clarinet, saxophone, bass, drums. Duke Ellington once said he wanted Louis Armstrong on every instrument.

Then, he was always himself. The first time he touched the trumpet he sounded great, I'm sure of that. The spirit was in him, and the understanding that comes from the Creator of humanity. His sound had a *light* in it. That's the only way I can describe it. You can't practice to get that. It's a spiritual presence, and when that light is in someone's sound—when you hear it, it draws, it attracts you.

The other person who seems to dominate the story of jazz, at least as we've told it, is Duke Ellington.

The most important things to know about Duke Ellington are that he loved people, he loved life, and he loved music. He understood

that anything is possible. He understood what it took to make something invisible visible, knew how to take what could be and make it what is. And he could do that in so many different ways. He showed the world how to orchestrate the sound of the blues for a large ensemble. The systems of harmonization and voicings that he alone invented only he knows. He could listen to a style and get to the very center of it, and take the meaning and the juice out of that style and put it into his own. People say that he wrote for his musicians and that that was the secret to his success. But I don't think that. I think that was the secret to *their* success, that they had him to write for them.

You don't get the same type of spiritual high-mindedness in his sound that you have in Louis Armstrong's. Duke Ellington, he's more of a late-night person. He's the person who understands the sensuous. That's in his music and it's in his sound. When he hits one or two notes on the piano, you know he's going to take you into a late-night room where something of interest is about to take place. He's like Bacchus or Dionysus. He loves things carnal. That's his domain. And he's there to let you know what you need to be doing and how you need to be doing it and what tempo you need to be doing it in. So he's indispensable.

The story of jazz and the story of race in America seem inextricably bound together.

Well, race is a . . . For this country it's like the thing in mythology that you have to do for the kingdom to be well. And it's always something you don't want to do. And it's always about confronting yourself, always tailor-made for you to fail in dealing with it. And the question of your heroism and of your courage in dealing with this trial is the measure of your success. Can you confront it with honesty? And do you have the energy to sustain an attack on it? And since jazz music is at the center of the American mythology, it necessarily deals with race because race is our black eye, to make a little pun. It's something that the more we run from it, the more we run into it. And it's an age-old story, if it's not race, it's something else. But in this particular instance, in this nation, it is race.

Now, jazz music is not race music. Everybody plays jazz music. Everybody has always played it. But when people teach the history of jazz, they always talk about white bands and black bands. Musicians don't learn that way. See, this is the big lie in the way that it's taught. Benny Goodman was going to learn the clarinet from whoever he could. Elvin Jones studied with a guy who played in the Detroit Symphony. Miles Davis went to Juilliard and studied with William Vachiano. Now, he didn't learn to play jazz from William Vachiano, but he's a trumpet player, so he's going to learn from whoever is there. Louis Armstrong's style is influenced by the style of cornet virtuosos like Bohumir Kryl and Herbert L. Clarke. Bunny Berigan is influenced by Louis Armstrong. Bix Beiderbecke is influenced by Louis Armstrong. Lester Young is influenced by Frankie Trumbauer. That's how music is. You hear something you like, and you want to play like that.

What was going on in those early years in Chicago, when young white kids including Bix Beiderbecke began traveling to the South Side to get in on the amazing new music being played by Armstrong and King Oliver?

Well, I think that with Bix Beiderbecke you have a prime example of a musician who's caught in the crossroads between the racial question and the question of jazz. Because you know, whenever you hear the question of race in jazz, you always hear it from one perspective. You always hear the same story of the white musicians coming in, playing and getting more credit from the media than the black musicians. And in general that happened. There's no doubt about it. It happens all the time. But you never hear the story from the perspective of the white musician. When these white kids came down to hear King Oliver and Louis Armstrong, we have to realize that this is some of the most abstract and sophisticated music that anybody has ever heard, short of Bach. Now, a musician loves music and loves that instrument. And when he hears someone who's great on that instrument there's a mixture of great envy, respect, and love. You're going out every night, you're hearing the greatest musician in the world play—Louis Armstrong—and all you want to do is be able to play like him. But you've been told, "Don't listen to them. These are niggers and they ain't playing nothing, and this is some coon music and it's all a joke." But you realize it's the most serious thing you've ever encountered in your life. And when you realize that, you realize that you, too, are a part of it. And that's got to be exhilarating and terrifying at the same time. Because to accept jazz music means that at a certain time you have to accept something about the humanity of the United States Negro.

This is something that goes back to Uncle Remus. But the difference is that old Uncle Remus was this helpless old "uncle" sitting down to tell the little white kids the ways of the world. Well, now this has been transformed because the men that these kids are looking at on the stage are well-dressed, sophisticated men, and Louis Armstrong is close to their age. There's the element of competition in there, as well as awe, as well as envy, as well as respect, as well as love, reverence, a lot of different feelings, all at once. Shame, too. Because these white kids have been taught these people are inferior their entire lives. Every magazine arti-

cle, every newspaper story, the whole mythology of America is saying, "A nigger ain't shit." That's what you have been taught. Now, you're standing up and you're looking at these men playing and you're saying to yourself, "Boy, I sure wish I could play like these guys." How does that make you feel? And when they go out and start learning how to play the music, what is society's response to them? Either they can make it and be known as the white this or the white that—which is not the thing that made them want to play the music in the beginning. Or else, they can be scorned by their parents, as playing dirty black music that's going to just make you be a drunk and in the gutter and have all kinds of good sex that you ought not be having. Or, they're going to grapple with the art form and learn how to play it and become as good as they can, but even if they become as great as they can possibly be, as Bix Beiderbecke did, they're still going to fall far short of Louis Armstrong. So, how do they, then, as men with the natural competitive drive that a man has, plus being white and therefore having been taught that they should be number one, how are they going to come to grips with this as they grow into manhood? That was the great question that confronted them throughout their lives.

You've argued that to play jazz you need to understand its history.

History is the playing field. That's true in all the arts. Shakespeare's dealing with themes that existed long before Shakespeare. Picasso used to say he could bring to life forms of art that had been dead for years—Sumerian art, Etruscan art. He could take these forms and bring them back to life and give them another flavor or feeling. That's the question of art; that's the fun of it. Do you want to play with the whole history of humanity? Or do you just want to play with the last ten years?

Jazz was most popular during the 1930s and early '40s, when it was played for dancers.

Jazz is dance music. The closer you get to the body response, the more the music is going to swing and the better it's going to feel. The further you get away from the body response, the less good it feels. When Duke Ellington would play a dance and play one of his slow pieces he could see the romantic effect that his music had, and on the up-tempo songs, he could see a whole floor of people dancing and juking to his music. But if you're playing in a concert hall sometimes people seem to be afraid even to tap their feet or move their heads. You say to yourself, "What's happening?" You don't know if you're swinging or not.

But there's the argument that jazz only matured when, after the advent of bebop, it became a more "intellectual" art.

I don't think that it ever was a question of it becoming more intellectual, because the wisest jazz musician in terms of just musical intelligence was Duke Ellington, and he never was attracted to that sound. So I don't think it became a thing where some tremendous amount of intellect was put into it to create a style that nobody could understand. That's what European music suffered from. Some of that music went into a direction that may have been mathematically sound but the audience just said no. Basically, you know, music deals with a man and a woman and men and women and their relationship to God. Now once you get out of that ballpark, you might come up with something hip and interesting for a little while. You might. You can pick your horn up and just play what you want to play with a group of musicians and it can be creative. They can play what they want. You can take a little theme and just play for an hour on it and you can play as loud as you want, you can express as much anger as you want, as much joy. It can be expressive and meaningful and you can have a great time doing it. But I don't think too many people are going to want to hear that for too long. So, to me, that's the

most elitist form of music. That's the ultimate elitist statement, which is, "This is what *I* want to do." And also you're not addressing form. It's like basketball, once the net is gone, once you don't have to stay in bounds, you're just out in the street dribbling. Which can be fun, but it ain't basketball.

You've said that jazz is for grown-ups, that it grows out of an adult sensibility.

Well, you never see a prodigy like Mozart, eight or nine years old, who is great in jazz music. Not that there are lots of Mozarts in classical music, but you do have people who come up who are precocious and who are on a professional level at a young age. You don't really get that in jazz. Jazz music is about how much you know about the human condition. What do you understand about old Uncle Ned, this dad that left his family? Or what do you understand about what your mother has to deal with? Or what do you understand about what the woman that you met on the bus told you? That's what comes out of your horn. What comes out of your horn is what you understand about life, the texture of it, the absurdity of it, and the beauty of it. And children don't think about that. They're too self-absorbed. We live in an age where there's a tremendous investment in the generation gap. Our music doesn't have that. When you're young, you try and learn how to play like people who can play. Nobody thirteen or fourteen is getting around Clark Terry and all these great musicians and telling *them* what the deal is. Whereas, if you go out and you talk to high school students, they'll ask, "What about what the kids are thinking?" As if, as an adult, your job is to relate to them, to try and figure out what they're thinking about, as if *that's* going to take you to another level.

When you talk about the message brought by great jazz musicians you definitely are talking about something that's spiritual. How many people did Louis Armstrong's music help to survive in the world? Jazz music is *existence* music. It doesn't take you out of the world. It puts you in the world and it says, "This is." It deals with the present and it says, "Yes, all of that is what happens." Somebody may be lying out drunk in the street. It might be the cat you've just heard playing. It might be Charlie Parker. But that fact doesn't alter the power of what he's saying, "Yes, I did that and I also do this." The whole range of humanity is in this music.

What does jazz tell us about our country right now?

Right now it's telling us that we need to learn how to listen. We don't listen, you know. It's like when I hear these young musicians play, the thing they all have in common is they don't listen to each other. First, they play too loud. When you're playing that loud, you just can't play with anybody else. And then it's telling us we need to listen and make an honest attempt to understand what somebody else is playing. If you're playing the trumpet and you don't understand what the bass is playing, you might be lost. If you don't know the chords the piano is playing, it's very hard to play with the piano. So part of your responsibility is to learn. You have to go and get with the drummer and say, "What is this rhythm?" "It's a five rhythm." "Okay, can you show me how to play that? How should I react to that?" You can't say, "Well, I'm African-American and you're Asian-American and you're Caucasian and you're Irish-American and I want ten percent of this and you can have the other ninety percent," because the music doesn't work that way. *Everybody* has to make the music. I can't say, "Well, I'm a trumpet player, I don't really have to know what the piano is playing. All I want is my space to solo." "Oh, I'm the drummer so I play louder than all of you all so do the best you can." You can't say, "Well, I'm the composer and I know more than all of you about music so play my music the way I want you to play it." You can't have that relationship to play jazz music. If you compose music, you have to write music the musicians can

play. Part of your success is to write something that they want to improvise on. If you are the trumpet player, you have to figure out how to play in balance with the saxophone. If you're the drummer, you have to figure out how to groove and swing and make everything feel right for everybody, how to push them along when they need help, how to back away when they don't need it, how to give 'em a little something. But you also have to listen to that bass and have the swing locked up. If you're the bass player, you've got to just do that workmanlike job and chip your two cents in whenever you can and come up with interesting ostinatos and grooves and take the music in different directions. So everybody has their little thing they have to do, but all the roles are interchangeable. It's a matter of the integrity and the intelligence of the group.

What would life be like without jazz?

You definitely can live without jazz. The only thing you need to live is water and some food. Art in general is nonessential to living. But now, the style that you're gonna be living in? Well, I don't know about that. You don't need a bed to sleep. You don't have to cook food to eat it. You don't have to have clothes of a certain style. You don't have to speak a certain way. Most of the things you are surrounded by you don't need. But when you have those things around you, it makes you feel good about living in the world. And it gives you something to look forward to, and it also gives you a way to connect with everything that has happened on earth. It's like real poor people in the country, on a Sunday, would get dressed up and they wouldn't have any money but just that little hat with the flower on it. You know, just what that flower represents. A certain thing. Just a little something to make you special and make you sweet. That's jazz music. That's what the jazz musician wants to give to the people.

OUR LANGUAGE

Jazz had been born in New Orleans and nurtured in Chicago and New York and on the West Coast, but by the mid-1920s, versions of it were being played in dance halls and roadhouses and speakeasies all over the country. The blues, which had once been the product of itinerant black musicians, the poorest of the southern poor, had become an industry, and dancing consumed a country that seemed convinced prosperity would never end. There were "all-girl" orchestras on the road now—including Babe Egan's Hollywood Redheads, a band billed as the Twelve Vampires, and the Parisian Redheads, all of whom actually came from Indiana. More than one hundred dance bands regularly crisscrossed the wide-open spaces between St. Louis and Denver, Texas and Nebraska, playing one-nighters. They were called

Pianist Ben Smith, center, and his Blue Syncopaters, 1928. Based in El Paso, Texas, Smith's outfit never recorded but, like scores of other so-called territory bands, they traveled thousands of miles every year bringing music—and more than a dash of elegance—to communities all across the plains and prairie states.

"territory bands"—the Coon-Sanders Nighthawks; the Alphonso Trent and Doc Ross and Troy Floyd and Benny Moten Orchestras; the Deluxe Melody Boys and Happy Black Aces; Jesse Stone's Blue Serenaders; George E. Lee and his Singing Novelty Orchestra; Walter Page and his Blue Devils; and Andy Kirk's Clouds of Joy. "People didn't think anything about going a hundred and fifty to two hundred miles to dance back in those times," one territory band veteran remembered. "We used to talk to a lot of people. They'd say, 'We came two hundred miles to see y'all.' "

Meanwhile, radio and phonograph records—Americans bought more than 100 million of them in 1927—were bringing jazz to locations so remote that no band could reach them. And the music itself was beginning to change—an exuberant, collective music was coming to place more and more emphasis on the innovations of supremely gifted individuals. Improvising soloists, struggling to find their own voices and to tell their own stories, were about to take center stage.

When Louis Armstrong returned to Chicago to play at the Dreamland Café in Novem-ber of 1925, he was startled to find a banner above the door proclaiming him "the World's Greatest Jazz Cornetist." His wife, Lil, had insisted on it, and Armstrong was embarrassed at first: "I never did want to be a big mucky-muck star," he said. But for him, there would be no turning back.

At first, Armstrong had loved playing with Fletcher Henderson, liked New York and the nightlife of Harlem, reveled in the reception he and the orchestra got whenever they went on tour. "We were the first colored big band to hit the road," he remembered proudly. "We went all through the New England states." But back in Chicago, leading her own band at the Dreamland Café, Lil Hardin Armstrong suspected that her husband was enjoying himself too well in Manhattan—word may have reached her that he was seeing a showgirl after hours—and she was dissatisfied in any case with the progress of his career. His New York sojourn had spread his reputation but Henderson was still unwilling to give him the star billing she was sure he deserved. In October of 1925, she talked the owner of the Dreamland into offering her husband seventy-five dollars a week and sent Armstrong a peremptory telegram, laying out the terms of the offer and the date she expected him to be back in Chicago. Then she added: IF YOU'RE NOT HERE BY THIS DATE, THEN DON'T COME AT ALL.

Armstrong came. After fourteen months in New York he had grown dissatisfied. Henderson was a weak disciplinarian. Some of his men drank too hard and arrived late—and sometimes did not arrive at all. "I was always *serious* about my music," Armstrong remembered. He resented the fact that no matter how well he played, he was never allowed to occupy the first trumpet chair—that position was the property of Elmer Chambers, whose refined "legitimate" tone Henderson had come to depend upon when playing for society dancers. (Armstrong later said Chambers sounded like a "nanny goat.") "Fletcher only let me play third cornet," Armstrong complained many years later. "The whole time I was in his band he'd only give me sixteen bars to get off with, but he'd let me hit those high notes that the big prima-donnas, first-chair men, couldn't hit." Armstrong saw himself as an all-around entertainer, too, someone who enjoyed getting laughs as well as applause, and he had been singing as well as playing since his days as an eleven-year-old tenor on the streets of black Storyville. Henderson didn't seem interested in those gifts. He disliked what he called Armstrong's "big fish horn voice" and thought his exuberant mugging style too black for white customers at Roseland. Armstrong's singing was largely confined to the band's more relaxed appearances in Harlem.

Above all, Armstrong never got over the sense that Henderson simply "didn't dig me" and continued to see him, despite his talent, as something of a dark-skinned rube. If Henderson did really feel that way—and years later he was still describing Armstrong as "pretty much a down-home boy in the big city"—the climax to the big farewell dinner he gave him at Small's Paradise in Harlem cannot have done much to change his mind. Speeches and a sump-

Small-time bands too poor to afford buses crowded into cars for the long jumps between engagements. Instruments traveled well enough when securely tied down outside or on top—provided it didn't rain.

The House of David, a Michigan-based sect whose founder believed himself destined to reunite the Lost Tribes of Israel, raised funds by fielding jazz bands as well as baseball teams during the 1920s. The sect's edicts against cutting one's hair evidently did not extend to women.

The Parisian Red Heads, who billed themselves as "America's Greatest Girl Band" and later changed their name to The Bricktops, 1929

The Erskine Tate Orchestra at the Vendome Theater on Chicago's South Side, 1925. Louis Armstrong sits fourth from the left. When Tate asked him to join his elegant organization, Armstrong wrote, "I like to have Fainted. . . . For anyone to play in *Tate's* band was Really, Really Somebody."

tuous dinner were followed by a jam session, all accompanied by bottle after bottle of champagne. Finally, Armstrong and Buster Bailey realized they'd had too much to drink and decided to make their way home. Armstrong lurched over to say a final good-bye to Henderson, he remembered, began to thank him for all his kindnesses, then leaned forward and gravely vomited all over the bandleader's "nice clean tuxedo shirt."

The Dreamland Café, at 3520 South State Street, was a comparative rarity in Chicago —an opulent, mirror-hung "black-and-tan" owned and run not by whites, but by a

prominent and well-connected black entrepreneur named Billy Bottoms. Pimps and prostitutes and the "fixers" who found black women for white men in more disreputable places were barred at the doors. "Residents and business men of the Race throughout the city," the Chicago *Defender* assured its readers, "could feel safe in taking their close friends and the members of the family there with the knowledge that nothing would be allowed, by word or act, to cause complaint." Just two weeks after the Armstrongs were reunited on its bandstand, the music critic of the *Defender* reported that the cornetist was "drawing many 'ofay' [white] musicians to the Dreamland nightly

to hear him blast out those weird jazz figures. This boy is in a class by himself."

The New Orleans pianist Richard M. Jones, now a producer of race records for the Okeh label, thought so too, and persuaded Tommy Rockwell, the executive in charge of the Chicago office, to record Louis Armstrong for the first time under his own name. On November 12, 1925, Armstrong and a pickup recording band he called his Hot Five—Kid Ory, Johnny Dodds, Lil Armstrong, and the banjoist Johnny St. Cyr— made the first three of some sixty-five recordings that would once and for all establish his as the most important solo voice in jazz. "When we made those records," Armstrong said much later, "it was just pick up them cats and do it. And we didn't want no royalties, just pay me, man, give me that loot. Got $50 each for each [tune]—just a gig to us and glad to do it so we could go up town and have a ball with the money. And now look at them records." Lil Hardin Armstrong agreed. "We had no idea in the beginning that jazz was going to be that important, that somebody would want to know how we started, what we did, what records we made, and it's amusing to read in books telling why we did this. I'm glad they know, because we didn't."

The Hot Five—and later, the Hot Seven— records are firmly rooted in the New Orleans tradition that had surrounded Armstrong from birth, but from the opening chorus of the very first side, an otherwise undistinguished tune by Lil Armstrong called "My Heart," something altogether new has been added. The familiar collective polyphony is still present and the only full-fledged solos are played by Dodds and the composer, but Armstrong plays the lead and a pair of breaks with such power and feeling that he *seems* to be soloing even when he is not. Over the next two years his role would steadily expand until, as the wife of his friend the drummer Zutty Singleton remembered, the rest of the musicians on his records became something like "a choir," present mostly to provide the background settings above which he could soar.

"I became more popular every night," Armstrong remembered, "and was the talk of Chicago." Within a month of his return and while still playing at the Dreamland, Armstrong accepted an offer from Erskine Tate, conductor of the pit band at the cavernous Vendome Theater, three blocks south on South State Street. This was a new kind of setting for Armstrong, a twelve-piece tuxedoed outfit, complete with strings and woodwinds, that accompanied silent films, and between screenings offered a full program of Broadway melodies and light classics culminating in what Armstrong remembered as "a red hot number." Arm-

strong was apprehensive at first, just as he had been when he got to Chicago and before he took his place on Fletcher Henderson's bandstand. His wife had to threaten to "skin you alive" just to get him to agree to go to his first rehearsal.

The job involved a great deal of sight-reading, and Tate also insisted Armstrong trade in what he called his "stubby little cornet" for a sleek new trumpet to match the one played by his section-mate, Tate's younger brother, Jimmy. (Armstrong would soon abandon the cornet altogether.) And when Tate tried to make him leave the orchestra pit and go onstage for his feature numbers, he balked. He didn't want to alienate the rest of the men in the band, he said. But they shone a spotlight down on him, anyway, and when it found his gleaming horn and he began to play, sometimes hitting fifty high C's in a row as the crowd counted along with him, and then climbing

to a high F, audiences went wild—and were unwilling to accept any substitutes, as young Adolphus "Doc" Cheatham discovered. Cheatham was fresh from Nashville, Tennessee, just twenty-one, and had only recently shifted from the saxophone to the cornet when Armstrong stopped him on a Chicago street corner.

[Louis] says, "How would you like to work for me at the Vendome Theater? I want to take off on a Thursday."

I says, "I'm very sorry, but I don't think I'm capable of filling in for you . . ."

[But] Louis insisted. . . . I didn't want to do it, but I felt that I needed some money in my pocket to eat on . . . and the musicians came in one by one until they were seated and then Tate came in with his baton. . . . When they got to Louis' part of his

The Pearl High School Orchestra in Nashville, Tennessee, 1918. Adolphus "Doc" Cheatham stands at upper left; he would soon trade in his alto saxophone for a cornet. His would be one of the longest careers in the history of jazz.

show, they played Louis' specialty, "Poor Little Rich Girl." This was a big band, fiddles and everything were going and [the audience] didn't notice me being there. I was sitting there with my cornet. And so, they came down to Louis' introduction and Tate's brother said, "That's you." So, I got up and blew on the cornet.

The people started screaming. You couldn't hear, I mean, I never saw anything like it in my life—for one second. Then it stopped, it died. The whole applause died, died right down . . . because they noticed that I wasn't Louis. I felt like dropping dead."

Musicians began paying their way into the Vendome just to see if Armstrong could make the high notes for which he was becoming famous. When he admitted to Lil that he sometimes worried he might fail, she was unsympathetic. He should just start practicing high G's at home, she said: "If you can hit G at home, you won't worry about an F at the theater." It evidently worked: asked by an interviewer late in life if he had ever missed any of those notes, Armstrong just laughed. "I had it in my pocket all the time."

All of Armstrong's innate showmanship was now on display. He danced and sang and clowned as well as played, loved to put on spectacles and a long-tailed coat and deliver mock sermons in the style of his favorite entertainer, Bert Williams, as a larcenous store-front preacher, "the Reverend Satchelmouth."

Some other musicians were upset by all the attention Armstrong was getting. Lil Armstrong remembered one evening when Freddie Keppard, the Creole cornetist who had been Joe Oliver's chief rival back in New Orleans, stormed into Dreamland, drunk and without his horn.

Freddie stood there by the bandstand and he listened for a while. Then he said to Louis "Boy, let me have your trumpet." So Louis looked at me and

Louis Armstrong's Hot Five, 1925. Left to right, Armstrong, Johnny St. Cyr, Johnny Dodds, Kid Ory, and Lil Hardin Armstrong. This publicity photograph was signed by Armstrong to one of the legion of young trumpet players, white and black, who had already begun to worship him, Chicago-born Muggsy Spanier.

I bowed my head, so Louis gave him the trumpet. So Freddie, he blew— oh, he blew and he blew and he blew. And then the people gave him a nice hand. Then he handed the trumpet back to Louis. And I said, "Now get him, get him!" Ooh, never in my life have I heard such trumpet playing. If you want to hear Louis play, just hear him play when he's angry. Boy, he blew and people starting standing up on top of tables and chairs, screaming. And Freddie eased out real slow. Nobody ever asked Louis for his trumpet again!

There were other challengers over the next few months, as well. According to Barney Bigard, Johnny Dunn, a suave performer in the staccato New York ragtime tradition, turned up another night and haughtily dismissed Armstrong's playing to his face: "Boy," he said, "you don't know how to do."

Armstrong "blew him out of the place," Bigard claimed. "They looked for Johnny Dunn when Louis was finished but he had skipped out. They never found him in there again."

Kid Ory remembered that roughly the same thing happened to the young fast-finger specialist Cladys "Jabbo" Smith when he came looking for Armstrong "with blood in his eye." Smith did his best, was overwhelmed, and left the club, muttering something about getting himself a trombone.

On February 26, 1926, Armstrong's "Hot Five" returned to the Okeh studio to record six more sides. All were further evidence of Armstrong's artistry; two made jazz history. "Cornet Chop Suey" was his first virtuoso masterpiece. Except for a leaden piano solo by his wife, Armstrong's cornet is the focus of the whole record—he states the melody with no accompaniment at all, leads the ensemble, plays a spectacular stop-time

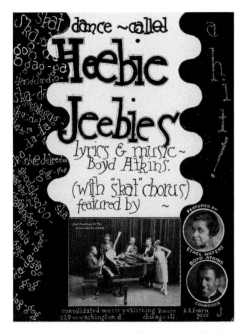

Louis Armstrong's success with "Heebie Jeebies" inspired other entertainers, including Ethel Waters, to record versions of their own.

solo, and ends with a cadenza all his own. Tommy Rockwell thought this recording so daring he did not release it until the sales of another side cut that day proved that Armstrong's name alone could sell records: when "Cornet Chop Suey" did reach the stores, aspiring cornetists all over the country struggled to memorize Armstrong's elegant dancing lines. In his native New Orleans one evening, a cutting contest—a musical showdown—between cornetists Edgar "Guy" Kelly and Henry "Red" Allen went to Kelly because Allen somehow forgot to play Armstrong's final cadenza.

The other historic side cut that day was a novelty tune called "Heebie Jeebies," on which Armstrong sang one ebullient chorus in nonsense syllables. The legend grew—eventually encouraged by Armstrong himself—that it was all an accident, that he had dropped the lyric sheet during the session and had begun "scatting" only because the record producer had signaled him not to ruin the take by stopping. No one else on the date remembered any such event and since Armstrong himself had

scribbled out the lyrics himself just moments before the session began as an aid to his memory and had already sung them correctly once, it is hard to see how he could have forgotten them. In fact, scat singing was a familiar practice in New Orleans—"We used to do that in the [boys'] quartet going down the street," Armstrong himself once admitted—and Don Redman had already recorded a scat chorus with Fletcher Henderson. But Armstrong brought to scatting an exuberant confidence and unpredictable rhythmic drive never heard before.

"Heebie Jeebies" was Armstrong's first hit, selling more than forty thousand copies within a few months, most of them in black neighborhoods. Mezz Mezzrow remembered driving fifty miles after midnight just to play the record for Bix Beiderbecke. "Bix kept chuckling as the record played over and over. . . . [Then he] tore out of the house to wake up everybody he knew . . . and make them listen to it. . . . For months after that, you would hear cats greeting each other with Louis's riffs. . . . 'I got the Heebies,' one would yell out, and the other would answer, 'I got the Jeebies,' and the next minute they were scatting in each other's faces. . . . Louis's [scatting] almost drove the English language out of the Windy City for good."

RIGHT UP MY ALLEY

Every evening during the summer of 1925, hundreds of young working-class white men and women could have been seen lined up at the entrance to the Midway Dancing Gardens, at Sixty-sixth and Cottage Grove on Chicago's South Side, impatiently waiting to pay their one-dollar entrance fee and get out onto the dance floor. Originally designed by Frank Lloyd Wright as an outdoor summer concert garden for the National Symphony Orchestra, it had been renovated for dancing in 1923 and became an instant hit with young people. "There is not a mature person to be found on the Midway Gardens

dance floor," reported *Variety.* "The youths in their inevitable high-waisted dark suits and with long funny hair and glossy with vaseline are perfect prototypes of the ballroom sheiks. The girls, most of them pretty and all of them endurance dancers, are dressed flashingly. In the daytime, their occupations probably range from dipping chocolates to taking dictation."

By 1925, America was dance-mad and dancers had strong opinions about the kind of music they wanted: "Where in former years they were content to dance to any old tin band," said the New York *Clipper,* "today they are unusually particular in the sort of music they 'hoof' to." And it was the sort of music played by the eleven-man Midway Gardens band that drew young Chicagoans. Smooth but unrelentingly animated—slow dancing was frowned upon and vigilant official chaperones moved constantly among the dancers looking for such inappropriate behavior—it was propelled always by what one newspaper called "a rhythm conducive to stepping." Three veterans of the New Orleans Rhythm Kings saw to that: pianist and musical director Elmer Schoebel, banjoist Lou Black, and drummer Frank Snyder. The band prided itself on being hotter than the more sedate orchestra in residence at the rival Trianon Ballroom, and much of its heat that summer was being provided by a sixteen-year-old clarinet prodigy named Benjamin David Goodman.

Bespectacled, taciturn, and still so young that he wore long trousers only when onstage, Goodman had been earning a living as a professional musician since the age of thirteen and was already good enough to have impressed another veteran of the New Orleans Rhythm Kings, the Chicago-born drummer Ben Pollack. Pollack was putting together a new hot band for an engagement in Venice, California, that summer, and sent his alto saxophone player and musical director, Gil Rodin, to look the boy over. Rodin liked what he heard well enough to take Goodman aside during a break and ask if he'd like to come west and join the band.

"O-o-oh, I'd love to come!" the boy answered, provided his parents approved.

David and Dora Goodman were Jewish refugees from Russian pogroms. Dora Goodman, who had been made to start earning her own living at the age of eight, could neither read nor write and rarely left her home. David Goodman was trained as a tailor, but in order to feed his family he often found himself toiling instead in the Chicago stockyards twelve hours a day, six days a week. Both the Goodmans had sacrificed greatly to ensure that all of their children—Benny was the ninth of twelve—would lead a life more comfortable and

more fulfilling than their own. But they also had made it clear to all their offspring that they had an obligation to find a way to support themselves just as quickly as they could.

As soon as Benny got a firm offer from Ben Pollack to go to California, he quit his job at the Midway Gardens so that his parents could not object too strenuously to his traveling so far from home. "Look," he remembered telling them, "I lost my job at the Midway Gardens. This other one [with the Pollack band] is the only one I've got." The Goodmans reluctantly agreed that he could go—and by doing so helped launch

one of the most extraordinary careers in American musical history.

Benny Goodman was one of the first true virtuosos in jazz, a master of his instrument, capable of elegant melodic improvisation even at breakneck speed. He was also a difficult and driven man, an aloof perfectionist whose implacable determination not only to try to be the best but to surround himself with the best first helped make him America's best-known bandleader, and then would impel him to become a somewhat reluctant pioneer, willing to defy racial conventions provided it would make his great orchestra still greater.

The Midway Gardens on the South Side of Chicago, photographed a few years before it was transformed into the vast outdoor ballroom where the young Benny Goodman shone

Benny Goodman at ten, and (below) the crowded neighborhood around Maxwell Street in which he grew up

Louis Armstrong delighted in reminiscing about his early days in the New Orleans neighborhood called "the Battlefield"; Benny Goodman would struggle all his life to distance himself from his youth. "I guess there are things that I simply want to block out," he admitted to one interviewer. "Probably because I never found it all that enjoyable. Growing up poor. Living in certain parts of Chicago. I'm not a great one for remembering."

The mile-square Maxwell Street ghetto in which Goodman was born on May 30, 1909, was more crowded, very nearly as poor, and almost as violent as Armstrong's Battlefield; Goodman himself remembered it as "pretty hopeless." A turn-of-the-century sociologist determined that if all of Chicago were as densely peopled as Maxwell Street, the city could accommodate the entire population of the Western Hemisphere. "The streets are inexpressibly dirty," wrote the reformer Jane Addams, who established Hull House nearby in part to provide at least

a little relief for the neighborhood's hard-pressed inhabitants, "the number of schools inadequate, sanitary legislation unenforced, the street lighting bad, the paving miserable and altogether lacking in the alleys and smaller streets, and the stables foul beyond description. Hundreds of houses are unconnected with the street sewer." It was called "Bloody Maxwell" because, the Chicago *Tribune* said, "it is the crime center of the country . . . [with] murders, shootings, stabbings, assaults, burglaries, robberies by the thousands . . . by people living in these areas in many instances more like beasts than human beings." Jewish gangs waged more or less constant warfare with one another and with the Irish, Italian, Polish, and Lithuanian gangs that held sway over the neighborhoods that surrounded it. The corner of Sangamon and Fourteenth Place, just a few blocks from Goodman's birthplace, was known as "dead man's corner" because it had seen more killings—of both criminals and lawmen—than any other spot in town. "Judging from the neighborhood where I lived," Goodman said, "if it hadn't

been for the clarinet, I might just as easily have been a gangster."

There was no such thing as privacy in any of the cramped cold-water tenement flats in which the Goodman family struggled to survive. The family was forced to move again and again when there was too little money to pay the rent, and the Goodmans spent at least one winter in an unheated basement apartment huddled together against the cold. Breakfast for adults and children alike was rolls and black coffee—there was no money for milk—and there were days, Goodman said, when "there wasn't anything to eat. I don't mean *much* to eat. I mean *anything.*" The hardship and crowding of his boyhood helped inspire in him a need always to remain a little apart from other people, a relentless drive to better himself, and a lifelong fear that all that he had achieved might somehow be taken away from him.

David Goodman was the central figure in his son's early life and Benny never forgot his father's coming home in the evenings, exhausted and still wearing the boots

The Hull House band in which Benny Goodman and his brothers played rehearses for an outdoor picnic in a suburb of Chicago. "After the concert was over," Goodman wrote, "we'd stuff ourselves on hot dogs, potato salad and . . . cakes—all we could eat. Then six or seven of us would go off in the woods and jam."

in which he had been shoveling offal at the stockyards all day. "The stink was awful. It was sickening. It smelled so bad." It was he who pushed his children hardest to do better. "Pop was always trying to get us to study," his son recalled, "so that we could get ahead in the world. He always envied people with book-learning and education. Whatever any of us amounted to may be pretty much traced to him."

And it was he who pointed his son toward music. When David Goodman learned that a neighbor's boys were earning extra money for their family by playing music in the neighborhood, he walked Benny and two of his older brothers down to the Kehelah Jacob Synagogue and signed them up for a boy's band right away. Instru-

ments were lent to them for a quarter a week and distributed strictly according to size: the biggest Goodman boy, twelve-year-old Harry, was given a tuba; Freddy, eleven, played trumpet; and Benny, the smallest at ten, got a clarinet. When the synagogue band dissolved after a year—the struggling congregation could no longer afford to underwrite it—David Goodman took his boys to Hull House, which, like the Colored Waif's Home that had given Louis Armstrong his start, had its own marching band that gave concerts in smart uniforms, marched in holiday parades, sometimes played church picnics, and—best of all from David Goodman's eminently practical point of view—provided serious professional training: Music at Hull House was more

than just a hobby, and those who studied it came from poor households all over the city. One of Goodman's fellow students was the future bassist Milt Hinton, whose parents had brought him north from Vicksburg, Mississippi, as part of the Great Migration.

The two older Goodman boys did well enough, but Benny seems to have been special from the first. Generally shy and reserved, his brother Freddy said, he was "never nervous" when it came to playing in public. When the Goodman boys heard jazz drifting through the doorways of ballrooms, Freddy continued, "It would be real exciting and we'd sneak in. . . . One time, Benny just jumped up onstage, grabbed the guy's clarinet and started to play. He was a natural, that's all. He could do whatever he pleased, whatever he felt like playing, even then." His precocity was not universally appreciated. The pianist Art Hodes, four years older than Goodman and a sometime visitor to Hull House, remembered him at eleven as having a "head that was outsized, [and] an ego that was outsized, too."

David Goodman recognized his son's remarkable gift and somehow managed to come up with an extra fifty cents a week to pay for private lessons with Franz Schoepp, a classically trained German-born clarinetist whose sole criterion in taking on a student seems to have been that he or she show a genuine gift for music. "I guess that sort of impressed me," Goodman remembered, "because there was plenty of prejudice about such things, even in Chicago." Two fully grown black jazz musicians were among his fellow students: the New Orleans master Jimmy Noone and Buster Bailey, with whom Benny sometimes played classical duets under Schoepp's critical eye. Noone would heavily influence Goodman's playing.

Schoepp was a stern Teutonic taskmaster—when Goodman asked why all his instruction books were in German, his teacher answered, "Dummkopf, soon *everyone* will speak German"—but he was a master teacher and he helped inculcate in his student a lifelong seriousness about his craft. Benny Goodman would practice every day, religiously, to the end of his life. "Some of the guys I played with . . . didn't go around learning more about their instruments from an intellectual point of view," he recalled. "All they wanted was to play hot jazz, and the instrument was just a means. . . . A lot of them criticized me—said my technique was too good. . . . But I've always wanted to know what *made* music. How you do it and why it sounds good. I always practiced, worked like hell." And there was another reason for his dedication, he admitted: "It was a kind of defense, . . . a way of getting away. . . . They couldn't talk to you if you were practicing."

Like Sidney Bechet before him, Goodman made money almost from the moment he began to play. At eleven, he won an amateur show at the Central Park Theater, wearing a bow tie, Buster Brown collar, and short pants and imitating the patented wobble of the novelty clarinetist, Ted Lewis. He did so well that when one of the vaudeville acts playing the theater fell ill, he was rewarded with a week's work. "The applause was nice," Goodman recalled, "but the five bucks they paid me was even better. . . . Nobody needed to remind us kids that someday we'd have to go out on our own and earn a living. The idea was with us almost from the time we were old enough to talk."

That idea would remain with him all his life. At thirteen, he was a member of the musician's union; at fourteen, he was running with the Austin High Gang, whose members were all a few years older than he, and trying hard to sound like Leon Roppolo of the New Orleans Rhythm Kings. Jimmy McPartland eventually began hiring him to play fraternity dances at the University of Chicago. "To be able to improvise in those days was quite an accomplishment," McPartland said. "Most musicians just sat down with the music stands in front of them and read off the notes, so if you could improvise and play a little jazz, you were really something and the college boys would hire you. [Frank] Teschemacher was our regular clarinetist, and he was good, but Benny was far ahead of him."

Goodman dropped out of high school after his freshman year; he was making fifteen dollars a night now, more than his father could earn all week, so much money that his mother had to be convinced that he had not secretly begun a career in crime. He played with nineteen-year-old Bix Beiderbecke aboard a Lake Michigan excursion boat, was dazzled by the beauty of Johnny Dodds's tone when they both played at the same amusement park ballroom, got fired from two different dance bands for playing too hot. "I was pretty restless," he

Benny Goodman at sixteen when he traveled to California to join the Ben Pollack Orchestra. He was "a skinny kid in short pants," he remembered, "with a clarinet and not much else in the way of baggage."

remembered, "and never stayed on a job very long if a new one came along where I might get a little more money or sit in with better players." Then, he landed the job at the Midway Gardens that brought him to the attention of Ben Pollack.

Gil Rodin had made California sound like paradise when he was trying to talk Goodman into joining Pollack's band, and when the boy first got there he was let down. The sunshine and the blue of the Pacific were more or less as advertised, but the Venice Ballroom stood on a shabby pier, flanked by a seedy beachside amusement park. "It was the sleaziest place," Goodman said. "Rides, roller coasters, . . . I just looked around and I thought, 'What the hell did I come *here* for?' "

Playing with the band quickly improved his spirits. A Chicago furrier's son, Ben Pollack was a good drummer with an extraordinary eye for talent. His outfit may not have been, as Goodman once said it was, "the first large white band that played real jazz," but it was certainly one of them. Its arrangements, by tenor saxophonist Fud Livingston and the youthful trombonist Glenn Miller, "left room for jazz improvisation," Goodman remembered, "which was right up my alley." He loved the band and loved being on his own—"I learned plenty about music—as well as other things—in those first few months," he said—but when Pollack took his men back to Chicago in January of 1926 and at first found work there hard to come by, Goodman deserted him for what he called "the hot work" in someone else's dance band.

Everything in his upbringing had told him the paycheck must always come first, and when Pollack was finally hired to bring his band into the Venetian Room at the fashionable Southmoor Hotel, Goodman wouldn't rejoin him for several weeks for fear it would fail. Pollack was so irritated he had to be talked into rehiring him. "Ben rather felt that I should have come on the job and done the opening with them," Goodman admitted, "and there wasn't the same closeness between us that there had been before." But on the bandstand, Goodman was a star performer, leaning so far back in his seat as he soloed that his feet sometimes rose off the floor, and he and Pollack—"the two Bennys," as the men called them—soon worked out a crowd-pleasing duet routine on up-tempo tunes like "I Want to Be Happy." "Pollack had a fly swatter and he'd lean over and be banging on the bass drum with it, yelling, 'Take another one, take another one,' and we'd keep on like that, generating a lot of steam. I must have enjoyed it, because we did it a lot. Nobody else at the time was doing it."

There was no need for Goodman's father to work now; Benny and his brother Harry (also in the Pollack band, now playing bass) were earning enough to feed the whole family. But David Goodman was a proud man and could not bear the idea of living off his boys. When his son suggested that he just retire and let his children take care of him,

he answered, "Benny you're a good boy. And that's very nice. But you take care of your life and I'll take care of mine." The boys helped their father open a newsstand at California and Madison, just to give him somewhere to go during the day.

On December 9, 1926, Benny Goodman joined the rest of the Pollack band in Chicago's Victor studio to record "'Deed I Do" and "He's the Last Word," on which he got to play a sixteen-bar solo. Even though Victor refused to release either side—the men had had too little time fully to master the elaborate arrangements—and the band would be asked to come back a week later to re-record them, nineteen-year-old Benny Goodman had become a recording artist.

David Goodman would never get to hear him. On his way home from his newsstand that same evening, at the corner of Madison and Kostner Streets, he was struck and fatally injured by a speeding automobile. He died the next day without ever having seen his boys play at the Southmoor. He'd been waiting, he'd told Benny, till he could afford a decent suit to wear so that he would not be too conspicuous among the well-dressed dancers. In later years, Benny Goodman could not mention his father's death without having his eyes fill with tears.

DOTTING IT DOWN

Passersby on Chicago's South State Street in the autumn of 1926 were treated to an extraordinary sight: a big gray mule picking its way through the busy traffic, hung with a sign advertising the Victor Recording Company's latest jazz offering, "Sidewalk Blues." Sitting on the mule's back and waving to the somewhat puzzled crowd was the elegantly dressed man who had recorded it, Jelly Roll Morton himself. It was a quintessential Morton moment—imaginative, colorful, and slightly old-fashioned, better suited to his hometown of New Orleans, where street advertising was a

way of life, than to the bustling up-to-date city of Chicago.

With the help of his publishers, the Melrose brothers, Morton had talked himself into a contract with Victor and begun to make records with a hand-picked group of Crescent City musicians he called the Red Hot Peppers. Exuberant and free-spirited, relaxed but hard-swinging, recordings like "Black Bottom Stomp," "The Chant," "Sidewalk Blues," "Dead Man Blues," "Grandpa's Spells," "Doctor Jazz," "Wild Man Blues," "The Pearls," "Georgia Swing," "Shoe Shiner's Drag" sound at first hearing like New Orleans collective improvisation at its best. In fact, they are meticulously arranged three-minute compositions in which everything but the breaks and brief solo choruses has been written down and repeatedly rehearsed.

"Nowadays," Morton said years later, "they talk about these jam sessions. Well, that is something I never permitted. Most guys, they improvise and they'll go wrong. . . . My theory is to never discard the melody. Always have the melody going some kind of way." Morton could think up a thousand ways to keep the melody going and in the process produced some of the most sophisticated and stirring recordings in jazz history. His object seems to have been to find the ideal equilibrium between arranged and improvised music, between the soloist and the group, the part and the whole—all within the New Orleans tradition he had helped create. Building upon the now traditional lineup—cornet, clarinet, trombone, piano, banjo/guitar, bass, and drums—he brought an astonishing array of colors and textures, moods and emotions to his evocation of life in the city of his birth. Like Duke Ellington—whom he detested as an imitator and who detested him as a braggart—he was able to incorporate everything he saw and heard around him into his music: ragtime and operatic strains as well as blues and Spanish rhythms, funeral parades and marching bands, and the street sounds of big-city

Jelly Roll Morton makes his wishes known to the members of his Red Hot Peppers in 1926. The musicians in this iteration of his band included clarinetist Omer Simeon, far left; banjo player Johnny St. Cyr, fourth from left; and trombonist Kid Ory, second from right. "Original Jelly Roll Blues" (below) was one of a dozen sides Morton cut that year.

remembered the first time he heard the rich, sophisticated, big-city sound of Morton's "Kansas City Stomps." "It made us feel hip, universal," he said. "We *walked* to the music . . . there was a sporty limp walk that you did."

Morton's growing celebrity only enhanced his ego. The New Orleans cornetist Lee Collins, who replaced Louis Armstrong in King Oliver's band, remembered once being summoned to Morton's Chicago apartment, where he found the great man "in bed with two women, one sitting on each side of him. . . . Jelly wanted to know was I going to stay in Chicago or run on back home like a lot of other New Orleans musicians did. Then he asked me to come to work with him. 'You know that you will be working with the world's greatest jazz piano player.' I told him I knew he was one of the greatest jazz pianists, but he said, 'Not one of the greatest—I am *the* greatest!' "

Morton was now well to do as well as famous. He was in demand for hotel ballrooms and college dances all over the Midwest, speeding from engagement to engagement in a gleaming black Lincoln, while a specially fitted-out band bus followed along behind, painted with a sign that read "Jelly Roll Morton and His Red Hot Peppers," though few of the men on board

America, church bells and streetcars and automobile horns, even snatches of vaudeville patter. His records showed the world a way that jazz might possibly have gone, had another son of New Orleans, Louis Armstrong, not already been at work in the same city in which Morton made them, rendering their infectious collective spirit instantly out of fashion.

For all his streetwise braggadocio, Morton's recording sessions were strictly businesslike. His men got paid five dollars a session for rehearsals—unheard of in that day and time, Johnny St. Cyr remembered—and Morton proved surprisingly willing to listen to his musicians. "Jelly was a very, very agreeable man. . . . He was fussy on introductions and endings and he always

wanted the ensemble his way, but he never interfered with the solo work. . . . He'd tell us where he wanted the solo or break but the rest was up to us." Still, there was never any doubt who was ultimately in charge. Once, when the trombonist Zue Robertson repeatedly refused to play a melody precisely as written, Morton pulled a revolver from his jacket and placed it on top of the piano; on the next run-through, Robertson never missed a note. "You did what Jelly Roll wanted you to do," Baby Dodds recalled, "no more and no less."

The Red Hot Peppers' records were an immediate success. The writer Albert Murray, then a small boy living in Magazine Point, Alabama, just outside Mobile,

had actually played on any of his records. (Hiring those high-priced musicians on a permanent basis would have cut too deeply into profits for Morton's liking.) He cemented his reputation as a flashy dresser, too—"the suit man from suit land," he called himself, with 150 suits and "too many shirts and socks and ties to mention"—and he wore diamonds on his fingers, on his garters and belt buckle, and had an especially large one implanted in a gold front tooth. (That was nothing, said Willie the Lion Smith, who never liked Morton much; he'd known a piano player who had a gold tooth with a diamond fitted into the mouth of his bulldog.)

Morton eventually married a tap-dancing showgirl named Mabel Bertrand, a beautiful Creole from New Orleans who evidently shared his own exalted sense of himself. She told an interviewer that he was so celebrated and "so well-liked by the white people that he never had to play a colored engagement; the colored places couldn't afford him. Only time colored people saw him was when he dropped into a cabaret for a drink, an announcement would be made and everybody would stand up to get a look at him. Really, Jelly Roll didn't like Negroes. He always said they would mess up your business. And Negroes didn't like him. I guess they were jealous."

Morton decided to pull up stakes and move to New York, confident that he could match his Chicago success in the center of the music business. His first engagement was a bit of a comedown—leading a pickup band at a Harlem dime-a-dance hall named the Rose Danceland—but he continued to tour and to make memorable records for Victor: "Shoe Shiners Drag," "Mournful Serenade," "Deep Creek, "Burnin' the Iceberg," "New Orleans Bump," "Blue Blood Blues."

Between engagements, Danny Barker remembered, Morton spent most afternoons at the Rhythm Club, a musician's hangout on West 132nd Street, "preaching in loud terms that none of the famous New York bands had a beat."

Jelly would drive up in front . . . and when the musicians saw him they would start to laugh, for they knew they could anticipate a show. . . . As Jelly would stop his large high-powered Lincoln car and step out onto the sidewalk, one of the group was sure to gleefully ask him, "Jelly what's that you say about New York musicians yesterday!" Jelly would prop up his lips and exclaim crisply, "What I said yesterday and today and on Judgment Day and also my dying day is that it takes one hundred live New York musicians to equal one dead police dog."

At home or on the road, Morton was always at work, thinking up new ways to keep his melodies going. "He used to wake up at two or three o'clock in the morning," his wife remembered, "and an idea would strike him and he'd get right by that grand piano. . . . He'd begin whistling and then go to dotting it down, dotting it down."

Max Kaminsky, left, in 1935, nine years after setting out to hear Bix Beiderbecke with the Jean Goldkette Orchestra, here with fellow members of the Tommy Dorsey band, including Dave Tough, closest to the camera, and Bud Freeman, right

BIX AND TRAM

On Monday evening, September 20, 1926—just five days after Jelly Roll Morton made his first recordings with his Red Hot Peppers—an eighteen-year-old Boston youth named Max Kaminsky set out from his home in Dorchester for a suburban dance hall named Nuttings-on-the-Charles in nearby Waltham. He was driving a brand-new Model T Ford, the down payment provided by his earnings as a dance band cornetist, and he was risking arrest by speeding at twenty miles an hour. A battle of bands was to begin at eight o'clock sharp and he didn't want to be late. The youngest of seven children born to Russian immigrants, Kaminsky had heard his first approximation of jazz—"Tiger Rag" by Ted Lewis—on a homemade crystal set seven years earlier, and, although he had been playing with local dance bands for several

years, his idea of good jazz was still the work of a bandleader named Pearly Breed, who broadcast from Shepherd's Colonial Tea Room in Boston a suitably decorous version of what he had managed to glean from listening over and over again to records by Bix Beiderbecke and the Wolverines. Now, Bix himself was coming to Waltham as part of the brand-new Jean Goldkette Orchestra, and Kaminsky was determined to hear him.

Nuttings-on-the-Charles was a big, ramshackle wooden dance hall built so haphazardly that its walls shook visibly whenever dancers took the floor. But it overlooked the Charles River, and on summer evenings, when its lights played on the water and music drifted out to the couples paddling slowly past in their canoes, it seemed wonderfully romantic. It was part of a chain of New England dance halls owned by two Boston-based brothers, Char-

The Jean Goldkette Orchestra on its New England tour, 1926. Arranger Bill Challis perches at the far end of the roof; Bix Beiderbecke sits fourth from the left, Frank Trumbauer crouches just above the windshield; and bassist Steve Brown occupies the hood.

lie and Sy Shribman, who loved jazz and wanted it to do well in their part of the country: Duke Ellington had twice played Nuttings-on-the-Charles that summer. Bringing the Goldkette Band all the way east from its home base in Detroit had been the Shribmans' idea, and to make sure it got a fair hearing in Waltham, they had billed Goldkette as "the Paul Whiteman of the West" and paired his band with two well-known local outfits, Mal Hallett's band—New England's Finest—and Barney Rapp and his Victor Recording Orchestra.

Hallett and Rapp played first, Kaminsky later wrote, mixing comedy routines with dance music. Then, the Goldkette band came on:

Charlie Shribman could have saved himself a lot of worry and expense. They opened with "Pretty Girl Stomp," went on to "Ostrich Walk," "A Sunny Disposish," "Clap Yo' Hands," and ended with "Tiger Rag," and they were such a stunning sensation that when the furor died down and it was time for Mal Hallett's band to play again, neither his musicians nor Barney Rapp's men [wanted to] pick up their instruments: "How can

you follow *that?*" Mal Hallett asked plaintively and the crowd wasn't bashful about letting him know they agreed with him. Nobody had heard anything like this music before.

Neither had I. . . . I just sat there, vibrating like a harp to the echoes of Bix's astoundingly beautiful tone. It sounded like a choirful of angels. When I did work up the courage to go over to speak to Beiderbecke during one of the intermissions, I was still so overcome I could hardly get a word out. After a few minutes I realized it was a tossup as to who was more shy,

Bix or me. He kept his eyes fixed on his shiny black shoes and solemnly nodded his round blond head at each halting word as I tried to tell him how wonderful the band sounded. It was like talking to an automated toy.

Kaminsky finally broke the ice by asking Bix if he'd like to go to a Braves baseball game. "Sounds fine to me," Bix said, and they spent the next few days together.

Kaminsky located a local source for bootleg alcohol for his hero, drove him from one Massachusetts engagement to the next—"I would have *made* a car if I didn't have one," he remembered—and, whenever he could, asked him about music. Bix was "gentle and silent," Kaminsky remembered, "with a dreamy, preoccupied manner. . . . All he ever seemed to care about were music and whiskey." But because of the spell his playing had cast, Kaminsky found himself irresistibly drawn to Bix, nonetheless. Beiderbecke painstakingly wrote out one of his solos for the youth to learn, explained what he called "anticipation—playing notes of the melody a hairsbreadth before the strict time"—and allowed him to listen in as he played a boardinghouse piano, puzzling out passages from the French impressionist composers Claude Debussy and Maurice Ravel, whose gauzy effects he vaguely dreamed of importing into jazz. "What's the difference?" he asked. "Music doesn't have to be the sort of thing that's put into brackets."

Beiderbecke had needed help to win a permanent place in the Goldkette band. Jean Goldkette himself was a French immigrant, a trained concert pianist who was now well on his way to making himself the dance king of the Midwest—he would eventually run a chain of ballrooms and some twenty different orchestras, including one of the leading black bands of the era, McKinney's Cotton Pickers, and a white group called the Orange Blossoms that would eventually become the Casa Loma Orchestra, another progenitor of big band swing. He hadn't initially much liked the idea of jazz—he had been among the musicians who quit Lamb's Café in Chicago rather than share the bandstand with Tom Brown's Band from Dixieland back in 1915—but he came to see "unlimited possibilities" in it, and was always on the lookout for hot soloists. He had lured Bix away from the Wolverines in the fall of 1924, only to fire him a few weeks later when he discovered Beiderbecke was unable to read music well enough to handle the kind of complex arrangements he favored.

Beiderbecke had been humiliated. In order to learn more about music—and perhaps to placate his disappointed parents, as well—Bix enrolled at the University of Iowa, only to be expelled just eighteen days later for taking part in a drunken brawl. Then, in the summer of 1925, the C-melody saxophone player Frank Trumbauer hired him for a new nine-piece band he was bringing into the Arcadia Ballroom in St. Louis.

Trumbauer—known as "Tram" to his friends and to the admiring young musicians who sought to imitate his poised, delicate sound—was, like the music he loved, a distinctively American blend: his great-granduncle on his mother's side was Charles Dickens; his father, who left the family when his son was ten, was half Cherokee. Born in Carbondale, Illinois, in 1901, Trumbauer was introduced to music by his mother, a pianist who accompanied silent films and squeezed in his first saxophone lessons between showings. At fourteen, he had his own schoolboy dance band, the Egyptian Jazzadores. By 1921, he was in Chicago, where he worked briefly with Isham Jones at the College Inn—and, he remembered, "had sense enough to watch the colored waiters and if they smiled at what I was playing then I was happy. Those boys know the score." He played for a time

Frank Trumbauer Orchestra in St. Louis, Missouri, 1925. Trumbauer sits behind the bass saxophone; Bix Beiderbecke is standing at his left. "This," Trumbauer remembered, "is where Bix and I got to know one another."

in the Edgar Benson Orchestra—a gim-micky traveling dance band in which he had to wear a Band-Aid across the bridge of his nose so that when dancers asked why, he could say that the band played so hot that without the Band-Aid the men would burst their blood vessels—and then went with Ray Miller's Orchestra to New York, where he'd first heard Bix play with the Wolver-ines. Wherever Trumbauer appeared, his sound stood out: "Sax men, in those early days," a fellow musician recalled, sounded more or less "like a buzz-saw going through a pine knot," but Tram was different, with his "easy flowing way of playing, . . . full of interesting little turns without destroy-ing the tune. . . . Just a beautiful tone!"

Friends had advised Trumbauer against hiring Bix Beiderbecke. "Look out, he's trouble," he was warned. "He drinks and you'll have a hard time handling him." But Trumbauer loved Beiderbecke's playing, that seemed so perfectly to complement his own, and was willing to take his chances. The two men were opposites in some ways: Trumbauer was tall, debonair, and busi-nesslike, while Bix was short, disheveled, and chronically disorganized. But they quickly became friends and musical part-ners, and during the eight months they spent together in St. Louis, Tram became a sort of surrogate older brother to Bix, dis-couraging his drinking, encouraging him to learn to read as well as play.

When I hired him, he told me he was a poor reader and he hesitated tak-ing the job. . . . We fixed up a book of regular trumpet parts and for hours on end I would work with Bix. I would teach him a tune. Note for note, and then hand him the part and we would follow it. Bix was a brilliant boy and it wasn't long before he could follow new parts. . . . [Soon,] Bix and I were thinking alike. I could stop on any note and Bix could pick it up and finish the phrase perfectly, and he

could do the same with me. We could play simultaneous choruses and never clash. . . . [T]his was the hap-piest and healthiest period in our lives. I made him assistant leader of the band. We played golf, rode horses, and he didn't have a drink for months at a time.

Beiderbecke loved playing with Trumbauer: "We have absolutely the hottest band in the country," he boasted to Hoagy Carmichael. "We're playing at the Arcadia [Ballroom] nightly and are panicking the town." And the feeling was mutual. When the ballroom closed in the spring of 1926, throwing Trumbauer's men out of work, and Jean Goldkette offered to make Tram the musi-cal director of his Victor Recording Orches-tra at Detroit's Graystone Hotel, Tram agreed to take the job only if Bix came, too.

The Goldkette band was a highly paid all-star aggregation. In addition to Bix and Tram, it was home at various times to trom-bonists Bill Rank and Tommy Dorsey, alto saxophonist Jimmy Dorsey, violinist Joe Venuti, guitarist Eddie Lang, and the New Orleans–born slap-bass specialist Steve Brown, who, Milt Hinton remembered, "was the one everybody listened to," and whose irresistible drive would help con-vince other bandleaders to abandon the tuba. Several arrangers contributed to the band's book, but the hardest-driving and most adventurous numbers were written by the saxophonist Bill Challis. Looking back, the clarinetist Artie Shaw, a perfec-tionist not given to extravagant praise, con-sidered the Goldkette orchestra "the first really great white big band. . . . unbeliev-able. They swung like mad."

The New England tour that had so thrilled Max Kaminsky had also won the Goldkette band an invitation to play at Manhattan's most prestigious ballroom, Roseland. They had been there a week by the evening of October 13, 1926, long enough to cause a stir among the city's musicians. But this

night seemed likely to be different. Fletcher Henderson was coming home to Roseland from a three-week stay at the Goldkette orchestra's headquarters, the Graystone Hotel in Detroit, for what was advertised in the *New York Times* as an evening of musical combat between "Two of the Finest —Unquestionably the Finest Dance Orches-tras in the World."

"The audience was a sea of white dress shirts," the architect and sometime guitarist Bill Priestley remembered, "all musicians from other bands on their way to their jobs, just hoping to catch the first set. That's the sort of reputation these bands had." Louis Armstrong had left Henderson more than a year earlier, but Henderson's band still included some of the best musicians in the country—Coleman Hawkins, Buster Bailey, Rex Stewart, cornetist Tommy Ladnier, and a young alto saxophonist named Benny Carter. "We were all very cocksure," Stew-art said, "up against a bunch of hicks from the sticks. Remember, we had those Don Redman arrangements and we tore into 'Stampede,' I think it was, and stood the place on its ear. There was no way they could top us."

Trumbauer knew enough not to try to follow "Stampede" with anything similar. Instead, Bill Priestley said, he started off with a brand-new Bill Challis arrangement of a pseudo-Spanish number in 6/8 *march* time, called "Valencia." "The Henderson band started to laugh when they heard the corny old tune," Priestley remembered, "but they stopped laughing when they heard the unison playing on what was a dia-bolically difficult chart. Christ! That brass section was like a machine-gun barrage, spraying out notes and cutting down the opposition. Then [the reed player] Don Mur-ray turned to Tram and said: 'Let's give it to them with both barrels,' and they lit into 'Tiger Rag' and blew the place wide open."

"They creamed us," Rex Stewart ad-mitted. "Those little tight-ass white boys creamed us. Don Redman said those Chal-lis charts cut us to ribbons. . . . their rhythm

BEAN

"I made the tenor sax," Coleman Hawkins said once. "There's nobody plays like me and I don't play like anybody else." All of it was true. More than anyone else, Hawkins was responsible for turning what had been a raucous novelty instrument into one of the central solo voices in jazz, by turns exhilarating and seductive, aggressive and infinitely tender.

He was born in St. Joseph, Missouri, in 1904—though in later years he liked to pretend he'd been born later for fear of scaring off younger women. Hawkins was a thoroughly schooled musician. His mother, who played the organ for her church, taught him to read music before he could puzzle out words. He studied cello, too—his father, a factory worker, worked two jobs to pay for his lessons—and he was a lifelong admirer of Pablo Casals. Then, his parents gave him a C-melody saxophone on his ninth birthday. It was used in vaudeville shows and marching bands then. "The funnier the noise," Hawkins remembered, "the better the playing." But he took to it right away. By the age of twelve he was playing at dances. In 1921, he joined Mamie Smith's Jazz Hounds in a touring tent show and soon thereafter shifted to the tenor saxophone. He was already supremely self-confident, and eager to challenge any musician willing to take him on. "When some young kid would come along," Hawkins remembered, "I'd have to go down and cut this boy. That's how Fletcher Henderson . . . happened to find me." Henderson offered him a job with his band in 1924. He stayed with it for more than a decade—and, inspired by what Louis Armstrong and Art Tatum were doing on their instruments, forever altered the way the saxophone was played.

He was given the nickname "Bean" because of the richness of the musical ideas that tumbled from his fertile brain. His sound was surging, virile, impassioned, filled with vibrato—and *loud*. As one of his disciples, Nick "Big Nick" Nicholas, said, "*All* of [Hawkins's] notes were big." Hawkins was of only moderate height but because of that huge sound and the self-assured way he carried himself he seemed far taller. The alto saxophonist Julian "Cannonball" Adderley, taken to see the Henderson band when he was a small boy, remembered Hawkins as "the most impressive looking jazz musician I've seen in my life. He just looked so authoritative. I kept looking at him. I never did look at Fletcher. I said, 'Well, that's what I want to do when I grow up.' "

Hawkins was a loner all his life; "a sometimes guy," the bassist Pops Foster said. "Sometimes he'd look right at you and didn't know you and sometimes he did." He loved fine clothes and good cognac and fast cars. During his years with Henderson, he speeded from engagement to engagement in his own Chrysler Imperial at better than one hundred miles an hour. He distrusted banks and some-

times carried thousands of dollars in cash. He was a prodigious eater. Johnny Williams, a fellow saxophone player in the Henderson band with a hearty appetite of his own, remembered dining with him: "We used to go in a restaurant together, and each of us would order two meals. The waitress would start setting up for four and Hawkins would say, 'No, Miss, it's just two of us.' " But otherwise, he kept largely to himself. His first wife left him when he seemed never to come home, and took with her almost all the furniture in his New York apartment. He didn't bother to replace it. He wasn't planning to be home much, anyway.

He lived for musical combat. "When we used to finish playing with the band," he remembered, "I'd make all the clubs. They all had little bands playing in them. So I'd hear something that sounded good. I'd come back to New York and have some new riffs."

In the 1920s the Hoofer's Club in Harlem sent out invitations to weekly "suppers," jam sessions meant to test players of a single instrument—pianists, trumpet players, trombonists, as well as saxophonists. No matter what the chosen instrument of the evening was, Coleman Hawkins would be there. "I just happened to stop by and had my horn," he'd say, and join right in. "You knew," a veteran of those sessions said, "he'd come in to carve somebody."

Several generations of saxophone players committed Hawkins's solos to memory, note for note, but he was himself never satisfied with his playing, was always eager to find out what younger musicians were up to and then try to beat them at their own game. He was "ashamed" of most of his earlier records, he once told a friend. Nobody should ever look back. Music, he said, should always be "an adventure."

Coleman Hawkins

The Jean Goldkette Orchestra advertises its willingness to take on all comers, New England, 1926.

[was] too strong, what with Steve Brown slapping hell out of that bass . . . and Frankie Trumbauer's inspiring leadership as he stood out front wailing on his C-melody." As for Bix, with whom Stewart happily shared a locker during their joint appearance at Roseland, he was a "once-in-a-million artist." Many years later, someone asked Benny Carter if the Goldkette band had been as good as some said it was. "Good, hell!" he said. "They were frightening." The two bands would meet again at Roseland the following January and battle to what Buster Bailey remembered as a hard-fought draw: "We weren't about to be taken twice. . . . You can bet there was a lot of great music that night."

A reporter for *Billboard* predicted on the basis of the Goldkette band's first performance at Roseland that it would soon be making records that "would scorch the wallpaper off the studio walls." But when the men actually got into the Victor studios, Edward King, the executive in charge, had something else in mind. King was unenthusiastic about jazz in general and brass players in particular and insisted on recording only strictly commercial arrangements. "Geez," Bill Challis remembered, "they picked out the *stinking-est* tunes for us. We really didn't get any good tunes to do. They didn't want any improvising. They were trying to make a hit, and in doing that they made us play the melody. . . . Bix used to steal in on the last eight bars of some of the tunes—even though they were real corny. . . . Bix would stand and improvise right over the band." The records sold well enough but failed to capture the excitement that those who heard the band in person never forgot. "I don't really know why [King] hired the band at all," the alto saxophone player Stanley "Doc" Ryker remembered.

"The stuff he *didn't* want . . . that was our style."

The chronic idiocies of race in America had a good deal to do with it. Most of the men who ran the record business thought sweet and sentimental tunes should remain the exclusive purview of white bands, while black orchestras had better stick with the blues and stomp numbers that supposedly came to them "naturally" and which the executives were convinced were all that buyers of race records could possibly want. Thus, white bands like Goldkette's and Ben Pollack's were rarely able to demonstrate on records how hard they could swing, while black bands like Fletcher Henderson's were kept from displaying the full scope of their skills. "Although the Henderson band played a variety of music on tours," Rex Stewart complained, "the record executives characterized [us] as a stomp band. They didn't accept the fact that a Negro band could play sweet, though as a matter of fact, we used to get tremendous applause at Roseland and other places for playing waltzes beautifully."

Meanwhile, a singer named Red McKenzie talked Tommy Rockwell—the same Okeh executive responsible for producing Louis Armstrong's Hot Fives—into recording Bix and Tram in a series of small-group recordings that eventually included "Clarinet Marmalade," "Ostrich Walk," "Riverboat Shuffle," "I'm Coming Virginia," and the closest thing to a genuine hit either man ever had, "Singin' the Blues."

"Singin' the Blues" had long been a favorite of both men and each had polished his playing of it to something like perfection before he reached the studio. Trumbauer's supple, relaxed opening chorus inspired a generation of young imitators, white and black. "*Everybody* memorized it," said the tenor player Budd Johnson; Trumbauer was "the baddest cat around and everybody was trying to play his stuff." And Bix's solo—bright and silvery, poised and carefully crafted—was memorized by brass players, as well. Fletcher Henderson admired "Singin' the Blues" so much that he would later hire Bill Challis to write an arrangement of it for his band in which the saxophones recreated Trumbauer's solo in unison while Rex Stewart played Beiderbecke's, note for note.

"Singin' the Blues" provided a sort of epiphany for the young clarinetist Artie Shaw. He was playing in a dance band then, and dissatisfied.

I was doing things you shouldn't do, but I didn't know who to follow, I didn't know who to copy. And finally I heard Bix and Trumbauer and . . . those were the guys. Being a white guy, I was subjected to white music and I heard Bix and Trumbauer and they were the exemplars. . . . And they played like they knew where they were going, there was a direc-

tion to what they did, there was a definition, a kind of discipline. . . . I knew that was the way to go.

Even "Singin' the Blues" failed to please Bix. For years, he had worked after hours on a dreamy piano piece of his own, a string of improvisational phrases rather than a full-blown composition but filled with pastel tone colors like those used by the French impressionists he admired. Rockwell encouraged him to record it, too. He ran too long on the first take, but Tram was there to give him a fifteen-second warning on the second and he got to the end without any trouble. Characteristically, he had never thought of a title for it and it was left to Trumbauer finally to come up with one. "Well, I thought to myself, Bix was certainly in a fog when he made it. And then it hit me. Fog. Mist. In a Mist. That's it—'In a Mist.' "

Jean Goldkette loved his flagship orchestra but he was also a businessman: the salaries he was paying its stars were outstripping his profits, and he could see no way to turn things around. And so, just nine days after Beiderbecke recorded "In a Mist," on the evening of September 18, 1927, the Goldkette band was back at Roseland for what would be its final performance. The pianist Irving Riskin remembered that all the men had tears in their eyes that night as they systematically played their way through the band's book in tribute to the arrangers who had helped make them sound so good. Every man took a solo on every tune, he said, and when they were finally finished and tried to leave the bandstand, the overflow crowd wouldn't let them go. "We started up again and played to almost frenzied cries from the audience. Many of *them* now had tears streaming down their cheeks. No one wanted this night to end." Finally, the manager of the ballroom called the local precinct and "soon dozens of policemen were pushing their way through, . . . making a lane for us to depart. . . . Even as we scurried through the long line of police offi-

cers, patrons tried to reach through and around the blue barrier just to touch us one more time."

The Goldkette men scattered in search of work. Bix and Tram would soon find it with the best-known, highest-paying bandleader in America, Paul Whiteman.

JUNGLE MUSIC

In New York that same fall, word spread that the gangsters who owned and operated Harlem's most opulent nightspot, the Cotton Club, were looking for a new band. The club had a colorful history. Built as a casino above the Douglas Theater on the northeast corner of 142nd Street near Lenox Avenue in 1918, it was run as the Club Deluxe by former heavyweight champion Jack Johnson before it was bought by a syndicate of mobsters headed by a British-born gangster with a high girlish voice and a long prison record named Owney Madden.

Harlem had become a magnet for wealthy whites eager to experience for themselves something of its supposedly "primitive" excitement, a turn of events that puzzled a good many Harlem residents. "What occasions the focusing of attention on . . . the Negro?" asked the writer Rudolf Fisher in the *American Mercury*.

Granted that white people have long enjoyed the Negro entertainment as a diversion, is it not something different, something more, when they bodily throw themselves into Negro entertainment in cabarets? Now Negroes go to their own cabarets to see how white people act. . . . And what do we see? Why, we see them actually playing Negro games. I watch them in that epidemic Negroism, the Charleston. I look on and envy them. They camel and fish-tail and turkey, they geeche and black-bottom and scrontch, they skate and buzzard and

A light-skinned performer dances for black and white customers at Small's Paradise in Harlem—while one anxious patron does his best to keep from being photographed in such surroundings, 1929. "The best of Harlem's black cabarets," wrote Rudolf Fisher, "have turned white."

mess-around—and they do them all better than I!

This interest in the Negro is an active and participating interest. It is almost as if a traveler from the North stood watching an African tribe-dance, then suddenly found himself swept wildly into it, caught in its tribal rhythm. . . . Maybe these Nordics at last have tuned in our wave-length. Maybe they are at last learning to speak our language.

"Harlem's night life now surpasses that of Broadway itself," wrote *Variety*. "From midnight until after dawn it is a seething cauldron of Nubian mirth and hilarity." "At this time Harlem was as white as it was black," the tap dancer Honey Coles remembered. "At night everybody from downtown came up, after everything closed downtown. Diamonds and minks and furs." No one knows how many speakeasies and cellar clubs and other drinking establishments then flourished in Harlem—estimates vary from five hundred to several thousand—but

by the late twenties a considerable number were doing well by catering to white thrill seekers. A card handed out to tourists on Manhattan street corners hinted at the excitement they would encounter uptown if they hired one of the advertiser's "Slumming Hostesses."

Here in the world's greatest city it would amuse and also interest you to see the real inside of the new Negro Race of Harlem. You have heard it discussed, but there are very few who

Seventh Avenue and 135th Street in 1928. The entrance to Small's Paradise—the second club of the same name run by a former elevator operator named Ed Smalls and popular with black and white patrons alike—is at the right. There, conventioneers attending the Elks rally welcomed on the banner hung across the street might have heard Willie the Lion Smith or Fletcher Henderson and would certainly have been served by waiters on roller-skates dancing the Charleston.

really know. . . . I am in a position to carry you through Harlem as you would go slumming through Chinatown. My guides are honest and have been instructed to give the best service. . . . Your season is not completed with thrills until you have visited Harlem.

No nightspot offered more thrills than the Cotton Club. Nostalgia for the antebellum South set the bizarre theme—the big stage was designed to resemble the veranda of a plantation house, complete with tall white columns and a painted backdrop of slave cabins and live oak trees draped with moss—and the main attraction was a lavish floor show in the Florenz Ziegfeld tradition that featured songs, dances, and lots of light-skinned, lightly clad chorus girls billed as "Tall, Tan and Terrific." Celebrities like Ethel Waters and Bill "Bojangles" Robinson were sometimes granted tables, but black patrons were generally barred; W. C. Handy himself, the "father of the blues," was once turned away. "It isn't necessary to mix with colored people if you don't feel like it," the author of a guidebook to Manhattan nightlife reassured his readers. At the Cotton Club "you have your own party and keep to yourself. But it's worth seeing how they step."

A leering reviewer for *Variety* gave a vivid sense of what brought most of the club's white patrons northward. "The almost Caucasian-hued high yaller gals look swell and uncork the meanest kind of cootching ever exhibited to a conglomerate mixed audience," he wrote. "The big attraction, of course, are the gals, 10 of 'em, the majority of whom in white company could pass for Caucasians, possessed of the native jazz heritage, their hotsy-totsy performance if working sans wraps could never be parred by a white gal. The brownskins' shivaree is worth the $2 couvert alone."

Still, despite the omnipresent gangsters, the whites-only seating policy, and the glorified minstrelsy, the Cotton Club also presented black entertainers as good-looking and glamorous. "On Sunday nights," Duke Ellington remembered, "when celebrities filled the joint, [the women in the chorus] would rush out of the dressing room after the show in all their finery. Every time they went by, the stars and the rich people would be saying, 'My, who is *that?*' They were tremendous representatives." And the music and choreography, costumes and stage sets rivaled the best of Broadway. In any case, it was the job every ambitious black bandleader in town wanted, including Duke Ellington.

Ellington was already on the rise. Four years playing just off Times Square at the cellar club first called the Hollywood Inn and then the Kentucky Club; three triumphant summer tours of New England ballrooms; a successful season playing for an all-black revue called *Jazzmania* at Harlem's Lafayette Theater; and a number of recordings that featured the startling, soulful growls of Bubber Miley had all helped see to that.

And he now had the help of a shrewd, tireless manager. Irving Mills was a squat, cigar-chewing Broadway operator, a one-time song plugger and vaudevillian fond of the royal "we": "We were very aggressive and colorful," he told an interviewer toward the end of his long life, "and up-to-the-minute with ideas and new things to do." Born on the Lower East Side in 1894, the son of Jewish immigrants, he had made himself one of the most successful music publishers in the business with a stable of songwriters and arrangers that would include Harold Arlen, Hoagy Carmichael, Dorothy Fields, James P. Johnson, Jimmy McHugh, Will Vodery, and Spencer Williams. When the blues became big business he began collecting them, too, sometimes for as little as fifteen dollars a tune.

At some point—Ellington and Mills themselves differed as to just when it was—Mills began to see that Ellington was somehow different from other bandleaders, that

something more might be made of him, to their mutual profit. "He used to come to the Kentucky Club often," Ellington remembered, "and one night he said he didn't know what we were doing with our music, but he liked it and would like to record some of it with our band. We jumped at the chance and this was really the beginning of a long and wonderful association. . . . He had the contacts. . . . We recorded for almost every existing label under different names: Duke Ellington on Victor, the Jungle Band on Brunswick, the Washingtonians on Harmony, the Whoopee Makers on Perfect, Sonny Greer and his Memphis Men on Columbia, the Harlem Footwarmers on Okeh."

Ellington and Mills would eventually form a partnership that in effect gave Mills and his attorney 55 percent of everything the orchestra earned. Some members of the band objected, especially when Mills's name began appearing as the co-composer of songs Ellington alone had written. But Ellington never publicly complained about

The door to the Cotton Club on 142nd Street at Lenox Avenue in Harlem, and a souvenir program that promises lurid goings-on inside

the bargain he had made, for he knew that in exchange, it had become Mills's mission to promote him as no black artist had ever been promoted before, as "a great musician who was making a lasting contribution to American music." The two men would eventually part, but Ellington refused to listen to others speak ill of Mills. "In spite of how much money he made on me," he wrote, Mills had been "the first to see our possibilities," and whatever the complications of their relationship, "I respected the way he operated. He . . . always preserved the dignity of my name . . . and that is the most anybody can do for anybody."

On November 29, 1926—ten weeks after Jelly Roll Morton began recording with his Red Hot Peppers, eleven days before Benny Goodman's recording debut and the death of Goodman's father—Duke Ellington recorded his first important original composition, "East St. Louis Toodle-o." Touring New England by bus the previous summer, the men in the band had passed so many billboards around Boston advertising "Lewando Cleaners" that they began to chant, "Oh, Lee-wan-*do*" whenever they saw another. Bubber Miley took up the phrase on his horn. Ellington shaped that kernel of an idea into a haunting theme, matched it with a second strain, then worked out with his men a carefully structured arrangement of the whole thing, along with a story to go with it. "In those days, . . . practically everything we wrote was supposed to be a picture of something," he said. "We were walking up Broadway one night after playing the Kentucky Club, and we were talking about this old man, after a hard day's work in the field, where he and his broken walk [are] coming up the road. But he's strong, in spite of being so tired because he's headed [home] to get his feet under the table and to get that hot dinner that's waiting for him. And that's the 'East St. Louis Toodle-o.' " (He had intended to call it "East St. Louis *Todalo*"—a todalo being a kind of halting dance—but the person who typed the copy for the record label evidently got the

Irving Mills

name wrong and it stuck.) It would be the band's theme song for the next fifteen years. "People heard it," Sonny Greer remembered, "and said, 'Here they come!' "

Ellington would follow that pattern again and again during his long career: an improvised melody developed by him or one of his men would be transformed under his direction into a full-scale arrangement that somehow also vividly evoked a scene from everyday American life. The difference between his and Fletcher Henderson's bands, Ellington once said, was that while Henderson's was "basically an ensemble group . . . in our band the solos . . . all the various stars we have had . . . always dominated everything." Ellington's boundless self-confidence was generally alloyed with becoming public modesty. His band would indeed always include extraordinary individual voices, each of which he carefully chose for precisely that reason, but it was his own genius, his own restless adventurousness and uncanny sense of form that made his music—and his orchestra—like no one else's.

In the autumn of 1927, Ellington recorded two more important pieces featuring Bubber Miley: "Creole Love Call," in which Miley shared solo space with an unearthly wordless vocal by the singer Adelaide Hall; and "Black and Tan Fantasy," an alluring blues-oriented piece that evokes the steamy atmosphere of places like the Cotton Club and then suggests—in a mournful but sly ending that quotes from Chopin's funeral march—that after all those good times the piper must inevitably be paid. It is filled with disparate elements—blues and spirituals, Chopin and King Oliver, and more than a hint of a New Orleans funeral parade—but it is also unmistakably Duke Ellington's.

It was shortly after recording "Black and Tan Fantasy" that Ellington and Mills got the news that the Cotton Club was looking for a new band. Mills urged the club's managers to hire Ellington. So did the songwriter Jimmy McHugh, who was writing the music for the club's next revue. But the manager insisted on holding auditions and wanted at least ten men, while Ellington, then playing at the Gibson Standard Theater in Philadelphia, still had only eight. Six other bands were scheduled to try out on the appointed day. "The audition was set for noon," Ellington said, "but by the time I had scraped up eleven men it was two or three o'clock. We played for them and got the job. The reason for that was that the boss, Harry Block, didn't get there till late either, and didn't hear the others! That's a classic example of being at the right place at the right time with the right thing before the right people." There was just one more obstacle. Ellington was under contract to finish out his run in Philadelphia. Owney Madden sent a go-between named Yankee Schwartz to see the theater manager there with word that he wanted Ellington for his club and he wanted him now: "Be big," Madden's agent is supposed to have said. "Be big or be dead." The manager wisely chose to be big.

In a still from a 1929 motion picture called *Black and Tan*, Duke Ellington and his orchestra preside over a stage show at the Cotton Club.

Duke Ellington and his orchestra opened at the Cotton Club on December 4, 1927, and stayed for almost four years. "When I began my work," Ellington recalled, "jazz was a stunt, something different. Not everybody cared for jazz and those who did felt that it wasn't the real thing unless they were given a shock sensation of loudness or unpredictability, along with the music." American popular music had always exploited the "exotic"—Oriental-sounding dances, songs with Hawaiian or American-Indian or African-American themes—anything that seemed to add novelty and spice. Cotton Club audiences now thought they heard in Ellington's new music, with its array of growls and moans and cries, its novel voicings and pervasive sensuality, echoes of Africa—which was just what they had trooped up to Harlem to hear.

Ellington fully understood the absurdity of much that went on at the Cotton Club. "That part was degrading and humiliating to both Negroes and whites," he said. "But there was another part of it that was wonderful." The Cotton Club was "a classy spot," he remembered; unruly guests were politely asked to be quiet and if they failed to take the hint were gently but firmly removed. (At the Kentucky Club they'd been given Mickey Finns.) He loved all the elegance, enjoyed meeting celebrities and getting to know the women in the chorus, even came to like playing cards after hours with the mobsters who ran the place. The club provided him with a priceless training ground, taught him how to produce on deadline, how to showcase talented people, even how to disguise the limitations of those less talented. "A lot of people worked as hard as hell to put those shows together," he remembered. "That was the Cotton Club spirit. Work, work, work. Rehearse, rehearse, rehearse. Get it down fine. . . . We knew we had a standard of performance to match every night. We knew we couldn't miss a lick. And we rarely did." In any case, nothing could demean Duke Ellington because he refused ever to be demeaned.

Even in the jittery old film of him enjoying his success at the Cotton Club, surrounded by dancers wearing some white choreographer's ludicrous notion of African costume, he remains somehow set apart at the piano in his white tails, invincibly dignified, in on the joke that is being played on everybody else. In 1929, when he appeared in a short called "Black and Tan," in which two black comedians performed stereotyped roles—stumbling, shiftless, illiterate, overly fond of alcohol—he was portrayed precisely as what he already was, a handsome, elegant, hardworking composer.

And, while the "jungle music" tag would remain with him for a time, neither distant Africa nor the perverse version of it that helped lure whites to Harlem was ever his source of inspiration. For that, he would always draw upon what he called "the everyday life and customs of the Negro," as the titles of the tunes that seemed to pour effortlessly from his pen during his Cotton

Newspaper advertisement for the second of two Cotton Club revues for which the Duke Ellington orchestra provided the music in 1928

15 Minutes in A Taxi Through Central Park
AND SEE
Dan Healy's New Fall Revue
"HOT CHOCOLATE"
Conceived and staged by Dan Healy now featured in "Good Boy"
Music by Jimmie McHugh; lyrics by Dorothy Fields — authors of "Blackbirds" — written exclusively for this Revue.

Cast of fifty! Beautiful girls! Sumptuous costumes! Lilting melodies! Fine voices! Witty lines! *Plus* **Duke Ellington's Recording Orchestra**

At the **Cotton Club**
Bradhurst 142nd STREET
7767-1687 at Lenox Avenue

Club years attest: "Black Beauty," "Jubilee Stomp," "New Orleans Low Down," "Swampy River," "Stevedore Stomp," "Dicty Glide," "Parlor Social Stomp," "Harlem River Quiver," "Harlem Flat Blues," "Memphis Wail," "Mississippi Moan," "The Breakfast Dance," "Rent Party Blues," "Saturday Night Function." Like his mother and father, like his teachers at William Lloyd Garrison High School in segregated Washington, Duke Ellington continued to manifest what he called "pride . . . the greatest race pride" no matter what else was going on around him. His goal was to write "Negro music," he said, to express "Negro feelings put to rhythm and tune." "I am not playing 'jazz,' " he told one of his first interviewers. "I am trying to play the natural feelings of a people." He was, in the admiring parlance of the time, a Race man.

Ellington's long-term residency at the Cotton Club made him the most celebrated black bandleader in New York, but it took the radio to introduce him to the whole country. The band first broadcast nightly from the Cotton Club on local station WHW. Then, at the urging of one of Ellington's most ardent admirers, the popular announcer Ted Husing, the brand-new Columbia Broadcasting System put him on the air nationwide several times a week, sometimes at midnight, sometimes at suppertime. "The world was *waiting* for that from coast to coast," Sonny Greer remembered. "[T]he people didn't get anything to eat till we came off. Cats working all day *starved* to death until we got off."

"We were very, very fortunate," Ellington said, "because . . . at that particular period all the other bands in the country were trying to imitate Paul Whiteman and naturally they were souped up with a lot of grandiose fanfares and all that sort of thing. But we had a very, very plaintive sort of style, and out of contrast alone we stuck out, and caught on."

In fact, some listeners were already hearing far more than mere "contrast" in

Ellington's music. The writer Ralph Ellison, then a high school student in Oklahoma City, remembered Ellington

first as a strangely familiar timbre of orchestral sounds issuing from phonograph records and radio.

Familiar because beneath the stylized jungle sounds (the like of which no African jungle had ever heard), there sounded the blues, and strange because the mutes, toilet plungers and derby hats with which I was acquainted as a musician had been given a stylized elegance and extension of effect unheard of even in the music of Louis Armstrong. It was as though Ellington had taken the traditional instruments of Negro American music and modified them, extended their range and enriched their tonal possibilities. We were studying the classics then, working at harmony and the forms of symphonic music. While we affirmed the voice of jazz and the blues despite all criticism from our teachers because they spoke to a large extent of what we felt about the life we lived most intimately, it was not until the discovery of Ellington that we had any hint that jazz possessed possibilities of a range of expressiveness comparable to that of classical European music.

At roughly the same time, R. D. Darrell, a New York critic writing for *disques,* a journal normally devoted only to the classics, was frank enough to admit that he had initially misjudged Ellington's music. "Black and Tan Fantasy" was the instrument of his conversion:

With the majority I did not recognize it when it first came to my ears in the form of the "hottest, funniest record you ever heard." . . . I laughed like everyone else over its instrumental wa-waing and garbling and gobbling, the piteous whinnying of a very

Duke Ellington during his Cotton Club days

ancient horse, the lugubrious reminiscence of the Chopin funeral march. But as I continued to play the record for the amusement of my friends I laughed less heartily and with less zest. In my ears the whinnies and wa-was began to resolve into new tone colors, distorted and tortured, but agonizingly expressive. The piece took on a surprising individuality and entity as well as an intensity of feeling that was totally incongruous in popular dance music. Beneath all its oddity and perverseness there was a twisted beauty that grew on me more and more and could not be shaken off.

A work like this was alien to all my notions of jazz. It had nothing of the sprightly gusto of Gershwin, . . . nothing of the polish of the Whiteman school, nothing of the raucous exuberance of the Negro jazz I had known. Nor was it in the heavily worked "spiritual" tradition except in that it sounded an equal depth of poignance. For all its fluidity and

rhapsodic freedom it was no improvisation, tossed off by a group of talented virtuosi who would never be able to play it twice in the same way. It bore the indelible stamp of one mind, resourcefully inventive, yet primarily occupied not with the projection of effects or syncopated rhythms, but the concern of great music—tapping the inner world of feeling and experience . . . seizing the human heart.

NEVER SATISFIED

On the afternoon of October 27, 1927, the day after Ellington recorded "Black and Tan Fantasy" in New York and a little over a month before he took his band into the Cotton Club, Bix Beiderbecke and Frankie Trumbauer stepped out of a taxicab in front of the Indiana Theater in Minneapolis and hurried inside. The Paul Whiteman Orchestra was appearing there as part of a forty-week cross-country tour. "The Whiteman band was to the music world what the 1927 New York Yankees were to baseball," its first trumpet player Charles Margulis remembered. "We were giants."

Bix and Tram agreed. "We found the stage door and stopped," Tram remembered. "The stage show was on. Never had we heard music like this before in our lives. We just stood there, like two kids. Oh, we had played with some good bands, that's true, but listening to the King made everything else seem small. . . . 'What music,' cried Bix. 'Aw, Tram, what the hell are we doing here, anyway?' "

In his dressing room at intermission, the huge Whiteman hugged them both—he was dripping with sweat, Trumbauer recalled— then hustled them right onstage, wearing borrowed crimson jackets and without any sheet music. Halfway through the first tune, Jimmy Dorsey poked Trumbauer with his clarinet to signal that Whiteman wanted him to take the next chorus.

Me? Oh, no! How did I get into this? What's the tune? The key? Where the hell's my horn? Oh yes, I'm holding it. . . . A great searing javelin of light from afar, away up somewhere, hit me in the face and I was on my feet and playing. . . . The band yelled! It broke up Paul, too. I felt a little better then and looked around at Bix. He was laughing, but I don't think he meant it because he knew that he was next. I gave him a familiar lead-in on the ending, and he picked up my phrase and carried on with a beautiful chorus. I dropped to my chair, amid the applause of the audience.

Whiteman took them out for dinner afterward, told them how delighted he was to have them in his orchestra, even urged them to record on their own: "If your records go over," he said, "we'll all benefit by them." Neither man could credit his luck.

Bix's father may still have disapproved of what his son was doing, but when the Whiteman orchestra played the Chicago Theater in Chicago that fall Bix got word that his mother was on her way to see him play. "Now he had been out the night before on a tear," Charles Margulis remembered, "and he looked in pretty bad shape, but by the time his mother arrived . . . he looked like Joe College. He was neat as a pin and all spruced up. His mother was very pleased that he had (in her words) made it to the top! She felt her son had reached the height of his career."

There is no reason to think Bix himself did not share that opinion, at least at first. He enjoyed the lush arrangements, the elegant variations on the classics, the cheerful antics of the singing trio called the Rhythm Boys—Harry Barris, Al Rinker, and Harry Lillis Crosby, whom the men in the band called "Bing." And Whiteman even encouraged him to compose—and perform—more of his impressionistic piano pieces. But the pressure of playing night after night took a steady toll. So did the admirers who lay in wait for Bix wherever Whiteman's tours took him. "There were always people in his room," his friend the clarinetist Pee Wee Russell remembered.

They would knock on the door even at six a.m. . . . I remember how, at one hotel, he used to leave word that he wasn't in. So some fellows would check into the hotel, take a room on the floor below Bix's room; then they'd come up and . . . pound on the door. . . . He even had a piano in the room, and when he had a spare moment, he'd try to get a composition started, but with all those people always hanging around he didn't have a chance. In a sense, Bix was killed by his friends. But I think the term is being used loosely. Because they were the kind of people who liked to be able to say, "Last night I was up at Bix's and oh, was he drunk. . . ." And Bix couldn't say no, he couldn't say no to anybody.

Beiderbecke began missing trains, hiding bottles beneath the bandstand, forgetting his cues. Many years later, a cornetist examining copies of Whiteman's sheet music discovered a notation in a sectionmate's hand: "Wake up Bix." He could now not bear to hear his own recordings; when an admiring musician borrowed his cornet and played his solo on the Wolverines' 1924 "Riverboat Shuffle," thinking he'd be pleased, Bix was just annoyed. "What on earth did you play *that* for?" he asked. He was merely "a musical degenerate," he had told a friend, still too ignorant about music ever to be able to express himself as he wished, unable to find in the kind of music he was playing the fulfillment he craved.

When the Whiteman orchestra came back to the Chicago Theater the following July, Louis Armstrong bought a ticket for the very first show and took his seat in the balcony. He remembered Bix both as a towheaded teenager back in Davenport and as a frequent visitor to the Chicago clubs in which he performed; he had especially admired "Singin' the Blues," and was now eager to hear him play with the best-known band in the country.

By now, the Whiteman orchestra had become a sort of traveling army. There were thirty-three men—and some 125 instruments—onstage for the second number, the *1812 Overture,* Armstrong recalled.

[Whiteman] had those trumpets way up into the air, just blowing like mad, and my man Bix was . . . blowing beautifully, and just before the end, they started to shooting cannons, ringing bells, sirens were howling like mad, but you could still hear Bix. The reason why I saw through all those different effects that were going on at the ending—well, you take a man with a pure tone like Bix's and no matter how loud the other fellows may be blowing, that pure . . . tone will cut through it all.

Armstrong went backstage to see Bix after the concert, he remembered, and "we hugged and kissed something wonderful." That night and for several nights that week, as soon as Whiteman's stage show was over, Beiderbecke would hurry down to the South Side café where Armstrong was playing and sit listening quietly until the last customers left at four a.m. "Then," Armstrong recalled, "we would lock the doors. Now you talking about jam sessions, huh, those were the things, with everyone feeling each other's note or chord, and blending with each other instead of trying to cut each other. We tried to see how good we could make music sound."

No one can ever know precisely what caused Bix Beiderbecke's rapid, steady decline into alcoholism and despair. Most of the reasons for it must lie buried in his boyhood. But some part of his chronic dissatisfaction with his own playing and with the music he was being asked to play may well have grown out of the maddening fact that the America of his time provided him with so few opportunities to play alongside the "real jazz niggers" who were the heroes of his boyhood, musicians like Louis Armstrong whose strengths might have helped him further develop his own. Many years later, Armstrong was asked what memories of Bix Beiderbecke remained with him: "Quiet," he said. "Never satisfied with his solos, and people raving. Always figured he had one better."

On November 30, Bix checked in to the Palace Hotel in Cleveland with the rest of the Whiteman orchestra for a weeklong run at the new Music Hall. Bix was now having more and more trouble controlling his drinking—and the depression that it seemed only to intensify. Onstage in Cleveland that evening, he passed out in the middle of a tune. His section-mate Charles Margulis managed to keep him from sliding off his chair but then, he recalled, Bix "was uncertain where he was, . . . took a

Sheet music used by the Paul Whiteman orchestra with "Wake up Bix" written in the hand of one of Bix Beiderbecke's long-suffering section-mates

HAPPY NEW YEAR
TO YOU

AND THIRTY-FOUR REASONS
WHY IT SHOULD BE A
HAPPY NEW YEAR FOR ME

AND HIS
GREATER ORCHESTRA

This greeting from Paul Whiteman to the readers of *Variety* appeared on the show business weekly's cover in 1928.

poke at me and sort of settled back into his haze." Whiteman had seen it all, and at intermission ordered Bix taken back to his hotel room. There, he suffered an attack of *delirium tremens* and smashed up the furniture. Whiteman had no choice but to put him under the care of a male nurse and move on to the band's next engagement.

"Bix still gone," Frankie Trumbauer noted in his diary the next day. "Stayed in Cleveland with DT's. I spent 4 years with him to no avail." He was hospitalized at the Rivercrest Sanitarium on Long Island, where he was found to have been suffering from pneumonia as well as alcoholism. Six weeks later, he left the hospital and checked into a hotel on Forty-fourth Street in New York, planning to rejoin the band when it got back to town the next day. But that night, accompanied by a friend, he visited

a speakeasy where, in an incident never fully explained, someone beat both men bloody and gashed Beiderbecke's thigh so badly with a broken bottle that he was left with a permanent limp.

This time, Whiteman made sure Bix went home to Davenport to recuperate. It was not a happy visit. A friend remembered Bix telling him that not long after he got there, he had discovered in a hall closet all the Paul Whiteman records he'd proudly sent home to his parents; his father had never even unwrapped them. If the story was true—and the family subsequently denied it—Bismarck Beiderbecke's apparent lack of interest in his work can only have served to reconfirm his own self-doubt. He was too good-natured ever publicly to criticize other musicians but, according to Frankie Trumbauer, only Louis

Armstrong among all the musicians in jazz now continued to hold his full interest.

When a reporter for the Davenport *Sunday Democrat* came to interview him as a local celebrity, Beiderbecke was both self-effacing and oddly ambivalent about the music he was playing. He enjoyed all the "traveling about" he got to do with the Whiteman band, he said, but jazz itself was "musical humor," nothing more. Yet, "even in the hands of white composers it involuntarily reflects the half-forgotten suffering of the negro," he continued. "Jazz has both white and black elements and each in some respects has influenced the other. Its recent phase seems to throw the light of the white race's sophistication upon the anguish of the black." Other than the short article the same newspaper had once run describing him as a promising pianist at the age of seven, this would be the only feature piece published about Bix Beiderbecke during his lifetime.

THE MOST DOG

Sidney Bechet remained Louis Armstrong's only serious rival as the most daring soloist in jazz. But, as Armstrong's fame continued to spread, Bechet's career was undercut again and again by the turbulent personality that found its best expression in his music. In the summer of 1925 he had opened his own Harlem cabaret on Seventh Avenue, the Club Basha—so-called because that was the way most New York musicians mispronounced his name—and was doing well, leading a house band that included one of his most avid admirers, nineteen-year-old alto saxophonist Johnny Hodges, until he got into a quarrel with his partner over the affections of a belly dancer and abruptly walked away from the business.

In September, he sailed for France with the all-black cast of a new musical, *La Revue Nègre,* which played Paris, Brussels, and Berlin. Bechet had only a small part: dressed as a peddler in a long duster, he

La Revue Nègre introduced Josephine Baker (above)—and the sound of Sidney Bechet—to thousands of Parisians in 1925. Later, Bechet moved on with Frank Withers's orchestra to Moscow, where the photograph on the opposite page was taken. Bechet stands at the center with his arm around a woman's shoulder. He and other members of the Withers and Sam Wooding bands spent a lot of time at the Moscow Artist's Club that winter, the reed player Garvin Bushell remembered, because "that's where the girls were."

pushed a brightly painted cart piled with artificial fruit onstage, then played a long improvised blues. But the show made an international sensation of the American dance the French called "le Charleston"—and an international star of its lead dancer, a long-limbed teenaged chorus girl from St. Louis named Josephine Baker. The French thought all the black performers wonderfully exotic. Critics called Baker "the black venus that haunted Baudelaire" and compared her to a snake, a giraffe, a kangaroo. When she began to parade along the boulevards with a live cheetah, admirers speculated as to which "animal" was more wonderfully "savage," the one at the end of

the leash or the one holding it. "The white imagination," Baker admitted privately, "is sure something when it comes to blacks."

After she left the show, the *Revue Nègre* collapsed and Bechet found himself touring the Soviet Union with a band led by the trombonist Frank Withers, an old friend from Will Marion Cook's Southern Syncopators. Then, he rejoined a much-reduced version of the original *Revue Nègre* that traveled to Berlin, Athens, Istanbul, Cairo, Oslo, Madrid, Prague, Rome. At the end, he admitted, the band was mostly made up of "Frenchmen, Germans and Cubans," but he still got star billing as "the Talking Saxophone," and he was bringing jazz to regions

so remote that people sometimes wet their fingers and rubbed Bechet's hand or cheek to see if the color came off.

Wherever he went, his competitiveness and quick temper went, too. Somewhere along the way he had picked up a dog, a blend of Doberman and bulldog, whose pugnacity was almost a match for his own. When he got to Berlin in 1926 and learned that the American reedman Garvin Bushell was also in town, playing with Sam Wooding's orchestra, and that Bushell was the proud owner of a Great Dane named Caesar, he lost no time in calling upon him.

About four o'clock one morning, Bushell heard a knock on his door. It was Bechet.

"Sidney what you want? It's four o'clock in the morning."

"Just open the door, I want to tell you something."

I opened the door and he had this squatty dog with him.

"I brought my dog 'round here," Sidney said, "and I really want to let you know just how much dog you don't have, and how much dog I've got. So come on out in the hall and let 'em fight."

By now, Caesar's clawing in the back, trying to get me out of the way to get to this Doberman. I said, "Would you take your dog and get away from here?"

"No, we gonna fight 'em out here this morning in the hall." Bushell closed the door and went back to bed.

Before long, Bechet was back in Paris, playing in a Left Bank nightclub, drinking and gambling with fellow expatriates—and soon in trouble again. "It's like there's somebody else inside a man," Bechet once admitted, "somebody that's not really that man, and when a thing happens, an anger, . . . that other person takes over. That's not to make excuses. I know well enough it's me all the time. . . . I can be mean. It takes an awful lot; someone's got to do a lot to me. But when I do get mean, I can be powerful mean."

Early one morning he got into an altercation at a café just off the rue Fontaine with a banjo player named Gilbert Michael "Little Mike" McKendrick. One eyewitness remembered that the trouble began when McKendrick dared question Bechet's knowledge of the chords of a song they'd just played. A piano player from Chicago named Glover Compton took McKendrick's side—although he would later claim the subject of dispute had actually been Bechet's chronic unwillingness to pay for a round of drinks—and accelerated things further by sneering at Bechet as "Dixie-boy."

Bechet went home, got his revolver, and came back. By now, the morning rush hour had begun and the streets were filled with Parisians on their way to work. "Mike had [a pistol] in his pocket but didn't nobody know it," Compton remembered. "Mike stepped out onto the sidewalk and I stepped out right behind him. That's when the shooting started." Pedestrians scrambled to get out of the way. McKendrick missed Bechet, whose own shots spun past his intended target: one smashed into Compton Glover's leg; others slightly wounded two women.

Bechet and McKendrick were arrested, tried, and sentenced to prison. Bechet got fifteen months but was released after eleven, provided he promised to leave France right away. The two men eventually became friends again. But Bechet never forgave Glover Compton for siding against him, and when rumors reached him that the pianist was thinking of going to court for compensation for his shattered limb, he sent word that if Compton dared try it, he should watch out for the welfare of his other leg. Compton dropped his plans to sue.

THE SUN'S EYE

Louis Armstrong, the man Bechet considered his greatest rival, was a hero now on the South Side of Chicago. "I became quite a figure," he said, "especially with the gals" who flocked to see him at the Vendome. One of them was Alpha Smith, a pretty nineteen-year-old nursemaid who came to the theater twice a week and always made sure she sat in the front row, "where I could get a look at her legs." Armstrong had grown unhappy at home. He didn't much

like being a sideman in his wife's band and was embarrassed when his fellow musicians called him "Henny," for henpecked. Lil's mother, who now lived with the Armstrongs and had never approved of jazz, thought Armstrong unworthy of her educated daughter and said so, loudly and often. "[T]here was no happiness there," he said. "We were always fussing and threatening to break up. If I sat on the bed after it was made up, why Lil would almost go into 'fits,' spasms, etc.—and poor Clarence, my adopted son with his nervous self used to almost jump out of his skin when Lil or Lil's mother would holler at him." And he had heard rumors that his wife had been seeing someone else while he was in New York. "Ever since I was a little boy in New Orleans hanging around those ole hustlers and pimps," he wrote, "they used to tell me, 'Never worry over no one woman—no matter how pretty or sweet she may be—Any time she . . . ain't playing the part of a wife, get yourself somebody else, also. And get another woman much better than the last one at all times.' Alpha commenced inviting me to her home." Soon he separated from Lil, took Clarence with him, and moved in with Alpha and her mother in their tiny apartment at Thirty-third and Cottage Grove. Both he and Clarence preferred it there, where no one nagged them, he said. They "didn't have to 'put on airs with a certain spoon for this and a certain fork for that.' . . . Alpha had fallen deeply in love with me by this time, anyway, and I was crazy about her."

In the spring of 1926, Armstrong had left the Dreamland, too, to join a band fronted by the violinist Carroll Dickerson at the Sunset Café, the most successful black-and-tan in town. It was billed as "Chicago's Brightest Pleasure Spot" and stood at the corner of Thirty-fifth and Calumet, just off the brightly lit South Side Stroll. Most of its customers were slumming whites, the pianist Earl Hines remembered. "Even the mixing

Alpha Smith, Louis Armstrong, and an unidentified friend mug for an amusement park photographer.

of white girls and colored pimps seemed to be an attraction." It was a tough place in a tough neighborhood. The owner of record was the mother of Joe Glaser, the crude-talking young man who managed it (and who would one day manage Armstrong himself), but it was really run by the mob and raided so often by the police, Hines said, that he used to run for the paddy wagon as soon as it pulled up in order to get a good seat. Al Capone—Armstrong remembered him as "a nice little cute fat boy"—was a frequent visitor.

Armstrong loved it. "I was young and strong, a flying cat, and God, I blew the people right out of the place. . . . The Sunset was packed every night. All the white people, all the nightlifers, the rich people from Sheridan Road and the big hotels would come out there on the South Side. . . . I'd

sing songs through a megaphone and four of us would close the show doing the Charleston."

Before long, Joe Glaser nudged Carroll Dickerson aside so that the band could be renamed "Louis Armstrong and his Stompers," and made Earl Hines its musical director. Hines was an innovator in his own right and played what came to be called "trumpet-style" piano, confidently spinning out complex, hornlike melodies with his right hand, while setting a looser rhythm with his left that helped push the music far beyond the strict beat of ragtime. He and Armstrong were rivals as well as friends, each spurring the other to greater heights. Together, they made an astonishing series of recordings—"Muggles," "Fireworks," "A Monday Date," "Skip the Gutter," "St. James Infirmary," "Basin Street Blues," "Save it Pretty Mama," "Beau Koo Jack," "Tight Like That," and an unprecedented trumpet-piano duet called "Weather Bird." "Making records we liked to do," Hines remembered. "Ideas used to come to us in the studio. . . . I think the public realized that we were really playing from the heart."

That "public" included the young white musicians who continued to come every night to play and learn. Armstrong called them "my boys." "I don't know how many musicians came to sit and jam with us," Hines said. "Whatever section they wanted to sit in, why a musician would step out from his chair. We all got a kick out of listening to each other, and we all tried to learn. We sat around waiting to see if these guys were actually going to come up with something new or different."

Armstrong was not the only great teacher at work at Thirty-fifth and Calumet. Joe Oliver was playing at the Plantation Café just across the street, and Jimmy Noone was appearing at an upstairs club called the Nest right next door to him. As many early mornings as they could manage, Eddie Condon and his friends headed for the Nest after the Sunset and the Plantation had closed. "We left our golf clubs there, our

The Carroll Dickerson band backs the floor show at Chicago's black-and-tan Sunset Café in 1922. Its leader stands at the center, his violin at his chin. When Louis Armstrong joined the orchestra four years later, Dickerson would be shunted aside in favor of the trumpet star.

instruments, our galoshes," he wrote. "There [we] listened to Jimmie Noone do things with a clarinet which no one had considered even probable. Jimmie was a chubby, congenial, gentle Negro. He had gold keys on his clarinet and almost every morning after one the clarinet was pointed

down at [Frank] Teschemacher, who sat smack up against the bandstand, staring up at Jimmie. Benny Goodman was there often, too." One night, a flutist with the Chicago Symphony brought Maurice Ravel to hear Noone spin out chorus after chorus of "Four or Five Times." "Impossible!" Ravel mut-

tered. "Then he tried to write down some of the runs Jimmie was playing, but he quickly gave it up," Condon said. "After that he just sat back like the rest of us, listening and staring at the gold keys."

When Joe Oliver first saw the sign go up outside the Sunset reading "The World's

The Plantation Café, where King Oliver led his Dixie Syncopators in 1926

Greatest Trumpet Player," he is supposed to have sent word to Armstrong to "Close those windows or I'll blow you off Thirty-fifth Street." The windows stayed open, Condon remembered, and, "with Louis and Oliver and Jimmie all playing within a hundred feet of each other . . . unless it happened in New Orleans I don't think so much good jazz was ever concentrated in so small an area. Around midnight you could hold your instrument in the middle of the street and the air would play it. That was music."

Louis Armstrong was walking through his South Side neighborhood with Bud Freeman one afternoon in the spring of 1928, when they stopped to listen to some street musicians play "Struttin' with Some Barbecue," one of the tunes recorded by the Hot Five. The trumpet player was laboring his way through Armstrong's own solo, note for note.

When the man had finished, Armstrong applauded politely, then stepped closer and murmured, "Man, you're playing that too *slow*."

"How would *you* know?" asked the trumpet player, indignant.

"I'm Louis Armstrong. That's my chorus you're playing."

When he passed by the next day, the musicians had put out a hand-lettered sign next to their tin cup: "Pupils of Louis Armstrong."

In a sense, all musicians now saw themselves as Armstrong's pupils, even the men who played the sweet, melodic dance music of Guy Lombardo. When Lombardo was working at the Granada Café on the North Side that same year, he made sure that Armstrong was not only admitted to the club—which otherwise had an exclusively white clientele—but that he was welcomed as an honored guest. "Louis said he was never treated any better anywhere in his life [than] he was by this famous orchestral group," a black newspaper reported after he and his friend, the drummer Zutty Singleton, had made a visit. "The Granada is one of the swellest night clubs in the country and is known from coast to coast. The minute the cornet king entered was the signal for the chord from the orchestra. . . . The boys were given a table in juxtaposition to the bandstand. They were wined and dined until the wee hours of the morning."

Armstrong would remain a lifelong admirer of Lombardo's orchestra. "I haven't heard no band that plays more perfect music," he said. No one else could play "that straight lead and make it sound so good."

All of Armstrong's records were now eagerly awaited by musicians, but one recording, made on June 28, 1928, would stand out above the rest. "West End Blues" was written by King Oliver and named for one of the resorts on Lake Pontchartrain that had played host to New Orleans bands like those in which he and his protégé had played back home, but Armstrong's treatment of it was unlike anything ever heard there—or anywhere else on earth.

It begins with an unaccompanied clarion cadenza, twelve seconds of bravura playing so dazzling that no other trumpeter has ever quite succeeded in replicating it, and so thrilling, the conductor and composer Gunther Schuller has written, that it "served notice for the first time that jazz had the potential to compete with the highest order of previously known expression." A reflective ensemble chorus follows; trombonist Fred Robinson has his mournful say. Then clarinetist Jimmy Strong restates the melody in his low register while Armstrong croons a heartfelt, wistful, wordless obbligato, as moving in its way as anything he

Earl Hines, 1928

ever played on the trumpet. Earl Hines adds an elegantly flowing piano chorus before Armstrong takes up his trumpet again and breaks into one of his most magisterial solos, beginning with a single note held without discernible effort for four measures, as if time itself meant nothing to him, and then plunging into the heart of the blues. "West End Blues" is one of the most sublime recordings in the history of music.

It almost didn't get made at all. According to Hines, when he and Armstrong and the other men got to the studio they knew only that Armstrong was going to open with his astonishing introduction and would need a rest soon thereafter to get his breath back. Having him scat a chorus solved that problem, but they still hadn't worked out a satisfactory finish. "We got to the end of it and Louis looked at me and I thought of the first thing I could think of, a little bit of a classical thing . . . and after I finished that I held the chord and Louis gave the downbeat with his head and everybody hit the chord on the end." But then, Zutty Singleton fumbled the final clop cymbal. The take was ruined. The engineers had to heat a new wax disc so that it would accept the imprint of the recording stylus, then start all over again. Singleton failed a second time. On the third take, he dropped his cymbal, which crashed to the floor. "So we spent hours in there with the hot wax," Hines continued, "and then sometimes after the hot wax was complete . . . the needle wasn't working. But it was a lot of fun—afterwards. . . . Louis and I stayed by that recording practically . . . two hours and we just knocked each other out because we had no idea it was going to turn out as good as it did."

"West End Blues" literally changed people's lives. Artie Shaw, then playing in a small-time dance band in Cleveland, heard the record and was so moved that in the summer of 1928 he resolved that he had to hear Armstrong play in person. By then, Arm-

Louis Armstrong's "West End Blues"

strong had moved on to headline at a splendid new South Side dance hall called the Savoy Ballroom. "I made a pilgrimage," Shaw recalled some seventy years later. "I took a week off and went up to Chicago . . . and I found my way to a place called the Savoy. And I sat on a bandstand which was about two feet off the ground . . . and just waited and he came on. And the first thing he played was 'West End Blues.' And I heard this cascade of notes coming out of a trumpet. No one had ever done that before. And so I was obsessed with the idea that this was what you had to do. Something that was your own, that had nothing to do with anybody else. . . . I was influenced by him, not in terms of notes, but in terms of the idea of doing what you are, *who* you are."

Young Max Kaminsky came to Chicago from Boston that same summer for more or less the same reason. He had dropped out of high school, he said, because he was usually too sleepy from playing somewhere the night before to pay attention to his teachers, and because none of his schoolmates—with the exception of his friend Harry Carney, who had now left school to join the Ellington band—"knew or cared

about the one thing I was interested in." He had no guarantee of work in Chicago, but he had heard Armstrong's Hot Fives and Hot Sevens—which, he said, had sounded like "just a lot of clatter" to most of the dance-band musicians with whom he'd been playing in New England—and decided that "if this was the kind of jazz going on in Chicago, then Chicago was the place to be."

A chance meeting with Bud Freeman introduced him to the ragtag crew of jazz-mad young whites whose version of New Orleans music the critics would eventually label "Chicago style." Since 1922, when the old Austin High Gang began haunting first the Friar's Inn and then the Lincoln Gardens, their numbers had grown steadily. The drummer Gene Krupa and cornetist Muggsy Spanier were both Chicagoans, but George Wettling, also a drummer, was from Topeka, Kansas; pianist Jess Stacy came from Bird's Point, Missouri, and had played on boats belonging to the same Streckfus line that had employed Armstrong and Beiderbecke. The cornetist Wingy Manone, who had lost his right arm in a childhood streetcar accident, hailed from New Orleans and remembered first hearing jazz on its "main stem—when the colored bands in trucks advertising a dance, battled it out."

"Though barely in their twenties themselves," Kaminsky wrote, "these men had been deeply immersed in the music for six or seven years, absorbing it firsthand from the New Orleans jazzmen while developing their own style and feeling, whereas I had heard it only in tantalizing dribbles and snatches." He somehow landed a job nonetheless, playing at a Chinese restaurant with Frank Teschemacher and George Wettling, with whom, he said, he "fitted in as naturally as a baseball bat fit into Babe Ruth's hands. . . . It seemed as if every day was the Fourth of July."

One evening, Wettling and Wingy Manone took him to hear Armstrong play

Arthur Arshawsky as a patriotic little boy in 1914, and (at the far left of the photograph at right) reborn as Artie Shaw, clarinetist in the Joe Cantor orchestra, one of several bands in which he would play before striking out on his own.

Arthur Jacob Arshawsky was born on the Lower East Side of Manhattan in 1910, the only child of immigrant dressmakers who eventually separated. When Arthur was seven, the family moved to New Haven, Connecticut, where the boy found himself an outcast, tormented by schoolmates who called him "sheeny" and "kike" and "Christ-killer." "My father'd left home," he remembered, "and I didn't like my life very much. I didn't like school, I didn't like anything. So it was a choice between getting a machine gun or an instrument. Luckily I found an instrument."

He visited a vaudeville theater and saw a musician in a snappy white-striped blazer kneel down on one knee in the spotlight and play "Dreamy Melody" on a shiny gold saxophone. "That did it," he remembered: music would be his way to fame and fortune. He worked in a grocery store to earn money for a saxophone, practiced so hard the inside of his lower lip bled, played amateur shows, and formed his own four-piece Peter Pan Novelty Orchestra, which earned him two dollars a night playing dances. School was

now only an interruption. "I was determined that I would play this instrument, so I managed to get flunked. I worked it out so that I got flunked two months in a row, and they threw me out. And despite my mother's pleas to the principal of Hillhouse High in New Haven, they wouldn't have me. So that meant I was free to play."

Like Benny Goodman, who would one day be his great rival, he adopted the clarinet, and joined a touring dance band as a full-time professional. Whenever he could, he went to Harlem to study with Duke Ellington's mentor, Willie the Lion Smith—whose fond nickname for him was "Snow White." His first musical models were Bix Beiderbecke and Frankie Trumbauer.

Eager to be accepted by audiences everywhere, and then "ashamed of being a Jew," he said, Arthur Jacob Arshawsky changed his name to Artie Shaw. He became one of the best-known bandleaders of the swing era but it was the challenge of improvisation that kept him fascinated:

You're aiming at something that cannot be done, physically can't be done. So you're trying to play a horn, and here's this clumsy series of keys on a piece of wood and you're trying to manipulate them with the reed and the throat muscles and what they call an embouchure, and you're trying to make something happen that never happened before. You're trying to make a sound that no one ever got before, or a combination of sounds creating an emotion. You're trying to take an inarticulate thing and take notes and make them come out in a way that moves you. If it moves you, it's going to move others. But very rarely does it happen, and when it does you remember it for the rest of your life. What can I say? It's the most exuberant experience you can have. It beats sex. It beats great food. It beats anything.

at the Savoy. As soon as they got inside, Armstrong came over to greet Wettling and Manone. They introduced their new friend, and Kaminsky and Armstrong shook hands. "From listening to his records I already had some inkling of the warmth and power of the man," Kaminsky wrote, "but I was totally unprepared for that remarkable penetrating awareness underneath the genial, easygoing manner. All his senses seem to receive impressions of you; you feel he's not so much sizing you up as opening his mind to you, like a receiver set. You can't fake it with Louis. He can tell."

Kaminsky wasn't prepared for the power of Armstrong's playing, either. The first number was "West End Blues," and when Armstrong began his bravura introduction, Kaminsky was literally stunned. "I sent one quivering look at Wingy and George and took my leave. The sheer loveliness of Bix's tone and feeling had captured me, but the combination of Louis's dazzling virtuosity and sensational brilliance of tone so overwhelmed me that I felt as if I had stared into the sun's eye. All I could think of doing was to run away and hide till the blindness left me."

MAY IT PLEASE YOU

At one-thirty in the morning on February 7, 1928, federal agents swooped down on a dozen of Chicago's leading North Side nightspots, took the names of every one of the hundreds of startled patrons caught with liquor on their tables, and padlocked the doors. A brand-new "hip flask" law now held that even those who provided ice and gingerale for patrons to mix with their own alcohol were liable to prosecution. Vice raids, launched by William Dever, Big Bill Thompson's Republican successor as mayor, had already closed several black-and-tans on the South Side. "Chicago was once the hottest café town in the United States," *Variety* reported, "famous for siz-

zling music, torrid night life, a great little spot for the great little guys. But that's history now. Night by night it gets tougher for the cabarets."

It got tougher for Chicago musicians, too. Some two hundred of them would lose their jobs by May. One hundred and fifty more were already out of work—or about to be—as popular enthusiasm for *The Jazz Singer* convinced theater owners to install equipment for talking pictures and dispense with the expensive orchestras that had accompanied the silents. Other musicians now felt themselves in actual physical danger. The music business in Chicago had often involved a certain amount of personal risk: a few years earlier, Bud Freeman had not been wholly reassured when the mobster who owned the club in which he was working took him aside and said, "Buddy, don't you ever worry about anybody in this here joint because nobody in this here joint will hurt you unless he gets paid for it." But now, as business slumped, Al Capone and his rivals began to war openly over the shrinking profits. Bombs gutted the Café de Paris and the Plantation Club, where Joe Oliver had been playing. An exodus of musicians began. Most headed for New York—Joe Oliver, Eddie Condon, Dave Tough, Gene Krupa, and Max Kaminsky among them.

The Ben Pollack Orchestra had led the way in February. Now billed as "The Big Band with the Little Leader," it played at a place called the Little Club at first, then at the Million Dollar Pier in Atlantic City, finally at the elegant Park Central Hotel, where the refugees from mob-run Chicago were made to feel more at home than they may have liked when the big-time gambler Arnold Rothstein, shot by persons unknown, staggered downstairs to die underneath the balcony on which they were playing.

Benny Goodman was still in the band, now playing alongside his old friends Jimmy McPartland and Bud Freeman as well as his brother, Harry. And Glenn Miller had been replaced by a big, bearlike, hard-

Jack Teagarden, 1924

drinking, hard-living young trombone player who was changing the way his instrument was played—Jack Teagarden.

Born and brought up in Texas cattle country, Teagarden began playing the trombone at the age of eight. His arm was then too short to manipulate the slide much beyond the bell, so he taught himself to reach low notes by developing a versatile embouchure that was the envy of every brass player who ever watched him on the bandstand. Once, when a pianist asked him "how come he never seemed to knock himself out going for low notes in fast passages," Teagarden answered, "Man, I don't like workin' that hard—I just use my lip." He had also still been just a boy when he learned to love the shouts and moans and bent notes that were the heart of blues music by listening night after night to Negro tent revivals held in a vacant lot just across the street from his family home. "The music seemed just as natural to me as anything. I could hum along with 'em with no trouble

The men of the Ben Pollack band—and a hotel bellhop—take their ease in Atlantic City, New Jersey, on a summer afternoon in 1928. Jack Teagarden sprawls at far left, next to the bellhop; Ben Pollack hugs his knees at the base of the flagpole; Benny Goodman is fourth from the right and his brother Harry right next to him.

at all." And he so revered Louis Armstrong that he and his friend Wingy Manone, having had a drink or two, buried a copy of Armstrong's "Oriental Strut" in the middle of the New Mexican desert so that it might be preserved forever.

Teagarden's playing, polished in the roadhouses and dance halls of the Southwest, seemed so relaxed, swung so hard, and was so deeply suffused with the blues, that once when he was playing Roseland with an otherwise undistinguished white band called the Scranton Sirens, Fletcher Henderson himself took him aside and said, "I have been listening to you. I don't see how any white man can play like you do. Tell me—and you have my strictest confidence—are you colored?" Teagarden, both flattered and embarrassed, shook his head no. Henderson was not convinced. "You can tell me," he said, walking away. "I won't say a word." For the rest of the engagement men in Henderson's band would call out to Teagarden, "Boy, what are you doing up there. Come on over with us where you belong."

On the morning of March 5, 1929, Teagarden found himself in the fastest possible musical company. Louis Armstrong was in New York playing a one-night stand in Harlem, where a banquet was given in his honor at which a good many of his old admirers from Chicago were present. "I had never seen so many good musicians, white and colored, in one place at the same time," Eddie Condon remembered, and he suggested to Tommy Rockwell—the producer of Armstrong's Hot Fives and Hot Sevens for Okeh, now stationed in New York—that he should take advantage of the occasion and make a record right away, before Armstrong returned to Chicago. Rockwell was nervous at first. "I don't know about a mixed group," he said. But he went ahead, anyway, and shortly after dawn, Teagarden, Joe Sullivan, and Eddie Lang joined Armstrong, Kaiser Marshall, and tenor saxophonist Happy Cauldwell in the Okeh studio to record a relaxed impromptu blues.

Teagarden and Armstrong had met eight years earlier in New Orleans but this was the first time Armstrong had heard the trombonist play. "It moves me," he said, putting his hand on his heart. "It moves me right through *here*." It had been a cold morning in Manhattan and the musicians had polished off a bottle of whiskey before they began to play. When the time came to give the tune a title, someone came up with "Knockin' a Jug." It remains a jazz masterpiece.

Like Louis Armstrong, Benny Goodman loved Teagarden's playing, but Teagarden was wary of Goodman at first. The clarinetist sat in front of him on the Pollack bandstand and whenever Teagarden played he would swivel all the way around and stare intently up at him. Finally, Teagarden asked what was wrong, had he offended Goodman in some way? No, Goodman answered; he was just listening. It was the first recorded instance of the intense expressionless stare that would make two generations of musicians who played with Benny Goodman uneasy. They called it "the Ray."

Having hired first-class musicians, Ben Pollack proved unable to handle them. "Ben was basically a good guy," one said, "but when he stuck a cigar in his mouth it was a signal that he was about to undergo a change of personality." His men resented it when he drove in a chauffeured limousine while they bounced from engagement to engagement in a rented bus; they were appalled when he abandoned the drums in order to stay in the spotlight full-time as conductor and crooner, could not understand why he so often made them record sweet arrangements instead of the hot ones they loved or why he insisted on ending each side with the same cloying signature— "May it please you, Ben Pollack." They cringed when he ordered the new drummer, Ray Bauduc, to wear a tiger head when the band played "Tiger Rag," and hated the number in which they were made to mince around the stage in hula skirts. "It was so stupid," Jimmy McPartland recalled. "We all wanted to quit. But that was New York for you. It was much more about business than Chicago. Chicago was freewheeling. New York was about making money."

A mutiny began to brew. Teagarden and McPartland were often too hungover to rehearse. One night, Harry Goodman smeared Pollack's megaphone with Limburger cheese to ruin his vocal. Another evening, already irritated by Benny Goodman's practice of taking more than his share of solos, Pollack was enraged to find out that after he had turned down an invitation to play a dance because the band had a prior engagement, his clarinetist had asked for a day off without telling him why he needed it, then secretly put together a band of his own and pocketed the seven-hundred-dollar fee. Goodman was unrepentant: "This was plenty good," he said, "much better than playing notes for someone else." He was already being eagerly sought out for record dates, usually as a member of one anonymous phantom group or another organized by record producers like Irving Mills—the Dixie Daisies, Kentucky Grasshoppers, Ten Blackberries, Whoopee Makers, and Mills Musical Clowns.

Tensions within the Pollack band finally exploded during a theater engagement in Brooklyn. Between shows, Goodman and McPartland liked to run up to the roof to play handball. In the course of one game they badly scuffed their white band shoes, then wore them onstage. After the curtain fell there was a confrontation with Pollack, McPartland remembered: " 'You're fired, McPartland,' he said to me. 'Look at your shoes!' Benny looked over and said, 'Did you just fire Jimmy?' He said, 'Yes, I did!' 'Well, look at *my* shoes,' Benny told him. 'I quit!' "

"It was hard leaving Gil [Rodin], Jack [Teagarden], my brother Harry and the others," Goodman remembered, "but I was feeling pretty confident at the time. . . . Pollack had done a lot for me . . . but I felt the time had come to go out on my own."

MY, MY, MY

In May of 1929, Louis Armstrong himself joined the stream of musicians moving from Chicago to New York. He was still a hero on the South Side: a columnist for the Chicago *Defender* had dubbed him "King Menilek," after the nineteenth-century ruler who had driven the Italians out of Ethiopia, because of the ease with which Armstrong had "slaughtered all the ofay jazz demons appearing at the Savoy recently." But even the Savoy had fallen on hard times—"Mr. Fagan [the manager] would come to us with a hard luck story every week," Armstrong recalled, "and the way he would lay this story on us, we just couldn't leave him that's all. . . . But [after a while it looked] like Mr. Fagan was laying that story on us a little too often." Then, Tommy Rockwell, who was now Armstrong's booking agent, had landed him a job in New York, playing for a brand-new musical with a plantation theme by Vincent Youmans called "Great Day."

Armstrong drove his own Hupmobile east—paid for with the proceeds from a new book of 125 transcribed breaks, meant for would-be cornet and trumpet players—at the head of a caravan of four battered cars carrying the ten members of the Carroll Dickerson band, with whom he'd been playing at the Savoy. There was no assurance of work for any of his friends, and Rockwell hadn't been told they were coming, but, as Armstrong explained, "we didn't want to leave one another so I took the whole band." "That was some trip," Zutty Singleton said. "We had a couple of vibraphones—tied them on the car and they got all rusty." One of the cars got into an accident and was simply abandoned; no one had cash for repairs. They took their time—stopping at Detroit, Toledo, Cleveland, and Buffalo, where they detoured to see Niagara Falls—and everywhere they went Armstrong was startled to find that his fame, spread by records and radio broadcasts from the Savoy, had preceded them into every black neighborhood. "We didn't

Louis Armstrong played into a Dictaphone all of the 125 cornet breaks that were carefully notated for this book published by the Melrose Brothers, but the recordings were subsequently lost.

know nothing about radio then," Armstrong said, "or how far it reached. So it was all fun. The cats were so glad to meet us that we didn't need spending money."

New York was different. The men had no cash left when they arrived. Tommy Rockwell was not pleased to find that he had a whole band on his hands. And Armstrong—and all the other black musicians whom Youmans had hired for his show—were summarily replaced with whites by the producer. Florenz Ziegfeld auditioned Armstrong and the band for *Showgirl,* a glossy new revue headed for Broadway, but picked the Duke Ellington orchestra to appear onstage instead.

Rockwell eventually got Armstrong and his men work at the Lafayette Theater and then at Connie's Inn, the Cotton Club's chief rival for the affection of monied thrill-seeking whites, at Seventh Avenue and West 131st Street. They were to play for a revue called *Connie's Hot Chocolates* with songs by Andy Razaff and the Harlem stride pianist Fats Waller. Two former delicatessen owners, George and Connie Immerman, were nominally in charge of the club, but the real owner—and one of Armstrong's most devoted admirers—was the murderous king of the New York numbers racket, Arthur Flegenheimer, better known by the nickname he chose because he thought it looked better in the headlines, Dutch Schultz.

The *Hot Chocolates* revue proved so popular that it soon moved downtown, to the Hudson Theater on Broadway, where it ran for 219 performances. Armstrong's perfor-mance of the show's biggest hit, "Ain't Misbehavin' "—singing and dancing now as well as playing, and from the stage, not the pit—regularly brought the house down. Nothing like him had even been seen on Broadway before.

Irving Kolodin, music critic for the *New York Times*, memorably captured the kind of show Armstrong was putting on for his audiences during these years.

He backs off downstage left, leans half-way over like a quarter-miler, begins to count (swaying as he does) "one, two, three" . . . he has already started racing toward the rear where the orchestra is ranged, and he hits four, executes a slide and a pirouette; winds up facing the audience and blowing the first note as the orchestra swings into the tune. It's mad, it's meaningless, it's hokum of the first order, but the effect is electrifying. No shabby pretense about this boy! He knows what his audience will take to their hearts and how he gives it to them. His trumpet virtuosity is endless—triplets, chromatic accented eerie counterpoints that turn the tune inside out, wild sorties into the giddy

Taking a break during the Atlantic City tryout of Vincent Youman's musical *Great Day* during the summer of 1929. The songwriter Harold Arlen stands second from left. Fletcher Henderson is at the wheel. The tall man in white is Will Marion Cook. Cornetist Rex Stewart sits at the far right. A few days later, the producers replaced all the black artists with white ones and Louis Armstrong, who had hoped to join them, had to look elsewhere for work.

Sheet music for Fats Waller's hit "Ain't Misbehavin'"

stratosphere . . . all executed with impeccable style and finish, exploits that make his contemporaries sound like so many Salvation Army cornetists. Alternately singing choruses and daubing with the handkerchief at throat, face, forehead (he perspires like a dying gladiator) the while a diamond bracelet twinkles from his wrist, he finally gets off the stage to rest.

Armstrong remained a hit on Broadway, but he still rushed north to Connie's Inn to do the whole show all over again after every performance, and sometimes squeezed in a star turn at the Lafayette Theater right next door, as well. "Had to get my sleep coming through the park in a cab," he remembered. "I was only [twenty-seven] years old. Didn't exactly feel I had the world at my feet, but it was very nice that everyone was picking up on the things I was doing, and all the bandleaders wanted me. Pretty soon I had to get in front of my own band. Nothing else I could do."

In Harlem, Mezz Mezzrow wrote, young men now began wearing wide-winged Barrymore collars and ties with oversized knots

because Armstrong wore them. "Louis always held a handkerchief in his hand because he perspired so much, onstage and off, and that started a real fad—before long all the kids on the Avenue were running up to him with handkerchiefs in their hands, too, to show how much they loved him. Louis always stood with his hands clasped in front of him, in a kind of easy slouch. Pretty soon all the kids were lounging . . . with their hands locked in front of them, and a white handkerchief always peeking out from between their fingers." And in far-off Missouri, Buck O'Neil, the future first baseman for the Kansas City Monarchs, remembered, whenever it rained he and all his young friends would drive around with their heads stuck out the window "so you could get hoarse [and] sound like Louis Armstrong." Fans and fellow musicians alike began to copy his distinctive vocabulary, too. He was the first to refer to a musician's skills as his "chops," the first to call people "cats." When he couldn't remember someone's name, he'd call them "Gate" or "Pops"—which would become the fond nickname his friends around the world called him until the day he died.

But for all his newfound fame he still was willing to take on any challenger who dared question his supremacy. He called it "defending myself." Jabbo Smith, already vanquished once in Chicago, met Armstrong again at the Rockland Palace, one of Harlem's biggest ballrooms. A capacity crowd of more than two thousand was on hand for the showdown, Rex Stewart remembered.

It was a beautiful sight—no flower garden could compete with the beauty of the gal's bonnets. There was also intense factionalism in the air because no one from Charleston, South Carolina, would concede Armstrong's superiority over their hometown boy, Jabbo. We musicians tried to tell the Charlestonians that while Jabbo was great, Louis was King. We

needn't have bothered. For weeks before the dance, arguments raged, bets were made, and, finally, the great moment came.

Smith played spectacularly, Stewart continued, "hitting high F's and G's and every time he'd fan that brass derby on a high F or G, his friends would yell, 'Play it, Jabbo! Go ahead, Rice!' " (Charlestonians routinely called each other "Rice"; it was a South Carolina nickname.) Then, Armstrong, "immaculate in a white suit," stormed on stage:

I've forgotten the tune but I'll never forget his first note. He blew a searing, soaring, altissimo, fantastic high note and held it long enough for every one of us musicians to grasp. Benny Carter, who has perfect pitch, said, "Damn! That's high F!" Louis never let up that night and . . . every time he'd take a break, the applause was thunderous, and swarms of women kept rushing the stand for his autograph. They handed him everything from programs to whiskey bottles to put his signature on. One woman even took off her pants and pleaded with him to sign them.

Louis Armstrong was now the greatest star in a music that had had no individual stars to speak of before him. Bandleaders had won a certain amount of fame, but individual soloists generally had not. People now paid to hear *him,* not his band, and he was venerated by musicians. "I'm very religious," Max Kaminsky once said. "I worship Louis Armstrong."

One Sunday evening in 1929, a delegation of white musicians who played downtown hotels and theaters and nightclubs trooped up to Connie's Inn to honor their hero at a dinner. Each of them had kicked in part of his earnings for an engraved gold watch, which Ben Pollack formally presented. It said, "Good Luck Always to Louis Armstrong from the Musicians on Broadway." In no other sphere of American life

Louis Armstrong, 1929

INTERVIEWER: What is jazz?

LOUIS ARMSTRONG: Jazz is what I play for a living.

in 1929 would such a ceremony have been held for a black person, in none other would the tribute have been so heartfelt, the love and respect been made so palpable, the recognition of a black artist's supremacy so unquestioned. Armstrong was delighted—and suggested they all play together after dinner: "And did we have a ball," he wrote years later. "My, my, my . . ."

THINGS CAN'T GO ON THIS WAY

"I guess I am a minus quality," Bix Beiderbecke wrote Frankie Trumbauer from his parents' home in Davenport in February of 1929. "I haven't had a drink for so long I'd pass on one." He complained of terrible pain in his knees that he blamed on his pneumonia, and begged for the loan of a little money and a new cornet so that he could practice. "I'll be back with you soon as my knees will work," he promised, "if Paul [Whiteman] will have me."

Whiteman welcomed him back in March, though his playing now seemed uncharacteristically listless. The orchestra spent a giddy summer at Universal Studios in Hollywood, where Whiteman saw to it that each of the thirty-five members of the band had the opportunity to buy his own brand-new Ford to drive around in. Other than play on the weekly Old Gold radio program, attend Hollywood parties, and spring practical jokes on one another, there was little else to occupy the musicians' time. They were supposed to be making a screen biography of their leader called *The King of Jazz,* but there was as yet no script. "With nothing to do, no commitments," a friend remembered Beiderbecke telling him, "the line of least resistance was to drink. He spoke with horror of the visions, snakes, animals, etc. [that *delirium tremens* caused him to experience]. Being disoriented and never wanting to go through it again."

Not long after the band finally got back to New York in September, the men assem-

LEON BIX BEIDERBECKE

Davenport Youth, Famed As Master of Trumpet Succumbs to Pneumonia

The Davenport (Iowa) *Democrat and Leader* announces the death of its local hero, Bix Beiderbecke, August 7, 1931.

bled in the studios of Columbia Records to record two new tunes. Bix made it through his eight-bar chorus on the first one, a ballad called "Waiting at the End of the Road." The second arrangement, "When You're Counting the Stars Alone," called for him to play another eight bars, but, although three folding chairs were lined up so that he could lie down and rest while the engineers got ready, in the end he was too weak even to try. Whiteman came to Beiderbecke's hotel room the next morning. "[Bix] was in bed," a friend remembered, "and told Paul he had been ill the previous day, but would be feeling better in a day or two. Paul took a step towards Bix and kicked an empty liquor bottle that was under the bed. Paul sat down on the bed and put his head in his hands, and said, 'Bix we've got to get you

straightened out, things can't go on this way.' " Whiteman finally told him to go home again; his job would be waiting for him whenever he thought he could handle it. But his drinking would have to stop.

On October 14, Bix Beiderbecke checked himself into the best-known alcoholism treatment center in America, the Keely Institute at Dwight, Illinois. Ten days later, on Thursday, October 24—"Black Thursday"—the stock market crashed, ushering in the Great Depression, ending forever the hectic, heedless Jazz Age Bix had seemed in part to embody. "The bottom," said *Variety,* "has dropped out of hilarity." Beiderbecke himself would die a little less than two years later at the age of twenty-nine, in the midst of yet another bout of *delirium tremens.* By then, the music he'd so loved to play would seem to be dying, too, overwhelmed by sweet dance music and sentimental crooners.

F. Scott Fitzgerald, who had given the vanished era its name, would also write its most eloquent epitaph:

Somebody had blundered and the most expensive orgy in history was over. . . .

Now once more the belt is tight and we summon the proper expression of horror as we look back on our wasted youth. Sometimes, though, there is a ghostly rumble among the drums, an asthmatic whisper in the trombones that swings me back into the early 'twenties, when we drank wood alcohol and every day in every way grew better and better, and there was an abortive shortening of the skirts, . . . and people you didn't want to know said, "Yes we have no bananas" . . . and it all seems rosy and romantic to us who were young then, because we will never feel quite so intensely about our surroundings any more.

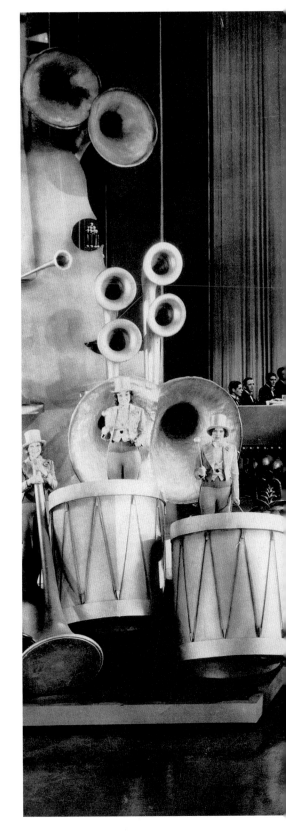

A still from the "Rhapsody in Blue" sequence from Hollywood's 1930 screen biography of Paul Whiteman, *The King of Jazz*. Much later, Whiteman wrote that the twenties had been "an era of wonderful nonsense . . . and I was a product of those times."

HARD, HARD TIMES

In 1928, the year before the Great Crash, Bessie Smith had recorded "Poor Man's Blues."

> *Mister rich man, rich man, open up your*
> *heart and mind*
> *Mister rich man, rich man, open up your*
> *heart and mind*
> *Give the poor man a chance, help stop*
> *these hard, hard times.*
> *Please listen to my pleadin', 'cause*
> *I can't stand these hard times long,*
> *Aw listen to my pleadin', 'cause I can't*
> *stand these hard times long,*
> *They'll make an honest man do things*
> *that you know is wrong. . . .*

She had been singing then about the plight of the people left behind by the prosperity of the

Andy Kirk's Clouds of Joy take time out along the road at Fort Smith, Arkansas, in 1929. Violinist Claude Williams kneels at the far left. Andy Kirk, second from the right, then still playing tuba, had only recently become leader. No band would work harder or travel more during the lean Depression years.

twenties. Now that the whole country was hurting, not even the blues seemed able to ease its pain. "Nobody wants to hear blues no more," Bessie Smith said. "Times is hard."

No crisis since the Civil War affected Americans more seriously than did the Great Depression. As the 1930s began, one out of every four wage-earners was without work, more than 15 million men and women. In Mississippi, on a single day in 1932, one quarter of the entire state went under the auctioneer's hammer. Thousands of jobless men wandered the landscape. Dust storms born in Texas and the Dakotas would soon begin to darken skies all the way east to Washington. Prices of wheat and corn and cotton fell so low that crops were left to rot in the fields. In Boston, children with cardboard soles in their shoes walked to school past silent shoe factories with padlocks on the doors. In New York, a jobless couple moved into a cave in Central Park and stayed there for a year. They could find nowhere else to live.

The music business came close to collapsing. Membership in the American Federation of Musicians fell by one third—even after their dues were cut in half, many musicians could no longer pay them. More than one hundred New York dance halls closed their doors and nearly half the theaters on Broadway were shut down or turned into movie houses. In Chicago, shivering jobless men burned old phonograph records to keep warm. American record companies, which had sold more than 100 million discs a year in the midtwenties, were soon selling just 6 million. Okeh, Gennett, and Paramount records all went out of business. The RCA Victor Talking Machine Company stopped making record players altogether for a time, and sold radios instead. Even Paul Whiteman had to lay off ten members of his thirty-man orchestra and ask the rest to take a 15 percent cut in pay.

"We . . . didn't realize how little chance we had in New York," Eddie Condon wrote. "The only place we could play was in our rooms, at our own request." He and Max Kaminsky were eventually locked out of their hotel in midwinter for failing to pay their rent. "We gnawed at each other's wrists," Condon recalled. "We bled to death in those years." When Kaminsky was finally lucky enough to land a job, he found himself running his own breadline every evening, passing out fifty-cent pieces to musicians less fortunate than he.

Hard times hit black Americans hardest. In some northern cities, six out of ten African-American workers lost their jobs. Poor southern migrants continued to come north, crowding into neighborhoods already packed with people, competing for the fast-dwindling number of jobs. Black businesses failed, crushing the entrepreneurial spirit that had been an essential element of the Negro Renaissance. The collapse of a black-owned bank in Chicago took with it all the savings of the musician's union's black local.

Harlem would never recover, but its speakeasies and dance halls, nightclubs and ballrooms continued to flourish for a time, as black residents and white visitors alike sought ways to forget their troubles, at least for an evening. The Cotton Club remained Harlem's most glamorous nightclub. But the community's biggest and most beautiful ballroom was the Savoy. It covered a whole city block on Lenox Avenue between 140th and 141st Streets, employed two bands at once so that the music need never stop, and was so popular with dancers that its maple-and-mahogany floor had to be replaced every three years. Just fifty cents on weeknights—seventy-five cents on Sundays—the Savoy billed itself as "the Home of Happy Feet." All the best bands appeared there. So did Harlem's most admired dancers. George "Shorty" Snowden was on the floor nearly every night. It was he who in 1928 had come up with the new dance filled with improvised "breakaways"—flinging his partner out and improvising solo steps before bringing her back again—which came to be called the lindy hop after the hero of the hour, Charles Lindbergh. Snowden's friendly rival, George "Twist Mouth" Ganaway, was also a constant presence; his long legs, spectacular dancing, and distinctive ensemble—blinding white from his shoes to the broad-brimmed hat he never took off—all helped distract lookers-on from the disfigurement that had prompted his

Music helped lift the spirits of a sharecropper's family in rural Louisiana during the Depression.

Chick Webb at work. "This man," the great drummer Jo Jones said of him, "taught me something that I had almost forgotten. He taught me how important the drum was."

Norma and Dorothy Miller, newcomers to Harlem

nickname. Snowden and Ganaway had staked out the northeast corner of the Savoy for themselves and the handful of dancers they thought worthy of appearing alongside them. They called it the Cat's Corner—and any fumble-footed amateur who foolishly persisted in intruding into it was liable to have one of the elect dance by and casually shatter his ankle with a kick. Savoy dancers were *serious*.

In the cold winter of 1929, Zalama Miller, a widow from Barbados, and her two daughters, Norma and Dot, had been forced to move out of their apartment across 142nd Street from the Cotton Club. As a little girl, Norma had loved dancing on the sidewalk to the music of Duke Ellington as it spilled out through the windows—the Charleston and the black bottom, the shimmy and the shim sham. But her mother could no longer come up with the rent.

Their new home was a third-floor flat on 140th Street, smaller than their old one but directly behind the Savoy. Norma Miller never forgot how it was to live within hearing of some of the finest music in the city.

The windows was wide open and so the music blasted right into our living room. Every night we heard this marvelous music. And, in those days, in the summer, the fire escape was where you sat to be cool. There was no air conditioning, nowhere. And our fire escape faced the back windows of the Savoy Ballroom, and you'd see shadows when people danced past the windows, figures dancing to that music. And my sister and I would respond to what we saw in the windows of the Savoy, and we would get into the living room and dance to some of the best bands in the world.

For months, Norma listened to the music and dreamed of going inside. Then, on Easter Sunday in 1931, she got her chance. She was twelve years old.

You know in those days, you always had a little new outfit to go out to church. Four o'clock, there's a matinee going to be at the Savoy Ballroom. After church I dashed up to Lenox Avenue. The people that went into the Savoy were sharp and we used to just stand outside to watch them. That's what I was doing. We started dancing outside the Savoy Ballroom and I heard somebody say to me, "Hey kid!" And I turned around and he said, "You, you." I recognized immediately who it was. It was the great Twist Mouth George in a white hat, white suit, white everything. Asking me, "Would you come and dance?" I said, "Would I!?" He grabbed me, we dashed up the stairs and I don't know whether I hit each step, 'cause he had such long legs. And I remember just flying up those stairs with him and you go through these doors and I think it was the most beautiful place I'd ever seen in my life, the reds and the greens and blues. And you turned around from the door, and that was the first time I ever saw a band on a bandstand. I mean, I'd been seeing the shadows and I'm so excited. He took me over in the corner and sat me down and brought me a Coke and said, "You sit here, and I'll come and get you." And finally, he came and got me—and I'll never forget that—he said, "Let's go!" And they hit that music, all I know is he just, he just threw me out. . . . My feet never touched the ground. The people were screaming and he put me on top of his shoulders, walked me around the Ballroom and the people is clapping and talking about Twist Mouth and he took me right around to the front, right outside, and put me back outside. . . . Greatest moment in my life! And I'm excited, and I'm going to go home and tell my mother and my sister . . . and then I said, "No, I better not say nothin!"

At roughly the same time, another young would-be dancer named Frankie Manning and five of his friends eagerly climbed the same stairs in search of the same excitement. Born in Florida and brought to New York by his mother as a small boy, Manning had yearned to see the Savoy for himself.

As we're climbing up the steps, I could hear this music coming down. And we started [saying], "Oh man! You hear that music? Wow!!" And we walked through the door . . . and we turned 'round. As you come up the steps, when you come through the doors, your back is to the bandstand. So, you turn around . . . and then you face the band, and as I turn around . . . the floor was full with people. And it looked like everyone on the floor was doing the Lindy Hop. Everybody was just bouncing up and down and the music was romping and stomping and

This 1932 cartoon, lovingly drawn by E. Simms Campbell and reprinted in African-American newspapers all over the country, only hints at the sheer density of music in Depression-era Harlem. The Sunday Matinee Club membership card at the right got eager young dancers into the Savoy Ballroom at a special rate.

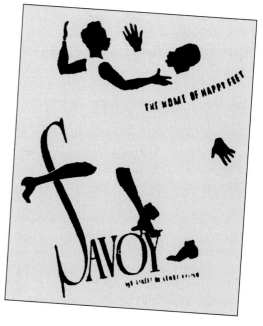

we . . . started looking at each other, "Hey, man, you hear this music! Look at all these people in this place dancing and jumpin'!" And the floor was, oh, . . . looked like the floor was getting into the mood of the dance, 'cause the floor was just bouncing up and down, you know, and the people were bouncing up and down and Chick Webb was on the bandstand wailing. Boy, it was just such a wonderful time in our life to come up there as youngsters and be exposed to this kind of music. Oh, wow!

Chick Webb, the man who most often made that kind of music at the Savoy, was born

with a hunchback, stood less than four feet tall, and lived all his life in constant pain. He was, as *Down Beat* crudely put it, "deformed, dwarfish, and delicate." But, his friend and sometime publicist Helen Oakley remembered, "self-pity was completely foreign to him." And, while he never learned to read music, he made himself into the most innovative drummer of his time. He could be explosive: "When he really let go," said Gene Krupa, "you had a feeling that the entire atmosphere . . . was being changed." But he also brought to the drums a new melodic conception; his breaks and solos were musical as well as exciting. Webb's body was so diminutive that when he stood up to play, as he sometimes did, fully half his height was hidden behind his big bass drum, but he had long arms, his hands and feet were outsized, his wrists and ankles were like iron, and he was a master showman. No one who ever saw him employ his especially slender sticks to whip his band along or watched him drive it using just his feet—while grinning and holding his motionless hands in the air—would ever forget it. "Before Chick," Doc Cheatham said, "drummers were essentially time-keepers." Webb was shy and amiable offstage, but once the "Little Giant" was seated behind his drums on the larger of the Savoy's two bandstands, it took a brave bandleader to dare lay claim to the other one. "He would just lay for other bands to come up there," the trombonist Dicky Wells remembered. "Ain't nobody," Webb told his men over and over again, "gonna cut me or my band."

AN END IN ITSELF

As the Depression settled in and more and more people found themselves without work or even the prospect of work, Duke Ellington continued to prosper. "We worked clean through the Depression," one band member said, "without even knowing there was one." Thanks to records and live broadcasts from the Cotton Club, Ellington was fast becoming one of the best-known bandleaders in America. And, backed by Irving Mills's relentless campaign to promote him as a serious artist, not merely an entertainer, he was also moving into worlds from which black entertainers had generally been barred. The band continued to play two shows nightly at the Cotton Club, but it also appeared onstage downtown as part of Florenz Ziegfeld's *Showgirl* revue. When Ellington's piano teacher from Washington, Miss Marietta Clinkscales, learned that her pupil was playing on Broadway she traveled to New York to see him, proudly fluttering her handkerchief from the mezzanine. Then, the French music hall star

Maurice Chevalier asked Ellington to play for his New York debut. The first half of the show was an hour-long concert by the Ellington orchestra and, according to Sonny Greer, the crowd was so loudly enthusiastic about their music on opening night that Chevalier tried to come on early for fear he would be overshadowed. Two weeks at the Palace followed. Ellington's was the first black orchestra ever featured at the nation's premier vaudeville house and was "the hit of the show," according to *Variety:* "his standing among the colored race in modern music is relative to that of the late Jim Europe."

"Of all our band leaders [Ellington] best succeeds in making jazz seem an end in itself," said a critic for the New York *Herald-Tribune,* "and not merely an invitation to dance." The effort Mills and Ellington were jointly making to present Ellington's music as dignified and distinctive was clearly paying off. And they had still bigger plans. In the summer of 1930, Mills arranged for the band to travel to Hollywood and appear in an RKO comedy called *Check and Double Check.* Its stars were Freeman Gosden and Charles Correll, veteran blackface comics who had made themselves the most popular radio performers in America playing *Amos 'n' Andy.* The

Duke Ellington in Hollywood, 1930

show's story line was supposed to be more or less up-to-date—its genial but dimwitted protagonists were Georgia-born African-Americans who had come north to Chicago's South Side to run a single-cab taxi company—but its humor harked back to the earliest days of the minstrel show. Five nights a week at seven p.m., the whole country stopped to listen to them. President Herbert Hoover's aides had orders not to disturb him when the program was on; factories rearranged their shifts so that workers wouldn't miss it; there were already

Duke Ellington flanked by his orchestra, 1930. First row, left to right, Freddie Jenkins, Charles "Cootie" Williams, and Arthur Whetsel (trumpets); Harry Carney, Johnny Hodges, and Barney Bigard (reeds). Second row, Joe "Tricky Sam" Nanton and Juan Tizol (trombones); Sonny Greer (drums); Fred Guy (guitar); Wellman Braud (bass)

Amos 'n' Andy records and an *Amos 'n' Andy* comic strip. Now, the duo was going to try the movies, and wanted to work with a black cast to lend authentic onscreen "atmosphere." "What irony!" Ellington's old friend Otto Hardwick would mutter some years later. "Couple of ofays put on black-face and win popularity for Negroes, give Negroes jobs. What irony!"

No irony was ever lost on Duke Ellington. But the stereotypical world of *Amos 'n' Andy* held no fears for him—he had already

transcended the strange expectations white patrons brought with them to the Cotton Club, after all—and he saw his Hollywood offer as the chance of a lifetime. In a world in which the roles usually offered to black performers were menials and buffoons, he and his men were being asked simply to be themselves onscreen.

There were twelve men in the band that traveled west that summer, all of them specialists in being themselves; that was the

profoundly American premise underlying all of Ellington's music. "The music," he said, "must be molded to the men." Only six of them had been with him when he opened at the Cotton Club. The rhythm section remained the same: Ellington himself at the piano; Freddie Guy on guitar; Sonny Greer still perched amid the most impressive set of drums and cymbals and bells and tympani in the country—three thousand dollars worth, he liked to boast; and bassist Wellman Braud driving the band with the same kind of big, clearly articulated New Orleans swing that Steve Brown had provided for Jean Goldkette: "When you got ready to blow a chorus," Ellington recalled, "Mr. Braud would already have established so compelling a beat that you could not miss."

Joe "Tricky Sam" Nanton had replaced Charlie Irvis on trombone by the time the band made its Cotton Club debut. A soft-spoken New Yorker of Caribbean descent, he had mastered Bubber Miley's growl and plunger skills and brought to them an emotional depth at least equal to Miley's own. "What [Nanton] was . . . doing," Ellington remembered, "was playing a very highly personalized form of his West Indian heritage. When a guy comes here from the West Indies and is asked to play some jazz, he plays what *he* thinks it is, or what comes from his applying himself to the idiom." Nanton would remain with Ellington until his own death, in 1946. Ellington's new section-mate, valve trombonist Juan Tizol, would stay still longer—a total of more than twenty years in two stints. Tall and bespectacled, a disciplined, classically trained musician from Puerto Rico, he was valued not for his improvisational skills—he claimed none—but for the apparent effortlessness of his playing, the beauty of his tone, and the emotional power he brought to stating the melody.

Max Kaminsky's Boston schoolmate Harry Carney had been just seventeen when he began his forty-six-year career with the Ellington band. Hired to play clarinet and alto saxophone, he soon turned to the baritone, and with his lyricism and huge, tumbling sound was already helping to transform it into a solo instrument—and an irreplaceable element of Duke Ellington's music. Now, he shared the reed section with two ardent admirers of Sidney Bechet: the Creole clarinetist Barney Bigard, who had his own version of the warm, woody New Orleans tone Ellington so admired; and a shy young Bostonian named Johnny Hodges, who would soon become one of the greatest alto saxophonists in jazz history, a mas-

Harry Carney, seen here in 1935, anchored Duke Ellington's orchestra for nearly half a century.

ter melodist with a tone so warm, so soulful, so seductive that one musician's wife begged her husband never to leave her alone with him; whenever she heard Johnny Hodges play, she confessed, she wanted "to open up the bedroom door."

There were three trumpet players now, and Bubber Miley, who had given the band its first instantly recognizable voice, was gone. He had started to drink heavily at the Cotton Club, and could no longer be counted on to turn up on time, or to be capable of playing well once he got there. Shortly before the band had begun broadcasting nationally, Ellington sadly let him go. His replacement was eighteen-year-old Charles "Cootie" Williams from Mobile, Alabama, who also became a master of the growl and brought to the band something of Louis Armstrong's style and passion. Freddie Jenkins, a graduate of Wilberforce University, was picked both for his musicianship

and for the flashy showmanship that won him the nickname "Little Posey." "He brought us a new kind of sparkle," Ellington said. "Even a cliché in his solos had an extra unique flair, a personality play." Arthur Whetsel, a Washington, D.C., minister's son and sometime medical student, was an old friend of Ellington's. Dignified, well-informed, and "aware of all the Negro individuals who were contributing to the cause by *commanding respect*," Ellington said, Whetsel played with such sweetness and refinement that he could evoke "big ole tears" from his listeners.

Like Frank Holliday's Washington, D.C., poolroom where the youthful Ellington first understood that "all levels could and should meet," Ellington's band would always be a gathering place for musicians of every class and kind. College men and school dropouts shared the Ellington bandstand, northerners and southerners, authentic New Orleanians and northern admirers of the New Orleans sound. Each was chosen because of his own distinctive voice; all would add luster to Duke Ellington's.

"Hollywood was fun," Sonny Greer remembered. Movie stars from other soundstages asked to hear their favorite tunes between scenes; there was plenty of time after hours to make the rounds of L.A. nightclubs; and excerpts from three numbers and a virtually unedited performance of "Old Man Blues" were included in *Check and Double Check*—and the latter became a hit record. Ellington cooperated cheerfully enough with the studio publicity department, posing for photographs that showed him implausibly standing on a chair to rehearse his men in the middle of a parking lot, grinning as he fled from a gaggle of beautiful dancers, even sitting at the wheel of a battered topless taxicab with the name of Amos 'n' Andy's fictional company—Fresh Air Taxicab Co. of America Incorpulated—scrawled on the side. Not even the timidity of studio executives, who insisted that the Creole Barney Bigard and Juan Tizol from

Puerto Rico be blacked-up for the cameras, so that the sensibilities of white southern moviegoers would not be offended, seems to have done much to spoil his mood.

The film died at the box office. Moviegoers found seeing as well as hearing Amos 'n' Andy disconcerting. Whatever the pair sounded like on the radio, onscreen they were unmistakably just two middle-aged white men in greasepaint. They would never make another movie. But Ellington knew that no other black bandleader had ever been given such a showcase, that Americans—all kinds of Americans—had seen him as he really was—handsome, elegant, dignified, and swinging.

Albert Murray, then still a schoolboy in Alabama, remembered in conversation with an interviewer how much Ellington was already beginning to mean to him:

When you saw the first pictures of Ellington he was very good looking, very hip, very well-dressed. You not only saw him on the entertainment pages of the Chicago *Defender,* the Pittsburgh *Courier,* the *Afro-American,* the Kansas City *Call,* you also saw him in magazines, very serious magazines like *Crisis,* which was the organ of the NAACP and *Opportunity* which was the organ of the Urban League. . . . Then, you also saw Duke Ellington in the movies and he was in top hat and tails. . . . And he was always serious. He had all this glamor-boy appearance, but the music had everything. It was as earthy as anybody else. Nobody could do blues pieces any better. Bessie Smith herself could hardly sing the blues better than Johnny Hodges could play the blues. So he transmuted everything, and people early on started saying, "Ah, you know, this is classical, this is classical." So that one of the interesting ironies about Ellington, is when he and his band would come to town, half the people

Duke Ellington: "I am trying to play the natural feelings of a people. . . . Some of the music which has been written will always be beautiful and immortal. Beethoven, Wagner and Bach are geniuses; no one can rob their work of the merit that is due it, but these men have not portrayed the people who are about us today, and the interpretation of these people is our future music."

would not dance, because as much as these particular people in this idiom love to dance, and as obvious as it is that this is dance-oriented music from the beginning—the whole conception is based on percussive dance-oriented statements—these people were so impressed with what Ellington was doing to the music that they'd dress up and just sit, and Duke wanted them to dance too. But people would say, "Yes, well I'll buy the record and dance to that at home but he's *present*." So, people anticipated him coming to town. It was like a sacred event.

As Ellington's fame grew, so did his popularity with women. He regarded them all as "flowers," his sister Ruth recalled, and they "fell on their faces in front of him." All of which angered his wife, Edna, and, when she discovered he was having an affair with a dancer at the Cotton Club, she slashed his cheek. He would carry the scar for the rest of his life, and deflected everyone who dared asked him about it. "Oh this?" he replied to one brash television interviewer much later in his life. "I have three stories. Taxi accident. What's the other one? Oh, Heidelberg. Heidelberg, you know—old Heidelberg. And sabers. You know, you stand toe-to-toe and the first one to move back loses? So, if you don't move back, you get the scar. . . . Then there's another one, too. I can't think of it at the moment. More personal."

Ellington and his wife never divorced, but they would never live together again, either. In 1931, he sent for his father and mother and sister to join him, his son, and his new love, a Cotton Club dancer named Mildred Dixon, in a big new apartment at 381 Edgecombe Avenue, in Harlem's best neighborhood, Sugar Hill. His father was reluctant at first—like Benny Goodman's father, he did not like the idea of living off his son—but his mother came right away. In Daisy Ellington's eyes, her son could do no wrong. Soon, she was happily cleaning

and cooking for him again, and longing for the moment each evening when he walked in the door and announced, "Mother, I'm home to dine." Ellington showered her with gifts and refused to listen to her protests at his extravagance: "Mother," he said, "if you don't take these things, I won't work." She received ropes of pearls, a fur coat, and a chauffeur-driven Pierce-Arrow so that she could follow her son from engagement to engagement. "After a couple of thousand people had stopped applauding," his sister remembered, "my mother was still applauding."

AIN'T THAT SOMETHING?

"Chicago's own Louis Armstrong and his orchestra are the current rage in New York," the columnist Dave Peyton assured the readers of the Chicago *Defender* early in 1929. "They have taken the city by storm." Armstrong was headlining in Harlem *and* playing on Broadway now, and his recordings were bringing him a still-broader audience. The breakthrough had been his version of a Jimmy McHugh–Dorothy Fields love song, "I Can't Give You Anything But Love." He had been playing such tunes in person for years—Art Hodes remembered having heard him improvise for thirty minutes on Noel Coward's "Poor Little Rich Girl" back at the Chicago Savoy— but black performers were only rarely given standard pop songs to sing on records. Soon, Louis Armstrong would record scores of such tunes—"Ain't Misbehavin'," "Stardust," "Some of These Days," "When You're Smiling," "Rockin' Chair," "Body and Soul" —transforming each into something altogether new, altogether his. In the process, he would revolutionize American singing, just as he had revolutionized instrumental jazz. He brought scatting into mainstream music; altered melodies and shifted rhythms to suit his own purposes; infused the most inane lyrics with honest feeling; and

brought to singing the same irrepressible sense of swing that had already changed forever the way instrumentalists approached their music. "Louis Armstrong," said Bing Crosby, "is the beginning—and the end—of American music."

He was a single act now. He had lost his job at Connie's Inn after his men failed once too often to turn up on time, and had then decided, under Tommy Rockwell's prodding, finally to break up the band and move out on his own.

Among the first Broadway tunes he had recorded was Fats Waller's "Black and Blue," originally written for *Hot Chocolates* as a complaint by a dark-skinned woman about her man's preference for lighter-skinned rivals. Armstrong transformed it, without a hint of self-pity, into a song about being black in a world run by whites. "In those days if one black man called another man 'black' that was fighting words," Arvell Shaw, Armstrong's bassist later in life, remembered. "But Louis was the first man I heard to say, 'You're black, be proud of it. You're black, you're not white, you're not yellow, you're black—be *proud* of it.' He was saying that when it was so very unpopular."

Armstrong was proud of his race, but unblinking about the reality of race relations in America. When a friend in California suggested that he come west on his own and try his luck in Los Angeles, he was initially apprehensive: "Naturally in those days," he wrote much later, "the minute a colored man gets off a train anywhere west or south he would have his head whipped worse than a kettle drum." But Armstrong went anyway and quickly found himself a hero in Los Angeles, just as he had been in Chicago and New York. He spent nearly a year there, fronting Les Hite's band at Frank Sebastian's New Cotton Club in Culver City, getting to know the movie stars who dropped in every night from the MGM studio lot right next door, and impressing West Coast musicians precisely as he had thrilled

Before the fall: Louis Armstrong in Culver City, 1930. Armstrong stands next to the owner of the New Cotton Club, Frank Sebastian, and the director of the band that backed him there, Les Hite. Lionel Hampton, then Hite's drummer, is third from the left.

their eastern counterparts. "Aspirants for Louis' coveted title" of trumpet king, reported a correspondent for the Pittsburgh *Courier,* "have sat around the Cotton Club night after night trying to figure out how the dark boys do it. Some of them are getting pretty good, but every time they think they have stolen his thunder Louis comes up with a brand-new lead." The trombonist Lawrence Brown remembered that "People used to come from way up around Seattle to hear him. Every trumpet player at that time tried

to play *one* of his choruses." There were more memorable recordings, too—including "Sweethearts on Parade," "I'm a Ding-Dong Daddy," "I'm Confessin', " "If I Could Be with You," "Shine," "Memories of You," "Just a Gigolo," and "Blue Yodel No. 9," on which he played obbligatos behind and around the vocal by the "singing brakeman," Jimmie Rodgers, demonstrating how closely allied are the blues and country-and-western traditions—a fact largely ignored by enthusiasts for both musics until Ray

Charles revealed the truth of it again more than three decades later.

Then, potential disaster struck. *Variety* reported the bare facts in March 1931.

Vic Berton, drummer with Abe Lyman's Band, and Louis Armstrong, colored trumpet artist in Sebastian's Cotton Club in Culver City, were arrested at the Cotton Club by narcotics officers and arraigned on charges of possessing marijuana, a dopeweed

In the lobby of the Royal Theater in Baltimore, Louis Armstrong distributes free coal to an unidentified woman, 1931. His manager, Johnny Collins, on the right, made sure his star got plenty of publicity out of his largesse, but Armstrong's generosity was genuine. "I came up through life the hard way just like those folks," he said. "And they made it their business to come backstage and thank me—of course, it caused me to stick out my chest with pride." The inscription on this copy of the photograph was written to the clarinetist Milton "Mezz" Mezrow, who supplied Armstrong and a good many other musicians with marijuana.

used in cigarettes. . . . Charge against them is a felony punishable by not less than six months and no more than six years in the penitentiary.

Armstrong had been an enthusiastic "viper" —marijuana-user—since returning to Chicago from New York in 1925. To him, pot was "an assistant, a friend, [and] a nice cheap drunk," safer than alcohol and akin to the natural herbs and grasses with which his mother had fed and cured him as a boy. Vic Berton had been sitting in with Armstrong's band at the New Cotton Club that evening—the former drummer with Bix Beiderbecke's Wolverines, he was so good that the band's young drummer, Lionel Hampton, had turned over his sticks to him the minute he walked in—and at intermission the two old friends had walked out into the parking lot to light up.

At that point, two policemen closed in, confiscated the evidence, and took them both into custody. Armstrong, with vivid memories of his own boyhood encounters with the New Orleans police, worried he would be beaten on the way to the station house and asked the officers not to "hit me in the 'chops.' " They turned out to be fans, and one told him that they would never even have been arrested had an envious bandleader playing nearby not turned them in.

Armstrong faced six months in jail and a thousand-dollar fine. As soon as Tommy Rockwell got word of his star's arrest, he dispatched a thug named Johnny Collins to see what he could do to get Armstrong out of jail. No one is sure what happened next. Some claimed that Collins used underworld connections to influence the judge. Vic Berton's brother, Ralph, suggested that it

was actually his brother's boss, Abe Lyman, who exercised political pull. In any case, Armstrong and Berton were given suspended sentences and released. "I went to work that night," Armstrong recalled, and "wailed—just like nothing happened. . . . I laughed real loud when several movie stars came up to the bandstand while we played a dance set and told me they thought 'marijuana' was a chick . . . that really fractured me!"

Armstrong left California for Chicago a few days later. Collins traveled with him and at some point evidently told Armstrong that Tommy Rockwell was no longer interested in acting as his manager. Armstrong signed on with Collins, instead. Nothing seemed to have changed since his release from the Waif's Home or the New Orleans Parish Prison. "If you didn't have a white captain to back you in the old days—to put his hand on your shoulder—you was just a damn sad nigger," he explained many years later. "If a Negro had the proper white man to reach the law and say, 'What the hell do you mean locking up MY nigger?' Then—quite naturally—the law would walk him free. Get in that jail *without* your white boss, and yonder comes the chain gang!"

Armstrong played a triumphant homecoming engagement at the Regal Theater, then took a ten-man band made up mostly of New Orleans musicians into a new West Side black-and-tan called the Showboat. There, new trouble started. Collins had lied to Armstrong: Rockwell had never intended to drop him; he still believed himself Armstrong's manager and in fact had signed him up for a return engagement at Connie's Inn in Harlem. Armstrong wasn't interested. He had not forgotten that Connie Immerman had fired him and his band the year before. "I did not want any part of those people ever again," he wrote. "I am just that way. If you kick my ass once you can bet I won't come back if I can help it so you can kick it again. . . . Connie's Inn was going down by degrees and at that time I was the Rage of the Nation."

But neither Rockwell—nor Connie Immerman's silent partner, Dutch Schultz—liked to be disappointed. First, two thugs tried and failed to shake Armstrong down. "We were just trying to get him to change managers," one of them told the policeman who arrested him. Then, someone started a fight in front of the bandstand. A woman was knocked senseless with a chair. Armstrong just kept playing. "Things like that never frighten me," he said. "I've seen so much of that bullshit during my days of playing music." Finally, a man with a revolver turned up in his dressing room. Armstrong was going to play Connie's Inn, the man insisted, and he was going to leave for New York the next day. Then, he marched Armstrong to a phone booth, where the voice of someone in New York—Armstrong later said he recognized it but would never tell anyone who it was—warned him not to fail to be on the morning train.

To get the menacing voice off the phone—and the gunman out of his dressing room—Armstrong said he'd be on it. He didn't mean it: "I ain't goin' to New York," he told Collins. "But get this straight—I ain't staying in Chicago neither. I'd rather take a walk through the cemetery at midnight." Instead, he and his band boarded a bus headed south the next morning. Behavior like that—open defiance of mobsters—at first seems out of character for the infinitely agreeable Louis Armstrong whom audiences thought they knew for nearly half a century. Max Kaminsky saw deeper, to the steel within.

This roly, rotund brown-skinned man with his marvelously expressive face, the comfortable broad-nostriled snub nose, the lips scarred from all that blowing, the wise, knowing, and innocent eyes, radiates warmth and energy like a cozy fireplace. But unaffected and unphony as he is, Louis has always been King. The white people didn't know about him for a long while, but he always had an enor-

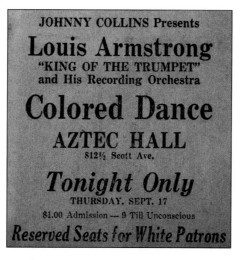

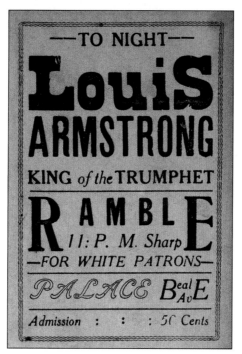

On Armstrong's 1931 tour of the Deep South white patrons were welcome at the dance heralded in the newspaper notice at the top—but only to watch. In Memphis, Tennessee (above), whites alone were allowed on the floor.

mous following among the colored people right from the start. He was always regal; from the very beginning, the musicians, colored and white, always came to *him,* and he'd hold court wherever he happened to be—

backstage at a theater or night club, between takes at a recording studio, or soaking in a steaming tub in his hotel bathroom. . . . Louis knows who he is. Not only that, he knows who you are, and though he is the most approachable, most genuine person in the world, and though his charity is legendary, you can't mess with Louis. . . . [His] trumpet comes first—that's Louis's first law. To him his playing is a gift, and he'll just sit there and think about the horn before he gets ready to play—accepting his gift he calls it. . . . Louis has never forgotten what he wants to do—just play that music—and in doing that he has done everything.

In June of 1931, Collins booked Armstrong into New Orleans. He hadn't been back to his hometown for nine years and wasn't sure what kind of reception he would get, but when his train pulled into the same station from which he had left to join Joe Oliver in Chicago, a huge cheering crowd and eight marching bands, led by his old neighborhood friends from the Zulu Social Aid and Pleasure Club, were waiting on the platform. "All in all," Armstrong recalled years later, "I think that day was the happiest day in my life."

He visited the Colored Waif's Home, where he had learned to play the cornet as a boy, delighted in a "Louis Armstrong Special" cigar specially manufactured in his honor, and outfitted a baseball team, Louis Armstrong's Secret Nine.

He had a three-month contract to play at the Suburban Gardens, a big restaurant on the edge of town with its own live radio program. Only whites were allowed inside, and several who had played with Armstrong as boys greeted him warmly. But some ten thousand blacks gathered along the riverbank in the darkness to hear their hero play through the open windows. And when the broadcaster who was supposed to act as master of ceremonies muttered

HOMECOMING

"The last of the magnolias were still on the trees, the smell of them on the air," Louis Armstrong remembered, when he returned to New Orleans in the spring of 1931. But it had been nine years since he'd gone north to join King Oliver and he wondered if people "had forgotten me in all the time I'd been away. But I soon found they had not. . . . As soon as I got off the train the crowd went crazy. They picked me up and put me on their shoulders and started a parade down the center of Canal Street. . . . My, my it is a wonderful feeling to go back to your home town and find that while you were away you have become a big man."

(Top, left) Louis Armstrong, mobbed by old friends and new fans in front of the Astoria Hotel at Rampart and Gravier Streets in the heart of the neighborhood in which he'd spent his boyhood. Armstrong is the blurred but grinning figure in the open collar standing at the left. (Bottom, left) Captain Peter Jones, the man who ran the Colored Waif's Home, welcomes back his institution's most celebrated inmate. (Below) A special five-cent cigar rushed onto the market in New Orleans just in time for its namesake's arrival

(Opposite, top left) Armstrong and the pianist in his band, Charlie Alexander, clowning at the WSMB microphone during their three-month engagement at the Suburban Gardens. (Opposite, right) Armstrong's Secret Nine, and its proud sponsor. Most of the players were fellow members of the Zulu Social Aid and Pleasure Club and their win/loss record was said to have been damaged by their reluctance to dirty their splendid white uniforms by sliding. (Opposite, bottom) Armstrong, center, and the members of his orchestra sit in with the latest version of the outfit that gave him his start—now renamed the Municipal Boys Home Band. Peter Davis, the band manager who had once thought Armstrong unfit to join its ranks, stands at the far right.

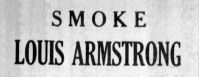

SMOKE
LOUIS ARMSTRONG

SPECIAL

Best 5c Hand Made Cigar
On The Market

LOUIS ARMSTRONG SPECIAL

into the microphone, "I just haven't the heart to announce that nigger on the radio," Armstrong did the honors himself, while the crowd cheered. "For the rest of that gig," he remembered, "I did my own radio announcing. That was the first time a Negro ever *spoke* on the radio down there. That other announcer? They threw him out the same night . . . ain't that something?"

Later that summer, Armstrong toured the South by bus. Johnny Collins and his wife rode along to help ease tensions over the segregation they encountered everywhere. In Memphis, Tennessee, the driver of a bus Collins had hired refused to carry the band once he saw that its members were black. The police were called. "Well now," Armstrong recalled, "one of the musicians was smoking a cigarette in a long fancy holder and this somehow didn't please the man, and he kept looking at my trumpet man, Zilner Randolph, who had some sort of French beret on. Zilner began to make it pretty clear that he wasn't standing for any of this shit." Then, the police spotted Collins's wife talking to Armstrong. It was more than they could stand. " 'Why don't you shoot him in the leg?' one officer asked another. More policemen arrived and most of the men were arrested. "We *need* more cotton-pickers down here," the officers said.

The desk sergeant who locked them up was even more belligerent. "You ain't gonna come down to Memphis and try to run the city," he said. "We'll kill all you niggers." When Armstrong's cell-mate, his valet "Professor" Sherman Cook, whispered that he was carrying "a great big joint all neatly wrapped," his boss said, "We can't be in any more trouble than we are in right now" and smoked away all the evidence—or so he later liked to remember. That same night, the manager of the Palace Theater, where they were booked, bailed out Armstrong and his men on the condition that they play over the radio for free to advertise his theater. When the broadcast began, Armstrong announced that he wanted to dedicate his first tune to the Memphis police department, then kicked off one of his most recent hits—"I'll Be Glad When You're Dead You Rascal You." Policemen pushed toward the bandstand. Armstrong braced for an attack. But the officers just wanted to thank him. "You're the only band that ever dedicated a tune [to us]," one of them said. Armstrong went right on singing.

OUT OF STYLE

On November 4, 1931, while Louis Armstrong continued his tour of the South, Buddy Bolden died of heart disease behind the walls of the Louisiana State Insane Asylum at Jackson. He was fifty-four years old. A quarter of a century earlier he had been the most celebrated cornet player in New Orleans—*King* Bolden—master of every kind of music—ragtime, waltzes, polkas, the blues—and among the first ever to perform the soulful amalgam called jazz. But he had been institutionalized ever since his nervous breakdown in 1907. His mother was now dead; his sister did not have the five dollars needed for a proper burial; and when the time came to escort his coffin to potters' field in New Orleans there was no marching band to play him home as he had played so many home in the old days.

Most of the New Orleans musicians who had once marched with him had passed on or moved elsewhere and were suffering, along with the rest of the country. The trombonist Kid Ory was in California, raising chickens. Johnny Dodds drove a taxi in Chicago and his brother Baby sometimes worked for a bag of groceries instead of cash. By the time Joe Oliver left Chicago for New York, he discovered, Louis Armstrong said, that "everyone was [already] playing him." He lost engagements because he refused to accept the lower fees club owners were now offering, and eventually found himself playing one-nighters through the South, best known as the onetime employer of Louis Armstrong.

Victor dropped Jelly Roll Morton from its roster. For better or worse, Armstrong's singular genius had tipped the balance toward the individual soloist and away from the exuberant collective polyphony both he and Morton had grown up with in New Orleans. Morton lost his bus, his trunks of finery, most of his diamonds. He called New York "this cruel city," and began to blame his decline on a West Indian voodoo curse. Younger musicians sometimes taunted him now

Jelly Roll Morton sets some musicians straight in front of the Manhattan Rhythm Club in a photograph by Danny Barker.

when he drove up to the Manhattan Rhythm Club, but he continued to insist that he was still "the master. *Anything* you play on your horn, you're playing Jelly Roll." "Some people thought he was old-fashioned," the guitarist Lawrence Lucie remembered, "but he was greater than we all thought he was. He'd been ahead of his time for a long time before times caught up to him."

Sidney Bechet had left Paris just as the Depression began, having done his time in a French prison for his shoot-out. He worked in Berlin for a time, then came home to America to join a big band led by Noble Sissle. Bechet hated ensemble playing, loathed the bright red jackets the men were sometimes made to wear, quit when Sissle wouldn't pay him as much as he was sure he was worth, and then found it hard to find other work. There were few jobs anywhere now, and most bandleaders insisted that musicians be able to read, as well as play—something Bechet still stubbornly refused to learn to do. He got a job at The Nest in Harlem, only to be fired for drinking and brawling, and found himself treated with less than reverence by the younger musicians with whom he played after hours: "It wasn't that Bechet wasn't playing good," the trumpeter Roy Eldridge remembered. "He was. But saxophone players like Coleman Hawkins and Benny Carter were attracting the attention of all the young cats, and those youngsters just weren't interested in anything that had happened earlier."

Finally, he and an old friend, the trumpet player Tommy Ladnier, formed their own sextet to play the kind of music they loved best. But when they opened at the Savoy, billed as "Ladnier and Bechet's New Orleans Feetwarmers—Dixie's Hottest Band—the Newest Note in Blazing Jazz" —the crowds were disappointing. Lindy hoppers found it hard to dance to their music. Jazz was maturing as an art form; it wasn't that Sidney Bechet was out-of-date, just that, like Jelly Roll Morton, he was out of style.

In the spring of 1933, Bechet and Ladnier gave up trying to make a living with their music altogether for a time and opened the Southern Tailor Shop at 128th Street and Nicholas Avenue in Harlem. Ladnier shined shoes. Bechet did the pressing and deliveries. But there were always jam sessions with old friends in the evenings. Bechet "would have a different wife every time I visited him," one recalled, "but he trusted none of them to do the cooking for his guests, and bristled alarmingly if anyone dared compare his gumbo to anyone else's. Not only did he insist that he was the greatest of all New Orleans musicians, he "wanted to be rated as the best Creole cook."

THE DISSIDENT

On "Makin' Friends," a record Jack Teagarden made with Eddie Condon, he had adapted an old blues lyric to speak for a good many jazz musicians who had traveled to New York only to find no work:

> I'd rather drink muddy water, sleep
> in a hollow log,
> Rather drink muddy water, Lord,
> sleep in a hollow log,
> Than be up here in New York treated
> like a dirty dog.

Twelve thousand of the fifteen thousand members of the American Federation of Musicians in Manhattan were jobless by 1933. There were still some positions for whites playing commercial music on the radio, but as Benny Carter remembered,

> radio staff and studio orchestras were closed to [black musicians] and these were steadier jobs paying hundreds of dollars weekly at a time when the union scale at places like the Savoy was thirty-three dollars. . . . Of course many white musicians, making more than we did, came to listen to us and play with us. We welcomed them and enjoyed the jamming. But we couldn't

John Hammond in his office at Columbia Records, 1939

go downtown and join them. We learned from each other and we didn't much blame the white musicians—we did envy them though. What was holding us back was not just the individual differences but a whole system of discrimination and segregation involving musicians, audiences, bookings, productions.

"The very fact that the best jazz players barely made a living, were barred from all well-paying jobs in radio and in most nightclubs enraged me," wrote John Henry Hammond Jr., in his autobiography. "There was no white pianist to compare with Fats Waller, no white band as good as Fletcher Henderson's, no blues singer like Bessie Smith, white or black. To bring recognition to the Negro's supremacy in jazz was the most effective and constructive form of social protest I could think of."

John Hammond was not a musician, did not own a record company or run a nightclub, or expect to profit from the work of the men and women he promoted so tirelessly, in print and in person. But few men played a more important—or more perplexing—role in the history of the music. Without him, Benny Goodman and Billie Holiday and Count Basie and a host of other stars might never have risen as far as they did. All of them would be grateful to him, but most would also come to resent his belief that he—and not they—always knew what was best for them.

He came by that belief naturally. Born in 1910, he was the great-grandson of Cornelius Vanderbilt, and was raised on Ninety-first Street just off Fifth Avenue in a mansion with sixteen servants and a ballroom that held 250 guests. Hammond's father was a taciturn and distant clubman, and the boy was closest to his mother, a fervent Christian Scientist with firm views about alcohol and tobacco and the improvement of other people's behavior. Hammond credited her with turning him into a "reformer, fired with her energy, certain in the right, . . . an inheritor of the guilt and therefore the obligations of wealth."

Both parents foresaw for their son a comfortable, conventional life very like their own. But at the age of twelve, while visiting London with his family, he heard his first live jazz—played by a white American outfit called Paul Specht's Georgians—and was entranced. He began collecting records, corresponded with adult jazz enthusiasts while still at Hotchkiss School, started slipping off to Harlem speakeasies at seventeen to sip lemonade and listen to black bands, and finally dropped out of Yale to try what only a handful of people had done—write seriously about jazz. At twenty, he was a correspondent for two British publications, *Gramophone* and *Melody Maker*.

It was not the fast life said to be led by musicians that drew Hammond to the music—he did not ever smoke, never drank in his youth, and was tongue-tied and clumsy around women. Instead, it was the opportunity to foster great music while helping to right what he saw as a great wrong. As soon as he came into his inheritance at twenty-one, he moved out of his parents' home and into a Greenwich Village apartment, asked that his name be removed from the Social Register because he was convinced it was anti-Semitic, and began

looking for ways to help the musicians and the music he loved. "I suppose I could best be described as a New York social dissident," Hammond said, "finally free to express my disagreement with the social system I was born into and which most of my contemporaries accepted as a matter of course."

Hammond had other causes—among them embattled coal miners in Kentucky, the Loyalist side in the Spanish Civil War, and the Scottsboro Boys, nine black youths falsely imprisoned for rape in Alabama; at twenty-five, he was a member of the national board of the NAACP—but scouting and promoting talented black artists always came first. To him, he once wrote, "jazz musicians *personified* . . . social injustice." His standards were lofty, for himself and for everyone with whom he dealt. He helped lease the Public Theater on the Lower East Side to provide jazz musicians with a dignified place to play, only to back out when the black manager his partner hired tried to bring in black vaudeville acts Hammond thought too commercial. Then, he organized live jam sessions on WEVD, a radio station whose call letters were the initials of the perennial Socialist presidential candidate, Eugene V. Debs, paying Benny Carter and Chu Berry and Chick Webb and others ten dollars a session plus carfare out of his own pocket to make their time in the studio worthwhile. These lasted only ten weeks because when the manager of the hotel in which the studio was housed began insisting that the musicians use the freight elevator, Hammond felt duty-bound to lead a walkout which eventually ended all jazz programming on the station. "Every place [John Hammond] goes," wrote the *New Republic* columnist Otis Ferguson, "he presently spies the taint of commercialism in art or the sordid hand of capitalism clutching workers. He burns. He speaks out. And then he *is* out."

"The times themselves imposed insurmountable odds," Hammond said, "particularly for Negroes, against achieving any

sort of recognition without help. The opportunities for me were clear." He continued to haunt Harlem nightspots, looking for new talent, but he also bought himself a Hudson convertible so that he could begin to scour the surrounding countryside as well, eventually driving thousands of miles from city to city, stopping in at burlesque houses and vaudeville theaters, speakeasies and roadhouses, anywhere he thought there might be someone worth hearing—and helping. (Hammond would wear out ten Hudsons in as many years, sometimes driving barefoot at night to keep himself awake behind the wheel.)

He got his first opportunity to record the kind of jazz he loved in 1932. Columbia Records was then moribund in America, but its recording director had a request for new jazz material from its parent company in London. Did Hammond have any ideas? Hammond did. He'd been writing as often as he could for his English readers about his favorite band. Now, he volunteered to bring Fletcher Henderson into the studio.

Henderson's orchestra had once been the band to beat. Its arrangements, by Don Redman and later by Henderson himself, were among the most adventurous in jazz and had helped set the pattern for the big swing bands that would within a few years conquer the country. Duke Ellington himself once admitted that in his early days "I tried desperately to try and sound like Fletcher Henderson." Few orchestras ever bested Henderson's once he'd called out to his men, "Come on—let's take charge." Coleman Hawkins, who was Henderson's tenor star for more than a decade, remembered his band as "the stompingest, pushingest band I ever heard. . . . They should have stomped all bands out of existence." Many of the musicians who moved through its ranks became stars in their own right—including Hawkins, Rex Stewart, Red Allen, Jimmy Harrison, J. C. Higginbotham, Dicky Wells, Buster Bailey, Roy Eldridge, Chu Berry, Ben Webster, and Benny Carter.

The Fletcher Henderson orchestra in Atlantic City during the summer of 1932. Banjo and guitar player Clarence Holiday, father of the singer Billie Holiday, is at the far left. Trombonist J. C. Higgenbotham is at the left of the pole in the center. Fletcher Henderson is to its right, followed by Edgar Sampson, alto saxophonist and arranger; drummer Walter Johnson; cornetist Rex Stewart; Russell Procope, clarinetist and alto saxophonist; Coleman Hawkins; and bassist John Kirby.

"Once you were selected by Fletcher Henderson," Carter remembered, "you had that as an imprimatur. Because all of the musicians that played with Fletcher Henderson at that time were highly respected musicians, not just jazz players. . . . And when I had the opportunity to be able to sit between Buster Bailey and Coleman Hawkins, I felt this is really *something*."

But Henderson had always been a detached and strangely lackadaisical leader, and a 1928 car accident, in which he suffered an injury to his skull, seemed only to exacerbate the problem. "Everything would seem comical to him," his wife, Leora, said, "and he never [aspired] to go higher than he was. He never had much business qualities, anyhow, but after that accident, he had even less. And worst of all, he would get careless." The Depression had only made things worse. Unlike Ellington, Henderson had no help setting up bookings. He often started off on tours without ensuring enough dates to make a profit possible. "We went out West from Memphis once," the trombonist Dicky Wells remembered:

Must have been going two days, and pulled up at this little place about eight o'clock for the dance at nine o'clock or ten o'clock: No lights. We began to get that feeling. There was a man inside sweeping the hall. "What time's the dance?" we asked.

"Dance," he said. "Oh yes, we had one last month."

Hard, Hard Times: 1929–1935   191

"No," we said. "When's the next one?"

"About a month from now."

Boy, that was a dismal day. It must have been six hundred miles. The cats said: "What, you brought us 'way out here!"

"Have another drink," [fellow trombonist] Sandy Williams says to the cats. . . . Then we were riding again.

Henderson never seemed able to make his band sound as good on records as it did in the ballroom, either, and he finally lost his home base at Roseland because he couldn't get his men to turn up on time. "Fletcher was never a natural leader," one of his musicians remembered. "If a man came in late Fletcher would just hang his head." Trumpet player Johnny Collins remembered wondering, when his fellow musicians arrived late or without the tuxedo that was one of the band's hallmarks, "How could they *do* this to this man?"

Henderson's men straggled into the studio so slowly for Hammond's recording date that they had to cut all three of the sides they'd planned in less than forty-five minutes. They were paid only union scale for their work. But the records sold well enough in England, gave at least a little boost to Henderson's demoralized orchestra, and established twenty-two-year-old John Hammond as a full-fledged record producer.

BLUE DEVILS

Bands all over the country were then struggling simply to survive. The Original Blue Devils, established in 1925 by the bassist Walter Page, had been one of the most successful of the Territory bands that roamed the Southwest. It played so many dates one year the men had just eight days off, and its ranks included so many fine musicians—including Page himself, known as "Big-un"

both for his bulk and for the sheer volume of sound with which he drove his band, the pianist Bill Basie, the trumpet player Oran "Hot Lips" Page, and the great singer Jimmy Rushing—that other bands shied away from engaging them in battle.

The Blue Devils wandered as far north as Minnesota and as far south as Galveston, Texas, in search of dancers, but their home base was Oklahoma City and, as the future novelist Ralph Ellison, then a schoolboy, remembered, they had always been a source of pride and inspiration to the Negro part of town.

> We had a Negro church and a segregated school, a few lodges and fraternal organizations, and beyond these there was all the great white world. We were pushed off to what seemed to be the least desirable side of the city . . . and our system of justice was based upon Texas law; yet there was optimism within the Negro community and a sense of possibility which, despite our awareness of limitation . . . transcended all of this, and it was this rock-bottom sense of reality, coupled with our sense of the possibility of rising above it, which sounded in [Jimmy] Rushing's voice.

Ellison lived four blocks from Slaughter's Hall, where the Blue Devils held forth on Saturday nights whenever they were in town, but lying in bed at night he never had any difficulty hearing every word Jimmy Rushing sang.

> Heard thus, across the dark blocks lined with locust trees, through the night throbbing with the natural aural imagery of the blues, with high-balling trains, departing bells, lonesome guitar chords simmering up from a shack in the alley, it was easy to imagine the voice as setting the pattern to which the instruments of the Blue Devils Orchestra and all the random sounds of night arose, affirm-

ing as it were, some ideal native to the time and to the land. When we were still too young to attend night dances, but yet old enough to gather beneath the corner street-lamp on summer evenings, anyone might halt the conversation to exclaim, "Listen, they're raising hell down at Slaughter's Hall," and we'd turn our heads westward to hear Jimmy's voice soar up the hill and down, as pure and as miraculously unhindered by distance and earthbound things as is the body in youthful dreams of flying.

> "Now, that's the Right Reverend Jimmy Rushing preaching now, man," somebody would say. And rising to the cue another would answer, "Yeah, and that's old Elder 'Hot Lips' signifying with him. . . ." And, keeping it building, "Huh, but though you can't hear him out this far, Ole Deacon Big-un . . . is up there patting his foot and slapping on his big belly [his bass] to keep those fools in line." And we might go on to name all the members of the band as though they were the Biblical four-and-twenty elders, while laughing at the impious wit of applying church titles to a form of music which all the preachers assured us was the devil's potent tool.

But after 1929, even the Blue Devils began to feel the sting of the Depression. Dance dates grew fewer and farther apart. The more successful Benny Moten Orchestra, based in Kansas City, lured away Bill Basie, Jimmy Rushing, Lips Page, and—eventually—even Walter Page himself, with offers of better pay and easier times.

The band struggled on, nonetheless, its numbers varying, according to the alto saxophonist Buster Smith, from fourteen to "three or four." "Nobody ever had enough money to amount to nothing . . . but we were just glad to be able to play music. Kept the band together." They were a so-called "commonwealth band"—a cooperative.

Bassist Walter Page and the 1931 version of his Blue Devils, at the Rite Ballroom in Oklahoma City. Trumpeter Oran "Hot Lips" Page is at the far left, Buster Smith, alto saxophonist and arranger, sits at the far right.

Everything—from hiring and firing to the cost of the oil and gas that kept their cars on the road in search of work—was shared equally. Their repertoire included waltzes and the square dances that appealed to the cowboy trade, but nine out of ten tunes were "jump numbers," riff-based blues with lots of room for soloing.

Without money to advertise themselves or big-time booking agents to smooth their way, the Blue Devils developed their own method of attracting a crowd. As soon as they pulled into a town, Smith remembered, the men split up to spread the word. Some talked up the band among what Buster Smith called "the upper classes"—"guys that went dressed up all the time. But we had some other boys that were liable to put on some overalls, get into town, go over and shoot pool around all the scallywags, . . . [saying] 'Well meet you at the dance,' and they'd all be there." They played county fairs and roadhouses and outdoor dances in East Texas that had to be lit by the head-

lights of the dancers' cars and paid for by the dollar bills the customers threw on the ground.

According to Buster Smith, he and Walter Page were strolling past a little upstairs club in Minneapolis one day in 1930, when they heard the sound of a tenor saxophone drifting down the stairs. The tune was familiar—"After You've Gone"—but the light, languid sound, swinging hard but without apparent effort, was different from anything they'd ever heard. "Who's that *fast* saxophone?" Page asked. "I'm going to get him in my band."

The mystery saxophonist was Lester Young. He had been born in Mississippi in 1909, but spent his earliest years living in Algiers, across the river from New Orleans, where he passed out handbills advertising dances just so he could walk alongside the trucks from which the ballyhooing bands played. When he was ten, his father, a school principal and music teacher, moved

the family to Minneapolis, remarried, and then took Lester, his brother, and his sister on tour with him in a circus sideshow band. Lester's mother and the wives of two cousins played saxophone. His younger brother, Lee, recalled that their father "did not want his kids to be a railroad porter, a redcap or a maid. You could not live in his house and not learn music." Lester played violin and trumpet first, switched to drums, then abandoned them at fourteen in favor of the alto saxophone because, he said, by the time he had packed the drums up after a performance, the girls he was most interested in had always gone home. Somewhere along the way he shifted to the tenor.

He seems to have been fiercely competitive from the first: fueled by canned pork and beans washed down with orange soda, he could play for hours. "I can play a hundred choruses," he liked to say, "and play different for every chorus." But he was also unusually sensitive, so resentful of his father's sporadic layings on of the razor strop he and his siblings called "Greasy Jim" that he ran away from home a dozen times in his teens. He was deeply affected by a camp meeting at which a white evangelist warned that those who did not come forward would be eternally damned—and then barred him and all the other African-Americans present from the mourner's bench. And when a Kentucky mob came for a cousin who had fought with a white man, it fell to Lester to smuggle him the pistol he needed to make his getaway. At nineteen, he ran away from home for good rather than accompany the family band on another southern tour.

By then he was already playing differently from anyone else. Coleman Hawkins had set the standard for most tenor men—swaggering, surging, big-toned. "The jazz world was under Hawk's spell," Young remembered. "But me, I couldn't imagine myself copying Hawk or anybody else." He had built his style in part on that of Frankie Trumbauer, whose records with Bix Beiderbecke he carried with him in his suitcase

The Blue Devils saxophone section in 1932. Alto players Theo Ross and Buster Smith flank the newest member of the organization, tenor saxophonist Lester Young, who then sometimes doubled on baritone.

before he'd come in with another." Young showed that understatement was compatible with swinging, that cool and hot could coexist, that a lope instead of a gallop might bring you first to the finish line.

"Originality," Young once said, "that's the trick." He was original in every other way as well. In an art form built in large part on individualism, no one was more individual than he. Heavy-lidded and slow-moving, he affected a strange, mincing pigeon-toed walk, wore distinctive clothes—a long black topcoat and a porkpie hat in his later years—and, for reasons no one ever entirely understood, held his saxophone at a forty-five-degree angle when he played. He had his own distinctive language, too. He called other musicians "Lady" this and "Lady" that. To fail was to "get bruised." "Can Madam burn?" meant "Can your wife cook?" He called white people "gray boys" and black people "Oxford grays." A woman was a "hat" and sometimes a "homburg" or a "Mexican hat"; and a pretty young woman was "pound cake." And if he sensed trouble anywhere nearby he would say, "I feel a draft."

It wasn't easy to talk him into joining the Blue Devils. He was in demand in Minneapolis, making five dollars a night at a time when, as one friend said, the cost of living was so low "he could have saved three dollars if he wanted to." But Buster Smith and another member of the band happened to have recently bought brand-new cars, Smith remembered, and Young was impressed by that: "He thought we was raising sin, making big money. . . . We looked around and here he come with his . . . suitcase and horn and got right on in the car."

Ralph Ellison first heard him play in an Oklahoma City shoeshine parlor. He was "jamming in a shine chair, his head thrown back, his horn even then out-thrust, his feet working on the footrests, as he played with and against . . . Ben Webster . . . and other members of the . . . Blue Devils. . . . With his heavy white sweater, blue stocking cap and up-and-out thrust silver saxophone,

wherever he went. He liked Trumbauer's spare way of telling "a little story," he said, and he admired his light, airy tone. "He played a C-melody saxophone. I tried to get the sound of a C-melody on a tenor. That's why I don't sound like other people. . . . I liked the way he slurred his notes." (Young liked Bix, too. "He sounded just like a colored boy sometimes. He was fine.")

Coleman Hawkins filled every moment with sound: "When I was playing one note," he once explained, "it was because I couldn't play but one. . . . When I can make two, I make two." Lester Young was among the first to demonstrate the power of silence. He had a very "spacey sound," the bassist Gene Ramey said. "He would play a phrase and maybe lay out three beats

Carving up the territory. Smiling Billy Stewart's Celery City Serenaders (top) were based in Florida but roamed as far west as Nebraska, where this photograph was taken. Zack Whyte (bottom) and his 1931 Chocolate Beau Brummels, based in Cincinnati, included two future jazz greats: arranger and trumpet player Sy Oliver and trombonist Vic Dickenson, fifth and second from right. When the Blue Devils got into trouble in West Virginia a few years later, it was Whyte who tried to snatch up the best of them.

[he] left absolutely no reed player and few young players of any instrument unstirred by the wild, excitingly original flights of his imagination. . . . Lester Young . . . with his battered horn upset the entire Negro section of town."

Clubs and theaters and dance halls closed, band uniforms grew threadbare, other Territory bands left the road, but the Blue Devils kept going for another two years. Then, as they toured Kentucky and West Virginia in the autumn of 1933, the Depression finally caught up with them. "The band was getting bruised," Lester Young remembered. "I mean really bruised, playing to audiences of three people." Their cars broke down and had to be abandoned, stranding them in Martinsville, Virginia, where they played in a tiny dance hall above a drugstore whose owner could never come up with enough money to pay their way out of town. Then, a youth from Beckley, West Virginia, turned up guaranteeing the men a salary if they would come and play there, at a roadhouse called the Black Knight. The thirteen Blue Devils hired two taxicabs to carry them across the Alleghenies, promising to pay their seventy-dollar fare just as soon as they got to Beckley. But the man who owned the Black Knight had never intended to pay anyone wages. The men were expected to "play for the door"—a percentage of paid admissions. Early snows kept at home the few jobless coal miners who might somehow have scraped up the entry fee.

There were no admissions. Days passed. Zack Whyte, leader of a rival band, got wind of their predicament and sent a bus from Cincinnati, with an offer of work for nine of the men. The commonwealth held together. "No, man," Buster Smith told Whyte's representative, speaking for all the Blue Devils, "if you're not going to take us all we're not going to go."

Meanwhile, Smith remembered, "the taxi drivers found out that two or three of the boys were going to sneak off anyway," went to the police, "and had our instruments attached." The sheriff seized everything, even their drums, returning them in the evenings just long enough for the men to play, then locking them up again until the next night. Then, the manager of the boardinghouse in which they'd been staying locked them out of their rooms.

It was the end of the Original Blue Devils. "We decided it was 'every tub,' " Lester Young remembered, "every man for himself." Hoboes showed them how to steal a ride on a freight train, but when Young and several other members of the band, without their instruments, managed to scramble aboard a moving boxcar—the trombone player nearly fell beneath the wheels—they found it already occupied by nineteen jobless white youths who had started a blaze to keep warm. They braced for trouble but the whites made room for them, and as the train rattled through the night, everyone, black and white, huddled together against the snow and the economic storm raging outside.

Lester Young resolved to get himself a new horn and start over in the town where times always seemed to be better—Kansas City.

K.C.

Kansas City, Missouri, was an economic oasis in the heart of the country, a mecca for migrants from the South and musicians in search of work. The man who ran it was the Democratic Boss of Jackson County, Tom Pendergast, an abstemious, church-going family man who was in bed every night by nine. His political power and immense fortune were built upon three things: total control of his party's political machine; ownership of the Ready-Mixed Concrete Company, which poured forth every cubic inch of material needed for the massive public works program he relentlessly sponsored for his city and county; and intimate links with organized crime that had helped to make the city he had been

running since 1926 the wildest place in America—filled with bars, brothels, and gambling dens in which, one reporter wrote, "the operators doctor the dice in such a manner as to make a loss to them a gravitational impossibility."

"If you want to see some sin, forget about Paris," said an editorialist for the Omaha *Herald,* "go to Kansas City." That kind of talk was calculated to appeal to every traveling salesmen and big spender between Chicago and Denver, Galveston and Minneapolis. Prohibition simply never existed in Kansas City. Not a single felony conviction for violating the Volstead Act was ever imposed on any of its citizens. Notorious fugitives like Pretty Boy Floyd and Baby Face Nelson danced unmolested in its nightclubs. Boss Pendergast's silent ally, Johnny Lanzia—"the Al Capone of Kansas City"—screened all candidates for the police force in order to weed out anyone who seemed overzealous, and policemen could be seen day and night rolling dice alongside civilian customers in the gambling establishments that lined Twelfth Street.

"Everything was wide open," Buck O'Neil of the Kansas City Monarchs recalled. "The sky was the limit, anything you were big enough to do and could afford, you *did* it. You could do it in Kansas City. Wide open!" There had been nothing like it in America since Storyville. No one knows how many clubs and cabarets and dance halls flourished in Kansas City—the Paseo Boulevard Room and the Pla-Mor Ballroom and the Reno Club; the Amos 'n' Andy and the Boulevard Lounge; Cherry Blossom and Chocolate Bar; the Lone Star and Elk's Rest and Old Kentucky Bar-B-Que; the Sunset and the Subway, Spinning Wheel and Hawaiian Gardens; Street's Blue Room, Hell's Kitchen, the Hi Hat, the Hey-Hay (where customers sat on hay bales), Dante's Inferno (where the waitresses wore devil costumes), and the Chesterfield Club (where the waitresses wore nothing at all).

Musicians like Lester Young, scrambling for work in the rest of the country, had no

A small sampling of K.C. nightclubs. In Kansas City, the bandleader Andy Kirk said, the stock market crash was "like a pin dropping: the blast of jazz and blues drowned it out."

Kansas City bandleaders built their reputations on musical combat. George E. Lee's Singing Novelty Orchestra (left)—featuring vocals by its leader and his sister, Julia—feared no band, black or white. Neither did Bennie Moten (right), whose outfit was the training ground for many of Kansas City's best musicians. "Moten," said the guitarist and arranger Eddie Durham, "was the king . . . the king all-out."

trouble finding it in Kansas City. It may have been a kind of hell for reform-minded citizens, but for the pianist Mary Lou Williams, it was "a heavenly city—musicians *everywhere.*" Like the men who played what critics would label "Chicago style," the musicians who became identified with Kansas City jazz came from everywhere. Bill Basie was from Red Bank, New Jersey; Lips Page was from Dallas; drummer Jo Jones was from Illinois by way of Birmingham, Alabama; tenor saxophonist Herschel Evans was from Denton, Texas; Mary Lou Williams was born in Georgia and raised in Pittsburgh; singer Jimmy Rushing was from Oklahoma City; and Jay McShann came from Muskogee.

As Albert Murray has written, what they had in common was a distinctly southwestern way of dealing with the blues.

The special drive of Kansas City music is . . . a device for herding or even stampeding the blues away. . . . [T]he KC drummer not only maintains that ever steady yet always flexible transcontinental locomotivelike drive of the KC 4/4, he also behaves for all the world like a whip-cracking trail driver. And so do Kansas City brass ensembles on occasion also bark and yap and snap precisely as if in pursuit of some invisible quarry, with the piano player siccing them on.

Kansas City musicians did not play the blues so much as stomp them, Murray wrote; Kansas City singers did not sing the blues, they *shouted* them.

There is no question about whether or not Jimmy Rushing and Big Joe Turner rode herd on the blue devils, spurring on the instrumental accompaniment as if from the saddle atop a quarter horse the while. . . . [S]ometimes it is also as if each Kansas City musician were riding the blues as if astride a bucking bronco. And come to think of it wasn't there something of the rodeo about the Kansas City jam session from the outset? The competition among the participants was incidental to the challenge of the music itself as the competition among cowboys for rodeo prizes was to the elemental contest between man and the wild animal.

Competition between Kansas City musicians ran especially deep. "For some reason," Claude "Fiddler" Williams remembered, "Kansas City was different from all other places because we'd be jamming all night. And if you come up here . . . playing the wrong thing, we'd straighten you out." "Regardless of how much anybody played or where they were from," said Mary Lou Williams, "when they came to Kansas City they found out how *little* they were play-

ing." The trumpet player Buck Clayton compared Kansas City musicians to gunfighters. Lips Page, he recalled, used to slip notes under the hotel-room door of visiting trumpet players reading, "Meet me tonight at such-and-such a club."

The pianist Sammy Price remembered going home at ten o'clock to change his clothes after playing at a session only to return to the club at one a.m. to find they were still playing the same tune. There were informal cutting contests for high school kids, free-for-alls for professionals, and the equivalent of heavyweight championship contests between the top musicians in town, often held at the Sunset or the Subway, the Reno or the Cherry Blossom. Kansas City jazz rewarded both individualism and the closest kind of cooperation. In order to provide a pleasing background for a succession of soloists, those waiting to play were expected to master complex harmonized riffs: "It showed a young guy that came in there," the bassist Gene Ramey recalled, "that he didn't just have to learn how to play a solo, he had to learn how to team . . . [how] to breathe at the same time." Kansas City jam sessions were most like camp meetings, Ramey continued, "completely imitated from one of those revival meetings, where the preacher and the people are singing, all that living, and there's happiness all around."

One evening in 1933, the great Coleman Hawkins himself was in town with Fletcher Henderson's band, on the last night of a week-long engagement, part of what would be one of the struggling band's final tours. After the show, he carried his horn into the Cherry Blossom at Twelfth Street and Vine, looking for challengers as he did wherever he went. Three of Kansas City's best tenor players were waiting for him: two whose styles owed much to his, Herschel Evans and Ben Webster—and twenty-four-year-old Lester Young.

By four o'clock in the morning they were looking for a fresh piano player. Mary Lou Williams was fast asleep at home.

Around four a.m., I awoke to hear someone pecking on my screen. . . . Ben Webster was saying, "Get up pussycat, we're jamming and all the pianists are tired out now. Hawkins has got his shirt off and is still blowing." Sure enough, when we got there, Hawkins was in his [undershirt], taking turns with the K.C. men. It seems he had run into something he didn't expect. Lester's style was light . . . it took him maybe five choruses to warm up. But then he would really blow. . . . That was how Hawkins got hung up. The Henderson band was playing in St. Louis that evening and Bean knew he ought to be on the way. But he kept trying to blow something to beat Ben and Herschel and Lester. When at last he gave up, he got straight in his car and drove to St. Louis. I heard he'd just bought a new Cadillac and that he burnt it out trying to make the job on time. Yes, Hawkins was king until he met those crazy Kansas City tenor men.

CARRYING THE FLAG

On June 2, 1933, John Hammond made his way to the Hudson River pier from which the S.S. *Olympic* was about to set sail for England. He was carrying a bulky parcel, a bon voyage gift for Duke Ellington, who was about to take his orchestra overseas for the first time. Ellington greeted Hammond politely enough, but when he unwrapped the package and saw that it contained a portable phonograph, he politely handed it back, telling his well-wisher he already had one. Both Ellington and Hammond were courteous, even courtly men, but there was never any love lost between them. Ellington did not appreciate the gratuitous advice that Hammond seemed compelled to offer: Hammond had already urged that Sonny Greer be replaced, suggested ways in which he thought the band's playing for dancers might be improved (though he could not dance himself), had even declared the silken sound of Ellington's latest addition to the band, trombonist Lawrence Brown, insufficiently "negroid." Now, Hammond's shipboard gift struck Ellington as just one more form of patronization.

As even Hammond had to admit, Duke Ellington was doing very well without his help. While other bands were faltering, his was moving from success to success. Readers of the Pittsburgh *Courier* proclaimed his the most popular black orchestra in the country. And he had won that popularity with music unlike anyone else's.

"We violate more laws of music than anyone else," Ellington told a reporter, "and then just go right along violating." Working always within the American jazz vocabulary that had first been developed in New Orleans—riffs, breaks, call-and-response—and never straying far from the blues that was always at the heart of his music, he cheerfully turned traditional ways of orches-

trating upside down. Even his men were sometimes baffled by what he asked them to do. "At first," Barney Bigard recalled, "I used to think everything was wrong, because he wrote so weird. It took me some time to get used to hearing all these things. He would make the chords all the wrong way, giving to someone else the part he should have given the clarinet player."

An otherworldly 1931 composition originally called "Dreamy Blues"—which Ellington claimed to have written in fifteen minutes while waiting for his mother to cook him dinner—provided an especially vivid example of what Bigard was talking about. The melody was stated by a trio—muted trumpet, muted trombone, and clarinet—but Ellington deliberately reversed the traditional roles of the trombone and clarinet so that Sam Nanton played the highest part while Bigard played the lowest. The eerie result—"a tone that's not there," Ellington called it, "an *illusion* of a tone"—was as otherworldly as the tune's title implied and caused a sensation when first performed on the radio. Retitled "Mood Indigo," it would be the band's first big hit, its most-requested number for more than forty years. Once, when an interviewer asked Ellington why he seemed so often to employ dissonance, he was unruffled: "That's the Negro's life. That's us!" he said. "Dissonance is our way of life in America. We are something apart, yet an integral part."

When Irving Mills suggested that Ellington enhance his reputation further by writing something longer than the usual three-minute dance tune, Ellington turned out "Creole Rhapsody" in a single night. More than six minutes long, filled with shifting tempos and changing moods, it took up two sides of a record and won for Ellington the first of hundreds of prizes he would garner over the years, the New York School of Music's 1933 award for the best composition of the year. The citation said "Creole Rhapsody" "portrayed the Negro life as no other piece had."

The youthful Albert Murray was also hearing echoes of the life he knew in Ellington's music.

One's earliest perception of Duke Ellington was that he was a transcendent figure in the music, because when you heard the earliest things [they] had so much of all the music that you knew about in it. For example, when I first heard "Mood Indigo," it sounded like somebody knew what to do instrumentally with a church quartet or a barbershop quartet that used to get together and harmonize popular songs or gospel songs on the corner. Everybody identified with that. It was as if we knew exactly where he got that from, some corner in Washington, just as we knew it from some corner in Mobile. And people would say it was like taking blues and making classical music out of it.

Ellington was eager to play overseas, but reluctant to sail because he had read newspaper accounts of the *Titanic* as a boy and had convinced himself that any boat on which he sailed would encounter an iceberg and sink. And there were other worries. No one was sure what sort of reception the band would get in London. Louis Armstrong had made a four-month visit to Britain and France the previous year, and, outside the world of British musicians, had not been an unqualified success. There had been no advance work—no one in London knew when Armstrong was arriving and it had taken a full day just to find a hotel that would rent a room to a black visitor—and local promoters had had to scurry around to come up with musicians capable of backing him up onstage. The editor of *Melody Maker* misheard someone using one of his hometown nicknames, "Satchelmouth," as "Satchmo" and the name stuck. The program Armstrong put on at the London Palladium, where he was billed as "the colored phenomenon"—the same kind of fast-paced show that had won him so much applause

Duke Ellington boards the S.S. *Olympic* for England, 1933.

back home—stunned the English. The mugging, perspiring onstage Armstrong, one British admirer wrote, seemed to have "only a tenuous connection with the creator of the moving music of 'West End Blues.' "

The Belgian poet and record collector Robert Goffin made a pilgrimage to London just to see his hero play. He had already dedicated his book, *Aux frontières du jazz,* to Armstrong as "the real King of Jazz," but was taken aback at first by seeing him perform in person: "The tempest of 'Rocking Chair' breaks loose and Louis plays, conducting with his eyes and sudden jerks of his hand, capers and contortions of his whole body, as though he wanted to terrify the three saxophones who find themselves called upon for a hot ensemble." Like a good many other enthusiastic writers about jazz, Goffin genuinely loved the music and genuinely misunderstood how it was made. Jazz, he was certain, proceeded directly

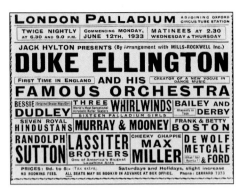

LONDON PALLADIUM ADJOINING OXFORD CIRCUS TUBE STATION
TWICE NIGHTLY AT 6.30 AND 9.0 P.M. | COMMENCING MONDAY, JUNE 12TH, 1933 | MATINEES AT 2.30 WEDNESDAY & THURSDAY
JACK HYLTON PRESENTS (By Arrangement with MILLS-ROCKWELL Inc.)
DUKE ELLINGTON
FIRST TIME IN ENGLAND AND HIS CREATOR OF A NEW VOGUE IN DANCE MUSIC
FAMOUS ORCHESTRA
BESSIE (Original Snake-Hips Girl) DUDLEY | THREE WHIRLWINDS World's Most Sensational Acrobatic Roller Skaters | BAILEY AND DERBY
SIXTEEN PALLADIUM GIRLS
SEVEN ROYAL HINDUSTANS | MURRAY & MOONEY | FRANK & BETTY BOSTON
RANDOLPH SUTTON | LASSITER BROTHERS | CHEEKY CHAPPIE MAX MILLER One of America's Biggest Laughing Acts | DE WOLF METCALF & FORD
PRICES: 9d. to 5/- (Tax extra) Saturdays and Holidays, slight increase
NO BOOKING FEES. ALL SEATS MAY BE BOOKED IN ADVANCE AT BOX OFFICE. Phone: GERRARD 7373

An advertisement for Duke Ellington's appearance at the London Palladium, and (below) Ellington himself, awash in British applause. "We were absolutely amazed," he wrote, "by how well informed people were in Britain about us and our records."

from the special "directness and spontaneity" of Armstrong's race. "Louis Armstrong is a full-blooded Negro," he assured the readers of a subsequent volume, and *therefore* able to "almost automatically enter into a trance and . . . express his sensibility by means of his instrument. . . . I know of no white musician who is able to forget himself, to create his own atmosphere, and to whip himself up into a state of complete frenzy." The curious notion that black musicians were more "primitive" than white ones and therefore freer to express emotion would continue stubbornly to persist in one form or another throughout jazz history, distorting the achievements of musicians of both races: nearly thirty years after Armstrong's death, his music was still sometimes subtly patronized as "instinctive."

Some Londoners simply walked out on Armstrong. "That man's mad!" one shouted. "He should be locked up!" A classical musician declared his stage show "a disgusting and abortive exhibition, likely to nauseate all decent men." Another called Armstrong "a purely freak musician." There were occasional shouts of "dirty nigger" from the galleries, and in one provincial British theater, tomatoes were thrown at the stage. And everywhere Armstrong went, his thuggish manager Johnny Collins made enemies. Frequently drunk, usually profane, and always grasping, Collins

wouldn't let Armstrong go onstage until he had the box-office proceeds in his hand. He was "a typical Yank that you'd see in these gangster films," a disgusted British musician recalled, "with a big cigar in the corner of his mouth." Armstrong had returned to America in November of 1932, just a few days after Franklin Roosevelt's election as President, pledged to "a New Deal for the American people" and an end to the Depression.

Thanks largely to Irving Mills, Ellington's reception in England was everything Armstrong's had not been. Mills and the British bandleader Jack Hylton saw to it that there were thirty-seven photographers and a big crowd at Waterloo Station when the band's train pulled in from Southampton, and, according to Barney Bigard, he and the other men were astonished to hear their British fans "calling everyone by their names: 'Here's Barney, here's Hodges, here's Cootie, here's Tricky Sam.' They

recognized everyone!" When the curtain rose on opening night at the Palladium and before a single note was played, Ellington marveled, there was "applause beyond applause." One opening-night critic declared that Ellington's music possessed "a truly Shakespearean universality . . . girls wept and young chaps sank to their knees," and another British writer, S. R. Nelson of the London *Era,* was very nearly undone by what he saw and heard that evening:

> Ellington the Amazing. Ellington the Musician. Ellington the Showman. Ellington the Artist. How can I . . . describe the unbelievable spectacle I have just beheld at the Palladium? . . . How to describe in so many words the most vital emotional experience vaudeville in England has ever known? . . .
>
> Where, oh where, are the renowned British qualities of aloofness, coldness, unemotionalism, self-restraint? I am not ashamed to say that I cried during the playing of "Mood Indigo." . . . Here was a music far removed from the abacadabra of symphony; here was a tenuous melodic line which distilled from the emotions all heritage of human sorrow which lies deep in every one of us. . . .
>
> Musically he is unique in the sense that as a composer, he has his own orchestra to play his compositions. It is doubtful whether any other orchestra in the world could interpret Ellington's music in the manner of his band.

London society took up the band. At one party, Edward Prince of Wales himself sat in at Sonny Greer's drums—and the prince professed to like it when Greer called him "Wales." They played a forty-five-minute program on the BBC, took thirteen curtain calls, and were made to play four encores at the Empire Theatre in Liverpool, where the Prince of Wales again led the applause.

The Ellington orchestra onstage in London. "After hearing what Ellington can do with four-teen players," wrote the British composer Constance Lambert, "the average modern com-poser who splashes about with eighty players in the Respighi manner must feel a little chas-tened. All this is clearly apparent to anyone who visits the Palladium, but what may not be so apparent is that Ellington is no mere band leader and arranger, but a composer of uncommon merit, probably the first composer of real character to come out of America."

So many people clamored for tickets to see them at the Salle Playel in Paris that two additional concerts had to be added to the schedule.

Best of all, according to Greer, Mills saw to it that an American flag flew above every hotel in which the orchestra stayed.

> In honor of us. Just like they flew the flag if a diplomat come and stay in the hotel. . . . We carried the flag and the prestige of my people. I am an American Negro. You hear the cats say, 'Black this . . .' I'm an *American Negro,* pal. We carried the flag for the American Negro . . . everywhere. We carried the flag for the dignity of the American Negro all over the world. We were treated with the utmost respect.

"The main thing I got in Europe was *spirit,*" Ellington told a reporter after he and the band got home that fall. "That kind of thing gives you the courage to go on. If they think I'm *that* important, then maybe . . . our music does mean something." Americans may still have seen him mostly as a bandleader, but some Europeans considered him a serious composer. "A musician," he said, "should have both Europe *and* America."

A twelve-week tour of the South followed the band's return. Even for men accustomed to the American road, the contrast was startling: "Of course all the places we played down there," Harry Carney said, "they were happy to hear the band. The drag was they'd be screaming and applauding and afterward you'd have to go back across the tracks. . . . In Europe we were royalty; in Texas we were back in the colored section. It was some adjustment, but we were young and could take it." The music critic of the Dallas *News* called Ellington "something of an African Stravinsky" who had "erased the color line" between jazz and classical music. But black fans in the South had to hear him from the balcony of the theaters he played; white hotels and restaurants excluded him and his band.

Daisy Ellington had taught her son from childhood simply to rise above all unpleasantness; after his southern tour, rather than again suffer the indignity of being turned away from hotels and restaurants, he and Mills arranged for the orchestra to travel in its own private Pullman cars so that the men could eat and sleep in the railroad yards, and saw to it that a fleet of taxicabs was waiting to ferry them to and from their appearances.

"They never *seen* nobody like us," Sonny Greer said.

> They had heard different colored aggregations that come through on a little raggedy-ass bus, but we had our own Pullman car, our own baggage car, . . . full possession of the diner, nobody could come in our Pullman car because the door stayed locked, because people autographing annoy you. . . . We had our own lighting equipment, own stage, one of the first bands to use a roll-down stage, . . . one of the first bands with all them overhead pinpoint lights, electrician. They never seen that. That's the way Irving Mills made us travel. . . . We didn't have to go through that junk— colored over this side, white over this.

"The natives would come by and they would say, 'What on earth is that?' " Ellington remembered. "And we would say, 'That's the way the President travels.' You do the very best with what you've got."

Ellington and his orchestra would always represent the very best, as the young Ralph Ellison remembered seeing for himself when the band turned up in Oklahoma City that year.

> Then Ellington and his great orchestra came to town—came with their uniforms, their sophistication, their skills; their golden horns, their flights of controlled and disciplined fantasy; came with their art, their special sound; came with Ivie Anderson and

Ethel Waters singing and dazzling the eye with their high-brown beauty and with the richness and bright feminine flair of their costumes and promising manners. They were news from the great wide world, an example and a goal, and I wish that all those who write so knowledgeably about Negro boys having no masculine figures with whom to identify would consider the long national and international career of Ellington and his band, and the thousands of one-night stands played in the black communities of this nation. Where in the white community, in any white community, could there have been found examples such as these? Who were so worldly, who so elegant, who so mockingly creative? Who were so skilled at their given trade and who treated the social limitations placed in their paths with greater disdain?

SOMETHING MUST BE DONE

In July of 1933, a month after Ellington's overseas tour began, John Hammond himself set sail for England, aboard the steamer *Homeric.* When he found that among his fellow passengers were Louis Armstrong and his companion, Alpha Smith, traveling abroad for a second time, he eagerly sought them out. One evening in Armstrong's stateroom Hammond was witness to a violent argument between him and his drunken manager, Johnny Collins, who was telling his star what he should and should not play onstage. Armstrong was resisting.

Collins became abusive. "Called me a nigger in the middle of the ocean," Armstrong remembered, "he's my manager and he's never done it before. But, you can see that 'nigger' brings out your fucking thoughts sometimes. I said, 'You know, Mr. Collins, I have been in show business for a long time. I'm an old hustler [from] way

hundred records, and appeared on countless radio programs, kidding his own music and everybody else's, too. No song was too dreary for him to make memorable.

But there was another side to Fats Waller, hidden from his fans. He was the favorite child of a mother whose early death he never quite got over and the son of a grim clergyman whom he permanently alienated when at the age of fifteen he chose to play what the old man called "the Devil's music." A white tough stabbed him when he was a boy; another shot and badly wounded his brother, standing right next to him; and a cross was burned on his lawn when he moved his family to Queens long after he became a recording star. His first marriage went bad and he twice did time for failing to pay alimony. A second liaison was

were the products of it. He grew bitter at h[...] his songs for so little money, and could [...] suade record executives to let him play on[...] that was his first love—the pipe organ. [...] recital at Carnegie Hall in 1942, but too [...] latory toasts before the performance und[...] that night, and reviewers were unforgiv[...] less high living caught up with him the fo[...] developed pneumonia while appearing a[...] fornia and died in his sleep aboard the tra[...] rying him home to New York. When Louis A[...] the news he cried all night. "Some little pe[...] in them," James P. Johnson remembered. "[...] all music—and you know how big he was.[...]

Thomas "Fats" Waller ate more food, drank more liquor, played as much piano—and seemed to be having more fun than any other musician of his time. He was a big man, nearly six feet tall, sometimes weighed more than three hundred pounds, and wore size fifteen shoes. He routinely downed three steaks for lunch, drank a quart or more of gin or whiskey at every recording session, and called the liquor he drank upon awakening each morning, his "liquid ham-and-eggs."

The stride piano master, James P. Johnson, was his friend and teacher, and he never lost the mighty, rumbling left hand Johnson had taught him. But the touch of his right hand was light, melodic, irrepressible. "Concentrate on the melody," he told one interviewer. "You got to hang on to the melody and never let it get boresome." He was never boresome. He sold some four hundred songs to publishers for as little as fifty dollars—and he sometimes sold them several times. "You had to buy them," said the music publisher Irving Mills, "even though you knew [he] probably had sold it elsewhere down the street or even across the hall." Waller's tunes included "Ain't Misbehavin'," "Honeysuckle Rose," "Squeeze Me," "I'm Gonna Sit Right Down and Write Myself a Letter," "Blue Turning Grey Over You,"

Fats Waller and the camera had a symbiotic relationship. (Top, left) He goes for a stroll i[...]

one evening, Fats Waller was playing in a New York club when he heard a stir in the audience. A large, heavy man was making his way among the tables. Waller stopped playing. "Ladies and gentlemen," he said. "I just play the piano, but *God* is in the house." Then he left the piano bench so that Art Tatum could take over. Tatum was the most admired, most imitated pianist of his generation but he was always something of a mystery, even during his lifetime.

He was born in Toledo, Ohio, in 1909, totally blind in one eye and very nearly sightless in the other. He began picking out tunes at home at three, was playing hymns in church at five, and trying to imitate the piano rolls his mother brought home for him to hear. According to his neighbor, the singer Jon Hendricks, he even mastered one lightning-fast duet, not knowing it had taken four hands to record the original. He had a memory for melody so photographic that he rarely had to hear a tune more than once to play it back with embellishments, and an ear for pitch so uncanny he could tell the denomination of a coin dropped on a table by the sound it made. By the age of seventeen he was working in small Ohio clubs—and dazzling visiting musicians with his artistry. When they urged him to come to New York, he would back off, saying he wasn't good enough yet.

But by the time the arranger Don Redman came through Toledo in 1931, the young man felt ready. "Tell them New York cats to look out," he told Redman. "Here comes Tatum!" He got to New York the following year as accompanist to the singer Adelaide Hall, but he stayed on as a soloist—and according to legend soon found himself being challenged by the three most respected pianists in town—James P. Johnson, Willie the Lion Smith, and Fats Waller. They met at a Harlem club called Morgan's. Each one played a favorite number. Each time, Tatum outplayed him. "He was just too good," Waller remembered. "He had too much technique. When that man turns on the powerhouse, don't no one play him down."

From then on, he was generally acknowledged as the most accomplished of all jazz pianists. His light, witty touch was unmistakable from the first note he played. He was as deft with his left hand as he was with his right, never lost the clarity of his conception no matter how fast he set the tempo, and seemed always to have in reserve a wealth of new melodic ideas, fresh harmonies, startling shifts in rhythm and dynamics, and unexpected quotations from other tunes to rivet the listener's attention. Like Earl Hines, who was his first musical hero, Tatum was at his best as a soloist. Other musicians tended to get in the way.

"The first time I heard Art Tatum I thought I was listening to four guys," the pianist Jimmy Rowles said. "Four people! That's what it sounded like. I mean, you couldn't

even see what he was doing. He was absolutely unbelievable." He influenced other kinds of musicians, as well. "He was the 'invisible man' of jazz," the trumpet player Roy Eldridge remembered. "Guys might not realize it, but after they heard Art he was always with them, in the way they thought about improvising."

Most of Tatum's life was music. He was married twice and had a son. He played a little pinochle, using a special light to squint at his hand and memorizing the cards others played as they were called out to him. He drank quart after quart of Pabst Blue Ribbon beer and followed the fortunes of the Cleveland Indians. Otherwise, he was at the piano, playing at one club, then moving on to close another and another, finally falling asleep for a few hours before starting in again. And he is said never to have turned away a challenge. According to the late trumpet player Harry "Sweets" Edison, when the Canadian pianist Oscar Peterson first brought his dazzling technique to New York,

a conclave of the city's best piano players one's apartment. Everyone was impress man's technique. Tatum followed him t "Oscar, that was very nice," he said. "No this song for you." And he played "Little N Busy Day."

Competition was never far from Tatu guitarist Les Paul recalled.

I remember one time we were driving tan, and he says, "Where are we now front of Madison Square Garden, Joe L ing," and we got to talking about that. "You know, I'd like to rent that place to take on all the piano players and f for all settle it. Rather than me go rou club to nightclub to beat these guys, I 'em all in one place and knock 'em a

back. I know that horn better than I know my wife.' "

Collins protested. *He* was in charge, he said; Armstrong had to do what he was told.

"I said, 'Listen, . . . you might be my manager and you might be the biggest shit, booking the biggest business in the world. But when I get on that fucking stage with that horn and get in trouble, you can't save me.' "

Collins bellowed that if Armstrong wouldn't follow orders, he would have to get off the boat.

Armstrong, tempted to hit him, thought better of it. "Now, I could bash his fucking brains out. . . . But it's a different story. It's a white man. So I don't fuck with Johnny. Then he got up—and walked right into a bucket of water."

John Hammond had been unable to contain himself. He upbraided Collins for his use of the word "nigger" and dressed him down for "his shabby treatment" of the man who was his "bread and butter." Collins, red-faced now and out of control, took a drunken swing at Hammond—who ducked and hit him back. Collins slumped. Armstrong could have broken his manager's fall, but he deftly stepped aside instead, and let Collins crash to the deck.

Hammond was sure Armstrong would always be grateful to him. "It was probably the first time a white man had thought enough of him to fight someone who abused him," he wrote. But Armstrong didn't see it that way; he was mostly pleased that by controlling his anger and avoiding further trouble he had achieved the desired result: "it was the same," he said, "as though I had hit him myself." Br'er Rabbit could not have done better. (Armstrong and Hammond would never be close, and Hammond's disappointment at what he saw as Armstrong's ingratitude eventually took the form of denigrating his genius: he would one day assure the readers of his autobiography that Joe Smith, Armstrong's decorous predecessor in the Fletcher Henderson band, had always been a greater trumpet player.)

Hammond stayed in England just long enough to get a contract from British Columbia to make some sixty sides with some of the musicians he most admired—Fletcher Henderson, Coleman Hawkins, Red Allen, Benny Carter.

The British were interested in Benny Goodman, too. Goodman was not then one of Hammond's favorites. "I felt that Benny was a good clarinet player, although no better than Jimmy Dorsey," he would write, "and less good than several black clarinetists I could think of." Nor had he pulled his punches when writing up a band Goodman had once too hastily organized to accompany the crooner Russ Columbo: "Mr. Goodman," he wrote, "I fear has forgotten all about the fact that there are actually *human beings* in the band. The result is painful and the band is merely another smooth and soporific dance combination."

But the British wanted Goodman, and Hammond dutifully went looking for him on West Fifty-second Street. Hammond knew the neighborhood well—his grandmother had once lived in a Fifth Avenue mansion just around the corner—and he also knew in which of the thirty-eight speakeasies on that single block between Fifth and Sixth Avenues Goodman was most likely to be found. The Onyx, at number 35, was known all over the city as a musician's hangout. Its password was "802," the number of the New York musician's local, and it was filled every night with musicians playing for one another. "It never ceased to amaze me," said the owner of the Onyx, "how [musicians] would come in complaining about how some leader kept them for rehearsals ten minutes longer than expected. Then they would stay in my place playing all night long—for free." Bix Beiderbecke had loved the Onyx. Art Tatum was often there. So were Willie the Lion Smith and Jack Teagarden and Tommy Dorsey, who for a time drove down from a Westchester ballroom after work nearly every morning, parked out front in his old Buick, listened until he heard a tune he

liked, then marched through the door playing his trombone.

Goodman was at the bar when Hammond entered, and not especially happy to see the man who had written so critically of him. When Hammond said that Columbia wanted to record him, Goodman called him a "goddamn liar"; Columbia was out of business, he said; everybody knew that.

Goodman was now one of the most successful freelance musicians in New York. Since leaving Ben Pollack in 1929—and despite the Depression and its impact—he had taken part in hundreds of record dates, and appeared often on the radio, as well. But by 1933, even he was finding it hard to get work and had begun to earn a reputation as sullen and difficult as well as gifted and versatile. A former prodigy who now found himself scuffling simply to survive, bored with the mostly humdrum music he was asked to play, he did not disguise his unhappiness from the men he worked for—and began to lose jobs because of it. "None of us had much use for . . . 'commercial' musicians," he recalled. "The saddest thing always was a recognized hot man who went in for that sort of work. . . . I guess I was doing something that didn't really satisfy me, and that's where a lot of the trouble came in."

Once Hammond made it clear that the offer was genuine, that it was *British* Columbia, not American, that wanted him, the offer seemed like a godsend. It would be Goodman's first chance to record the kind of music he loved best under his own name. But there was an initial hitch. Hammond wanted him to record with Coleman Hawkins and Benny Carter. Most of Goodman's first musical mentors had been black. He loved sitting in with black bands, and jamming with musicians of both races in clubs like the Onyx; had even adopted a hip, pseudo-black way of talking to identify more closely with his heroes. But making a living came first. "If it gets around that I recorded with colored guys," he told Hammond, "I won't get another job in this town."

"It can't be that bad," Hammond protested.

"John, you don't know," said Goodman. "It's that bad." And, Hammond admitted, "he was right." Scrambling for work in the depths of the Depression, white musicians wanted no new competition.

Hammond rounded up an all-white group that included Jack Teagarden, Gene Krupa, and Joe Sullivan to record with Goodman. The record that resulted—"Ain't-cha-Glad," backed with "I've Got a Right to Sing the Blues"—sold five thousand copies, a respectable figure for a jazz record in 1933—and established Goodman for the first time as a bandleader. He never forgot the thrill of walking into the Commodore Music Shop on East Forty-second Street and seeing the record displayed with a hand-lettered sign saying: "Benny Goodman and His Orchestra."

Hammond continued to provide work for the black artists he loved best. On the morning of November 27, 1933, he recorded two tunes with the Broadway star and former blues singer Ethel Waters, and immediately afterward brought into the same studio his latest discovery, an eighteen-year-old singer he could not seem to stop talking about. He had found her earlier that year singing in a Harlem nightspot called Monette's, had been embarrassed by the bawdy songs she was then performing, but dazzled by the way she looked and sang. "I heard something that was completely new and fresh," he recalled, "the phrasing, the sound of an instrumentalist." "This month there has been a real find in the person of a singer named Billie [Holiday]. . . . Although only 18," he had written in *Down Beat,* "she is incredibly beautiful . . . and sings as well as anybody I ever heard. Something must be done about her for gramophone records."

Enthusiasm like that about another singer was not calculated to please Ethel Waters, whose tolerance for an attractive competitor half her age was predictably low. When Holiday arrived, Waters settled into a chair in the back of the studio to hear for herself just what Hammond was so excited about.

Billie Holiday had a tiny voice—barely a full octave. "It just go up a little bit and come down a little bit," she once told an accompanist. "This voice of mine's a mess, a cat got to know what he's doing when he plays with me." And she chose to lead a life so full of self-abuse that it was a wonder among her friends that she managed to survive even to the age of forty-four. The sordid details of her private life, chronicled in lurid books and twisted into soap opera by Hollywood, have too often been allowed to obscure the fact that somehow, out of it all, she managed to make unforgettable art; that she was, after Louis Armstrong, the greatest singer in jazz history.

She was born Eleanora Fagan in Philadelphia in 1915 and brought up in Baltimore, the illegitimate daughter of an illegitimate mother. She yearned all of her girlhood for her mostly absent father, Clarence Holiday, a big-band banjo player and guitarist whose flashy example helped lure her into the music business but whose hustling ways were mirrored in many of the predatory men she would later call "Daddy." As a girl, she was farmed out among relatives whose feelings for her seem to have been more dutiful than loving, could not be made to stay in school, and spent her tenth year in the House of the Good Shepherd for Colored Girls, a Dickensian institution run by nuns where she may have been molested by older inmates. She was released at eleven only to be raped by a neighbor, then locked up again in the House of the Good Shepherd as a material witness against her attacker. At twelve, she was working as a prostitute in Alice Dean's waterfront whorehouse and earning extra money singing along with the Victrola in the parlor—Bessie Smith and Louis Armstrong were her favorites, and became the primary sources of her style. "I always liked the big volume and the big sound that Bessie Smith

Eleanora Fagan at three

got," she once told an interviewer. "[B]ut . . . I heard a record Louis Armstrong made called 'West End Blues,' and he doesn't say any words, you know? . . . and I reckoned he must have been feeling awful bad. I liked the feeling I got from it. So I wanted Louis Armstrong's *feeling.*"

She moved to New York with her mother at thirteen or fourteen, worked in another brothel and did time in the workhouse on Blackwell's Island for prostitution, then began singing for tips at house parties and small clubs—the Yeah Man, the Hot-Cha, Pod's and Jerry's Log Cabin, the Alhambra Grill, and a dozen more. Most of the places she sang were subterranean and small. Often there was only a pianist to accompany her and she was expected to work the whole room without a microphone, stopping at each table to sing a chorus or two, shifting her delivery slightly with each stop to encourage bigger tips. It was the best possible training for someone who all her life would consider herself an improvising jazz musician before she was a singer. "I don't think I'm singing," she told an early interviewer, "I feel like I am playing a horn." And she could never bear to sing a song exactly the same way twice: "I just can't do it. I can't even copy me." She began to build a reputation among musicians—Hammond brought Benny Goodman to hear her, and they dated for a time, to the horror both of his siblings and her mother—and she began experimenting with new names: Billie *Halliday*, first, after her favorite movie star Billie Dove, and then Billie *Holiday*, after her absent, longed-for father.

Benny Goodman escorted her to the recording studio Hammond had booked—his having recorded successfully under his own name had evidently emboldened him to record with black as well as white musicians—but she was nervous when she got there. She had never sung into a microphone before. Ethel Waters was glaring at her. All but one of the musicians in the nine-piece studio group was white. Joe Sullivan, the pianist on the date, told her just to close her eyes and sing. "You're not going to let these people think you're a square, are you?" he said. The forgettable novelty tune recorded that afternoon was "My Mother's Son-in-Law." "I get a big bang out of [hearing it]," Holiday told an interviewer toward the end of her life. "It sounds like I'm doing *comedy*. My voice sounded so funny and high. . . . I sounded like I'm about three years old. But I don't like any of my records, to be truthful with you. Because it's always something you *should* have done. Or you should have waited *here;* or you should have phrased . . . well, you know how it is."

She was paid thirty-five dollars. The record went nowhere. Ethel Waters felt she had nothing to worry about; Hammond's discovery, she would say later, sang as if her shoes were too tight. Holiday returned to performing in Harlem wherever she could find work. But John Hammond remained determined to make her better known in the wider world.

LET'S DANCE

On December 5, 1933, eight days after Billie Holiday's first recording session, the Twentieth Amendment was repealed. Prohibition was over at last. "The speakeasies," Eddie Condon remembered, "unlocked their doors and fresh air hit the customers for the first time in thirteen years." But when speakeasies reopened as legal nightclubs, business was mostly poor: with neighborhood liquor stores now open, people saved money by drinking at home. "Prices went down," Condon continued, "musicians were out of work, and the weather turned cold." "B'way Niteries Praying for Good Ol' Prohi Days. Ain't No Drinkin," said *Variety*. To get back their customers, the clubs needed to offer new excitement, new distractions. A noisy showman and sometime songwriter named Billy Rose, already the proprietor of a flashy club called the Casino de Paree, announced plans to open a still more lavish one on Broadway, complete with midgets, fire-eaters, a waterfall, a trained seal, nude showgirls—and room for one thousand patrons. Rose wanted a dance band, too, and Benny Goodman was determined to provide it.

There were a number of black bands already playing the kind of music Goodman had in mind, but Rose insisted upon a white outfit and there were just two of those: one led by the talented but quarrelsome Dorsey brothers, Jimmy and Tommy, and the crisp, disciplined Casa Loma Orchestra, then broadcasting weekly over the CBS network from the Glen Island Casino in Westchester.

Billie Holiday, photographed between performances behind the Apollo Theater in Harlem with, clockwise from left, Ben Webster, "Shoebrush" (possibly a stagehand), saxophonist Johnny Russell, and pianist Ram Ramirez, 1935

The permanent cast of the *Let's Dance* program assembled in NBC's cavernous Studio 8H, big enough to play host to three orchestras plus professional ballroom dancers and an audience of one thousand. Benny Goodman and his band are at the far left, Xavier Cugat holds the baton just above the microphone, surrounded by members of his Latin orchestra, and beyond him (also with a baton) is Kel Murray and his orchestra, specialists in sweet commercial dance music.

Both were managed by the powerful Rockwell-O'Keefe agency, run by Louis Armstrong's onetime manager, Tommy Rockwell, and his partner, a veteran dance-band booker, Francis "Cork" O'Keefe.

Goodman was just twenty-three and had no manager, but the records he had made under his own name had encouraged him to see himself as a potential bandleader and he began to think he could outdo both the Dorseys and the Casa Loma orchestra. He knew what kind of band he wanted:

> I was interested only in jazz. I wanted to play dance music in a free and musical style—in other words, in the way that most good musicians wanted to play, but weren't allowed to on the ordinary job. . . . My feeling was that the kind of music I liked to play (and did, whenever I had the opportunity) was something real and genuine which the public would go for if they had a chance to hear it. Certainly if musicians who worked six or eight hours a night would go out of their way to hear a band that played as if it enjoyed its work (like Duke's or Fletcher's) then certainly the public ought to like it, too. . . . [N]o white band had yet gotten together a good rhythm section that would kick out, . . . or swing . . . using arrangements that fit in with this idea, which would give the men a chance to play solos and express the music in their own individual way.

With John Hammond's help, he began to round up young musicians who shared his passion for what he called "genuine" jazz and put them all through rigorous rehearsals. "Nothing less than perfection would do," he said. "I lived that music and expected everybody else to live it, too." At their first audition, Billy Rose was not impressed but he agreed to hear them again. Meanwhile, Goodman found himself a seventeen-year-old singer named Helen Ward. Her attractive presence helped per-

suade Rose to give Goodman his chance. The club opened in June of 1934, Goodman remembered, and "the band got a few favorable notices here and there in the papers," even if most of the customers seemed unsure just how to dance to the music it made. But then the mobsters who had provided Rose with his backing decided Goodman and his men were being paid too much. They were given notice.

Goodman was devastated: "This was probably the toughest blow I ever received," he said. Another disappointment followed hard on its heels. John Hammond came to him with a visionary proposal. He was in the process of creating a "real all-star band" for a tour of the British Isles, he told Goodman: "His idea was to pick the best men, regardless of color, . . . the first mixed band in jazz history." He had already signed up the drummer Gene Krupa and the pianist Teddy Wilson, saxophonists Benny Carter and Chu Berry, trombonists Jack Teagarden and J. C. Higginbotham, and trumpet players Charlie Teagarden, Doc Cheatham, and Henry "Red" Allen. Nothing like it had ever been attempted before. Would Goodman agree to front the band? He eagerly said yes, and got himself a passport. Hammond drummed up British excitement about the tour by writing about it anonymously in *Melody Maker.* "This combination is the most significant which the world has ever known," he assured his English readers, "and its educational value for British musicians is beyond dispute." But in his impetuous zeal, Hammond had neglected either to get a firm commitment from English booking agents or to consult the British musician's union, which saw the arrival of American bands, whatever the color of the men playing in them, as a threat to its membership. Times were hard in Britain, too. "Finally, just as everything seemed set and we were practically ready to get on a boat," Goodman remembered, "the scheme collapsed, and fourteen guys were brought down as they never had been before." The British Ministry of Labour had refused permission for the tour. Hammond was so embarrassed by this failure that when he came to write his autobiography he left out all mention of it.

Still looking for work, Goodman approached Tommy Rockwell for help. Not a chance, Rockwell told him. He and O'Keefe already managed Jimmy Dorsey (now separated from his brother, Tommy) and didn't need another band led by a reed player.

Meanwhile, Goodman had learned that the National Broadcasting Company was planning a new three-hour Saturday night radio program called *Let's Dance*. The show needed three bands—one to play rhumbas and tangos, one to play sweet dance music, and one to play the kind of hot music the Casa Loma Orchestra was already broadcasting on CBS, the kind younger dancers seemed to like, the kind Benny Goodman was still determined to play. Again, there were several black bands—Chick Webb's, Fletcher Henderson's, and Benny Carter's among them—that could have filled that bill but the network studios were closed to them.

Goodman regrouped, rehearsed, auditioned, and—after a straw vote among the younger employees of the advertising agency that was handling the show—landed the job. It was his big break: weekly network appearances could make his a national name.

The orchestra now included a number of first-class musicians, among them the drummer Gene Krupa, reedmen Toots Mondello and Art Rollini, and, off and on, the brilliant but hard-drinking trumpeter Bunny Berigan, who, Louis Armstrong believed, "can't do no wrong in music." (The feeling was mutual: all a trumpet man really needed on the road, Berigan once said, was a toothbrush and a photo of Louis Armstrong.) But Goodman was still worried. On a visit to his friends, the singer Mildred Bailey and her husband, the xylophone player Red Norvo, Goodman complained that the band still sounded too much like

This ad for the *Let's Dance* radio program came from a pamphlet put out by its sponsor, Nabisco's Uneeda Biscuits.

the one led by the Dorsey brothers and that it had nowhere near enough arrangements to fill all the airtime he was about to be given. Bailey agreed: what Goodman needed was "a Harlem book." She urged him to talk with Fletcher Henderson.

By the time John Hammond approached him on the band's behalf, Goodman remembered, "Fletcher was pretty much up against it"—he was bankrupt, in fact, and had had to break up his orchestra for the time being—and he was happy to sell Goodman a few of his charts, and to write new ones for him, as well. "The first two arrangements we got from Fletcher," Goodman remembered, "were ones that he had been using in his own band—[Jelly Roll Morton's] 'King Porter Stomp' and his brother Horace's 'Big John Special.' As far as I know, it was the first time they had been played by a white orchestra, and it was one of the biggest kicks I've had in music to . . . dig the music out of them, even in rehearsal."

Just as important for Goodman's future, Henderson turned out to have a genius for

turning popular songs of the day—"melodic tunes," Goodman called them—like "Can't We Be Friends," "Blue Skies," "I Can't Give You Anything But Love," "Sometimes I'm Happy"—into big-band standards. "Song is the wind-chime of memory and these were our songs," the writer James T. Maher recalled. "They were part of the daily ordinary and this is what took Benny over the gap, out of jazz, into the American parlor. He arrived with 'Blue Skies.' Well we knew 'Blue Skies.' I mean everybody knew Irving Berlin so that we were home free. 'This is our guy,' we said."

"*These* were the things, with their wonderful easy style and great background figures, that really set the style of the band," Goodman said.

Up to that time the only kind of arrangements that the public had paid much attention to, so far as knowing who was responsible for them was concerned, were the elaborate ones such as Ferde Grofé's for Whiteman. But the art of making an arrangement a band can play with swing . . . one that really helps a solo player get off and gives him the right background to work against—that's something very few musicians can do. The whole idea is that the ensemble passages where the whole band is playing together or one section has the lead, have to be written in more or less the same style that a soloist would use if he were improvising. That is what Fletcher really could do so wonderfully . . . so that the whole thing really hung together and sounded unified.

Other arrangers would write for Goodman, including Benny Carter, Jimmy Mundy, Gordon Jenkins, Edgar Sampson, Fletcher Henderson's brother, Horace, and a Mormon saxophone player named Spud Murphy. But, Goodman said later, "Fletcher's ideas were far ahead of anybody else's. Without Fletcher I probably would have had a pretty good band but something quite different from what it . . . turned out to be."

Spurred by an unprecedented advertising campaign, which called upon Nabisco customers to hold Saturday-night dance parties in their living rooms, *Let's Dance* was a hit—young Americans began planning their Saturday nights around the show. Its original thirteen-week contract was renewed for a second thirteen weeks. The Goodman band made a series of records for Victor, and they started to sell. Benny Goodman's reputation was spreading fast.

The tenor saxophonist Jerry Jerome was then a pre-med student in New York. "I'd never heard a clarinet like that," he remembered, "nothing like what Benny played. And the band too. Playing Fletcher Henderson's kind of music with a tremendous beat. I would be studying pathology, and I dropped my books Saturday night at 12 midnight and put that show on. Forget about pathology, I gave my good cells a chance to work out listening to that kind of music. It was fabulous, just wonderful."

WHAT I WANTED TO PLAY

Not long after his battle with Lester Young in Kansas City, Coleman Hawkins had sailed for Europe. He'd been playing in Fletcher Henderson's band for more than a decade, had grown weary of watching Henderson pass up opportunities and bungle bookings, and, when he heard of the reception Duke Ellington and others had received abroad, decided to try his luck overseas, as well. He sent a cable to the British bandleader and booking agent Jack Hylton: I'M INTERESTED IN COMING TO ENGLAND. COLEMAN HAWKINS. When Hylton responded with an offer of fifty pounds a week, Hawkins asked Henderson for a couple of months' leave and set sail for England. He would not return to America for more than five years.

Lester Young was hired to take Hawkins's place. It didn't go well. The men in the band couldn't get Hawkins's huge sound out of their heads. "The whole band was buzzing on me because I had taken Hawk's place," Young remembered. "I didn't have the same kind of sound he had. I was rooming at the Henderson house and Leora Henderson would wake me up in the morning and play Hawkins's records for me so I could play like he did. . . . I just listened. I didn't want to hurt her feelings." The hostility of his fellow musicians was wounding. "I had in mind what I wanted to play and I was going to play," he recalled. "That's the only time that ever happened, someone telling me to play differently from the way I wanted to."

Life was made a little more bearable by Billie Holiday, who met Young at a Harlem jam session, fell in love with his light, laidback sound that seemed so like her own, and took him home for a time to live with her and her mother. But Young refused to alter his style to suit anyone. Finally, reluctantly, Henderson decided Young would never fit into his band; the other men remained too hostile. "I'm going to let this boy go," he told his reedmen, "because he'll have no peace around here. But before I do, I just want to say this. He can outplay you—and you—and *you!*" Young boarded a train and headed back to Kansas City, but he would be back, and when he returned he would upset the world of jazz just as he had once upset the Negro section of Oklahoma City.

LOST IN A WILDERNESS

In early 1934, Duke Ellington's mother, Daisy, had been diagnosed with cancer. She had always been the center of her son's world and he sought out the finest specialists in the country to help her. But they could do nothing. Ellington was at her side, his head resting next to hers on the pillow, when she died on May 27 of the following year.

For her funeral in Washington, D.C., her son filled the church with three thousand flowers and asked Irving Mills to buy the most splendid casket he could find. Then, he collapsed in grief. "After my mother passed," he remembered, "there was really nothing, and my sparkling parade was . . . at an end." He drank heavily for a time, saw no one, refused to leave the apartment they had shared. "His world had been built around his mother," Mercer Ellington remembered, "and the days after her death were the saddest and most morbid of his life." And when he did return to the road he could not bring himself to compose as he once had. "The bottom's out of everything," he said. "I have no ambition left. When mother was alive I . . . could fight with anybody, against any kind of odds. . . . Now what? I can see nothing."

Then, slowly, he began to work again, on a tribute to his mother. As he wrote and

Daisy Ellington (left), her husband, J.E., and her daughter Ruth, about 1932

rewrote in his train compartment, he remembered, tears stained the music sheets. He called the piece "Reminiscing in Tempo." "It was written in a soliloquizing mood," he once explained. "My mother's death was the greatest shock. I didn't do anything but brood. The music is representative of that. It begins with pleasant thoughts. Then something awful gets you down. Then you snap out of it." It was the most ambitious music he had yet written, in three movements, thirteen minutes long, covering both sides of two records, nearly twice as long as "Creole Rhapsody."

Most critics weren't sure what to make of it. But John Hammond had no doubts: he hated it. He had not forgotten the icy courtesy with which Ellington had returned his farewell gift. Hammond's sympathy for musicians rarely extended to those who functioned independently of him, and he reserved for himself the right to decide what artists should do and not do with their talents. In an article for the Brooklyn *Eagle* entitled "The Tragedy of Duke Ellington, the 'Black Prince' of Jazz: A Musician of Great Talent Forsakes Simplicity for Pretension," he declared Ellington's tribute to his beloved mother "vapid . . . without the slightest semblance of guts . . . formless and shallow." The cause, he continued, was the composer's character.

> He suffers abuse and exploitation with an Olympian calm and fortitude, never deigning to fight back or stand up for even his most elemental rights. Unpleasantness of any sort he flees from; he would greatly prefer not seeing the seamier side of existence, and has spent most of his recent years in escaping from the harsh reality that faces even the most secure among Negroes. . . .
>
> The real trouble with the Duke's music is the fact that he has purposely kept himself from any contact with the troubles of his people or mankind in general. It would proba-

bly take . . . a Langston Hughes to describe the way he shuts his eyes to the abuses being heaped upon his race and his original class. He consciously keeps himself from thinking about such problems as those of the southern sharecroppers or the Scottsboro Boys . . . though he is too intelligent not to know that these all do exist.

Ellington rarely replied to criticism directly. "I have always been a firm believer in experimentation," was all that he would say. "To stand still musically is equivalent to losing ground." But this marked the beginning of his lifelong dislike of music critics.

"There were two worlds of jazz," James T. Maher remembered many years later, "the world of the musician and the world of the writer, observer, critic. The critic frequently is defining jazz, telling the musician what he could play, what he couldn't play or should play, or shouldn't play. These were the people who established what is the canon of jazz: what jazz is, what it isn't. Who's good, who's bad. Who's a hero, who's a bum. . . . I often [felt that] musicians going through the years reading this stuff must have felt they were absolutely lost in a wilderness."

THE BEST FRIEND
I EVER HAD

Louis Armstrong's second overseas tour, that began in July of 1933, had been at least as eventful as the first. His midocean confrontation with Johnny Collins had only been the beginning. He discovered that Collins had been cheating him steadily, had failed to pay British taxes due after his first visit, had even pocketed money that had been earmarked for his estranged wife, Lil. And he had offended British fans everywhere Armstrong appeared. Armstrong fired him and a drunken Collins sailed for

Publicity photograph of Louis Armstrong, distributed when he was still under Johnny Collins's management

home, carrying with him Armstrong's passport. When Collins sobered up, he realized he had lost his big attraction and sent him a telegram declaring himself STILL ALL FOR YOU. Armstrong threw it in the wastebasket. "Never, never, never," he said.

He played London's Holborne Empire Theatre, where the audience loved him but critics accused him of including too much show business and too little memorable music, then undertook a frantic tour of other British cities and a triumphant visit to the Continent—Holland, Sweden, Norway, and Denmark, where ten thousand fans turned out to meet him at the Copenhagen railroad station, so many that he was at first convinced they must be waiting for someone else. He was billed as "The Messiah of Jazz," "The Superhuman of the Trumpet," "The *Real* King of Jazz."

With the British bandleader Jack Hylton as his temporary booking agent, he returned to London in December, for another week-long appearance at the Holborne

Louis Armstrong on his own in London

Chicago summit: a party for Duke Ellington and Louis Armstrong, held at Tony's Tavern at 52 West Thirty-first Street, February 14, 1935. In addition to the guests of honor, seated side by side on the left side of the table, the party included Armstrong's companion Alpha Smith, just beyond him, the trumpet player Punch Miller, waving his instrument, and, across from Armstrong, Wellman Braud, who was Ellington's bassist and an old friend of Armstrong's from New Orleans.

Empire, playing a breathtaking version of "Shine" that ended each night with seventy high C's in a row, followed by a climactic high F. One evening in midsolo he split his lip—"blood all down in my tuxedo shirt, nobody knew it. Just bowed off the stage . . . and didn't go back for four months." He spent some time resting in London—where he and Alpha found a restaurant that prepared reasonably authentic red beans and rice, his favorite New Orleans dish—then moved on to Paris where delirious French admirers followed him everywhere and he "had to take so many bows until I wound up takin' 'em in my bathrobe." Afterward, he started off on another tour—Belgium, Switzerland, and Italy, this time—but his lip, badly callused and liable to infection after years of outperforming other trumpet players, continued to plague him. "His lips were as hard as a piece of wood and he was bleeding," the trombonist Arthur Briggs remembered. "We thought he had some very sad disease."

Finally, in January of 1935, he sailed for home—and into a world of trouble. Each of his ex-agents was suing him for breach of contract, and Collins was threatening bodily harm, as well. His estranged wife, Lil, was threatening to take him to court for back maintenance. Alpha Smith was insisting he get a divorce and marry her. And when he got back to Chicago he couldn't seem to find steady work, was forced to sell his thirty-two-hundred-dollar car to raise a badly needed three hundred dollars. Even Louis Armstrong had finally hit hard times. "Couldn't go no further with all them shysters yipping at me," he recalled.

Then, Joe Glaser reentered his life. Glaser had been the manager of the Sunset Café in 1926 and 1927, and Armstrong had been impressed by him, "had always admired the way he treated his help," he said. "He seemed to understand colored people so much." He was also, Armstrong said, both a tough "crude son of a bitch" and well connected in the underworld—strengths, not weaknesses, to someone who had grown up working in New Orleans tonks and who had as yet seen no evidence that it was possible for any lone black man, no matter how celebrated or gifted, to get a fair shake unaided. The son of a well-to-do Chicago doctor, Glaser had once planned to become a physician himself, but had become a front man for the Capone mob, instead. He managed prize fighters—and fixed fights; ran a brothel, and was taken to court twice for sleeping with underaged girls. But Repeal had now broken organized crime's grip on Chicago. Al Capone himself was in federal prison—and minor hoodlums like Glaser found themselves hard pressed to make a living.

Both men agreed that Armstrong sought Glaser out in the spring of 1935, but otherwise their accounts differ as to how their new association began. Glaser claimed Armstrong had been desperate when he came to see him—"broke and very sick. He said, 'I don't want to be with anybody but you. Please Mr. Glaser, just you and I. You understand me and I understand you.' And I said, 'Louis you're me, and I'm you.'" Then, Glaser said, he gave up all his other flourishing enterprises in order to focus exclusively on Armstrong's career.

Armstrong contended that it was Glaser who had been "down and out . . . raggedy ass," when he asked him to become his manager, and that at first Glaser had said he couldn't do it because he was penniless. "That don't make no difference," Armstrong said he told him. "You get me the jobs, you collect the money. You pay me one thousand dollars every week free and clear. You pay off the band, the travel and hotel expenses, my income tax, and you take everything that's left."

Whatever really happened during their first discussion—and it seems clear that each man really did need the other—Glaser quickly put Armstrong's house in order. He placated both of Armstrong's ex-managers and his wife, arranged for him to front a big

Louis Armstrong and Joe Glaser

band directed by the trumpet player Zilner Randolph, and negotiated for him a lucrative contract with Jack Kapp of Decca Records, the same brand-new firm that was now producing hit after thirty-five-cent hit for Bing Crosby. He also made the bookings, arranged bus and hotel rooms, kept the books, paid the bills, and sometimes rode along with the band when it went south to ensure that his star and his band were treated properly. The two men are thought never to have had a written contract, and Glaser may have pocketed as much as half of Armstrong's earnings over the next three decades. But, as Johnny Williams, a bass player in the Russell band remembered, while he would eventually manage a whole

stable of black stars, "Mr. Glaser would tell all of the other entertainers in his office, 'Louis Armstrong comes first, everybody else is second.' "

By midsummer of 1935, thanks largely to Glaser's genius at publicity, Armstrong was back on the road and back on top. August 18, the Pittsburgh *Courier* reported, was "Louie Armstrong day up and down the [Monongahela] Valley. . . . Wherever you go you can hear a Victor record with Armstrong . . . warbling his ditties and blowing his trumpet to reach notes no other trumpet player can ever hope to attain. From Rankin, East Pittsburgh, Homestead, Duquesne, Clairton, McKeesport, Mon City, Monessen, Donora and other neighboring

towns and villages, they're planning motor cavalcades." Two weeks later, a correspondent for the same paper reported, Armstrong was breaking records at the Howard Theater in Washington, D.C. "Never has Washington given an artist a greater ovation than was accorded Louie here. Milling crowds followed him everywhere, autograph hunters keeping him busy, the man who played before . . . titled heads . . . who came to the U.S. and went into seclusion in Chicago, only to be brought out by his lifelong friend and advisor Joe Glaser . . . presented a musical unit . . . as distinctive . . . as any ever presented to an American public starving for something new."

Glaser brought to his new job the menacing air he'd learned on Chicago's South Side. "You don't know me," he liked to say when beginning negotiations with someone new, "but you know two things about me; I have a terrible temper and I always keep my word." He was "the most obscene, the most outrageous and the toughest agent I've ever bought an act from," one New York club owner said, and the impresario George Wein, who dealt with him in later years, developed a grudging admiration for his "wonderful ability to lie with total impunity."

To some observers with no firsthand knowledge of the world from which Armstrong had come, Glaser seemed uncomfortably overbearing and Armstrong strangely passive in his presence. But things were never quite as they seemed. Armstrong drew some lines over which even the man he always called "Mr. Glaser" dared not step: he would not forswear marijuana, for example, no matter how often his manager told him he must do so. And whenever Glaser proved too slow paying the bills, Armstrong managed to get his way by gently suggesting that if they weren't taken care of right away he just might not be able to make some of the bookings his manager had made for him. And when necessary, Armstrong could be very tough indeed. He

THE MUSIC OF THE DEGENERATE

Jazz music, built upon the principle of free expression, has always made dictators uncomfortable. The Soviet regime was ambivalent about jazz, at first. Ragtime had been popular under the last czar and touring American musicians like Sidney Bechet were still warmly received in the years following the Revolution. Things changed when Josef Stalin took power. In a 1928 article for *Pravda* entitled "The Music of the Gross," the novelist Maxim Gorky laid out the party's new position. Jazz was capitalist poison being deliberately spread among black Americans to keep them from dwelling on their status as slaves of the System.

> [T]here are rumblings, wails and howls like the smarting of a metal pig, the shriek of a donkey, or the amorous croaking of a monstrous frog. This insulting chaos of insanity pulses to a throbbing rhythm. Listening for a few minutes to these wails, one involuntarily imagines an orchestra of sexually driven madmen conducted by a man-stallion brandishing a huge genital member. The monstrous bass belches out English words; a wild horn wails piercingly, calling to mind the cries of a raving camel; a drum pounds monotonously; a nasty little pipe tears at one's ears; a saxophone emits its quacking nasal sound. Fleshy hips sway, and thousands of heavy feet tread and shuffle. The music of the degenerate ends finally with a deafening thud, as though a case of pottery had been flung down to earth from the skies.

Jazz and jazz dancing were now seen as anti-Soviet. Schoolchildren who confessed to liking jazz were made to confess their errors in front of their classmates. Anyone caught playing American jazz records was subject to six months in jail.

Then, in 1933, Adolf Hitler came to power in Germany. Within weeks, the Nazis banned what they called "Nigger-Jew" music from the radio. Brownshirts broke up jazz concerts. National contests were organized to find a suitably Aryan substitute for jazz—Neue Deutsche Tanzmusik—"New German Dance Music." The result was leaden and cloying, without a hint of improvisation. Jews were eventually driven from the musician's union. Records made by artists identified as black or Jewish were dropped from some German record catalogues. Benny Goodman's records were formally banned when the Nazis learned that he was Jewish in 1937, but Artie Shaw went right on selling because the propaganda ministry had somehow become convinced that he was the son of the Irish writer George Bernard Shaw.

As the Nazis railed against the jazz "baccilus," the Soviet Comintern radically altered its attitude toward the music, even organized its own unwieldy forty-three–man State Jazz Orchestra of the Soviet Union. American Communists fell into line. For a time, the American party called for a Black Republic of the South, stretching from Virginia to Texas. African-Americans were henceforth to be seen as a *colonized* people, and jazz was officially declared a worthy folk music, expressive of their victimization. "Jazz has its roots in the oppressive measures of the southern plantation owners against the Negro masses," wrote Charles Edward Smith in the *Daily Worker*. "It is specifically a folk music. . . . That hot jazz continues to flourish and that at least some of those who produce it are beginning to realize its class content is another indication of the growing class consciousness of the masses." (Never mind that jazz had always been urban, not rural; that it was joyous and affirming rather than tragic; that most musicians, black as well as white, saw playing jazz primarily as a way to make a living.)

Entartete Musik, (Degenerate Music), catalogue of a Munich exhibition organized by the official Nazi cultural watchdog, Dr. Hans Severus Ziegler, in 1937

is said at least once to have threatened to cut Glaser's throat if he ever heard that his manager was pocketing money to which he, Armstrong, was entitled.

But in the end, he told one interviewer, he would always be grateful to Glaser for making it possible for him to focus on what he loved best—his music.

> So all those headaches of keeping a band, keeping musicians, paying them, watching the box office, commissions, paying taxes, picking songs to record—I don't bother with it. Joe just gave me so much every month, and took care of the rest. Maybe I'd be rich now if I'd tried to get the whole hog in one—but I just want to do the things I know how to do. Always looked to me like everybody who made a lot of money didn't do nothing but die and leave it—and rushed themselves into the cemetery. . . . And I'm going to send *everybody* flowers. I come from the old hustling territory, you know. Like the old Creole horn player, [Buddy] Petit, used to say every time we meet a parade or a funeral, "Won't never let this horn kill *me*. I'm going to kill *it*."

In his elliptical memoir, *Music Is My Mistress,* Duke Ellington captured something of the complicated relationship between the two men.

> Louis Armstrong and Joe Glaser; Joe Glaser and Louis Armstrong. Don't put the cart before the horse, they say, and at first glance you might think Louis was the horse doing all the pulling while Glaser was in the driver's seat of the cart. Obviously, a cart is a most convenient place to stash the gold. Then you realize that in spite of how well Joe Glaser did for himself, Louis still ended up a very rich man. . . . Joe Glaser watched over Louis Armstrong like the treasure he was.

SUCH AN AMERICAN THING

Around two-thirty in the afternoon on March 19, 1935, a sixteen-year-old Puerto Rican boy was caught trying to steal a ten-cent pocket knife from the S. H. Kress Five-and-Dime Store at 125th and Lenox Avenue. In the scuffle that followed he bit the hand of a clerk. The police were called and hustled the boy into the basement for questioning. A crowd began to gather. An ambulance arrived. Then, a hearse happened to pass by. Rumors spread, first that the boy was being beaten, then that he had been killed by the store clerks. Protesters began to harangue the police and were arrested. Someone hurled a brick through the Kress window.

Two days of rioting followed. Harlem became "a bedlam of missiles," wrote Alain Locke, "[of] shattered plate glass, whacking night sticks, mounted patrols, police sirens and police bullets." Scores of shop-windows were smashed; store shelves were emptied. One suspected looter was shot dead; one hundred more were injured. Even the Savoy Ballroom was damaged, and had to close briefly for repairs.

In the wake of the riots the editors of the New York *Daily News* sought to foster racial harmony in the city—and sell more newspapers—by sponsoring a Harvest Moon Ball, in which couples of all races from all five of the city's boroughs could compete in the waltz, tango, rhumba, fox-trot—and the lindy hop.

Herbert White—"Whitey" to admirers and enemies alike—was the bouncer at the Savoy. An ex-sergeant in the Hellfighters and the founder of a gang called the Jolly Fellows, whose members prided themselves on both their dancing and their street-fighting skills, he was also a sharp-eyed entrepreneur. The craze for lindy hopping had spread across the city, and Shorty Snowden and Twist Mouth George Ganaway

were already doing a brisk business entertaining at downtown parties. White wanted a piece of the action, too, and when Snowden and Ganaway rejected his offer to become their manager, he hand-picked six of the Savoy's best young dancers, and began drilling them over and over again for the *Daily News* contest. A well-publicized victory for a group of Savoy dancers whom he controlled could make him a rich man.

Norma Miller and Frankie Manning, both now well known at the Savoy, were among Whitey's chosen few, and the Harlem semifinals held at the Savoy turned out to be child's play for them. "Chick Webb's band played like they never had before," Norma Miller recalled, and the downtown judges were so dazzled that all three couples were sent on to the finals at Madison Square Garden.

Whitey gave them a pep talk at the Savoy before heading downtown: "We've got to show them what the lindy hop is all about," he said. "That we are the champs. You have

Frankie Manning, at right, urges dancers to perform one of the aerial maneuvers he pioneered at the Savoy.

The people for whom blues music was created in the first place . . . are dance-oriented people. They are dance-beat-oriented people. They refine all movement in the direction of dance-beat elegance. Their work movements become dance movements and so do their play movements; and so, indeed, do all the movements they use every day, including the way they walk, stand, turn, wave, shake hands, reach or make any gesture at all. So, if the overwhelming preponderance of their most talented musicians has been almost exclusively preoccupied with the composition and performance of dance music, it is altogether consistent with their most fundamental conceptions and responses to existence itself.

—ALBERT MURRAY

The lindy hop is said to have been born at the Manhattan Casino in 1928, but it reached its peak of perfection at the Savoy Ballroom in Harlem where these photographs were all taken during the 1930s.

Whitey's Lindy Hoppers. "Whitey"—Herbert White—is the man in the middle; Norma Miller stands to his right. The troupe was performing at the New Cotton Club in Culver City, California while filming *A Day at the Races* with the Marx Brothers in 1937.

got to bring back that Championship. You are the flag-bearers of the Savoy, and you know what we expect. . . . Let the *Daily News* report that we took it all, first, second and third! We want all three. Remember, we don't take out any other prizes. All we got is the lindy hop so you better make sure it belongs to us. Do you dig?"

"We dig!" the dancers answered in unison.

At the Garden, the Abe Lyman Orchestra and the newly reconstituted Fletcher Henderson band were to take turns on the bandstand. The program began with a Grand March around the dance floor as the big crowd applauded, Norma Miller remembered. "The noise increased as the lindy hoppers, the last in line, entered. We could hear the audience was with us, and we responded to their yells by swinging when we walked. Harlem was on parade."

The more traditional ballroom dancers came first, and Miller couldn't help thinking as she watched them glide past that while the steps they were doing were beautiful they "all had their roots in a foreign country, but the lindy hop was created in New York. In Harlem. . . . It was an American dance created by Americans. It had soul, and it had swing."

White lindy hoppers from elsewhere in the city went on first. "They seemed clumsy to us," Miller said. "Watching them butcher our dance made our tempers flare, and this made us even more determined to take the crown." Then, as the Henderson band tore into an up-tempo number, the Savoy dancers finally got their chance to take the floor, whirling, leaping, flying into the air—

and bringing the crowd roaring to its feet. When it was over, Norma Miller, Frankie Manning, and their friends had won first *and* second *and* third place, just as Whitey had hoped they would.

As members of Whitey's various traveling troupes—Whitey's Hopping Maniacs, Whitey's Lindy Hoppers, and the Jive-A-Dears—Norma Miller and Frankie Manning would become full-time professional dancers, delighting every kind of audience, appearing in the movies, everywhere spreading the message they had learned at the Savoy. Interviewed together many years later, they reflected on what they had learned on its dance floor.

NORMA MILLER: We lived in a very segregated country. But the most amazing thing about the [Savoy] Ballroom was it was the first building in America, ever in the world, that opened its doors, completely integrated. At the time we didn't understand that. See, the whole time of the years of our dancing, black and white danced together in the Ballroom. It never dawned on us, at least not on *me,* that there was a situation about black and white, 'cause we always had white competitors. We couldn't go to the Roseland [where black dancers were still barred]. But the Roseland could come to our Ballroom. So it was a normal thing for us, any night of the week you would see some of the great white stars come into the Ballroom, all kinds of white musicians. I saw Leopold *Stokowski* in the Savoy Ballroom! So I was raised in an integrated dance world. I didn't know about the other until I went outside the Ballroom. So, my first experience as far as dancing was concerned, was always integrated.

FRANKIE MANNING: Well, I'll tell you, when I was going to the Savoy, I wasn't realizing that white people

and black people were going there. All I could think about was *dancers* were going to the Savoy Ballroom. And whether you were black, green, yellow, or what, if you walked in the Savoy, the only thing we wanted to know is: Can you dance? And if you came in there, it wasn't like a white person walking in, and everybody turn around and look at them. We'd say, "Hey, he can *dance! Right! OK."* You know. But we didn't look up at his face to say he's black, green, yellow or what.

NORMA MILLER: And everybody came to dance. Swing has a marvelous thing of bringing people together.

FRANKIE MANNING: Oh. You said it.

NORMA MILLER: Ah, you *know* it. . . . We had white dancers in the Savoy Ballroom.

FRANKIE MANNING: Oh, yeah.

NORMA MILLER: And I'm telling you they were good.

FRANKIE MANNING: Oh, man, were they ever.

NORMA MILLER: They were so good that you wanted to *hit* 'em. But see, that was such an American thing. We had Italian boys that used to come from the Bronx. You had the Jewish boys that come from Brooklyn, and this melting pot—

FRANKIE MANNING: Oh, man—

NORMA MILLER: —of everybody trying to outdance each other. We didn't know how rich we were in relationships but fifty years ago, when we look back, we realize we had a wonderful thing going with all races and that's what made the Savoy such a wonderful place.

CAN'T YOU BOYS PLAY ANY WALTZES?

"Benny Goodman and his *Let's Dance* band are a great medicine," said *Metronome* in April 1935, "a truly great outfit—fine arrangers and musicians who are together all the time—they phrase together, they bite together, they *swing* together." Things looked bright for Benny Goodman that spring. Thanks to his weekly appearances on network radio and the records his band had begun to make, he was getting a name for himself among young people who loved to dance. And a series of unheralded appearances at the Savoy playing opposite Chick Webb, had, according to Goodman, given his men "a wonderful opportunity to compare our playing with his, to try to match some of the guts he got into the music."

Then, workers at Nabisco went out on strike. All baking stopped. With no biscuits to sell, the company canceled the show.

Goodman had a booking agent now. Willard Alexander, who worked for the Music Corporation of America agency and was himself just out of college, had been willing to gamble that college-age dancers would prefer Goodman's music to that being played by any of the otherwise uniformly sweet dance bands that made up the MCA roster. Alexander hastily arranged an engagement at the Roosevelt Hotel in Manhattan, home of Guy Lombardo. "We wanted to get work for the band," Alexander remembered. "Hell, we would have booked them into the Holland Tunnel." It was a disaster; Lombardo's fans could not abide Goodman's music. The waiters held their fingers in their ears. One indignant customer sent Goodman a scrawled note: "Just by way of *contrast,"* it said, "why not play something sweet and low?" The band was let go after just two weeks.

Meanwhile, determined to keep the Goodman band together, Alexander arranged a cross-country summer tour for the band,

Singer Helen Ward, Benny Goodman, and the Goodman orchestra surrounded by a sea of dancers at the Steel Pier in Atlantic City in 1936, the summer after their big breakthrough. Left to right, Chris Griffin and Ziggy Elman (trumpets), Gene Krupa (drums), Red Ballard (trombone), Hymie Schertzer (alto saxophone), Bill De Pew (reeds), Helen Ward, Benny Goodman, Murray McEachern (trombone), Zeke Zarchey (trumpet), Vido Musso (tenor saxophone), Arthur Rollini (baritone saxophone), Harry Goodman (bass), Jess Stacy (piano)

to end at the old Rainbow Gardens in Los Angeles—now refurbished and reopened as the Palomar Ball Room. Goodman was not pleased. "The West had a reputation for being corny," he remembered. "So I said, 'Well, this has got to get worse the farther west we go. I don't see any future in this at all.' "

Nonetheless, he and his band set out across the continent in July, playing one-nighters as they went for as little as $250. There was no money for a bus, so the musicians had to drive themselves. Enthusiastic dancers greeted them in Pittsburgh and Milwaukee. But in Denver, where they were scheduled to play for two weeks, the manager of a dance hall called Elitch's Garden demanded they leave after hearing them for just half an hour. "I hired a *dance* band," he said. "What's the matter—can't you boys play any waltzes?" Goodman managed to hold on to the job by sending out for stock arrangements and playing them absolutely straight. But he felt so humiliated at doing so that he wouldn't come out of his hotel room during the day. Things went from bad to worse. In Grand Junction, Colorado, the band played behind wire netting to keep from being hit by whiskey bottles hurled by disappointed dancers. A big crowd was waiting for them at MacFadden's Ballroom in Oakland and seemed to like their hot numbers but Goodman suspected it was a fluke. And at Pismo Beach, Helen Ward recalled, "We played in a fish barn. I mean that literally. The place *stank* of fish," and almost no one danced.

As Goodman's little caravan of cars rolled toward Los Angeles, he realized that if their luck didn't change, it was unlikely he could hold his orchestra together. "I thought we'd finish the engagement," he remembered, "then take the train back to New York and that would be it. I'd just be a clarinetist again."

They reached the Palomar on August 21. It was a cavernous place, larger than any ballroom Goodman had ever played before, and hundreds of young people had crowded the dance floor. "We took things a little easy with the opening sets," Goodman recalled, "sticking to the softer arrangements." The crowd seemed familiar with the music, but they were also unresponsive and oddly restive. "This went on for about an hour." Then, according to one member of the band, the trumpet player Bunny Berigan called out, "Let's cut the shit, Benny," meaning that the band should play the kind of arrangements they really liked. Goodman didn't need much urging: "I decided the whole thing had gotten to a point where it was make or break. If we had to flop, at least I'd do it in my own way, playing the kind of music I wanted to. For all I knew this might be our last night together, and we might as well have a good time. . . . I called out some of our big Fletcher arrangements."

Although Goodman didn't know it then, that was exactly what the young Californians had been waiting for: local disc jockeys had been playing his hottest records over the radio for weeks. "To our complete amazement, half the crowd stopped dancing and came surging around the stand. . . . After traveling three thousand miles, we finally found people who were up on what we were trying to do. That first big roar from the crowd was one of the sweetest sounds I ever heard in my life—and from that time on the night kept getting bigger and bigger as we played about every good number in our book."

The music Goodman and his men were playing was not new. Fletcher Henderson and Duke Ellington, Benny Carter, Chick Webb, the Casa Loma Orchestra, and others had been playing their version of it for years, but this well-rehearsed, hard-driving new outfit appealed as nothing else had to youthful white dancers. The swing era was about to begin—and jazz music would come as close as it ever would to becoming America's popular music.

REMINISCING
IN TEMPO

DAN MORGENSTERN

Though I was born in Europe, I'm a child of the swing era. Even in Vienna, home of the waltz, where I spent my earliest years, the sound of American popular music was heard. For me then, the main source of music was not the radio, which was for grown-ups to listen to news on, but the phonograph, with which I began a lifelong love affair as soon as I was old enough to master the mechanics of winding up the spring-driven motor and making the turntable start and stop.

The world has long since become spoiled in its easy consumption of recorded music, but I had to work for my magic sounds. My mother's portable phonograph had to be rewound after every three-minute 78 side—unless you liked the effect of the music gradually slowing down, which could be fun, especially when it came to the human voice. And 78s, made of shellac, were quite heavy for a small child to handle—and breakable. Before I began to make my own acquisitions, the "libraries" at my disposal consisted of the records my mother and her younger siblings had danced to as teenagers, from the early 1920s through the mid-1930s, when I began to get interested.

In retrospect, there wasn't much that could qualify as real jazz. The closest was "Georgia on My Mind" by the British trumpeter, singer, and Armstrong acolyte Nat Gonella—my first, indirect contact with the master. There was "Crazy People" by the Boswell Sisters, which I liked, and "St. Louis Blues" by Abe Lyman's Californians, which I didn't (and I was right—it's corny and loud). Early favorites were "Singin' in the Rain" and "Nobody But You" by Fred Rich's orchestra. As I discovered much later, this was a studio group including the Dorsey brothers, who were responsible for the good if brief jazz solos after the inevitable vocals that conditioned my young ears to English with an American accent.

There were a few classical records as well, and from an early age I was taken to Sunday symphony concerts for young people. But it wasn't until one of my father's closest friends, the great composer Alban Berg, presented me, on my sixth birthday, with two beautiful, shiny twelve-inch discs of Mozart's *Eine kleine Nachtmusik,* performed by members of the Berlin Philharmonic under Erich Kleiber, that this kind of music got through to me. I loved this piece, soon knew it by heart, and was shaken by Berg's sudden death just two months after he gave me this gift.

About a year later, much against my will, I started violin lessons. Like most kids, I'd been banging on pianos and enjoyed the effect, but Nathan Milstein had come to visit and proclaimed that I had the hands of a violinist. And our grand piano was no longer accessible to me. My father had lost his job as Viennese cultural correspondent for a major German newspaper in the wake of the Nazi takeover, and we had to take in a lodger—a famous but ill-tempered cellist, who needed the piano to rehearse and teach. Maybe it was because our tenant played a stringed instrument that I didn't take to the fiddle, but in any case, we soon had to leave Vienna. One of the ugliest and most unmusical sounds I'd yet heard was that produced by the crowds greeting the arrival of Hitler in the city where he had learned to hate Jews.

For years I was certain that my first taste of live jazz was in Denmark, where my mother and I found a haven after the Anschluss (my father wound up in France). But when I heard a record by Jack Hylton's band (Hylton was England's Paul Whiteman) called "Ellingtonia," I suddenly recalled that I had seen them in Vienna and heard this medley of "Black and Tan Fantasy," "It Don't Mean a Thing," "Mood Indigo," and "Bugle Call Rag." It was "Mood Indigo" that triggered my memory. For this number, the houselights had gone down and pin spotlights had picked up three instrumentalists at center stage: trumpet, trombone, and clarinet. The two brass horns had sparkling mutes in their bells, and the effect, combined with that haunting melody, was magical.

The jazz I heard and saw in Copenhagen, however, was something else. It came in the person of none other than Fats Waller, who gave a series of concerts in the Danish capital in the fall of 1938. My mother, bless her, took me to one of them, and I was fascinated by this huge black man who played the piano and sang, moved, and talked with such enormous energy and good humor that it was impossible to keep still (it mattered little that I understood only a word or two of his lyrics and patter).

Of course I had to have some Waller records, and by then I'd also taken a liking to Ella Fitzgerald and the Chick Webb band—in particular, the song "The Dipsy Doodle," which had a childish vocal that I enjoyed, though less than the Sandy Williams trombone solo that followed it. In those days, we listened to records in a different way than we do now. They were usually acquired one at a time, and one would listen again and again to each three-minute side. It was, I think, a good way to learn how to appreciate nuances.

In addition to Waller, I also got to see the Mills Brothers, that unique vocal quartet which then still had considerable jazz in its repertory. I was particularly taken with their "Tiger Rag." And while they were not American, the Quintette du Hot Club de France, which I also saw in concert, had jazz of a high order to offer in the persons of Django Reinhardt and Stephane Grappelli. Though I admired Grappelli's supple fiddling, it was the Gypsy guitarist Django, with some of the same vitality that Waller gave off, who got to me.

Soon afterward, World War II broke out, and there were no more foreign visitors. By then, I'd been in a boarding school outside Copenhagen for some time. It was run by a progressive educator who had a warm personality and all sorts of ideas about teaching kids, but no business sense whatever. The turnover of students and teachers was fairly constant, and the food pretty awful (rare for Denmark), but I had a good time. Discipline was lax, and the older kids liked me because I had my little record collection, by now including Benny Goodman and Artie Shaw, which I let them borrow to dance to, provided they'd let me kibitz. There was an older boy who knew a lot about jazz and had many more records than I; he had almost all the Goodman small-group sides and also liked the great Danish violinist Svend Asmussen. He was a loner, but sometimes he invited me to his room to listen. He chided me for letting other kids borrow my records—he was my first encounter with the odd species called the collector.

It was young Dan Morgenstern's dream to see Fifty-second Street by night when he reached America in 1947. Here it is in broad daylight the following year.

The boarding school came to a sudden and dramatic end during the war's first winter, which was uncommonly cold. There was no money for heating, so all classes were held in the big dining room, which had a fireplace that was fed by chopped-up furniture. Eventually the septic tank burst, and when a huge mound of frozen sewage decorated the backyard, the authorities swiftly closed the place. I was back in Copenhagen by early April, when, for the second time in my short life, I was awakened by Nazi-generated noise. This time it wasn't hysterical screaming but airplanes filling the sky. I had a good view of them from my slanting bedroom window. They were flying low enough that the swastika tail emblems were perfectly visible. Fortunately, they were dropping leaflets, not bombs, and despite my mother's entreaties, I rushed out to read the message. In very bad Danish, the leaflets informed the populace that the Germans had arrived to "protect" them.

As an unintended result of the Nazi occupation, jazz became more popular than ever—a phenomenon universal to countries under the Hitler jackboot. In France, Django Reinhardt enjoyed the greatest acclaim of his career, and even in Germany there were clandestine groups of jazz fans who'd meet to listen to records. Jazz was anathema to the Nazis, who considered it a mongrel affront to Aryan "culture," the product of an unholy alliance between Africans and Jews. But to those who hated the Nazis, jazz stood for freedom, for democracy, and for the spirit of America, which, especially after Pearl Harbor, seemed to embody hope for a better future. In Denmark, Asmussen became so popular that the Gestapo arrested him and took him to Berlin for questioning. When they eventually released him, he fled to Sweden, where I also wound up, after the Danish underground had ascertained that the Nazis were about to round up all Jews for deportation. The story of our rescue has been told often (if

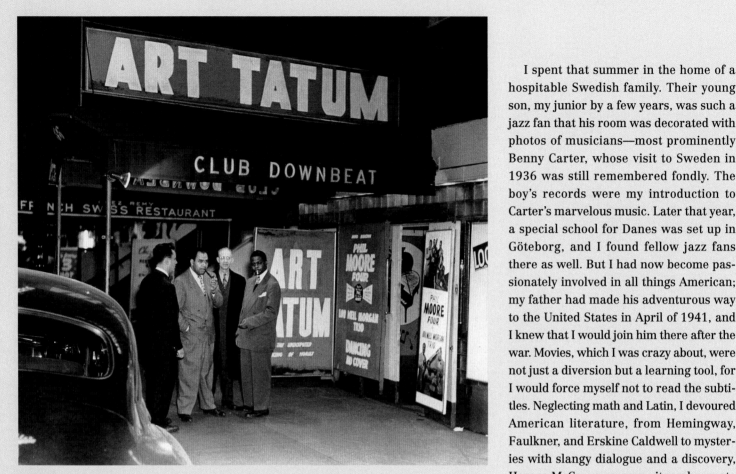

The Club Downbeat on Fifty-second Street. The man with the pipe is pianist and arranger Phil Moore, who during this engagement had the thankless task of playing on the same bill as Art Tatum.

I spent that summer in the home of a hospitable Swedish family. Their young son, my junior by a few years, was such a jazz fan that his room was decorated with photos of musicians—most prominently Benny Carter, whose visit to Sweden in 1936 was still remembered fondly. The boy's records were my introduction to Carter's marvelous music. Later that year, a special school for Danes was set up in Göteborg, and I found fellow jazz fans there as well. But I had now become passionately involved in all things American; my father had made his adventurous way to the United States in April of 1941, and I knew that I would join him there after the war. Movies, which I was crazy about, were not just a diversion but a learning tool, for I would force myself not to read the subtitles. Neglecting math and Latin, I devoured American literature, from Hemingway, Faulkner, and Erskine Caldwell to mysteries with slangy dialogue and a discovery, Horace McCoy, a screenwriter who wrote in a tough, Morse-code style. And, of course, I loved to hear jazz singers, who weren't always easy to decipher.

Much of our spare time, however, was now spent listening to war news on the radio. There was the BBC, of course, but also clandestine stations broadcasting anti-Nazi propaganda in German, and Radio Moscow in English and German. Not long after V-E Day, I was back in Denmark, where our neighbors had preserved our apartment and its contents—not a fork was missing, and the plants had been watered—again, as if that were simply the natural thing to do.

Though I was delighted to be in Copenhagen—a city I still love—my thoughts for the future were focused on America. It would be a while; my father had to become a U.S. citizen before my mother and I could be admitted. Meanwhile, my thus far rather scattershot interest in jazz began to become a bit more directed. I read a somewhat superficial history by Hugues Panassie; unfortunately, no one turned me on to a remarkable Danish book—Sven Møller Kristensen's *Hvad Jazz Er* (What Jazz Is), published in 1938—that was far better than Panassie or, for that matter, anything by then published in English. I also started to collect records seriously. I couldn't afford the specialist stores,

not often enough); what seems most remarkable about the experience is that the Danes who risked their lives to save strangers did so as if it were the most natural thing to do—a ray of light in the darkness of the twentieth century.

Sweden had no blackouts, as we'd had in Denmark, and there were new American movies and recent jazz records by way of England. Along with a bunch of other refugees, I soon found myself at a boarding school outside Stockholm that specialized in kids from upscale broken homes. One of my roommates, luckily, was a jazz fan with a small but distinguished stash of records. One of the best was "Bugle Call Rag" by a group generically known as The Rhythmmakers. Assembled by the enterprising Eddie Condon in the depth of the Depression, this joyful, integrated session featured Red Allen's trumpet, Pee Wee Russell's clarinet, Joe Sullivan's piano, and a super-caloric rhythm section anchored in Zutty Singleton's drums. Whoever woke up first would activate the turntable, and those swinging sounds would promptly dispatch any cobwebs. They were still lingering in my ear when, on June 6, 1944, the morning's first class was interrupted to bring us news of D day.

but I found a basement shop that was a marvelous jumble of secondhand records, books, and magazines. Not having yet discovered Charles Delaunay's *Hot Discography,* I was pretty much on my own, and would certainly have passed up a disc by the Mound City Blue Blowers if not for a notation on the label that said "Coleman Hawkins," a name I was aware of, mainly from the beautiful "Heartbreak Blues" I had already acquired. The Blue Blowers included not only Hawkins, whose "Hello Lola" and "One Hour" solos were landmarks in his career, but also Pee Wee Russell, already known to me from "Bugle Call Rag."

The first individual artist I collected was Duke Ellington, starting with the Okeh "Black and Tan Fantasy." Every Ellington record seemed to be different; nothing was predictable. My first Armstrong was a good one: the Hot Five's "Basin Street Blues." That, of course, is a blues in name only, but Muggsy Spanier's "Relaxin' at the Touro" was really the blues—one of my great early favorites. On occasion, I'd get some new records—British imports—at a fine, big music store, where a friendly jazz-minded salesclerk would give me some guidance (and in those days, of course, you could listen to a new record before you bought it). One fine day he persuaded me to purchase a book, American and very expensive but a good investment. This was *The Jazz Record Book,* published in 1942, which not only was an annotated guide to hundreds of records, from country blues to swing bands, but also contained a concise and well-written survey of jazz history. (Years later I came across a contemporary review by Barry Ulanov in *Metronome,* already the leading journal of jazz modernism, which castigated it for praising the music of Jelly Roll Morton and, in particular, Sidney Bechet. But in Denmark I was still blissfully unaware of journalistic infighting in the jazz world, and in any case I had found out about Bechet on my own, via a friend from school who owned the gorgeous "When the Sun Sets Down South.")

There was good Danish jazz as well—from Asmussen, still very popular, and from trombonist Peter Rasmussen, who could hold his own with the best Americans. I was still too young—and too broke—to hear live jazz in nightclubs, but there was the occasional concert, and also some fine programs of jazz films. The biggest event of my European phase, however, was the first visit of an American jazz band to Copenhagen since the prewar years. This occurred in the fall of 1946, and the band was Don Redman's, the last to be fronted by this big-band veteran who'd made history in the 1920s as Fletcher Henderson's chief arranger. It had been put together mainly to perform for U.S. servicemen and -women still stationed in Europe, with the assistance of Redman's friend the Danish jazz baron Timme Rosenkrantz.

The star soloist was Don Byas, a master of the tenor sax, who remained in Europe for the next twenty-six years and, as a result, did not achieve the wider critical recognition he deserved. Byas had been a member of the first group to play bebop on Fifty-second Street, but he was not stylistically a bopper. Nor were the other Redman stars—trombonist and vibraharpist Tyree Glenn, trumpeter and singer Peanuts Holland, and the twenty-five-year-old pianist Billy Taylor—but they were certainly at the cutting edge of swing. The band's two genuine boppers, interestingly, were its only white members, trumpeter Allan Jeffreys and trombonist Jack Carmen. The singer was Inez Cavanaugh, Rosenkrantz's companion and also an accomplished journalist.

I attended two of the four concerts and was swept away by Byas's huge tone and show-stopping balladeering on "Laura," the band's punch and swing on the up-tempo numbers, and Holland's playing and singing, influenced by Armstrong and Hot Lips Page. One of the band's most interesting numbers was "For Europeans Only" by Tadd Dameron, staff arranger for the Billy Eckstine and Dizzy Gillespie bands, whom Redman hailed as "a young man you will be hearing from." But it was the total impact of this genuine American jazz orchestra—with its rhythmic drive, individual virtuosity, and showmanship (the big production number was "Stormy Weather," featuring Cavanaugh, the band as a glee club, and several tempo changes; it brought down the house)—that was a taste of things to come.

On April 22, 1947, my mother and I arrived in New York. I hadn't seen my father since the spring of 1939, when I'd briefly visited him in Paris. He had a small radio, and on my first night in New York, when I couldn't sleep, I turned it on in search of what I expected to find in abundance: jazz. It took quite a while. There was lots of talk, not all of it in English, and much pop music, but no jazz. Finally, near the end of the dial (strictly AM in those days, of course), I caught the last notes of something jazzy, followed by the husky, black-sounding voice of the disc jockey, which I found hard to understand. He referred to himself by the unlikely name of Symphony Sid. What was even harder to comprehend was the music that followed: a version of a tune I gradually came to recognize as "I Can't Get Started," which I knew from Bunny Berigan's famous, triumphantly accented record. This version also featured a trumpet, but it was dirgelike, with an oddly mournful backdrop, and, to my naive ears, out of tune. (I knew dissonance from modern classical music but was unaccustomed to it in jazz.) This, of course, was Dizzy Gillespie's unique interpretation—an appropriate introduction to jazz in New York.

But I hadn't finally reached Manhattan to listen to jazz on the radio—or on records. While most first-time visitors wanted to see the Statue of Liberty (arriving by ocean liner, I'd already seen it) or the Empire State Building, I wanted to go to Fifty-second Street, that legendary block of jazz clubs I'd read so much about. It wasn't much to look at from the outside, though the names on the various marquees and sandwich boards made me drool. History tells us that by the spring of 1947 the street was well into its decline and fall, and to be sure, there were signs touting strippers and comedians. But having Sidney Bechet, Charlie Parker, and Billie Holiday all on the same block wasn't shabby.

I soon discovered that it was possible to hear a lot of music from outside the clubs, if there wasn't too much traffic noise and the doormen didn't chase you away. Eventually I learned how to nurse a beer through several sets of music by drinking from the bottle, which was opaque, instead of using a glass, which the bartender could easily spot when empty, or, if I wanted to stick around all night, to tip the bartender well on the first transaction, after which he'd leave me alone with my empty bottle.

I learned these tricks from a man who became my jazz Virgil—an unsung trumpeter named Nat Lorber, whom everyone knew as "Face." Nat did indeed have a striking visage: a big head with the broad features of his Russian-Jewish peasant ancestors. Both his parents were born in the old country and still spoke Yiddish at home. Nat, the oldest of three siblings, was born in 1920—in Harlem, as he liked to point out—and reared in the Bronx (where a neighbor was fellow trumpeter Milton Rajonsky, later known as Shorty Rogers) and then Brooklyn, where his father, a garment cutter, rented a modest house near Coney Island. Nat knew New York—all of it—like the back of his hand, and he knew where to find jazz off the beaten path.

I met Nat on Fifty-second Street at the White Rose, a bar where drinks were cheap and there was a so-called free lunch—pickled herring, beets, onions, cheese, pickles—and where the musicians hung out between sets when working or just anytime. We were introduced by a pretty girl who'd befriended me at a Greenwich Village left-wing gathering, and who'd taken me on my first visit to Harlem, to see Dizzy Gillespie's big band, with Chano Pozo, at the Apollo Theatre—an unforgettable event. Pozo, who would soon die, was something to see as well as to hear. She also took me to the Royal Roost, predecessor of Birdland as the home of bebop in New York. There I got to tell Tadd Dameron, whose band included Fats Navarro on trumpet, that I'd heard his music performed in Denmark. Tadd was the only musician who was interested in and nice to me—the others were attentive only to the ladies—and he and I became lifelong friends.

That same girl also introduced me to Randy Weston, the world's tallest pianist (and one of the best), who, happily, is still around.

In those early days he was still managing his father's candy store in the Bedford-Stuyvesant section of Brooklyn, where I spent a fabulous New Year's Eve at a local dance, with Randy's band supplying the music. It included the excellent guitarist Rector Bailey, never heard to advantage on records—the first of many musicians I was to come across who don't show up in the history books but could outplay many who do.

Nat Lorber was one of them. He couldn't read music, and his knowledge of harmony was rudimentary. He was mainly self-taught, though he took a few lessons from Charles Colin, a renowned trumpet teacher. He had one of the biggest sounds ever coaxed from a trumpet, and it was an attractive sound. He adored Louis Armstrong and knew everything there is to know about his records. When I met Nat, he was a protégé of another of his idols, Hot Lips Page, who always tried to find him jobs, though he had a hard enough time getting decent gigs for himself.

Lips was not very tall, but had an inch or more on Nat, whom he affectionately dubbed "Shorty" (which, with Lips's Texas accent, came out "Shawty"). Lips, whom I came to know through Nat, was the veritable incarnation of the spirit of jazz. A master of the blues instrumentally and vocally, he would, I'm sure, have finally found the fame he so richly deserved in the wake of Ray Charles's success, but it was too late for Lips by then—he died of a heart attack in 1954, at the age of forty-six. Though he was a consummate showman in the Armstrong mold (Lips came closer to Louis in certain ways than any other trumpeter-singer) and knew how to put together swinging bands, big and small, his true métier was the jam session. He was a master at setting riffs, a skill he no doubt had honed in Kansas City, and at beating off the right tempos. He could, when challenged, outblow all comers. In the words of Dizzy Gillespie, "When it comes to the blues, don't mess with Lips—not Louis, not Roy [Eldridge], not me, not anybody." Truth be told, it wasn't just the blues. Lips knew his changes, though he was anything but orthodox. And he was a great teacher of session etiquette. Bandstand boors would get their comeuppance in various ways, all designed to let them make fools of themselves. But he could also be kind and patient when it was called for.

Going uptown with Lips and Nat was a treat. Between them, they knew every joint where there might be some music. The wide variety of venues ranged from the Lotus, a workingman's bar equipped with a turnstile so no one could leave without having paid (Lips referred to it as "a bucket of blood," but I never witnessed any mayhem there), to the glamorous after-hours place in the basement of the Braddock Hotel, adjacent to the famous Minton's. Perhaps my fondest memory is of one so-called social

The interior of Condon's, owned and run by the guitarist Eddie Condon, who can be glimpsed through the cigarette smoke, keeping rock-steady time at the left side of the stage

club, after-hours but semi-legitimate. You had to sign up at first visit and receive a membership card, and only then would a door leading down a flight of stairs be opened. Greeted by the good uptown smell of chicken in the basket, we spotted Billie Holiday at a table consuming some of it as she listened to Art Tatum, seated at an upright piano. On the floor, sitting cross-legged, were Charlie Shavers and Joe Bushkin, gazing up at Art, who taunted Charlie: "Any note you can play, I'll play figure eights around it!"

When the music and the socializing ended, often after dawn, one might repair to Jenny Lou's (immortalized in Louis Jordan's "Early in the Morning"), a sparkling little restaurant appointed in southern style, where such simple things as eggs with grits and biscuits tasted like manna from heaven and the coffee too was out of this world. Harlem was also the home of marvelous ribs and the best potato salad I've ever tasted.

The Apollo was a trip. No other audience was so attuned to what transpired onstage, be it music, dance, or comedy. When B. B. King gave out with one of his long, suspended guitar notes, a perfectly placed comment from the audience rang out: "Take your time—this is my day off!" Pandemonium. When the Ellington band was in residence, one waited for the moment when Duke

would introduce Johnny Hodges. The always expressionless alto genius would slowly make his way to the solo mike (not that he needed it). When that first golden, glissandoed note issued forth, all the ladies would utter a collective sigh. And then there was the time when Dinah Washington and party were in the house, front row center, and we were seated right behind them, having come early to catch Redd Foxx in his favorite lair. Don't ask me to recall the repartee (in any case, not printable, even today), but I do know my gut was sore for days from laughing so hard.

Except for an occasional elbow at the bar, I never experienced any hostility in Harlem, even in later years, when the music scene, or what was left of it, had changed and the Apollo no longer was what it used to be. For a while, starting in the later fifties, there was a little bit of Harlem in midtown Manhattan. The Metropole on Seventh Avenue, between Forty-eighth and Forty-ninth Streets, which previously had featured Gay Nineties–style vaudeville entertainment, decided to switch to jazz. At first, it was sort of Dixieland, but then, starting with Max Kaminsky and Sol Yaged, it veered more toward what by then was called mainstream jazz; that is, latter-day swing. Red Allen was soon ensconced on the world's most peculiar bandstand, running above the nearly block-long bar (I never figured out how they got the upright piano into place; it was hard enough for the drummers), with mirrors both behind and across from the band. Music was continuous from three in the afternoon, when a trio began playing for five hours; after that two bands would alternate until closing time, between three and four in the morning.

Aside from Allen's band, which most often included Buster Bailey on clarinet, J. C. Higginbotham on trombone, and the great Cozy Cole on drums, there would be Roy Eldridge and Coleman Hawkins, when they were not touring with "Jazz at the Philharmonic," or Charlie Shavers and Budd Johnson, or any of a host of great musicians. Once Shavers sent Dizzy Gillespie in as a sub, and it was a kick to hear Dizzy with New Orleans veteran Tony Parenti on clarinet—they got along just fine. Twice each night both bands would play; this was the so-called jam session, and mostly it would be a fairly routine run-through of "When the

Saints Go Marching In," on which each hornman was also supposed to sing a chorus—something Hawkins steadfastly refused to do. On occasion, there'd be some sparks, such as when Red got ambitious and challenged Roy Eldridge, who smote him. But the most memorable jam was when Dinah Shore was in the house, Roy and Charlie Shavers were leading the bands, and "Dinah" was aptly chosen as the jam vehicle. Roy had his flügelhorn that night, and when he and Charlie got into trading eights and fours—look out!

Though the Metropole was kind of funky, celebrity visitors were not uncommon. And there were always musicians in the crowd. Miles Davis came by more than once to dig Roy and Hawk, and Roy insisted that this was where Miles picked up on the flügelhorn. John Coltrane came to check out Hawk, and stayed all night. And Benny Goodman came in to visit with his old friend Buster Bailey; they'd shared the same clarinet teacher in Chicago ages before.

Between sets one would repair across the street to the Copper Rail, a bar where the drinks were bigger and cheaper than at the Metropole, and where on a given afternoon and night one might encounter a veritable who's who of musicians. This was especially so after the Rail began to feature soul food, cooked up by a lady named Della, who, according to far-better-versed experts than I, was an artist without peer. Having been introduced in my early New York period to chitterlings—by a friend who cleverly didn't tell me what they were until I'd decided that they tasted good—I was ready to experiment, though my standbys were such things as chicken and dumplings, or smothered pork chops. Once, when I was checking out pig's tails, Ben Webster walked in, looked at my plate, and picked me up from the stool, holding me in the air and announcing to all present what I was dining on. (I also remember Ben, who himself had a reputation for being difficult when inebriated, trying his level best to restrain Oscar Pettiford, who was four sheets to the wind.)

Perhaps my most glorious night at the Copper Rail was when Louis Armstrong's All Stars did a one-night stand at the Metropole and the musicians threw a party for Pops across the street. This was just after "Hello, Dolly!" and there was a banner that read: "You Beat the Beatles!"

My first encounter with King Louis had come about fifteen years before, also through my friendship with Nat, who'd introduced me to a very special lady named Jeann Failows. (Incidentally, women on the jazz scene were generally much hipper than the men—musicians, of course, excepted.) Jeann, who'd been a WAC during the war and worked in publicity (she promoted a now exceedingly rare paperback called *To Be or Not to Bop*, an informal history of bebop by a young man named Nard Griffin; had done work for Musicraft Records; and produced jam sessions at various venues, including the Club Harlem on 145th Street), was a member of Armstrong's inner circle. At the time I met her, she was entrusted with Louis's voluminous fan mail from all over the world, which she would answer with Pops's personally autographed diet pointers, and, if need be, responses to often arcane questions.

Louis and the All Stars were appearing at the Roxy, a long-gone Times Square landmark, the biggest movie-and-stage show palace after Radio City Music Hall. Nat and I met Jeann at the backstage entrance and were escorted to Louis's dressing room. Wrapped in a white bathrobe, with that famous handkerchief tied around his head, he greeted us warmly. Jeann had to repeat my name, adding that I'd recently arrived from Denmark. Louis weighed "Morgenstern" and "Scandinavia," coming up with "Smorgasbord," his name for me from then on. But when he signed a photo for me, he made it out to Dan; it was the first of many. He had an astonishing knack for making you feel at ease in his presence; it quickly seemed as if you were an old friend. Someone who really was soon dropped in, Joe Bushkin, who presented Pops with a red rose, a gift from fan Tallulah Bankhead, who'd sent it with her love . . . and something else as well. Pops smelled the rose, broke into a smile, and extracted from the yet unopened blossom an elegantly rolled large reefer. Also present was an even older friend, June Clark. June, who was Louis's age, had been a prominent trumpeter on the New York scene in the 1920s, but tuberculosis had put an end to his career, and, as he often said, there was no reason for him to go on with the trumpet after what Louis had accomplished. For a time, he'd been Louis's road manager; later he would become Sugar Ray Robinson's right-hand man.

After a while, Louis excused himself, saying he wanted to catch a nap before the next show. He and June disappeared behind a partition, and Jeann gestured to us to be quiet. Soon we heard the most beautiful whistling: it was Louis's solo from the 1930 recording of "Sweethearts on Parade," note-perfect, with all the right inflections. June now emerged, saying, sotto voce: "He's asleep." It was a very special lullaby. Jeann informed us that June could whistle almost all of Louis's famous solos.

Half an hour later, it was time to wake Louis, who demonstrated his lifelong talent for going to sleep in seconds and waking up alert and refreshed regardless of the length of the nap. While Pops was getting dressed, trombonist Jack Teagarden dropped in to discuss a musical point. The rapport between the two was evident, but I was amazed at Jack's eyes; in the words

Nighttime on Fifty-second Street

of a famous blues song, they looked like cherries in a pool of buttermilk. The stage manager arrived to give the five-minute warning, and Pops promptly entrusted us to him, with firm instructions to find us places from which we could see well, leaving us with "Enjoy the show!" As you may well imagine, we did; as Mezz Mezzrow put it, "Them first kicks are killers." I would, thankfully, share many more times with Louis, and the magic never wore off.

Like the Ancient Mariner, I could go on and on. When I was "hanging out," I had no intention of becoming what people call a jazz "critic" (most who write about jazz aren't critics but, at best, reviewers, or reporters, editors, etc.). Since I was friendly with musicians, I shared their often jaundiced view of that other breed, very few of whom I ever encountered in my nocturnal pursuits of the muse. I haven't told of my encounters with a more modern breed of players, such as the time when I had a one-on-

one with Charlie Parker in the little bar next to Birdland called the Magpie. It was late afternoon; nobody in the joint; waiting to meet a friend. In walks Bird; it was the time when, briefly, he was using a cane, but he looked well and rested. He sat down next to me—a nice gesture, since there were many empty stools. "Mr. Parker," I said, "can I buy you a drink?" "Why don't you let me buy *you* one," he responded, and I noticed, as I had before when hearing him speak, how much he sounded like my main men, the guys from the generation before him. Not knowing what to say, I brought up Hot Lips Page, who had often talked about Bird and loved his playing. His face lit up at the mention of Lips's name, and he asked me when and where I had last seen him and to give Lips his best. I wish I could remember the rest, but there wasn't much, since Bird's date soon arrived and he said goodbye. I never had a chance to buy him that drink back.

Life moves in strange ways, and sometime after embarking on a journalistic career, I was urged by Stanley Dance—who was then visiting the United States and kept encountering me at the Copper Rail and at recording dates I was attending at the musicians' invitation—to send a monthly news column to the British magazine *Jazz Journal.* "They can't pay," he said, "but they'll give you records and books, and it would be a service to the musicians." Before that, I'd written about jazz a bit in the college paper I edited at Brandeis University, mainly to make propaganda for some jazz concerts we were producing—most memorably, a solo recital by Art Tatum (who told us, when we drove him back to Boston, where he was appearing with his trio, that this had been the very first time he'd done a concert all by himself, and he thanked us, which floored me, though I'd soon enough learn more about such injustices)—and a short review or two in the New York *Post,* where I was an editorial assistant, but this was a challenge.

My most enthusiastic early readers were my musician friends, and one thing led to another. What has served me best, I hope, is that I learned about the music not from books but from the people who created it, directly and indirectly. The greatest compliment I ever got was from Louis Armstrong. I had sent him an advance copy of the special issue of *Down Beat* we had prepared for his seventieth birthday, and for which we had gathered warm greetings from more than eighty musicians, covering the length and breadth of the music. Within days, a letter arrived in that familiar hand (Pops always addressed his envelopes himself). "I received the magazine," it said, "and it knocked me on my ass!" No raves from "critics" could ever top that.

THE VELOCITY OF CELEBRATION

In November of 1935, a young freelance writer from Toronto named Helen Oakley was living in Chicago, where she was disappointed to find very little of the jazz music she loved. She had expected to find the city where King Oliver and Louis Armstrong had first become famous a thriving jazz community. Instead, she remembered, it had become a "musical wilderness" in which jazz musicians were "looked on very poorly—even by their wives." With a friend from the suburbs, Edwin "Squirrel" Ashcraft III, she helped found the Chicago Rhythm Club to keep the music alive through a series of informal jam sessions.

Benny Goodman's weekly Let's Dance *broadcasts in 1934 had meant a great deal to her and her friends; they "lightened our hearts," she*

The Erskine Hawkins orchestra played for Americans of all kinds at the Savoy Ballroom during the late 1930s. Hawkins, always a favorite in Harlem, would eventually replace Chick Webb as the leader of the house band. The secret of his success, one of his veterans said, was that he "kept it simple" and never strayed too far from the blues.

remembered, offering hope that the near-total monopoly of sweet dance bands and saccharine crooners might one day be broken. And when she and Ashcraft learned that Goodman was about to follow his triumph at the Palomar Ballroom with a month at the Urban Room of the Congress Hotel—where no jazz had ever been played before—they determined to do all they could to make his homecoming a spectacular success.

First, they persuaded so many of their wealthy young friends to go to the Urban Room that dancing to Goodman's band became fashionable as well as fun. Then, Oakley herself went backstage with a scheme to garner for the band still more publicity. She proposed something never attempted before in America, a Sunday-afternoon benefit concert at the hotel, intended not for dancers, but for real jazz fans. Goodman was against it at first: "Hell, no!" he said. "After all, this is just dance music. What's the use of trying to make something fancy and formal out of it?" It just seemed like extra work to him. But he finally reluctantly agreed to try it. Oakley and Ashcraft sent a phalanx of debutantes out to sell tickets and in the end, eight hundred eager, mostly well-to-do jazz lovers crowded into the Urban Room on December 8, not to dance but to hear the band play. "Gene Krupa said it was the biggest thrill he'd had so far, for the people just to *listen* to them," Oakley recalled. "It was Chicago society and even Benny was a little impressed."

All the city papers ran enthusiastic stories. So did *Down Beat,* for which Helen Oakley was then writing. More important, a reporter for *Time* had been in the audience, and wrote up the concert for the January 20, 1936, issue of the magazine: "spectacled clarinetist Benny Goodman," he reported, "is the Man of the Hour to thousands of jazz fans," living proof that "jazz was reaching a second peak in U.S. musical history."

The band's one-month engagement at the Urban Room was extended to six, and

Goodman began to be billed as the "King of Swing." He hadn't liked the label at first. He knew that his music was little different from that already being played by Chick Webb, Fletcher Henderson, and others, and did not see himself as the "King" of anything. Also, he was worried about having the word "swing" applied to his music. "I didn't know how long this was going to last, and I didn't want to be tied down to something people might say was old-fashioned just because they got tired of the name."

But a new name for the music had been badly needed. For most Americans, mired in the Depression, "jazz" was an unhappy reminder of the years everyone wanted to forget, the era of frantic excess that had preceded the Crash. Swing became the word of choice, though even musicians were hard-pressed to provide a definition. "It's a livelier tempo," said Wingy Manone, "you know, swingy-like." Fats Waller called

For more than a decade, the Benny Goodman Orchestra would remain one of the most popular in the country. It topped the bill at Pittsburgh's Stanley Theatre in 1936 (opposite page), and ten years later (below), six thousand New York bobby-soxers still turned out at the 17th Regiment Armory to dance to Goodman's music and clamor for his autograph.

it "two-thirds rhythm and one-third soul." Chick Webb said it was "like loving a special girl; and you don't see her for a year, and then she comes back—it's something inside you." Duke Ellington defined it as "that part of rhythm that causes a buoyant, terpsichorean urge." Louis Armstrong, whose rhythmic innovations were at its heart, saw nothing new in swing: "They used to call it ragtime. Later on . . . it was called jazz music, hot music, gutbucket, and now they've poured a little gravy over it and called it swing music."

Laymen were understandably still more confused. The same *Time* article that hailed Benny Goodman's arrival reported as further evidence of a jazz renaissance the staggering popularity of a novelty tune called "The Music Goes 'Round and Around."

The music goes 'round and around,
Whoa-ho-ho-ho-ho-ho. . . .
And it comes out here . . .

Introduced by trumpet player Eddie Farley and trombonist Mike Riley at the Onyx Club on Fifty-second Street—once the favorite downtown speakeasy of New York musicians, now a legitimate nightclub—the song sold better than 100,000 records. In response to listeners' requests, one New York radio station played it twenty-eight times in a single evening. A rival station recorded it in eleven languages and dialects—including Polish and pig latin. It was a "nut song," in the goofy American tradition of "K-K-K-Katy," and "Yes, We Have No Bananas," with only the most tenuous link to jazz or to the brand of music Benny Goodman played, but *Time* gravely declared it "fundamentally a 'swing' tune," nonetheless.

Whatever swing was—and the word would eventually be used to describe everything from simple-minded novelty tunes aimed at teenagers to the sophisticated, richly textured creations of Duke Ellington's adult sensibility—it would catch on as no other music ever had before, would become the defining music for a whole generation of Americans. And jazz music, which had

been born in adversity and had already come to symbolize a certain kind of American freedom, would be called upon to lift the spirits and raise the morale of a frightened country. In the process it would also at least begin to break down some of the barriers that had separated Americans from each other for more than three hundred years.

Goodman's December concert had been so successful that three months later Helen Oakley and Squirrel Ashcraft organized another one in the same room. Fletcher Henderson was featured this time. He, too, drew a capacity crowd, and at the end invited Goodman and Gene Krupa to come up and play with a small group that included Chu Berry and the fiery young trumpeter Roy Eldridge. Goodman would later claim that this had been "the first time, probably, that white and colored musicians

Teddy Wilson. "America is the whole world," he wrote, and once he and Lionel Hampton joined the Goodman band—led by a Jewish immigrant's son, and made up of blacks as well as whites, northerners as well as southerners—it seemed to him something like the whole world, too.

had played together for a paying audience in America." It wasn't. Whites and blacks had worked together in Fate Marable's early bands on the Streckfus boats, Bubber Miley had played with Leo Reisman's orchestra after Duke Ellington fired him (though he had had to do so while dressed as an usher who just happened to have brought his horn to work), Benny Carter had briefly played as well as arranged for Charlie Barnet's orchestra, and no one will ever know how many light-skinned Creoles had been quietly performing alongside whites all along. But it was virtually unprecedented in a hotel ballroom setting, and the enthusiasm the Chicago audience had shown for seeing Goodman, Krupa, and the Henderson men jamming together emboldened Oakley to make yet another unwanted suggestion. There was to be a third Goodman concert on Easter Sunday, April 12. For that one, she told Goodman, he should import from New York the pianist Teddy Wilson, whose deft, lyrical, utterly confident touch had already helped account for the success of four sides cut earlier by the Benny Goodman Trio.

Theodore Shaw Wilson was the reserved, urbane son of a professor of English and a librarian at Tuskegee College. He had majored in music theory at Talladega College, before playing with Jimmie Noone, Louis Armstrong, and Benny Carter. Wilson admired Art Tatum and Fats Waller, but it was Earl Hines whose style seems to have meant the most to him. Hines had developed his "trumpet style" in the age before microphones, Wilson once explained, and in order to be heard had had to work out the long melodic lines he played with his right hand using octaves, not single notes. "But when I came up, the microphone was being used to amplify the piano so it wasn't necessary to have all the power that Hines used. This enabled me to do a lot of running in the right hand." Wilson's right-hand "running"—poised but endlessly inventive, succinct but always swinging—was an ideal match for Goodman's clarinet. Each was a

perfectionist. "Teddy is as nuts about accuracy as I am," Goodman once said. "He'll never let a note get away from him if he can possibly help it."

The two had played together as part of small studio bands organized by John Hammond back in 1934, but the idea of a trio recording had come about more or less by accident. Not long before Goodman began the tour that ended at the Palomar, he had gone to dinner again at Mildred Bailey's house in Forest Hills, New York. Wilson had happened to be there, too, and after everyone had finished eating, Bailey suggested that the two men play together while her young cousin kept time with a pair of whisk brooms on a kitchen chair. It was as if he and Wilson had been working together for years, Goodman remembered. "I don't know how many tunes we played that night, but when we finished everybody said it was a shame we didn't have records of what we played."

John Hammond remedied that right away. Just before Goodman left New York, Wilson cut four sides with the Benny Goodman Trio—"After You've Gone," "Body and Soul," "Who?" and "Someday Sweetheart." (Gene Krupa played drums.) Goodman loved the records—they were "just like chamber music," he said. But now, when Helen Oakley suggested that he include Wilson on the next concert program in Chicago, he was against it. "I'm not such a fool," he told her. "I'm making good. This is gonna be my career. I don't want to wreck everything to present a black talent in the middle of everything." Again, Oakley talked him into taking the chance, and again, it all went beautifully: "The three of us worked in together as if we had been born to play this way," Goodman said. "What surprised us was the great response from the audience."

Teddy Wilson became a permanent part of the Goodman organization, but as a separate attraction and a member of the trio, not as the regular pianist—that was Jess Stacy's job. (In congratulating Goodman for

The Benny Goodman quartet at the Paramount Theater in New York, 1937. Left to right, Teddy Wilson, Lionel Hampton, Gene Krupa, and Goodman himself. "The quartet is a beautiful thing all through," wrote Otis Ferguson in the *New Republic*, "really a labor of creative love."

hiring "a colored boy of great talent," *Down Beat* was careful also to praise Stacy for his "noble gesture" in being willing, even for a few numbers every night, to live "in the shadow of the colored man.") Goodman and Wilson were never personal friends—their relationship was "one of mutual respect," Wilson said. "They could never have been buddies," Helen Oakley explained, because of personality and class, not race. Wilson's parents were academics; Goodman's mother could not even read. "I'm sure Teddy must have sized Benny up and found him lacking in many ways," she said.

"Benny still had a lot of rough edges. . . . He was very unpolished and sometimes quite coarse. . . . Teddy's own background was so different."

Politics and civil rights never interested Goodman much. It was music that obsessed him. He wanted the best musicians he could find for his band. Black musicians were among the best. "They were the only ones that could outplay him," Helen Oakley recalled. "Nobody else could. They were the only ones that Benny would take seriously," and he now saw no reason why mere cus-

tom and prejudice should keep him from having them in his orchestra.

In Los Angeles the following summer, he hired twenty-eight-year-old Lionel Hampton, a master of an instrument relatively new to jazz, the vibraphone. Born in Louisville and raised in Chicago, Hampton had been a professional drummer since the age of fourteen. Like Teddy Wilson, he had played with Louis Armstrong—it had been Armstrong, in fact, who had urged him to take up the vibraphone—and, like Armstrong, he was a showman, dancing and singing as well as playing with an infectious

Do you remember what it was like? Maybe you do. Maybe you were there. Maybe you were there in New York two-thirds of the way through the 1930s, when there were so many great bands playing—so many of them at the same time. You could choose your spots—so many spots.

—George T. Simon

Midtown Manhattan at the height of the swing era

drive matched by few players in the history of the music.

The Goodman trio became a quartet. "That quartet was a beautiful sight," John Hammond remembered: "Teddy, cool, correct, the impeccable piano; Gene, with the chomping jaw, shaking head and falling lock of hair, crouched over his powerful drums—he had a heavy foot, did Gene, but an urgent, pulsating drive; Benny with clarinet an inch or two from his mouth so he could smile beatifically at some little four-mallet riff of Lionel's, then answering with one of those perfectly controlled, razor-edged, scintillating Goodman runs. I tell you those were lovely times!"

The quartet's first record, "Moonglow," swept the country. Some promoters still worried that integrating the organization would, in time, hurt business, and even Goodman thought it best not to include Hampton and Teddy Wilson when the band opened in Dallas. But after some patrons walked out, demanding their money back because the quartet had *not* appeared, he made sure that Hampton and Wilson were featured in every show. The question of whether white audiences would stand for seeing blacks and whites play together—at least when it came to the best-known band in the country—seemed to have been answered.

"Stand for it?" Otis Ferguson wrote in the *New Republic.*

The people stand up from their tables just to hear it better. They play every night, clarinet, piano, vibraphone, drums—and they make music you would not believe . . . not a false note, one finishing his solo and dropping into background support, then the other, all adding inspiration until . . . they get going too strong to quit. . . . This is really composition on the spot, with the spirit of jazz strongly over all of them but the iron laws of harmony and rhythm never lost sight of; and it is a collective thing, the most beau-tiful example of men working together to be seen in public today.

Goodman could be very tough with people who tried to come between him and the perfection that was his perpetual goal. Lionel Hampton remembered sitting with Wilson and Goodman in a club one evening when a drunk stumbled over to their table and asked, "Benny, what are you doing with these niggers in your band?"

"If you say that again," Goodman answered, "I'll take this clarinet and bust you across the head with it." The drunk backed off.

Goodman himself was always a little baffled by all the fuss made about his decision to bring Wilson and Hampton into his organization. "I never thought it was brave. . . . We just did it. . . . [T]hat was the way it was supposed to be. How can you play if you're gonna worry about a guy's color? It's tough enough just to *play.*"

THE KINGDOM OF SWING

People who had never listened to jazz before now were filling ballrooms all over the country—the Aragon in Chicago, the Arcadia in Detroit, the Alcazar in Baltimore, and the Ali Baba in Oakland; the Cinderella in Appleton, Wisconsin, and the Million Dollar Pier in Atlantic City; the Twilight in Fort Dodge, Iowa, and the Moonlight in Canton, Ohio, and hundreds, perhaps thousands, more. Big band swing became a hundred-million-dollar industry. Between thirty thousand and forty thousand musicians would find work playing swing music after 1935. Another eight thousand men and women were needed just to manage, book, and promote their appearances. Swing rescued the recording industry; only six million records had been sold in the United States in 1933; by 1939, that number would grow to fifty million, and three-fifths of them were being played on some 300,000 jukeboxes, pro-viding the accompaniment for a host of dances—the big apple and little peach, the shag and Susy Q, and the dance that had started it all—the lindy hop.

It took time for some jazz musicians, accustomed to small-group fare, to adjust to the demands playing in a swing band made on them. Max Kaminsky joined Tommy Dorsey in 1935.

All the years before, we had just played songs as we felt them, but now a whole new era of arranged section playing was starting, and reading the parts and counting the rests was a completely different feeling from the free-swinging improvisation I had been used to. It was a big thing to get used to sitting in a band and playing for a while and then just sitting there waiting for your turn to play again. And this was a different kind of arranged music which—thanks to Fletcher Henderson, Don Redman, . . . Duke Ellington, and all the other Negro bandleaders who had figured it out years ago—enabled the big bands to swing. Formerly the big dance bands would have one section playing at a time, so that the arrangements were really a series of section solos, but five saxes playing instead of one, and none of them swinging. But now, with one section playing against another section, and within the riffing of phrases, and by using jazzmen who gave the music a hot, driving tone, the whole band swung.

Hundreds of bands were on the road now, and young Americans followed the careers of the men who played in them just as they followed those of athletes and movie stars. The writer Elizabeth Hardwick was a Kentucky high school girl in those years and later remembered the matter-of-fact way in which she and her young friends had received the comings and goings of the great bands and the miraculous music they made.

[T]here was a dance place just outside of [Lexington] called Joyland Park. In the summer the great bands arrived, Ellington, Louis Armstrong, Chick Webb, sometimes for a Friday and Saturday or merely for one night. When I speak of the great bands it must not be taken to mean that we thought of them as such. No, they were part of the summer nights and the hot dog stands, the fetid swimming pool heavy with chlorine, the screaming roller coaster, the old rain-splintered picnic tables, the broken iron swings. And the bands were also part of Southern drunkenness, couples drinking coke and whisky, vomiting, being unfaithful, lovelorn, frantic. The black musicians, with their cumbersome instruments, their tuxedos, were simply there to beat out time for the stumbling, cuddling fox-trotting of the period.

The band busses, parked in the field, caravans in which they suffered the litter of cigarettes and bottles, the hot, streaking highways, all night, or resting for a few hours in the black quarters: the Via Dolorosa of show business. They arrived at last, nowhere, to audiences large or small, often with us depending upon the calendar of the Park, the other occasions from which the crowd would spill over into the dance hall. Ellington's band. And what were we doing, standing close, murmuring the lyrics?

At our high school dances in the winter, small, cheap, local events. We

Jimmie Lunceford, center, once said that "A band that looks good, goes in for better showmanship, and seems to be enjoying its work will always be sure of a return visit." Lunceford's orchestra demonstrated those truths night after night for more than twenty years. He had fine soloists, but it was the band's showmanship, its astonishing ensemble precision, and the irresistible arrangements of Sy Oliver that brought dancers to their feet wherever it played.

Charlie Barnet, shown here fronting his band in an RKO film called *Music in Manhattan*, dropped out of Yale to play tenor saxophone like his idol, Coleman Hawkins. Lena Horne would be his singer for a time, and he fought hard to integrate the music business. When a fire destroyed all his arrangements in 1939, Benny Carter and Duke Ellington would ship him new ones to keep the band going.

(Below) The Casa Loma Orchestra at the Steel Pier in Atlantic City, 1931. An offshoot of the Jean Goldkette Orchestra and named after a Toronto ballroom, the band was a cooperative led by an elected "president," alto saxophonist Glen Gray (with moustache, seventh from the left), and was the first swing band to have its own commercially sponsored radio program, the Camel Caravan, beating Benny Goodman to the microphone by nearly two years.

Black bands generally were not signed to the kind of long-term contracts the most popular white orchestras enjoyed, but there were exceptions. The Earl Hines Orchestra (above) presided over the Grand Terrace Ballroom in Chicago for ten years, while the singer-showman Cab Calloway (below, with baton) made New York's Cotton Club his headquarters all through the 1930s. The trumpeter in the foreground is Doc Cheatham.

(Left) A dance at the Knights of Columbus Annex in Gary, Indiana, in 1934. A local band, Rupert Harris and His Black Diamond Orchestra, provided the music.

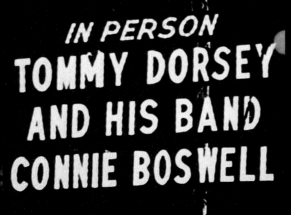

Clarinetist, saxophonist, and sometime singer Woody Herman and his 1937 "Band That Plays the Blues" (above), the first of a long succession of hard-swinging orchestras he would organize and lead over three decades. Musical tastes changed drastically during that time, and hundreds of musicians passed through his bands, but they always echoed Herman's own infectious love of playing. "My business," he said, "is excitement."

Tommy Dorsey, wearing the light suit (below), was billed as "the Sentimental Gentleman of Swing." His singing tone on the trombone was perfectly suited to the ballads in which his band specialized, but there was nothing sentimental about the man himself. He was combative and tight-fisted, a hard-drinking taskmaster who created his own band mostly because he could no longer bear to play alongside his brother, Jimmy, and took pleasure in publicly berating his men for their mistakes and then could not understand why they didn't like him. But his band was hugely popular and through its ranks moved such stars as Bunny Berigan, Dave Tough, Bud Freeman, Buddy Rich, and a skinny singer from Hoboken, New Jersey, named Frank Sinatra.

Artie Shaw (left) was Benny Goodman's greatest rival—and his own worst enemy. Gifted and articulate, he won an enormous following for his music—and his good looks. But he was "cursed," he said, "with serious-mindedness." He disliked autograph-seekers, disdained jitterbugging, and was made so uneasy by his own success that he repeatedly walked away from the business. "The basic truth," he concluded, "is that popular music has little or nothing to do with musical values at all."

The Glenn Miller Orchestra (below) at the Meadowbrook Ballroom in Cedar Grove, New Jersey, in 1939. Miller, here in the light suit, playing trombone, had no illusions about art. He couldn't understand why he was criticized as a musician. "All I'm interested in is making money," he once told John Hammond. He and his orchestra would turn out a string of hits, including "String of Pearls," "Little Brown Jug," "Moonlight Serenade," and "In the Mood," that would be among swing's most familiar anthems.

had our curls, red taffeta dresses, satin shoes with their new dye fading in the rain puddles; and most of all we were dressed in our ferocious hope for popularity. This was a stifling blanket, an airless tent; gasping, grinning, we stood anxious-eyed, next to the piano, hovering about Fats Waller who had come from Cincinnati for the occasion. Requests, perfidious glances, drunken teenagers, nodding teacher-chaperones: these we offered to the music, looking upon it, I suppose, as something inevitable, effortlessly pushing up from the common soil.

THE ENERGY IT TAKES

Benny Goodman's favorite orchestra was Duke Ellington's, he said, both because "the flavor of Duke's music is entirely different than anything else in jazz," and because his soloists seemed to have such a deep personal commitment to what they were playing.

For his part, Duke Ellington rarely complained about Goodman's coronation by the press as "The King of Swing" or the enormous popularity of the new, mostly white bands that followed in his wake. After all, Ellington had written the tune that gave the new music its name—"It Don't Mean a Thing If It Ain't Got That Swing"—three years before Goodman hit it big at the Palomar, and he didn't much like the term, himself. "Jazz is music," he said. "Swing is *business*."

Ellington continued on his own independent course, refusing as always to be categorized. By doing so, Rex Stewart remembered, "he could stand above his contemporaries . . . in the manner of a god descending from Olympian heights. And why not?" Stewart continued. "He had removed himself. Let the world catch up."

Duke Ellington at the microphone: "The master of them all is still . . . Ellington," wrote Aaron Copland in 1938. "The others, by comparison, are hardly more than . . . arrangers."

When hits for the full orchestra proved few and far between, he formed small groups within his band, just as Benny Goodman did, and wrote or arranged some 140 pieces to showcase his stars. Other bands would eventually follow suit: Tommy Dorsey's Clambake Seven; Bob Crosby's Bob Cats; Woody Herman's Four Chips; Artie Shaw and his Gramercy Five; Chick Webb and His Little Chicks. Ellington also tried having two basses for a time, to give his band a little extra lift; and he continued to experiment with longer forms, as well, most notably a two-part piece called "Diminuendo in Blue" and "Crescendo in Blue" that took up both sides of a 78. "Like all of our compositions," he said, these pieces "concern themselves with capturing and revealing the emotional spirit of the Race."

Eventually, there were new popular hits, as well—Juan Tizol's "Caravan," "I Let a Song Go Out of My Heart," "Prelude to a Kiss," "Jeep's Blues." And again and again—in Dallas and Chicago and Memphis and half a dozen other towns—Ellington and his men found themselves playing theaters and ballrooms that had previously been closed to black bands. When an overly familiar interviewer asked Ellington how he felt about the fact that he could neither dine nor stay in some of the hotels in which his band played, Ellington characteristically deflected the question. "I took the energy it takes to pout," he said, "and wrote some blues."

Benny Goodman was not the only white bandleader to revere Ellington. No one admired him more than Charlie Barnet, and when he opened at a club on New York's Fifty-second Street Barnet invited him down to hear his men play Ellington's music. Ellington hesitated. The club did not normally welcome black patrons, and he asked Helen Oakley, now in Manhattan and working for Irving Mills, to scout the territory on his behalf. "Duke was terribly careful, *extremely* careful about what he called 'situations,' " she remembered. "He never got into situations. Fifty-second Street was making all their money on black talent and keeping out black customers. But they told me that they would be very pleased if Duke Ellington would come. They'd have a table ready." Ellington asked her, " 'Is it all right?' " she remembered, "and I told him, 'Yes, yes it was.' And it was all right. They received him at the door and they had a special table and Charlie was in seventh heaven." Ellington sat quietly, sipping his drink and smiling appreciatively as Barnet and the band outdid themselves playing his music. But at one point he quietly turned to Oakley and murmured, "Hmm, they even *fluff* where we do."

CUTTING BUTTER

John Hammond, who had been partly responsible for putting together the Benny Goodman band which had ushered in the swing era, now had a new mission. He had been in Chicago in the winter of 1936, recording boogie-woogie piano players during the day and listening to the Goodman band at the Congress Hotel at night. One evening, he wrote later,

> Having heard enough of Goodman's music, . . . I went out to my car, . . . not quite decided where to go next. It was cold as only January in Chicago can be, and I turned on the car radio. I had a twelve-tube Motorola with a large speaker . . . I spent so much time on the road that I wanted a superior instrument to keep me in touch with music around the country. It was one o'clock in the morning. . . . [T]he only music I could find was at the top of the dial, 550 kilocycles, where I picked up W9XBY, an experimental station in Kansas City. The nightly broadcast by the Count Basie band from the Reno Club was just beginning. I couldn't believe my ears.

Hammond had heard Basie during a brief visit to New York with the Bennie Moten band several years earlier. He had been a powerful but busy pianist then, a stride player with a rumbling left hand. But now, he had developed what Hammond called "an extraordinary economy of style. With fewer notes he was saying all that Waller and Hines could say pianistically, using perfectly timed punctuation—a chord, even a single note—which could inspire a horn player to heights he had never reached before."

Despite the cold, Hammond slipped out to his car every night that week to listen in to Count Basie and his band. One evening, he insisted that Benny Goodman join him between sets to hear them. Goodman was

unimpressed. "So what's the big deal?" he said, shivering in the car.

"I suppose I was asking too much of Benny. There I was in the parking lot of the Congress, telling him that a nine-piece group in Kansas City was the best I had ever heard, while across the street he was enjoying a triumph with one of the smash bands of the country." Hammond was undeterred. He was now determined to bring Count Basie to New York.

William James Basie had given himself his title. "I knew about 'King' Oliver and . . . that Paul Whiteman was called the 'King of Jazz,' " he remembered. "Duke Ellington was also . . . one of the biggest names in Harlem. . . . So I . . . had some little fancy business cards printed up to announce it. 'Count Basie,' it said, 'Beware the Count Is Here.' " It was a rare moment of immodesty. Count Basie's career seemed to build almost in spite of himself—or so he always liked to make it seem.

He was born in Red Bank, New Jersey, in 1904, the son of a coachman. His mother took in laundry to pay for his piano lessons. As a boy, he had dreamed of joining a circus and running away to see the world. He dropped out of school at fourteen, planning to become a drummer. Then young Sonny Greer, who would soon spark the Ellington band, came to town and outplayed him so badly he was driven back to the piano. In 1924, he had moved to Manhattan, where he learned all he could from the Harlem stride specialists—James P. Johnson, Willie the Lion Smith, and his own contemporary, Fats Waller—and paid his bills by accompanying silent films.

Then he went on the road, playing burlesque and vaudeville theaters with Katie Krippen and Her Kiddies, Liza and Her Shufflin' Six, and a troupe called Gonzelle White's Big Jazz Jamboree—which ran out of money when it reached Kansas City in 1927. "There we were," Basie remembered, "with no show and no loot and no job." He played organ in the Eblon movie theater for a while, but for the first time in his life wherever he went in Kansas City he found himself surrounded by the blues. "Eighteenth Street, at that time, was blazing," he remembered. "I mean, everything was happening there, beautiful . . . you could hear the blues from any window or door. Right away I knew that was for me." The blues would be at the heart of everything he did for the rest of his life, specifically the irresistible Kansas City style of *stomping* the blues that his friend the writer Albert Murray, quoting Duke Ellington, has called "the velocity of celebration." "I really don't know how you would define stomp in strict musical terms," Basie once said. "But it was a real thing. What I would say is if you were on the first floor and the dance hall was upstairs, that was what you would hear, that steady, *rump, rump, rump, rump,* in that medium tempo. It was never fast."

Basie spent several months on the road with Walter Page's Original Blue Devils, but when they began to have trouble finding dates, he returned to Kansas City and went back to working at the Eblon, moving from club to club after it closed, listening and sitting in. At about five o'clock one morning in 1929 he saw a big crowd on Eighteenth Street. "When I asked about them, somebody said that they were the wives and sweethearts and . . . relatives and friends and followers waiting for the Bennie Moten Band that was due back in town from a long tour out in the territory. . . . It was kind of like standing around waiting for the hometown team." Eventually, the band pulled up in two gleaming Chryslers. Bennie Moten and his brother Bus were waving from the first one. "They had a special kind of class," Basie said, "and they also looked like they had it made in some ways, while the Blue Devils were still out there struggling from gig to gig."

Basie wanted to sign on right away, but there was a problem. The band already had a piano player—Bennie Moten himself. It seemed hopeless, Basie recalled. "But I have always been a conniver, and began saying to myself, I got to see how I can connive my way into that band." Basie could read little music but he had plenty of arranging ideas and managed to talk the trombonist, guitarist, and arranger Eddie Durham into working some of them out with him on paper, then passing them along to Moten. Moten liked them, asked for more, and when he went away on a brief business trip, let Basie sit in at the piano. Dancers loved him. After that, Moten played only an opening number or two at each show, then turned the keyboard over to Basie. The Moten band recorded for Victor, and traveled all the way east to New York City where they played at the Savoy and were not disgraced in a battle of the bands with Chick Webb. Playing with Moten's band night after night for five years, Basie said, made him realize that music mattered more to him than show business.

Then, in 1935, after Bennie Moten died on the operating table during a botched tonsillectomy, his band disintegrated and Basie began putting together a nine-piece outfit of his own—"Count Basie and the Barons of Rhythm." Their home base was the Reno Club at Twelfth and Cherry Streets. It was a rough place, with a tiny bandstand. Imported Scotch was fifteen cents a shot, domestic whiskey just a dime. Food came from a hot-dog stand next to the bar. Blue clouds of marijuana smoke hung perpetually above the balcony where the white customers sat, and taxi dancers and their clients climbed constantly up and down a separate staircase that led to bedrooms on

Kansas City's best. The Bennie Moten band at Philadelphia's Pearl Theater during a 1931 foray to the East Coast. The twin keyboards are manned by Count Basie, left, and Bennie Moten. The singer Jimmy Rushing is at the far left.

The Count Basie band as it looked at the Meadowbrook Lounge in Meadowbrook, New Jersey, in 1937. By then, it had been expanded from nine to thirteen men and its rhythm section included the infallible guitarist Freddie Green, behind Basie's piano, between drummer Jo Jones and bassist Walter Page.

the second floor for two dollars a trip. "I liked the atmosphere down there," Basie said. "There was always a lot of action."

The band's nine members would eventually include five fellow veterans of the Blue Devils and Bennie Moten bands: Walter Page, Jo Jones, Buster Smith, Lips Page, Herschel Evans, and Lester Young. But Basie was firmly in charge. "I . . . had some pretty clear ideas about how I wanted the band to sound," he remembered. "I knew how I wanted each section to sound. . . . I had my own way of opening the door for them to let them come in and sit around awhile. Then I would exit them."

"A band can really swing when it swings easy," Basie said, "when it can play along like . . . cutting butter." The rhythm section was the heart of that conception, and Basie's was perhaps the greatest in jazz history. Walter Page's bass provided the powerful "walking" 4/4 pulse that allowed Jo Jones, himself a former tap dancer, to keep time on the high hat and ride cymbals and

abandon the heavy, thumping, insistent emphasis on the bass drum that had characterized much jazz drumming. The result was light and relaxed, fluid and shimmering, less the ticking of a rhythmic clock than a surging wave of percussion, on top of which soloists seemed able to float without apparent effort. "When [Jo Jones] came out with the Basie band," the drummer Louie Bellson said, "it was as if we had been *waiting* for him." And Basie's piano provided the perfect complement. With Page and Jones at work, he had long since given up the steady, four-beats-to-the-bar left hand that the masters of Harlem stride had taught him in favor of spare, witty fills and asides that commented on the music being played and spurred his men to greater effort. Even a single note, Count Basie said, can swing.

His band caught on fast. Soon, a crew from radio station W9XBY was turning up at the Reno Club several times a week to broadcast its music as far east as Chicago.

Like most Kansas City outfits, the Basie band specialized in "head arrangement," worked out informally without sheet music. Buster Smith remembered how one of their favorites came about: "We were fooling around at the club and Basie was playing along in F. That was his favorite key. He hollered that he was going to switch to D-flat and for me to set something from [another tune called 'Six or Seven Times'] on alto. Lips Page jumped in with the trumpet part without any trouble and Dan Minor thought up the trombone part. That was it—a 'head.' "

Basie and his men called the arrangement that resulted "Blue Balls." The band was about to play it with just a few minutes to fill before they went off the air one morning, when the announcer asked Basie for the name of his next tune. Its informal title clearly wouldn't do for the radio audience. He looked up at the studio clock and said, "Call it 'One O'Clock Jump.' " He would play it night after night for the next fifty years.

THE ROAD

Swing musicians spent most of their lives on the road. Even for the best-paid bands, like Benny Goodman's and Duke Ellington's, it was wearying. Some bookers insisted that they cover five hundred miles between dates and work seven nights a week until the union finally managed to get it decreased to six nights and four hundred miles. "When I left Duke," one longtime Ellington trumpet player remembered, "I slept almost a whole year." Max Kaminsky played first trumpet for Tommy Dorsey for a time and endured weeks of one-nighters, traveling through the icy winter dark in an unheated bus. "You'd get through playing . . . at one a.m., grab something to eat before riding all night in that frigid torture chamber until anywhere from eight to eleven the next morning, stumble . . . into some ratty little hotel, fall like a corpse onto a bed until it was time to get up and rehearse, and then you'd eat, shave, bathe, put on your band uniform and play again until one a.m. and then repeat the whole routine, week after week, month after month. . . . You'd begin to ask yourself, if you were still on speaking terms with yourself, why in the name of sanity you were doing this."

For those working for less well known outfits, life was a good deal harder. Some bands were too poorly paid to afford even a bus. As many as ten musicians packed into a single touring car and hauled their instruments in a trailer. Sometimes, stranded between engagements, they would simply pull into a roadhouse, begin to play, and hope to raise enough cash to buy dinner by passing the hat.

There were compensations, of course. "To be factual," Rex Stewart remembered, "all of the fellows had little black books crammed with addresses and telephone numbers of fillies from coast to coast," and there seemed always to be women gathered around the bandstand who were, as he said, "ready, willing and eager." "The men didn't have to run after the girls," remembered Myra Taylor, vocalist with a Kansas City–based territory band called Harlan Leonard's Rockets. "The girls ran after the men, and I used to call 'em 'chili bandits.' Because that was about the best that they were going to get was a bowl of chili and a pop, you know. And they would go to the motels and things with these fellows. They played very hard out there on the road, . . . because sometimes they didn't get to see their wives for two months, three months maybe, before they would get back home, so, they had a very nice time."

Black musicians faced obstacles unknown to their white counterparts. Barred from restrooms, white hotels, and restaurants, they had to rely on the black community for help. It was not always forthcoming. "We'd go to some towns," Doc Cheatham remembered, "where they had black restaurants. The minute we'd get there, they'd change the menu, and put the prices up." But in most

places the men received nothing but hospitality. A network of celebrated cooks waited to welcome them. "They cooked for you like they'd cook for their family," one band member remembered. "And they didn't mind filling your plate up." One Atlanta landlady named Mom Sutton served musicians at a table that "looked like a mile long," another man remembered, "everything you could name—sausages, bacon, eggs, biscuits, corn bread, homemade pies—all for just fifty cents." There were black hotels and rooming houses in most big towns, although sleeping on the bus was sometimes preferable. Everyone who checked into the sole black hotel in Macon, Georgia, for example, was issued a baseball bat by the manager. "You might get some rats in your rooms," he said, "and they're often quite big ones, so keep this beside your bed."

Cab Calloway's band, like Duke Ellington's, often traveled from city to city by private Pullman, but when they performed in small southern towns the men had to go by bus. "We'd get in town just in time to get the instruments out and set up the bandstand and go to play," Milt Hinton said.

Hadn't had anything to eat, had no place to stay, or anything. We up there playing and the people crammed in there, and my wife Mona would be the only girl traveling with the band. She would go around to the black neighborhoods and talk to the ladies. She'd say, "One of the musicians is my husband, and we haven't had anything to eat and we haven't any place to stay." And these ladies were always so nice, they would get together and call one another and say, "Well, Miss Jones will take two of them at this house. And Miss Smith, she'll take two." We on the bandstand playing like

The Don Albert Orchestra, led by its trumpet-playing star, at left, traveled all over the southwest and midwest in this brightly painted band bus. According to at least one authority, by billing itself as "America's Greatest Swing Band," Albert's outfit was the first to use the word "swing" in its title.

crazy, and [Mona would] say, "Well, look, they haven't had anything to eat. If I go and get five or six chickens can I pay you to help me fix a little food for them?" By intermission time, Mona would come down to that bandstand with a great big basket of chicken and potato salad and a list of names, "Dizzy you and he are staying over at Mrs. Jones's house, Charlie you and so and so over at Mrs. Smith's house." And this is the way we survived.

Looking back, Andy Kirk, whose Twelve Clouds of Joy played one-nighters for twenty years, had little patience with those who remembered only the bleak side of life on the segregated road. "If it hadn't been for one-nighters," he wrote,

> I wouldn't have met Mrs. Mary McLeod Bethune and Dr. George Washington Carver. We couldn't stay in the white hotels. . . . I'm glad now we couldn't. We'd have missed out on a whole country full of folks who put us up in their homes, cooked dinners and breakfasts for us, told us how to get along in Alabama and Mississippi, helped us out in trouble and became our friends for life. . . . If it hadn't been for one-nighters, I wouldn't have known there were other people but rednecks in the South. I wouldn't have found out that not all white southerners wanted to put their foot on me. I wouldn't have found out there were Whites in the South I could talk to person to person, man to man.

Black musicians, like the members of the Cab Calloway band photographed here by Milt Hinton in 1940, routinely transcended such Jim Crow indignities as (right) the Oklahoma road sign and (top) being forced to enter the Atlanta railroad station through the official "Colored Entrance." (Above) Left to right, Calloway, tenor saxophonist Chu Berry, and trombonist Tyree Glenn bring a taste of the wider world to two awestruck boys in Durham, North Carolina.

Basie himself later claimed he would have been happy enough if he'd stayed in Kansas City forever. But John Hammond's vociferous public enthusiasm for the band made the move east almost inevitable. It seemed to Hammond that the Basie band—blues-based, loose but hard-swinging, with plenty of soloing room—had everything the big commercial bands lacked. "I want to say categorically and without fear of ridicule that Count Bill Basie has by far and away the finest dance orchestra in the country," he wrote in *Down Beat.* "And when I say this I am fully aware of Benny Goodman, Fletcher Henderson, and Chick Webb. . . . He has excellent soloists . . . and a driving rhythm section more exciting than any in American orchestral history."

Enthusiasm like that inevitably attracted the interest of others. Before Hammond could sign Basie for Columbia, Dave Kapp, the brother of Jack Kapp, the head of Decca Records, turned up in Kansas City. Claiming to be Hammond's friend, he talked Basie into agreeing to make twenty-four sides a year for a total of $750—less than union scale and without the promise of so much as a penny for royalties. Joe Glaser came to town, too, and hired away Lips Page—then put him under wraps for a time so that he could not challenge Louis Armstrong's trumpet primacy. Page's replacement in the Basie band was Buck Clayton, a master melodist who had begun life in Kansas but honed his skills in California and in a hotel dance band in Shanghai. Hammond convinced Willard Alexander to book the band but Alexander, in turn, insisted that it be expanded immediately from nine to thirteen men in order to compete with the big swing bands back east.

Duke Ellington happened to be in town on October 31, 1936, the night Basie and his men boarded their secondhand Greyhound bus for the journey east. "Go ahead," Ellington assured Basie. "You can make it." Basie himself was not so sure. As he set off, he knew that his band, which had been small and tight, was now ragged, unwieldy, and under-rehearsed.

Its first engagement—at the Grand Terrace in Chicago—did not provide much encouragement. The Basie men already played the blues better than anyone else in the country, but management insisted they also master more complicated arrangements to accompany an elaborate floor show. (Basie didn't even attempt the special arrangement of *The Poet and Peasant Overture* he was handed, he remembered; a "lady pianist" had to be called in just to play it.) Only the dancers seemed to like the band: "Why don't you just lay off," one told her boss when he complained about Basie's men. "Take it easy. These are just a nice group of country boys. . . . My God, one of these days you might be trying like hell to get them back in here. Just wait and see." They played a one-nighter in Buffalo on their way to New York, Basie remembered, and Mal Hallett's orchestra—the same outfit that Jean Goldkette's band had so badly intimidated in Massachusetts in 1926—"ran us out of there."

"Basie, who'll be in a New York ballroom by the time this gets into print hasn't been . . . impressive," the critic George T. Simon wrote in *Metronome* that fall. "True, the band does swing, but that sax section is so invariably out of tune. And if you think that sax section is out of tune, catch the brass! And if you think the brass by itself is out of tune, catch the intonation of the band as a whole! Swing is swing, but music is music. Here's hoping the outfit sounds better in person."

The band's first appearance in Manhattan, at Roseland, was little better. Basie's men knew no waltzes, no tangos, few standards. The young clarinetist and bandleader Woody Herman, making his own New York debut at Roseland that week, kindly lent Basie several of his own arrangements. "[Basie] was so green," Helen Oakley recalled. "Lester's saxophone was tied with string. And Basie had his back to the [crowd]. . . . He was afraid of the people."

Humiliated, Basie determined to take hold. He commissioned arrangements of current tunes, replaced some of his men, tightened discipline among the rest, and spent most of the next year and a half on the road, trying to make his orchestra better.

Meanwhile, the Great Depression, which had showed signs of lifting, suddenly deepened instead. The stock market collapsed again. In less than six months, four million more men and women lost their jobs. One-third of the people of Akron, Ohio, were thrown onto the relief rolls. When funds ran out in Cleveland, sixty-five thousand men, women, and children found themselves without any money for food or clothing. Poor Chicago children scavenged for food in garbage cans. Sharecropper families huddled along Missouri roads in makeshift tents, driven from their homes by landlords for daring to talk of organizing. It was called the "Roosevelt Recession," the steepest economic decline in American history. Things got so bad in Basie's native New Jersey that the state began issuing licenses to beg. If ever the country needed the healing power of the kind of blues Basie and his men played it was now—blues born in the dance halls and roadhouses and juke joints of Texas and Oklahoma, Kansas and Missouri; pulsing and stomping and played by men who had honed their skills in cutting contests that sometimes went on all night.

SCARY

On the morning of March 3, 1937, the Benny Goodman orchestra was to begin a two-week run at the Paramount Theater on Times Square. The movie, a dour Pilgrim-era drama called *Maid of Salem,* went on first, and by the time Goodman and his men took their places on the movable orchestra pit and the elevator began its slow rise, every seat in the house was filled. As the band came into view, playing its theme song, "Let's Dance," it was greeted by a roar so loud and so prolonged, Goodman said,

A security man struggles to keep an overexcited New York fan from getting to Benny Goodman in 1939. The trumpet star Harry James looks on warily, just over the intruder's head.

that it seemed "like Times Square on New Year's Eve . . . exciting, but also a little frightening—scary." The applause did not let up for four or five minutes, Goodman remembered. "We looked at them . . . as if they were the show and we were the audience." Soon, the audience *was* the show— or at least a large part of it. As the band resumed playing, and despite efforts by an army of uniformed ushers to stop them, young people leaped from their seats, filled the aisles, even jumped onto the stage to dance. (Much later, a Goodman publicist admitted that the first two dancing couples had been plants, but there was nothing orchestrated in the response of the rest of

the audience, which had started lining up that morning at seven o'clock.)

Until then, Goodman's high school–age fans had had to content themselves with hearing their hero on records. His band had traditionally played hotels and ballrooms, where alcohol was served, prices were high, and the customers were mostly adults. But before noon at the Paramount, anybody with a quarter was welcome. By three that afternoon, 11,500 teenagers had paid their way inside; by closing time that evening the number had risen to 21,000, and the aisles had been alive with dancers all day.

The Paramount appearance set a strange sort of benchmark for Goodman

and his rivals. If they couldn't get their audiences up and dancing no matter where they played, they had failed. "We'd go to another place like Philadelphia or Detroit," Goodman said, "and the manager would say, 'What about the kids dancing in the aisles?' . . . He would be rather disappointed if the whole theater didn't . . . dance, whereas we were always trying to curtail it and avoid it because it did interfere with the actual program that was going on."

Swing music had been growing in popularity for years, but it was adolescents— working-class adolescents, for the most part—who now turned it into a national craze. In spite of the Depression, trumpet sales doubled, while sales of clarinets—Artie Shaw's and Benny Goodman's instrument—tripled. There was an unofficial swing "uniform": boys dressed in sport jackets and slacks, like the ones their heroes wore on the bandstand; girls favored bobby socks and saddle shoes, blouses and sweaters, and pleated skirts that flared when they got onto the dance floor.

Young fans had their own language, too, and Cab Calloway lent his name to a *Hepster's Dictionary* to aid the uninitiated. A hot number was a "killer-diller." "Armstrongs" were musical notes in the upper register. "Swingaroos" or "hep-cats" were divided between "jitterbugs"—who danced —and "ickies"—who didn't, but stayed on the sidelines shouting encouragement to the musicians and clapping, usually just off the beat. Young women showered the best-looking players with letters and telephone numbers and some waited at the stage door, as one Goodman saxophonist fondly remembered, willing to "do anything" to meet their heroes.

Swing inevitably had its critics. When bandleaders began "swinging the classics"—rifling well-known works by everyone from Bach to Stephen Foster in search of familiar airs that could be turned into danceable hits—some radio stations barred the results altogether as artistic desecration. After a Detroit station cut the singer Maxine Sullivan's swing version of the traditional Scottish ballad "Loch Lomond" off the air, Sullivan sent Eleanor Roosevelt the titles of other familiar songs she hoped to record to see if the First Lady was in any way offended. "My dear Miss Sullivan," Mrs. Roosevelt replied from the White House, "I can't imagine what the songs you mention would be like in swing tempo, but there is nothing wrong in doing it. If people like it, and you succeed, you will be doing other things. You cannot please everyone all the time."

The sweet bandleader Blue Barron denounced swing as "nothing but orchestrated sex . . . a phallic symbol set to

sound." The Catholic archbishop of Dubuque called it a "communistic endeavor," a pretext for "cannibalistic rhythmic orgies." To others, it seemed a "mass contagion . . . musical Hitlerism." Dr. A. A. Brill, a Manhattan psychiatrist, went before newsreel cameras to declare that "Swing music represents our regression to the primitive tom-tom-tom, a rhythmic sound that pleases savages and children. . . . It acts as a narcotic and makes them forget reality. They forget the Depression, the loss of their jobs. . . . It is like taking a drug." There was nothing new in any of this. The sight of white youths enthusiastically adopting dances that had been born in the black community had always alarmed their elders. "If they'd been told it was a Balkan folk dance," Duke Ellington said, "they'd think it was wonderful."

Still, even musicians sometimes grew alarmed at the unbridled enthusiasm of their fans. Jerry Jerome, who played tenor with Benny Goodman for a time, remem-

bered what it was like. "They'd scream and yell and dance and carry on and enjoy themselves," he said. "I was shocked when I stood up to take a tenor solo, there was such a scream, and I realized they didn't hear one note of my solo. They were there because someone stood up, 'He's with the band,' you know. 'He's a soloist.' But what he played? They weren't listening."

They *were* listening at the Savoy. It was still Harlem's best-loved ballroom, still home to the most demanding dancers in the country. "The lindy hoppers up there made you watch your p's and q's," Dicky Wells recalled. "The dancers would come and *tell* you if you didn't play. They made the guys play, and they'd stand in front patting their hands until you got the right tempo." Frankie Manning and his dancing partner Frieda Washington had now added "air steps" to the lindy, lifting their partners over their shoulders, sliding them between their legs, hurling them high in the air. And Chick

The Goodman band drives dancers back out into the aisle during a return engagement at the Paramount in 1938.

Webb was still in charge. On the night of May 11, 1937, Benny Goodman himself ventured uptown to challenge him at what was billed as the "Music Battle of the Century."

Webb considered the Savoy his personal territory, to be defended against all invaders, but he also had far bigger dreams. "You know something, man?" he once told Artie Shaw. "Someday I'm gonna be walkin' up the street one way and you gonna be comin' down the other way, and we gonna pass each other and I'm gonna say, 'Hello, best white band in the world' and you gonna say, 'Hello, best colored band in the world.'" Webb had scrimped and sacrificed to keep his men together, sometimes using his rent money to buy arrangements, and he was never able to pay his men enough to fend off job offers from more successful bandleaders. (Whenever he spotted Fletcher Henderson at the Savoy, he would call out, "Well, who do you want this time?")

It was not lost on Webb that Benny Goodman's band had succeeded spectacularly with music that greatly resembled his own. ("Stompin' at the Savoy," and "Don't Be That Way," both big hits for Goodman, had in fact been written and arranged for Webb's band by its alto saxophonist, Edgar Sampson.) Nor had he forgotten those evenings back in 1934 when Goodman had brought his brand-new band up to the Savoy, hoping his men would learn how to play with what Goodman called the same sort of "guts" Webb's men employed. Now he called special afternoon rehearsals. The brass, reed, and rhythm sections each went through its precise paces in a separate room. "Fellas, [this] is my hour," Webb told his men as they took the bandstand. "Anybody misses notes—don't come back to work!"

Four thousand fans had jammed into the ballroom on that May evening, and mounted policemen had to be called to control the crowd of five thousand more who couldn't get in and refused to go home. Among those who managed to squeeze through the door were Norma Miller and

Showdown at the Savoy

Frankie Manning, professional lindy hoppers now, who had been taking on all comers in dance contests across the country. Now, they had come home to the Savoy to see their hero face the best-known band in the country.

FRANKIE MANNING: This was an electrical night. I mean, here's Benny Goodman, the king of swing, and here's . . .

NORMA MILLER: . . . Chick Webb, the king of swing.

FRANKIE MANNING: The king of swing, you know as far as *we* are concerned. We knew about Benny Goodman. A lot of people may not realize that a lot of arrangements that Benny Goodman had, Chick Webb had the same arrangements and when they get on a bandstand, now this is when you can know which band is the best—by listening to them play the same

arrangement. And to me, Chick Webb outswung Benny Goodman that night.

NORMA MILLER: I say the same thing, yeah.

FRANKIE MANNING: That was my feeling. I'm not saying this because . . .

NORMA MILLER: . . . Not being prejudiced.

FRANKIE MANNING: I feel that Chick Webb outswung Benny Goodman that night, you know, because I saw guys on Benny Goodman's bandstand when Chick Webb was playing. I seen guys on there, . . . they just shook their heads.

The Goodman band was routed. Gene Krupa bowed low before the man who had beaten him. Chick Webb, he said later, had "cut me to ribbons." "Nobody," one of Webb's men remembered, "could have taken it away from Chick that night."

A week after joining the
Count Basie band, Billie
Holiday sings at the Apollo,
1937. "That's where Billie
really starred," Basie
remembered. "She just
couldn't get off the stage."

DON'T-CARISH

In March of 1937, the same month Benny Goodman opened at the Paramount and two months before Goodman was vanquished by Chick Webb, Count Basie hired Billie Holiday to sing with his band. She called him "Daddy Basie." He called her "William," and understood both her talent and her temperament. "You know the kind of people that say, 'I'm going to get cussed out anyway, so what's the difference? What the hell?' " a woman who'd known Holiday since the age of twelve once asked. "Well, [she] went out and done what she felt like doing, 'cause she was just *don't-carish.*" She would remain don't-carish all her life—cursing, drinking, brawling, pursuing partners of both sexes, and unwilling to make the kind of compromises with public taste and racial custom that other performers routinely made in order to get ahead.

Nonetheless, John Hammond had remained determined to make her a star. In the summer of 1935, he arranged for the first of a series of recording sessions for her, singing with small groups led by Teddy Wilson. Many of the tunes—"What a Little Moonlight Can Do," "A Sunbonnet Blue," "Miss Brown to You"—were throwaways, but she managed to make them memorable with her bright, mocking voice and her trick of singing just behind the beat. "She enjoyed singing so much," Wilson remembered. "She was bubbling at those record dates. . . . In those days there was none of the blues and despairing, none of the stuff that came out [later]." She began to play better clubs, too, and to garner some good reviews. "Billie Holiday," wrote Ted Yates in the *Amsterdam News,* "the torch singer . . . can be heard in the popularly frequented 'hot spots' [around Harlem]. You should hear the buxom lass go to town with . . . very fine recordings [like] 'Miss Brown to You.' "

But trouble seemed to follow her wherever she went. She lasted only four days at the Famous Door on Fifty-second Street;

furious when she was told she couldn't sit with the white customers, she walked off the job. "When she walked in," the manager's wife remembered, "she walked in with her head high. . . . If you asked her for a request, she *might* sing it if she was good and ready. That was her way. She sang what she wanted to sing." She appeared at Chicago's Grand Terrace with Fletcher Henderson, but lost that job after hurling a chair at the manager when he dared tell her she was singing "too slow." Even Joe Glaser had no luck trying to make her over. Once, when he suggested she sing a little faster, she turned on him. "Look, you son of a bitch," she said, "*you* sing it. I'm going to sing *my* way, you sing your way."

On the road with the Basie band, Holiday drank and cursed and gambled with the men on the bus as if she were one of them—and won so much money shooting dice that when Christmas came she had to lend the losers cash to buy presents for their families back home. "She was like a man," Harry "Sweets" Edison said, "only feminine." She had an affair with guitarist Freddie Green, who she later claimed was the only man she ever really loved. But on the road and off, she was closest with Lester Young, whom she had first befriended during his brief New York sojourn as Coleman Hawkins's replacement in the Fletcher Henderson band. They gave one another nicknames. She was "Lady Day" to him, and he was "Prez" to her (named after President Franklin Roosevelt, whom she called "the top man in this country"). They would be friends most of their lives, though never lovers.

John Hammond had brought them, other members of the Basie band, and Teddy Wilson together in the recording studio for a series of small-group sessions that were among the most memorable in jazz history: "This Year's Kisses," "Why Was I Born?" "I Must Have That Man," "I'll Get By," "Mean to Me," "Foolin' Myself," "Me, Myself, and I," "A Sailboat in the Moonlight," "The Very Thought of You," "With-

out Your Love," and more. The best jazz is built upon shared communication—musicians listening and responding to one another and in the process creating something greater than any of them could ever achieve alone. The music offers no better example than these recordings on which Billie Holiday and Lester Young seem almost to meld, languorous voice and languorous saxophone weaving in and out of one another, as if completing one another's thoughts, sharing one another's souls, having a wonderful time.

A WHORE IN CHURCH

On the evening of January 16, 1938, Benny Goodman was scheduled to make still more jazz history. Paul Whiteman had presented a program of his symphonic version of the music at Aeolian Hall almost fourteen years earlier. Now, Goodman was to offer up the real thing, a celebration of two decades of authentic jazz. As usual, he'd been reluctant to break new ground and, again, Helen Oakley and John Hammond had had to talk him into it. He had been so worried that no one would turn up to hear what the world still considered dance music that he asked the British comedienne Beatrice Lillie if she would appear on the bill as an added attraction. She sensibly declined.

He needn't have worried. The house was sold out weeks in advance. Seats for one hundred overflow onlookers were set up onstage, and Goodman himself had to go to a scalper to get tickets for members of his family from Chicago, who decided at the last minute to attend.

On the evening of the concert, Roman Catholic picketers, bundled against the cold, marched up and down in front of the Fifty-seventh Street entrance, their placards denouncing Goodman for having played at a benefit concert for the Spanish Loyalists. Backstage, Goodman's men were nervous. Peeking out through the curtains, Harry James muttered that he felt "like a whore

Carnegie Hall billboard for Benny Goodman's concert, January 16, 1938. Appearing there, Goodman recalled, "was the thrill of my life."

in church." But when they had all filed onstage and Goodman appeared, clarinet in hand, wrote Olin Downes of the *New York Times,* "he received a real Toscanini send-off from the excited throng. There was a quivering excitement in the air, an almost electrical effect."

The opening number was Edgar Sampson's arrangement of "Don't Be That Way." The men, still unsettled by their surroundings, sounded strangely tentative until Gene Krupa took it upon himself to wake them up with a thunderous drum break. Goodman had commissioned nothing new for the occasion, but he had planned a tribute to "Twenty Years of Jazz." "I didn't have the

idea of putting across a 'message' or anything like that," he wrote. "I was just satisfied to have the kids in the band do what they had always done, and the way they did it was certainly wonderful. . . . We were playing for 'Bix' and the fellows on the riverboats, in the honky tonks and ginmills."

They began with a doggedly faithful rendition of the Original Dixieland Jazz Band's "Sensation Rag." The twenty-three-year-old cornetist Bobby Hackett played "I'm Coming, Virginia" in honor of Bix Beiderbecke. Goodman himself gently parodied his first idol, Ted Lewis. Harry James paid florid tribute to Louis Armstrong. Then—since only Ellington men could fully capture the distinctive Ellington sound—Johnny Hodges, Harry Carney, and Cootie Williams were featured on one of Ellington's loveliest pieces, "Blue Reverie." There was a jam session in which Ellington's musicians as well as Count Basie and several of his men—including Lester Young—took part. Goodman played beautifully with his trio and quartet—and the crowd gasped with pleasure when Krupa accidentally knocked one of his cymbals from its stand and Lionel Hampton snatched it from the air and stroked it with his mallet without losing a beat. As they played, young people and older concertgoers alike got up and danced in the aisles of the staid old hall.

Critics weren't quite sure what to make of it all. Olin Downes was baffled that while he was utterly unmoved, his teenaged daughter, seated next to him, had been unable to sit still. The Carnegie Hall concert actually lost Goodman money—rehearsal time and guest stars had eaten up all the profits—but it opened the New York concert stage to the new music: there would be four more evenings of jazz at Carnegie Hall before the year was over. And a live recording made that night but then forgotten and not released for a dozen years captured the Goodman orchestra at something like the peak of its powers. "I think the band I had at Carnegie Hall . . . was the best . . . I ever had," Benny Goodman remembered.

THE SWINGINGEST BAND

Count Basie and his men had not stayed around for the finale at the Goodman concert. They hurried uptown, instead, to the Savoy Ballroom, where Chick Webb and his orchestra were waiting for them. As soon as the concert ended, Benny Goodman and most of his men raced north, too, to see whether the new band from Kansas City could out-swing the band that had trounced them the year before.

A writer for the New York *Amsterdam News* offered a blow-by-blow description of the contest that followed.

> Throughout the fight, which never let down in its intensity during the whole fray, Chick took the aggressive, with the Count playing along easily and . . . more musically, scientifically. Undismayed by Chick's forceful drum-beating, which sent the audience into shouts of encouragement and appreciation and caused beads of perspiration to drop from Chick's brow onto the brass cymbals, the Count maintained an attitude of poise and self-assurance. He . . . parried Chick's thundering haymakers with tantalizing runs and arpeggios which teased more and more force from his adversary.

Although a judge declared Webb the official winner, the house remained divided, and for more than sixty years, surviving band members would debate who had actually come out on top that evening. "At least we didn't get run out of there," Basie remembered, and "we didn't have to run up against those babies anymore." His men had held their own in combat with the hardest-swinging outfit in New York, but he still felt that the band was not as tight as he wanted it to be. He needed a new base of operations, a place where he could stay for a while and work with his men, just

The Basie band during its triumphant summer-long 1938 residence at the Famous Door. Left to right, Walter Page, Jo Jones, Freddie Green, Benny Morton, Basie himself, Herschel Evans, Buck Clayton (who entirely obscures Dan Minor), Dicky Wells, Earle Warren, (who mostly obscures Ed Lewis), Harry "Sweets" Edison, Jack Washington, and Lester Young

as he had done at the Reno Club back in Kansas City.

That spring, Willard Alexander and John Hammond approached the owners of a tiny club on West Fifty-second Street called the Famous Door to see if they would agree to hire the Basie band for the whole summer. It was a shoebox of a place; no more than sixty customers could squeeze inside and the bandstand was smaller than the one at the Reno Club. The owners thought the whole idea was crazy. No big band had ever

played there and, to make matters worse, since there was no air-conditioning, there was also almost no summer business. But Basie's boosters persisted; Fifty-second Street—"Swing Street"—was now the most important street in jazz, and the CBS radio network had offered to broadcast from the club for thirty minutes every weekday night. The club owners finally relented, after Alexander and Hammond agreed to loan them the money they needed to have the place air-conditioned.

Basie called rehearsals every afternoon.

The band was still "pretty rough," Dicky Wells remembered, and its arrangements remained mostly heads. Wells recalled his first day in the band:

> "Come on," Basie said, "take your ax out and sit down and blow with the cats. See if you like it."
> "Where's my music?" I asked.
> "Sit in and see what happens. . . . Grab a derby and start fannin!"
> [It] was the swingingest band I had been in since Fletcher's. Basie would

Lester Young (above) takes off in front of the Count Basie band. (Below, left) Occupants of some of the higher-priced seats. Nearly twenty-five thousand swing fans were on hand from all five boroughs of New York City as well as Connecticut and New Jersey. (Below, right) Ivie Anderson sings "St. Louis Blues" with the Duke Ellington orchestra.

In January 1938 a young German Jew named Henry Ries, in flight from the Nazis, managed—after two attempts—to reach sanctuary in the United States. Anti-Semitic laws in Germany had barred him from studying music, his first love, but he now hoped to pursue a career as a photographer. On Sunday, May 29, he took his camera out to Randalls Island in the East River. There, Martin Block, a disc jockey for radio station WNEW, was to host twenty-five bands in a daylong Festival of Swing.

Ries had never seen or heard anything quite like it. The music was amazing, he remembered sixty-two years later, but still more amazing to him was the nature of the crowd that gathered to hear it. "It was fully integrated. I can only remember seeing one black person in my life before that day and that was Jesse Owens at the Olympics in Berlin. I was there when Hitler refused to shake his hand." More astonishing still was the fact that when the Duke Ellington band broke into a new number called "Diminuendo and Crescendo in Blue," black dancers first, and then white ones, leapt from their seats and began to dance while the police stood by and watched. "I was fresh from Germany under the Nazis, remember," Ries said, "where you had to ask permission to go the bathroom. That kind of freedom was simply unthinkable. I never forgot it." Ries went on to serve in the U.S. army during the war and then became a well-known New York photographer. These images, shot that day on Randalls Island, have never before been published.

(Top) Ellington's "Diminuendo and Crescendo in Blue" brings dancers out of their seats and onto the field. (Below, left) Ellington in charge. (Below, right) Woody Herman and his band.

start out and vamp a little, set a tempo and call out, "That's it." He'd set a rhythm for the saxes first, and Earle Warren would pick that up and lead the saxes. Then he'd set one for the bones, and we'd pick that up. Now it's our rhythm against theirs. The third rhythm would be for the trumpets, and they'd start fanning with their derbies. . . . The solos would fall in between the ensembles, but that's how the piece would begin, and that's how Basie put his tunes together. He had a big band, but he handled it as though it were six pieces.

It remained a rough, hard-drinking, hard-living, good-time outfit. The titles of some early Basie recordings testify to the kind of Kansas City customs his men had brought east with them. "Taxi War-Dance" was both a reference to a recent struggle within the New York taxi industry and to the fierce competition among the men for the favors of the taxi dancers who worked the clubs at which they had played; "Shorty George" was the band's name for "the other man," who might take a musician's wife or girlfriend if he stayed out on the road too long (as in, "Hey man; wonder if Shorty George is in your house now"); and "Swingin' at the Daisy Chain" was a hymn to a notorious uptown whorehouse that catered to patrons of every sexual persuasion, often all at once. And the men could be tough on each other. Lester Young kept a little bell on the bandstand to ring if anyone played a wrong note, and Jo Jones would often echo it by playing a little figure—"bing-bing-bing"—on the rod of his cymbal.

That summer, everything seemed to come together. The heart of the band remained its "All-American rhythm section," now including the steadfast guitarist Freddie Green, who would remain with Basie for forty-six years and virtually never lose the beat—or take a solo. Basie himself was the key, Sweets Edison said. "He was the greatest for stomping off the tempo. He

Jimmy Rushing romps with the Basie band at the Apollo, 1937.

noodles around on the piano until he gets it just right. Just like you were mixing mash and yeast to make whiskey, and you keep tasting and tasting the mix to make sure you've got the ingredients . . . to the point where you know it's going to be all right. [Walter Page and] Freddie Green and Jo Jones would follow him until he hit the right tempo and when he started it, they *kept* it."

So did the rest of the band. There were three trumpets—Ed Lewis, Buck Clayton, and Sweets Edison; three trombones—Benny Morton, Dan Minor, and Dicky Wells; and four reeds—Earle Warren, Jack Washington, Herschel Evans, and the incomparable Lester Young. Having Young in the band, one musician remembered, was "like having a pixie with a blowtorch," and the jousting between him and his friendly rival Evans was like having a Kansas City jam session onstage every night. Out front, at the microphone, was Jimmy Rushing, the singer whose huge joyful voice Ralph Ellison had heard from his Oklahoma City bedroom as a boy, and whose ever-expanding bulk would soon earn him the nickname "Mr. Five-by-Five."

"What a thrill it was to play in that band!" Sweets Edison remembered. "We couldn't wait to get on the bandstand at night. It was just like a horse prancing to get out on the racetrack." According to one steady customer that summer, the men in the band were now working together so well that Basie himself sometimes stopped playing and just "sat listening to them with a slight incredulous smile." "Those guys didn't just play together," Willard Alexander said. "They used to *breathe* together. . . . In that small place fourteen playing as one! You could feel the pulsations inside you." Those pulsations could be painful. In order to sound right on the radio, Basie ordered his men to blow with full force in the tiny, low-ceilinged room when they were broadcasting; during those thirty minutes patrons were asked to carry their drinks outside and listen from the street until they signed off again. Nobody seemed to mind.

Kansas City stomp was at last being heard all across the battered country.

COMMODORE

The day after Benny Goodman's triumph at Carnegie Hall and Count Basie's closely fought battle with Chick Webb at the Savoy, jazz history of another kind was made in a dingy recording studio at 1780 Broadway in Manhattan. Goodman's pianist Jess Stacy was there, his fingers still sore from the previous night's concert. With him were five veterans of the early days of jazz in Chicago —the guitarist Eddie Condon, drummer George Wettling, trombonist George Brunies, saxophonist Bud Freeman, and clarinetist Pee Wee Russell. Joining them were two men equally fond of the kind of small-group jazz they had first known as youths: bassist Artie Shapiro and the cornetist Bobby Hackett, in whose playing could be heard echoes of both of his boyhood idols, Louis Armstrong and Bix Beiderbecke. As Eddie Condon's Windy City Seven they cut five sides that day—"Love Is Just Around the Corner," "Beat to the Socks," "Carnegie Jump" and "Carnegie Drag" (both named in honor of Benny Goodman, who had granted permission for Stacy to be there), and "Jada." The records were loose and lively, true to the spirit of the twenties, but with a relaxed, swing-inspired beat. And they were superbly recorded. The producer, a record-shop operator named Milt Gabler, had gone to extraordinary lengths to achieve the proper balance. Since the music he was recording was collectively improvised, he wanted to be able to hear each instrument clearly all the time. It was the first recording session for his brand-new label, Commodore Records, and he was determined to get it right. New Orleans may have been "the cradle of jazz," Gabler said, but he wanted Commodore to be its "iron lung."

He was banking on the fact that big band swing had not captured the heart of every

jazz fan. Some found it too regimented, too commercial, agreeing with Sidney Bechet that "big swing bands . . . leave a [musician] with nothing to say and no way to say it. . . . If you know in advance every note you're going to play and just the way you're going to play it, there's no need to have feelings. . . . Music like that you could almost make a machine play it for you." Others were simply nostalgic for the small-group sounds of their youth. Still others had persuaded themselves that jazz was proletarian "people's music," worth listening to only when played by black musicians whose "natural" gifts were unsullied by musical literacy; one of their journals declared Art Tatum a sellout and pronounced Benny Goodman "the poorest musician in America. An uncreative riffmaster." Less than twenty years after the first recordings, jazz was already being seen as important enough to argue about, an art form with a history. Whatever their motivation, record collectors had begun haunting junk shops and canvasing black neighborhoods in search of rare Gennets, Okehs, Perfects, Harmonys, Crowns, Melotones, Silvertones, Vocalions.

Gabler ran the Commodore Music Shop on East Forty-second Street. It was just nine feet wide, but a mecca for collectors from all over the country. "It's a shrine," said Eddie Condon, "the crummiest shrine in the world." Thousands of records lined its floor-to-ceiling shelves, and jazz classics—Bix Beiderbecke's Wolverines, Louis Armstrong's Hot Fives and Hot Sevens—poured nonstop from a loudspeaker above the door. Gabler sold every kind of jazz, but he personally preferred small groups to big bands, and was happiest when listening to what he called "an informal gathering of temperamentally congenial jazz musicians [playing] unrehearsed and unscored music for their own enjoyment." In 1935, working with an eager young jazz enthusiast from Yale named Marshall Stearns, Gabler had founded the United Hot Clubs of America (UHCA) to reissue records the major labels had long since dropped from their

Milt Gabler, right, and his staff at the Commodore Music Shop

catalogues. They were sold through the mail with the personnel for each session carefully printed on the label.

To boost sales and to promote small-group jazz in general, Gabler and his friend John Hammond also persuaded a host of eminent musicians into playing free for his customers at Sunday-afternoon jam sessions. Benny Goodman and Gene Krupa volunteered their services; so did Artie Shaw and Chick Webb, and members of the Count Basie band. Gabler rented empty recording studios for his sessions, until so many fans turned out that the fire department called a halt to them. Then, he moved them to Fifty-second Street, first to the Famous Door, then to a slightly bigger place called Jimmy Ryan's. Max Kaminsky, who frequently took

part, was somewhat unnerved by the character of the crowds that turned out to hear them. "We were suddenly besieged," he wrote, "by a strange new breed of fan—the record collector. Pale, intense, studious-looking young men buttonholed us . . . and plied us with questions about who had played what instrument in some pickup band recorded twenty years earlier."

By late 1937, Gabler's UHCA program had proved so successful that the major labels began reissuing their old records themselves. He then decided to start a new label and make recordings of his own. The music was alive, not dead, after all, and he was dedicated to it—he lived for what he called the "thrill" he got from "not knowing what's going to happen next" in the stu-

dio—but in the end he might not have made a go of it without the help he got from Eddie Condon.

Condon was never more than a good rhythm guitarist—he refused ever to solo—and he drank staggering amounts of Scotch. "I can't stand the customers when they're drunk if I'm sober," he once explained, "so I drink, too. It creates a mutual tolerance." His cure for a hangover began, "Take the juice of two quarts of whiskey." But he was also an able organizer of musicians and a genius at publicity. Funny and fast-talking, he managed to get himself and other like-minded musicians more or less steady work on Fifty-second Street when the conventional wisdom was that only swing would sell. He talked friends at *Life* magazine into covering a Commodore session and then publishing a lavish picture-story announcing the rebirth of traditional jazz. He spread his message still further through a monthly series of radio broadcasts from the stage of Town Hall, even though the audience for the first concert was so small that he greeted it with "Good evening lady and gentleman." Condon made a sort of fetish of disliking big bands. Any group with more than eight musicians, he said, was just a "sales conference," and he would prove still less tolerant of later musical developments. When a waiter dropped a tray filled with glasses while he was playing in the Greenwich Village club he ran during the late 1940s, he is said to have shouted, "Boys, none of that 'progressive' jazz in here!" Critics tended to lump Condon in with what would come to be called "the Dixieland Revival," but he and his cohorts hated the phrase and were in fact not reviving anything. They were simply continuing to play the kind of joyous, collective music they had always played. Condon's guitar now helped set a relaxed 4/4 rhythm rather than the tighter ragtime-derived beat of his Chicago days, and he was just as likely to call for a recent tune by George Gershwin as an old one by Jelly Roll Morton. Condon and his friends knew as Max Kaminsky knew—and as Morton him-

In August of 1939, a little over a year after Eddie Condon, fourth from left, ever-present drink in hand, staged the all-star jam session for *Life* magazine that helped launch the so-called traditional jazz "revival," he organized this musical get-together. Among those taking part: Bud Freeman and trombonist J. C. Higginbotham, at left, Billie Holiday, and trumpeter Max Kaminsky, here playing drums so that a French visitor can try out his horn. Intended for the magazine's weekly "*Life* Goes to a Party" feature, the pictures of this session by a former guitarist named Charles Peterson never ran.

self had suggested long before—"it's not *what* you play but how you play it."

Commodore became closely identified with Condon and his kind of music. But Milt Gabler's sole criterion for recording musicians was that he like the way they played. Jelly Roll Morton and Sidney Bechet and Willie "the Lion" Smith and Tom Brown, the trombonist who had first brought New Orleans music to Chicago in 1915, recorded for him. But so did Billie Holiday and Lionel Hampton, Chu Berry and Roy Eldridge, and Coleman Hawkins. On September 27, 1938,

Gabler recorded four tunes with the Kansas City Six—Count Basie's rhythm section minus Basie himself, with Eddie Durham on electric guitar, trumpeter Buck Clayton, and Lester Young, who played clarinet instead of tenor on "I Want a Little Girl" and "Pagin' the Devil," simply because Milt Gabler thought it would sound great. It did, and the four sides cut that afternoon are among the most justly celebrated in small-group history.

Soon, Commodore would have competitors, including Steve Smith's H.R.S. (Hot

Record Society), Bob Thiele's Signature, and Blue Note, the best-known and longest-lasting of the independents, created by two refugees from Nazi Germany, Alfred Lion and Frances Wolff. The sort of small-group jazz that Milt Gabler and his independent rivals recorded in the shadow of the big bands would prove some of the most exciting music of an exciting era.

Jelly Roll Morton relished the brief renewal of interest in him and his music that his Commodore recordings inspired. He had

Helen Oakley, in the light dress, then working for Irving Mills, organized this 1937 jam session at the Brunswick recording studio in New York to help launch the Master and Variety record labels. Chick Webb, Artie Shaw, and Duke Ellington all volunteered their time. Milt Gabler kneels behind Ellington; Oakley's British-born future husband, the jazz historian Stanley Dance, stands against the far wall.

had far less attention than he'd liked since Victor dipensed with his services in 1930. He had moved to Washington, D.C., tried and failed as a fight promoter, taken up with another woman without bothering to tell his wife, gone through all of his money, and had to sell off all his diamonds except the one that glittered from his front tooth. He finally opened a dingy little place variously called The Music Box, The Blue Moon Inn, and The Jungle Club. Only his ego had remained intact. When he heard a radio announcer introduce W. C. Handy as "the Father of the Blues and Jazz," he dashed off an angry letter to *Down Beat* in which *he* claimed to be the creator of jazz. Just to make things perfectly clear he signed it "Very Truly Yours, Jelly Roll Morton, Originator of Jazz and Stomps, Victor Artist, World's Greatest Hot Tune Writer." That

same spring, the folklorist Alan Lomax sought him out and encouraged him to play and reminisce into a wire recorder at the Library of Congress. The heavily edited result, a book called *Mr. Jelly Roll,* constituted a gaudy but priceless record of the music's early days in New Orleans.

Morton was thin and frail by the time Commodore and Blue Note and Victor asked him to record again, but he was just as demanding of other musicians as he had been in the old days. He was soon back on the street again, threatening lawsuits against ASCAP and former managers who he believed had misappropriated his music and fulminating against the younger musicians who ignored him. When he finally died in Los Angeles in 1941, four well-known black bandleaders, including Duke Ellington and Jimmy Lunceford, happened

to be playing nearby. Not one attended his funeral. And the night before he was to be buried, according to one of the few friends who remained loyal to him, someone slipped into the funeral home and chiseled his last diamond from his tooth.

THE RAY

Benny Goodman's band was never quite the same after Carnegie Hall. Gene Krupa would soon leave to form his own orchestra; so would other stars—Teddy Wilson and Harry James and Lionel Hampton—forcing Goodman to rebuild the most popular orchestra in America.

Personnel was never Benny Goodman's strong point. Singer Helen Ward had been one of the band's prime attractions—and she was in love with its leader. When an admirer urged her to leave the band early on, Goodman had assured Ward he planned to marry her. Then, not long after she turned her suitor down, Goodman explained that he had had second thoughts. He was too young to get married, after all. When she finally told him over dinner that she planned to leave the band anyway, he threw his menu in her face.

All through the years, Goodman's musicians would find him distant, preoccupied, so obsessed with making music that he sometimes couldn't even remember their names. Stories about his odd behavior are legion. Offstage, he was simply oblivious. Helen Ward also remembered rehearsing with him at his home on a cold winter's day and complaining that there wasn't enough heat. "You know, you're absolutely right," Goodman said, and went and got himself a sweater. The singer Peggy Lee recalled getting into a taxi with Goodman at a Manhattan stoplight. Goodman was silent, lost in thought. The light changed. He still said nothing. Finally, the driver asked, "Where to?" Startled, Goodman reached for his wallet and asked, "What do I owe you, Pops?"

The tenor saxophonist Zoot Sims played for Goodman in the late 1940s. One day he brought to rehearsal a bright shiny apple and put it on his music stand to eat during a break. "Benny had a habit of grabbing your cigarettes or anything," he remembered, "and I saw him looking at that apple. I said, 'Oh, oh. There goes my apple.' I had a solo coming up. So Benny grabbed my apple. I stood up to take my solo, and it's the longest solo I ever had with Benny Goodman. . . . He kept signaling 'one more,' until he finished the whole apple. Then he said, 'That's enough.'"

On the bandstand, "Benny wanted perfection," Helen Ward remembered, "and he got it." Anything less yielded the disconcerting owlish stare that his sidemen called "the Ray."

Helen Oakley suggested that Goodman simply couldn't help himself.

Benny got such a bad name for himself. But what people didn't realize about Benny was that he had a God-given gift, and he never to his dying day realized that other people didn't have that same gift. He didn't know. He turned the "Ray" on the guys in the band. He didn't know it was the "Ray." But he would simply turn his eyes on you, and look at you as though asking, "Are you real?" "Did you really do that?" "Couldn't you have done better?" And they withered. His guys were terrified. But until he read about it, he didn't even know he did it.

One musician who had spent several unhappy months with the band, trying to figure out just what it was his leader wanted from him and always seeming to fall short, finally stormed into Goodman's dressing room. "That's it, Benny!" he said. "I can't take this anymore. I'm quitting!"

He slammed the door on the way out.

"Who *was* that?" Goodman asked his manager.

In rebuilding his band, Benny Goodman would often have more help than he liked from John Hammond. In 1939, Mary Lou Williams told Hammond about a twenty-three-year-old musician from Oklahoma City who, she said, had figured out how to bring something of Lester Young's light, loping, rhythmically surprising style to the electric guitar. His name was Charlie Christian. He was the son of a blind, itinerant blues singer, and had been a local hero since his school days when he played a homemade instrument and, Ralph Ellison remembered, "No other cigar box ever made such sounds."

Without hearing Christian and without consulting Goodman, Hammond arranged for the young guitarist to board a train for Los Angeles, where Goodman was playing with his band. The next night, when Goodman got to work at the Victor Hugo Restaurant, he found Christian's amplifier already set up onstage and Christian himself waiting in the wings, wearing an outfit of his own design that featured a purple shirt and yellow shoes. "Goodman watched Charlie approach the bandstand," Hammond recalled, "looked around the room until he spotted me, and zapped me with the famous Goodman 'Ray.'"

Goodman's quintet was onstage. He called for "Rose Room." Christian fell right into the tune as if he'd been rehearsing it for days. "All he had to do was hear the melody and chord structure once and he was ready to play twenty-five choruses, each more inventive than the last," Hammond wrote. "Benny would play a chorus or two, Lionel would answer him, and their talent would inspire Charlie to greater improvisations of his own. Before long the crowd was screaming. . . . 'Rose Room' continued for more than three-quarters of an hour."

Goodman hired Christian right away. The Benny Goodman Quintet became a sextet. Before tuberculosis and too many good times cut short his career at twenty-five, Charlie Christian would bring a new, experimental spirit to the Goodman band—and to the guitar. More than anyone else, he would make it a solo instru-

Charlie Christian, wearing dark glasses, says goodbye to Oklahoma City friends and family before setting out for Los Angeles to join Benny Goodman in August of 1939.

YOU'LL GET THROUGH

"Why is it," *Down Beat* once asked, "that outside of a few sepia females the woman musician never was born capable of sending anyone further than the nearest exit? . . . You can forgive them for lacking guts in their playing but even women should be able to play with feeling and expression and they never do it." That kind of complacent chauvinism has characterized jazz since the beginning.

The trumpet player and singer Valaida Snow was the best-known female soloist of the thirties, both at home and in Europe, where she settled in 1936. Billed as "Queen of the Trumpet" and "Little Louis," she was especially admired in Paris and Scandinavia, where, a friend remembered, she was driven around in an "orchid-colored Mercedes Benz, her pet monkey rigged out in an orchid jacket and cap, with the chauffeur in orchid as well."

But with a handful of exceptions like Snow, only female pianists and singers have found a consistent welcome in the jazz world. Still, a number of women's bands—"all-girl orchestras"—did take to the road during the swing era. Ina Ray Hutton and her Melodears were perhaps the best-known. "We played the provinces," their leader remembered. "I guess I saw all the men in America out front. Some of them tried to get backstage—some sent mash notes. But I kept the sex in the saxophones."

The Melodears' success inspired Laurence C. Jones, the principal of a threadbare Mississippi school for poor and orphaned black children, to form his own band, the International Sweethearts of Rhythm, and use it to raise funds. (The band was "International," one band member explained, because "we had Mexican and Chinese" as well as black girls.) The Sweethearts quickly outgrew Piney Woods. Professional musicians, black and white, signed on, and they found themselves playing top ballrooms all over the country. "You could put those girls behind a curtain," one bandleader said, persuaded he was being flattering, "and people would be convinced it was *men* playing."

That kind of attitude was all too familiar to the pianist, composer, and arranger Mary Lou Williams, but she did her best to ignore it. "As for being a woman, I never thought much about that one way or another," she said, looking back over her long career. "I never thought about anything but music." She earned the respect of every man with whom she played.

She was born Mary Scruggs in Atlanta in 1910 and was raised in Pittsburgh. "Jazz is a self-taught art," she remembered, "and I was a loner." A child prodigy, at the age of six she was already helping to support her ten half-brothers and -sisters by playing piano for parties, and she was playing hopscotch in the backyard when her first offer to play the carnival and tent-show circuit came. It was "a terrible life," she remembered, but she stuck with it, at seventeen married a saxophone player named John Williams, and eventually found work doing double duty as pianist and chauffeur for one of the best of the riff-based territory bands, Andy Kirk's Twelve Clouds of Joy. Between engagements she drove a hearse. When Kirk's band settled in Kansas City in 1928, the Williamses moved there, too. Soon, she was the band's full-time pianist, with a sure touch and a feeling for the blues rarely matched by any pianist, male or female. "Women during that era were not really allowed to be in with a group of men," she remembered. "That made the people scream and carry on because they saw a woman that weighed about ninety pounds—to hear me play so heavy, like a man, that was something else." Soon, she was being billed—accurately—as "The Lady Who Swings the Band." She was also its top arranger, and by the mid-thirties was writing for other big bands, as well—Louis Armstrong, Earl Hines, Benny Goodman, even Duke Ellington—often working furiously by flashlight at night as the Kirk band bus hurtled down the highway.

Later, she moved to Manhattan and become a musical mentor to younger musicians, including the modernist masters Dizzy Gillespie, Bud Powell, and Thelonious Monk. "You've got to play, that's all," she said. "They don't think of you as a woman if you can really play. . . . No musician ever refused to play with me. No one ever refused to play my music or my arrangements. . . . A woman I know once came to me and said, 'They won't play my arrangement because I'm a woman.' I said, 'Do your work to the best of your ability, and you'll get through.' "

Mary Lou Williams

ment that could hold its own with brass or saxophones. "After I heard him, I could forget about everybody else," one younger guitarist remembered. "Charlie Christian was *it.*"

Not long after Hammond surprised Goodman with Charlie Christian, Goodman would surprise Hammond by marrying Hammond's own sister, Alice Hammond Duckworth, the divorced wife of a British member of parliament. Soon, the pseudo-black accent Goodman had developed while still a struggling musician in Chicago was replaced with a new one, "Long Island lock-jaw," his old friend James T. Maher would call it, better suited to the new life the boy from Maxwell Street now found himself leading among New York patricians. Being a member of the family did not immunize Goodman against Hammond's hectoring criticism. "Benny is still a great musician," his new brother-in-law wrote not long after the wedding, "but he is no longer an inno-vator or a musical radical. . . . [I]t is the increasing conservatism of a man who has made his pile and who no longer wishes to buck popular prejudice."

SCENT OF MAGNOLIAS

In 1938, Count Basie had fired Billie Holi-day. He later said they'd disagreed over money; she claimed John Hammond had insisted she sing the kind of blues Bessie Smith had sung a decade earlier, she had angrily refused, and Basie had too meekly sided with Hammond.

Then, Artie Shaw asked her to join his band. Black singers with white bands were almost unheard of, although Jimmy Dorsey had featured a singer named June Rich-mond for a time. Shaw's musicians were delighted. Max Kaminsky, now playing first trumpet in the band, remembered how Hol-iday "stood up in front of the mike, listening sort of dreamily [and] came sliding in, in the

nick of time, like a lazy ball player starting to lope around the bases but taking his own good time because he knows the ball he just hit is *never* going to stop sailing."

The reaction of dancers and hotel own-ers was more problematic. In Toronto, one musician's wife recalled, there was no prob-lem about finding Holiday a hotel room. "She took it as she should have taken it, that it was her right." But in her own country, she was often turned away from the hotels in which the other musicians stayed, and in some places she even had to leave the band-stand between numbers.

She hadn't been sure she should accom-pany the band when it went south, Artie Shaw remembered.

On the way down below the Mason-Dixon line, that mystic line, she said, "You think I should come down?" I said, "Yeah, Billie, I think it's impor-tant that you do this." I wasn't think-ing in terms of black-white. I was thinking it important that she come and stay with this band. And every-thing was fine and they loved her until one night she sang a tune and after the tune was over, some redneck in front of the band hollered up, "Have the nigger wench sing another song." She was a pretty hot-tempered girl, and she looked over at him and you could see her flushing under the tan, and calling him a "Mother-fucker." So, a little turmoil arose out there and I was prepared for it, and I had a couple of cops in the wings, just in case, and they hustled her off into the bus and drove her away.

Things were almost as bad in New York City, the town Holiday now considered home. When the band appeared twice weekly on network radio, the sponsor, Old Gold cigarettes, insisted that only the band's white singer, Helen Forrest, perform on the air. And when the band played the Hotel Lincoln, Holiday was ordered to use the

freight elevator so that other guests wouldn't assume blacks were staying in the hotel. She spent most of the engagement holed up in her room.

Holiday finally left Shaw. Both he and Basie, she told *Down Beat,* were prisoners of "too many managers, too many guys behind the scenes who told everybody what to do." She returned to the clubs she knew best, vowing never to travel with a dance band again. "She did what she liked," a club owner remembered. "If a man she liked came up, she'd go with him; if a woman, the same thing. If she was handed a drink, she'd drink it. If you had a stick of pot, she'd take a cab ride on her break and smoke it. If you had something stronger, she'd use that. . . . When she told you off, you were damn well told—white, black, rich, poor."

On December 30, 1938, Café Society, a nightclub like no other, opened its doors just off Washington Square in Greenwich Vil-lage. It was the creation of an ex–shoe salesman named Barney Josephson, who hoped—with John Hammond's help—to demonstrate that New Yorkers would turn out to hear jazz presented "with dignity and respect" before a genuinely integrated audi-ence. He billed it as "The Wrong Place for the Right People"—and it was a hit, not only with those who shared his liberal politics but even with some of the society people its slogan was meant to lampoon.

Billie Holiday was on the first bill—Hammond had convinced Josephson to hire her—and she stayed for almost nine months, doing three shows a night backed by the trumpeter Frankie Newton's band. In April 1939, a young, leftist high-school teacher named Abel Meeropol turned up at the club to see her. He had written a poem and set it to music, he said. Would she sing it? It was about lynching, and the picture it painted—of innocent victims of southern mob violence hanging from poplar trees, faces distorted in death, blood spattered on the roots—was brutal in its candor:

Billie Holiday records "Strange Fruit" for Commodore Records, April 20, 1939. The guitarist is Jimmy McLin.

walked out. One woman who cried out, "Don't you dare ever sing that song again. Don't you dare," turned out to have witnessed a lynching as a little girl and had found it unbearable to be reminded of it in a nightclub. Even John Hammond, now at Vocalion Records, thought the song too inflammatory for its catalogue, but agreed to allow Holiday to record it for Milt Gabler at Commodore. Backed by "Fine and Mellow," a blues she and Gabler put together, "Strange Fruit" reached number sixteen on the record charts in April of 1939—and transformed Holiday's career. From then on, she would be the musical and emotional focus of every record she made, no longer just another soloist who happened to be singing, not blowing. She never sang another explicitly political song, but she did also gradually alter her repertoire, de-emphasizing the kind of sly upbeat tunes that had won her her first following, in favor of increasingly dolorous songs, such as "Lover Man," "I Cover the Waterfront," her own bitter "God Bless the Child," and "Gloomy Sunday"—subtitled "The Hungarian Suicide Song."

Holiday would consider "Strange Fruit" her own for the rest of her life. "It's my song," she said. "It has a way of separating the straight people from the squares." She sometimes claimed to have written it herself. Once when the folksinger Josh White dared perform it at Café Society, she threatened to slit his throat if he ever tried it there again.

TAKE CARE OF ELLA

When the Count Basie and Chick Webb bands had warred at the Savoy, dancers had been divided about the overall outcome, but there had been no doubt whose band singer they liked best. Billie Holiday had still been Basie's vocalist then, but she lost out three to one to Webb's twenty-one-year-old singer, Ella Fitzgerald, already the favorite singer of Harlem lindy hoppers and

Scent of magnolias, sweet and fresh.
Then the sudden smell of burning
    flesh.

Holiday called herself "a Race woman," but she was frankly reluctant to try the song at first. It was completely different from anything she'd ever sung before, and it was grim beyond measure. "I was scared people would hate it," she said. "The first time I sang it I thought it was a mistake. . . . There wasn't even a patter of applause when I finished. Then a lone person began clapping nervously. Then suddenly everyone was clapping."

Soon, Barney Josephson recalled, she was singing it at the end of every set.

I made her do it as her last number, and no matter how thunderous the

applause, she had orders from me not to return for even a bow. I wanted the song to sink in. . . . The room was completely blacked out, service stopped—at the bar, everywhere. The waiters were not permitted to take a glass to the table, or even take an order. So everything stopped—and everything was dark except for a little pin spot on her face. That was it. When she sang "Strange Fruit," she never moved. Her hands went down. She didn't even touch the mike. With the little light on her face. The tears never interfered with her voice, but the tears would come and knock everybody in that house out.

The song and Holiday's chilling rendition of it caused a sensation. A few customers

Ella Fitzgerald and Chick Webb
at the Apollo, 1939

soon to become first "the First Lady of Swing," and eventually "the First Lady of Song."

Fitzgerald's childhood had been nearly as bleak and troubled as Holiday's. Her parents never married. Her stepfather abused her. Her mother died when she was fourteen. She dropped out of high school, then ran away from the Colored Orphan Asylum in Riverdale to which the court sent her for truancy. For nearly two years she was homeless, living on the Harlem streets, dancing and singing for tips, sometimes supporting herself as a numbers runner or a lookout for a brothel. Her dream was to be a dancer.

On the evening of Wednesday, November 21, 1934, she was scheduled to dance in an amateur show at the Apollo Theater in Harlem. But when she learned that two already well-known dancing sisters were to close the show, she decided she'd try singing, instead.

She was overweight and awkward, wearing secondhand clothes and men's boots as she stepped into the spotlight. And she was terribly nervous—she knew Apollo audiences could be brutal. Somehow she started by singing off-key. The crowd grew restive. The master of ceremonies stopped her. "Folks, hold on now," he said. "This young lady's got a gift she'd like to share with us tonight. She's just having a little trouble getting it out of its wrapper. Let's give her a second chance."

That was all she needed. Backed by the Benny Carter Orchestra she sang two songs—she and Carter both remembered them as "Judy" and "The Object of My Affection"—and she did so in the style of her favorite singer, Connie Boswell of the Boswell Sisters. Boswell "did things that no one else was doing at the time," Fitzgerald said much later, she phrased like a horn player, shifted rhythms, rearranged melodies. Fitzgerald brought down the house and was awarded the first prize of ten dollars, which was supposed to carry with it a week's salaried work onstage. But the

manager of the Apollo reneged. He didn't think Ella Fitzgerald good-looking enough for show business. She returned to the streets, entering other amateur shows when she could, sometimes singing without pay for local bands.

Meanwhile, Chick Webb, still seeking a way to reach the huge white audience that Benny Goodman and Artie Shaw and other bandleaders now commanded, resolved to find what was then called "a girl singer" or "canary," someone who could sing but also be a decorative addition to his band. His male vocalist, Charles Linton, was assigned the task of scouring the city for likely candidates. Linton brought back Ella Fitzgerald.

Webb was appalled: "You're not putting *that* on my bandstand," he whispered. "No, no, no. Out!" But Linton threatened to quit if she weren't given a chance and Webb relented. It was the best decision he ever made. Fitzgerald's flawless ear and perfect pitch astonished other musicians; her girlish voice and ferocious sense of swing delighted the public. One of their first records together, "Sing Me a Swing Song (and Let Me Dance)" got the Webb band onto the hit parade for the first time in its history. Soon his orchestra—featuring Ella Fitzgerald—was appearing regularly on the radio and in ballrooms all over the country, with hit after hit on the jukebox.

In 1937, still just twenty, she won the Number One Female Vocalist poll in both the country's leading jazz magazines, *Down Beat* and *Metronome*. The following spring, she and Chick Webb recorded an old nursery rhyme, "A-Tisket, A-Tasket," and turned it into a swing anthem. It reached number one and stayed there for seventeen weeks. By autumn, Webb and Fitzgerald had three more novelty tunes on the charts—all at once.

Down Beat now called the Chick Webb orchestra "one of the best known and most popular swing bands in the country." But Webb was paying a price for his new success: the spotlight was on his young singer

now. His band was taking a back seat, its jazz quotient leached away in favor of bouncy commercial swing arrangements of popular songs. "Chick had been totally immersed in the *band*, and the guys stood behind him 100 percent," Helen Oakley recalled. "But after he got Ella it was different." Over the next few months, Webb issued just fourteen instrumentals and more than sixty vocals, almost all of them by Ella Fitzgerald. Billie Holiday, who had faced Ethel Waters's scorn at the beginning of her own career, now showered some of her own on the newcomer. One member of the Orchestra recalled that she came into the Savoy several times wearing a big fur coat, muttered "A great band like that with Ella—that bitch," turned around, and stalked out.

Then, Webb's lifelong physical frailty began to grow worse. His kidneys weakened, complicating his struggle against the spinal tuberculosis that had plagued him since childhood. He collapsed several times after performances and was finally confined to a Baltimore hospital. "Anything happens to me," he told a friend, "take care of Ella." He died on June 16, 1939, not yet thirty. Thousands filed past the casket at his family's church. Gene Krupa sat next to it all day, weeping. Most of the mourners wept during the funeral service when Fitzgerald sang "My Buddy." Webb's band stayed together but changed its name to "Ella Fitzgerald and Her Famous Orchestra." She didn't need anyone to take care of her.

BROWN SUGAR

"When I was a kid," Louis Armstrong once wrote a friend, "my grandmother used to say to me that the only person that makes money sitting on his ass is a shoemaker." During the swing era, Joe Glaser made sure Armstrong was perpetually on the move. Glaser was convinced that Armstrong, already a big star, could be still bigger if he would focus as much of his energy on show-manship as he did on music.

Armstrong needed little urging. He had always seen himself as an all-around per-former—his passport listed his profession as "actor and musician"—and his show business hero was Bill "Bojangles" Robin-son, who danced and sang and cracked jokes, and did them all superlatively well and without blacking-up. "People love me and my music," Armstrong once said. "The minute I walk on the bandstand . . . they know they're going to get something good. *I see to that.*"

He was playing differently now—there were fewer high-note flights—but his tone was even warmer than it had been before, if anything, and by hewing more closely to the melody, paraphrasing rather than recomposing, he somehow seemed still more magisterial. Asked to record every kind of material, he happily obliged. "There are no bad songs," he once said, and he approached each one as if it could be made into a masterpiece. Nor did the big band craze ever hold any terrors for him. The first records that brought him fame had been made with small New Orleans–style groups but he'd been playing with large orchestras off and on ever since taking his seat with Fletcher Henderson in 1924, and it was he who had first brought the whole notion of "swinging" to New York. He pro-duced spectacular new big-band versions of old favorites like "Struttin' with Some Barbecue," as well as brand-new hits like "I'm in the Mood for Love," "You Are My Lucky Star," "Jubilee," and his own "Swing That Music." He cut two comedy records as "Elder Eatmore," a version of the sticky-fingered preacher he had first impersonated for South Side audiences back in Chicago. On several sides, he thoughtfully softened his playing so as not to overwhelm the Mills Brothers' imitations of musical instruments, and, with an all-white choir, he recorded spirituals, on one of which —"Going to Shout All Over God's Heaven" —he struck a characteristically sly blow

On a Hollywood soundstage tricked up to look like a white set designer's notion of a Harlem street, Louis Armstrong plays a tune called "Public Melody Number One" for a corked-up Martha Raye in the 1937 film, *Artists and Models.*

against the racial expectations of his pro-ducers. While the chorus determinedly murmurs a stereotyped "hebbin, hebbin, hebbin" in the background, Armstrong clearly sings out "Heaven, Heaven, Heaven."

Glaser arranged appearances for Arm-strong in big-budget Hollywood films, too: *Pennies from Heaven,* with Bing Crosby, *Every Day's a Holiday,* with Mae West, *Going Places* (in which he plays a groom named Gabriel and sings "Jeepers Creep-ers" to a horse), and *Artists and Models,* in which his trumpet playing drives the blacked-up comedienne Martha Raye to dance so frantically that *Variety* warned her never to do such a thing again. "While Miss Raye is under cork, this intermingling of the races isn't wise, especially as she lets her-self go into the extremest manifestation of Harlemania torso-twisting and gyrations. It may hurt her personally." (It didn't.) All of the roles Armstrong played were stereo-typical—such parts were virtually all that 1930s Hollywood offered black perform-ers. In each of them, however, he remains uniquely himself: funny, guileful, supremely gifted, and utterly undisturbed by anything going on around him. Armstrong was writ-ten up in *Esquire* and *Vanity Fair* and in 1936 he published a book called *Swing That Music,* a sanitized version of his life that was nonetheless the first jazz autobiogra-phy ever to appear anywhere. That same year, he became the first black performer to host his own national sponsored radio program, substituting for Rudy Vallee on *The Fleishmann's Yeast Hour.* And when he was not making movies or records or appearing on the radio, Armstrong was on the road, fronting the big Luis Russell band that included several old friends from New Orleans.

His battered lip continued to plague him from time to time and in 1937 Glaser added Henry "Red" Allen to front the band at each performance until it was time to showcase its star. There were new challengers now, as well. Young Roy Eldridge could play faster and higher than Armstrong could, and most white fans were said to prefer Harry James, who said he felt embarrassed being mentioned in the same sentence with the man he very nearly worshiped. (When James won the *Down Beat* reader's poll for trumpet in 1944, he said, "That's ridiculous, Louis Armstrong is Number One," and to the end of his life, he would preserve a torn fragment of brown paper bag because Armstrong had once scrawled a few encouraging words to him on it.)

The road itself was wearing. As Pops Foster remembered,

> It was tough traveling through the South in those days. We had two white guys with us—the bus driver and Joe Glaser. If you had a colored bus driver back then, they'd lock him up in every little country town for "speeding." It was very rough finding a place to sleep in the South. You couldn't get into the hotels for whites, and the colored didn't have any hotels. You rented places in private homes, boarding houses and whorehouses. The food was awful and we tried to find places where we could cook. We carried a bunch of pots and pans around with us.

But for all the problems that afflicted his lip, for all the rival trumpet players now attracting attention, and for all the hardships encountered along the way, Armstrong remained a hero in black neigh-

borhoods all over the country. The bassist Johnny Williams remembered the crowds that gathered to see Armstrong off the morning after every performance. There were usually fifty to sixty people on the street to say good-bye no matter where they were, he said, including old friends as well as complete strangers, "a fellow sitting in a wheelchair, or on crutches, a woman— whatever." As his bus waited, Armstrong would go slowly down the line slapping backs, shaking hands, and giving out cash to anyone with a hard-luck story. "You know, not saying, 'Look, look, look, look, look, I'm giving this.' [He'd just] ball it up, put it in their hand, and say, 'Please take care of yourself.'"

In September 1937, Armstrong and his band were in Savannah, Georgia, when they suddenly came upon Joe Oliver standing by the side of the road, peddling tomatoes and potatoes from a vegetable stand. As Armstrong went from triumph to triumph, his old mentor had gone from bad to worse. His music had long since fallen from fashion. A crooked manager had collected deposits on all the dates he'd set up for one tour, then run off with the money. There were troubles on the road, too, as his saxophone player Paul Barnes noted in his diary.

> November 1—having bus trouble. Stay on road all night. Weather cold. Orchestra makes bonfire with bus tire. Get help next morning.
>
> November 7—Bus seized by clothing store, finally redeemed. . . . too late for Orchestra to make date in Cumberland, Kentucky. Woman proprietor of Southern Hotel holds King Oliver's trumpet for rent.

Even Oliver's diet had betrayed him: years of eating slice after slice of bread heaped with sugar caused him to lose all his teeth. He was fitted with dentures but afterwards found it impossible to play for more than a

Louis Armstrong onstage and in command, at the Apollo, 1939. "For me," said Duke Ellington, "he's the epitome of the kind of American who goes beyond the rules."

few minutes at a stretch and had been forced to take the job selling vegetables just to keep going.

"He was standing there in his short-sleeves," Armstrong said. "No tears. Just glad to see us. Just another day. He had that spirit." Armstrong gave him all the cash he had on hand—some $150—and took up a collection among the other New Orleanians in the band. "That night we played at a dance and look over and there's Joe standing in the wings," Armstrong wrote. "He was sharp like the old Joe Oliver of 1915. He'd been to the pawn shop and gotten . . . his suits and all—Stetson hat turned down, high-button shoes, his box-back coat. He looked beautiful and he had a wonderful night."

Armstrong and his men moved on the next morning. Oliver remained stranded in Savannah. "I'm still out of work," he wrote his sister from there three weeks later. "Since the road house close I haven't hit a note. But I've got a lot to thank God for because I eat and sleep. . . . Soon as the weather can fit my clothes I know I can do better in New York."

An old admirer eventually took pity on him and gave him a job.

Dear Sister:

I open the pool rooms at 9 a.m. and close at midnite. If the money was only ¼ as much as the hours I'd be all set. But at that I can thank God for what I am getting. Which I do night after night. . . .

Now Vick . . . I'm going to tell you something but don't be alarmed. I've got high blood pressure. Was taking treatment but had to discontinue . . . because it cost $3.00 per treatment. Now it begins to work on my heart. . . .

Should anything happen to me will you want my body? Let me know because I won't last forever. . . .

Don't think I am afraid because I wrote what I did. I am trying to live near[er] to the Lord than ever before. So I feel like the Good Lord will take care of me. Good night, dear.

Joe

Joe Oliver died on April 10, 1938. The headline of the Savannah *Tribune* read:

"DADDY" JAZZ MUSIC PASSES
KING OLIVER, NOTED BAND LEADER
FOUND DEAD IN BED
WAS THE DISCOVERER OF LOUIS ARMSTRONG

His funeral was held in Harlem, paid for by the Negro Actor's Guild. Louis Armstrong attended, along with a host of Oliver's old friends, and never forgave the presiding clergyman, Adam Clayton Powell Jr., for feeling called upon to draw moral lessons from the fact that Oliver had once had money but had been unable to hold on to it. "Just because the Guild buried him was no reason for rubbing it in," Armstrong said.

———————————

Louis Armstrong breaks it up at Connie's Inn, 1936. "When I commenced to put a little showmanship in with the music," he said, "people appreciated me better."

Lucille Wilson as a chorus girl at the Cotton Club where, Louis Armstrong remembered, "I paid strict attention to her . . . looking beautifuler 'n beautifuler every night."

Late in the summer of 1938, Lil Hardin agreed to grant Armstrong a divorce. They had spent most of their fourteen-year marriage apart. A few days later, on tour in Texas, he finally married Alpha Smith, with whom he'd been living off and on for nearly ten years. Lil claimed he had begged her *not* to give him his freedom and that she'd done so only to spite him, knowing that Alpha was threatening a breach of promise suit if he didn't wed her right away. In any case, it was not a happy match. "[Alpha's] mind was on furs, diamonds and other flashy luxuries and not enough on me and my happiness," Armstrong said later of his third wife. "I gave her all the diamonds she thought she wanted, but still she wanted other things. She went through all my money."

That fall, he opened at the new Cotton Club, located on Broadway at Forty-eighth Street, sharing the stage with his old idol, Bill Robinson. There, he spotted Lucille Wilson, a beautiful twenty-four-year-old dancer in the chorus line. "Maybe her color had

something to do with my falling in love with [her]," he wrote later. "Ever since I was old enough to feel a desire for women I've been drawn to those of darker hue. Lucille was the first girl to crack the high yellow color standard used to pick girls for . . . the Cotton Club."

Wilson sold cookies backstage to supplement her income and support her family—she was the daughter of the owner of a taxi fleet who had fallen on hard times— and Armstrong began his pursuit of her by buying up all her cookies, then passing them out to children in Harlem. She did her best to avoid him, nonetheless, until he cornered her backstage one day and said, "See here, little girl. I know all the cats are sharking after you; I just want you to know I'm in the running, too." He began calling her "Brown Sugar," started taking her for long rides in the chauffeured Packard Joe Glaser had bought for him, asked her if she would learn to cook him red beans and rice.

She said she would. "It seemed to me Lucille was the ideal girl for me," he remembered. "Good common sense . . . not particular about showy people." But the future remained cloudy. So long as he kept bringing money home, Alpha showed no signs of leaving him, and Lucille was not interested in a relationship with a married man.

A VERY DIFFERENT WORLD

In March 1939 Duke Ellington and his orchestra set sail a second time for Europe, this time aboard the *Île de France*. The continent was already moving toward war and the ship's hold was filled with parts for French fighter planes. There had recently been great changes in Ellington's life, as well. Both his parents were now gone: his father had died of tuberculosis in 1937. At thirty-nine, he had fallen in love with a beautiful Cotton Club dancer named Evie Ellis. He left Mildred Dixon and moved in

with Ellis. She would remain loyal to him all his life and even sometimes call herself Mrs. Ellington, but he would never agree to divorce his wife in order to marry her. Then, he had abruptly ended his long partnership with Irving Mills. Ellington never revealed the reason for the break. One story suggested that he had examined the books and found that when his mother died Mills had failed to follow his orders to buy her the finest casket in Washington, D.C. But Ellington may also have been reacting to stinging attacks on his closeness to Mills in the black press. A writer for the Pittsburgh *Courier* denounced Ellington for permitting Mills to write the words to his songs when deserving black lyricists were without work, and the Reverend Adam Clayton Powell Jr. had called him "just a musical sharecropper," dependent for his livelihood on "Massa Mills." Ellington's son, Mercer, believed his father's reputation was simply so well established by 1939 that he no longer needed Mills's services. Whatever the reason, the two men parted company.

The European tour had been Mills's idea, but even he could not have foreseen the sort of impact it would have—on European fans or on Ellington himself. The mass popularity of other bandleaders may have temporarily eclipsed him in the United States, but in Europe he remained supreme. Crowds met his ship at Le Havre with "such adoration and genuine joy," Rex Stewart remembered, "that for the first time in my life I had the feeling of being accepted as an artist, a gentleman, and a member of the human race." Everywhere Ellington went, people paid to hear his music played from the concert stage, not the bandstand. A Paris critic declared that Ellington's music was "related to the rhythm of the atom" and revealed "the very secret of the cosmos." Big crowds turned out in Brussels, Antwerp, The Hague, Utrecht, Amsterdam, Copenhagen, Oslo, and fifteen cities in Sweden, where admirers filled the platforms of every station through which Ellington's train passed in

Duke Ellington enjoying himself at the Savoy in the company of two of the finest singers in jazz, Ivie Anderson, left, who sang with his own orchestra, and Ella Fitzgerald, 1939

hopes of getting at least a glimpse of their hero. "The orchestra's refined appearance made a deep impression," wrote a critic for the Stockholm *Dagens Nyheter* on April 17, 1939, "and was a decided contrast to those slovenly, indifferent, clowning orchestras, which belong in the cheap cabarets, and never have anything of musical quality to offer." Ellington was still in Stockholm on April 29, his fortieth birthday. A sixteen-piece local band woke him that morning and admirers filled his hotel room with flowers. That evening, the whole audience rose to sing him happy birthday.

But not even he—with his highly developed skill at refusing to acknowledge unpleasantness—could overlook the evidence of the mounting crisis all around him. The Nazis had barred jazz music and frowned upon black foreigners, and when the train carrying the band across northern Germany was delayed for six hours at Hamburg, uniformed soldiers patrolled the platform. Barney Bigard saw them shove around "like dogs" an elderly Jewish couple who tried to enter the dining car. In Paris, the band performed in a new underground theater, built to withstand the Ger-

man bombs the French feared would soon be falling. And when their train crossed Holland, Bigard remembered, "we could see out of the . . . windows that they were putting machine-gun posts in all the haystacks and in the ditches. It was kind of scary."

As the *Île de France* steamed into New York harbor in May, Bigard said, "I was never so glad to see that old Statue of Liberty." Ellington was happy to be home, too, but he had also once again been energized by the respect given to his music and his musicians abroad. "Europe is a very different world," he told a friend. "You can go anywhere and talk to anybody and do anything you like. It's hard to believe. When you've eaten hot dogs all your life and you're suddenly offered caviar it's hard to believe it's true." He was about to begin one of the greatest creative periods in his career.

STILL THE BOSS

Two months later, with war in Europe just weeks away, Coleman Hawkins, too, came home to New York. Other American musicians had toured overseas; Hawkins had lived there for more than five years. Appreciative audiences in Britain, France, Scandinavia, and Holland treated him more like a concert artist than an entertainer; he sometimes appeared onstage with symphony orchestras, playing rhapsodic chorus after chorus. He had a good time offstage, too. He loved good food and drink but "girls were his hobby," one Dutch fan remembered. "He used to serenade them with his sax."

His return was "like God coming home," Milt Hinton remembered. Hawkins immediately set out to see for himself whether he could still outplay the younger musicians who had risen to prominence while he was away. After listening in all over town, he was reassured. "I'd been over there for so long . . . I thought by the time I came back . . . the musicians here would be further advanced. . . . But it was just like . . . when I *left*. . . . They're not going to cut me playing that."

Above all, he wanted another shot at Lester Young. At around three o'clock one morning, he found his way to Puss Johnson's basement club in Harlem where a jam session was being held, attended by both Young and Billie Holiday. Word spread fast, and soon, Rex Stewart remembered, the club was filled with musicians eager to see what would happen when the two giants of the tenor saxophone faced off again, six years after they had first met in Kansas City.

Coleman Hawkins sipping tea in London. "He was an aristocrat," a young admirer remembered. "I couldn't take my eyes off him."

[Hawkins] strode in, unpacked his sax and joined them. . . . [W]hen Billie finished, she announced to the house that it had been a pleasure to have had the world's greatest tenor saxophonist backing her up—Lester Young!

You could have heard a pin drop after that remark, but the Hawk ignored it . . . [and began to play]. The tempo Hawk set was almost unbelievable, it was so fast. And he had the tune all to himself. Then he sauntered to the bar, had a big drink, and waited to see how the cats would follow his avalanche of virtuosity. For some reason nobody felt like blowing at the moment. So Coleman picked up where he had left off, this time with a ballad, finishing up with an incredible cadenza, to thundering applause.

Lester sat on the sidelines, drinking with Lady Day, and I must say that

he kept his cool. I heard [some musicians talking to one another], "Well, that's that. Coleman is still the boss."

But when *Down Beat* reported that Hawkins had been the victor that morning, Holiday indignantly telephoned the editor to object: "Young really cut the Hawk," she said. "Most everyone there who saw them tangle agreed on that."

A few months later, Hawkins went into the studio with a nine-piece group and recorded four sides, including "Body and Soul," a ballad he had been playing for years as "an *encore*," he said, just "something to get off the stage with." Like Louis Armstrong's "West End Blues" eleven years earlier, Coleman Hawkins's "Body and Soul" shook the musical world. It was in three parts: a tender, elliptical two-bar hint of the melody; two surging choruses that build to a thrilling crescendo; a gorgeous falling unaccompanied cadenza. Except for a brief piano introduction and some gentle supportive chords from the rest of the band, it was all Hawkins's huge, warm, all-encompassing sound.

"Body and Soul" sold astonishingly well for a disc by a jazz soloist in which melody played such an insignificant part. Hawkins claimed not to be surprised. "Gracious," he said, "I play like that all the time!" He had approached "Body and Soul" the same way he approached every ballad, he assured the young singer Thelma Carpenter. "First, you have to tell them the story," by which he meant state the melody. "Then, it's like making love. . . . You must romance her." The climax of the solo is "when you're having the orgasm," he said. And the cadenza? "Well, now that's the *satisfaction*." But musicians heard much more than eroticism in "Body and Soul." Hawkins's startling improvisation would help inspire a whole generation of young musicians to become what one saxophonist called "chord conscious," to see if they could take jazz in a different direction.

DEDICATED TO CHAOS

By 1940, the Great Depression had finally ended. The economy had begun to boom again, as the country readied itself for what growing numbers of Americans saw as inevitable—U.S. entry into World War II. But the swing music that had helped keep American spirits up during the lean years still seemed to be everywhere. Bandleaders like Benny Goodman and Artie Shaw and Glenn Miller were earning as much as $20,000 a week. Cab Calloway and Duke Ellington and Count Basie were doing well, too. But most black bands were no longer sharing in the good times. "Are Colored Bands Doomed as Big Money Makers?" asked Down Beat, *and then answered: "Negro Leaders Could Make More Money Running a Rib Joint."*

The old racial stereotyping that had made it difficult for men like Fletcher Henderson to show all that they could do on records at least had

Somewhere in France. The sounds of swing bring G.I.s together, courtesy of a USO entertainer, 1945.

helped reserve for black musicians—who were supposed to have a natural affinity for it—the kind of hard-swinging music Goodman and his rivals now routinely performed. Their success—as Goodman was always careful to concede—was due in part to the behind-the-scenes contributions of black arrangers. Even many of the snappy onstage routines fans of bands like Glenn Miller's most enjoyed—choreographed derby work by the trumpet section; trombones blaring right and left, up and down, in perfect unison; reedmen leaping up and down to solo—had been pioneered by black bands and carefully taught to them by veterans of those outfits, such as Eddie Durham.

Civil rights legislation did not help, at least at first. New public accommodations laws in northern states initially reduced opportunities for black musicians. Many all-black theaters closed. A good many white club and hotel owners, now forbidden to discriminate openly against black customers, kept them out anyway by refusing to hire any more black bands. While the top white bands wintered in New York, Chicago, and other large cities, playing so-called location jobs at the best hotels and promoting themselves on the radio, all but a handful of black orchestras were forced to stay on the road year-round simply to survive. Few complained: "You may have holes in your shoes," Earl Hines (who himself managed to land a long-term stint at the Grand Terrace in Chicago) often told his men, "but don't let people out front know it. Shine the tops."

White bands like Tommy Dorsey's, which could play a broad spectrum of music, were hailed for their versatility. Their black counterparts who sought to do the same were often indirectly accused of trying to get above themselves. Black bandleaders who larded their music with showmanship—such as Louis Armstrong, Cab Calloway, and Lionel Hampton—continued to do well. Those, like Teddy Wilson and Benny Carter, who focused mostly on their music and pol-

ished it to a fine gloss, foundered. *Their* music, Thelma Carpenter remembered hearing on Fifty-second Street, was "too white."

The lyricist Andy Razaf had seen it all coming back in 1932 and, in three verses of doggerel printed in the *Amsterdam News,* had tried to warn his fellow Harlem musicians:

You're a novelty no longer,
They have copied all your tricks;
'Till white bands can pass for colored
With "gut-bucket" blues and "licks."

Once they marveled at your ragtime
And you gladly showed them how,
So they've mastered all your rhythms;
They don't really need you now.

If you want to hold your places
You had better do your stuff;
Keep rehearsing and rehearsing,
You can never learn enough.

For the "ad lib" days are over,
Noise and faking are passé;
If you feel that you are rusty
Get that music book today.

Studying that music book had not been enough. "The truth is," said *Down Beat* in the spring of 1940, "the public will absorb only a very limited number of Negro bands." A new kind of swing was in favor now, said *Variety.* It was "sweet hot" or "swing sweet," a "white man's style of swing, retaining the Negroid bounce but coupling it to more respect for the melody."

Meanwhile, some black bandleaders felt themselves under the threat of still another kind of siege. In October of 1940, Benny Goodman hired away Duke Ellington's trumpet star, Cootie Williams, for an additional twenty-five dollars a week. Ellington was unruffled. He helped Williams negotiate his contract with Goodman. And he replaced Williams the night after he left with another fine trumpet player, Ray Nance, who, Ellington said, "never played a bad note in his life" and also danced, sang, and played the violin. Williams himself saw the move as a great opportunity: Goodman's was the greatest *swing* band he'd ever heard, he said. And Goodman, in his turn, did his best to soften Jim Crow's impact on his new star. Williams's friend and section mate, Jimmy Maxwell, was assigned the task of checking them both in whenever they reached a strange hotel. "It cost me a fortune [to live] with Cootie," Maxwell remembered, "because I wouldn't eat in the dining room if he couldn't, so we both ended up getting room service. When there were black waiters, though, if you ordered a steak, they would bring you three."

After the United States entered World War II in 1941, venues like the Forest Park Ballroom in Marshalltown, Iowa, would find it more and more difficult to keep their doors open.

Cootie Williams working
with Harry James and
Benny Goodman, 1941

But Williams's departure from the Ellington orchestra was bittersweet news in the music business. The bandleader Raymond Scott even wrote a mournful tune about it, "When Cootie Left the Duke," and while Dan Burley of the *Amsterdam News* applauded Goodman's "sense of justice in giving Negro musicians the chance they so richly deserve in playing the music they originated," he also thought it a bad precedent, sure to weaken further the already precarious position of the black bands.

To dangle such tempting bait as fat salary checks, plus a chance to play in swing music's big leagues, is to the colored musician what a chance to pitch for the Brooklyn Dodgers in the major baseball circuit would be to a member of the N.Y. Black Yankees. In such an instance the athlete would drop his colored league connections in such a hurry it wouldn't even be funny. The Negro musician figures to do the same thing. . . . The future isn't as bright as we'd like to see it for the *average* musician buried in a Negro band. . . . The Negro has a definite place in swing music—to originate, not to profit. . . . The other fellow will tolerate him only so long as he can learn something new.

Other white bandleaders were now hiring other black stars, as well, and dealing as best they could with the trouble their new men often encountered on the road. Artie Shaw canceled thirty-one one-nighters in the South rather than give in to a contract that required him to seat Lips Page a minimum of fifteen feet from the rest of the band. He hadn't done it for "civil rights," he said later, "I did it for sanity." And Gene Krupa was briefly jailed for punching a Pennsylvania restaurant owner who had allowed all of his men except Roy Eldridge through his door.

With the exception of Sidney Bechet and Coleman Hawkins, Eldridge may have been the most competitive musician in jazz history. "When I was young," he said, "I used to go around looking for every jam session. I used to stand out on the sidewalk, smoking, listening to the band inside, summing up the opposition. Eventually, I'd walk in and try to cut them. All my life, I loved to battle. And if they didn't like the look of me and wouldn't invite me up to the bandstand, I'd get my trumpet out by the side of the stand and blow at them from there." And even as an old man, when he was introduced to the youthful Lester Bowie and told Bowie was a fellow trumpet player, he narrowed his eyes: "Be ready," he said. "He wanted to play better than anybody," remembered one of his most ardent admirers, John Birks "Dizzy" Gillespie, "just to *wipe out* everybody else." Born in Pittsburgh in 1911 and dubbed "Little Jazz" by Otto Hardwick, he was short and chesty, a veteran of the Teddy Hill and Fletcher Henderson bands, as well as the hero of countless early morning cutting contests. He played with astonishing speed—a by-product, he said, of having closely studied Coleman Hawkins and other saxophonists—and with titanic emotion, producing long, involved lines that sometimes seem about to careen into chaos, only to be snatched back just in time.

But for all his power and combativeness, Eldridge was also a proud and sensitive man. In the end the effort required to maintain his composure in the face of the daily indignities he experienced as the sole black musician in a white band would prove more than even he could bear:

I knew I'd have to be awful cool; I knew all eyes were on me. . . . All the guys in the band were nice, and Gene [Krupa] was especially wonderful [but when] we headed west for some one-nighters, winding up in California, that was when the trouble began. We arrive in one town and the rest of the band checks in. I can't get into their hotel, so I keep my bags and start riding around looking for another place, where someone's supposed to have made a reservation for me. I get there and move all my bags in. Naturally, since we're going to be out on the coast several months, I have a heavy load—at least a dozen pieces of baggage. Then the clerk, when he sees that I'm the "Mr. Eldridge" the reservation was made for, suddenly discovers that one of their regular tenants just arrived and took the last available room. I lug that baggage back into the street and start looking around again. By the time that kind of thing has happened night after night, it begins to work on my mind; I can't think right, can't play right.

When we finally got to the Palladium in Hollywood I had to watch who I could sit at the tables with. If they were movie stars who wanted me to come over, that was all right; if they were just the jitterbugs, no dice. And all the time the bouncer with his eye on me, just watching for a chance. On top of that, I had to live way out in Los Angeles while the rest of the guys stayed in Hollywood. It was a lonely life; I'd never been that far away from home before, and I didn't know anybody. I got to brooding.

Then it happened. One night the tension got so bad I flipped. I could feel it right up to my neck while I was playing "Rockin' Chair." I started trembling, ran off the stand, and threw up. They carried me to the doctor's. I had a 105 fever; my nerves were shot.

Things got worse in the South. In Norfolk, Virginia, Eldridge and the white singer Anita O'Day had to perform their hit duet "Let Me Off Uptown" from opposite ends of the stage. He found himself barred from the men's room and expected to make do with a bucket. When he joined the rest of the band on the deck of a ferry boat, the captain ordered him below, and when

Roy Eldridge in full cry at the Arcadia Ballroom in New York in 1939, in front of the band he led until he joined Gene Krupa two years later. When he wasn't onstage himself, one trumpeter remembered, Eldridge would search out young trumpeters in other clubs, then "take out his horn at the door . . . start on a high B-flat and just come walking in."

Krupa intervened, insisting his star be allowed to stay where he was, the captain said, "Well, if you can stand him it's all right with me." "Just as if I had leprosy," Eldridge remembered.

He loyally stayed with Krupa till that band broke up. In 1944, he accepted an offer to join Artie Shaw and again met with trouble in California.

We got to Del Mar. I got in the hotel all right but couldn't eat in the dining room. Some of the guys who knew I liked Mexican food suggested that we go to a little Mexican joint. When *they* refused to serve me, all the other guys walked out with me, but it still started to put me in that mood again. [Then,] I went to the place where we were supposed to play a dance and they wouldn't even let me in. . . . "This is a white dance," they said, "and there was my name right outside: "Roy 'Little Jazz' Eldridge" and I told them who I was. When I finally did get in, I played that first set, trying to keep from crying. By the time I got through the set, the tears were rolling down my cheeks—I don't know how I made it. I went up to a dressing room and stood in a corner crying and saying to myself "Why the hell did I come out here again when I knew what would happen?" Artie came in and he was great. He made the guy apologize who wouldn't let me in, and got him fired. But finally I left the band in San Francisco. . . . Man, when you're on the stage you're great, but as soon as you come off, nothing. It's not worth the glory, not the money, not worth anything. Never again!

In fact, he would rejoin Gene Krupa five years later. By then, thanks in part to his courageous pioneering, integrated bands were no longer so great a novelty and conditions on the road had at least begun to change.

JIGSAW

"The most significant thing that can be said about Swing music today," Duke Ellington had written in 1939, "is that it has become stagnant." To be sure, "the myriad of bands throughout the country . . . who are modeling themselves along the lines of a Benny Goodman . . . rather than along the lines of any out-and-out popular dance band are cultivating a higher standard of musicianship than that heretofore required." But popular success inevitably rewarded artistic timidity: "It has thwarted the improvement of many good bands, which for commercial reasons remain in the same uninspired groove and refuse to risk rising above the current public taste."

Ellington could afford to be critical. His own popularity had never been greater and his music had never been more rich, more daring, in part because of a series of new additions to his band. Just before he sailed for Europe the spring before the war broke out in Europe, he had played the Stanley Theater in Pittsburgh. Black Pittsburgh was the realm of Gus Greenlee, the numbers king. Greenlee owned boxers, nightclubs, apartment buildings, and the champion Negro League baseball team, the Pittsburgh Crawfords—as well as Greenlee Stadium, in which they played. And so, when Greenlee's nephew suggested in the presence of his uncle that Ellington take a few moments to listen to a local pianist who was a friend of his, he knew that even the Maestro dared not say no.

The piano player did not look like much. Billy Strayhorn was just twenty-three years old, barely five feet tall, bespectacled, and still partly supporting himself as a drugstore

Duke Ellington and Billy Strayhorn, 1960. "Music. That's it," a friend remembered, trying to explain their relationship. "Duke lived, breathed, ate and drank music. That's all that really mattered to him—nothing else. That's what he loved. And he loved Billy Strayhorn because they made music together."

clerk despite having achieved some success arranging for local bands and playing piano around town. But he performed Ellington's "Sophisticated Lady" with such flair and originality, and had already written such interesting tunes of his own, including the ballads "Lush Life" and "Something to Live For," that Ellington asked Strayhorn to come see him when he got home. "I would like to have you in my organization," he said. "I have to find some way of injecting you into it. I have to find out how I do this after I get back to New York."

Ellington scribbled out instructions on how to reach his Harlem apartment by subway and when the two men next met, Strayhorn had composed and arranged a brand-new piece based on them. "It was

like writing a letter to a friend," Strayhorn remembered. "Take the 'A' Train" eventually became Ellington's theme and Strayhorn became his lifelong collaborator, called "Strays" and sometimes "Swee'pea," because of his imagined resemblance to the ageless single-toothed baby in the "Popeye" comic strip.

At first, they seemed unlikely partners. Strayhorn was warm, gregarious, and openly homosexual in a time when most gay people remained grimly closeted. Ellington was private, enigmatic, and a flamboyant ladies' man. But he was also profoundly worldly: "Pop never cared one bit that Strayhorn was gay," Ellington's son, Mercer, remembered. "He was never prejudiced against anyone he thought was really worthy. . . . It was nothing new to him. . . . Pop knew the story. He backed up Strayhorn all the way."

Strayhorn's talent was what counted. Ellington said he was "my right arm, my left arm, all the eyes in the back of my head; my brainwaves are in his head, and his in mine." He once tried to explain to an interviewer the nature of their collaboration.

Oh, Billy Strayhorn is my writing and arranging companion. I may be somewhere, like in Los Angeles, and he's in New York, and I get to the 17th bar of a number and I decide, well, I think rather than sit here and struggle with this, I'll call Strays and I'll call him and say, "Look, I'm in E flat someplace and, and the mood is this and you know, this man is supposed to be walking up the road and he reaches a certain intersection and I can't decide whether he should turn left, right, go straight ahead, or make a U-turn." And he says, "Oh, yes, I know what you mean," you know? And "Well, I think you could do that better than I could"—that's his first response, you know? And all the time, he's thinking about how he can outdo me, you know? And then, and very often without any more than that, we come up with practically the same thing.

For almost three decades Ellington and Strayhorn would dedicate themselves to the same all-consuming goal: the greatness of the Duke Ellington Orchestra, of Duke Ellington's music, and of Duke Ellington himself.

Ellington's music had always been a blend of personal voices and regional styles—the eastern ragtime of his early teachers, the New Orleans music he first heard from Sidney Bechet and Louis Armstrong, the smooth sinuous sounds he'd perfected at the Cotton Club and on Broadway. Now, two new men brought to the band something of the same stomp-style blues

that Count Basie had introduced to the country. The first was the bassist Jimmy Blanton. He was just twenty-one years old when Sonny Greer took Ellington and Strayhorn to hear him in a St. Louis club. "All my life I'd never heard nobody like this guy," Greer said. Ellington agreed, and hired him on the spot. Blanton would die of tuberculosis within three years, but that was time enough for him to revolutionize bass playing. Blanton had a huge, warm sound, a buoyant beat, and a gift for placing "those precision notes in the right places," Ellington wrote, "so that we could float out on the great and adventurous sea of expectancy with his pulse and foundation behind us." But beyond that, he was more harmonically sophisticated than any of his predecessors and capable of melodic flights—both plucked and bowed—that no bassist before him had ever come close to matching. Ellington already had a very good bass player named Billy Taylor and was happy to have both men provide what he called the "foundation-and-beat" for his band, until Taylor suddenly quit one evening in Boston, saying, "I'm not going to stand up here next to that young boy playing all that bass and be embarrassed." It was only after the advent of Blanton—and the opportunities Ellington provided for him in recorded piano-bass duets like "Pitter Panther Patter" and "Sophisticated Lady" and in arrangements for the full band such as "Jack the Bear" and "Sepia Panorama"— that the bass began to be taken seriously as a solo instrument.

Then, in January of 1940, Ben Webster joined the band, becoming the fifth member of the reed section and Ellington's first tenor saxophone star. No one in the Ellington orchestra ever played more beautifully—or caused more trouble. A former pianist who had got his start on saxophone playing alongside Lester Young in the Young Family troupe, he was a native son of Kansas City and a hard-drinking veteran of the all-night tenor battles that characterized musical life there. One of his nick-

names was "the Brute." "If he had a few drinks in him," his friend Milt Hinton remembered, "he was an animal. I've gone with him to his house in Kansas City. His mother was a schoolteacher, and when he was in his mother's house he was like little Lord Fauntleroy. We would go right around the corner and have a beer and he'd knock four people down before we got out of the

Ben Webster backstage in 1949. By then, he had been gone from the Ellington organization for six years but wherever he worked for the rest of his life—he lived until 1973—he would tape up a photograph of Ellington labeled "The Governor."

door." Both sides of Webster's turbulent personality were expressed through his horn. On up-tempo tunes like "Cotton Tail" and "Conga Brava" he was all swagger and drive, roaring as few other saxophonists have ever roared, "buzzing and growling through chord changes," as Rex Stewart wrote, "like a prehistoric monster challenging a foe." But when given ballads like "All Too Soon" and Billy Strayhorn's "Chelsea Bridge," he could croon with a warmth and tender, breathy intimacy that even his section mate Johnny Hodges had a hard time matching.

Lovers of Ellington's music enjoy debating which of his bands was the best. But no one denies that the orchestra he led between 1940 and 1943 (when Ben Webster left to try and make it on his own) produced an astonishing body of music: "Jack the Bear," "Ko-Ko," "Chelsea Bridge," "Conga Brava," "Concerto for Cootie," "Cotton Tail," "Never No Lament" (later retitled "Don't Get Around Much Anymore"), "Harlem Air Shaft," "All Too Soon," "Sepia Panorama," "In a Mellotone," "Warm Valley," "Take the 'A' Train," "Jumpin Punkins," "Rain-Check," "Just a-Sittin' and a-Rockin'." These and other pieces are often praised as "three-minute masterpieces." There is no doubt that they are masterpieces, but they run just three minutes mostly because that was all the music that could be squeezed onto one side of a 78 rpm record; air-checks from those years show that, in live performance, during which soloists were given more room to blow, these same arrangements often stretched more than twice as long.

During Ellington's half century on the road, scores of musicians would appear with his orchestra and some stayed with him for most of that time. But none was ever allowed to get too close. He "was a miraculous jigsaw," one friend said, "and seldom did anyone pick up more than a few pieces at a time." He seemed the epitome of self-confidence, but he was also a lifelong hypochondriac who lugged with him a doctor's bag filled with a pharmacopoeia of vitamin pills wherever he went. His closest friend was his physician, Dr. Arthur Logan, and no matter where in the world he happened to be, he would telephone his doctor to "see how I'm feeling today." For years he refused to fly, and after the international demand for his music made it impossible for him to remain grounded any longer, he never boarded a plane without first clutching a gold cross his sister had given him to wear around his neck after their mother died. He wouldn't wear a watch because, he said, he didn't want to "rush through life"; insisted that every window be closed during a rainstorm for fear lightning might enter the room; would not tolerate peanuts or newspapers or whistling backstage; never again wore a jacket from which a button had dropped off; refused to wear brown because he had been wearing it the day of his mother's death; and loathed the color green because, he said, ever since the age of eight it had reminded him of grass—and cemeteries.

He was a man of enormous appetites, all of them demanding instant gratification. A French reporter once asked Tricky Sam Nanton if his boss was a genius. "He's a genius all right," Nanton answered, "but Jesus, how he eats!" He dumped packet after packet of sugar into the Coca-Colas he now guzzled in place of the hard liquor that had once fueled him, is said once to have wolfed down thirty-two sandwiches at intermission during a dance in Brunswick, Maine, and often ate three quarts of ice cream at a sitting—one chocolate, one vanilla, one strawberry.

He had catholic tastes in women, too. "I'm seldom alone," he once told a radio interviewer. "I'm extremely partial to extremely pretty people." He was still living with Evie Ellis, but she would never be the sole woman in his life. "I think Evie was his protection," said the publicist Phoebe Jacobs. "In other words, every time he got too involved with another woman, he'd

Duke Ellington and his orchestra at the Oriental Theater in Chicago in the autumn of 1940. Left to right, Juan Tizol, Tricky Sam Nanton, Lawrence Brown, Fred Guy, Johnny Hodges, Barney Bigard, Ellington himself, Ben Webster, Sonny Greer, Otto Hardwick, Jimmy Blanton, Harry Carney, Wallace Jones, Rex Stewart, Ray Nance

always say, 'Well, I have to go back to Evie.'" "It was shocking" how women threw themselves at him, his sister remembered, but he was never an innocent bystander and routinely employed lines that would have gotten a less magnetic man laughed from the room. "I'm so jealous of your dress," he'd say to a woman he'd never met before, and when she asked him why, he'd answer, "Because it's closer to you than I will ever be." And before allowing his son Mercer (who was prematurely gray) to join the band as road manager and sometime trumpet player, Ellington insisted his son never publicly call him Pop, for fear it would disillusion the women who continued to crowd his dressing room.

But his greatest hunger was always for his music—writing it, orchestrating it, then hearing it played back to him right away by the men around whose unique strengths and weaknesses it was always carefully constructed. He wrote everywhere, every day, and all the time, aboard trains and buses, in cars racing down the highway, on restaurant napkins and nightclub matchbooks, even in his bedroom. "After you've absorbed the day and you get all settled down," he said, "you're quiet and you're all ready to go to sleep. You turn out the light and you put your head on the pillow and you get your sleeping stance together and there's the idea you've been looking for all day long and you get up and put the light on, get the paper and the pencil, jot it down, and usually before you go to sleep, you got the next part of it."

Since every note he wrote was meant to be played by a specific musician, he is often said to have "cast" his compositions the way a director casts a play. A better analogy might be to a playwright crafting a vehicle for one or another member of a permanent all-star cast. He had meticulously built his band out of distinct individuals—"eighteen maniacs," he once said. Over the years, there would be drunks and drug addicts among Ellington's men, and at least one kleptomaniac who raided his fel-

Duke Ellington works to get what he wants from Johnny Hodges, tenor saxophonist Al Sears, and multi-reedman Jimmy Hamilton at a 1944 recording session for RCA.

low musicians' belongings on the bus or in the dressing room nearly every night. Some of his men routinely failed to turn up on time, and occasionally had to be bailed out of jail. Rex Stewart had only rarely spoken to Cootie Williams when he was in the band; Barney Bigard refused to talk with Lawrence Brown; Brown would not speak to Ellington himself.

Ellington seemed to ignore it all. "Why deal with unpleasantness?" he asked. What discipline there was came indirectly. He rarely said a word if a musician showed up late or had been drinking, but during that evening's performance, he could be counted on to set a breakneck tempo, then call on

the guilty party for chorus after solo chorus. Nor did he generally fire anyone, though as Rex Stewart said, "once he has decided on a change, a change happens." "Even his most loyal followers couldn't understand how the band could be so great with such seeming lack of discipline," Stewart continued. "They wondered how all of this inventiveness and beautiful music could be produced as bandsmen drift on- and off-stage, yawn, act bored, apparently disdaining the people, the music, and the entire scene."

None of that mattered much to Ellington—provided his men could play when called upon. And when it came time to work out a new arrangement he seemed always able to get all of the disparate elements to come together for the greater good. The setting never seemed to matter, either, as one prewar visitor to Ellington's hotel room in Los Angeles remembered:

Duke was in the bathtub. Beside him was a stack of manuscript paper, a huge container of chocolate ice cream, a glass of Scotch and milk and Jonesy [Richard B. Jones] . . . his valet, and his job was to keep adding warm water and let out cooling water to maintain a constant temperature in the tub for the Maestro. And Duke was serenely scribbling notes on the paper and then calling to Bill Strayhorn. Billy would take the notes and play them on the beat-up old upright piano in Duke's room. Duke would listen and then write more notes, which he would give to Strayhorn. The band seemed to be all on the same floor of the hotel—like a very long railroad flat—and the sound of Strays at the keyboard was like some kind of signal. Pretty soon you'd hear Ben Webster playing the line, then Ray Nance would start tootling from somewhere down the hall, Sonny Greer would come in with his sticks, and the music would start to form. . . . Duke writing more and more notes for Swee'-pea . . . Jonesy keeping the water just right.

SWINGING WITH CHANGE

By late 1940, as Hitler's armies continued their relentless drive across Europe and Nazi bombs fell on London, a new club called Minton's Playhouse on 118th Street in Harlem had begun to attract some of the most adventurous musicians in jazz. It was cramped and dingy—it had been the dining room of the Hotel Cecil—but two things made it popular. The owner was Henry Minton, the very first black delegate in the New York musician's union. Nobody who came there to jam was going to be fined for playing without pay. And it was managed by the former bandleader Teddy Hill, who had come up with the idea of making Monday evening (the musician's traditional night off) "Celebrity Night," with free food and drink for anyone willing to come in and play.

Minton's was about music, not dancing or entertainment. "There was complete quiet," the guitarist Danny Barker remembered, "very little talking, no glasses clinking, no kinds of noises." Soon, the all-night sessions at Minton's were attracting some of the best musicians in jazz—sometimes thirty at a time: Chu Berry, Don Byas, Coleman Hawkins, Milt Hinton, Billy Strayhorn, Art Tatum, even Benny Goodman. Ben Webster and Lester Young "used to tie up in battle" there, the bartender remembered, "like dogs in the road. They'd fight on those saxophones until they were tired out; then they'd [call] Kansas City, and tell *them* about it." Sometimes, Mary Lou Williams remembered, "you couldn't get into Minton's for musicians and instruments."

Many of the music's most established stars did cheerful battle on Minton's bandstand, but something else was happening, as well. It was at Minton's—and in another after-hours Harlem night spot, Clark Monroe's Uptown House, as well as backstage among young musicians playing in big bands here and there all across the country—that a new style was beginning to evolve out of swing, filled with passion but cerebral and demanding, too, and relentless in its intensity. Its creators were mostly black and in their early twenties (some were even younger). They were well-schooled musicians who had grown up listening to and playing swing music but, as one of them remembered, "Benny Goodman had been named the 'King of Swing.' . . . We figured what the hell, we can't do no more than what's been done with it, we got to do something else . . . some other kind of thing." They were eager to explore new rhythm patterns and fresh harmonies and they were dissatisfied, both with the dance music they were expected to play night after night and with the way their music was being presented in America. The public still saw them as entertainers; they wanted to be seen as artists.

The new music began, as most new developments in jazz have begun, in the rhythm section. Two especially adventurous young musicians—the drummer Kenny Clarke and the pianist Thelonious Monk—were at the heart of the Minton house band.

Kenny Clarke, who played with everyone from Sidney Bechet and Louis Armstrong to Billie Holiday, had extended Jo Jones's innovations on the drums, keeping time mostly on the ride cymbal while urging on the soloists with what he called "bombs" on the bass and snare drums. It earned him the nickname "Klook-mop," eventually shortened to "Klook." His style puzzled some musicians—"he breaks up the time too much," one complained—and lost him at least one big band job, but Clarke was sure he was on to something. "If you are playing, the tempo should be in your head," he told musicians. "Don't depend on me." He had found a way to turn the old church-based call-and-response that had first characterized the relationship between individual instruments in New Orleans music and then been echoed by the brass and reed sections in the swing bands into a continuous back-and-forth conversation between drums and horns. Charlie Christian found Clarke's drum style so ideally suited to the long, supple, unpredictable eighth-note lines he liked to play on the guitar that he kept an extra guitar amplifier on the Minton's bandstand.

Thelonious Monk delighted in unconventional rhythms, too, but his most significant contribution to the new music would be harmonic. Born in North Carolina but raised on New York's West Side, he was just twenty-three years old in 1940, but had already written several of the venturesome

Visionaries: Kenny Clarke (top) and Thelonious Monk

tunes, filled with unusual chords and voicings, that would become staples of postwar jazz—"'Round Midnight," "Epistrophy," "Ruby, My Dear," "Well, You Needn't." Monk's music was thoroughly grounded in all that had gone before. His heroes were James P. Johnson, Fats Waller, and Duke Ellington; as a youngster, he had toured the country playing gospel music for a female evangelist billed as "the Texas Warhorse," and echoes of stride, gospel, and the blues can all be clearly heard in everything he ever played. But some musicians found his distinctively percussive piano playing, with its sudden starts and stops, its silences and jagged rhythms, its use of "flatted fifths"—unusual intervals which suggested bitonality—"weird" at best, sinister at worst.

Others were entranced. Danny Barker remembered the impact of first hearing Monk and Clarke play together. "Monk started," Barker said. "Klook fell in, dropped in, dived in, sneaked in; by hook or by crook, he was in. . . . You would look, hear the off-, off-, off-beat explosion and think 'fireworks,' and then the color patterns formed in the high sky of your mind."

The new music had no name as yet. They called it simply "playing modern." Among those who heard it early on was Ralph Ellison, now living and working in New York, and a frequent visitor to Minton's. Raised on the straightforward 4/4 stomp of Walter Page's Original Blue Devils, whose headquarters, Slaughter's Hall, had been within earshot of his home in Oklahoma City, he found some of the new music he heard at Minton's as disquieting as it was exciting.

It's been a long time now and not many remember how it was in the old days, not really. Not even those who were there to see and hear it as it happened, who were pressed in the crowds beneath the dim rosy lights of the bar in the smoke-veiled room, and who shared, night after night, the mysterious spell created by the talk,

the laughter, grease paint, powder, perfume, sweat, alcohol, and food—all blended and simmering, like a stew on the restaurant range, and brought to a sustained moment of elusive meaning by the timbres and accents of musical instruments locked in a passionate recitative . . . at Minton's Playhouse. . . . It was an exceptional moment, and the world was swinging with change. . . . Usually, music gives resonance to memory . . . but not the music then in the making. . . . Its rhythms were out of stride and seemingly arbitrary, its drummers frozen-faced introverts dedicated to chaos. And in it the steady flow of memory, desire, and defined experience summed up by the traditional jazz beat and blues mood seemed swept like a great river from its old, deep bed. We know better now, and recognize the old moods in the new sounds, but what we know is that which was then becoming.

Whenever he was in town, Roy Eldridge made a point of turning up at Minton's. The fresh pace set by Clarke and Monk did not intimidate him, and he was always on the alert for new challengers. It was there one evening that, after weeks of trying, a young trumpet player from the South, who had regarded Eldridge as his hero, finally managed to best him. "There was this one guy that I remember that came on the stand and played and when he played I looked up," the guitarist Johnny Collins recalled. "And he was different. That was Dizzy Gillespie."

John Birks Gillespie was born in Cheraw, South Carolina, in 1917, the youngest of nine children of a bricklayer and sometime musician who beat all his offspring every Sunday morning whether or not they'd done anything wrong. "Papa believed a hard head made a soft behind," Gillespie remembered. "He turned me into a tough little rebel." He would remain a rebel into his adult years, resentful of every kind of

John Birks Gillespie, photographed before moving to New York. "I could get over my horn better than the average cat," he wrote of himself in those days, "and had a lot of fire."

authority, unwilling to alter his ideas of how music should be played to suit anybody else, but also willing—even eager—to share all that he knew with others. Like Jelly Roll Morton, Dizzy Gillespie would be a theorist and teacher as well as a groundbreaker. And he would struggle all his life to keep alive the link between jazz music and ordinary people that his heroes from an older generation had always represented, the link that his own innovations would inadvertently help to destroy.

His father died when the boy was ten. That tragedy was followed by another: shortly after the 1929 Crash, the president of the town's only bank fled with most of the money in its vaults, including the Gillespie family savings. His mother had to take in washing to keep food on the table. Her son was sent into the cotton fields—and resolved right away that cotton picking was not for him. He was a combative hyperactive youth—"fidgety and frisky," one Cheraw woman remembered. He dodged buckshot to steal watermelons from a local farmer, regularly battled—and beat—boys bigger than himself, and refused to treat white people any differently than anyone else. When a white woman insisted he call her "ma'am," he stopped mowing her lawn, even though by doing so he cut the family's income by fifteen cents a week.

"I always knew I was something special," he said, but precisely what special path he would take was unclear until he entered the third grade at the Robert Smalls school and came under the influence of Alice V. Wilson, one of those extraordinary teachers to whom an underfinanced, segregated school system seems simply to have been a spur to greater effort. She could not read music—everything her pupils performed was in B-flat because that was the only key she knew on the piano—but she organized her boys and girls into a band that played at the beginning of class each morning using a miscellaneous collection of battered old instruments given to the school by the state. "[John] just went crazy!" Miss Wilson remembered. "They didn't want him to have a horn at first, you know, he was so little. But he was so persistent, 'I can play it! I can play it!'" Gillespie tried trombone first, even though his arm was too short to reach all its positions, then got hold of a trumpet. After that, there was no stopping him. "He didn't care about anything but music. He would come to school every morning with his horn under his arm, instead of books," and he played scales so relentlessly that she once had to take the horn from his mouth so that his fellow students could hear her teach. Gillespie would later credit Miss Wilson with turning "an ornery cuss . . . not worth a dime" into someone eager to make something of himself.

His resolve was strengthened in the summer of 1933 when he briefly went to work digging ditches for the Works Progress Administration (WPA). "It struck me at that time how illiterate our people were," he wrote. "It really hurt me to see my brothers on the WPA gang walk up to the table to get their pay and have to make an X because they couldn't write their names. That made a deep impression on me. Before then, I'd never really seriously considered becoming a professional musician." After that, he seems never to have considered anything else. At fifteen, he won a musical scholarship to the Laurinburg Institute, a North Carolina trade school for Negroes. There, he sat in with any touring band that came to town, never missed a broadcast by Duke Ellington or Cab Calloway, and spent most of his time at the keyboard rather than playing the trumpet. The piano "has all the various combinations of notes and chords . . . right there in front of you like no other single instrument," he said, and it was at Laurinburg that he developed his lifelong fascination with theory and composition.

At sixteen, he was already good enough at trumpet for King Oliver to offer him a job traveling with one of his last threadbare bands. Gillespie turned him down because, he said, he'd never heard of the old man.

He himself was then still trying to play like Louis Armstrong, according to a fellow student, but by the time he moved to Philadelphia with his family in 1935, he had found a new hero, Roy Eldridge, whom he called "the Messiah of our generation." His first grown-up jobs were with Philadelphia bands, playing Eldridge-style solos—but even faster, a fellow musician said, "like a rabbit running over a hill. Any key, it didn't

Gillespie—now nicknamed "Dizzy"—as a member of the Cab Calloway orchestra, photographed by his bandmate, Milt Hinton. "Even back then," Hinton recalled, "he was playing way ahead of the times."

make a difference." He was excitable—standing up and dancing when others soloed, sometimes pushing the pianist aside in the midst of one of his own solos to play chords with one hand while continuing to finger the valves on his trumpet with the other—and he was already experimenting with the music: "Playing chord changes, inverting them and substituting different notes," he said, "trying to see how different sounds led naturally, sometimes surprisingly into others." His fellow musicians "didn't know if I was coming by land or sea." They called him the "Cheraw Flash" at first, and then "Dizzy," which stuck.

He moved to New York, toured the British Isles, and performed in Paris with Teddy Hill's band, and in 1939 he began two years with Cab Calloway's orchestra. Its arrangements were mostly conventional, meant to provide the proper background for its leader's manic singing and dancing—but Calloway was a stickler for polished performance, and the men who played for him over the years were some of the best in the business: Chu Berry, Danny Barker, Milt Hinton, trumpeters Jonah Jones and Mario Bauza, and the drummer Cozy Cole.

Gillespie quickly made his presence felt. "From time to time," said the pianist Bennie Payne, "Dizzy would just take off in double time. Man, it was wild. . . . Cab was very meticulous about music and he'd get mad as hell. 'What the hell you tryin' to do with my band?' Cab would holler at Dizzy. Dizzy would just smile and all Cab would say was 'Just play it the way it's written.'" Calloway dismissed Gillespie's more adventurous playing as "Chinese music," eventually turning more and more of his solos over to his able but more predictable section mate Jonah Jones. Gillespie grew bored by the arrangements he was made to play, and was made restless by the kind of discipline Calloway insisted upon. "He used to drive Cab crazy," Milt Hinton remembered. "We'd get on the stage and Cab would be singing a ballad—'I love you my dear . . .'—and Dizzy would act like he'd looked out in the audience and seen somebody that he knew and waved at them. And the people in the audience would start laughing and when Cab looks around to see what's happening, he sees that our eyes are all closed, like we're in church."

Gillespie lived for the jam sessions at Minton's and Monroe's, where he was free to experiment with fast tempos, fresh harmonies, unfamiliar keys. "We used to play unusual substitute chords and extensions of the chords to throw off some of the other musicians who came up to sit in," he said. "I can remember when nobody except us played the chord progressions A-minor seventh to D seventh to D-flat." Milt Hinton sometimes collaborated with Gillespie in the search for fresh chords that baffled musicians at Minton's.

> We had such fun together. He would show me so many things. When we were on intermission we'd go up on the roof of the Cotton Club. I'd squeeze my bass up the fire escape and he would show me these different new modern changes that he was talking about, and we'd play them and he'd say, "Now, tonight when we get off we're going to go down to Minton's and those guys down there are waiting to play with us, and we got these new changes and we gonna lose 'em. Get 'em lost." So, when we got out at four o'clock in the morning, we stopped at a bakery and get a quart of milk and six donuts and eat them on the way, get to Minton's, and all these young kids is out there waiting for us to come in. They say, "What you guys gonna play?" We'd say, "I Got Rhythm." And they'd start out and we put these crazy changes on them and they couldn't play 'em. And they would see that they would have to leave and let us have our own fun.

Gillespie's reputation for having his own fun wherever he was eventually lost him his job. On Sunday, September 21, 1941, the band was performing at the State Theater in Hartford when Calloway saw a spitball arc into the spotlight. It had clearly been thrown by someone in the band. Jonah Jones was the real culprit, but when the show was over, Calloway stormed backstage, loudly accused Gillespie of disrupting one too many performances, and raised his hand as if to slap the troublemaker. Gillespie pulled the carpet knife he always carried. A scuffle followed, and when Calloway got back to his dressing room there was blood on his vanilla-colored suit. "This kid cut me!" Calloway said. He told Gillespie to "get your horn and get out."

Gillespie would never lose his ebullience, his humor, or his high energy, but when the time came for him to lead his own groups he would be a disciplined professional. Marriage in 1940 to a practical-minded dancer named Lorraine Willis had helped to steady him, but looking back, he said it had been his time with Calloway that had taught him that vital lesson. "Discipline! That's the word—with no deviation from it. . . . Working in [Calloway's] band taught me to do what I was supposed to do."

He spent the next fifteen months taking jobs wherever he could find them. He worked with Charlie Barnet and Ella Fitzgerald, sold arrangements to Jimmy Dorsey and Woody Herman, and played in Benny Carter's sextet at Kelly's Stable and at the Famous Door on Fifty-second Street. "I was asked to get rid of him," Carter said, "because he was playing augmented ninths. They thought he was hitting bad notes. . . . [But] I saw that he was groping for something. And he knew his music. . . . I stood up for him." It was an invaluable experience for Gillespie. He was given more solo room than he had ever had before, and night after night he got to play next to Carter, who was a master of musical logic. But when Carter went on tour with Billie Holiday, Gillespie was left on his own again, still looking for congenial company in which to make the audacious music he felt certain he was meant to play.

Poster for *Jump for Joy*

SOLDIERS OF MUSIC

The same summer that Gillespie lost his job with Cab Calloway, Duke Ellington and his orchestra had come to rest momentarily in Hollywood. They were working on something altogether new, an all-black musical—"a sun-tanned revue-sical" called *Jump for Joy*. There was to be no shuffling, no dialect, no blackface comedy. It was meant to honor the Negro contribution to the country—an attempt, Ellington said, to give "an American audience entertainment without compromising the dignity of the Negro people. . . . This is the problem every Negro artist faces. . . . The American audience has been taught to expect a Negro on the stage to clown and 'Uncle Tom,' that is to enact the role of a servile, yet lovable inferior."

The show opened to rave reviews: "In *Jump for Joy*," said the Los Angeles *Tribune*, "Uncle Tom is dead. God rest his bones." Those in the cast—they included Dorothy Dandridge and Herb Jeffries, Ivie Anderson and the great Kansas City blues shouter, Joe Turner—never forgot its liberating power. "Everything," one dancer recalled, "every setting, every note of music, every lyric, *meant* something." And, Ellington recalled, when he insisted to the comics that they go onstage without blacking-up, they "came offstage smiling, and with tears running down their cheeks." "It was well done," he said, "because we included everything we wanted to say without saying it. Which is the way I think these social significance things should be handled. . . . Just to come out onstage and take a soap box and stand in the spotlight and say ugly things is not entertainment." But *Jump for Joy* ran only eleven weeks and never made it to New York. Broadway wasn't ready for what Ellington called a "special significance show." Besides, the country's attention was now focused elsewhere.

On December 7, 1941, America found itself at war. Jazz went to war, too, and overseas, swing—still America's most popular music—would serve to remind the men and women of the armed forces of home. "Bandsmen today are not just jazz musicians," said *Down Beat,* "they are soldiers of music."

On the home front, the music industry found itself struggling once again. Blackouts and late-night curfews darkened some nightclubs and dance halls. A 20 percent entertainment tax closed ballrooms all across the country. The rationing of rubber and gasoline eventually drove most band buses off the roads, and servicemen now filled the Pullman trains, making it difficult for musicians to get around by rail. A shortage of shellac, which was used in the manufacture of records, curtailed the recording of music, and companies stopped making jukeboxes and musical instruments altogether for a time because they were deemed unnecessary to the war effort.

The draft stole away good musicians—Jack Teagarden lost seventeen men to the army in just four months—and bandleaders were forced to pay their replacements more for less talent. "I'm paying some kid trumpet player $500 a week," Tommy Dorsey complained, "and he can't even blow his nose." With so many male musicians in uniform, more than a hundred "all-girl" bands were on the move across the country, playing for dances, helping to sell war bonds.

By October 1942, *Down Beat* was running a regular column headed "Killed in Action." At one point during the fighting, there were thirty-nine bandleaders in the army, seventeen in the navy, three in the merchant marine, and two more in the Coast Guard. Glenn Miller, whose infectious hits like "In the Mood" epitomized the war years, disbanded his own hugely successful orchestra, enlisted, and formed an all-star air force unit that some believe was the best band he ever led—and died in 1944, when his airplane disappeared over the English Channel.

Benny Goodman was kept out of the service by a chronic back injury, but he and many other musicians volunteered for the USO, and made special "V Discs" for the armed forces. Artie Shaw led a navy band that toured the South Pacific—playing in jungles so hot and humid that the pads on the saxophones rotted and horns had to be held together with rubber bands. He and his men were bombed or strafed seventeen times by Japanese planes. "There were times when it was really very moving," he remembered.

You'd play three notes and the whole audience was instantly roaring with you. They knew the record and you got the feeling that you'd created a piece of durable Americana that was speaking to these people. I remember an engagement on the USS *Saratoga,* this huge carrier. And we were put on the flight deck and we came down into this cavernous place where there were three thousand men in dress uniforms. And, you know the reverse of the Paramount [Theater], where you were on a stage and moved up. Here we came down and we were playing my theme song and a roar went up. I tell you, it really threw me. I couldn't believe what I was seeing or hearing, I felt something extraordinary. I was by that time inured to success and applause and all that. You'd take that for granted after a while. You could put your finger out and say, "Now they're gonna clap." But this was a whole different thing. These men were starved for something and to remind them of home and whatever—"Mom and apple pie." And the music had that effect I suppose. All I know is that when we played the "Star-Spangled Banner" afterwards, it was moving to me. And that's not a very good piece of music, as you know.

African-Americans rallied to the flag just as they had twenty-four years earlier. A million black Americans served in the armed forces before the fighting ended—nearly half a million of them overseas. But there was a new and growing impatience in black America, a determination that its sacrifices not be repaid with renewed mistreatment as they had been after World War I. "Though I have found no Negroes who want to see the United Nations lose this war," said the president of the Brotherhood of Sleeping Car Porters, A. Philip Randolph, "I have found many who, before the war ends, want to see the stuffing knocked out of white supremacy. . . . American Negroes . . . are confronted not with a choice but with the challenge both to win democracy for ourselves at home and to help win the war for democracy the world over." Even before the fighting began, Randolph had forced Franklin Roosevelt to issue an executive order opening up jobs in defense industries by threatening a hundred-thousand-man march on Washington if he failed to act.

No one willing to look could miss the hypocrisy of being asked to fight bigotry abroad while experiencing it at home. "The nation cannot expect colored people to feel that the United States is worth defending," Eleanor Roosevelt wrote early in the war, "if the Negro continues to be treated as he

Music and mail call in the South Pacific, 1944. Servicemen, one of them wrote, wanted music that "reminds them of home, that brings back something of when we were happy and free."

MEN HAVE DIED FOR THIS MUSIC

Nothing the Nazis could do in occupied Europe could crush the music that propaganda minister Joseph Goebbels called "the art of the subhuman." Jazz stayed stubbornly alive, a bright symbol of resistance. When the Germans barred even the use of the *word* "jazz," the Hot Jazz Club of Belgium renamed itself the "*Rhythmic* Club"— and kept on swinging. And when the Germans banned the performance of all American music in Paris, local musicians simply changed the titles of the tunes they loved: "In the Mood" became "Ambiance"; "Holy Smoke" became "Joyeuse fumée"; and Count Basie's "Jumpin' at the Woodside," turned into "Dansant dans la Clairière." "Swing!" the French jazz enthusiast Charles Delaunay recalled. "This magic word became the watchword for young people everywhere. Swing was on everyone's lips, you swore by it. Everything that was at all original or redolent of American life was baptized 'swing.' "

In 1942, Goebbels changed tactics. Realizing that he could not do away with jazz, he resolved to turn it to the advantage of the Reich, and ordered his ministry to organize its own radio swing band, then aim its broadcasts of familiar American tunes like "Makin' Whoopee" at the Allies with new and poisonous anti-Semitic lyrics added.

> Another war, another profit, another Jewish
>   business trick,
> Another season, another reason for makin'
>   whoopee!
> We throw our German names away,
> We are the kikes of USA.
> You are the goys, folks,
> We are the boys, folks—
> We're makin' whoopee!

In Germany itself, young fans called "swing kids" continued to defy the Gestapo all through the war, to meet in secret, play records, tune in to Allied radio, and dance. The German-born jazz pianist Jutta Hipp later struggled to explain to an American interviewer how important the music had been to her and to her friends during the massive Allied bombing of Germany. "You won't be able to understand this because you were born [in America] but to us jazz is some kind of religion. We really had to fight for it, and I remember nights when we didn't go down to the bomb shelter because we listened to [jazz] records. We just had the feeling that you were not our enemies, and even though the bombs crashed around us . . . we felt safe."

To divert attention from their crimes, the Nazis eventually made a propaganda film intended to demonstrate to the world their supposed "kindness" to the Jews. The infamous Terezin Concentration Camp outside Prague was dressed up as a model "village," and its occupants given new clothes. They were then filmed being "entertained" by inmate musicians, including a jazz band called the Ghetto Swingers. Once the filming was over, the musicians' reward was to be sent to the death camp at Auschwitz, along with hundreds of thousands of other innocent people.

Long after the war, an interviewer asked Dizzy Gillespie if jazz should be considered "serious" music. "Men have died for this music," he said. "You can't get more serious than that."

In a rare frame from a sequence shot for a Nazi propaganda film and now lost, an inmate band called the Ghetto Swingers ostensibly entertains at Terezin concentration camp in 1944. The band's leader, right, is clarinetist Fricek Weiss, who modeled his style on that of Benny Goodman. He and his parents were subsequently gassed at Auschwitz.

THE GYPSY

Django Reinhardt

The hero of French jazz lovers under the Nazis, the personification of the stubborn individualism that had always been at the heart of the music, was an illiterate and contrary gypsy, to whom politics and patriotism were largely irrelevant. The guitarist Django Reinhardt was born in a horse-drawn wooden caravan in Belgium in 1910, the illegitimate son of a circus clown. His mother, so dark-complected that her nickname was Négros, moved Django and his younger brother back and forth across Western Europe during World War I, trying to keep out of the line of fire of both sides. In 1918, her caravan finally came to rest just outside Paris, where her son began eking out a living playing *muzette,* the music of the French working class. In 1928, he burned his left hand so badly that he lost two digits and the use of the thumb. It took him eighteen months to work out a new and distinctly unorthodox way of fingering. Meanwhile, a friend played him a record of Louis Armstrong's "Dallas Blues." It was the first jazz he had ever heard. He wept at the beauty of it and determined to learn to perform this astonishing music for himself.

By 1934, he and the French violinist Stéphane Grappelli were leading a quintet sponsored by a band of well-to-do jazz enthusiasts who called themselves the Hot Club of France. Their hard-swinging music, influenced by Armstrong and by records they had heard featuring the violin-guitar duo of Joe Venuti and Eddie Lang, caught on quickly all over Europe. Reinhardt's cascades of single

notes poured forth with such power and imagination that the great classical guitarist Andrés Segovia is said once to have demanded to know where he could get a copy of the music the gypsy was playing.

"You can't," Reinhardt laughed. "I just made it up."

Reinhardt and Grappelli were in Britain when the war began. Grappelli decided to stay there. Reinhardt returned to Paris and, after the German occupation began, found himself the toast of the city, the best jazz musician in a town starved for jazz. No matter how celebrated he became—and he was a favorite of both French citizens and German officers on leave—he remained a gypsy at heart, wandering off to play billiards while audiences waited in their seats, demanding vast sums before he'd perform, then playing just down the street for free, insisting that restaurateurs serve him gypsy fare like roasted hedgehog, sometimes disappearing altogether for weeks at a time. He managed to avoid ever being made to perform beneath a Nazi flag, and when, in the summer of 1943, he learned that the Germans were planning to send him on a tour of army bases he determined to escape. He made his way to the border of neutral Switzerland and tried to cross the Alps to safety. A German patrol stopped him before he got very far. He was sure he would be shot or sent to one of the concentration camps to which gypsies less celebrated than he were now routinely condemned. But the officer in command turned out to be a fan, asked for his autograph, and sent him back to Paris.

After France was liberated and the war ended, he toured the United States briefly with Duke Ellington. Reinhardt's playing was wonderful, Ellington remembered, but he had never been certain his guest star would be on hand when the curtain rose. "You had to stay with him every minute because if a chick went by, he'd be behind her, if [he] was coming down the elevator and he saw a sharp chick, oh, man! He'd get in the cab with her. Django was too much!"

Backstage between sets in New York, Reinhardt watches fellow members of the Duke Ellington band Al Sears, trumpeter Shelton Hemphill, and Lawrence Brown play cards. Bassist Junior Raglin, Harry Carney, and Johnny Hodges also look on from the sidelines.

GLENN MILLER

ARMY AIR FORCE BAND

RCA VICTOR
LPM-6700

Music at war. The last known photograph of Glenn Miller (top, left), taken in London just before his plane disappeared over the English Channel, and the cover of the best-selling album made by his Army Air Force Band that was released afterwards. Members of the Count Basie Band (above) surrounded by officers and men at the Tuskegee Army Air Field at Tuskegee, Alabama, in 1943. The musicians visible are, left to right, tenor saxophonist Don Byas, Sweets Edison, Basie, Jimmy Rushing, trumpeter Al Killian (partially obscured), and alto saxophonist Jimmy Powell. The USO staged the servicemen's dance (below) in New York's Central Park. (Opposite) Artie Shaw and his orchestra perform aboard a warship in the South Pacific, 1943.

Members of a U.S. Navy band. President Franklin D. Roosevelt shrank from integrating the armed forces but, he said privately, "there's no reason . . . why we shouldn't have a colored band on some of [our] ships, because they're *darned good at it.*"

is now." But even A. Philip Randolph was unable to persuade President Roosevelt to integrate the armed forces. Black Americans served throughout the war on a strictly segregated basis. Blood supplies for saving the lives of the wounded were carefully separated by race. On one base, a schedule listed separate services for "Catholics, Jews, Protestants, and Negroes." Some commanders forbade black troops to read black newspapers. There were violent confrontations between black and white troops at

military installations. Off-base, American soldiers whose skin did not happen to be white were harassed, beaten, even refused service at restaurants where German prisoners of war were allowed to eat. The Pittsburgh *Courier* mounted a "Double-V" campaign, calling for simultaneous victories over the nation's enemies abroad and discrimination at home. Heavyweight champion Joe Louis got in trouble with his black fans when, after defeating Buddy Baer, he donated his purse to the navy,

when that branch of the armed forces still restricted most African-American sailors to menial tasks.

No one felt more alienated from the war effort than young black musicians. They knew that once drafted they were likely to be sent to the Jim Crow South for basic training, where the relative freedom they had experienced in the North would vanish, and when that ordeal was over, they were less likely than their white counterparts to be offered jobs in military bands.

THESE THINGS CAN'T HAPPEN

Swing had been America's favorite music all through the thirties and no location had been too remote for the radio to reach. The future pianist Dave Brubeck, born in 1920, was a California rancher's son then. His mother wanted him to play classical piano but his rancher father hoped that he would follow in his footsteps, and as a boy Brubeck spent hours on horseback, mending fences and driving cattle. But even as he rode, he had reveries of playing in a swing band. "My dream was that the Benny Goodman Band Bus would want to get through the cattle and I wouldn't let him through unless they let me get on the bus and play with them. In my mind, someday I'd be heard with some band going through there."

Benny Goodman never turned up, but Brubeck's father eventually relented, and he was studying music in college when America entered the war. Graduated in 1942, he joined the army as a rifleman, married a fellow student on a three-day pass, and shipped out to Europe in the summer of 1944, fully expecting to go right into combat with General George Patton's Third Army. Instead, he was picked to lead a band entertaining the men in the field. The United States Army may have been segregated, but Dave Brubeck's Wolf Pack Band was not. The master of ceremonies—named Gil White—was African-American;

so was the trombonist, Jonathan Richard Flowers. The men ate, slept, and lived together, and shared adventures they would never forget. They once played so close to the front lines that German planes swooped down to strafe them—and the whole audience rushed for their weapons to shoot back. During the Battle of the Bulge, Brubeck and his men got lost and found themselves deep in German territory. It was hours before they found their way back to the American lines.

The Wolf Pack Band stayed with Patton's Third Army until the war in Europe finally ended on May 8, 1945. Through it all, the band had remained integrated. But when the men eventually got home the following year, nothing in America seemed to have changed. "When we landed in Texas we all went to the dining room to eat, and they wouldn't serve the black guys," Brubeck remembered. "They had to go around and stand at the kitchen door, and this one guy said he wouldn't eat any of their food and he started to cry and he said, 'What I've been through and the first day I'm back in the United States, I can't even eat with you guys.' He said, 'I wonder why I went through all of this?' "

As the leader of his own quartet, Brubeck would eventually become one of the best-known musicians in jazz. He refused ever to play anywhere audiences were segregated and once walked off a network television show when he saw that the director planned to shoot his group so that his bassist Gene Wright, who happened to be black, would never appear onscreen. To him, jazz would always represent "the music of freedom." His wartime experiences had something to do with that. So did an experience from his boyhood: "The first black man that I saw," he remembered, "my dad took me to see a friend of his and asked him to 'Open your shirt for Dave.' " More than half a century later, Brubeck's eyes filled with tears at the memory. "There was a *brand* on his chest. And my dad said, 'These things can't happen.' *That's* why I fought for what I fought for."

Above) Young Dave Brubeck rides the range and (below) performs for the troops with his Wolf Pack band.

At lunchtime on a summer's day in New York City's Times Square in 1944, a navy marching band waits its turn while a swing orchestra helps dedicate a giant cash register meant to record the progress of the Fifth War Loan Campaign.

Many musicians served, anyway. But some simply kept moving, hoping their draft notices would never catch up with them, and a few feigned homosexuality or pretended to be psychotic or addicted to drugs to avoid conscription. The trumpet player Howard McGhee said he won an exemption by assuring an army psychiatrist that if inducted he would *ask* to be sent South so that he could organize black soldiers to shoot whites: "Whether he's a Frenchman, a German or whatever . . . how would I know the difference?" Those attitudes only hardened as musicians became special targets of white policemen and white servicemen who objected to their good clothes, their hipster language, their new assertiveness. "The enemy, by that period, was not the Germans," Dizzy Gillespie said, "it was above all white Americans who kicked us in the butt every day, physically and morally. . . . If America wouldn't honor its Constitution and respect us as men we couldn't give a shit about the American way. And they made it damn near un-American to appreciate our music."

REACH

On January 9, 1942, a little over a month after the Japanese attack on Pearl Harbor, Lucky Millinder's orchestra was well established on the Savoy Ballroom bandstand once held by Chick Webb. His band, propelled by the piano of Bill Doggett, the bass of George Duvivier, and the drums of Panama Francis, was a special favorite with Harlem dancers, and when a new outfit from Kansas City led by Jay McShann arrived to play opposite them in a battle of the bands that evening, Millinder's men were not worried. The sight of the out-of-towners—all young, all dressed in cheap Sears and Roebuck suits, all badly rumpled after the cross-country trip by car— appalled the Ballroom's manager. It was "the raggediest looking band" he'd ever seen, he told McShann. "This is New York

City, boy, this isn't Kansas!" And, just before the contest began, one of Millinder's elegantly outfitted musicians sent McShann a note meant to rattle him further: "We're going to send you hicks back to the sticks."

For three half-hour sets, the two bands played more sedately than usual, each listening carefully to the other, assessing strengths and weaknesses. "We just kinda laid back," one of McShann's men said. Then, Millinder launched into a series of elaborate arrangements meant to show up the out-of-towners. "Heavy stuff," McShann said, but "Lucky wasn't swinging." It was the opening McShann had been waiting for. "As soon as he hit his last note we fell in," he said. "When Jay turned his boys loose," one New York saxophonist remembered, "he had hellions working. Just roaring wild men." McShann's band, like Count Basie's, stomped the blues and specialized in loosely organized head arrangements that could be expanded almost infinitely as long as dancers were responding. "This was a thirty-minute number," McShann said, "and the people screamed and hollered for *another* thirty minutes." Millinder and his men stood by helpless and fuming as the Savoy dancers called for encore after encore by the band their leader had dismissed as "those western dogs."

The McShann band was tight, the blues it played irresistible to dancers. But its skinny, twenty-three-year-old alto saxophonist, Charlie Parker, was something else again. He had not yet fully developed the style that would make him the most influential soloist since Louis Armstrong. But he already sounded very different from Benny Carter and Johnny Hodges, the alto saxophone masters musicians then most admired. His sound was harder than theirs, virtually without vibrato, and he had found a fresh way to phrase the inexhaustible musical ideas that already seemed to tumble from his horn without apparent effort. The pianist and composer John Lewis was in the army, about to go overseas, when he heard Parker over the camp radio on a

live pickup from the Savoy. "Nobody knew him. . . . It was literally astounding to everyone. . . . He played perfectly. There was no fumbling, no note you could do without. All complete ideas. He kept arriving at complete wonderful ideas."

Musicians hurried to the Savoy to hear him. When "Charlie got up and played," recalled Howard McGhee, then a youthful high-note specialist in Charlie Barnet's band, "we all stood there with our mouths open because we hadn't heard anybody play a horn like *that*." He "was playing stuff we'd never heard before," Kenny Clarke remembered. "[He] was running the same way we were, but he was way out ahead of us."

"He had a completely different approach in everything," said Jay McShann, who had been among the first to recognize his talent. "Everything was completely different, just like [when] you change the furniture in the house and you come in and you won't know your own house."

After the arrival of Charlie Parker, the house of jazz would never be the same. Kenny Clarke had worked out a new way to play the drums. Dizzy Gillespie, Thelonious Monk, and their youthful cohorts were already seeking novel ways of working with melody and harmony, and Parker would contribute greatly to that search. But his greatest innovation would be to what the late jazz historian Martin Williams called "melodic rhythm," not the basic time but "the rhythm that the players' accents make as they offer their melodies." Building largely on the quarter note, Louis Armstrong had shown the world how to swing. By basing his improvisations primarily on eighth notes and developing altogether fresh methods of inflecting, accenting, and pronouncing phrases, Charlie Parker showed it could be done another way. The density and harmonic sophistication of Coleman Hawkins, the loose-limbed melodic sense of Lester Young, and even something of the supremely self-confident phrasing of Louis Armstrong can all be heard in Parker's playing. No one understood his importance better than did Dizzy Gillespie, who had already heard Parker once in Kansas City while with the Calloway band. "He had just what we needed," he said. "He had the line and he had the rhythm. The way he got from one note to the other and the way he played the rhythm fit what we were trying to do perfectly. We heard him and knew the music had to go his way. . . . He was the other half of my heartbeat."

Parker's genius was incontestable. So was his maddening personal complexity. A musician who'd known Parker well suggested that he should have been nicknamed "Chameleon." Even in his photographs he seems to have been several people all at once: now slender and boyish, then bloated and middle-aged, then youthful and lively again; sometimes wide-eyed and apparently innocent, sometimes sly and knowing, as often with a deadened gaze that seems to

Charlie Parker in Kansas City, 1940

foretell the tragedy that eventually befell him. The scattered interviews he gave are contradictory, too. Sometimes he said his music grew directly out of swing; at others that it was "something entirely separate and apart from jazz." Parker "stretched the limits of human contradiction beyond belief," Ralph Ellison wrote. "He was lovable and hateful, considerate and callous; he stole from friends and benefactors and borrowed without conscience, often without repaying, and yet was generous to absurdity. He could be most kind to younger musicians or utterly crushing in his contempt for their ineptitude. He was passive and yet quick to pull a knife and pick a fight. He was given to extremes of sadness and masochism, capable of the most staggering excesses and the most exacting physical discipline and assertion of will."

Only Louis Armstrong and Duke Ellington can be said to have made greater contributions to the music, and no one will ever know what further heights Charlie Parker might have reached had he not allowed his own relentless hungers finally to consume him.

Charles Parker Jr. was born in 1920 in Kansas City, Kansas, and raised just across the Kaw River, in Kansas City, Missouri. His father was a tap dancer turned Pullman chef, who drank too much and deserted his wife and son before the boy was ten. His mother spoiled her only child while also demanding much of him, insisting that he wear a suit and tie to school, and that he hold her hand whenever they went out together. Abandoned by his father, smothered by his mother, "Charlie was always old," Rebecca Ruffin, the high school sweetheart who became his first wife, remembered. She did not deny his mother's single-minded devotion to her son, Ruffin told the writer Stanley Crouch, but believed she had been more dutiful than affectionate, nonetheless. "He wasn't loved, he was just given. . . . It seemed to me like he needed. He just had this need. It really

touched me to my soul." "He couldn't fit into society," an old friend remembered, because "his mother babied him so much that he . . . was expecting that from everybody else in the world."

The boy had few friends, kept his own counsel, played alto and baritone horn in the school band, but was so often truant that he would eventually be forced to repeat his freshman year in high school. At eleven, after hearing Rudy Vallee on the radio, he talked his mother into getting him a horn like Vallee's, only to lose interest and loan it to a friend for two years before taking up music again.

Then, everything seemed to happen too fast. Barely an adolescent, he began to hang around the doorways of the bars and nightclubs that flourished just a few blocks from his home, steeping himself in the blues. By fifteen, he had begun his lifelong obsession with getting high. He used nutmeg at first; then Benzedrine dissolved in wine or cups of black coffee that allowed him to play night after night without sleep; then marijuana; finally heroin. At sixteen, he married Rebecca Ruffin, and soon prepared for the birth of his first child, a son. He also began playing with a group of slightly older musicians in a local dance band called "the Deans of Swing." Its trombonist, Robert Simpson, became his closest friend and Parker was devastated when Simpson died suddenly at twenty-one. Years later, he would explain to a fellow musician that he never allowed himself to get too close to anyone because "once in Kansas City I had a friend who I liked very much, and a sorrowful thing happened. . . . He died."

At about the same time, and before he was really ready, he plunged headlong into the cutting contests that were the proving ground for any Kansas City musician on the way up. He "used to come to our jam sessions," Fiddler Williams remembered. "And he kept his saxophone and instruction book in a sack. And, he could play anything in the instruction book, play it backwards. But he didn't have himself together, couldn't run

The Jay McShann band broadcasting live from the Wichita, Kansas, studios of station KFBI in 1940. Charlie Parker is seated fourth from the left, Jay McShann is at the piano.

out of a major into a minor, or a diminished into an augmented chord." One night at the Reno Club, sitting in with members of the Basie band, the sixteen-year-old Parker found himself in over his head, unable to make the right changes at the breakneck speed at which the older men were playing. Jo Jones hurled a cymbal at his feet to get him off the bandstand. Angry and humiliated—and determined that nothing like that would ever happen to him again— he got a job with a dance band in the Ozarks and spent every spare moment practicing and listening again and again to records made by his heroes, Chu Berry and, later,

Lester Young. Like Sidney Bechet and Bix Beiderbecke before him, Parker would essentially teach himself to play; unlike them, he tried to learn all there was to know about the music that had become his life. When he mastered a new tune he would teach himself to play it in all twelve keys so that no one would ever again be able to dismiss his playing, and he sought out older musicians who could answer any questions he was unable to answer himself. "I lit my fire," he remembered, "I greased my skillet, and I cooked."

On Thanksgiving Day 1936, the car in which Parker and two other young musi-

cians were riding to an engagement skidded on a patch of ice and overturned. One passenger was killed. Parker's ribs were broken and his spine fractured. He spent two months recuperating in bed, easing his pain with regular doses of morphine. His drug use evidently accelerated after he got back on his feet. He stayed away from home for weeks at a time, sold his wife's belongings to buy drugs, pressured her to give him a divorce. "If I were free," he told her, "I think I could be a great musician." He would be addicted to heroin for the rest of his life.

In 1937, he went to work for one of his idols, altoist Buster Smith, a veteran of Walter Page's Original Blue Devils, who was a master of what was called "doubling up," playing solos at twice the written tempo. "He always wanted me to take the first solo," Smith said. "I guess he thought he'd learn something that way. . . . But after a while, anything I could make on the horn he could make too—and make something better of it."

No matter how intricate and fast-paced Parker's music became, the Kansas City stomping brand of blues would remain at its heart. "What you hear when you listen to Charlie Parker," wrote Albert Murray, "is not a theorist dead-set on turning dance music into concert music. What you hear is a brilliant protégé of Buster Smith and an admirer of Lester Young, adding a new dimension of elegance to the Kansas City drive, which is to say to the velocity of celebration. Kansas City apprentice-become-master that he was, Charlie Parker was out to swing more, not less. Sometimes he tangled up your feet but that was when he sometimes made your insides dance as never before. At his best he could make your insides cut all the steps that your feet could not cut anyway."

Parker's appearance with Jay McShann at the Savoy had not been his first visit to New York. After Buster Smith went east to help Count Basie whip his band into shape at the Famous Door in the summer of 1938, Parker followed him to Harlem. His old mentor put him up until his wife got tired of having him around. He wandered the Harlem streets, stared up at the marquee of the Savoy Ballroom, and dreamed of playing there some day. He took a nine-dollar-a-week job washing dishes at a little club just so he could hear another of his idols, Art Tatum, play piano every night. He sometimes ventured up to Monroe's Uptown House, but his perennially disheveled looks and the frantic pace at which he already liked to play put off a good many musicians. Some had then thought him a dope dealer masquerading as a musician. But one night that December, he later told an interviewer,

jamming with an unremarkable guitarist named Biddy Fleet at Dan Wall's Chili House, on Seventh Avenue between 139th and 140th Streets, he had made a personal musical discovery. Intrigued by the sophisticated chord changes of Ray Noble's "Cherokee," a recent hit for the Charlie Barnet orchestra, he kept thinking there "must be something else. I could hear it sometimes but I couldn't play it." Then, he found he could develop a fresh melody line using the higher intervals of a chord while Fleet backed them with related changes. A few days later, a telegram from his mother telling him that his father had been stabbed to death brought him home to Kansas City before he could share his secret with anyone else, and it was more than two years before the Jay McShann band brought him back to Harlem again.

It was while playing with McShann that he got his distinctive nickname, "Bird." When the car in which he and McShann were riding hit a stray chicken, a *yardbird*, Parker insisted they pull over so that he could have it fried up by his landlady. The story got around and the name stayed with him. "He was an *interested* cat in those days," McShann said, eager to help work out riffs for the saxophone section, grateful for every chance to solo, sometimes playing a single tune backstage for hours at a time with instructions to anyone who played with him to alert him whenever he inadvertently repeated himself. "We used to have an expression when a cat's blowing out there, the cats'd holler, 'Reach! Reach!' " McShann continued. "What we meant by that, we know that a cat knows his potential, what he can do. If you keep hitting on *Bird* like that, Bird would just do the impossible. He was that type of person. He would do the impossible. You'd make him do the impossible . . . because he always had enough stored back here, that he never did run out."

He was the baby of the band and at first the older men all loved him for his musicianship and his energy. Bassist Gene

Ramey remembered that the McShann organization had been "the only band I've ever known that seemed to spend all its spare time jamming or rehearsing. We used to jam on trains and buses; and as soon as we got into town, we'd try to find somebody's house where we could hold a session. All this was inspired by Bird. . . . Naturally we petted and babied him, and he traded on this love and esteem we had for him until he developed into the greatest con man in the world." He borrowed money and failed to pay it back, nodded off on the bandstand, disappeared for days at a time.

Jay McShann was a gentle taskmaster. Like Duke Ellington, he was willing to put up with pretty much anything from his musicians, provided they turned up on time to play. But Parker constantly tested his patience. In an effort to keep dealers from getting to his alto saxophone star, McShann left standing orders that no strangers be allowed through the stage door between sets. They got to him anyway, and after Parker collapsed from an overdose during a Detroit appearance, McShann finally, reluctantly, let him go. The bandleader Andy Kirk, who happened to be in Detroit that evening, gave Parker a lift to New York, where he began looking for steady work. (The McShann band itself dissolved shortly afterward when its leader was drafted right off the bandstand.)

Then, in late 1942 or early 1943, as American G.I.'s fought German troops for the first time in North Africa, Charlie Parker joined Dizzy Gillespie in a new big band led by Earl Hines. Since making "West End Blues," and other historic sides with Louis Armstrong in the late 1920s, Hines had spent most of his time in Chicago, presiding over an orchestra at the Grand Terrace Ballroom, owned and operated first by Al Capone and then by his brother, Ralph. But in 1940, he had bought himself out of that long-running contract and started touring.

By 1943, his band was filled with young modernists. Besides Gillespie and Parker

The Earl Hines band at the Apollo, 1943. Billy Eckstine is at the microphone with Hines just behind him. Dizzy Gillespie plays at the far left while, at the far right, Charlie Parker listens and grins. Sarah Vaughan is at the piano.

(who agreed to play tenor because Hines already had two altoists), it included trumpet player Benny Harris, trombonist Benny Green, and a teenaged Sarah Vaughan, hired both to sing and to share piano-playing duties with Hines; she was known as "Sailor" then for the richness of her vocabulary and her fondness for good times. The band's big draw was a handsome baritone named Billy Eckstine, billed as the "Sepia Sinatra," who had just had a big hit with a soulful double entendre blues called "Jelly, Jelly."

Hines had Gillespie write arrangements of several of his own tunes for the band, including "Night in Tunisia" and "Salt Peanuts," even though he didn't personally much like the new sounds his young men were making. "It was getting away from the melody a lot," he said. But he had been an innovator himself, he remembered, knew "these boys were ambitious and [therefore] always left a field for any improvement if they wanted to do it." They did want to do it. They also made it clear that they were not content to endure with-

out complaint treatment that, after more than two decades as a black entertainer playing for white audiences, their leader had come to see as routine. When a man Billy Eckstine remembered as an "old, rotten cracker" amused himself by repeatedly throwing chicken bones into the Jim Crow car in which the members of the band were riding north through Virginia, Eckstine waited till the train reached Washington, D.C., stopped the man on the platform, demanded to know why he'd done it, and, when he didn't answer, hit him so hard he hid beneath the train, begging for mercy. "Another thing that used to make me mad was pianos," Eckstine recalled. "Here we come to some dance with Earl, the number one piano player in the country, and half the keys on the goddamn piano won't work. So when we were getting ready to leave I'd get some of the guys to stand around the piano as though we were talking, and I'd reach in and pull all the strings and all the mallets out. 'The next time we come here,' I'd say, 'I'll bet that son-of-a-bitch will have a piano for him to play on.'" "[Eckstine] used to have me so nervous!" Hines said. "I never liked to say anything because I was always thinking that I'd come back to one of those joints and they'd think I'd done it. But those guys of mine . . . they didn't care."

They did care about their music. Gillespie and Parker were now playing together every day. "We were together as much as we could be under the conditions that the two of us were in," Gillespie recalled. "His crowd, the people he hung out with, were not the people I hung out with. And the guys who pushed dope would be around, but when he wasn't with them, he was with me." Parker had brought all his old habits to the band along with his artistry. He borrowed money constantly, missed dates, and learned to sleep onstage, wearing dark glasses, and with his cheeks puffed out, as if he were playing. According to Stanley Crouch, he also gave a pin to one of his section mates with orders to jab him in the thigh whenever it was his turn to solo. Parker was perpetually voracious and in a hurry—"always on a panic," as he himself said—and his ravenous appetite extended to every area of his life. The same hunger that drove him to devour drugs, alcohol, and food and to pursue women at a pace that astounded even his streetwise compatriots also allowed him to amass little-known facts on every subject from auto repair to nuclear physics and to memorize the most complicated charts after a single reading.

On Valentine's Day 1943, the Hines band appeared in Chicago at the Savoy Ballroom, the same cavernous South Side nightspot at which Artie Shaw had first heard Louis Armstrong fifteen years earlier. The engagement was memorable for two reasons. Three customers were shot on the dance floor during a single set that evening. And the next day, in Room 305 of the Savoy Hotel, the band's road manager, Bob Redcross, plugged in a portable disc recorder to capture for the first time the sound of Parker and Gillespie playing together. The bassist Oscar Pettiford had walked his instrument three miles across the city just to play with them that day, but he can barely be heard as the two musical companions tear their way through an eight-minute version of "Sweet Georgia Brown." Gillespie builds his solo with almost audible care, each chorus unfolding separately, resolving itself logically. Parker, still playing tenor rather than his customary alto, hurtles seamlessly through chorus after chorus, spilling out long ribbons of eighth notes as if they were in limitless supply. "I think I was a little more advanced, harmonically, than [Parker was]," Gillespie later wrote. "But rhythmically, he was quite advanced, with setting up the phrases and how you got from one note to another. . . . Charlie Parker heard rhythms and rhythmic patterns differently, and after we started playing together, I began to play, rhythmically, more like him. In that sense he influenced me, and all of us, because what makes the style is not what you play but how you play it." Their combined talents released so much musical energy—"fire," one musician called it—that the other men in the band confessed they sometimes felt left behind.

But except for Bob Redcross's homemade discs (which would not be heard for decades beyond his circle of friends), Parker's and Gillespie's earliest innovations went unheard on record. Earl Hines never got into a recording studio during the time they

were with him. On August 1, 1942, the American Federation of Musicians had ordered its members to stop making records—other than the "V discs" intended only for servicemen—until the record companies agreed to pay them when their music was played in jukeboxes or on the radio. Capitol and Decca settled within a year, but Victor and Columbia held out until November 1944. And so, except for a handful of dedicated collaborators and a few devoted fans, the new music Parker and Gillespie and their cohorts were developing remained largely a secret.

Frank Sinatra during his days with Tommy Dorsey

The recording ban had another indirect impact on American popular music, perhaps still more important to the history of jazz. Singers were not members of the musician's union and were therefore exempt from the recording ban. To stay in business, record companies produced a steady flow of a capella records—vocal quartets or solo singers backed by choruses. The tunes were most often peppy novelties meant to boost the anxious country's spirits or sentimental songs ideally suited to men and women kept apart by war. Young people loved them—and the singers who sang them.

On December 30, 1942, Benny Goodman returned to the Paramount Theater on Broadway, the same theater in which, five years earlier, he had set his fans to dancing in the aisles and first came to understand how much his band—and the swing music it represented—had meant to young people. As usual, the name of the movie being shown at the Paramount (a musical called *Star-Spangled Rhythm*) came first on the marquee, but the Goodman orchestra, featuring the singer Peggy Lee and the Goodman sextet, came next, followed by two comic acts. At the bottom of the bill, as an added attraction, was Tommy Dorsey's one-time singer, Frank Sinatra. He had already outpolled Bing Crosby to become the nation's number one vocalist in both *Billboard* and *Down Beat,* but Goodman, whose world did not extend much beyond his own orchestra and the music it played, evidently knew very little about him. As the slight, slender, visibly nervous Sinatra approached the microphone, a great collective shriek went up from hundreds of teenaged girls who had paid their way in to see him. The sound momentarily bewildered Goodman. "What the hell was *that?*" he asked into the microphone.

The squealing and shouting went on for nearly five minutes. It was the sound of the future. "Before," said the veteran tenor saxophonist Ted Nash, "people went to see the band, and then they'd listen to a solo now and then or a singer here and there. The singers were strictly secondary. But when Frank hit that screaming bunch of kids, the big bands just went right into the background." In Sinatra's wake, other band singers became single acts: Perry Como, Doris Day, Helen Forrest, Dick Haymes, Peggy Lee, Jo Stafford. Singers would now reign over American popular music. The day of the instrumentalist as matinee idol was coming to an end.

NO YARDSTICK TO MEASURE IT BY

On the evening of January 23, 1943, Duke Ellington appeared for the first time at Carnegie Hall. The event was billed as his "Twentieth Anniversary Concert"—it had been two decades since he had opened at the Hollywood Club—and the program included hits both old and new. But Ellington also introduced musical portraits of three great black entertainers—comic Bert Williams, dancer Bill Robinson, and singer Florence Mills, each of whom had brought a new kind of dignity to the stage. And he introduced his most ambitious musical undertaking to date, a forty-four-minute extended composition called *Black, Brown and Beige*, and subtitled *A Tone Parallel to the History of the Negro in America.*

It had been more than ten years in the making, and was a musical manifestation of the "Race pride" that had been taught to him as a boy in Washington and that had sustained him during the Cotton Club years. "I contend," he had told a black congregation in Los Angeles just before the war broke out,

that the Negro is the creative voice of America, *is* creative America, and it was a happy day in America when the first unhappy slave was landed on its shores. We stirred in our shackles, and our unrest awakened justice in the hearts of a courageous few, and we recreated in America the desire

The program for Duke Ellington's first appearance at Carnegie Hall, 1943

for true democracy, freedom for all, the brotherhood of man, principles on which the country had been founded.

We were freed, and as before, we fought America's wars, provided her labor, gave her music, kept alive her flickering conscience, prodded her on toward the yet unachieved goal, democracy—until we became more than a part of America! We—this kicking, touchy, sensitive, scrupulously demanding minority—are the personification of the ideal begun by the Pilgrims almost 350 years ago. . . .

We are more than a few isolated instances of courage, valor, achievement. We're the injection, the shot in the arm, that has kept America and its forgotten principles alive in the fat and corrupt years intervening between our divine conception and our near tragic present.

The composition was in three parts. "Black" was a portrait of slavery times. "Brown" alluded to the Negroes who fought first to liberate America in the Revolution, then to liberate themselves in the Civil War, and who then survived the complicated mix of hope and betrayal that followed Emancipation. The final movement—"Beige"—was meant to be a complex, composite portrait of black American life in the twentieth century. "I have shown [the Negro American] as he is supposed to be—and as he is," Ellington said. "The opening themes of the third movement reflect the supposed-to-be-Negro—the unbridled, noisy confusion of the Harlem cabaret which must have plenty of 'atmosphere' if it is to live up to the tourist's expectation. But there are, by numerical count, more churches than cabarets in Harlem, there are more well-educated and ambitious Negroes than wastrels. And my fantasy gradually changes its character to introduce the Negro as he is—part of America, with the hopes and dreams and love of freedom that have made America for all of us." The piece ends by restating the theme of *Black, Brown and Beige,* which, Ellington pointed out, was "still 'Red, White and Blue.' "

The audience at Carnegie Hall—which included Eleanor Roosevelt—loved Ellington's new work and the concert earned more than five thousand dollars for Russian War Relief. But some jazz critics dismissed it, again accusing Ellington of having abandoned the music that had made him famous. "It was unfortunate that Duke saw fit to tamper with the blues form in order to produce music of greater 'significance,' " John Hammond wrote. "I hope that some day he will be able to find himself once again and continue his contributions to the folk—or people's—music of our time." Most classical critics didn't like it either. "Mr. Ellington was saying musically the same things he had said earlier in the evening," wrote John Briggs of the New York *Post,* "only this time he took 45 minutes to do it." Paul Bowles, writing for the *Herald Tribune,* was still

Duke Ellington, photographed by Gordon Parks during his six-month reign at the Hurricane Ballroom in New York City in 1943. The band broadcast live from the Hurricane every Sunday evening and as a result Ellington's asking price for theater appearances had nearly doubled by the time he moved on, finally making him one of the best-paid bandleaders in the country.

more dismissive: " 'Black, Brown and Beige' lasted the better part of an hour and contained enough bright ideas for several short pieces. But presented as one number it was formless and meaningless. Nothing emerged but a gaudy potpourri of *tutti* dance passages and solo virtuoso work . . . unprovoked modulations . . . [and] recurrent clichés. The whole attempt to view jazz as a form of art music should be discouraged."

They had missed the point. Ellington admired European composers, but saw no need to emulate them; he was not interested, when composing music meant to deal with life in the New World in the twentieth century, in using forms developed in the Old World in the seventeenth and eighteenth. As always, he was seeking new ways to use the elements that made up what he called "the American idiom"—work songs, blues and spirituals, Caribbean dances, call-and-response, vamps, section writing, breaks, riffs, improvised solos—to explore new worlds, convey ever more complex emotions, tell ever more involved stories. "Jazz is like the automobile and airplane," he told a reporter for the New York newspaper *PM.* "It is modern and it is American. . . . The Negro element is still important. But jazz has become part of America. There are as many white musicians playing it as Negro. . . . We are all working together along more or less the same lines. We learn from each other. Jazz is American now. *American* is the big word."

He would eventually become almost impervious to critics. "I don't respect criticism," he told one interviewer, "because . . . the critics of jazz are not like the critics of the symphony. When a critic hears jazz, he's hearing it for the first time . . . and he has no yardstick to measure it by." He felt the same way about uninformed praise as he did about critical attacks. Once, after a friend read aloud to him a review which gravely praised him for doing things in his music that actually had never crossed his mind, he said, "That kind of talk stinks up the place."

Ellington never presented *Black, Brown and Beige* in its entirety again, but he would introduce five more extended works at Carnegie Hall over the next five years: *New World A-Coming*, *Perfume Suite* (co-composed with Billy Strayhorn), *Deep South Suite*, *Liberian Suite*, and *The Tattooed Bride*. Neither patronizing critics nor commercial considerations nor the minute-by-minute distractions of life on the road would ever slow his pen. "Ellington always feels that he has found sanctuary when he boards a train," wrote Richard Boyer, who accompanied the band for months in order to write a three-part profile of him for *The New Yorker* in 1944.

He says that then peace descends and that the train's metallic rhythm soothes him. He likes to hear the whistle up ahead, particularly at night when it screeches through the blackness as the train gathers speed. "'Specially in the South," he says. "There the firemen play blues on the engine whistle—big smeary things like a goddam woman singing in the night." . . . Frowning, his hat on the back of his head, swaying from side to side with the motion of the car, occasionally sucking his pencil and trying to write firmly despite the bouncing of the train, humming experimentally, America's latter-day Bach will work through the night.

THAT'S MY HOME

Louis Armstrong was forty when the war began and, like Duke Ellington, too old for the army, but he did what he could, playing army camps and navy training stations, insisting that he be allowed to entertain both black and white units, and visiting military hospitals, where black and white wounded alike begged him to sign their casts "Satchmo."

His courtship of Lucille Wilson remained

Louis Armstrong and friends, somewhere on the road not long before he wed Lucille Wilson in 1942. The woman at the right is Velma Middleton, who would sing with Armstrong's groups for nearly three decades.

stalled so long as he stayed married to his third wife, Alpha. Then, Alpha ran off with Cliff Leeman, the drummer in the Charlie Barnet band. "Thank God," Armstrong wrote a newspaper columnist. "If I could only see him and tell him how much I appreciate what he's done for me by taking that chick away." A Chicago judge granted Armstrong a divorce on October 2, 1942. Ten days later he and Lucille were married. There was no honeymoon; Armstrong began a six-month tour of one-nighters that very evening. Lucille knew enough not to complain—she alone, of all the women he had known, Armstrong said, understood "my horn comes first."

They were still on the road as Christmas approached, and Lucille bought and decorated a small Christmas tree for their hotel room. "I gave him his Christmas present," she remembered, "and we finally went to bed. And Louis was still laying up in bed watching the tree, his eyes just like a baby's eyes." When she reached over to turn off the lights, he stopped her. "No, don't turn

them out. I have to just keep looking at it. You know, that's the first tree I ever had." And when they packed to leave the next day, he insisted she bring the tree along, too. "I kept that tree until way after New Year's," she said, "putting it up every night and taking it down every morning, in a dozen hotels. And then when I did take it down for the last time, Louis wanted me to mail it home."

In fact, there was no home to which to send it. Lucille soon wearied of the road and took the train to New York, determined to find a house in which they both could live. She found a narrow three-story house in a working-class neighborhood in Queens.

When Armstrong's tour ended in March 1943, and his taxi pulled up in the middle of the night to the front door of his new house, he couldn't believe it was his. "*One* look at that big *fine* house and right away I said to the driver, 'Aw, man, quit kidding and take me to the address I'm looking for.'" The cabbie insisted Armstrong was home. "I got up enough courage to get out of the

Armstrong at the Apollo

cab and rang the bell. And sure enough the door opened and who stood in the doorway with a real thin silk nightgown and her hair in curlers? To me [Lucille] looked just like my favorite flower, a red rose."

For the rest of his life, Lucille Wilson Armstrong would provide him with the permanent home for which he'd yearned since his boyhood on the streets of New Orleans. Arvell Shaw, who played with Armstrong for many years, thought he heard something special when his boss sang one of his most frequently requested songs, "That's My Home." "I listened not so much to the timbre of the voice but to the *feeling*," he said, "because it was something that went deep inside. When he would do a tune like 'That's My Home' and sing, 'I'm always welcome back no matter where I roam,//We call it home sweet home,' so help me I'd have to fight back the tears. Now *every night* we'd do that!"

THE STREET

On April 21, 1943, police officers padlocked the doors of the Savoy Ballroom. Both city and military authorities claimed that armed forces personnel had contracted venereal diseases from women they had met there. Angry Harlem residents charged that the real reason was that blacks and whites had not just danced together at the Savoy, but had gone home together afterward. "Hitler has scored a Jim Crow victory in New York," the Reverend Adam Clayton Powell Jr. told his congregation. Closing down the Savoy was "the first step toward segregation" of the city.

There were race riots over jobs and housing all across the North that summer, and in August violence again came to Harlem. Six were killed, seven hundred injured, and nearly fifteen hundred mostly white-owned shops were damaged or destroyed. The old dreams of the Harlem Renaissance were deferred once again. Harlem had already begun to get a repu-

tation among whites as a dangerous place— so dangerous that many jazz fans hesitated to visit it anymore, and the mob-connected men who ran some of its biggest clubs had long since fled downtown to start all over again.

Since the mid-1930s, the living heart of jazz in New York had been two blocks of old brownstones on the West Side—Fifty-second Street, between Fifth and Seventh Avenues. Never, not even in New Orleans at the turn of the century or along the brightly lit Chicago Stroll in the 1920s, had so much great jazz been concentrated in so small a space. Seven jazz clubs still flourished there in the early 1940s. The Spotlite, the Yacht Club, and the Three Deuces were on the south side of the block between Fifth and Sixth; Jimmy Ryan's, the

Onyx, and Tondelayo's were right across the street. And there were two more clubs a block further west—Kelly's Stable and the Hickory House.

The Street's unofficial queen was Billie Holiday. It had seemed like "a plantation" to her when she and Teddy Wilson were working there in the mid-1930s, she remembered, but now black musicians were everywhere, black and white customers mingled fairly freely, and the level of musicianship that surrounded her was simply astonishing. Her very first engagement at Kelly's Stables included on the same bill a quartet led by Coleman Hawkins; the hardest-swinging violinist in the history of the music, Stuff Smith (who sometimes fined the members of his quintet ten dollars if they *didn't* come to work high); and at inter-

A rainy night on New York's Fifty-second Street (left), mecca for jazz fans like the rapt duo shown below. Signs for Jimmy Ryan's, Leon & Eddie's, and the Orchid can be seen on the left side of the street facing the marquee for The Famous Door. "Fifty-second Street was total friendship," the songwriter Alec Wilder recalled. "It was the last time that an American street gave you a feeling of security and warmth and the excitement of musical friendship."

Session at Ryan's. On the afternoon of Sunday, February 1, 1942, a New York jazz fan could go and hear this all-star lineup in person: right to left, Al Morgan, Earl Hines, Marty Marsala, Pete Brown, Lips Page, Kenny Hollon, Jack Bland (partly hidden), Red Allen, Zutty Singleton, Max Kaminsky. The identity of the trumpeter at far left is unknown. It all cost just one dollar, and if you missed it there was likely to be another session just as good the following Sunday. Milt Gabler, the man who made it all possible, is at the far left with his finger to his lips.

mission, the pianist Nat "King" Cole and his trio. And competing clubs up and down the Street featured attractions only slightly less stellar.

To a jazz fan like the future impresario George Wein, then a teenager living in Boston, it was an irresistible magnet. "I was just a kid thirteen or fourteen years old and my brother was three or four years older," he remembered, "and we would come down the West Side Highway and we'd get off at Fifty-second Street, and drive. Before we checked into a hotel, we would drive straight across town down Fifty-second Street. . . . It was like being in a candied heaven, and the candy was the jazz that you could grab onto. That night, we would take ten or fifteen dollars that my father had

given us to go out, and I'd go into these bars where I couldn't drink and I would spend a dollar for a ginger ale. We'd go to five clubs. It was just the greatest feeling that one could have, particularly at three o'clock in the morning. I was half-asleep but I wasn't asleep. You were alone, maybe there were three or four couples, and you felt that the musicians were playing for you."

The musicians were playing for one another, too. "We were a brotherhood," one remembered. They moved from club to club to sit in, and crowded the bandstand at Milt Gabler's Sunday-afternoon jam sessions at Ryan's. Sidney Bechet and James P. Johnson and Hot Lips Page and Roy Eldridge and Coleman Hawkins were all regulars. "Eight tenormen could be around at the same

time," a small-time saxophonist named Art Engler remembered.

The courtesy that was shown to each man blowing was unbelievable. If you got a groove going, they'd encourage you, "Take another chorus! Keep going, man!" I remember a session at Ryan's when all the great tenor men in town seemed to be around—Ben Webster, Chu Berry, you name them. I was there, too, and I was scared stiff. But I *had* to play. I forget the tune but suddenly, somebody doubled up the time. And with all these great cats around me, I couldn't hold back. I was so excited, I just started blowing and I blew beyond what I could normally play. I could hear Chu, Ben, and the others urging me on. And soon there were three tenors going like mad, me in the middle, God, you'd come out of a session ten feet off the ground.

When one club owner complained to Jack Teagarden that his nightly habit of picking up his trombone between sets and ambling up or down Fifty-second Street to play somewhere else was cutting into business, Teagarden said he was "just being neigh-borly," and kept right on doing it. "It was beautiful because you'd play all kinds of music," the drummer Shelly Manne said. "It was like a history of jazz on one street. . . . It was really healthy for musicians. . . . I think that was the most creative time in jazz. If you were a jazz historian, you could have gone down there and seen and heard, with your own ears, the evolution of the music, right there on the street, and it all made sense."

————————

In December 1943, something new was added to the rich musical mix on Fifty-second Street. Dizzy Gillespie and Oscar Pettiford brought a quintet into the Onyx. (Gillespie, Billy Eckstine, Charlie Parker, and four other musicians had all recently left Earl Hines rather than undertake another tour of the Jim Crow South. Gillespie had hoped to have Parker with him on Fifty-second Street, but a telegram inviting him to join them was evidently never received.) Nineteen-year-old Max Roach

Members of the Billy Eckstine band onstage in Pittsburgh in 1944: Lucky Thompson, Dizzy Gillespie, Charlie Parker, and Eckstine himself. "I can truthfully say . . . without any type of conceit," its leader remembered, "there was no band that ever swung like that band . . . but we never could get anywhere because [nobody could] hear it."

played drums at the Onyx. Don Byas was on tenor for a time, followed by Budd Johnson. George Wallington played piano.

They were an astonishment. The pace at which they played was often furious. Max Roach's drumming—full-force but filled with subtle changes in pitch and timbre and unexpected shifts between sound and silence—was startling. Even their tunes were different. "We'd take the chord structures of various standard and pop tunes and create new chords, melodies and songs from them," Gillespie wrote. "We . . . added substitute chords to songs like 'Night and Day,' 'How High the Moon?' 'Lover,' 'What Is This Thing Called Love?' . . . We added and substituted so many chords that most people didn't know what song we were really playing. 'How High the Moon?' became 'Ornithology,' 'What Is This Thing Called Love?' was 'Hothouse.' " (If customers were sometimes confused, so was ASCAP, which would otherwise have had to be paid for the use of the original songs when the time eventually came to record.)

Above all, there was the sound of the young Dizzy Gillespie, memorably evoked by *The New Yorker* writer Whitney Balliett: "[He] never merely started a solo, he erupted into it. A good many . . . solos began with four- or eight-bar breaks, and Gillespie . . . would hurl himself into the break after a split second pause, with a couple of hundred notes that corkscrewed through several octaves, sometimes in triple time, and well into the solo itself. . . . Gillespie's style at the time gave the impression —with its sharp, slightly acid tone, its cleavered phrase endings, its efflorescence of notes, and its brandishings about in the upper register—of being constantly on the verge of flying apart. However, his playing was held together by his extraordinary rhythmic sense."

The Onyx engagement "was the thing that put us on the map," Gillespie wrote. It was then, he said, that the new style got its new name. For most tunes, he said, "we just wrote an intro and a first chorus. I'd

say, 'Dee-da-pa-da-n-de-bop.' And we'd go on into it. People, when they'd want to ask for one of those numbers and didn't know the name, would ask for 'bebop.' "

The war years had brought more than musical change to Fifty-second Street. New York was the jumping-off place for thousands of soldiers and sailors about to go overseas, and the Street was a natural gathering place. Music lovers were eventually outnumbered by servicemen and the people who catered to them—strippers, B-girls, pimps.

Servicemen about to ship out found Billie Holiday's languorous, melancholy singing perfectly suited to their mood. "I gave so many going-away parties at the Famous Door, I lost count," she said. "It was always the same: three or four young boys would spend the whole night in the joint; we'd lock up, have a final drink, and they'd walk off. A few weeks later, I'd get a letter from some damn island. . . . Some of the letters would break your heart."

Most of the white soldiers and sailors who crowded the Street during the war were just looking for a good time, but as Gillespie noted, there were also some who'd "come down to the Street to start some shit," and the sight of well-dressed black musicians in close proximity to white women seemed especially to enrage them. Gillespie and Oscar Pettiford were once assaulted simply for walking down the block with the light-skinned, red-haired singer Bricktop. Curses were exchanged. A sailor swung at Pettiford, who swung back. More sailors swarmed the musicians. In the near-riot that followed, Gillespie managed to cover Pettiford's escape by wielding his carpet knife with one hand and swinging his trumpet with the other—being sure to use the valves and not the fragile bell to beat off his attackers. Then he started his own run for the subway, holding his hand over his mouth so that his lip would not be injured. He made it down the steps with the sailors pounding after him, vaulted the

turnstile, then climbed onto a narrow cat-walk next to the train tracks and crouched there until his drunken pursuers lost interest and stumbled away.

In the spring of 1944, Charlie Parker and Dizzy Gillespie found themselves together again, back playing one-nighters as part of a brand-new band led by Billy Eckstine. It was a modernist orchestra with distinctly modern attitudes: Gillespie remembered that when the manager of the Plantation Club in St. Louis insisted that the band enter through the back door, "we just walked in with our horns, in front"—and got fired. Its music—much of it arranged by Gillespie— was daring, too. It was a "fantastic" band, its drummer Art Blakey recalled, a nurturing ground for bebop. At various times, Eckstine's band included Sarah Vaughan, trumpeter Fats Navarro, alto saxophonist Sonny Stitt, tenor saxophonists Budd Johnson, Gene Ammons, and Dexter Gordon, and Leo Parker on baritone. But it only made a few instrumental records and they were "sadder than McKinley's funeral," according to Blakey, only a pale reflection of what the men could do in person.

By winter, Parker and Gillespie had left Eckstine and were appearing together frequently as part of a quintet at the Three Deuces on Fifty-second Street. "They played very, very fast," the drummer Stan Levey said. "They had great technique, great ideas. They ran their lines through the chord change differently than anybody else. Prior to them, it was Roy Eldridge, Coleman Hawkins, that type of thing. This was a complete left-hand turn with the music. It was wonderful. When I heard this thing, I said it was for me. I got connected."

"It was the height of the perfection of our music," Dizzy Gillespie remembered, "on fire all the time. Sometimes I couldn't tell whether I was playing or not because the notes were so close together. He was always going in the same direction as me." Nothing quite like it had been seen or heard since Louis Armstrong and King Oliver

Fans line up outside the Classic Theater in Dayton, Ohio, to see Louis Jordan in 1945. Black and white teenagers alike had already begun to shift their allegiance from jazz to rhythm and blues.

had seemed uncannily able to complete one another's musical ideas at the Lincoln Gardens more than twenty years before. Musically, it was a perfect partnership; personally, things were more complicated. Parker was often late and sometimes absent. When Gillespie confronted him about it, Parker denied he was using drugs. Gillespie knew he was lying. There would always be tension between them.

There was tension with some older musicians, too. The drummer Dave Tough, who had learned to play jazz in Chicago during the 1920s but had easily made the transition to big band swing and was always interested in what younger musicians were doing, found Parker and Gillespie intimidating at first. "As we walked in . . . these cats snatched up their horns and blew crazy stuff. One would stop all of a sudden and another would start for no reason at all. We never could tell when a solo was supposed

to begin or end. Then they all quit and walked off the stand. It scared us."

The next summer, Gillespie took an eighteen-piece bebop big band on the road, touring the South as part of "Hep-sations '45," a variety package that featured comedians, acrobats, singers, and the tap-dancing Nicholas Brothers. He had thought they were to be booked into theaters where his music—"geared for people sitting and listening"—might have had a chance of finding an audience. Instead, he recalled, "all we were playing was dances" and southern dancers were unmoved by "Salt Peanuts" and "Shaw 'Nuff," "Bebop" and "Night in Tunisia." They wanted blues and most of the young men in Gillespie's band now considered blues a reminder of the bad old days, a legacy of Jim Crow and even Uncle Tom. "The bebop musicians wanted to show their virtuosity," Gillespie wrote. "They'd play the twelve-bar outline of the

blues but they wouldn't blues it up like the older guys they considered unsophisticated. They busied themselves making changes, a thousand changes in one bar."

Changes didn't interest southern dancers. "They couldn't dance to the music, they said," Gillespie remembered in 1979. "But I could dance my ass off to it. They could have, too, if they had tried. Jazz should be danceable. That's the original idea, and even when it's too fast . . . it should always be rhythmic enough to make you wanna move. When you get away from that movement, you get away from the whole idea. . . . But the unreconstructed blues lovers down south couldn't hear nothing else but the blues. They wouldn't even listen to us. After all these years, I still get mad just talking about it."

The fact was that jazz was no longer the music of choice for young black dancers, north or south. Wartime defense jobs had pulled great numbers of black men and women off the land and into the urban industrial world for the first time. The circumstances of their lives had altered, but their tastes had not. Born and brought up on the blues and with more money to spend than ever before, they constituted a fast-growing market looking for down-home excitement, the kind of music that the singer and alto saxophonist Louis Jordan was now making.

Jordan had worked with Chick Webb when Ella Fitzgerald was with the band. He loved playing jazz with an orchestra, loved singing the blues, too; but he had grown up in show business—his father had led the band for a celebrated vaudeville troupe called the Rabbit Foot Minstrels—and he never lost his delight in entertaining people. He also had a shrewd business sense, and as the popularity of the big bands began to fade, he remembered, "jazzmen played mostly for themselves. . . . I still wanted to play for the people, for millions, not just hep cats." Starting in 1942, he had begun to do just that, exploiting some of the most crowd-pleasing aspects of jazz—an infectious beat, suggestive but good-natured novelty lyrics, and his own bluesy saxophone solos—to produce hit after hit with his Tympany Five: "I'm Gonna Move to the Outskirts of Town," "That Chick's Too Young to Fry," "Choo Choo Ch' Boogie," "Ain't Nobody Here but Us Chickens," "Saturday Night Fish Fry," and "Caldonia (What Makes Your Big Head So Hard?)." "With my little band," Jordan said, "I did everything they did with a big band. I made the blues jump." Other jazzmen, including Lionel Hampton and Cootie Williams, Lucky Millinder and Erskine Hawkins, were now seeking to make the blues jump, too. The result would eventually become known as rhythm and blues.

ONE MAD NIGHTMARE

To Lester Young, the world beyond the sound of his horn had always seemed more or less irrelevant, even unreal. And so, when draft notices began to arrive, he simply ignored them. In August 1944, as he had been preparing to appear in a short film by the photographer Gjon Mili, the FBI caught up with him. Young was "actually crying in that film," according to Jo Jones, "because he didn't want to go into the army."

Young did all he could to stay out, carefully noting on his induction form that he smoked marijuana regularly. The army took him anyway. Since his boyhood encounter with a white mob, he had always tried to avoid the Deep South. Now, he was sent to Fort McClellan in Alabama. The black warrant officer in charge of the regimental band was a former college professor who scorned jazz and refused to permit him to play. Instead, he was ordered to perform endless hours of KP, under a white sergeant from rural Georgia with little patience for a black soldier who lived up North and insisted on speaking a strange language of

Lester Young and Jo Jones, newly captured by the draft, pose for an army cameraman at Fort Ord in California, 1944.

his own. And when the sergeant found a photograph of Young's first wife, who had been white, in his trunk, he evidently saw to it that Young was brought up for court martial for possession of marijuana. An army psychologist diagnosed him as in a "constitutional psychopathic state, manifested by drug addiction, chronic alcoholism and nomadism." He was dishonorably dis-

charged, nonetheless, and sentenced to a year in the stockade. He tried to run away once only to return, he said, when he saw "all those cats with guns." He was permitted to play in the barracks band; later, he would tell Zoot Sims that he had made "those sad motherfuckers swing."

He otherwise rarely talked about his time in the army. "It was a nightmare, man," was all he would say, "one mad nightmare." When he finally got back to the music world, he remained a master of his instrument, as deep an influence on the next generation of saxophonists as his older rival Coleman Hawkins had been on his, and his idiosyncratic sense of humor remained intact. "He'd walk by you while you were sitting in a booth, talking to somebody," the pianist Jimmy Rowles remembered, "and as he went by he'd just kind of brush you with his finger. 'Bob Crosby's in the house.' And keep going. That meant that the fuzz was there and if you had any marijuana, you better watch it. And he was way too slick for any of those guys. He could spot a Bob Crosby anywhere. And the reason why he called them Bob Crosby—sometimes there would be two in a club, he'd say, 'Bing is here, too'—he had [been] arrested one time in Kansas City, or Minneapolis or someplace, by some policeman that looked just like Bob Crosby."

But even before the army took him, his music had begun to change, and afterward, the celebrated silences in his playing grew longer, the whisper-to-a-shout shifts more startling, his sound darker and more anguished. There were fewer jump tunes, too, and more introspective ballads. The effect was world-weary and often extraordinarily moving. Young's personality changed, as well. Always shy and detached, he became wary and reclusive after the war, retreating still further behind his hipster facade, fending off strangers with opaque responses to their unwanted questions—"bells" or "ding-dong." He began to drink too much, also, and over the years, he would grow bitter that younger saxophone players whose styles had clearly grown directly out of his—"the other Ladies," he called them—often seemed to be having more success than he was. "It was pitiful," a friend remembered, "to see him . . . hearing all those young kids playing the ideas he had discarded. . . . You could see him wondering where to turn."

NOW'S THE TIME

On November 26, 1945, at the Savoy recording studios in midtown Manhattan Charlie Parker was at last scheduled to make his first recordings under his own name. He and Gillespie had appeared together on Fifty-second Street that January, and he was now known and admired among musicians. "There was a revolution going on in New York," one saxophone player remembered, "a rebellion against all those blue suits we had to wear in the big swing bands." "It was a cult," another recalled, "a brotherhood." Soon, a third remembered, "there was everybody else and there was Charlie."

But beyond the world of music he was still mostly unknown. At first, the session seemed likely to be a debacle. Bud Powell, the pianist Parker had wanted, had disappeared. Powell's replacement, Sadik Hakim, turned out to be unsure of the chord changes, so Dizzy Gillespie sat in at the piano on the first three tunes, "Billie's Bounce," "Now's the Time," and "Thriving on a Riff." Curley Russell played bass; Max Roach played drums; and nineteen-year-old Miles Davis played trumpet on all three. But the fourth tune was "Ko Ko"—not Duke Ellington's composition but a Parker original, based on the changes of "Cherokee"—and it began with a complex, blistering introduction, which so intimidated Davis that Gillespie stood in for him, then raced back to the keyboard while Parker soloed.

"Ko Ko" would astonish those who heard it for the first time, just as the first records Louis Armstrong made under his own name had astonished people twenty years before. With Max Roach boiling along in the background, Parker and Gillespie leap into their furious eight-bar unison chorus. Then, each plays a dazzling eight-bar arabesque before Parker launches into two ferocious, plunging, note-filled choruses that sound like nothing ever heard before on records. " 'Ko Ko' may seem only a fast-tempo showpiece at first," Martin Williams wrote, "but it is

not. It is a precise linear improvisation of exceptional melodic content. It is also an almost perfect example of virtuosity *and* economy. Following a pause, notes fall over and between this beat and that beat; breaking them asunder, robbing them of any vestige of monotony; rests fall where heavy beats once came, now 'heavy' beats come between beats and on weak beats. . . . [It] shows how basic and brilliant were Parker's rhythmic innovations, not only how much complexity they had, but how much economy they could involve."

Other records had hinted at what was to come, and, thanks in large part to Gillespie's willingness to share his discoveries with anyone who asked about them, big bands like those led by Woody Herman, Boyd Raeburn, and Stan Kenton had already incorporated elements of the new music into their arrangements. But these Savoy sessions were unadulterated bebop—intricate unison themes, dissonant chords, and the most demanding kind of virtuosic solo playing, all driven by bold, assertive drumming that both helped set the ferocious pace and provided a sort of running commentary on everything the soloists were doing. Charlie Parker's secret was out.

"Ko Ko" by Charlie Parker's Ri Bop Boys, the record that let the world know what Parker, Dizzy Gillespie, and their cohorts had been up to during the wartime recording ban

WHITE NOISE AND WHITE KNIGHTS: SOME THOUGHTS ON RACE, JAZZ, AND THE WHITE JAZZ MUSICIAN

GERALD EARLY

REBELS AND RACE

Jazz is the product of the whites. . . . It is the progeny of the blacks.

—Tenor saxophonist Archie Shepp,
Down Beat, December 16, 1965

By 1938, when *Life* magazine published a feature article on jazz and thus conferred middlebrow respectability on a music that fifteen years earlier most mainstream publications considered degenerate, whites dominated the scene. Although not always the music's most original thinkers (and one wouldn't expect it of the majority in any genre) they certainly were its most public personalities.

There was no particular reason in 1938 to think that whites would not always continue to dominate jazz, but this is not quite what happened. After World War II, the critical and historical tides turned strongly toward seeing blacks as the art's major innovators and seeing the music as an expression of certain black aesthetic principles involving the elements of swing and the blues. Doubtless, the civil rights movement had something to do with the change, as African-Americans became an assertive political and moral force in American society and racist attitudes were no longer given social or intellectual credence. Some whites, of course, continued to do very well financially and to receive, at times, considerable public acclaim as players, but it is noteworthy that, of the jazz movements that have sprung up since World War II, the ones most denigrated or dismissed by critics and looked upon with the greatest suspicion by most of the jazz-loving public are the ones most dominated by or identified with whites: cool or progressive or West Coast or third-stream jazz, as well as fusion or jazz-rock, genres generally held in lower esteem than the once-controversial avant-garde of the 1960s. To be sure, a good deal of the music made within these movements hasn't aged well, but a lot of hard bop and soul jazz is just as dated and unlistenable today.

Meanwhile, the critics argued that jazz was always hip, on the cutting edge, with an air of rebellion about it. This certainly seemed to be what jazz audiences believed after World War II, when the notion was popular enough to become a selling point used by the music industry itself. But however much jazz critics may have exaggerated the extent of this rebellion, it is clear that jazz has generally followed the path of other art forms, where both rebellion and reverence, the anxiety of influence and the need for tradition, exist in a state of continual tension. Tradition is both inspiration and a form of oppression and repression. Rebellion is at once the release of new energy and fresh ideas and an impulse to commit fraud through self-indulgence and novelty for novelty's sake. The traditionalist accuses the rebel of lacking craft and discipline; the rebel accuses the traditionalist of being a reactionary formalist.

It is still true that more whites than blacks play jazz and today black audiences show little interest in it except for the highly commercialized and groove-based "smooth jazz" played by black and white musicians like Kenny G, George Benson, George Duke, Joe Sample, Marcus Miller, and Larry Carlton. Indeed, jazz has become global music, a craft practiced by highly skilled musicians all around the world. But even in this age of diversity and multiculturalism we still seem bedeviled with the question of whether whites can play jazz, whether blacks are more gifted jazz players, whether whites have ever done anything truly innovative in jazz. The legendary Bix Beiderbecke, the only white who could be considered a figure in jazz approaching the stature of Louis Armstrong, Charlie Parker, or Miles Davis, exists not as a paradigm, in the end, but as something of an anomaly. The white player is caught in a curious kind of trap. He is condemned—if he plays something called "white" jazz—for being unable to swing (the music's *sine qua non*), and therefore of being inauthentic. He is equally inauthentic (and a thief, besides) if he plays something called "black" jazz. Within these strictures, therefore, it would seem impossible to be white and play jazz on any terms.

Richard Sudhalter has tried to come to the white musicians' rescue with his recent volume, *Lost Chords: White Musicians and Their Contribution to Jazz, 1915–1945,* a long mess of a book that is neither serviceable nor kind to its reader. There has been a certain amount of unavoidable anger over its publication. Some think that the white jazz musician, after all, has gotten more than his due in the amount of money, publicity, and pop culture legitimacy he has garnered over the years and in the greater number of jobs and venues that were open to him but closed to black musicians. (Some will cynically but rightly say that "Crow Jim," or favoritism for black jazz musicians, came in only when jazz seemed to be dying and there was no place to play it anymore.) To write a book such as Sudhalter's (even, as he protests, in the name of the true multicultural nature of jazz), that is a defense of white people in their whiteness, is, for many, racism trying to disguise itself as an exploration of diversity.

Nonetheless, Sudhalter raises very important points. No one would argue that saxophonists like Lee Konitz, Art Pepper, Paul Desmond, and Bud Shank are as important to the history of jazz as Charlie Parker or John Coltrane or Coleman Hawkins or Lester Young, but are they not as important as Eric Dolphy or Sonny Rollins or Sonny Stitt or Pharoah Sanders or Cannonball Adderley or Dexter Gordon or Jackie McLean? If musical evidence shows that they are, then in any responsible history of the music, these white saxophonists ought to be discussed alongside the black ones. Should we know about Papa Jack Laine, a drummer, who was considered the father of white New Orleans jazz and helped develop such famous white musicians of the early period as Nick LaRocca, Paul Mares, Raymond Lopez, and Leon Roppolo? Is he as important as someone like Art Blakey, who over three decades developed a host of hard-bop black musicians? Sudhalter also brings up the more problematic question of how to define jazz. Are swing and blues the essential elements? Are these the elements that blacks contributed to this music? Is white jazz largely understood as jazz that does not swing and is not blues-based? (I think it is.) Are these divisions accurate at all in characterizing the relationship of race to this music?

The careers of two of the most influential and successful white jazz musicians to appear since 1940, bandleader Stan Kenton and pianist Keith Jarrett, may help us understand better the white musician's perception of himself and how he is perceived by others. The two men are very different: they were reared on opposite coasts (Jarrett on the east and Kenton on the west); each emerged during a distinctly different era of jazz and of American social history (Kenton during the Depression, Jarrett during Vietnam and Watergate); each plays a different style of music; and each approaches the piano in a distinctive way. Even physically, the men are opposites: Kenton was very tall with very long arms; Jarrett is sinewy and short with very muscular hands. Yet there are a number of similarities: both have been accused of arrogance, of musical self-indulgence, of recording too much, of pretentiousness, of lack of originality. Both have intense, cult-like followings that view them as almost superhuman and certainly as compellingly original. But among casual jazz fans and music lovers their music generally goes unrecognized and unheard. Both achieved considerable success for people playing complex instrumental music that is rarely played on the radio today, and both did so with little regard for the fickle desires of the marketplace. And both forcefully articulated principles for playing jazz.

BALBOA AND BEYOND

We were wired, that first summer at Balboa. We were glued in. . . . I was so wrapped up in the music, I didn't even know I was married! We used to follow Stan around. He was like a god to us!

—Bassist Howard Rumsey, in Carol Easton's *Straight Ahead: The Story of Stan Kenton*

Jazz is finished.

—Stan Kenton, *Down Beat,* April 23, 1964

In 1964, Stan Kenton voted for Barry Goldwater for president. In 1968, he voted for George Wallace. It can be assumed that his politics were not simply conservative but far right-wing. It can also be assumed that Kenton did not think much of the civil rights movement. A jazz record producer told me that Kenton's records still have enormous appeal to the members of the NRA. Oddly, toward the end of his life—he died in 1979—he had attracted two very different audiences: old fans who remembered the glory days of progressive jazz and cherished the memory of a band that was loud and aggressive; and young kids, reared on hard rock, who appreciated the Kenton band for precisely the same qualities.

When Kenton read the results of the 1956 *Down Beat* critics' poll, in which guitarist Tal Farlow and clarinetist Benny Goodman were the only white musicians to win in any of the "established talent" categories, he fired off this angry telegram to the editor.

JUST SAW YOUR FOURTH JAZZ CRITICS POLL. IT'S OBVIOUS THAT THERE IS A NEW MINORITY GROUP, 'WHITE JAZZ MUSICIANS.' THE ONLY THING I GAINED FROM STUDYING THE OPINIONS OF YOUR LITERARY GENIUSES OF JAZZ IS COMPLETE AND TOTAL DISGUST.

In an open letter to Kenton, published the following month, jazz critic Leonard Feather responded in kind:

You conveniently ignore the theory, long held among most musicians and jazz authorities . . ., that almost every major development in jazz history has been the work of Negro musicians and that even the few exceptions such as Bix, Benny Goodman, and [Lenny] Tristano admit that they leaned heavily on the inspiration of Negro predecessors.

Doubtless, it came as news to Stan Kenton that for the past twenty years he had been performing a Negro art form. He thought of jazz as simply American, and he said as much in interviews over the years. It must be noted that Feather uses the word "theory," not "fact," in talking about the importance of blacks in the history of the development of jazz. Although he seemed not to realize it, Feather was defending the poll results on political and moral, not musical, grounds by accusing Kenton of racism. "Nobody heard you complain when you were winning," he wrote Kenton, who had received just 10 votes to Count Basie's winning 223. But for all his bitterness, Kenton was right in asking for a musical justification for the selections. If, as he said he always believed, "a man's a man" and the individual counts for everything, and if at least as many whites were playing jazz professionally as blacks, why should blacks so dominate the polls?

"The fact that most of the winners in this critics' poll happened to be coloured," Feather wrote, "had nothing whatever to do with any racial attitude, conscious or unconscious, on the part of the voters." But Feather couldn't possibly know this. If whites had done very well in past polls—and they had dominated them all during the 1930s—why should they now be seen as worse than black players? When did this "theory" arise of blacks as the major innovators in the music, and why had it won the hearts and minds of most critics?

As a result of this controversy, Kenton was seen by some as the last great defender of white jazz, the ultimate white jazz musician. His music became, even more intensely, the embodiment of jazz as the great lost cause of whiteness in American culture. His best biographer, Carol Easton, described the source of Kenton's racial views:

> Stan has periodically been accused . . . of discriminating against black musicians. He has. But in their haste to label him racist, his detractors reveal their own ignorance of the Gestalt that is Stan Kenton.
>
> No man can be expected to be any more or less than the environment that shapes him. Stanley is his mother's son. From early childhood, he was indoctrinated with Stella's philosophy of absolutes: right-wrong, good-evil, black-white, democracy-communism. Scratch the superficial veneer of sophistication and you find, at the core of the man, the provincial, chauvinistic, myopic, unshakable values of the quintessential WASP. . . . Morally, he has no peripheral vision; a social conscience is "that liberal crap."

Kenton did hire black musicians, including Ernie Royal, Karl George, Jesse Price, Jimmy Crawford, Curtis Counce, Kevin Jordan, Jean Turner, Julius Watkins, and Don Byas, a point that comedian Mort Sahl, like other Kenton champions, has made. But blacks never had a real presence in his bands nor any impact on the nature of the music. The *character* of the band was always overwhelmingly white, inasmuch as it is legitimate to describe the character of a band in racial terms. Kenton racialized his music conceptually, or certainly his public thought he did, and many may have found this an appealing aspect of it—which is probably why his defenders like to bring up those blacks who occasionally played with him. (In a March 1958 interview with *Down Beat,* Kenton said this about an important nonwhite music's relationship to jazz, "In the future, Afro-Cuban rhythms are going to loom big in modern jazz; so big that people will stop thinking of them as strictly Afro-Cuban. One day, American music will have swallowed up completely the Cuban rhythms." Leftists see white imperialism in these remarks, while the right sees good old American enterprise and artistic Manifest Destiny.) One finds occasional articles about his band's appearances in the black press of the 1940s and 1950s, but it isn't likely that many blacks joined the Stan Kenton Fan Club in those days; it put "KKK" on all its letters, which stood for "Keep Kenton Kicking."

Unlike Keith Jarrett, who was a child prodigy, Kenton was a tall, ungainly youth with no particular aptitude for anything. But he burned with an adolescent's egotism, a belief that he deserved a better life and that he had something to offer the world. He discovered music as a teenager and made it his mission, his calling. He clung to it for dear life and dear identity, banging heavy-handedly for hours on the piano. He felt that if he did not make a go of it in music there would be nothing for him—there would, in fact, be nothing of him. As he said of his youth:

> I had a very hard time becoming a part of anything. I felt I had no right even to *be* here. I was afraid of people. I was very awkward and clumsy, uncoordinated. I couldn't run or play basketball. I was no good at baseball. Scholastically, I was no great shakes. But I wanted so terribly to *be* somebody, to do something important. Then the music came along, and I went after it desperately, was really *driven* into it, because I was so hungry to identify with *something*. . . . At that particular time, it could have been anything. It just happened to be music.

Kenton's big break came in 1933 when Everett Hoaglund, a leading musician in southern California, hired him to play with his band at the Rendezvous in a town called Balboa, a name that became almost mystically meaningful to him. No matter how far or how much he was traveling, Balboa would become synonymous with Kenton; it was his professional and spiritual home.

Kenton took over saxophonist Vido Musso's orchestra in 1938 and organized his own band two years later. In the summer of 1941 his band was booked into the Rendezvous. There, the Kenton sound was born—unbearably loud, rhythmically overwhelming, made up of ponderous blocks of sound. The young people who heard it went crazy. It seemed like Benny Goodman at the Palomar all over again.

By the mid-1940s, Kenton was playing what he called progressive jazz, filled with dissonance, atonality, and other techniques borrowed from European composers like Milhaud, Stravinsky, and Shostakovich. If you were a white composer or arranger with a yen for twentieth-century European music and a love of big bands, you went, composition paper in hand, to Stan Kenton. His band played places like the Philadelphia Academy of Music and Symphony Hall in Boston that almost never permitted nonclassical performers. Despite the disputes that his music generated—no one was neutral about Kenton; he was either loved or hated—he achieved a great deal of respect as a composer and bandleader among a good many young white musicians, his legion of ecstatic fans, and some critics as well. *Down Beat* and *Metronome* usually wrote about him favorably. He also made a great deal of money with hits like "Eager Beaver," "Peanut Vendor," "Intermission Riff," and a slew of songs whose titles started with "Artistry."

Stan Kenton and college-age fans

In the late 1940s, Kenton put together a new band, the Innovations Orchestra—forty pieces, including sixteen strings—and performed highly experimental pieces like Bob Graettinger's "City of Glass," which seemed to bewilder and stun audiences. His music grew ever more grandiose. (Bassist Howard Rumsey was onto something when he called Kenton "the Wagner of American jazz," but there was also something about him of Paul Whiteman.) The Innovations Orchestra gave way eventually to his twenty-seven-piece Mellophonium Orchestra (named for the four obscure French hornlike instruments it featured, which the other horn players charged had poor tone and threw them off pitch). It, in turn, was replaced by his Neophonic orchestra (Kenton himself coined the name). His staunch admirers stayed with him through it all, but the general public eventually fell away. In the 1955 film *Blackboard Jungle*, the rebellious students destroy their teacher's Stan Kenton records. Things had changed since 1941.

Kenton's music was white jazz—in some ways the apotheosis of white jazz. Swinging was beside the point. To put it crudely,

in the Kenton worldview, blacks had rhythm but whites had theory. Glenn Miller had put it this way in 1940: "I haven't got a great jazz band and I don't want one. Some of the critics, *Down Beat*'s among them, point their fingers at us and charge us with forsaking real jazz. . . . It's all in what you define as 'real jazz.' It happens that to our ears harmony comes first. A dozen colored bands have a better beat than mine. Our band stresses harmony." Kenton reiterated that notion in 1965: "It's time that we get away from that hackneyed part of the field of jazz music. I have always maintained that a thing doesn't necessarily have to swing all the time to be jazz, because there's a certain way of playing music that came from the jazz conception that can be applied to rubato movement in music or any sort of time, any conception of time. It doesn't have to be always a swing thing."

Kenton had a tempestuous personality—he married three times, talked wildly of becoming a psychiatrist, announced that jazz was "neurotic," then "dead," then reborn. By 1975, illness had forced him to give up the road but he continued to conduct hundreds of clinics at high schools and colleges. He left all his music to North Texas State University. Like so many Americans in the modern age, he believed in the efficacious power of education, that jazz was a sort of creed to be passed on.

Stan Kenton and his orchestra in 1946. Shelly Manne is on the drums.

great white knight of American music, but it is difficult for me to tell at this distance whether he was slaying dragons or simply tilting at windmills.

KUNDALINI

Jazz is one of the least learnable art forms.
—Keith Jarrett, *Jazztimes,* May 1999

Keith Jarrett has been accused many times of making music that is not jazz and that certainly does not, in any conventional sense, swing. He has issued solo improvisations on pipe organ, piano, and clavichord, an early album of pop tunes (an effort best forgotten), and another, called *Spirits,* which sounds like Native American music, and on which Jarrett plays all the instruments, including a variety of flutes and drums. But of all the many records that he has made, and he has been staggeringly prolific, none seems stranger than his 1980 album, *Sacred Hymns,* a recording of music by the spiritualist G. I. Gurdjieff. Jarrett's choice of material seems especially bizarre because the music is uninteresting harmonically, simplistic and lifeless, intended not for listening but as accompaniment to ritual dancing. Its tediousness had to be apparent to Jarrett himself, so the album must have been made for extra-musical, or philosophical, reasons. It exists only as programmatic to a set of ideas that have little to do with music but everything to do with consciousness. To a musician as obsessed with the mythological and romantic significance of bringing music into being as Jarrett is, this is certainly a valid enough reason to record it.

Kenton's music may not be listened to much these days, but his reach extends far beyond the people who still buy his records. The white jazz musicians who played with Kenton make an impressive list: Maynard Ferguson, Art Pepper, Laurindo Almeida, Mel Lewis, Charlie Mariano, Anita O'Day, June Christy, Bob Cooper, Shelly Manne, Howard Rumsey, Kai Winding, Shorty Rogers, Lee Konitz, Frank Rossolino, Bud Shank, Stan Getz, Zoot Sims, Pepper Adams, and Sal Salvatore. Among the arrangers who worked with Kenton were Bill Holman, Gerry Mulligan, Bill Russo, Johnny Richards, and Pete Rugolo, all among the most famous of the post–World War II era. When one thinks about all the clinics Kenton held and all the high school and college bands in the country today that play Kenton arrangements, it is easy to see that his impact on American music is very wide. There might, indeed, be less than six degrees of separation between any white jazz musician today and Stan Kenton, perhaps between him and any jazz musician. In this sense, he remains an institution. Unlike Keith Jarrett, who thinks of jazz as something intuitive, Kenton always believed that jazz could be "learned," although he also always feared that it might become "over-intellectualized" and lose its "heart" and "validity."

I saw his band perform at Glassboro State College in New Jersey in 1972. My ears did not stop ringing for two days after the concert; my chest pounded during the performance—whether from excitement or from anxiety I'm not sure. Stan Kenton was the last

Making such an album reaffirmed certain important self-concepts that have been essential to the Jarrett myth: the primacy of process in the making of music; the refusal in any way to compromise with market taste or with the expectations of his fans, thus intensifying his sense of integrity; the idea, widely held in the sixties when he was making his way as a professional musician, that music is a representation of something spiritual and philosophical. Like John Coltrane, the spiritual and musical hero for many musicians of his generation, Jarrett increasingly saw music as a pervasive force that did more than just accompany or induce certain moods. It was capable of producing both large-scale social change and consciousness-altering personal awareness. Having grown up with those ideas, Jarrett extended them so far that he was able to play music that clearly was not jazz without much compromising his standing as a jazz musician among listeners of his own generation.

What brought Jarrett to the attention of thousands of listeners, many of whom had no interest in jazz, was his series of solo piano concerts, long blocks of improvised music—no recognized tunes or songs—performed on a grand piano. Neither the critics, the public, nor Jarrett himself saw it as jazz in the traditional sense. During these performances, which lasted anywhere from sixty to ninety minutes, Jarrett combined snatches of Celtic, Indian, and gospel music, as well as blues and jazz, with moments of haunting lyricism. Somehow, the results never seemed a mere pastiche of effects or influences or whims, but rather were highly conceptualized presentations of real music-making.

Jarrett had three things going for him to make what would seem so unpromising a project a great commercial and critical success. He was unquestionably a virtuoso on his instrument; he produced enough interesting, even challenging music during most of these concerts to overcome the boring, tedious, repetitious, or overly ardent passages; and he played the piano in an energetic manner—his detractors would say it was histrionic and ostentatious—to convey to his audience that he was dramatically seized, possessed by the entire process of music-making, and that what he was doing not only required great inspiration but great physical stamina. (These acrobatics struck the more mystical among his fans as physical reenactments of the drama of Kundalini—the energy that certain Yogis believe lies dormant at the base of the spine until it is activated and channeled through the seven chakras, or spiritual centers of the body.) There was always a sense of uncoiling or unfurling about Jarrett's concert performances, which is what Kundalini—the name under which he published his music for several years—means.

Of course, the gyrations were good showmanship, too, and some came to see him as the Gene Krupa of the keyboard. His playing of classical music (which he was to do with increasing frequency after 1980) did not seem to require them. This made the solo concerts seem to Jarrett's admirers not mere music-making but rather a spiritual event, as if Jarrett were a shaman calling upon the spirits, so shamelessly and vigorously did he demand the favor of his muse. In interviews he said such self-important things about the meaning of these concerts (he had to empty himself of music before he began playing, he said; death surrounded his appearances because he was so vulnerable, so open, when at the keyboard) that they also took on significance as demonstrations of a philosophical proposition about music.

Jarrett's thinking in this regard may have been influenced by Karlheinz Stockhausen, the composer-visionary who argued for what he called, in a 1971 lecture, "intuitive music."

> There are certain abilities required . . . in order to play this sort of music . . . that the traditional musician has never learned. . . . The most profound moments in musical interpretation and composition are those which are not the result of mental processes, are not derived from what we already know, nor are they simply deducible from what has happened in the past. Musicians must learn to become the opposite of egocentric; otherwise you only play yourself, and the self is nothing but a big bag full of stored information. Such people are closed systems. But when you become like what I call a radio receiver, you are no longer satisfied with expressing yourself. . . . You become a medium.

The solo concerts, then, had the appearance of being deep music, while remaining accessible to the large audience they generated, an audience that, by and large, did not care for mainstream jazz. Because Jarrett's highly rhythmic music did not swing, one might say that Jarrett succeeded in apotheosizing white jazz or what most people have come to believe constitutes white jazz. The irony is that during the early 1970s, a good many of Jarrett's listeners thought he was black or biracial, which added a kind of sexiness to white jazz that no one ever thought it could have.

So, this complex set of characteristics, along with the fact that solo piano records were cheap to make—one musician, one instrument—and that Jarrett started these grand piano meditations when most younger jazz musicians were still intrigued by electric or rock-oriented music of the kind that Jarrett himself had played in an early edition of Miles Davis's electric band, helped assure his financial success. The company that recorded him, ECM (Editions of Contemporary Music), first released a three-record set of two solo piano concerts, performed in Bremen and Lausanne, that did very well; then a two-record set of just one concert, in Köln. This became not only Jarrett's most popular record but the most popular solo piano record in the history of American music, probably because it is the most insistently lyrical, the prettiest of all his solo efforts. Finally, in the middle 1970s, came a ten-record set of performances in Japan called *Sun Bear Concerts*. No jazz musician, no musician of any genre, had ever before put out such a massive set of original, totally improvised music. Even this sold well, making the top-ten *Billboard* jazz chart for a time.

As Jarrett's fame grew through the solo concerts, skepticism mounted among some critics: Whitney Balliett was gently dismissive in the *New Yorker,* and Gary Giddins in the *Village Voice* expressed unease with what he called Jarrett's "homesick lyricism." It is hard to say how well the solo concerts will hold up as the years go by but it seems likely that, like Thomas Wolfe's novels, Jarrett's solo concerts go down best with the young. I daresay Jarrett's reputation ultimately will not rest on them. Indeed, had he produced solo concerts alone he probably would have been dismissed by the jazz establishment, especially since they helped to spawn a new genre in popular music: the New Age piano solo—sentimental, simplistic, vaguely tied to nature—played by and sold almost exclusively to whites, seemingly meant only to relieve stress while drinking expresso. (The New Age pianist George Winston has, in fact, replaced Jarrett as the best-selling solo pianist in the United States.)

But Jarrett is also a jazz composer of considerable ability, and during the seventies he wrote music for two quartets, one made up of American musicians, the other of Europeans. The music that Jarrett produced with these groups was simply astonishing, a mix of influences that included Ornette Coleman, John Coltrane, Dave Brubeck, Bill Evans, George Gershwin, the Beatles, and Miles Davis, made richly original through the alchemy of his imagination. At least eight of the albums he made with these groups—*Birth, Death and the Flower, Backhand, Shades, Belonging, My Song, The Survivors' Suite, Personal Mountains*—are among the best jazz records of the 1970s; some are clearly among the best small-group jazz records since World War II. (To my mind, "Blossom," from the album *Belonging,* may be the most moving instrumental jazz ballad ever recorded.)

Since the early 1980s, Jarrett has played and recorded concerts with a trio that performs nothing but standards from the Great American Songbook. This series, too, has produced a number of very fine jazz recordings—especially *The Cure, At the Deer Head Inn,* and *Standards, Vol. 2*—that stand among the best of their era. In addition, Jarrett has recorded classical works by composers ranging from Bach to Shostakovich. Indeed, the solo concerts, even if one thinks of them as absolutely fraudulent as jazz, constitute only a small part of his recorded output. Jarrett deserves to be considered one of the major American musicians of the last thirty years for the astonishing variety and quality of his jazz and classical work. He also deserves credit for being a major force in returning younger jazz musicians to acoustic music, by showing there was an audience for it.

It is difficult to say how much race has affected Jarrett's reputation. Would he be more highly regarded if he were black? Does he enjoy the generally good reputation he does in part because he is white? Would he have been given the opportunity to record

Keith Jarrett, 1968

the same sorts of projects with ECM or any record company had he been black? How much did confusion about his race help him in the early days of his career before it became commonly known that he was of French-Hungarian extraction? How much did he exploit the fact that he had wiry hair puffed like an Afro? Jarrett certainly knew that his racial background was of some interest, as he said in a 1972 interview in *Down Beat.* "All music that is important and valuable comes from exactly the same source. It's just a question of the heredity or ancestry of the people. That's why people have trouble with me, trying to figure out what I am because if you can get to the source of all that music, you can play all that music."

The issue of race was raised more recently in an interview with the *New York Times Magazine.* In it, Jarrett lashes out at Wynton Marsalis, who is unquestionably the most famous jazz musician of our era, with a reputation with the general public that far exceeds Jarrett's own:

For a great black player who talks about the blues—I've never heard Wynton play the blues convincingly, and I'd challenge him to a blues standoff any time.

In the 1960s, the only people who had trouble with my being white were whites. Some kinds of playing, taken to their logical extremes, can be the realm of black players, and others maybe of white players, but the whole situation wasn't so—well, so black and white back then. I played

with Miles, and he used to tell me I had to be black in some places. It was so free. It was up to us what we did and who we were, and so much of it happened in private.

One's immediate response to Jarrett's remarks was that he was jealous because Marsalis had achieved the fame Jarrett felt he himself deserved and, worse still, that he believed Marsalis had acquired this acclaim largely because he is black and the public, both black and white, demands a black musician to be the authenticator of jazz. This reduces Jarrett to being the equivalent of a disgruntled white man who is upset because he believes some prominent black is where he is because of affirmative action, not merit. I take him at his word when he said in a subsequent interview: "I don't feel envious of Wynton Marsalis. I feel sorry for him. He was too young to know how to handle what happened." But I think his remarks do reveal a distinct frustration with being a white musician in such a starkly racialized field, in some ways, more repulsively racialized than in the 1920s or 1930s. Jarrett exists in a sort of cul-de-sac without the range of influence or impact that a person of his achievement should have in his field.

His remarks about Marsalis grow from his general disappointment with the current jazz scene, which Marsalis symbolizes more than anyone else and which seems to be producing, to Jarrett's mind, little vital music. It must be remembered that in the 1970s, when Jarrett was at the height of his compositional

powers, he was writing music that was not a recapitulation or a reclamation of the jazz that had gone before but, rather, struck out for his own territory on his own terms. There was little in Jarrett in his early years of success that seemed in any way worshipful of the jazz tradition; he did not even want to be called a jazz musician, and, ironically, it was that attitude, more than anything, that made him most true to the tradition of jazz as freedom and individuality, as attitude and ego, as rebellion and jousting with father figures, than I think he is given credit for. For Jarrett, jazz is not simply a body of music or a set of techniques; it is a psychological stance toward music-making. Therefore it must be seized, confronted, doubted, blasphemed, willed, accepted. But it cannot be learned as a set of rules, as a doctrine, as the unfolding of some predestined historical process. To his mind, to "learn" jazz is, in effect, to put the critics on the bandstand, to make the preoccupations of musicians identical with theirs: interpreting and protecting canons. The British writer T. E. Hulme once said, "There are certain catchwords which, while they embody truth, at the same time kill it." It is perhaps Jarrett's view that current jazz is much like the catchword that is killing the truth it embodies.

What Jarrett says about Marsalis is, in one sense, no worse than what many famous jazz musicians have said about their colleagues in interviews over the years. Jarrett is no harsher than, say, Miles Davis was with Oscar Peterson, whose playing he loathed.

But what is disturbing about Jarrett's remarks is that he makes an issue of both his race and Marsalis's. Marsalis is condemned for being an inauthentic *black* player. Marsalis is "jazzy," Jarrett continued, "the same way someone who drives a BMW is sporty"; in other words, he is a bourgeois black making bourgeois jazz. Jarrett claims that as a white, he can outplay Wynton in a blues contest. The concern is not that this childish boast was made, but that Jarrett made a specific issue of his whiteness as proof that blackness is no authenticator of jazz-playing ability. The point about blackness is well taken; the implicit defense of his whiteness is both gratuitous and irrelevant. Jarrett, thus, wavers between offering a critique and making a racial insult that all arises not over Marsalis's abilities but over Jarrett's self-consciousness about being white. Even in this age of diversity and multiculturalism, the chasm between black and white in jazz remains wide if the work of the most accomplished black musician of his generation is so thoroughly dismissed because he is not "really" black, and if the work of one of the most accomplished white musicians in the history of jazz is not given its proper place in the tradition because he is white.

JAZZ

RISK

The singer Jon Hendricks had served in the wartime army and was on a troopship coming home from Europe when he first encountered the new music that had been developing while he was overseas. "I suddenly heard this song over the ship's radio," he said. "It was frenetic and exciting and fast and furious and brilliant and beautiful and I almost bumped my head jumping off my cot. I ran up to the control room and said to the guy, 'What was that?' He said, 'What?' I said, 'That last song you just played, the one you just played!' He said, 'I don't know.' I said, 'Where is it?' He said, 'It's down there on the floor.' I looked down there on the floor, the floor's covered in records. I said, 'Come on, what color was the label?' He said, 'It's a red label.' So I began to sort them out and I would come across red labels and I would ask him, 'Was it this one?' And he said,

Bassist Tommy Potter, Charlie Parker, Dizzy Gillespie, and a very young John Coltrane at Birdland, the New York club named for Parker. "The first time I heard Bird play," Coltrane recalled, "it hit me right between the eyes."

'No.' Finally, I found it. It was a Musicraft label and it was called 'Salt Peanuts.' And it was Charlie Parker and Dizzy Gillespie. And I gave him thirty dollars and I said, 'Play this for the next hour!' "

The war had transformed the lives and elevated the expectations of millions of African-Americans. "I spent four years in the army to free a bunch of Dutchmen and Frenchmen," another black veteran said, "and I'm hanged if I'm going to let the Alabama version of the Germans kick me around when I get home. . . . I went into the army a 'nigger'; I'm coming out a *man*." Bebop was a musical development, not a political statement. Its message was one of accomplishment, not anger. But something of the spirit of that ex-soldier—self-assured, impatient, uncompromising—would nonetheless be mirrored in the new music.

"Your music reflects the times in which you live," Dizzy Gillespie wrote. "My music emerged from the war years . . . and it reflected those times. . . . Fast and furious, with the chord changes going this way and that way, it might've looked and sounded like bedlam, but it really wasn't." Gillespie was right. America and its indigenous music were both entering a new age in 1945. Jazz had always involved risk. To create art on the spot—to step forward and express oneself—had meant taking enormous chances. But now, Gillespie and Charlie Parker and their youthful companions were taking a still greater gamble. Determined to free the music from what they considered the tyranny of popular taste, to strip it of every vestige of the minstrel past, they would try to build a brave new musical world in which talent—and only talent—would count.

SO TOUGH

In the first week of December 1945, just a few days after recording "Ko Ko," Dizzy Gillespie and Charlie Parker boarded a train for Los Angeles. Billy Berg, the pro-prietor of a new Hollywood nightspot, Billy Berg's Swing Club, had invited Gillespie to bring a group west to introduce to California the kind of music that had been causing such a sensation on Fifty-second Street. Berg had asked for five musicians, but there were six men in the party: Gillespie and Parker, bassist Ray Brown, pianist Al Haig, drummer Stan Levey, and vibraphonist Milt Jackson. Gillespie—who knew Parker's habits all too well—had added Jackson to make sure that even when Parker failed to turn up, as he knew he sometimes would, there would still be five men on the bandstand, as called for in the contract.

Stan Levey had been under Parker's spell ever since he first played with him a year or so earlier. "Charlie Parker . . . was the Pied Piper of Hamelin. I was working on Fifty-second Street with different people, Ben Webster, Coleman Hawkins. And this guy walks down, he's got one blue shoe and one green shoe. Rumpled. He's got his horn in a paper bag with rubber bands and cellophane on it and there he is, Charlie Parker. His hair standing straight up. He was doing a Don King back then. Well, I says, 'This guy looks terrible. Can he play? What?' And he sat in and within four bars, I just fell in love with this guy, the music,

"Salt Peanuts" by Dizzy Gillespie and His Orchestra

you know. And he looked back at me, you know, with that big grin, with that gold tooth, and we were just like that. From that moment on, we were together. I would have followed him anywhere, you know? Over the cliff, wherever."

Somewhere in the Arizona desert, the train stopped to take on water, Levey remembered, "and I look out the window and I see this spot out there carrying . . . a little grip, and I'm saying, 'What the hell is that?' And I look closer; it's Charles Parker." Suffering from withdrawal and desperate for drugs, Parker had jumped down from the train and was wandering off into the empty desert in search of a fix. "Dizzy turned to me, he said, 'What's that?' and I said, 'I think it's your saxophone player.' So he said, 'Go get him.' So I ran out real quick and grabbed him, and I said, 'Where are you going?' "

Parker said, "I got to get something out here somewhere."

Levey managed to talk Parker back aboard the train. They still had twenty hours to go. When they finally reached their destination, an admirer was at the station to warn Parker that heroin was costly and hard to come by in Los Angeles. That was only the beginning of the problems he and Gillespie and their companions faced in bringing bebop to the West Coast.

Jazz had flourished in California since Freddie Keppard, Jelly Roll Morton, Kid Ory, and other New Orleans musicians began drifting there before the First World War. Like New York's Fifty-second Street, the heart of black Los Angeles—Central Avenue between Forty-second and Vernon—was home to a host of clubs: the Down Beat and Club Alabam, the Last Word and Lovejoy's, the Memo, and Ivie's Chicken Shack, a restaurant run by Duke Ellington's onetime singer Ivie Anderson.

Billy Berg's club was different. It was on North Vine Street in Hollywood, for one thing, and was meant to be a sort of Cali-

Dizzy Gillespie on the
corner of Sixth Avenue and
West Fifty-second Street

fornia version of Manhattan's Café Society, offering jazz and welcoming black as well as white patrons—something otherwise unheard of in Hollywood, where black citizens just driving through town were routinely pulled over and searched.

Young musicians who had already been experimenting locally with the kind of sounds Gillespie and Parker were playing turned out to hear them. Howard McGhee was there on opening night. So were bassist Charles Mingus, tenor saxophonist Dexter Gordon, and pianist Hampton Hawes. The reed player Buddy Collette recalled Gillespie and Parker's initial impact on him and his friends: "This was for real. The stuff that you heard on records that you didn't believe, you . . . had to believe because you saw people standing playing it. . . . It was kind of scary to hear, because they were playing so fast that we didn't understand what they were really playing. . . . They were using notes that we didn't even dare to use before because it would be considered wrong. And those stops and gos between Dizzy and Bird. . . . You know, you'd look at everybody and say, 'Can you believe what we just heard?' "

A good many ordinary customers were asking one another the same question. But they seemed more "dumbfounded" than excited, Gillespie remembered. The music the young musicians loved struck many of the others in the room as frantic, nervous, chaotic. Sometimes they asked the men to sing.

Nothing could have been more insulting to musicians who wanted to be seen as serious artists, not performers; who were determined to simply play their music, not to put on a show. It was bad enough, from their point of view, that they had to share the stage every evening with Slim Gaillard and Harry "the Hipster" Gibson, musical comedians who, like Cab Calloway, specialized in novelty tunes that capitalized on the latest inner-city slang for the delectation of mainstream white audiences. Gaillard drew upon a lexicon of laid-back nonsense syllables he called "vout" to produce hits like "Flat Foot Floogie" and "Cement Mixer (Put-Ti-Put-Ti)," while Gibson's best-known number was called "Who Put the Benzedrine in Mrs. Murphy's Ovaltine?" Theirs was precisely the kind of entertainment Gillespie and Parker most despised, and the two were furious when Gaillard began billing himself as "the bebop bombshell," fearing that their music and his comedy routines would become confused in the public mind. They were right to be afraid. When *Time* got around to noticing bebop that spring, it defined the new music as "hot jazz overheated with overdone lyrics full of bawdiness, references to narcotics and double-talk."

Martin Williams, destined to become one of the most perceptive of all jazz historians, was still in the navy—and still in the grip of his Virginia boyhood—when he went to hear Parker and Gillespie at Billy Berg's. Their music, he remembered, had seemed to him then not merely novel but "arrogant" and "uppity." "What struck me even more than the music," he recalled, "was the *attitude* coming off the bandstand—self-confident, aggressive. It was something I'd never seen from black musicians before."

"Nobody understood our music out on the Coast," Parker said, by which he meant music fans, not musicians; "they *hated* it." Gillespie agreed: "They thought we were playing ugly on purpose. They were so very, very, very hostile! . . . Man, they used to stare at us so tough."

When Dizzy Gillespie and the rest of the sextet boarded the plane to fly back to New York on February 9, 1946, Charlie Parker was not with them. He had traded his ticket for cash with which to buy drugs. It had taken him weeks to locate a steady source of heroin: the disabled proprietor of a shoe-shine stand named Emery Byrd but known to his customers as "Moose the Mooch." Parker was so grateful to have found him that he signed over to him half his future royalties in exchange for a guar-

anteed supply and wrote a tune in his honor.

He worked with Howard McGhee at the Club Finale on Central Avenue. He recorded a solo on "Lady Be Good" alongside Lester Young at a "Jazz at the Philharmonic" concert that became a standard in the repertoire of aspiring saxophonists all over the country. And he recorded for a new label called Dial several of his own tunes, including "Yardbird Suite" and "Ornithology."

Then, in April, the police arrested Moose the Mooch. He was sent to San Quentin, and Parker was once again without heroin. To compensate, he began drinking as much as a quart of whiskey a day. Soon he was living in a converted, unheated garage, with only his overcoat for bedding.

Howard McGhee found him there and arranged for him to record again for Dial on July 29. But Parker arrived so drunk the record producer had to help hold him up in front of the microphone. A psychiatrist gave Parker six tablets of phenobarbital to bring him around, and he managed to stumble through a troubled take of "Lover Man." (Although Parker himself later said the recording should be "stomped into the ground," the producer released it anyway, and some of Parker's acolytes dutifully committed it to memory, note for unsteady note.) That night Parker twice wandered into the lobby of his hotel wearing only his socks, then fell asleep while smoking and set his bed ablaze. The firemen had to shake him violently to wake him, and when he protested, the police hit him with a blackjack and put him in handcuffs. He spent ten days in jail, charged with indecent exposure, resisting arrest, and suspected arson, and was then transferred to Camarillo State Hospital. He would spend six months inside its walls, tending a lettuce patch, putting on weight, playing C-melody saxophone on Saturday nights in the hospital band. His third wife, Doris Sydnor, who had met him when he was playing the Famous Door, where she was the hatcheck girl, came to California and took a job as a waitress so that she could visit him three times a week. Eventually, he would write a tune about his new home: "Relaxin' at Camarillo."

THAT'S WHAT MUSIC IS FOR

The end of World War II had marked the beginning of the end for the big swing bands. Tastes were changing. Sentimental singers now outsold instrumentalists, and young people flocked to see and hear them. Musicians' salaries, which had risen dramatically during the war, remained so high that it was nearly impossible to draw big enough crowds to meet them. The wartime tax on entertainment remained in effect, too, keeping nightclub prices high, encouraging people to stay at home, forcing ballrooms to close. Duke Ellington and Count Basie managed to stay on the road, but by Christmas of 1946, eight of their best-known rivals would announce that they were at least temporarily leaving it: Les Brown, Benny Carter, Tommy Dorsey, Woody Herman, Ina Ray Hutton, Harry James, Jack Teagarden, even Benny Goodman. Great jazz soloists like Coleman

Hawkins abandoned dreams of heading up big bands of their own and retreated to nightclubs—places too small for dancing. All kinds of jazz were still being played everywhere at the war's end. But whatever the style, the jam session was becoming the model: freewheeling, competitive, exacting—the kind of jazz that musicians had always played to entertain themselves after the squares had gone home.

Louis Armstrong was still touring with his big sixteen-piece band, though the fees he was getting—sometimes as little as $750 a night—were less than half what he'd

Louis Armstrong, still on the road with his big band during the early 1940s

earned a few years earlier and barely covered the cost of the all-night bus travel that took him and his men from one gig to the next. In a letter to a friend written from his hotel room in Tulsa, Oklahoma, he reported on his most recent travels.

> November we leave San Francisco on tour.
>
> Sacramento (26th). Army camp. Concert and a dance.
>
> Los Angeles . . . (28th). Elks Ballroom. Was real groovie indeed.

Phoenix . . . (29th). Mixed dance.

El Paso . . . (30th). White dance. Colored spectators. After the dance we went across the Border to Juarez, Mexico. I gotten real high off tequila. And tried to eat up all the Mexican food I could find. Haw haw haw.

Denver . . . (December 2). Mixed dance, and how.

Tulsa . . . (December 4). All colored dance. . . . We are leaving at ten o'clock in the morning for Tampa. That is over thirteen hundred miles. Goodness, have to be real troupers to get with those long jumps. . . . But it's great fun, b'lieve that.

Armstrong loved his men, but privately even he had begun to see that something needed to be done. "They were a nice bunch of cats," he remembered, "and I didn't want to see them all out of work. But the trend was changing."

As the popularity of the big bands waned, and the new music of Charlie Parker and Dizzy Gillespie spread, interest in early jazz flourished as well. In New York, Eddie Condon and his hard-drinking cohorts continued to play and record their updated version of the music they'd first played in the twenties. On the West Coast, a band led by trumpet player Lu Watters and featuring trombonist Turk Murphy reached still further back into jazz history: they were big band veterans, but their models were the earliest New Orleans bands, and they played tunes no newer than Jelly Roll Morton's. Condon dismissed them as "archaeologists." The drummer Dave Tough, who, like Condon, had first played jazz in the Midwest in the early twenties but had moved on to the big bands, was now dismissive of both his old friends and the much younger West Coast purists. "Dixieland jazz was once revolutionary stuff," he said. "But now it's just a straight Republican-ticket kind of music. . . . All it is is a bad copy of

the music white Chicago musicians played, who were in turn doing bad imitations of the music they had heard from the musicians who came from New Orleans." Nonetheless, the so-called Dixieland Revival would retain a sizable following over the years, both in America and abroad.

For those who believed that jazz had steadily deteriorated since its earliest days, a savior had seemed to appear in the early 1940s. Even better, he had emerged from the cradle of jazz itself. Bunk Johnson had been a well-respected New Orleans cornetist in the early years of the century. Sidney Bechet had played with him in the Eagle Band. But after a 1931 brawl in which a friend was stabbed to death on the bandstand next to him and Johnson's teeth were badly damaged, he had abandoned his horn and become a day laborer in the rice fields, sometimes supplementing his income by whistling at local carnivals.

Two young jazz enthusiasts—Fred Ramsey Jr. and Charles Edward Smith, then at work on a history to be called *Jazzmen*—tracked Johnson down, had him fitted with

Bunk Johnson, photographed at home in New Iberia, Louisiana, just before he was brought north to restart his career

dentures by Sidney Bechet's dentist brother Leonard, and, with help from Louis Armstrong, bought him a trumpet. He was recorded twice in New Orleans, playing with a band of veterans that included the clarinetist George Lewis, and was eventually brought north to play what his admirers were sure would be "authentic jazz," unsullied by commerce or what they believed to be the pernicious influence of schooled musicians.

Things did not work out quite as they had hoped. Johnson turned out to be a teller of tall tales. He claimed to be ten years older than he was, and said he had been Louis Armstrong's teacher. Armstrong was characteristically generous about him, telling one interviewer that in the old days Johnson had had "a better tone than anyone" in New Orleans. (He waited until after Johnson died to say that Johnson hadn't actually *taught* anybody anything. "Bunk never had time for us kids, always [going] to and from the Eagle Saloon, where he drank a whole lot of port wine. You could *smell* it coming out of that horn.") Johnson's long layoff turned out to have impaired his playing some, but it had not altered his old habits. In 1945, he played in Boston as part of a group led by his old friend Sidney Bechet, also now benefiting from the resurgence of interest in New Orleans music. It did not go well. Johnson drank—and complained—continuously. The tempos were too fast, he said; he hadn't come all the way from Louisiana just to play what he called "racehorse Dixieland." Bechet was too loud and he took too many bows. And Johnson even made it known that he was weary of playing the old songs. He preferred popular tunes of the day, he said—and he wanted to play them with schooled swing musicians. It wasn't what the revivalists had had in mind; Bunk Johnson did not fit their stereotype. Bechet let him go. Johnson made more recordings, but the high life took a heavy toll, and his lip began to bother him. He turned up two and a half hours late for a Chicago concert and then could barely

Pops Foster, Bunk Johnson, and Sidney Bechet during their turbulent Boston sojourn, 1945. "People, they was paying to hear certain things," Bechet recalled, "and hell, we had to give it to them. But whatever it was we were playing . . . it wasn't nothing to what it could have been."

play. "The picture of the old trumpet player was a pitiful and tragic one," wrote one critic. "For those who were there . . . the name Bunk Johnson lost its magic and its meaning." Johnson eventually went home to Louisiana.

Bunk Johnson's second career did not last long, but in 1946 Hollywood tried to cash

in on the renewed interest in early jazz he had helped to spark with a dreadful film called *New Orleans*. Advertised as "the Low-down on Wicked Old Basin Street! . . . and the Music That Made It Wicked!" it was actually a standard movie love story with jazz only as background music. Billie Holiday was in it—playing a maid. So was Louis Armstrong, who found himself performing

onscreen with a small group of old friends from New Orleans, again playing the kind of music with which he'd grown up. The film did provide him with a hit, "Do You Know What It Means to Miss New Orleans?" whose popularity suggested to two of his friends—a jazz-loving publicist named Ernie Anderson and the cornetist Bobby Hackett—that their hero might insure his

The 1947 Town Hall concert that changed the course of Louis Armstrong's career. Left to right, Jack Teagarden, Dick Carey, Armstrong, Bobby Hackett, Peanuts Hucko, Bob Haggart, and Sid Catlett. "Ain't a trumpet player that don't play a little something I used to play," Armstrong told one interviewer. "That's all right. Makes me feel good."

future by reminding the public of his past. They managed to persuade Joe Glaser to let Armstrong play a concert with a small group rather than his big band.

On the evening of May 17, 1947—a little over a month after Jackie Robinson took the field for the first time as a member of the Brooklyn Dodgers—Armstrong appeared at New York's Town Hall with a small, integrated group of his own that included Hackett and the drummer Sid Catlett. Jack Teagarden played trombone. "I've been waiting about twenty years for this," he said from the stage. "I'm really in heaven tonight." The Town Hall concert sold out, critics loved it, and on the strength of its success, Armstrong formed the first version of his All Stars. It included Catlett, Barney Bigard, the pianist Dick Cary, bassist Arvell Shaw, and Teagarden. When Armstrong warned Teagarden that he might encounter trouble on the road because he

was white and traveling with black musicians, his old friend is supposed to have reassured him: "You're a spade, and I'm an ofay. We got the same soul. Let's blow."

Louis Armstrong and his All Stars opened on August 10, 1947, at Billy Berg's Hollywood club, where Charlie Parker and Dizzy Gillespie had made their troubled debut two years earlier. Again, they were a hit. The personnel would shift over the next twenty-four years. Earl Hines would be part of the ensemble for a time. So would pianist Billy Kyle, the Louisiana-born clarinetist Edmond Hall, and the trombonist Trummy Young, who abandoned modernism to spend twelve years with Armstrong because, he said, he was "the greatest teacher you can find."

The reductive categorization that would eventually divide the jazz community into warring camps was already well under way by 1947. Bands were expected to play

either Dixieland or bebop or swing. But Louis Armstrong, like Duke Ellington, remained "beyond category." The instrumentation of his All Stars mirrored the New Orleans ensembles of his youth, but the rhythm was based on the kind of 4/4 swing he had brought to Fletcher Henderson's orchestra almost a quarter of a century earlier. And while he invariably opened with "Indiana" and closed with his theme song, "Sleepy-Time Down South," the tunes he and his men played in between ranged from what Armstrong called "the good old good ones" to brand-new hits, which in the coming years would include everything from "Ç'est Si Bon" and "La Vie en Rose" to "Blueberry Hill" and Kurt Weill's "Mack the Knife." "We've got to keep it rolling," he liked to say, and his carefully crafted appearances included a good deal of genial hokum: stage jokes, set routines, eye-rolling, and toothy grins—all part of the total entertainment package that had always been Louis Armstrong. He had long since abandoned the high-note acrobatics that he now admitted had primarily been meant to cow "the musicians in the house," preferring instead to follow the counsel of his mentor, King Oliver: "High notes is all right. You hit 'em and they sound like some-thing. But the notes in the staff is more valuable." But his ability to imbue every note he sang or played with joy and life remained undiminished, and he took understandable pride in the All Stars' impact on audiences no matter where they appeared. "These same people may go around the corner and lynch a Negro," he wrote to a friend. "But while they're lis-tening to our music, they don't think about trouble. What's more, they're watching Negro and white musicians play side by side. And we bring contentment and plea-sure. I always say, 'Look at the nice taste we leave.' It's bound to mean something. That's what music is for."

Louis Armstrong and Billie Holiday during the filming of *New Orleans*, 1946. The man at the far left in the straw hat is bassist Red Callendar; Charlie Bear plays piano; Kid Ory sits at center with his trombone on his lap; the guitarist is Bud Scott; and the bald man at the right is Barney Bigard.

THE EMBODIMENT OF THE AMERICAN EXPERIENCE
An Interview with Albert Murray

The essayist, novelist, and teacher Albert Murray has been listening to and thinking about America's music since his boyhood in Alabama, where he was born in 1916. Educated at the Tuskegee Institute (where he later taught English), he is a retired major in the U.S. Air Force and the author of nine books—three volumes of essays and three novels as well as Good Morning Blues: The Autobiography of Count Basie *(as told to Albert Murray) and* Stomping the Blues, *a seminal work in the history of jazz, which he prefers to call "blues music." Coproducer Lynn Novick interviewed Albert Murray twice for the* Jazz *film project. The following was gleaned from those conversations.*

What is jazz?

Jazz is a music played by Americans to get rid of the blues. Once you had a group of people here who defined themselves as Americans, there was going to be an American culture. And the musical synthesis of all of the imported sounds plus the indigenous sounds added up to jazz. This synthesis, ironically, was made possible by the people who came here as captives from Africa. They were slaves but they were also the freest people in America when it came to absorbing all the different elements that were brought over by people from other cultures.

They didn't bring over the music as such but they brought over an emphasis on percussive musical statement because they were dance-beat oriented. Everything they heard they turned into a dance beat. It was as if every instrument became a drum. They were wide open to all the influences that were here—Gregorian chant, Christmas carols, Scotch highlanders' songs, German music, Italian, march music—and they heard it all as *American* music. Everything they made was an American synthesis, a music truly indigenous to American experience. What came out of that was the extension, elaboration, and refinement of a truly vernacular or native culture from a folk level through a pop level to a fine art.

Now, a work of art is a statement which encapsulates the artist's basic attitude toward experience. So if the definitive nature of American culture has to do with freedom, then, if you stylize American attitudes, it would be a stylization of freedom. Nothing embodies that with greater comprehensiveness and wider appeal, or greater profundity and more precision, than jazz.

What's your first memory of the music?

Blues music is so much a part of my experience, it's impossible to know when I first heard it. It was as if I was born knowing the blues. One image which comes to me is hearing the blues from somebody's Victrola in an adjoining neighborhood, hearing Ma Rainey and Bessie Smith. I knew these were living people. Then there was a guitar player who used to come up out of the railroad bottoms around twilight. Mr. Chaucer—of course people in our neighborhood used to say "there comes old Mr. Choicy"—he'd come strolling up the street by our house and he would be warming up his guitar on the way to some juke joint. I didn't live very far from a place called Soda Waters and there were various honky-tonks down the street in this sawmill and railroad section on the outskirts of Mobile.

When you realize that blues music was basically juke joint music or good-time music, you are right at the core of what the music is about. Now, any church member in the neighborhood that I grew up in would hear sermons against it on Sunday mornings. So a honky-tonk was a sinful ritual. That's why people speak of the Sunday-morning service and the Saturday-night function. The Saturday-night function was for having a good time, but what was so mature about it was that you were having a good time by acknowledging the actualities of life and the contingencies of love. The lyrics were about negative experiences but the whole ambiance of a juke joint was downright aphrodisiac—and that's the opposite of despair.

But it was always secular music, and the communities that I grew up in were as religious as they were secular, so there was a sort of division. The Sunday-morning service had to do with getting down on your knees to propitiate God and to profess your unworthiness and to prepare for life beyond this vale of tears, life in the world to come. Whereas blues music was concerned with coming to terms with the everyday problems of life and creating a basis of continuity.

When did you first hear music you'd call jazz?

As I grew up, I became more interested in instrumental music. There were bands connected with dance hall dances and Mardi Gras. There were local bands, bands from New Orleans, and bands for baseball games. By the 1930s, we began to get jazz not only on records but on the radio. The records that dominated everybody's thinking were the records of Louis Armstrong. We knew those records note for note, everybody's part on every record, all the solos, all the jive talk. By high school, we were listening to the great bands—Fletcher Henderson, Duke Ellington, Jimmie Lunceford, and Earl Hines.

Not only did we hear the music all the time on records, but the bands were very real to us. The great bands were also road bands and so you got a chance to see these people. Cootie Williams was in Ellington's band and he was from Mobile. And Louis Armstrong was little old fat Louis from down in New Orleans and people knew him. It went together with the touring baseball teams. You would see at some rooming house that there would be a bus out front and you knew it was either a baseball team or a band.

What was the impact of seeing and hearing those great musicians?

Even the guitar players and local honky-tonk players represented style, elegance, sophistication. And when the big bands came along, as Count Basie used to say, "None of that ring-around-the collar stuff." Those men always had to be sharp. They were style setters.

What about Duke Ellington?

Duke Ellington's music represented the musical equivalent of the American spirit of affirmation in the face of adversity. It was constantly creative, it generated resilience that made an experimental attitude possible, and he did it all by dealing with the idiomatic elements that he knew most about—the blues and popular songs. The synthesis that Ellington made was American, the interaction of the learned tradition and the vernacular tradition that adds up to an American form, that qualifies as fine art. That's what Louis Armstrong represented, too. Ellington represented a richer orchestration, but the basis was already laid by Armstrong. Ellington was Armstrong multiplied by fifteen. He could use more instruments to say it than Armstrong could, but the implications were there.

What did Count Basie mean when he said "Nothing's too fast or too slow to swing."

Nothing is too fast to swing, too big or too small to be elegant. Swinging is the elegant response to chaos. In this music, you know its aesthetic if it's swinging. If you can make the mood specific enough, what could be more practical? It's more practical than a checkbook.

The Basie repertory became part of the ambiance of my college years. When I graduated, the tempo, the beat, the pulse of the United States that I wanted to be able to cope with was "Doggin' Around." Can you solo on "Doggin' Around?" Can you reach the state of resilience, the state of flexibility, the position that will enable you to be as stylish as that music made you feel?

You have a special love for Lester Young.

Lester is the embodiment of the blues idiom as I define it. There is an element of melancholy but it's overcome by elegance. He's laid back, at the same time here's a guy who has been hurt. Like a combat veteran, he's got a sporty limp walk because he's been through something, and with those trumpets shouting all around, at all sides, he's got that parade-ground strut of a guy who's been wounded. I grew up in that context. If you are going to be a football player, one of the badges of honor is to come limping into the dining room. People know that you had to pay a price for that. Lester Young's music makes me feel that he's paid the price but he's more elegant as a result. That I take as a human triumph of ultimate proportions.

What about Charlie Parker?
To appreciate Parker it's absolutely essential to remember that he's a Kansas City musician, therefore he's a blues musician. The journalistic approach to music became very abstract in his time, and they started talking about flatted fifths and diminished ninths and then lost track. But just get into a dance hall or into a jam session and start that stuff out and see where it goes and then you get it. Parker's music was based on the simplicity, the stripped-down efficiency that had come from Count Basie. So a very pragmatic way of approaching Charlie Parker is to realize that if you took the straight melody and then listened to Basie play it, it's as if he was subtracting. Then you get to Charlie Parker, and it's as if you had a rococo multiplication on the subtraction. What is getting to you is the emotional impact of blues music hitting you with a new form of elegance.

Talk a little about jazz criticism.
Historically, jazz has been appropriated by various political groups for their own purposes and, unfortunately, much jazz criticism at the beginning had less to do with the music than with what critics were interested in. They were enthusiastic about it but condescending, too. Very few editors seemed to see it as something that required first-rate minds. When they thought of brown-skinned Americans, they wrote about problems and victims, protest and suffering, and although they themselves would have a good time listening to it, the one thing they didn't notice was that the people playing it and in the venues where it was played, got dressed up and were out to have a good time; not to be confused with the awkward abandon of over-enthusiastic visitors out to take off their shoes, undo their hair, and let everything hang out.

American criticism of the arts in the twentieth century has been very much caught up in the idea of avant-gardism and has to do with embracing innovation, the pursuit of something new, something rebellious. But an avant-garde is a military metaphor. It has to do with the advance party, the shock troops, the expendable troops that establish the beachhead in order to bring up the main body. They very seldom get on the beach and of the few that do, maybe half are sent back to the veteran's hospital wounded. Or they retire, shell-shocked, or maybe they're just dead. And when the main body comes up and starts dating the girls, what's left of the avant-garde is

Saturday-night function. Itinerant farm workers shed the blues in a tent near Bridgeton, New Jersey, 1942.

back stateside. American art critics act as if a whole career could be built on that, but an avant-garde not followed by the main body is a lost legion.

Art has to do with security against chaos. What we want are durable forms, things that endure, that go beyond a local situation, a given time, a given circumstance, an approach which addresses itself to humanity, to the whole human proposition. To me there's nothing more boring than the pursuit of novelty.

Ornette Coleman comes up and says, "This is free jazz." But what is freer than jazz? As soon as you *say* jazz, you are talking about freedom of improvisation. The whole thing is about freedom, about American freedom. So why would anybody want to free it from its forms? The whole idea of art is to create a form that is a bulwark against entropy or chaos. Jazz is not meant to be formless and absolutely self-indulgent. That's like embracing the waves in the sea. You cannot embrace entropy. You cannot embrace chaos.

That is where we have come in American jazz criticism. People are praised for being innovative but not for [having] a profound impact. It's simply, "This is new, you should get with it." But true artists are not taken in by that because any really serious artist knows that the creative act itself involves avant-gardism—meaning, to make

that which is out there your own. Giving your own take on it. So each new, creative achievement is, in effect, avant-garde, because if it's powerful enough other people will identify with it. If you make other people want to take something from what you have established, well, that is the *true* avant-garde.

What is it about jazz, after nearly eighty-five years of hearing it, that gives you the most pleasure?
Jazz is the embodiment of the American experience, the American spirit, the American ideal. That's why it means so much to me as a writer to experience people responding to it. They want to move, they want to do something in a certain way, and the best jazz always moves in the direction of elegance, which is the most civilized thing a human being can do. The height of human development is elegance, the ultimate extension, elaboration, and refinement of effort where just *doing* it gives pleasure of itself. That's about as far as we get with life. It's what Ernest Hemingway called the sweat on a wine bottle. If you don't enjoy how those beads of sweat look when you pour the wine out and you taste it and how your partner looks and how the sunlight comes through, well you missed it!

SHOWING YOUR ASS

Most critics remained wary of the new music Charlie Parker and Dizzy Gillespie were making, and the strict traditionalists among them, who had already pronounced swing inauthentic, found bebop still harder to swallow. The *Jazz Record* charged Gillespie with seeking to "pervert or suppress or emasculate jazz." Outnumbered, the youthful champions of modernism, in turn, denounced the opposition as "Moldy Figs." The argument was conducted mostly on the periphery of the music. Ben Webster and Don Byas and other giants of the swing era sought out beboppers with whom to play. Coleman Hawkins recorded with Gillespie and Parker, worked with Howard McGhee, and included Thelonious Monk in one of his groups even when club owners wanted him replaced. Bebop, Hawkins said many years later, was what musicians "*should* have been playing when I came back [to America] in '39."

But there were musicians to whom bebop really did seem little more than noise. When McGhee shared a bill with Kid Ory in Los Angeles, Ory stormed out after one set, saying, "I *will* not play with this kind of music." "We don't flat our fifths," said Eddie Condon, "we drink 'em." Tommy Dorsey denounced Parker and Gillespie as "musical Communists." "Of all the cruelties in the world," said Fletcher Henderson, "bebop is the most phenomenal."

The embattled boppers gave as good as they got. Gil Fuller, who had arranged for Gillespie's big band, said comparing what had gone before with the music he and his

The Dizzy Gillespie All-Stars play New York's Town Hall, May 16, 1945. Gillespie listens as Charlie Parker solos. Harold "Doc" West is on drums. Slam Stewart plays bass. Al Haig (not visible here) played piano that evening and Curley Russell, not Stewart, was on the bass for most of the concert.

associates produced was like equating a "horse and buggy with a jet plane." Gillespie himself once likened earlier jazz to "Mother Goose rhymes. It was all right for its time, but it was a childish time." And the "progressive" bandleader Stan Kenton charged that the trouble with Armstrong and the other members of his generation was that they played without what he called "science."

No one was more offended by remarks like that than Armstrong himself. "These young cats now," he said, "they want to carve everyone because they're full of malice, and all they want to do is show you up, and any way will do as long as it's different from the way you played it before. So you get all them weird chords which don't mean nothing, and first people get curious about it just because it's new, but soon they get tired of it because . . . you got no melody to remember and no beat to dance to. . . . They'll come back to us when all the shouting about bop and science is over, because they can't make up their own tunes, and all they can do is embroider it so much you can't see the design no more. . . . So they're all poor again and nobody is working, and that's what modern malice done for you."

Dizzy Gillespie wanted to bring his audiences what Louis Armstrong called "contentment and pleasure," too. He had helped create the modernist music he called bebop in part to protest against the imperative to entertain with which black musicians had always had to contend. But he had now also encountered audiences that were not just indifferent but openly hostile to it. "Sea to sea," he wrote later, "America in 1945 was as backward a country musically as it was racially. Those of us who tried to push it forward had to suffer." For all his earnestness about his music, he was himself a born entertainer as well as a consummate musician, a product of the swing era who had never lost his love for the power and dynamic range of big bands and who saw no inherent contradiction between demanding

music and a good time being had by all. And he was, as Stan Levey said, "voracious in his drive to succeed."

As soon as Gillespie got back to the East Coast, he began, with help from Billy Shaw of the William Morris Agency, to build himself a new orchestra. "We wanted it to sound like what Dizzy and Bird were doing," said Gil Fuller, "but . . . translated into a big band sound." With arrangements by Fuller, Tadd Dameron, George Russell, John Lewis, and Gillespie himself and tunes like "Ow!" "Oop Bop Sh'bam," "One Bass Hit," and "Things to Come," they succeeded in doing precisely that. Over the next few years, the Dizzy Gillespie band would include an extraordinary number of young musicians who would go on to make names for themselves: Ray Brown, Kenny Clarke, John Coltrane, Kenny Dorham, Paul Gonsalves, Jimmy Heath, Milt Jackson, Yusef Lateef, James Moody, Cecil Payne, and Sonny Stitt.

Few bands in history have matched Gillespie's for sheer excitement. "The power, the rhythm, the harmonies," Kenny Clarke remembered, "were something I'd never heard before. You can't imagine what it was like to play in it." "From the first note to the last note," Milt Jackson agreed, "you could hear that happiness, that togetherness, you can hear it all in that music." The reeds tore through long, intricate lines without so much as a hint of vibrato. "The brass had high notes and lots of 'em," Ray Brown remembered. "Just screaming figures. . . . And after about half an hour of that, you'd look over at the trumpet section, and everybody's lip is hanging down, looking like ground meat." To give the brass section a chance to recover, Jackson and the rhythm section would take over for fifteen minutes or so in mid-performance. (This quartet would later form the first incarnation of the longest-lived combo in jazz history, the Modern Jazz Quartet.)

Gillespie also incorporated something new into the music for his band. Ever since the days when he had played alongside the

Chano Pozo

Cuban-born Mario Bauzá in Cab Calloway's trumpet section, Gillespie had wanted to find a way to bring back into jazz the contagious but complex rhythms of the Caribbean that Jelly Roll Morton had insisted were essential to the music as "seasoning." But Gillespie had something more than spice in mind. He wanted literally to combine the two forms, playing jazz on top of authentic—and authentically complicated—Afro-Cuban polyrhythms. To do it, he needed someone steeped in those rhythms. In 1947, Bauzá told Gillespie of an extraordinary conga player recently arrived from Cuba named Chano Pozo. Pozo spoke virtually no English. "Dizzy no peaky pani," Gillespie claimed he liked to say, "I no peaky engly, but boff peak African." And Pozo was a rough customer—a brawler who carried a bullet lodged too near his spine to be removed, he would soon be murdered by a cocaine dealer with whom he quarreled. But with his help Gillespie produced a series of so-called Cubop recordings that caught on all across the country. The best-known were "Cubana Be–Cubana Bop" and "Manteca" (Spanish for "greasy"), which Gillespie, Pozo, and George Russell put together in December 1947. Both included impassioned drumming, African-style chanting, and trumpet solos by Gillespie based not on chords but on basic scales called modes—an innovation first heard in Duke Ellington's "Tattooed Bride" and that would not be encountered again in jazz for more than a decade.

The impact of these records, Gillespie wrote, "was similar to a nuclear weapon when it burst on the scene. There'd never been a marriage of Cuban music and American music like that before." "Manteca" would remain Gillespie's theme song all his life. Its success helped inspire other bandleaders like Stan Kenton to add Cuban-tinged arrangements to their books, and sent Gillespie and his orchestra on a tour of Scandinavia, Belgium, and France. Everywhere he went in Europe, Gillespie was hailed as a hero. When he borrowed a battered horn to play a Paris concert, young French musicians began distressing their instruments. "They thought they'd get my sound if their horns were beat-up," he said, shaking his head in wonder and delight. "Bebop, the most recent evolution in the history of jazz, has conquered Paris," wrote the poet Boris Vian. "Thanks to Dizzy Gillespie."

Duke Ellington believed that the impact of his own work had been lessened by its having been categorized as "jazz," and he warned Gillespie not to let his music be limited by anyone else's label. But in his eagerness to win a big following and keep his band together, the younger man paid no attention. "If you've got enough money to play for yourself," he said, "you can play anything you want to. But if you want to make a living at music, you've got to sell it." Nobody ever worked harder to sell his music than Gillespie did. He was a dervish onstage, hurtling through breakneck solos

Dizzy Gillespie and his big band at the Orpheum Theater in Los Angeles, 1949. Despite the orchestra's early success, Gillespie wrote, "we were stuck with the old bebop dilemma, whether jazz is primarily a music for dancing or listening."

Bebop as big business. (Above) The opening spread of the 1948 *Life* feature that made Dizzy Gillespie a celebrity—and helped turn his music into a fad; and (below) a Los Angeles appearance at which worshipful dress-alike fans surround their hero

in the highest register, then jitterbugging, singing, swapping jokes with comedians, wearing funny hats. "Comedy is important," he explained many years later. "As a performer, when you're trying to establish audience control, the best thing is to make them laugh if you can. . . . When you get people relaxed, they're more receptive to what you're trying to get them to do. Sometimes, when you're laying on something over their heads, they'll go along with it if they're relaxed." Gillespie did so much to make them laugh during one concert at Carnegie Hall that Louis Armstrong came backstage afterward to tell him he was overdoing it. "You're cutting the fool up there, boy. Showing your ass."

For better or worse, Gillespie allowed himself to become the public face of bebop. The Morris agency billed him as "The Mad Genius of Music" and encouraged the press to write colorful stories about his dark-rimmed glasses and goatee, his berets, the leopard-skin jackets he sometimes wore onstage, the cheeks that puffed alarmingly when he played, and, later, the distinctive upthrust bell of his trumpet, which he said helped him hear himself better—everything except his music. When *Life* planned a big picture story on the new music for the autumn of 1948, Gillespie proved all too willing to play along and even helped persuade the uniformly dignified Benny Carter to cooperate for the camera.

> They made us perform a bebop greeting for them. "Hi-ya, man!" "Bells, man where you been?" Giving the sign of the flatted fifth, a raised open hand.
>
> "Eel-ya-da!" We gave a handshake sign that we were playing triplets, ending with an elaborate handshake. That was supposed to be the bebopper's greeting, but there was no such thing in real life. It was just a bunch of horseplay we went through so they could pretend we were something weird.

Gillespie even pretended to be a convert to Islam, posing in his bedroom with his head bowed toward Mecca because a small but growing number of his contemporaries had become Muslims. He understood the impulse that had made some young black musicians turn eastward—"They've been hurt," he told one writer, with tears in his eyes—and he later bitterly regretted having participated in what he called "blasphemy."

But by 1948, Gillespie's salesmanship seemed to be working. "Dizzy's male fans," wrote *New Yorker* writer Richard Boyer,

> most of whom are in their late teens or early twenties, express their adoration for Gillespie by imitating him. They try to walk with his peculiar loose-jointed, bow-legged floppiness; try to force their laughter up into a soprano squeak; wear blue berets and shell-rimmed spectacles, as he does; smoke meerschaum pipes as he does; and assiduously cultivate on their own lower lips replicas of the tuft of hair that Dizzy wears on his. . . . He knows that his slightest mannerism of action or dress may be reproduced on an international scale. . . . In St. Louis he was photographed with the bottom buttons of his uniform, by chance, unfastened. After the picture appeared in a jazz music magazine, beboppers . . . began leaving their shirts partly unbuttoned.

At one New York club where the Gillespie band played, the owner did a brisk business selling paste-on goatees to female admirers—and to male fans still too young to grow their own.

Like swing music a decade earlier, bebop seemed to be becoming a saleable commodity. "That's right, man!" said a newspaper advertisement for a Chicago tailor, "Bop King Dizzy Gillespie and his great band are another addition to the steadily growing number of top musicians who have made the switch to FOX BROS. for the greatest uniforms and accessories. You dig?" New York's Swing Street had deteriorated steadily since the war—most jazz clubs had been turned into strip joints and Chinese restaurants—but new nightspots, catering primarily to bop fans, now began to open up nearby on Broadway: the Royal Roost, Bop City, the Clique.

The leaders of other big bands, looking for a way to survive in a world increasingly dominated by crooners, thought they saw salvation in Gillespie-style music as well. Woody Herman formed a new band of eager young musicians—his so-called Second Herd—with what he called "the bebop revolution" at its core. Its most memorable recording was Jimmy Giuffre's blistering "Four Brothers," featuring one of the ablest reed sections in jazz history: Stan Getz, Zoot Sims, and Herbie Steward on tenor and Serge Chaloff on baritone. "In the Herman band," bassist Chubby Jackson remembered, "the Marines were coming."

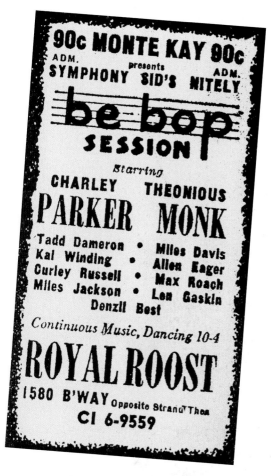

Advertisement (above) for a jam session organized by the jazz disc jockey Symphony Sid Torin; and (below) the marquee of the short-lived Bop City, on Broadway

Ella Fitzgerald enthralls a Manhattan audience that
includes Duke Ellington and Benny Goodman, 1948.

Benny Goodman, too, launched a new bop-tinged band that year. It featured Wardell Gray on tenor saxophone, and arrangements by Chico O'Farrill. Bebop "certainly deserves to be encouraged," Goodman said. "They're doing something different, not copying." He especially liked Gillespie and Parker. But "it's nervous music more than exciting music. If some of [the boppers] would just try to simplify their arrangements and solos, they'd come off much better. It seems that they're all trying to outdo and outstartle each other." Still, he said, "I think something good will come out of all of this."

TRYING TO PLAY CLEAN

When Charlie Parker returned to music after his long stay at Camarillo, he was not pleased by the kind of attention Dizzy Gillespie had been getting—or by the eagerness with which Gillespie had seemed to seek it. Parker had brought bebop with him from Kansas City in 1942, he assured one interviewer, implying that no one else had had a hand in its creation. Gillespie's big band was a bad idea, he told another, because it was forcing his old partner to stagnate: "He isn't repeating notes yet, but he is repeating patterns." Parker was still more unhappy with the cultish aura that now surrounded the music. "Some guys said, 'Here's bop.' Wham!" he told another interviewer, shaking his head sadly. "They said, 'Here's something we can make money on.' Wham! 'Here's a comedian.' Wham! 'Here's a guy who talks funny talk.' " The word "bebop" bothered him, precisely as "jazz" had bothered Duke Ellington. "It's just *music*," he said. "It's trying to play clean and looking for the pretty notes."

Parker formed what came to be called his classic quintet, with Max Roach on drums, Tommy Potter on bass, Duke Jordan on piano, and a still-youthful Miles Davis on trumpet. (Later, Davis would be replaced by Kenny Dorham, Al Haig would substitute for Jordan, and Roy Haynes would replace Roach.) Parker played with more assurance and clarity than ever, but he remained perpetually unsatisfied. He was also embarrassed by the acolytes who followed him from bandstand to bandstand, carrying disc recorders, which they turned on whenever he stepped forward to solo and clicked off again the moment he had finished. When someone asked him which three of his records a collector should buy first, Parker told him to save his money.

Meanwhile, young admirers continued to hang on his every note. "When Charlie Parker came on the scene," said Sweets Edison, "he made such an impression on the musicians that if he would play a melody wrong, and if you told one of his disciples that melody was wrong, you might get knocked out."

When the alto saxophonist Art Pepper was introduced by a friend to a recording by Parker, Pepper was as thrilled and thunderstruck as Max Kaminsky had been upon first hearing Louis Armstrong's "West End Blues." "I just got deathly sick," said Pepper. "I couldn't stand any more, and [my friend] was going to play something else [by Parker], and I said, 'No, no, I can't stand it. I can't listen to any more.' "

No one was more eager to follow Parker's lead than a Harlem high school boy and would-be saxophonist named Jackie McLean. He first idolized Lester Young, even bought himself headgear that looked something like Young's trademark porkpie hat. Then he heard Charlie Parker. "As a very young musician," he recalled,

that's how I wanted to play, exactly. I didn't care if someone said I sounded like him. That's what I wanted to do. And that was all I dreamt of doing. I didn't want to be original; I wanted to play like Charlie Parker. This week that he was playing at the Apollo was

perfect for me and the only way I could get to see him would be not to go to school. So, a few of my friends and I would leave home in the morning, and go down in the subway, but instead of going to the Bronx to our school, we would go down to 125th Street and put our books in one of those lockers in the subway and go get in front of the theater and there would be nobody there 'cause it would be so early in the morning like nine, nine-fifteen, something like that. . . . We would sit and watch the movie and then we would wait until it was time for the stage show and then the curtain would come back and there he'd be. And of course, we heard all of this great music that we had heard on these recordings and we would enjoy that show and then we'd get up when the movie came on and dash, sneak out of an exit on the side, so we could see Bird when he came out to get a breath of air and he would just say, "How you guys doing? Aren't you supposed to be in school today?" We'd

The youthful Jackie McLean

say, "Yeah, Bird, but, but like, we came down here to see you."

McLean persisted, playing Parker's records over and over again and following him all over the city, trying to stay as close as he could to the great man. One day, it paid off:

I came home from school and my mother said to me, "You're not going to believe this but I got a phone call from Charlie Parker today." And I said, "What?" I was very excited. "Well, what did he say?" She said, "Well, he wants you to come down to this place called Chateau Gardens tonight and wear a blue suit, shirt and tie, and play for him until he gets there." Man, I immediately went in the room, began to practice to get ready for this big night for me. When the curtain went back, the people were very disappointed, I might add. I began to play through the tunes that I knew like "Confirmation" and "Now's the Time" and "A Night in Tunisia" and "Don't Blame Me" and the things that Bird played. Then, I looked and saw this crowd surge to the back and I saw Bird come in. I saw a saxophone case up in the air. The people were so close around him that he was holding his saxophone case over his head. And then they followed him all the way to the stage. He took out his horn and walked out there and he said, "Play one with me," and we did one together, and then he told me to go sit down.

FROM THE HEART

In February 1949, Louis Armstrong was back home in New Orleans at Mardi Gras. The Zulu Social Aid and Pleasure Club had invited him to reign as its king in the annual parade, and he had eagerly accepted. It was the fulfillment of a "lifelong dream," he said, the most vivid possible evidence of

Charlie Parker and the rhythm section of a 1949 all-star band chosen by the readers of *Metronome:* left to right, guitarist Billy Bauer, bassist Eddie Safranski, Parker, and pianist Lennie Tristano

the love and respect the men and women among whom he'd grown up in the streets of black Storyville still held for him. He spent all day and half the night on the mule-drawn Zulu float, drinking champagne, greeting old friends, and hurling some two thousand specially painted coconuts to the crowds that lined the narrow streets. When a fistfight broke out between a by-stander and the "mayor" of Zululand, he just smiled. "My, my, just like old times," he said. The All Stars rode with him and, Arvell Shaw remembered, "people from all over the world—his fans—had come to see him. I've never seen anything this beauti-ful in my life."

The Zulu float remained what it had always been, a gaudy parody of the whites who ran both the city and the rest of the festivities. But to young African-Americans, especially those living elsewhere in the country with no knowledge of the event's complex dou-ble meanings, the sight of Louis Armstrong in blackface, wearing black tights, crimson feathers, and a cellophane grass skirt, seemed bizarre, a degrading throwback to minstrel times. Dizzy Gillespie, for one, saw it that way. "Louis," he told a reporter, "is the plantation character that so many of us . . . younger men . . . resent." Even some old friends seemed hard put to defend him. "I love Pops," Billie Holiday said. "He Toms from the heart." That anyone could dare suggest that Armstrong was Tomming because "he didn't act 'dignified' enough" enraged Max Kaminsky. "Dignity was their new password, their god, while many were carrying on in ways that had nothing to do with dignity."

Armstrong still delighted white fans—the news that he was to reign as King of the Zulus had helped put him on the cover of *Time* wearing a crown, the first jazz musi-cian ever to appear there—but the black crowds that had once packed every place he played had begun to drift away. He saw it as desertion. He had pulled himself out

(Above) Louis Armstrong, center, as King of the Zulus during the 1949 Mardi Gras parade in New Orleans; and (below) a collage he created later to commemorate his reign. It includes a roster of all his predecessors as king as well as his lifetime membership card in the Zulu Social Aid and Pleasure Club.

of poverty as great as that encountered by anyone of any color in America, and he had done so without ever putting on airs. He was who he was—"always the same man, offstage or on," according to Barney Bigard —and to have his own people criticize him for remaining true to his New Orleans upbringing seemed hard.

He was especially bitter about one appearance in Dallas where his capacity crowd had been almost entirely white, while just down the street Louis Jordan— "one of them zoot-suit saxophone players playing all that jungle joogie," Armstrong called him privately—had packed another theater with young black fans. When Armstrong said he wanted to play Harlem's Apollo, where he had once been a top attraction, Joe Glaser told him not to bother; it was just another small theater, he said, no longer worth his while. Armstrong had insisted: "Those are my people." But when he finally opened, "he didn't fill the theater," one of his wife's close friends remembered. "And Lucille told me he cried many nights up there, that hurt him so."

Louis Armstrong was now one of the best-known Americans in the world and certainly the best-known African-American, yet the people he had always considered his own were turning their backs on him. It was a wound that would never fully close.

DRASTIC STUFF

In May 1949, a delegation of American musicians landed in Paris for one of the first international jazz festivals ever held anywhere. Sidney Bechet was the best known to French fans, but Charlie Parker had been invited as well. There continued to be dark murmurings in the jazz press that traditional and bebop musicians were mortal enemies. Bechet had told an interviewer that bebop was already "as dead as Abraham Lincoln," and he and Parker had only recently been pitted against each other in a broadcast "Battle of Music," advertised as a "showdown" by its organizer, the writer Rudi Blesh. In fact, they got along fine, once Bechet figured out how to open the dressing-room window to let out Parker's marijuana smoke. Not given to compliments, he nevertheless told Parker how much he admired "those phrases you make," and in the jam session that ended the final day of the festival these two masters—the white-haired New Orleans pioneer and the twenty-nine-year-old architect of bebop—found instant common ground in the blues, the music that was at the heart of everything either man ever played.

Bechet's appearance at the festival marked a triumphant return to the country from which he'd been exiled twenty years before, and he was so well received that he eventually decided to settle in Paris permanently, becoming a revered elder statesman of jazz, known to his legion of admirers as "Sidney Nationale."

To his surprise and pleasure, Charlie Parker, too, found himself a hero to the French, hailed as a worthy successor to Bechet, Armstrong, and Ellington, sought out by Jean-Paul Sartre and other intellectuals, and treated for the first time in his life not as a performer but as an artist. He had already begun to talk of broadening his horizons still further, but when he got back to New York and tried to interest the producer Norman Granz in commissioning works for him to record with a forty-piece orchestra, Granz instead hired dance-band arrangers to produce lush settings for popular standards. The result—an album called *Charlie Parker with Strings*—was disliked by most critics, who found the arrangements bland and unimaginative and accused Parker of selling out, precisely as they'd once scolded Louis Armstrong for abandoning his New Orleans repertoire in favor of popular songs. They failed to see that, as Parker himself said, a performance should be judged "good or bad not because of the kind of music—but because of the quality of the musician." Parker's long, hard-edged, bluesy lines unfurled beautifully above the strings, and

Charlie Parker and Sidney Bechet traveling together to France in 1949, and (below) Bechet striding past the corner of rue Bechet and rue Armstrong in Paris eight years later

Opening night at Birdland, December 15, 1949. The spectacularly eclectic bill included, left to right, Max Kaminsky, Lester Young, Lips Page, Charlie Parker, and Lennie Tristano.

on "Just Friends"—the best-selling of all his recordings—he produced one of the most haunting improvisations of his career. Of all his records, he said, it was the only one he ever really liked.

In December, two weeks after Parker made his first recordings with strings, the refurbished Clique Club on Broadway, renamed Birdland in his honor, opened its bright-red doors for the first time. The opening bill was a smorgasbord of stylists: Max Kaminsky and Hot Lips Page, as well as Lester Young, Charlie Parker, and a little-known singer named Harry Belafonte. "Feelings between the boppers and the traditional jazzmen were strained, to put it gently," Kaminsky wrote. Some of the younger musicians had

been openly disrespectful of Page, and Page had been wounded by their derision. "But Charlie Parker," Kaminsky said, "who was rated the great genius of all that [modern] music, liked my band better than anything else he heard there. We had nothing else in common; I couldn't drink the way he did, and I didn't know his friends and never went out with him on any parties, but musically we became good friends."

Nothing musical was ever alien to Charlie Parker. He often drank at a midtown bar whose jukebox was stocked in part with country music. When one of his acolytes asked why he liked to hear songs they all thought corny, he answered, "Listen. Listen to the stories." A friend remembered leaving him transfixed in a Manhattan

snowstorm late one night, unable to tear himself away from the thump and blare of a Salvation Army band. Another told of driving with him through the countryside when someone remarked idly that livestock loved music. Parker asked the driver to stop, assembled his horn, stalked into a field, and gravely played several choruses to a bewildered cow.

"Jazz has got to go on from here," he had told trumpet player Red Rodney. "We just can't stop with this." And when Rodney asked him who would show the way, he answered, "I'd like to be the one to do that." Like Bix Beiderbecke before him, he began to look to European composers, not American sources, for inspiration. The future, he told one interviewer, lay in finding a way to blend the complex harmonies of modern European music with the emotional color and dynamics of jazz. But, also like Beiderbecke, he knew he lacked the grounding in music theory that would have allowed him to bring about the kind of meeting of musical traditions he had in mind. To rectify that, he sometimes spoke wistfully of returning to France to study composition with Nadia Boulanger, enrolling at the Conservatoire Nationale de Musique, or taking instruction in orchestration from Edgard Varèse. "I only write in one voice," Varèse said Parker told him. "I want to have structure. I want to write orchestra scores."

Parker seemed finally to have found a little domestic peace. His marriage to Doris Sydnor had ended, but he had moved in with a woman named Chan Richardson and adopted her daughter. "He was irresistible," Richardson remembered. "He had a life force, an incredible life force. Bird was a giant. . . . He had a maturity beyond his years. In fact, he said to me one day, 'I'm not one of those boys you're used to.' And I went 'Ooooh!' " They would have two children together, Pree and Baird, and would live for a time on Manhattan's Lower East Side, where Parker led a life that on the surface seemed very like that of his neighbors: breakfasting with the children, strolling to the corner for the morning paper, watching westerns on television.

But with Charlie Parker, nothing was ever quite as it seemed. On the bandstand, he was usually able to discipline his furious talent. But offstage he was all too often out of control. "*This* is my home," he told a friend as he rolled up his sleeve to inject himself. The pianist Hampton Hawes remembered watching in disbelief one evening as Parker, chain-smoking marijuana, first downed eleven shots of whiskey and a handful of Benzedrine capsules, then shot up: "He sweated like a horse for five minutes, got up, put on his suit, and half an hour later was on the stand playing strong and beautiful."

There would still be nights when he'd pull himself together to play strongly and beautifully, but they would grow fewer and further between as the years went by, and the appetites that always gnawed at him would prevent him from seriously following any of the new musical paths of which he'd spoken, precisely as similar hungers had kept Beiderbecke from following his. "Bird tried to kick many times while he was with me," Chan Parker recalled, "sometimes very successfully. But he told me once, you know, you can get it out of your body but you can't get it out of your brain."

"Jazz was born in a whiskey barrel," said Artie Shaw, "grew up on marijuana, and is about to expire on heroin." Alcohol had always been part of the jazz world, helping to relieve the stress of life on the road and the strain of performing every night, and marijuana had been part of it since the twenties. Louis Armstrong continued to smoke it nearly every day. But heroin was different—"drastic stuff," Armstrong called it—and it soon seemed to be everywhere, dumped by organized crime into black big-city neighborhoods, where it found a ready-made market among youthful newcomers from the South who found in it momentary relief from dislocation and disappointment. "Heroin came on the scene like a tidal

Billie Holiday in performance, 1949

wave," Jackie McLean remembered. "I mean, it just appeared after World War II. And I began to notice guys in my neighborhood nodding on the corner, and so we all began to find out that they were nodding because they were taking this thing [we] called 'horse.' " McClean himself would be engulfed by it, and would remain addicted for eighteen years.

One by one, many of the most gifted musicians in jazz would be lost for a time to narcotics, among them Art Blakey, Chet Baker, John Coltrane, Tadd Dameron, Dexter Gordon, Stan Levey, Gerry Mulligan, Fats Navarro, Art Pepper, Max Roach, Sonny Rollins, Sonny Stitt, and eight of the sixteen men in Woody Herman's band. The tenor saxophonist Stan Getz tried to support his habit by holding up a drugstore, spent six months in jail, and returned to drugs and alcohol almost the moment he got out.

Each man's demons are derived differently, of course; no two musicians fell prey to drugs for precisely the same reasons. But there were common threads. To begin with, as Blakey explained, "it makes you feel good. . . . I started it because I liked it. There isn't any other reason." Heroin extended the natural high that playing produced, stretched out the process of winding down after performing. It served to soften the edges of the gritty world in which musicians were forced to earn their living. And, some said, it also seemed to slow things down, made it easier to perform at the accelerated pace the new music often demanded. It didn't help anyone to play better, Blakey said, but it did "make you *hear* better."

Above all, perhaps, there was the example set by Parker, whose genius every aspiring musician envied. Trying to match his dazzling technique, his frantic tempos, his overflowing ideas, worshipful musicians began consciously to emulate his addiction as well as his music, partly in the hope that by sharing it they could somehow share his

genius, too. "Bird was like fire," John Lewis remembered. "You couldn't get too close."

Dope undercut professionalism and served to split the jazz community between users and non-users. "Heroin was our badge," Red Rodney remembered, "the thing that made us different from the rest of the world. It was the thing that said, 'We know. You don't know.' It was the thing that gave us membership in a unique club, and for this membership we gave up everything else in the world. Every ambition. Every desire. Everything. It ruined most of the people."

It would help to ruin Billie Holiday, too. In 1941, she married a sometime marijuana dealer named Jimmy Monroe and began smoking opium. Then she moved in with Joe Guy, a good-looking trumpet player who had once been in Minton's house band. He was addicted to heroin, and soon, she was using it, too. When her mother, Sadie, died suddenly of a stroke at forty-nine, Holiday was devastated. She had often quarreled with her mother but had also relied on her for emotional support. Now she felt abandoned, terrified of being alone. Her casual drug use became complete dependence. She missed dates, fought with accompanists and club owners, and spent virtually all of her income paying for drugs for herself and Joe Guy. Finally, Joe Glaser, now her manager, insisted she have herself hospitalized for six weeks to end her habit. It didn't work.

On May 19, 1947, narcotics agents arrested Holiday and Guy in their New York hotel room and charged them with possession. She pled guilty and was sentenced to a year and a day in the Federal Reformatory for Women at Alderson, West Virginia. At Guy's trial, she refused to say whether or not he had purchased the heroin the agents had seized. He went free. While she was locked up, her New York cabaret card was revoked; she could still give concerts in New York when she got out but was no longer allowed to perform in clubs. Old

friends stopped seeing her. Even Lester Young had drifted away.

Beyond the damage dope did to the lives of the individual musicians who became its victims, it did still more to the jazz world as a whole. Eager always for sensational stories, the press exaggerated the already sordid details until even musicians who had nothing whatsoever to do with narcotics—and the overwhelming majority of musicians did not—came under suspicion. The old link between musicians and the black community was further weakened as well. Before the narcotics plague hit, Dicky Wells remembered, "when word spread that the band was in town, doors flew open." But afterward "they [flew] shut—wham, wham—twice, so they [would] stay closed."

IT REALLY BROKE MY HEART

"BOP IS A FLOP—COMMERCIALLY," *Variety* reported in late 1949. "The musical style is dying almost as fast as it began, according to maestros who employ it, agents who book it and recording companies which grabbed fast a few months ago to corral its exponents." In the end, their brief foray into bebop could not save the big bands. Charlie Barnet broke up his orchestra, admitting that the small crowds who'd turned out to hear him in recent months had "a legitimate beef," because the band's new bop-based arrangements hadn't been "particularly good for dancing." Woody Herman, $175,000 in debt, disbanded his Second Herd. Count Basie temporarily gave up his orchestra in favor of an octet. Benny Goodman surrendered, too, never again to lead a full-time band of his own, and would later blame the new music for his failure. "The damn monotony of it got to me," Goodman remembered. "Bop was mostly publicity and people figuring angles."

The men in the Duke Ellington band were eventually forced to swap their private Pullman for a bus but the orchestra never left the road. Here, in 1961, more than a decade after most of the big bands had broken up, high-note trumpet star William "Cat" Anderson, an unidentified friend, and Johnny Hodges pass the time playing cards as their bus takes them across America.

Dizzy Gillespie's band had fallen on hard times as well. For all his success, his payroll continued to outpace profits. Music lovers clustered around the bandstand wherever he appeared, but the big crowds of dancers the band needed to stay afloat stubbornly failed to materialize. During one southern tour, even the sight of Gillespie and guest star Ella Fitzgerald doing the lindy together had not been enough to persuade other dancers to join in. "They didn't care whether we played a flatted fifth or a ruptured 129th," Gillespie wrote. "They'd just stand around the bandstand and gawk." Frankie Manning, once one of the best-known professional jitterbuggers at the Savoy Ballroom, admitted to having been stumped by Gillespie's music, too. After five years in the army and off the dance floor, he formed a dance troupe called the Conjurors and tried to go back to doing what he did best.

> I worked with Dizzy's band in Washington, D.C. . . . We went on the stage. I gave him my music, "Jumping at the Woodside"—Count Basie—and he's got this drummer up there, and he's giving me all this "chuck-a-bong pim, chick-a-pim" and I usually hear "chick-a-chu, chick-a-chu, chick-a-chu." When we finished the act and I came off, I said to Dizzy, "What the ———is this you're doing?" It was different from when I used to see kids out there on the floor, *swinging.* Eventually, I got to understand the music, but it was not music for dancing. And that is the thing that I had been used to, music for *dancing.*

Finally, in March 1950, Lorraine Gillespie gave her husband an ultimatum: "You got a hundred musicians or me! Make up your mind." Gillespie reluctantly let all of his men go. "Everybody was sorry about that, man," he said many years later. "Cats were crying. . . . So was I. The fad was finished."

EXTREME JAZZ:
THE AVANT-GARDE

GARY GIDDINS

For many jazz lovers, the avant-garde is an inferno that reproaches the musically decorous while derogating mainstream orthodoxy. Though its audience is international, its achievement vast, its influence sweeping, its history fully half as long as that of jazz proper, it is often regarded as a thing apart—a separateness sanctioned by those avant-garde enthusiasts who listen to nothing else. Like much of jazz history, this schism has a precedent in European classical music: the divisive reaction—augured by Shavian critics who championed radical Wagner at the expense of reserved Brahms—to serialism, which begat converts and antagonists but few neutrals.

The avant-garde has been treated as a metaphor rather than as music by proponents and enemies alike. The former have adapted it to suit social and political movements as various as Marxism, mysticism, pacifism, internationalism, black nationalism, and integration, implying at times a revolutionary-cause-du-jour applicability. As a result, the avant-garde is not infrequently characterized as a music of the left. But so is jazz itself—"a people's music," in Sidney Finkelstein's 1940s phrase. Detractors revile avant-gardists as both elitist and barbarous: on the one hand, as insulated academics who hijacked jazz and turned it into a nearly occult pursuit only they can comprehend; on the other, as charlatans who clothe their ineptness in rhetoric and noise. Either way, naysayers invariably insist, the avant-garde alienated the very "people" it hoped to liberate.

I offer two anecdotes to confirm and muddle prejudices in each camp. At a Finnish jazz festival in the early 1980s, two saxophonists from East Berlin, performing outside the wall for the first time, spoke poignantly of jazz's liberating power and then embarked on a fusillade of shrieking high-note blasts. After several minutes of this, a notable American avant-gardist turned to me and said, "Let's go. This stuff is a lot more fun to play than to listen to." At a rehearsal by a New York jazz orchestra a few years later, musicians bitterly groused when it was announced they would be conducted by a famous avant-gardist in a program of his music: "He can't play," "It's a mockery," etc. When the guest conductor arrived and the musicians read his scores, they marveled at his craftsmanship and, having assured themselves of his skill, earnestly embraced the rigors of his music. After the concert, the most outspoken of the early skeptics conceded to me, "He's a brilliant guy. I wish we played more music like that."

If we are to rescue avant-garde jazz from parochialism of any kind, we need to define the term. The dictionary is the place to begin: "n. 1. A group, as of artists and writers, regarded as preeminent in the invention and application of new techniques in a given field. 2. The admirers of such a group and critics acting as its spokesmen. adj. 1. Of or relating to the vanguard, as in the arts. 2. Ahead of the times." All these definitions are useful, but quite obviously too general. A distinction must be made between a universal avant-gardism and a school of jazz known as the avant-garde. I emphasize "known," because most innovators resist the pigeonhole; indeed, they vigorously resent a characterization of their music that presumes complexity and mayhem, virtually warning their potential audience to exercise caution.

Jazz has always had a vanguard, performers who propelled the music in new directions, dismaying generations of fans content with what they already knew. Louis Armstrong, Jelly Roll Morton, Duke Ellington, Bix Beiderbecke, Earl Hines, and Coleman Hawkins were among the jazz pioneers of the 1920s, each in his way an avant-garde musician who helped relegate customary jazz, rag, and blues styles to the dead ends of the past. Their innovations were perceived not as assaults on convention, but as the kind of ingenuity that enhances traditions without undermining them. Yet in raising jazz to a new plateau of emotional and technical expression, they precipitated the greatest schism of all, delivering art music from folk music and dividing artists from journeymen. Since we venerate them much more than we do their dimly remembered predecessors, we do not burden them with the stigma of otherness often associated with the avant-garde, but rather honor them as forebears.

Nor do we think of the swing era as avant-garde. The Basies, Goodmans, Shaws, and Luncefords were undeniably "pre-eminent in the invention and application of new techniques," and conservative critics predictably assailed them for enfeebling and commercializing classic jazz, but you can hardly call them "ahead of the times"; they *were* the times. Lester Young may have been considered too far out for New York in 1934, yet two years later countless musicians, and not just tenor saxophonists, were trying to play like him. Staunch anomalies such as Red Norvo's "Dance of the Octopus," Coleman Hawkins's "Queer Notions," or Duke Ellington's "Reminiscing in Tempo," though avant-garde for the day, were too singular to suggest a movement or even a style.

Bebop created a greater divide, splitting the jazz world in two and engendering as much contumely, ridicule, and recrimination as the avant-garde school born in its wake. The methods of Charlie Parker, Dizzy Gillespie, Bud Powell, Thelonious Monk, and dozens of others—a peer group in thrall to a new music and

An evening in Cecil Taylor's Manhattan loft, sometime during the 1980s. The tenor saxophonist is Henry Threadgill; Jerome Cooper plays drums.

a new way of thinking about music—were quintessentially avant-garde, except for one thing. Even as contemptuous pundits poked fun at alleged bebop manners, the musicians supplanted their predecessors almost as completely as Armstrong's generation superseded the raggy beats and polyphony of Dixieland. Armstrong and swing didn't disappear with the advent of bebop, however, but were pressed into a historical frame. Like Bach overlooking Mozart overlooking Beethoven, jazz had now established a history of unceasing revision; it was an expanding and developing art that continued to infuriate the musically complaisant while keeping the adventurous, if not on the dance floor, then certainly on their toes.

Aspects of the avant-garde jazz movement can be traced back to every other kind of jazz. Consider, for example, its reintroduction of polyphony—one of the dominant strengths of the avant-

garde. Bebop evolved from the past with an attitude of determined modernism, setting itself in opposition to the clichés and styles of the past; the avant-garde opposed clichés but not styles, accepting the entire canvas of jazz history as its platform. Still, its direct roots lie in bebop, which raised issues about harmony, melody, rhythm, and instrumentation that succeeding generations could scarcely fail to explore. Charlie Parker said he came alive when he realized he could improvise on the higher intervals of chords. His successors expanded that quest, exploring the limits of chords, then dispensing with them altogether. Even as bop introduced a categorical, tight-knit virtuoso style, it encouraged innovations that challenged its own precepts. Was bop an obstacle course of refined chord changes? George Russell composed a piece for Dizzy Gillespie's orchestra ("Cubana Be/Cubana Bop") that eschewed chords in favor of modes or scales. Were bop's rhythms of such velocity that only cymbals could mark the beat? Gillespie and Parker introduced Afro-Cuban rhythms and Latin percussion instruments. Was bop hot? Miles Davis gave birth to the cool. Were bop variations so cunning they obscured the themes? Monk stressed thematic variations.

Monk was branded a charlatan for his unconventional style as pianist and composer. George Russell's "A Bird in Igor's Yard," which meshed jazz and classical techniques, and Lennie Tristano's "Digression," a "free" group improvisation (without pre-stated melody, harmonic structure, or tempo), were considered so avant-garde in 1949 that Capitol Records refused to release them. Yet, again, these were isolated performances, and though they heralded jazz schools (third stream, the Tristano cult), they were not the stuff of a movement. That came later, triggered by musicians who came of age during the bop era but were regarded as outcasts by their contemporaries. Considering the number of directions jazz took in the fifties—cool, hard bop, third stream, soul, modal—and the remarkable range of personalities that flourished, a player would have to be fearsome indeed to earn a nearly unanimous disrespect. Happily, a few were.

After three years at the New England Conservatory, Cecil Taylor relocated to New York and was laughed off bandstands until he began to attract like-minded musicians, even disciples. In 1956, at age twenty-seven, he recorded his first album, *Jazz Advance*. Not exactly a salvo, it introduced a startling new voice, that of a pianist who played at and around chords while sidestepping the kind of linear melodies that were the foundation of practically all modern jazz improvisation. His touch was so brisk and percussive, he seemed to be beating drum patterns on the keyboard. On "Rick Kick Shaw," he offered a template for a piano style redolent of diverse jazz and classical influences without quite deferring to any of them. The album was largely ignored or patronized.

At the same time, John Coltrane, an apparently insignificant tenor saxophonist who had worked with Gillespie and Johnny Hodges but was not above playing low-rent bar gigs, experienced a musical and personal rebirth and dedicated himself to the compulsive study of scales. At thirty, he was hired by Miles Davis and revealed a keening high-register sound and a prolix style that crammed so many notes into a chord he left nothing for his accompanists to play. After he recruited a scorching rhythm section—McCoy Tyner, Jimmy Garrison, Elvin Jones—Coltrane developed his music with astonishing fervor, winning and losing audiences along the way. One initially admiring critic described his approach as "sheets of sound," only to dismiss "Chasin' the Trane" as an "airleak" a few years later.

At the same time, in Los Angeles, Ornette Coleman—who, to hear him tell it, was run out of his native Fort Worth for playing alto saxophone in a way that made usually peaceable musicians resort to violence—was attracting followers willing to put their preconceptions on hold, notably Don Cherry, Charlie Haden, and Billy Higgins. Desperate for work, he offered his compositions, singular melodic inventions that could be immensely moving and wittily tumultuous, to Contemporary Records. The label surprised him by signing him to play them. His first album, recorded at age thirty, proffered the exclamatory but reasonable title *Something Else!!!* Its successors were more insurgent: *Tomorrow Is the Question, The Shape of Jazz to Come, Change of the Century*. Coleman's ebullient if raw quarter-tone pitch conveyed the primitivism of rural blues and, at the same time, a shocking modernist mockery.

If Taylor, Coltrane, and Coleman represented the beginnings of a new jazz movement, it was unprecedented in several regards. For one thing, they were making an impact at relatively advanced ages; Louis Armstrong and Charlie Parker effected revolutions at

Pharoah Sanders

twenty-five. For another, they tended to eye each other cautiously, from a distance. Unlike the progenitors of swing or bop, who frequently performed and recorded together, these three offered widely disparate approaches to a new kind of jazz. Coltrane recorded once with Taylor and once with Coleman's band, but never with Coleman, who in turn never recorded with Taylor. Each man was a school unto himself. Their divergent musics reflected uncommonly diverse backgrounds. Parker, Gillespie, and Powell came from different points on the map, but all were spawned by jazz. By contrast, Taylor was classically trained and Coleman apprenticed himself in rhythm and blues; only Coltrane issued directly from jazz.

That they signaled the beginnings of a musical movement did not become clear until the early 1960s, when the attention they garnered encouraged numerous other musicians to join them on the jazz fringe. Unlike musical uprisings of the past, this one did not admit of a generational divide. Eric Dolphy, a late bloomer from California and an accomplished technician by any standard, moved to New York to play with the Charles Mingus Quartet and instantly attached himself to Coltrane and Coleman. Mingus himself, the superb bop bassist who now publicly criticized musicians in his own band for relying on bop's clichés, cast a wary eye at the newcomers but was himself liberated by the spirit of radical adventurism. Jimmy Giuffre, the tenor saxophonist who wrote Woody Herman's "Four Brothers," organized a free-form trio with bassist Steve Swallow and the influential pianist Paul Bley, who had worked with Coleman and was developing his own approach to free or spontaneous improvisation. Sun Ra, born in 1914 and an alumnus of jazz's first great orchestra, Fletcher Henderson's, moved his much recorded but neglected Arkestra to New York in 1960 and emerged as a dynamic mobilizer of the new music.

In 1960, Coleman recorded his double quartet, *Free Jazz,* and gave the movement a name, though ultimately one of limited utility. Free-form improvisations unquestionably accounted for much of the new jazz; they marked an inevitable response to the highly structured patterns of bop. The year before, Miles Davis enjoyed immense success with *Kind of Blue,* one of the most iconic of jazz LPs, popularizing a modal approach to improvisation. "So What" is commonplace in form (AABA, thirty-two bars), but instead of a system of chord changes, the harmony consists of one scale (D minor) for twenty-four bars and another a half step higher for the release. A few weeks later, Coltrane, who played on that session, recorded *Giant Steps,* taking the opposite tack on the title piece, which has two chords to every measure. Davis winnowed bop's harmonies to encourage original improvisations, and Coltrane

maximized them for the same reason. Coleman took the next step: complete freedom from fixed harmonic and, for that matter, rhythmic patterns. He focused on melody, allowing harmonies to emerge serendipitously. His music had a buoyantly swinging rhythmic pulse but abrogated the steady demarcations of a 4/4 beat. You couldn't listen with half a mind, because there were no familiar resolutions; you had to concentrate on the escapade of Coleman's solo and the way the ensemble accompanied it.

The new music took a major leap in 1962, when Cecil Taylor's trio—altoist Jimmy Lyons, drummer Sunny Murray—performed and recorded at Club Montmartre in Copenhagen. In addition to abandoning fixed harmonies once and for all, Taylor pushed further than Coleman had in liberating rhythm. Coleman's beat was rootless, but the pulse was relatively regular. Taylor, with Murray's support, allowed the rhythmic pulse to permutate, moment by moment, as a consequence of whatever he played; the energy of his attack governed the time. Swing was no longer a downbeat you could follow with your foot, but a percussive wailing you followed as closely as you might a melodic variation. Taylor also shared the Club Montmartre bandstand with Albert Ayler, a young tenor and soprano saxophonist, recently discharged from the army, whose ballistic harmonics, sing-song themes, and otherworldly solos were so startling, some thought he had to be kidding.

Meanwhile, Coltrane continued to speed into the stratosphere of musical expressionism. Cynics could deride Ayler and Coleman as fakes, and Taylor and Dolphy as virtuoso aesthetes; Coltrane, however, had come through the ranks. Though one critic branded him "anti-jazz," no one questioned his technical command of jazz harmony and rhythm, the exquisite pitch-perfect beauty of his sound, the emotional resolve of his ballads and blues, or his sincerity. If he chose to play free, committing himself to a new music that alienated so many, he had to be taken seriously.

By 1963, the avant-garde had the verve and brawn of a genuine crusade. A year later, a series of six concerts produced by thirty-nine-year-old trumpeter, composer, and educator Bill Dixon at New York's Cellar Cafe brazenly proclaimed the new order as nothing less than "The October Revolution in Jazz." And a whole generation of players was ready to storm the gates, among them Archie Shepp, Milford Graves, Roswell Rudd, John Tchicai, Marion Brown, and Pharoah Sanders. Two record labels announced their commitment to the new music. The independent ESP-Disk, originally created to promote Esperanto, got off to a heady start with Albert Ayler's *Ghosts,* and introduced new musicians on an almost monthly basis, including a few who considered the avant-garde a musical option, not a religion: pianist Don Pullen, who created one of the major ensembles of the eighties, linking avant-

Lester Bowie

garde and mainstream techniques; bassist Eddie Gomez, who enjoyed a long association with Bill Evans; and Bob James, the godfather of "jazz lite." The most widely distributed avant-garde label was Impulse, a subsidiary of ABC-Paramount, which signed Coltrane and bannered its gatefold covers with the slogan "The new wave of jazz is on Impulse!"

The movement had a profusion of competing names: free jazz, the new wave, the new music, the New Thing, black music, revolutionary music, fire music, out music. That the term "avant-garde" remained after the rest faded into a miasma of 1960s oratory may be attributed in part to its prevailing, inoffensive meaning. But it also came into play because of the strange circumstances that followed the music's ostensible acceptance, when in spite of its expanding influence, the avant-garde showed signs of corruption and a general languishing.

Avant-garde jazz reflected the turmoil of the 1960s. It was a minority music, expressing euphoria and sadness and daring and resentment and anger and other feelings through styles so extreme as to utterly alienate most of the traditional jazz following—itself a withering minority in the age of rock. The rhetoric for and against was often ugly, as it had been during bop, though now you also heard accusations of racism, tomming, and worse. Most of that passed quickly enough, though a lingering distrust continued to rend the jazz audience. Veteran musicians felt that

their art had been fatally subverted, and some tried to make common cause with rock, while others accepted private students or joined school faculties, and still others sought studio or pit-band work until the storm abated. The avant-garde players, as always, had an even rougher time. After the novelty value waned, not even the innovators sold enough records to maintain a vivid presence. Many of the most critically admired avant-garde works sold a couple of thousand copies at best.

And yet the influence of the avant-garde was everywhere. Established musicians were responding to its musical challenges and emotional immediacy. They adapted, in their different ways, what they found viable, even if it was nothing more than license to go overboard. I recall musicians in the mid-sixties expressing astonishment at how "inside" Coleman sounded, when only a few years earlier he had seemed impenetrably "outside." Small wonder. In the interim, the avant-garde rubbed off on almost everyone who didn't bolt from jazz entirely. A new genre appeared: the ultramodern album by mainstream-modern musicians to the right of the avant-garde, who could not resist testing its turf. Consider Sonny Rollins's *Our Man in Jazz,* Jackie McLean's *Destination Out,* Charles Mingus's *Black Saint and the Sinner Lady,* Andrew Hill's *Point of Departure,* Stan Getz's *Sweet Rain,* Tony Williams's *Lifetime,* Sam Rivers's *Fuscia Swing Song,* Wayne Shorter's *The All-Seeing Eye,* Roland Kirk's *Rip, Rig and Panic,* Modern Jazz Quartet's *Space,* Jaki Byard's *Sunshine of My Soul,* Miles Davis's *Miles in the Sky,* and Gil Evans's *Blues in Orbit,* among many others, all of which partake of the avant-gardism rife in the 1960s. Rock groups also borrowed licks from the new jazz; by the mid-seventies, the studios were rampant with Coltrane imitators—you heard them on pop records, in TV bands, and in film scores.

Still, with all this going on, the avant-garde appeared to curl up in hibernation. Coleman's label, Atlantic, dropped him in 1961, and he recorded erratically in the years to come, often traveling in the opposite direction of free jazz, with notated works for string quartet, symphony orchestra, rock band, and other ensembles. His unique sound and attack, however, abided. Inexplicably, Ayler, whose finest work was lavishly flamboyant in the best sense, began to record hippie fusion anthems before his tragic death in 1970. Of the major avant-garde figures, Taylor, like Monk before him, had to wait the longest for acceptance. Between 1962, when he recorded at the Montmartre, and 1973, his only records were two stunning 1966 Blue Note LPs, *Unit Structures* and *Conquistador!,* a concerto written for him in 1968 by twenty-four-year-old Mike Mantler (recorded by his Jazz Composer's Orchestra), and a taped concert from Europe in 1969. Taylor spent a few of those years teaching at colleges in the Midwest.

Coltrane's death in the summer of 1967 had a baleful impact on all of jazz, but it marked the beginning of the Coltrane legend. A church was consecrated in his name in San Francisco, and his record sales—mostly modest during his life—began to soar. His passing symbolized jazz's capitulation to rock in the late sixties, though there was really nothing symbolic about it. ESP-Disk became a reissue operation, as did Impulse, despite a series of ambitious recordings by Archie Shepp and Sam Rivers. Record labels folded, and clubs went dark. The next few years were a rough patch in jazz history.

But jazz came roaring back in the mid-seventies. It was a period in which a slew of not-very-old masters—among them Rollins, Mingus, Dexter Gordon, Sarah Vaughan, Gerry Mulligan,

the Modern Jazz Quartet, James Moody, Hank Jones, Red Rodney, and Phil Woods—tired of their sabbaticals and side trips and returned to action with new energy, helping to refuel the mainstream audience. It was also the period in which a new coterie of avant-garde musicians took much of the jazz world by surprise, thoroughly overturning some of the assumptions generated by their predecessors. They had a broader agenda, and they interpreted the idea of freedom as the capacity to choose between all the realms of jazz, mixing and matching them not only with each other but with old and new pop, R&B and rock, classical music and world music. Lester Bowie recorded an unaccompanied trumpet fantasy called "Jazz Death?" in which he interrupts his purple mosaic of a solo to ask if jazz is indeed dead; at the end, he answers cavalierly, "Well, I guess that all depends on what you know."

These musicians ambushed the national press because they had been honing their music not in New York, where much of the press and the record industry resides, but in points west, especially Chicago, St. Louis, and Los Angeles. Some had toured Europe, and several had recorded for small labels, little more

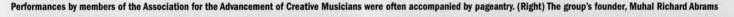

Performances by members of the Association for the Advancement of Creative Musicians were often accompanied by pageantry. (Right) The group's founder, Muhal Richard Abrams

than vanities for the most part, with the noted exception of Chicago's Delmark Records. On that label, one began to hear of a cooperative called the AACM (Association for the Advancement of Creative Music) and to hear the music of its guru, Muhal Richard Abrams, an erstwhile bop pianist, and its younger members, including Bowie, Roscoe Mitchell, Joseph Jarman, Leroy Jenkins, Henry Threadgill, Anthony Braxton, Chico Freeman, Steve McCall, George Lewis, and Leo Smith. Before long, many relocated to New York, where seemingly overnight new venues—in many instances, apartments or lofts (hence the phrase "loft jazz")—opened shop to present their wares.

This was all pretty astounding, sociologically and musically. Instead of lone paladins arriving from different cities, hoping to sit in, win recognition, and make a name, here came gangs of accomplished players, some just getting started, others past forty. In addition to the AACM players, there was the Black Artists Group from St. Louis, including Julius Hemphill, Oliver Lake, Hamiet Bluiett, and Bakaida Carroll. A kind of offshoot of the AACM developed in New Haven, where Yalies Anthony Davis and George Lewis worked with Leo Smith and Fred Anderson. From Los Angeles came a network of players without an acronym but with a history of working together, ranging from John Carter and Bobby Bradford—associates of Coleman long before he came to New York and now in their forties—to Arthur Blythe, a veteran of Horace Tapscott's Los Angeles band, to college students James Newton, Mark Dresser, and David Murray.

It is impossible to overstate the degree to which all these players countered the most meretricious effects of fusion and sparked a renewed hunger for creative jazz, setting the stage for the return of many of the aforementioned mainstream jazz stars. They were a new breed of musician, often doubling as painters and poets and entrepreneurs. They formed small bands that lasted for years, decades, including the trios Revolutionary Ensemble and Air, and the ongoing Art Ensemble of Chicago. They defied expectations; Threadgill's Air played free and used hubcaps for percussion but also cannily interpreted tangos and Scott Joplin. Many musicians harbored big-band ambitions and eventually realized them, energizing orchestral jazz for the first time in a decade. Yet they also performed in any way that was economically feasible, pioneering solo wind concerts and duets. They made it a point of honor to write original music but were not averse to playing standards. Though contentious rhetoric was occasionally heard, it was usually a benign expression of black pride; this music was more often satirical than angry. Arthur Blythe arrived in New York with a nickname given him by friends as a young man, "Black Arthur." One critic attacked him for the moniker alone, assuming him to be a crazed militant. When Blythe played his alto, however, he produced a dynamic, brittle, pear-shaped sound, sweet and sour, that hadn't been heard in jazz since Benny Carter, and that perfectly reflected the man.

Free jazz to these musicians was not a specific, aharmonic way of approaching improvisation, but one style among many. Even when they played free solos, they often couched them in contexts that were scrupulously notated. The more important point is that they were not limited by the artificial boundaries of idiom. Sun Ra, long a Midwesterner, understood this all along, and at his concerts in the 1980s, he typically combined impetuous blowouts with complex arrangements, visual spectacle, blues and tap-dance rhythms, a sermon, a Fletcher Henderson arrangement, and "Hello, Dolly!." It was not uncharacteristic for a pianist like Anthony Davis to play Ellington one season and compose an opera the next; for Muhal Richard Abrams to orchestrate an Ellington piano piece at one concert and employ ripped newspapers as voicings at the next; or for Julius Hemphill to record aggressive unaccompanied sax solos one year and devise a theatrical pageant the next.

Perhaps the most resourceful of the younger players was tenor saxophonist, bass clarinetist, composer, and bandleader David Murray, who at twenty paid homage to Albert Ayler, identifying himself with the avant-garde tradition, and before he was thirty added homages to Hawkins, Young, and Paul Gonsalves. Murray never had one band when he could have several, so you could hear him with a quartet, his widely celebrated octet, his big band, as well as solo and in duos and trios. With Hemphill, Bluiett, and Lake, he created the World Saxophone Quartet, which at first played free because they had nothing written, but soon built up a superb book of original pieces. In the late nineties, Murray played with jazz musicians from every generation, as well as rock, hip-hop, gospel, European, and African musicians.

Wave after wave of avant-garde musicians continue to show up, bringing to bear the influences of whatever musics they know and adapting them into the broadest possible jazz context. In New York, they now appear regularly at places like the Knitting Factory and Tonic. Dozens of labels—the most prominent include the pioneering Black Saint and Soul Note in Italy, DIW in Japan, and the expanding Knitting Factory Records in New York—record them. The names and faces change, but they continue to explore avant-garde traditions. Joe Morris plays Ornette Coleman on guitar, and John Zorn's Masada explores Jewish themes in a context directly related to Coleman's sixties quartet. There is hardly a pianist, no matter how exquisitely trained, whose attack hasn't been affected by the belling cascades of Cecil Taylor. David S.

The World Saxophone Quartet: David Murray, Julius Hemphill, Oliver Lake, Hamiet Bluiett

Ware's quartet, one of the most highly regarded ensembles of the decade, is made up of two Taylor alumni (Ware and the ubiquitous bassist William Parker) and a pianist, Matthew Shipp, who extends Taylor's methods in an entirely personal direction. The Rova Saxophone Quartet transcribed and recorded, note for note, Coltrane's *Ascension*, which thirty years ago was considered the most exhilarating or appalling assault on musical conventions ever played. Several avant-garde players routinely join with mainstream musicians; competence is rarely an issue.

The avant-garde is no longer a jazz school, like swing or bop, and cannot be supplanted. It is rather a kind of parajazz, which has evolved in various directions over the past forty years, blending with every other kind of jazz and every other kind of music, including R&B, klezmer, electronic, country, Bulgarian folk songs, koto, gamelan, Mahler—you name it, you can find it. Though the avant-garde enjoys a predictably narrow following, the audience is constant in the United States and even more so in Europe, where fusions between jazz and classics are more readily assimilated. Most avant-garde jazz is clearly anchored in jazz; some of it is just as clearly anchored alongside. Though no longer an exclusive territory of innovators, gadflies, and prophets, it remains a loose confederation of individualists who take nothing—not even swing or blues—for granted. Like jazz, parajazz offers something for everyone.

THE ADVENTURE

On February 24, 1952, Dizzy Gillespie and Charlie Parker appeared together on a television variety show called Stage Entrance. The kinescope made that day is all that we have of Parker in public performance, and the Down Beat awards ceremony that precedes it provides an excruciating example of the kind of condescension often displayed toward jazz and jazz musicians, even by those who believed themselves boosters. The critic and composer Leonard Feather delivers a stiff little speech about brotherhood, then hands the host, Broadway gossip columnist Earl Wilson, a pair of wooden plaques to present to Parker and Gillespie. Wilson greets the musicians, offers up the plaques—making fun of Gillespie's nickname as he does so—and then asks, "You boys have anything to say?"

Don Cherry, left, and Ornette Coleman at New York's Five Spot

For once, Gillespie is speechless. Parker, his face without expression, his voice low and icily polite, replies: "They say music speaks louder than words, so we'd rather voice our opinion that way." During that voicing—an abbreviated version of the bop anthem "Hot House"—Parker's face remains impassive, his fierce eyes and the movement of his big fingers on the keys the only outward signs of the effort required to yield such brilliant, jagged cascades of sound, the sound itself the most eloquent possible response to patronization.

The end of the Gillespie big band had been more than a personal disappointment for its leader. It also marked the end of an honorable but doomed effort to build a bridge between the new music and the old jazz audience. Similar efforts by other musicians would be made over the years to come. None would entirely succeed. For better

Pee Wee Ellis and Ron Carter playing for "listeners only" at the Pythod Club in Rochester, New York, 1958

or worse, jazz seemed on its way to becoming an art music, meant for concert halls and nightclubs, not ballrooms—adventurous and demanding; intended for aficionados, not ordinary people; infused with the every-musician-for-himself spirit of the jam session; aligned not with the American mainstream but with the growing counterculture for which commercial success was evidence of corruption, of "selling out." "Our dislikes followed a pattern . . . ," the jazz writer Barry Ulanov once confessed, "which began with our celebration of an unknown musician, singer or band, and ended with our derogation of the same musician, singer or band when he, she, or they had achieved popularity."

No one present at the music's birth in New Orleans could have foreseen that any of this would happen. But then, nothing about the trajectory of jazz had ever been predictable. First, America's most important music had been created by African-Americans, a people from whom little or nothing had been expected by the country's white majority. Then it had been nurtured by the marketplace, which, according to modernist theory, should have been inimical to art. Most of the great figures in jazz's first half century—Buddy Bolden, Jelly Roll Morton, and King Oliver; Louis Armstrong and Duke Ellington; Bix Beiderbecke, Coleman Hawkins, Lester Young, Benny Goodman, and Count Basie—had managed to make unforgettable music while pleasing dancers for a living. "If I hear a sigh of pleasure from the dance floor," Ellington once said, "it becomes part of our music."

"The kind of jazz we [all] played had a functional base," Max Kaminsky remembered. "We . . . played to provide the music for dancing. Before our time, jazz had been played in marching bands, in street parades, at picnics, funerals, weddings. Before that, jazz had been evolved from blues and work songs [and from the churches]. All this was in the music. It came out of the raw stuff of life." But now, Kaminsky continued, everything seemed to be changing.

Jazz, like Dr. Frankenstein, had all unwittingly created a monster in its own image—the jazz addict—who, in becoming all hopped up about . . . its significance as an art form, very nearly snuffed the life out of it. . . . [J]azz no longer belonged to the musicians and the dancers; it was taken over lock, stock, and barrel by the fans, the addicts, the record collectors, the amateur critics, the recording companies, the promoters, the nightclub owners, the A&R men, the lecturers and writers. These were the people who now decided what was jazz and what wasn't, who dictated how it should be played and on what instrument, and specified who could or could not play "real" jazz.

There was more to it than that. Jazz had started out as an exuberant ensemble form, its impact derived in large part from the cooperative spirit of the musicians, their ability simultaneously to play and to listen to one another. A man's reputation then had rested on his individual sound and the imagination and rhythmic sophistication he brought to the two- and four-bar breaks that Jelly Roll Morton said were essential to the music. In the early 1920s, the singular genius of Louis Armstrong had brought the soloist front and center and established once and for all the notion of the improvising jazz musician as romantic hero. But until the early 1940s, even the most celebrated soloists had still been expected to work their magic within a carefully arranged framework. Solos remained relatively brief. A premium was put on telling one's story with economy as well as with emotion and imagination. And the theme on which the improvisation was based was often as familiar to the listener as it was to the musicians.

The music that Parker and Gillespie pioneered was deliberately different. Tunes were either wholly new or consciously disguised. Ensemble passages were almost

Sonny Stitt, 1953. No one had a harder time dealing with Charlie Parker's legacy than this superb musician, whose sound and ideas on alto saxophone sounded so like Bird's that he switched to tenor in order to be seen and heard as his own man.

beside the point. Everything depended on the energy and ideas of the improvisers. If that energy and those ideas seemed inexhaustible—as they routinely did when bebop's creators were on the bandstand—the sheer momentum and creative power let loose had the potential to thrill anyone willing to listen. But even when Parker and Gillespie were playing, there was always the risk that, by pouring forth so much unrelenting musical complexity, they would eventually inundate even their admirers. (Parker himself understood this. "More than four choruses," he once warned Milt Jackson, "and you're just practicing.") And over a long evening, in the hands of less talented musicians, the standard bebop format—ensemble theme, string of solos, ensemble theme—could exhaust the patience of even the most earnest audience.

"COOL"

"Bird and Diz were great," Miles Davis remembered, but "if you weren't a fast listener you couldn't catch the humor or feeling of their music. Their music wasn't sweet and it didn't have harmonic lines that you could easily hum with your girlfriend trying to get over with a kiss." He would be among the first musicians to begin looking for ways to broaden the music's appeal and restore some balance between the soloist and the ensemble.

In the winter of 1947–48, Davis was part of a steady stream of musicians who filed in and out of an apartment building on East Fifty-fifth Street in Manhattan at all hours of the day and night. The pianist John Lewis often dropped by when he was not on the road with the Gillespie band. So did Max Roach and Kenny Clarke, trumpeter-arranger Johnny Carisi and composer George Russell, trombonist J. J. Johnson, alto saxophonist Lee Konitz, and the lanky, red-haired baritone saxophone player and arranger Gerry Mulligan.

Their goal was the one-room basement home of Gil Evans. Born in Canada of Australian parents in 1912, he had been raised in the American West and learned to love jazz listening to Louis Armstrong and Duke Ellington over the radio. He had for several years been working as an arranger for the Claude Thornhill orchestra, a distinctly unorthodox dance band that featured dreamy, slow-moving arrangements with instrumentation then unusual in jazz: French horns and tuba, flute and piccolo. New York musicians had been mightily impressed by the fresh ways Thornhill had found to apply that sound to bop standards like "Thriving on a Riff," "Yardbird Suite," and Miles Davis's "Donna Lee." Except for the Billy Eckstine band with Charlie Parker, Davis said, Thornhill's was the best band in "these modern times."

But Evans was no longer writing for it. The Thornhill orchestra had gradually become a caricature of itself, he remembered, finally so slow-moving it put even him to sleep, and he was now scuffling, along with most of the musicians who hung out in his apartment, and taking part in a sort of informal round-the-clock music seminar for which his door was always open. Sometime that winter, Evans, Davis, Mulligan, and their friends began to talk of organizing a nine-piece rehearsal band—trumpet, alto saxophone, French horn, tuba, trombone, baritone saxophone, piano, bass, and drums—the smallest number of instruments that could capture the sound and harmonies of the Thornhill orchestra at its best. Evans had hoped Charlie Parker would take part, he recalled, but Parker wasn't willing "to use himself as a voice, as part of an overall picture instead of a straight soloist."

Miles Davis was more than willing. The band would have remained only idle talk if he hadn't been involved. "He took the initiative and put the theories to work," Mulligan remembered. "He called the rehearsals, hired the halls, called the players, and generally cracked the whip." He also talked the Royal Roost into giving the Miles Davis Nonet a two-week run in the summer of 1948—and made sure that the sign outside credited the arrangers by name, something that may never have been done before.

The music of the nonet was carefully organized, supple and smooth whatever the tempo; soloists faded almost imperceptibly in and out of ensemble passages. Count Basie topped the bill at the Royal Roost while the nonet was playing there. It sounded "strange and good," he remembered. "I didn't always know what they were doing, but I listened and I liked it." Walter Rivers, an executive at Capitol Records, liked it, too, and recorded twelve sides. Gerry Mulligan wrote five of the arrangements (John Lewis, Gil Evans, Miles Davis, and Johnny Carisi wrote the others), but there would have been no nonet and no recordings without Miles Davis.

Davis would always want to be in charge. Modernist critics who saw special virtue in newness and record company executives who saw commercial advantage in novelty would insist on portraying him as a great innovator—"the most consistently innovative musician in jazz from the late 1940's through the 1960's," according to *The New Grove Dictionary of Jazz*—and he liked to see himself that way as well. In fact, he was something more complex, more interesting: a master consolidator, able without apparent effort to incorporate other people's discoveries, alter and arrange them to suit his own fierce musical intelligence, and repackage them in ways that made them unmistakably his own. The results were simultaneously admired by other musicians and appealing to a good many listeners who might otherwise have been uninterested in jazz.

He developed his own instantly identifiable trumpet sound by bringing to the complexity of Dizzy Gillespie's music something of the lyricism and simplicity of statement of the trumpet players of an earlier era. Like Duke Ellington, he was a lifelong tal-

Early Miles. (Above) At thirteen, far left, with his sister Dorothy, brother Vernon, and mother Cleota Davis; and (below) the trumpet player farthest from the camera, as a seventeen-year-old member of Eddie Randle's Rhumboogie Orchestra in St. Louis

ent scout, always on the lookout for musicians who sounded "different from everybody else," he said, and then—also like Ellington—capable of creating an altogether fresh collective sound out of those individual differences. Davis's seductive trumpet playing and brooding good looks— "the difference between me and other musicians is that I've got charisma," he once told an interviewer—combined with the peculiarities of his personality and the unique opportunities presented by the changing times through which he lived, allowed him actually to become the sort of musical superstar Parker and Gillespie could only dream of being. But the price of sustaining that success would eventually be the abandonment of the music that made him great.

He was born on May 26, 1926, in Alton, Illinois, and raised in East St. Louis. His full name was Miles Dewey Davis III, but, because he was the son of a well-known dentist and gentleman farmer with the same name, he was known to everyone in town as "Junior." Small and dark and so good-looking that schoolmates called him both "Inky" and "Pretty" just to annoy him, Davis was raised in the kind of cushioned comfort few of his fellow musicians ever knew: a big house in town, as well as a two-hundred-acre farm with a cook, a maid, and a stable of riding horses. He delivered newspapers as a boy, not because he needed the money, but because his parents thought it would be good for him to earn a little on his own. His slight appearance and the relative affluence of his upbringing would eventually embarrass Davis, who wanted above all to be accepted by the street-smart jazz fraternity. To compensate, he would adopt an exaggerated toughness that he never abandoned.

His parents quarreled constantly—they would divorce in 1944—and his father gave him his first trumpet when he was thirteen, Davis said, mostly because his mother wanted him to play the more genteel violin. His first idol was Harry James, whose fat, romantic sound, filled with vibrato, he dreamed of emulating. His trumpet teacher, Elwood Buchanan, worked hard to get him to stop what he called "all that shakin' he's doing. Man, he's gonna shake enough when he gets old." "In high school," Davis told an interviewer many years later, "I was the best in the music class on the trumpet and I knew it, but all the contest prizes went to the boys with the blue eyes. It made me so mad I made up my mind to outdo anybody white on my horn. . . . [P]rejudice and curiosity have been responsible for what I've done in music."

Jazzmen became his heroes: "I was fascinated by the musicians, particularly guys who used to come up from New Orleans and jam all night. I'd sit there and look at them, watch the way they walked and talked, how they fixed their hair, how they'd drink, and of course how they played." One of his idols was a local star, Clark Terry, who would one

day play with Duke Ellington and Count Basie. Davis landed jobs with two local groups, Eddie Randle's Rhumboogie Orchestra and Adam Lambert's Six Brown Cats. Each specialized in small-group swing for dancing, with a heavy emphasis on the blues. When the Billy Eckstine Band came to St. Louis in the summer of 1944 and the third trumpet fell ill, Davis got a chance to sit in for a week. He was a good sight reader and had no trouble with the arrangements, he remembered, but he had barely been able to bring himself to play "because I was listening to what everybody *else* was playing. . . . Bird was unbelievable. . . . [Eckstine's] band changed my life. I decided right then and there that I had to leave St. Louis and live in New York where all these bad musicians were."

He was growing up fast—at eighteen he was already supporting a wife and baby

daughter—but his decision to move to New York to seek out his idols, made a few weeks after sitting in with the Eckstine band, was bitterly opposed by his mother. Like the parents of Bix Beiderbecke, Fletcher Henderson, and Teddy Wilson, she had hoped for a more sedate future for her boy, beginning with a university education at Fisk, and she agreed to his departure only after he promised to attend classes at the Juilliard School of Music.

Though he did develop a lifelong interest in music theory at Juilliard, Davis would spend just one semester there. He found the unrelenting emphasis on the classics wearying; disliked the sort of tone his trumpet teacher insisted upon; was wary of his fellow students, all but a handful of whom were white; and had no faith that any symphony orchestra was going to hire him, no matter how well he played. Instead of attending classes, he spent much of his time and all of his first month's allowance trying to track down Charlie Parker. Eventually, he persuaded his hero to move in with him. Parker's music continued to enthrall him, but he was soon put off by the older man's personality—what he called his "greed." Davis came home from work one evening to find that most of his belongings had disappeared, pawned by Parker to raise money for drugs. Davis was furious, so furious, he said, that he got his knife and went looking for his lodger. When he found him, Parker was on the bandstand, wearing Davis's best suit, though its trousers barely reached his ankles and its sleeves ended inches above his hands. Davis started toward the bandstand, then stood transfixed. "You couldn't believe what he was playing," he remembered. "You couldn't believe what was coming out of his horn. You had to love him."

Davis continued to love Parker, continued to hang around his bandstand wherever he played. "Miles Davis was cocky," Stan Levey recalled. "Always dressed in a Brooks Brothers suit and standing around the Three Deuces when we were

Young Miles Davis, second from the left, in the fastest possible company. Charlie Parker, Allen Eager, and Kai Winding at New York's Royal Roost, 1948

Juliette Greco and Miles Davis in Paris. "Music had been my entire life until I met [her]," Davis recalled. "She taught me what it was to love someone."

there with a matchbook, copying down chord changes." Soon Davis was appearing regularly alongside Parker in clubs and recording studios, doing his best to play in the fleet style of Dizzy Gillespie and his most virtuosic disciple, Fats Navarro.

Then, in the spring of 1949, he traveled to Paris in the same troupe as Parker and Sidney Bechet. Davis had not been prepared to be impressed by the Old World. Still young and unsure of himself, he compensated by trying to appear impervious to everything. But the trip "changed the way I looked at things forever," he remembered. "Paris was where I understood that all white people weren't the same." He met Picasso and Sartre and Albert Camus, and had a brief, heady romance with the singer and actress Juliette Greco. "I had never felt like that in my life," he said. "It was the freedom . . . of being treated like a human being, like someone *important*."

"I was so depressed coming back to this country on the airplane that I couldn't say nothing all the way back," he recalled in his

autobiography, and he claimed that his subsequent addiction to drugs had been caused by the stark contrast between the way he had been treated in France and his experience scrounging for jobs back home. "In Paris," he said, "whatever we played . . . , right or wrong, was cheered . . . and we came back over here and couldn't even find . . . work, international stars and couldn't get jobs." But in an earlier interview Davis stated things more starkly. He got hooked, he said then, because "I got bored and was around cats that were hung."

Whatever the truth of the matter, Miles Davis turned to heroin—first snorting it, then injecting it directly into his veins. His marriage ended. To support his habit—"to feed the beast," as he called it—he stole from friends, pawned his horn, even became a pimp. He was briefly jailed for possession in Los Angeles but beat the charge. Then his own father, desperate to make him quit his habit, had him arrested again in the hope that he would commit himself for treatment. Davis refused to sign in, cursed his father, returned to heroin. He was beginning to earn a reputation as difficult, unreliable. Jobs grew still more scarce. "It was bad enough playing the kind of music that we played," he remembered, "but with a habit it was worse. People started looking at me another way, like I was dirty or something. They looked at me with pity and horror, and they hadn't looked at me that way before." Miles Davis then seemed likely to be just one more promising musician devastated by drugs.

JAZZ GOES TO COLLEGE

The twelve sides cut by the Miles Davis Nonet never sold particularly well as singles and when they did finally appear on a twelve-inch LP in 1957, the album was titled *Birth of the Cool* by executives at Capitol Records seeking to cash in on the pub-

lic's current fascination with what jazz journalists were variously calling "cool" and "West Coast" jazz. In fact, the records didn't represent the birth of anything. There had been cool players since the days of Frankie Trumbauer. Nor did the musicians who played on them ever consider themselves members of any "school." But, like Davis, they were all interested in solving the problems that had inspired them to flock to Gil Evans's apartment in the first place: how best to bring what Evans called the "rhythmic and harmonic revolutions" of bebop to a larger and more receptive audience, and how to bring about a better balance between the soloist and the group.

Gerry Mulligan was among the first to offer a solution. A fine musician, capable of brilliant improvisation in the baritone's rarely heard upper range, he was also a skilled arranger. After working with Davis and Evans, he had moved on to California, where he had shown that even the overbearing Stan Kenton orchestra could *almost* be made to swing if given the right charts. Then, in early 1952, he put together a quartet of his own at the Haig, a small club on Wilshire Boulevard in Los Angeles. On trumpet was Chet Baker, with a pensive sound something like the one Miles Davis had begun to develop. Chico Hamilton was on drums, Bob Whitlock or Carson Smith on bass. There was no piano, but Mulligan didn't seem to need one. The horns played counterpoint. The drums and bass played melodic lines, as well as rhythm, and the rhythm itself shifted effortlessly from Dixieland two-step to 4/4 swing to bop-style polyrhythms and back again. The quartet's sound was rollicking, breezy, and good-humored, inviting to those who found bebop forbidding. It began to build a small but enthusiastic local following. Then, just as had happened to Benny Goodman with such happy results in Chicago in 1936 (and to Parker and Gillespie with such disastrous ones in 1945), a writer for *Time* happened by the club and wrote up the group. Its sound, he said, was "just about unique in

Gerry Mulligan in the recording studio

"What we wanted to do," said the drummer Shelly Manne, "was write some new kind of material for jazz musicians, where the solos and the improvisation became part of the whole, and you couldn't tell where the writing ended and the improvisation began. The spaces were right, it was lighter, maybe a little more 'laid-back.' "

Eastern jazz journalists—and there were virtually no western ones—generally derided West Coast jazz as tepid and derivative, best understood as background music for life in a region where the sun never seemed to stop shining. But a large part of the mostly white record-buying, concert-going public loved it. During the mid-fifties, *Down Beat* readers voted Chet Baker the best trumpet player in the country, ahead of Miles Davis, Louis Armstrong, and Dizzy Gillespie, precisely as their parents had preferred Benny Goodman to Count Basie and Duke Ellington during the late 1930s. Shelly Manne later maintained that *Birth of the Cool* had been the "main influence" on the growth of West Coast jazz. Gillespie disagreed: "Miles wasn't cool . . . like that. . . . Miles is from the part of St. Louis where the blues come from. Just part of his music is played like that, cool. They copped that part—the cool—but let the rest, the blues, go, or they missed it."

The Modern Jazz Quartet's music had all the intricacy and subtle dynamics of the most sophisticated chamber music, but the blues were never out of earshot. Its musical director, John Lewis, another veteran of the *Birth of the Cool* sessions, had always loved Charlie Parker's music but loathed the corrupting influence of Parker's addictions and the terrible damage they had done to the reputation of jazz and the men who played it. And, like Miles Davis and Gerry Mulligan, he saw no reason why the chaos of the jam session should remain the paradigm for small-group jazz. "I think the audience . . . can be strengthened," he once told an interviewer, "if we strengthen our work with structure."

the jazz field. . . . In comparison with the frantic extremes of bop, [Mulligan's] jazz is rich and even orderly, . . . marked by an almost Bach-like counterpoint. As in Bach, each Mulligan man is busily looking for a pause, a hole in the music which he can fill with an answering phrase." Soon there were long lines outside the Haig waiting to get in, and recordings by the quartet—"Line for Lyons," "Bernie's Tune," "My Funny Valentine"—made for a Los Angeles label called Pacific were being heard on the radio. Gerry Mulligan and Chet Baker found themselves stars.

Other California musicians—many of them alumni of the Kenton and Herman orchestras, including clarinet and tenor saxophone player Jimmy Giuffre, flutist and alto saxophonist Bud Shank, and trumpeter Shorty Rogers—were conducting similar experiments, and the jazz press began to write about a new West Coast "cool" school.

The Modern Jazz Quartet grew directly out of the Dizzy Gillespie big band. Lewis, vibraphonist Milt Jackson, bassist Ray Brown, and drummer Kenny Clarke had begun playing together nightly as a sort of entr'acte, mostly to give the winded Gillespie brass section a chance to regroup after one or another of the taxing flag-wavers for which the band was famous. After the orchestra broke up in 1950, they recorded as the Milt Jackson Quartet—the "MJQ." Shortly thereafter, Brown went on the road with his wife, Ella Fitzgerald, and was replaced by another outstanding bassist, Percy Heath. The group recorded again, began to attract some attention, and, since none of the four men wanted to acknowledge any of the others as leader, resolved to stay together as a cooperative renamed the Modern Jazz Quartet in order to retain the initials by which they were already beginning to get known. Connie Kay joined the group after Kenny Clarke moved permanently to Europe in 1955.

John Lewis served for a time as president of the summer music school at Lenox, Massachusetts, headquarters of the "third stream movement," which sought to blend jazz and classical music into something altogether new. He would compose pieces with foreign-sounding names—"Vendome" and *Django,* the "La Ronde Suite" and "Jazz Ostinato"—many of which were filled with fugal passages and counterpoint. And the quartet developed its first following playing concert halls in Europe. But Duke Ellington and Count Basie remained at the heart of Lewis's music. Ellington was his idol—his initial interest in fugues grew out of hearing Ellington's "Fugue-a-ditty" at Carnegie Hall in 1946—and he wanted the quartet to have the same sort of impact Basie's first band had had. Basie, he said, had managed to "integrate ensemble playing which projected—and sounded like—the spontaneous playing of ideas which were the personal expression of every member."

Not since Jelly Roll Morton's Red Hot Peppers thirty years earlier had a small

Members of the so-called cool school got the most critical attention in California during the 1950s but they were never alone on the Pacific Coast, as this souvenir of an all-star jam session at Jimbo's Bop City in San Francisco in 1952 attests. Tenor saxophonists Dexter Gordon and Jimmy Heath are in the left foreground; Heath's brother, Percy, plays bass, Milt Jackson is to his left; Roy Porter is on drums; Hampton Hawes is at the piano; and alto saxophonist Sonny Criss is second from the right. The club owner "Jimbo" Edwards is in the right foreground.

jazz group achieved such an exquisite equilibrium between written and improvised passages, between the soloist and the ensemble, the part and the whole. It was an ideal assemblage of personalities. Lewis's own playing was clear, concise. Milt Jackson, who began his musical life singing in a gospel quartet, was one of the greatest masters of blues feeling in jazz. Percy Heath and Connie Kay played together as if they were joined at the hip; and Kaye was a supremely tasteful drummer, capable of swinging hard using only a set of tiny bells. "Collectively, the group has no peers, past or present," wrote Whitney Balliett. "It exudes tact, understanding, sympathy, and a loyalty that conceals all inward friction, if any. Indeed, its members, having attained a utopian selflessness, listen to each other more than to themselves."

The members of the MJQ wore tuxedoes onstage, did not banter with the crowd, and made it known that they preferred respectful concert hall audiences to raucous night-

clubs—facts that caused writers with short memories to dismiss them as ostentatious and overly solemn. In fact, as Milt Jackson patiently explained, the group's demeanor grew directly out of the prewar African-American jazz tradition: "We wanted to bring back a level of dignity that we all remembered from watching all those great bands in the swing era. That was a very important part of jazz that I think we lost somewhere along the way." "I am an American Negro," John Lewis once said. "I'm proud of it and I want to enhance that position." He and the Modern Jazz Quartet would continue to do precisely that for some forty years.

On Monday evening, March 2, 1953, snow blanketed Tappan Square in downtown Oberlin, Ohio, and the students headed for the big Romanesque-style chapel named for the abolitionist president of Oberlin College, Charles Grandison Finney, were bundled against an icy wind. The Dave Brubeck

Quartet was to appear there that evening, and as the concertgoers filed through the doors, stomping snow from their boots, slipping out of coats and scarves, settling into the yellow-oak pews, neither they nor the musicians nervously waiting backstage were quite sure how the evening would go. Jazz concerts on campuses were still relatively rare in the East, and Brubeck had been told he might find the audience in Finney Chapel especially unresponsive, since it was sure to include music students from the Oberlin Conservatory—*serious* musicians, he was warned, who "don't understand jazz."

No one was more serious about music than the pianist himself, and no one knew better than he how wide the traditional gulf still was between jazz and classical music. When he was an undergraduate at the College of the Pacific before the war, some members of the faculty treated him with open contempt for wanting to play jazz. But afterward, at Mills College, he studied with the French composer Darius Milhaud, who had incorporated elements of jazz into his own music as early as 1923, and whose attitude was very different. When Milhaud asked on the first day of class if there were any jazz musicians in the room, Brubeck was initially afraid to raise his hand. "I'd been so used to being put down for being a jazz musician," he recalled. "Most conservatories in the United States still wouldn't let you play jazz, even in a practice room." He lifted his hand anyway, and

The Modern Jazz Quartet: Percy Heath, Connie Kay, John Lewis, and Milt Jackson. Their music was "tintinabulous," wrote Whitney Balliett. "It shimmers, it sings, it hums. It is airy and clean. Like any great mechanism, its parts are as notable as their sum."

The classic Dave Brubeck Quartet—drummer Joe Morello, bassist Gene Wright, Brubeck, and Paul Desmond—performs at the New York World's Fair in 1964.

so did several others. Milhaud told them that George Gershwin and Duke Ellington were the two most important American composers, and that "if you're going to express America, you've got to have the jazz idiom in your music." Anyone who wanted to write his homework in fugue and counterpoint as jazz was free to do so.

That was all the encouragement Brubeck and his friends needed. They formed an octet in 1946 that employed modernist elements borrowed from European music, including the unusual time signatures that would remain hallmarks of Brubeck's music for half a century. After college, Brubeck formed a trio, then a quartet, and began gathering a following on California campuses. Dance bands had visited colleges since the early days of jazz, but students who wanted to listen rather than dance had been forced to go far afield. Beginning in the 1950s, musicians like Brubeck began to take jazz to them.

Journalists sometimes classified Brubeck with other West Coast musicians because he came from California and enjoyed mak-

ing musical reference to the classics, but there was nothing remotely cool about his playing. He was a fiery, uncompromising improviser—dissonant, unsentimental, rhythmically daring. Some writers dismissed him as ponderous and heavy-handed. "The word 'bombastic' keeps coming up," an exasperated Brubeck once told a friend, "as if it were some trap I keep falling into. Damn it, when I'm bombastic, I have my reasons. I want to be bombastic. Take it or leave it." In any case, his style was perfectly complemented by the playing of alto saxophonist Paul Desmond: light, lyrical, floating, more like Lester Young than Charlie Parker—like the sound, Desmond himself famously said, of a dry martini. "The things I'm looking for musically," Desmond once told an interviewer, "are clarity, emotional communication on a not-too-obvious level, form in a chorus that doesn't hit you over the head but is there if you look for it, humor, and construction that sounds logical in an unexpected way. That, and a good dependable high F-sharp, and I'll be happy."

Each made the other better, and at Oberlin that evening in 1953 they outdid themselves. The audience—including the conservatory students—responded with ovation after ovation. The concert was recorded, and the album that resulted— *Jazz at Oberlin*—helped build enthusiasm for Brubeck. He was signed by Columbia, the nation's biggest label; made another live album, called *Jazz Goes to College;* and soon found himself the leader of the most popular jazz group in the country. Black as well as white fans followed the quartet during the 1950s. It was named the favorite group of the readers of the Pittsburgh *Courier,* and Brubeck never forgot that when Willie the Lion Smith heard one of his records in a blindfold test, Smith had said, "He plays . . . like where the blues was born. . . . He has heavy hands but hits some beautiful chords. . . . You could put this on at anybody's house, and they'd dance all night."

The Dave Brubeck Quartet would introduce hundreds of thousands of young people to jazz over the coming years.

FIFTY-TWO WEEKS
A YEAR

The Oberlin Conservatory students had loved the Brubeck concert, but like other music schools all across the country, the conservatory itself was slow to warm to jazz. When Duke Ellington and his orchestra arrived for a concert on the same Finney Chapel stage three years later, the gleaming grand piano traditionally used by visiting artists was gone, replaced by a smaller, scarred-up instrument. Where was the grand piano? the embarrassed president of the jazz club asked. Back in storage, a custodian explained. The conservatory had a standing rule: jazz musicians were not to play the good pianos; they might hurt them. Ellington, betraying not even a flicker of annoyance, strode onstage, seated himself at the battered piano, and launched into the introduction to "Take the 'A' Train" as if he were seated at the finest instrument on earth.

On Thursday, November 4, 1954, Dave Brubeck was in San Francisco nearing the end of a tour as part of a Norman Granz "Modern Jazz Concert" package that included Gerry Mulligan and Stan Getz, as well as the Duke Ellington Orchestra. No one understood better than Brubeck the debt he owed to earlier generations of black musicians, and he considered Ellington both a good friend and the greatest of all American composers. That morning, Brubeck remembered, "I heard a knock on my hotel room [door] at seven o'clock and it was Duke, and he said, 'Dave, you're on the cover of *Time* magazine.' And my heart sank. . . . I wanted to be on the cover *after* Duke. The worst thing that could have happened to me was that I was there before Duke and he was delivering the magazine to me, saying, 'Here.' "

Ellington, long accustomed to seeing the spotlight trained on other musicians, was characteristically gracious about Brubeck's good fortune and was genuinely fond of him

personally. Toward the end of Ellington's life, after Yale University had given him an honorary degree and set up a fellowship in his name, he would ask his son Mercer to make sure that Brubeck and his onetime drummer Louis Bellson were both made Ellington fellows. "I don't want people to think I only had black friends," he said.

Ellington's creativity had not slowed. The bebop revolution had not directly affected his orchestra, in part because his own music had always been at least as harmonically rich as that of the boppers. Earlier records like "CottonTail" and "Main Stem" had presaged a good many of the changes they had made; but several of his new men, including the trumpet player Clark Terry and the tenor saxophonist Paul Gonsalves, were fully familiar with the style. The long-playing record, introduced by Columbia in 1948, seemed made for Ellington, who could now move beyond the limitations of the three-minute 78. In 1950, he recorded *Masterpieces by Ellington,* concert-length versions of four favorites, including "Mood Indigo." He followed that two years later with *Ellington Uptown in Hi-Fi,* including a definitive thirteen-minute performance of his *Tone Parallel to Harlem,* a richly colored, wonderfully various portrait of the neighborhood he loved, which many believe to have been the finest of his extended works.

But ballrooms continued to close all across the country as Americans turned in ever-growing numbers to television for their entertainment. In February 1950, *Down Beat* presented Ellington with a special award simply for still being in business. By then, every one of the big bands that had appeared in the 1949 readers' poll had left the road but his; even Count Basie had now been forced to give up his orchestra in favor of an octet, before forming what Albert Murray called his "New Testament" band and starting all over again two years later.

The Ellington Orchestra no longer sounded quite the same. Drummer Sonny Greer had left, replaced first by Louis Bellson and eventually by Sam Woodyard. Two

Dave Brubeck on the cover of *Time*

of the most familiar Ellington "voices," Lawrence Brown and Johnny Hodges, also went out on their own for a time. Ellington could no longer afford the sleek private Pullman that had carried his men everywhere —he was frequently working for the same fees he had received twenty years earlier— so he and Harry Carney drove together across the continent in Carney's Cadillac while the rest of the men traveled by bus. Feeling it necessary to scotch persistent rumors that he, too, would be forced to abandon his orchestra, he explained that he was paying his bills with the earnings from his songs. "The . . . reason we're still in it is . . . artistic interest. We're not one of those people who stay in the business only so long as business is good. We stay in it fifty-two weeks a year. . . . The fun of writing and participating in music is the motivating force that keeps us going on and on."

But he was struggling now, as he had not struggled since his early days in the business. Frank Schiffman, proprietor of the Apollo Theatre in Harlem, kept an index card on every artist who ever appeared on his stage, assessing his or her act and detailing how many tickets they had sold. An entry he made in 1954 provided a stark summary of the situation in which Duke Ellington found himself: "Unchanged pattern. Fine personality. Good band. Mediocre draw."

MY NAME IS BIRD

On the night of October 30, 1954, with Dave Brubeck's owlish *Time* cover portrait soon to begin peering out from every newsstand in New York, Charlie Parker appeared at Town Hall. Thelonious Monk was on the bill that evening. So were several of the most promising of Parker's young admirers: tenor saxophonist Sonny Rollins, trumpet player Art Farmer, pianist Horace Silver. But the publicity for the evening had been poor, more seats were empty than filled, and at intermission the musician's union seized half of Parker's earnings as a penalty for having failed to follow its rules. Several weeks later, the record producer Ross Russell went to see Parker play at an Eighth Avenue spot called Le Club Downbeat. Parker's suit was dirty and unpressed, Russell said, and he was wearing carpet slippers instead of shoes: "His face was bloated and his eyelids so heavy that only half the pupils showed. The first five minutes of the set were spent in slowly assembling his saxophone while fellow musicians, all of them unknown, stood nervously on the bandstand. When Charlie got around to playing it was evident that he was having trouble getting air through the horn."

Parker was clearly spiraling downward. In March he had been in Hollywood when he received word from Chan in New York that their two-year-old daughter, Pree, was dead of pneumonia. The night he got the

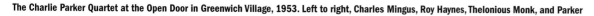

The Charlie Parker Quartet at the Open Door in Greenwich Village, 1953. Left to right, Charles Mingus, Roy Haynes, Thelonious Monk, and Parker

THE ARCHITECT

No more mysterious man ever played jazz than Thelonious Sphere Monk. And few created more memorable music. At first, casual listeners noticed only Monk's eccentricities. He had his own way of dressing and styles of headgear. He went for days without speaking to anyone. He sometimes got up in midperformance to dance in apparent ecstasy and rarely played anyone else's music, he once explained, because he was determined to create a demand for his own. And, though his first label, Blue Note, sought to capitalize on his strangeness by billing him as a "mysterious character . . . a strange person . . . the High Priest of Bebop," he intensely disliked being categorized as part of any "bebop movement." He was always Thelonious Monk, his own man.

Even his distinctive, splay-fingered, stride-based percussive keyboard style caused talk. "Thelonious would wait a minute before he hit a key," recalled Loraine Gordon, whose husband, Max, owned the Village Vanguard where he often played, "and I'd say, 'Oh, my God. Is he going to make it?' . . . And I used to sit there saying, 'Oooh, where's it going to land? Where's it going to?' And it was always right. He always landed on the right note."

In 1951, New York police found narcotics in a parked car in which Monk and his fellow pianist Bud Powell were sitting. The drugs actually belonged to Powell, but when Monk refused to testify against his friend, he was denied a cabaret card and so was forbidden to play anywhere within the city where alcohol was served. Monk refused to consider leaving town. Nor would he take a day job. Instead, for six long years he mostly stayed at home in his crowded apartment, making an occasional date in the suburbs and recording from time to time for Prestige, but otherwise bent over his keyboard, working on the music that was his obsession. His wife, Nellie, supported the family.

Finally, in 1957, Riverside Records issued *Brilliant Corners*, an album on which he played his own compositions with a small group that included the tenor saxophonist Sonny Rollins and the drummer Art Blakey. The jazz writer Nat Hentoff gave it an enthusiastic review in *Down Beat*. Then, with the help of his manager who swore (falsely) that Monk used no drugs, he finally obtained a new cabaret card in time to take a quartet into the Five Spot, then located in Cooper Square in Greenwich Village. Big crowds followed, suddenly eager to hear the man the critics had once scorned. Monk had not changed. He still lapsed into long silences, still broke into dance on the bandstand, still played tunes whose logic was so intricate, the tenor saxophonist John Coltrane remembered, that when his musicians got lost it was "like falling into an empty elevator shaft." It no longer mattered. The jazz public was beginning to learn what musicians had known all along: There was method in his alleged madness, a powerful musi-

cal logic into which all the sudden stops and starts, the angular rhythms and dissonant passages and unanticipated intervals that had once so alarmed his audiences

effortlessly fit. "I felt I learned from him in every way," John Coltrane recalled. "Working with Monk brought me close to a musical architect of the highest order."

Thelonious Monk, rehearsing in a New York loft with saxophonists Phil Woods and Charlie Rouse, 1959

Bud Powell

Erroll Garner was the most popular jazz pianist of the period, but Bud Powell was the most influential among other piano players. He, too, was a child prodigy, but there the similarities ended. Powell was the son of a New York stride piano player who saw to it that he had a firm grounding in the classics before he began to play jazz. The fleet, flowing style of Art Tatum was a powerful influence upon his own playing, but Thelonious Monk was his protector when he first began to appear in New York nightclubs as a teenager, already displaying two distinctive characteristics: astonishingly fast right-hand runs—"he almost plays off the end of the piano," another pianist marveled—and strange, sometimes belligerent behavior whenever he swallowed more than a sip of alcohol, an early warning of terrible trouble to come.

During a murky encounter with Philadelphia police in the spring of 1945, Powell was beaten repeatedly over the head. His injuries seem to have intensified his mental problems. He spent ten months in an institution on Long Island, returned to the clubs, then suffered a second breakdown, after which he was locked up for eleven months. Electric shock treatments calmed his outbursts but they also damaged his memory for much more than music. He drew a keyboard on the wall of his cell, ran his fingers silently over it, then asked bewildered visitors how they thought he sounded. He lived and performed in France for several years but was never entirely rational again; he spent time in and out of institutions, sometimes stopped playing for minutes at a time to stare into the audience. He died at forty-two. But Powell was, as Dizzy Gillespie said, "the definitive pianist of the bebop era," and his playing—urgent and acrobatic, elegant and anguished by turns—influenced the way a whole generation of musicians would approach the keyboard.

news, Parker sent four telegrams, each more incoherent than the last.

> MY DARLING. MY DAUGHTER'S DEATH SURPRISED ME MORE THAN IT DID YOU. DON'T FULFILL FUNERAL PROCEEDINGS UNTIL I GET THERE. I SHALL BE THE FIRST ONE TO WALK INTO OUR CHAPEL. FORGIVE ME FOR NOT BEING THERE WITH YOU WHILE YOU ARE AT THE HOSPITAL. YOURS MOST SINCERELY, YOUR HUSBAND,
> CHARLIE PARKER.

> MY DARLING, FOR GOD'S SAKE HOLD ON TO YOURSELF.
> CHARLES PARKER.

> CHAN, HELP.
> CHARLIE PARKER.

> MY DAUGHTER IS DEAD. I KNOW IT. I WILL BE THERE AS QUICK AS I CAN. MY NAME IS BIRD. IT IS VERY NICE TO BE OUT HERE. PEOPLE HAVE BEEN VERY NICE TO ME OUT HERE. I AM COMING IN RIGHT AWAY. TAKE IT EASY. LET ME BE THE FIRST ONE TO APPROACH YOU. I AM YOUR HUSBAND. SINCERELY,
> CHARLIE PARKER

He managed to get through the funeral but then seemed unable to hold himself together. An engagement with a string section at Birdland ended in disaster when he drank too much and tried to fire the band. The manager fired him instead. He went home to Chan, quarreled with her—and tried to kill himself by swallowing iodine. Ambulance workers saved him. He twice had himself committed to Bellevue Hospital for psychiatric help, began riding the subways all night, often seemed frightened, suspicious even of his admirers. "They just came out . . . to see the world's most famous junkie," he told a friend.

The man who had hoped to demonstrate that jazz need not be linked to show business had himself become a public spectacle. "No jazzman," wrote Ralph Ellison, "struggled harder to escape the enter-

tainer's role than Charlie Parker. The pathos of Bird's life lies in the ironic reversal through which his struggles to escape what in Armstrong is basically a *make-believe* role of clown—which the irreverent poetry and triumphant sound of his trumpet makes even the squarest of squares aware of—resulted in Parker's becoming something far more 'primitive': a sacrificial figure whose struggles against personal chaos, on stage and off, served as entertainment for a ravenous, sensation-starved, culturally disoriented public which had but the slightest notion of its real significance."

One evening, Parker made his way into a club where Dizzy Gillespie sat listening to a band. Parker was disoriented: "Why don't you save me, Diz?" he said over and over again. "Why don't you save me?" "I didn't know what to do," Gillespie remembered. "I just didn't know what to say." Parker stumbled back out onto the street.

"I ran into him one night about three in the morning," the writer Nat Hentoff recalled. "I was going downstairs into Birdland. Bird was coming up. We didn't [really] know each other. I'd interviewed him a couple of times on radio. And tears were streaming down his face. He said, 'I've got to talk to you, I've got to talk to you.' I said, 'Fine, there's an all-night coffee shop on the corner.' 'No, no. I'll call you tomorrow.' Well, he never called. I could have been anybody, I think."

On Saturday, March 5, 1955, Parker was booked into Birdland again, this time as leader of a quintet that included Art Blakey, the trumpet player Kenny Dorham, bassist Charles Mingus, and the troubled pianist Bud Powell. Parker arrived late, then fled the bandstand when he saw that Powell was so drunk he could barely stay on the piano bench. When Parker came back for the second set and called the first tune, Powell insisted on playing another, then slammed the keyboard shut and walked off while Parker stood at the microphone helplessly calling after him, "Bud Powell," "Bud Powell," over and over again. Finally, Mingus pushed him aside. "Ladies and gentlemen," he told the crowd, "please don't associate me with any of this. This is not jazz. These are sick people."

The night after the Birdland debacle, Parker and a group of friends turned up at the Open Door to hear young Jackie McLean. Ordinarily, McLean would have been thrilled that his hero was showing interest in him. But not this time. "I had rented this horn and used it," he remembered, "and one night I was getting in a cab and I had been drinking a lot and Bird was helping me to get in the cab with some other people, and he said, 'Here, let me take this.' And he took the horn. And of course, about two or three days later, when I saw him, he didn't have the horn. It was in the pawn shop. I was a little angry at him about that, so when he invited to drop me home after the job was over, I said, 'No, that's okay. I'll get a cab.'"

On the evening of March 9, George Wein, now grown up and the owner of a Boston club called Storyville, was expecting Parker to turn up for an engagement that was to begin the following day. "I came into the club about eight o'clock," he recalled, "and Bird was not there. And somebody said, 'Bird's on the telephone.' And I picked up the phone and I dialed the number and a recorded voice said there was a yellow-tipped swallow seen this morning at the Ipswich marshes. It was the Audubon Society. Somebody played a joke on me, you know, to call 'Bird.' . . . And I hung up. I laughed. And Bird never showed up. So far as we were concerned, 'What the hell, Bird goofed again.' But it was his last goof."

Parker had packed his bag that evening, intending to leave New York for Boston. But on the way to Grand Central Station he dropped by the Stanhope Hotel on upper Fifth Avenue to see his friend the Baroness Pannonica de Koenigswarter, a member of the Rothschild family and a generous patron of jazz and jazz musicians. Parker was

Broadway in 1957. The Alvin Hotel, which would one day become the last home of Lester Young, is at the left, just across the street from Birdland.

clearly ill when he got there, and soon began vomiting blood.

Alarmed, the baroness called a doctor. The doctor asked Parker if he drank. "Sometimes," Parker answered, "a sherry before dinner." The doctor urged that he be hospitalized. Parker refused. He'd had enough of hospitals. The baroness and her daughter agreed to do what they could for him.

On Saturday evening, March 12, still at the Stanhope, Parker turned on the television to watch *Stage Show,* the Dorsey brothers' weekly variety program. He had always liked the sound of Jimmy Dorsey's saxophone. The first act was a comedy juggler. Parker laughed, choked, then collapsed. By the time the doctor could get there, he was dead. The official cause was pneumonia, complicated by cirrhosis of the liver. But Parker had simply worn himself out.

"I bought a New York *Post,*" Jackie McLean remembered, "and I sat down on the bus and I rode for several blocks before I opened it, and then when I opened the paper and looked inside, I saw that Bird was dead, that he had passed away at the Baroness's. Of course, I was in tears. I felt especially bad because I had just seen him at the Open Door and, being angry about the horn, I had missed [having] one more moment with him, you know, if I hadn't been over-reacting. Everybody was crushed when Bird died. I didn't go to his funeral. I couldn't, I just couldn't go, couldn't be a part of that."

Although the coroner had estimated Parker's age at between fifty-five and sixty, he was just thirty-four when he died. At thirty-four, Louis Armstrong still had thirty-seven years of music-making ahead of him. At the same age, Duke Ellington had only begun to write the extended works that would help win him his place among America's most important composers. Parker's innovations had been enormously important, but his weaknesses had insured that his dreams of moving jazz in still more new

It seemed to many critics eagerly looking for an heir to Charlie Parker during the late 1950s that Sonny Rollins must be that man. He grew up on the West Side of Manhattan, a neighbor of Thelonious Monk, Bud Powell, and the great Coleman Hawkins, whose huge aggressive tone he would incorporate into his own. Rollins's wellspring of ideas seemed bottomless. He played always with wit and exhilaration and titanic energy and impressed the drummer Art Blakey as being the most determined man he'd ever known. His best-known album from that period was *Saxophone Collossus*—and he seemed the living embodiment of that word. "Every place I went," he remembered, "it was 'Sonny Rollins . . . he's the cat to see.' Which was good, except that I didn't have that feeling within myself. . . . I felt that I disappointed the people."

And so in 1959, he stopped performing for more than two years. At night he would make his way out onto the Williamsburg bridge and play into the wind. "We have to make ourselves as perfect as we can," he said. "I liked to practice there because I could play as loud as I wanted and just go through anything I wanted to do."

When he came back in 1962, to many he seemed more powerful and inventive than ever, pouring forth musical ideas in solos that sometimes stretched on in clubs or onstage for an hour and more. A fearless modernist, Rollins is profoundly old-fashioned in his disdain for recording. Performing before an audience, he said, is "like having sex live"; playing in the sterility of the studio is like "cybersex." And when he is playing, nothing is allowed to get in his way. Once, at an outdoor concert at Saugerties, New York, in the summer of 1985, after playing for nearly fifteen minutes and wanting "to get closer to the people," he jumped off the high stage and shattered his heel. The pain was so great he couldn't get back onto his feet, but he went right on playing from the ground, "not just because the show must go on," he explained, "but because I still was able to blow."

Sonny Rollins

directions would in the end have to be realized by others.

By the time he was buried in Kansas City, admirers had already covered walls in Greenwich Village with the slogan "Bird Lives." For better or worse, he had become the apostle of hipness to some, and his early death only seemed to seal that misapprehension. Beyond his contributions to the music, Ralph Ellison wrote, Parker's "greatest significance was for the educated white middle-class youth whose reaction to the inconsistencies of American life was the stance of casting off its education, language, dress, manners and moral standards: a revolt, apolitical in nature, which finds its most dramatic instance in the figure of the so-called white hipster."

No one loved—or misunderstood—bebop more deeply than the Beat poets. "Jazz," Allen Ginsberg was still saying shortly before he died in 1998, "gives us a way of expressing. It's the spontaneous motions of the heart. The devotions that we feel. The ecstasies that we feel. The transcendence over the material absurdity of mechanized life that everybody's trapped in. It's like a fountain of instantaneous inspiration that's available to everybody. All you've got to do is turn on your radio or put on a record or pick up an ax yourself and blow."

The music of Parker and Gillespie and their peers was complex, sophisticated, exacting—only the most highly skilled musicians were capable of playing it. Yet the Beats insisted it was simple, spur-of-the-moment—*anybody* could do it. They would see themselves as the musician's natural allies, fellow outlaws, kindred spirits in the search for spontaneous expression. In fact, they were simply subscribing to a new version of an old misunderstand-ing: the same misunderstanding that had made Jim Europe's men hide their music in order to fulfill the white audience's expectation that they were "natural" musicians who simply let their feelings flow through their horns; the same one that suggested that Louis Armstrong's music derived from instinct while Bix Beiderbecke's was drawn from his intellect; the one that led the patrons of the Cotton Club to see Duke Ellington's complicated, worldly compositions as primitive "jungle music"; and the same one that had frequently limited black bands to recording up-tempo tunes for which they were believed to have an inborn gift. Sadly, that misunderstanding would persist through the whole history of the music, and jazz would never entirely shake the reputation for alienation and "weirdness" born out of the era of bebop and the beats.

In the hard-living world of jazz, Clifford Brown stood out. Drugs and alcohol didn't interest him, nor was he temperamental. He routinely arrived an hour early for recording dates to clean his horn and ready his mind. And he always seemed to have time for younger players eager for advice. His only vice was chess.

"Clifford was a profound influence on my personal life," Sonny Rollins remembered. "He showed me that it was possible to live a good, clean life and still be a good jazz musician." As much as his fellow musicians admired Clifford Brown's character, they were awed by the warmth and richness of his tone and the long, melodic, dancing lines that seemed to flow effortlessly from his horn.

Dizzy Gillespie had heard the nineteen-year-old Brown play and began talking him up in New York. In 1954, in California, Brown joined forces with Max Roach. For more than two years their quintet was one of the most widely admired in jazz, and it seemed to many that Clifford Brown was destined to join the ranks of the greatest of all trumpet players: Louis Armstrong, Roy Eldridge, Dizzy Gillespie, Miles Davis.

On the evening of Monday, June 25, 1956, at the end of a rare day off spent with his wife and infant son, Brown took part in a jam session in Philadelphia. He hadn't wanted to be there but, characteristically, was doing a favor for a friend. Now he would be forced to drive through the night to get to his next gig in Chicago. It was after midnight before Brown and the pianist Richie Powell finished playing. They took off in Powell's new car with Powell's wife, Nancy, at the wheel. It began to rain. Suddenly the car skidded out of control, flew over an embankment, and turned over. All three passengers were killed instantly.

Dizzy Gillespie was about to go onstage at the Apollo Theatre in Harlem when he heard the news that Clifford Brown was dead. When the curtain rose, most of the men in his band were in tears. "For his artistry," Gillespie said, "there can be no replacement."

"'ROUND MIDNIGHT"

"I don't go with this bringing 'dignity to jazz,'" Miles Davis once told an interviewer. "The way [the Modern Jazz Quartet] brings 'dignity' . . . in their formal clothes and the way they bow is like [asking Sugar] Ray Robinson [to bring] dignity to boxing by fighting in a tuxedo." The middleweight champion was one of Miles Davis's heroes. He admired Robinson's clothes, his grace and good looks, the beautiful women who clustered around him wherever he went. "But when he was training for a *fight*," Davis remembered, "he didn't have no women around . . . and when he got into the ring . . . he never smiled . . . he was all serious business."

Inspired by Robinson's seriousness about his craft and finally weary of the life his addiction was forcing him to lead, Davis resolved to kick his habit. Characteristically, he determined to do it on his own. He had just finished an engagement with Max Roach in Hollywood. He rode the bus halfway across the continent to his father's farm outside East St. Louis. His father told him he could do nothing for him except offer his love: "The rest of it you got to do for yourself." Davis did. He moved into a two-room apartment on the second floor of the family guest house and locked the door. For seven days, as the craving for drugs raged, he neither ate nor drank, shivering with cold and struggling to keep from screaming with the pain that tortured his joints. Then, he remembered, "one day it was over, just like that. . . . I walked outside into the clean, sweet air over to my father's house and when he saw me he had this big smile on his face and we just hugged each other and cried."

In fact, it wasn't quite over. There would be a good deal of backsliding with heroin and other controlled substances over the years, but when Davis returned to New York in February 1954 he was clean. "All I could think of," he recalled, "was playing music and making records and making up for all the time I had lost." That year alone, he recorded one album for Blue Note and five for Prestige as a leader, using a shifting cast of gifted young musicians. One all-star session that included Kenny Clarke, J. J. Johnson, Horace Silver, and tenor saxophonist Lucky Thompson yielded two of the greatest extended blues performances in jazz history, "Walkin'" and "Blue 'n' Boogie." To the pianist Dick Katz, they constituted "an amazing seminar . . . a sort of summing up of much of what happened musically to the players involved during the preceding ten years. It is as if they all agreed to get together to discuss on their instruments what they had learned and unlearned, what elements of bop they had retained or discarded." If Miles Davis's nonet recordings had suggested to some that the blues might profitably be sacrificed in the interest of broadening the music's appeal, these sessions went a long way toward restoring them to their rightful place.

Davis's own sound was now unmistakable. He had neither the technique nor the temperament for playing in the aggressive Gillespie mode. Instead, he had developed his own spare, introspective style, often employing a stemless Harmon mute to add intensity. It retained the older man's harmonic sophistication but relied more on distillation than on speed or long lines; on playing only what he called "the most important notes." "I always listen to what I can leave out," he once explained. He brought back into the music something of the shrewd, relaxed phrasing of Billie Holiday and Lester Young, and something as well of the emotional dynamism of earlier trumpet players that had been overlooked in the onrushing pyrotechnics of early bebop. He also brought with him an almost androgynous tenderness that, like Ben Webster's breathy intimacy, belied his sometimes belligerent public personality. By 1955, wrote Martin Williams, "one passionate note from Miles Davis seemed to imply a whole complex of expressive sound, and three notes a ravishing melody."

It was becoming fashionable among journalists to see jazz as a sort of musical relay race in which one Great Man handed the baton of innovation on to the next while everyone else faded conveniently into the background. The annual summer jazz festivals held at Newport, Rhode Island, beginning in 1954 should have demonstrated conclusively how misguided this notion was.

Newport was a seaside town of mansions and green sloping lawns, the summer retreat of some of the East Coast's wealthiest old families and about as far from the places where jazz began as it was possible to get. Two local jazz lovers, Elaine and Louis Lorillard, came up with the idea of the festival, but George Wein made it happen. "I felt that jazz could use a coming together," Wein remembered. "Economically, jazz musicians could not draw large crowds as individuals, not since the big band days. Jazz had become a club music. Jazz musicians needed a festival. By bringing many groups together we could draw many kinds of jazz fans. It became a great source of public relations for the music. People wrote about festivals because they were happenings. They were important events, successful from the start."

Wein insisted that every kind of musician be invited. Jazz should be a family affair, he said. Everyone who played it well should be welcome. Eddie Condon's Chicagoans were asked to come. So was Dizzy Gillespie. Count Basie, Stan Kenton, Dave Brubeck, Louis Armstrong, Pee Wee Russell, and Stan Getz were all going to be there. Roy Eldridge and Coleman Hawkins agreed to appear as well—though Eldridge couldn't resist kidding his old friend about playing under a tent again after nearly forty years on the road.

In 1955, Miles Davis wanted to be invited, too. "I hadn't thought of using Miles," Wein recalled, "because Miles was difficult. You'd call him and he'd say, 'Aw, I don't know if I want to do that.' I knew him. He'd worked in my club and we weren't that friendly, and he treated me like he treated everybody else." But they saw one another in New York that spring and Davis asked, "You gonna have that jazz festival up in Newport?" "Yeah, Miles," Wein replied. "You can't have a jazz festival without me," Davis said.

Wein eventually agreed. Davis would appear on the final night with an all-star group of modernists: Thelonious Monk, Gerry Mulligan, Zoot Sims, Percy Heath, and Connie Kay. "It was a difficult festival because our sound system wasn't very good," Wein recalled. "But Miles put his [muted] horn right in the microphone and

Workin',' one of four superb albums Miles Davis made for Prestige in just two days in 1956. It was not released for four years.

the only thing that came through the whole festival was his playing ''Round Midnight.' It was so beautiful that everybody wrote about it. I mean, it changed his whole life. And all I can remember when he came off is that he said to me, 'Tell Monk he plays the wrong changes on "'Round Midnight."' 'Lots of luck,' I said. 'Miles, he wrote the song, what do you want from him?'"

Davis's soft, fragile-sounding solo turned out to be the highlight of the weekend. The crowd stood to cheer him. On the strength of the Newport performance and his recent spate of extraordinary records, he won first place among trumpet players in the annual *Down Beat* Critic's Poll, nosing out Dizzy Gillespie. Davis professed to be surprised at all the fuss: "You'd think I'd been on the moon. What are they talking about? I just played the way I always played."

But George Avakian of Columbia Records had been in the audience that evening, scouting for new talent that would appeal to the same kind of college-educated audience with which Dave Brubeck was now having such success. Not only had Davis played with remarkable lyricism, he noticed, but the crowd had seemed unable to take its eyes off him, even when he was not playing. Columbia offered a contract, and Davis eagerly accepted. "The real money," he said, "was in getting to the mainstream of America," and that was where Miles Davis now wanted to be. Columbia had all the resources to get him there, to make him a jazz star on a scale not seen in jazz since the swing era. But he could not begin officially to record for his new label until he had produced four more albums for Prestige. He was so eager to move on that he managed to make them all in just two daylong sessions. All four—*Cookin', Relaxin', Workin'*, and *Steamin'*—were masterpieces.

They also helped to introduce the Miles Davis Quintet, the second group with which Davis would make jazz history. None of its members was well known when Davis found him; each would become a major figure in the music. Bassist Paul Laurence Dunbar Chambers (his middle names given in honor of the turn-of-the century poet) was just twenty, but already possessed of a huge warm sound and a rich melodic imagination. The drummer Philly Joe Jones was so obscure when Davis hired him that he was still sometimes confused with Count Basie's great drummer, Jo Jones, but he played with a rare combination of swing and simplicity, and had an uncanny ability to predict precisely where a soloist was heading and then to be waiting with the perfect support when he got there. Like all the members of the quintet except its leader, Jones was hooked on drugs and sometimes less than reliable. Davis didn't seem to care. "Look," he told one writer, "I wouldn't care if he came up on the bandstand in his BVD's and with one arm, just so he was there. He's got the fire I want. There's nothing more terrible than playing with a dull rhythm section. Jazz has got to have *that thing.*"

Pianist Red Garland was a former boxer—he had once lost to Davis's hero, Sugar Ray Robinson—possessed of an impeccable touch, a distinctive block-chord style, and a willingness to take direction. Dorothy Davis, Miles's older sister, had introduced her brother to the music of Ahmad Jamal, a Pittsburgh-born pianist popular with the public and (in part because of that) unpopular with most jazz

With Percy Heath and Gerry Mulligan, Miles Davis makes musical history at the Newport Jazz Festival in 1955.

CAFÉ
RESTAURANT
BOHEMIA

MILES DAVIS
QUINTET
TEDDY CHARLES

His career reborn, Miles Davis takes a break in front of
the Café Bohemia in Manhattan in the autumn of 1955.

writers, who dismissed him as a coy cocktail lounge entertainer rather than a serious musician. But Davis heard something else in the sound of his trio: the power of understatement, a confident willingness to let silence speak—"space breathing through the music," Davis called it—qualities he wanted to adopt for his own group and which Red Garland was able effortlessly to assimilate into his playing.

The most controversial member of the quintet was the tenor saxophonist John Coltrane. A tailor's son, born in Hamlet, North Carolina, in 1926, he was the grandson of ministers, and before he fell under the spell of Charlie Parker and performed in Dizzy Gillespie's big band and with Johnny Hodges, he had made his living playing the blues. The earnest exhortation of the preacher and the intensity of the blues were both evident in everything he ever played. He was unable to stop thinking about music when not onstage; he and his friend and sometime rival Sonny Rollins would phone one another late at night, play a phrase or two into the receiver, then hang up and wait for the other to call back with a musical answer of his own. He was so determined to play every note that crowded into his head that he often did not know when to stop. Once, at the Apollo, he continued to solo for so long that the stage manager ordered the curtain closed; Coltrane kept right on playing. Some jazz writers found his relentlessness off-putting; one compared his onrush of ideas to "epileptic fits of passion." Davis himself sometimes wearied of Coltrane's protracted playing and once asked a friend to find out why he felt it necessary to go on so long. The saxophonist answered a little sheepishly that he simply didn't know how to quit. "Tell him," Davis said, "to try taking the horn out of his mouth." But when other musicians suggested that Davis find a saxophone player better able to edit himself, he remained loyal: "I didn't understand this talk of Coltrane being difficult to understand," Davis said. "What he does is to play

John Coltrane listening to a play-back, 1957

five notes of a chord and then keep changing it around, trying to see how many different ways it can sound. It's like explaining something five different ways."

Davis understood that Coltrane's volubility was the perfect foil for his own lean, laconic approach. The Miles Davis Quintet had everything. It played standards with which most Americans could identify: "If I Were a Bell," "Surrey with the Fringe on Top," "Bye Bye Blackbird," "Some Day My Prince Will Come," "My Funny Valentine." Garland, Chambers, and Jones worked so well together that they became known independently as "The Rhythm Section." Each performance involved a five-man conversation in which each musician listened as well as stated his case. And in the amiable ongoing contest between Miles Davis and John Coltrane, listeners could witness a painter of miniatures pitted against a muralist, rapier against broadsword, haiku versus epic poetry. "All the logic of the bebop group concept had found a kind of resting point, a balance in this band," wrote the critic and pianist Tom Piazza, "a sort of miniature golden age before the assumptions of the music began to be questioned again."

OOFTAH

On the evening of April 3, 1956, a little over a month before Miles first recorded with his new quintet, twenty-one-year-old Elvis Presley was scheduled to perform on the Milton Berle television program. It was not his first television appearance; he had made his debut on the Dorsey Brothers' *Stage Show* (the program Charlie Parker had been watching when he died), performing his own versions of rhythm and blues hits first recorded by the titanic Kansas City blues shouter Joe Turner, "Shake, Rattle, and Roll" and "Flip, Flop and Fly." But the Berle show was the big time. Its star had slipped a little since he was known as "Mr. Television" because of the number of sets people had bought in order to see him, but millions still tuned in each week. This program was to be broadcast live from the deck of the U.S.S. *Hancock,* anchored in San Diego harbor. A septet led by Harry James was also on the bill, and they were openly scornful of Presley when he turned up for rehearsal with his guitar and no arrangements. The drummer Buddy Rich traced the form of a square in the air behind the singer's back and muttered, "This is the worst." James nodded agreement. The audience was filled with sailors' wives and girlfriends, who never stopped shrieking with excitement as Presley performed "Heartbreak Hotel," but after the show, James still assured a friend that this hillbilly had no talent and no future. It was wishful thinking. "Heartbreak Hotel" was already at the top of *Billboard*'s pop, country, *and* rhythm and blues charts; Presley's version of "Blue Suede Shoes" was climbing the same polls fast; his first long-playing album was on its way to becoming RCA Victor's first million-dollar seller; and he had just signed a Hollywood contract. Millions of adolescents, the fortunate beneficiaries of unprecedented American prosperity, with tens of millions of dollars of their own money to spend, were about to transform the music business; every year between

1955 and 1959, American record sales rose 36 percent. The audience for jazz was about to shrink still further. The age of rock 'n' roll had begun.

So had the modern civil rights movement. Just as the 1920s were caricatured as an era of unrelieved hedonism, the fifties have often been misrepresented as a decade of smug tranquility. They were undeniably boom years. The gross national product grew by better than a third between 1950 and 1960. Americans achieved the highest standard of living in the history of the world. The suburbs nearly doubled in size, and by the decade's end, one-quarter of all Americans lived in them.

But black Americans had emerged from the war years with greater expectations for themselves than ever before, just as other Americans had. Racial justice had not been high on the national agenda when the fifties began. Neither the executive nor the legislative branch of government could be made to show much interest, and so, with backing from the NAACP, black citizens took their struggle against segregation into the courts in Texas, Oklahoma, Virginia, Delaware, the District of Columbia, South Carolina, and Kansas, where a Topeka welder and part-time preacher named Oliver Brown and twelve other black parents sued the board of education for forcing their children to travel to distant schools when all-white public schools were closer. On May 17, 1954, the United States Supreme Court ruled in *Brown v. Board of Education* that "in the field of education the doctrine of 'separate but equal' has no place. Separate educational facilities are inherently unequal." When southern legislators urged defiance and southern school boards proved slow to act, the Court issued an order requiring them to make a prompt and reasonable start toward full compliance with "all deliberate speed."

White southerners responded with fury. Nineteen of twenty-two southern senators and eighty-two of 106 southern congress-men signed a "Southern Manifesto" that accused the Supreme Court of "clear abuse of judicial power" and promised to resist implementation of its desegregation order by "all lawful means." Eight black men were lynched in 1955, at least two of them simply for insisting on exercising their right to vote. A young black woman who attempted to enroll at the University of Alabama was manhandled by a mob and then formally "expelled." The Ku Klux Klan experienced a rebirth. Some half a million men and women joined the White Citizen's Councils of America, pledged to maintain segregation at all costs.

Bebop, rhythm and blues, and rock 'n' roll, the head of the North Alabama White Citizen's Council assured his followers, were all part of an NAACP plot to "brainwash" white youth. "Negro music appeals to the base in man," he said, "[and] brings out cannibalism and vulgarity." It was the duty of every white patriot to help stamp it out.

On April 10, 1956, just a week after Elvis Presley appeared on the Milton Berle program, Nat King Cole, the jazz pianist who had transformed himself into one of the most popular crooners in the country, was to perform with the Ted Heath Orchestra on the stage of the Birmingham Municipal Auditorium. There were to be two shows that evening—white fans at eight o'clock, black ones at ten.

As Cole strolled into the spotlight for the first show, singing his latest hit, "Little Girl," five white men leaped onto the stage. All were members of the White Citizen's Council. One hit Cole in the mouth, knocking him back over his piano stool. Another grabbed his foot and began to twist it. Eight police officers, posted in the wings in case of trouble, rushed onstage, flailing at Cole's attackers with their nightsticks. Lee Young, Cole's drummer, shouted to Ted Heath to strike up the national anthem to keep the brawl from getting bigger, but Heath was English and launched into "God Save the Queen" instead of "The Star-Spangled Banner." Cole's assailants were eventually handcuffed and taken to jail. The mayor came to the singer's dressing room to apologize. White fans shouted their regret, and Cole limped back onstage and received a long standing ovation. But he refused to sing again until the black crowd waiting anxiously outside was allowed in at ten o'clock. "Man, I love show business," he told a friend that evening, "but I don't want to die for it."

Such events not only embarrassed people of good will at home, but also grievously damaged the country's reputation overseas. The cold war had become a permanent part of life. The United States saw itself as the leader of "the free world," and Soviet propagandists delighted in spreading news of American shortcomings. Under prodding from Adam Clayton Powell Jr., now a Democratic congressman, the U.S. State Department began to seek out jazz musicians to send abroad in the hope that visits by black and white Americans making music together would help offset the bad press.

First to go was Dizzy Gillespie, who in early 1956 found himself once again in front of a big band, subsidized this time by the State Department, and scheduled to appear before jazz-hungry audiences in South Asia and the Middle East. Gillespie was an ambassador unlike any ever seen before. At an embassy garden party in Ankara, Turkey, he refused to perform until street children peering over the compound wall were allowed inside. "Man," he said when the ambassador protested, "we're not over here to play for any elites!" Everywhere he went, he remembered, reporters "asked us a lot of questions about racism in the United States. But they could see it wasn't as intense [as they'd been told] because *we* had white boys and I was the leader of the band. That was strange to them because they'd heard about blacks being lynched and burned and here I come with half whites and blacks and a girl [trombonist Melba Liston] playing in the band. And everybody seemed to be getting along fine. . . . I didn't try to hide anything, I said,

HERE WE ARE

Beginning in 1944 and continuing for nearly two decades, the California-born promoter Norman Granz led his integrated all-star Jazz at the Philharmonic troupe all over the country and overseas as well. He had two goals in mind: to broaden the audience for the music and to do so without compromising equal treatment for his musicians. He saw his programs as "a variety show of the finest jazz."

Some of the biggest names in the music were part of his package at one time or another: Dizzy Gillespie and Roy Eldridge, Charlie Parker and Benny Carter, Coleman Hawkins and Lester Young. Granz's idea of a good show, Gillespie remembered, was getting musicians "out there to battle one another's brains out onstage." The evening-long, all-star jam sessions—terrific one night, cacophonous the next—always placed a heavy emphasis on stirring up the crowd. The musicians sometimes grumbled, but Granz was unrepentant. "I may give the audience honk-

ing," he said, "but it's the best honking there is. . . . Jazz has always been, to me, fundamentally the blues and all the . . . emotions it arouses. . . . My concerts are primarily emotional music."

Granz's deep commitment to ending discrimination was never questioned. "Jazz is America's own," he said. "It is played and listened to by all peoples—in harmony, together. Pigmentation differences have no place. . . . As in genuine democracy, only performance counts." Anywhere Granz's people played, if airlines or hotels or restaurants dared try to discriminate against any of them, he did not hesitate to cancel. "He would just check everybody into the Hilton Hotel," Stan Levey remembered. "We'd all show up in the lobby and [there'd be] a lot of, you know, throat-clearing, and he'd say, 'This is our group. Let's have our rooms.' He was terrific. Norman really broke a lot of barriers. We just showed up: 'Here we are.' "

In October of 1955, only weeks before Rosa Parks refused to give up her seat on a city bus in Montgomery, Alabama, five members of the Dallas, Texas, vice squad slipped backstage at a Jazz at the Philharmonic concert. They were supposedly searching for drugs, but were actually looking for some way to show Norman Granz what they thought of his integrationist principles. They found Dizzy Gillespie and the tenor saxophone star Illinois Jacquet shooting dice in Ella Fitzgerald's dressing room and arrested all three of them. When one officer asked Gillespie his name, he answered, "Louis Armstrong." Another officer headed for the bathroom. Granz hurried after him, sure he was planning to plant narcotics. The policeman pulled his revolver. "I ought to kill you," he told Granz. "They took us down[town]," Fitzgerald remembered, "and then when we got there, they had the nerve to ask for an autograph."

Jazz at the Philharmonic troupe photographed on arrival at the Honolulu airport, 1952. Standing, Ray Brown, pianist Oscar Peterson, guitarist Barney Kessel, Norman Granz, unidentified Hawaiian promoter, Roy Eldridge, pianist Hank Jones, Lester Young. Seated, alto saxophonist Willie Smith, tenor saxophonist Flip Phillips sharing his garland with trumpeter Charley Shavers, Ella Fitzgerald, drummers Buddy Rich and Gene Krupa, and clarinetist Buddy De Franco.

'Yeah, there it is. We have our problems but we're still working on it. I'm the leader of this band, and those white guys are working for me. That's a helluva thing. A hundred years ago, our ancestors were slaves and today we're scuffling with this problem, but I'm sure it's gonna be straightened out someday.' "

Benny Goodman followed in December, fronting a new band for a tour of eight Southeast Asian nations. In Bangkok, he went directly from the airport to the royal palace, where the saxophone-playing king of Thailand was waiting to play duets with him. ("Pretty good player," a tactful Goodman said afterward, "for a king.") Twenty-five thousand Cambodians turned out to hear his band play "Blue Skies." He, too, was asked about the progress of civil rights at home. "I didn't have anything particular to say," he remembered, "other than that we've had colored musicians in the band for twenty-five years."

In the spring of 1956, the State Department turned to Louis Armstrong. He had never been more popular. He'd recently published a second memoir, a vivid account of his early years, *Satchmo: My Life in New Orleans;* he'd made best-selling albums of music by W. C. Handy and Fats Waller; he'd scored a top-40 hit with a buoyant version of "Mack the Knife" (a musical portrait of a fictional pimp and cutthroat who, but for having been born in London instead of Storyville, might have been a figure from Armstrong's own boyhood); and, simply by being himself, he had stolen the movie *High Society* from its ostensible stars, Grace Kelly and Bing Crosby. Wherever he played, as guitarist Danny Barker told jazz historian Jason Berry, his dressing room was filled with people from every part of his remarkable life.

He'd be sitting down in his underwear with a towel around his lap, one around his shoulders and that white handkerchief on his head and he'd put that grease around his lips. Look like a minstrel man, you know . . .

and laughing, you know, natural the way he is. And in the room you see, maybe, two nuns. You see a street walker dressed all up in flaming clothes. You see maybe a guy come out of the penitentiary. You see maybe a blind man sitting there. You see a rabbi, you see a priest, see. Liable to see maybe two policemen or detectives, see. You see a judge. All of 'em different levels of society in the dressing room and he's talking to all of 'em. "Sister So and So, do you know Slick Sam over there? This is Slick Sam, an ole friend of mine." Now the nun's going to meet Slick Sam. Ole Notorious, been in nine penitentiaries. "Slick Sam, meet Rabbi Goldstein over there, he's a friend of mine, rabbi, good man, religious man. Sister Margaret, do you know Rabbi Goldstein? Amelia, this is Rosie, Goodtime Rosie, used to work in a show with me years ago. Good girl, she's a great performer. Never got the breaks." Always a word of encouragement, see. And there'd be some kids there, white and colored. All the diverse people of different social levels . . . and everybody's looking. Got their eyes dead on him, just like they was looking at a diamond.

The State Department asked Armstrong to take his All Stars to the Gold Coast, the first African colony to win its freedom and about to become the republic of Ghana. More than a score of would-be trumpeters met his plane at the Accra airport, blaring a tumultuous version of a local song called "All For You." Seventy tribal chieftains received him at the University of the Gold Coast, each with his own band of drummers and dancers. Later, more than a hundred thousand people turned out to hear the man most of the world now regarded as the living symbol of jazz. And everywhere, he saw people who looked so much like him and the other members of his family that he

came to believe his own ancestors must have come from the Gold Coast. He looked "very wistful," Arvell Shaw remembered. " 'I saw a lady just looked exactly like [my sister] Mama Lucy and somebody like my mother,' he said. 'This is truly where I'm from.' " But a CBS film crew traveling with Armstrong captured something else. When the All Stars played at one large gathering and he invited everyone to dance, no one even tried until Armstrong's wife, Lucille, got up to show them how. They loved seeing Armstrong, and were caught up in the spirit of undiluted joy and celebration he was able to communicate to any audience anywhere, but they also clearly considered the music he was playing *American* music, not their own.

Armstrong now had a new honorary title, "Ambassador Satch," and the following year, when the Soviet Union itself agreed to receive a jazz band, he seemed the logical choice to take America's music behind the Iron Curtain for the first time. But events intervened. As the school year began that September, in open defiance of a federal court order, Governor Orville Faubus of Arkansas sent National Guard troops to block eight black children from entering Little Rock's Central High School. Meanwhile, white mobs jeered at and spat on other African-American children trying to attend schools in Clinton, Tennessee, and Charlotte, North Carolina, and beat a minister in Birmingham, Alabama, to the ground for attempting to enroll his daughter. All of it was covered on television. Washington had so far refused to intervene.

On September 18, Armstrong was on tour in Grand Forks, North Dakota, when a local reporter dropped by his hotel room. Armstrong was shaving—and outraged by what he'd been seeing on the news. President Dwight Eisenhower had "no guts," he told his visitor. Faubus was "an uneducated plowboy." "The way they're treating my people in the South, the government can go to hell," he said. "It's getting so bad a colored man hasn't got any country." He would not go to Russia for the State Department. The reporter asked him if he was willing to be quoted. He said he was.

His road manager was appalled, afraid Armstrong had ruined his career, and hurried to tell the press Armstrong was "sorry he spouted off." When a television newsman with a camera crew caught up with Arm-strong as he was about to board an airplane the next morning, he made it clear that he was not at all sorry. "What are you going to tell the Russians when they ask you about the Little Rock incident?" he was asked. "It all depends what time they send me over there," Armstrong answered, his eyes invisible behind dark glasses, his face without a trace of his usual public smile. "I don't think they should send me now until they straighten that mess down South. And for good. I mean not just to blow over. To cut it out. . . . Because they've been ignoring the Constitution. . . . They're taught it in school, but when they go home their parents tell them different. Say, 'You don't have to abide by it because we've been getting away with it a hundred years. Nobody tells on each

Trummy Young, Louis Armstrong, and Edmond Hall bring America's music to West Africa, 1956.

Louis Armstrong preparing himself to go onstage in Paris, 1960

other. So don't bother with it.' So, if they ask me what's happening if I go now, I can't tell a lie. . . . [That's] the way I feel about it."

Critics, both black and white, attacked him. An old friend from New Orleans took him aside. "Nigger," he said, "you better stop talking about them white people like you did!" Adam Clayton Powell Jr. denounced Armstrong for embarrassing the government. Sammy Davis Jr. said that since Armstrong was still willing to play for segregated audiences, he "did not speak for the Negro people." Station WBKH in Hattiesburg, Mississippi, banned Armstrong's music. The Hearst columnist Jim Bishop called for a boycott of Armstrong's concerts. And not one of the younger musicians who had accused him of Tomming in the past publicly came to his defense.

Armstrong never backed down and in the end lost just one gig—at the University of Arkansas. When Eisenhower did finally send in the 101st Airborne to insure that black children got to and from their school in safety, Armstrong sent the president a congratulatory telegram: "IF YOU DECIDE TO WALK INTO THE SCHOOLS WITH THE LITTLE COLORED KIDS, TAKE ME ALONG DADDY. GOD BLESS YOU."

On January 7, 1959, Armstrong and Dizzy Gillespie would appear side by side on the CBS-TV *Timex All Star Show,* playing and singing a jubilant version of one of Gillespie's favorite numbers, "Umbrella Man." They were near-neighbors now in Queens, their wives were close friends, and it is clear from the fun they had working together onscreen that old arguments had long since been forgotten. Later in the year, when Armstrong suffered a heart attack in Italy, the Gillespies were among the first to hear from him. "Ole Sidney Bechet and Big Sid Catlett [both of whom had recently died]," he wrote, "were trying to get me to come up there with them and hold that 1st chair down on the trumpet. Probably they would have had a little luck if they weren't so damn cheap. Huh—they only wanted to pay me union scale. . . . I got more than that when I first came up North from down in Galilee."

Years later, in his autobiography, *To Be or Not to Bop,* Gillespie explained his change of heart: "If anybody asked me about a certain public image of him, handkerchief over his head, grinning in the face of white racism, I never hesitated to say I didn't like it. I didn't want the white man to expect me to allow the same things Louis did. Hell, I had my own way of 'Tomming.' . . . Later on, I began to recognize what I had considered Pops's grinning in the face of racism was his absolute refusal ever to let any-

thing, even anger about racism, steal the joy from his life. . . . Coming from a younger generation, I misjudged him."

The actor Ossie Davis had a similar conversion experience while working with Armstrong on an otherwise forgettable film, *A Man Called Adam.*

One day at lunch, everybody'd gone out. The set was quiet. As I came back to the set I looked up and there was Louis Armstrong sitting in a chair, the handkerchief tied around his head, looking up with the saddest expression I've ever seen on a man's face. I looked and I was startled and then I started to back away because it seemed such a private moment, but he heard me backing away and he broke out of it right away, "Hey, Pops, looks like these cats are going to starve old Louis to death, hey, man, wow. . . ." And everything you know, I went into it with him but I never forgot that look and it changed my concept of Louis Armstrong. Because I, too, as a boy had objected to a lot of what Louis was doing. I figured all them teeth and that handkerchief— we called it "ooftah," by which we meant you do that to please the white folk. You know, you make them happy and all that stuff, make us look like fools. But it was only then I began to understand something about Louis. He could put on that show, he could do that whole thing, because in that horn of his he had the power to kill. That horn could kill a man. So there was where the truth of Louis Armstrong resided. Whatever he was, the moment he put the trumpet to his lips, a new truth emerged, a new man emerged, a new power emerged and I looked on Louis for what he truly was, after that. You know, he became an angelic presence to me after that moment.

FIRE!

Dizzy Gillespie was not an admirer of West Coast jazz. "There was no guts in that music," he said, "not much rhythm either. . . . This music, jazz, is guts. . . . I guess the idea was not to go 'savage' with it, biting, like we were. But that's jazz to me. Jazz to me is dynamic, a blockbuster."

Jazz was a blockbuster to Art Blakey, too. He wanted to provide a hard-swinging antidote to the cool music then so popular: critics, looking for a label, called the music he and others began to play "hard bop." "Fire! That's what people want," he said. Blakey had begun his career as a pianist and had launched his own big band at fifteen, switched to the drums after being outplayed by the youthful Erroll Garner, and soon developed his own distinctive thunderous, roiling style. He played with Fletcher Henderson, Mary Lou Williams, and Billy Eckstine. "It was like a school to me," he said of his time with Eckstine, "and that's when I realized that we had to have bands for young black musicians—big bands, little bands, a whole lot of bands— because this music is an experience."

He had put himself through every kind of experience, survived every kind of trouble. He was so short—less than five feet— that one critic dismissed him early on as a "pygmy." ("At least she spelled my name right," Blakey said.) A Georgia policeman beat him so badly that he had to have surgery on his skull. His first wife died. Heroin was a frequent companion, and he refused to be apologetic about it. He adopted Islam, renaming himself Abdullah Ibn Buhaina, and traveled to West Africa to learn more about traditional drumming. But jazz, he would always maintain, "is American music. There's nothing like it anywhere on the planet. People are always trying to connect it to something else, to African music, to Latin music. It's not. It's American music. . . . Now, they say, 'Art Blakey, he's black. That makes him an

African.' I'm not. I'm an American and this is American music."

In 1955, Blakey and the pianist and composer Horace Silver established a quintet they called the Jazz Messengers and began to record for Blue Note. "They used fixed arrangements and they brought in gospel influences, blues influences," the record producer Michael Cuscuna remembered, "things that people could relate to who were not deeply into modern jazz. And it caught on very quickly. The message of the group was 'We swing, we're earthy, we play the blues. You can walk away humming it, but we're not going to cheat on the quality of the music or the creativity.' And they found a way to do everything."

"When we're on the stand," Art Blakey said, "and we see that there are people in the audience who aren't patting their feet and who aren't nodding their heads to our music, we know we're doing something wrong. Because when we do get our message across, those heads and feet do move."

When Silver left to form a group of his own, Blakey kept the Messengers name and for forty-five years traveled the world joyfully spreading his message. Two generations of future stars would get their start or hone their skills with Blakey: pianists Joanne Brackeen, John Hicks, Keith Jarrett, Geoff Keezer, Bobby Timmons, Cedar Walton; saxophonists Benny Golson, Branford Marsalis, Jackie McLean, Hank Mobley, Wayne Shorter; trumpet players Donald Byrd, Kenny Dorham, Freddie Hubbard, Brian Lynch, Wynton Marsalis, Lee Morgan, and Woody Shaw.

"The Messengers were the training ground for a lot of great musicians," Wynton Marsalis remembered, "because [Blakey] would put his swing up underneath you so that you could learn how to play, and he would tell you you were sad. And when I first sat in with him, I knew I wasn't playing nothing. He said, 'Man, you sad, but that's all right.' And when you were around him, you were around the essence of jazz music. So he put that in us. 'If you want to

Art Blakey at work. "To me the bandstand is hallowed ground," he said. "You come up here, you're supposed to play. A musician is supposed to play, if he gets up off his deathbed, he's supposed to play."

play this music, you have to play it with soul, with intensity, and every time you touch your horn, you play your horn. You know, this is not a game.' "

Blakey was not a sentimental man. "I'm always kicking them in the ass," he said. "It's as much as anyone can do to keep up with me. . . . I'm not running a post office." "Everybody had to do their job or you were replaced," Jackie McLean remembered. "And in every city that we went to, if there was a star alto player there, Art would invite him to come and play with the band and that was always to keep me on notice that there was always somebody waiting in the wings." On the road, Blakey was indefatigable, the living, laughing symbol of the music's extraordinary resiliency. Even when growing deafness made it hard for him to hear his soloists, he continued to outswing musicians half his age. "Music," he told his audiences nearly every night, "is supposed to wash away the dust of everyday life from your feet."

DIMINUENDO AND CRESCENDO

In the summer of 1955, Duke Ellington was reduced to accompanying ice skaters at a Long Island rink. The following summer he was on the cover of *Time,* his career in high gear again. Newport, which had helped to re-ignite Miles Davis's career the year before, did the same for Ellington.

It was the orchestra's first appearance under the festival's striped tent—Ellington had been asked only to be a master of ceremonies the previous year—and he was anxious to do well. His mood was not improved when he was asked to open the last evening of the festival with the "Star-Spangled Banner" and four of his men failed to turn up on the bandstand. Then, after just two tunes, Ellington was waved off the stage to make way for other performers and had to wait more than three

When Duke Ellington sought to cause a stir at the New-port Jazz Festival on the evening of July 7, 1956, he turned to "Diminuendo and Crescendo in Blue," the same driving two-part piece that eighteen years earlier had brought dancers out of their seats at the Randalls Island Festival of Swing. At Newport, he had important help from two individuals: tenor saxophone star Paul Gonsalves (opposite), who played twenty-seven furious choruses, and a woman from New Bedford (opposite, bottom) whose dancing helped whip the normally sedate crowd into a frenzy. (Below) An exuberant Ellington urges the band to take its bows.

Duke Ellington at the 1960 Monterey Jazz Festival

hours before his band could get back on. "What are we, the animal act? The acrobats?" Ellington asked. Tenor saxophonist Paul Gonsalves remembered that the band was "angry" when it finally went on again shortly after midnight.

George Wein had urged Ellington to compose something new to thwart the critics who were now writing that he had grown stale, and he had put together a new three-part work called *The Newport Festi-*

val Suite. The suite went over well enough with the audience, but it began to drizzle, and after two more numbers, "Sophisticated Lady" and "Day In, Day Out," people began heading for the parking lot.

To get them back, Ellington called for one of his old standbys, "Diminuendo and Crescendo in Blue," written in 1937. The band hit so hard, the rhythm section rocked so powerfully, that people stopped, listened, and hurried back to their seats. Ellington

himself usually played a solo between the piece's two parts. This evening he turned over that duty to Gonsalves, whose big, furry tone and affinity for the blues echoed those of his hero, Ben Webster. After four choruses or so, the crowd began to roar. "People sat in reserved seats normally," Wein remembered, "and then they sat and watched the concert and once in a while they'd stand up and cheer and give a standing ovation. But a woman started to dance.

Everybody crowded around to see the dancing of this woman, a blond woman from New Bedford."

"She was quite attractive," Clark Terry said, grinning at the memory, "and Ellington kind of enjoyed that, and it inspired him, and he in turn inspired the band. [Drummer] Sam Woodyard started pounding a little heavier. Things begin to build up to a real frenzy." Gonsalves dug in, one furious chorus following another. "Ellington caught that spirit," Wein remembered; "he kept playing that piano, comping and comping and keeping it going, and you could see in his face the joy and the excitement."

The audience became so enthusiastic that Wein, afraid of a riot, began frantically signaling Ellington to cut the number short. But Ellington refused. "Don't be rude to the artists," he shouted, waggling his finger. Gonsalves didn't stop for twenty-seven choruses.

The crowd demanded four encores. A few weeks later, Ellington finally made his long-awaited appearance on the cover of *Time.* An LP of the Newport appearance sold hundreds of thousands of copies, more than any other record he ever made. "Every time I saw Duke after that," Wein recalled, "he would say, 'I was born at Newport in 1956.' Lots of luck—he'd only created the whole history of American music prior to 1956. But the band was working more. They were getting more money. People were calling for the band, and Duke felt a new surge in his life."

During the next few years, Ellington would produce an astonishing body of work, including *Such Sweet Thunder,* an extended suite based on the works of Shakespeare; *The Queen's Suite,* inspired by having been formally presented to Queen Elizabeth II in 1958 (an event so memorable for him that he refused ever to discard the shoes he had worn that evening); *Night Creature,* a work for jazz and symphony orchestras; and a television extravaganza called *A Drum Is a Woman,* a history of jazz in music and dance, for which he used his unrivaled manipulative skills to transform Clark Terry into Buddy Bolden. As Terry recalled it:

He knew how to psychoanalyze everybody, he knew how to psyche you into doing what he wanted you to do. He said to me, "Sweetie, you're gonna portray the role of Buddy Bolden." And I said, "Well, Maestro, *you* don't even know that much about Buddy Bolden," I said, "What do *I* know about Buddy?" He said, "Oh sure you know about Buddy Bolden. . . . He was suave. He was debonair and he was dapper and he was always accompanied by charming ladies. . . . And as a matter of fact he had such a big fat sound, when he tuned up in New Orleans, he would break glasses across the river in Algiers. He was fantastic with diminishes and bent notes. Oh man, could he bend a note!" So he said, "Play me some bent notes." So I played a few bent notes . . . when you vary the pitch, go from the center below, or above. He said, "That's it. Now play me some diminishes." I [tried it and] he said, "That's it! You *are* Buddy Bolden!" And I thought I *was* Buddy Bolden there for a minute. So what you heard on the record of *A Drum Is a Woman* is what he actually extracted from me through psychology.

April 29, 1959, was Ellington's sixtieth birthday. Friends gathered in New York and presented him with twenty-four specially made leather-bound albums containing the lovingly transcribed music for some seven hundred of his pieces. Ellington thanked everyone profusely, his friend Dr. Arthur Logan remembered, "but the sonofabitch didn't even bother to take them home." They were reminders of his past. He wanted to look only to the future, and was off the next morning for Ishpeming, Michigan, where the movie director Otto Preminger was filming a courtroom drama, *Anatomy of a Murder.* Ellington had been asked to compose the score. By evening, he and Billy Strayhorn were at work on the lounge piano in their hotel, setting out to conquer still another musical field. "It has nothing to do with money," he said once, trying to explain why, even when things were going well, he seemed unable to stop taking on new projects. "I like to solve problems."

That same spring, Ellington replied—indirectly, as always—to a French writer who had chastised him for having "debased" one of his earlier masterpieces by rerecording and reorchestrating it:

I don't want to be modern . . . futuristic . . . and neither do I want to be hung by the plaintiveness of something we might have done years ago, even with success. I don't want to feel obliged to play something with the same styling that we became identified with at some specific period. I have no ambition to reach some intellectual plateau and look down on people. And, by the same token, I don't want anyone to challenge my right to sound completely mad, to screech like a wild man . . . or to write a song that praises God, if I so desire. I only want to enjoy what any other American artist wants—and that is freedom of expression and of communication with our audience.

SEPARATE WAYS

Billie Holiday had been released from the Federal Reformatory for Women in 1948 but, under New York's bizarre cabaret law, still remained barred from city clubs because of her conviction for narcotics possession. "I can play Carnegie," she complained, "but I can't play the crummiest gin joint in New York." There were more arrests, more headlines, more good-looking but violent men. In rare, tranquil moments she was wistful about missed opportunities.

"My former wife was pregnant," the writer Nat Hentoff recalled. "And we saw Billie . . . on the street, and she just kept rubbing her hand over the stomach, feeling what was underneath there, because she'd never had a child and she'd wanted one."

The index cards kept by Frank Schiffman at the Apollo tersely traced her decline.

5/25/50

Unless a miraculous change takes place, Billie's value to us is lost. She has lost her public favor. . . . Seems unable to remain away from stimulants.

8/14/53

Terrible! She was sick, but she was also under the effect of stimulants. Only a miracle can restore this girl and make her worthwhile playing here again.

9/16/55

Very indifferent lackadaisical performance. Although she was not troublesome as when under the influence of stimulants, proved absolutely valueless to the box office.

Holiday (like her sisters in misery, Judy Garland and Edith Piaf) had long since begun to attract a following more interested in her troubles than her music. In 1956, raddled by heroin and alcohol and desperate for money, she agreed to tell her own story to William Dufty, the husband of a friend and a newspaperman who evidently believed that any double-checking of the gaudy tales she told him would be seen by her as an act of betrayal. The lurid result, *Lady Sings the Blues,* proudly billed by its publisher as "the most shocking autobiography of our times," portrayed her mostly as a helpless victim of malevolent men and endemic racism, idiotic laws and an uncaring public, and would later serve as the basis for an overwrought Hollywood film starring Diana Ross that further muddied the waters.

Billie Holiday at New York's Town Hall toward the end of her career. "Some say that what Billie does now is no longer singing," wrote Dan Morgenstern in *Down Beat* in 1958. "Whatever it is, it sure as hell communicates."

The fact that she was an artist, fully conscious (except when her addiction temporarily befogged her mind) of the effect on her audience of every precisely enunciated syllable, every languid rhythm and shrewdly slurred phrase, was largely overlooked during her last years. Her voice did crack and thicken with time, and at the Newport Jazz Festival in 1957 she seemed a caricature of herself, her delivery blurred, stumbling over lyrics she had sung a thousand times before, abandoned even by the uncanny sense of time that had always been hers to use. But several rehearsal conver-

toward the very end, when in the presence of musicians whose quality matched hers—Ben Webster, Sweets Edison, Jimmy Rowles—she could sometimes pull herself together long enough to demonstrate that she was a more moving singer than she had ever been, not because she had suffered so but because onstage and in the sound studio, if not in life, she had learned how to transcend her suffering and transform it into art.

On December 6th, 1957, the writers Whitney Balliett and Nat Hentoff helped gather an extraordinary group of musicians for a one-time-only, live program on CBS called *The Sound of Jazz*. Nothing like it had ever been tried before on American television. It was an all-star assemblage: Jo Jones and Count Basie, Thelonious Monk and Coleman Hawkins, Gerry Mulligan and Ben Webster. Lester Young and Billie Holiday were there, too. They had made their first unforgettable records together twenty years earlier and had subsequently fallen out, most likely over Holiday's drug use. "They had grown way apart," Hentoff said, "and when we were there for the blocking and the sound check, they very carefully were on different sides of the studio." Young was too weak to play in the big band section of the show, so Hentoff told him he should save his strength for a small-group session with Holiday. "And you can sit down. You don't have to stand."

They were to perform "Fine and Mellow," Holiday's own song and one of the very few blues she ever recorded. Gerry Mulligan played the first solo, in double time. Ben Webster came next, blowing a single breathy, heartbreaking chorus. "Then, Lester got up," Hentoff remembered, "and he played the purest blues I have ever heard, and [he and Holiday] were looking at each other, their eyes were sort of interlocked, and she was sort of nodding and half-smiling. It was as if they were both remembering what had been—whatever that was. And in the control room we were

all crying. When the show was over, they still went their separate ways."

Lester Young was now living in the Alvin Hotel on Fifty-second Street. He had moved there from Long Island, telling his second wife that he could not bear any longer to be so far from the world of jazz that had always been his real home. Alcohol had destroyed his health. Younger musicians did what they could for him. "I'd come in and call Prez's room," Jackie McLean recalled, "see if he wanted me to go to the store or anything for him. I loved Lester Young so much. . . . Sometimes he would say, 'Yeah, come on up,' and I'd go up to his room and go buy him some cigarettes or something like that. It was kind of sad. He

Lester Young, left, and Billie Holiday confer with another musician in the CBS television studio, New York, December 6, 1957.

sations between her and her accompanists recorded at about the same time still show a perfectionist at work, adjusting and readjusting old arrangements, trying out new ones, changing time, key, instrumentation, determined always to make a good song better, a great song greater still. And even

Lester Young in Paris

used to sit at the window and look across at Birdland, at the people coming and going." Young still managed to play whenever he was asked, but he spent his time between dates moving from movie house to movie house on Forty-second Street or listening to his record player—other people's music, never his own. He died in his room at the Alvin on March 15, 1959, hours after returning from an engagement in Paris. By then, his influence was everywhere. Allen Eager, one of his most devoted disciples, said simply, "Anyone who doesn't play like Lester is wrong."

Billie Holiday attended Young's funeral and asked to be allowed to sing. She was refused permission by his widow, began to weep and curse, and finally had to be led from the chapel. She herself now had only three months to live. She was almost unrecognizable—thin, drawn, haunted. She had sold off even her mink coat to support her habit—and to buy food for the chihuahua that was her only consolation. On May 30, she collapsed and was rushed to the hospital. Somehow, someone managed to smuggle heroin into her room. A nurse discovered it. Holiday was placed under arrest. Police were stationed at the door. She died at forty-four on July 17, 1959. The official cause was cardiac failure. The real cause, said Joe Glaser, who paid for her funeral as he had paid for Charlie Parker's, was "a concoction of everything she'd done in the last twenty years."

"I still play her records now," the former baseball star Buck O'Neil remembered almost half a century later. "When you saw her, it was just so different than any other person you'd seen onstage singing. The way she would sell a song—anybody else could sing that song, and when Lady Day sang it, it was a different song altogether. It just made you feel good all over or she'd make you want to cry. It'll bring back to you great moments in your life and it might bring back the saddest moments in your life. This was Billie Holiday."

MILES AHEAD

"That group I had with Coltrane made him and me a legend," Miles Davis remembered. Boastful as that sounded, it was the unadorned truth and it was only the beginning. Between 1957 and 1960, he would release eight albums for Columbia. Three of them—*Miles Ahead, Porgy and Bess,* and *Sketches of Spain*—were collaborations with his old friend Gil Evans: lush, moody, richly textured orchestral arrangements that showcased Davis's dark but lyrical sound on flügelhorn. All three were hugely popular among young record buyers seek-

ing romance; with Miles Davis playing softly on the turntable, almost anyone "could get over with a kiss." (Louis Armstrong, Evans's first hero, heard *Porgy and Bess,* and was so impressed he asked the arranger to provide a similar setting for him. Thrilled, Evans hurried to see Joe Glaser. "Who the hell are you?" Glaser asked. That ended the discussion.)

In March of 1959, Davis brought the members of his current small group into the Columbia studios to make another album. There had been changes in personnel. Philly Joe Jones had been replaced by Jimmy Cobb. Red Garland was gone, too.

His replacements were Bill Evans and, on one tune, Wynton Kelly. The alto saxophonist Cannonball Adderley had been added to make it a sextet. Davis asked them to play five original tunes they'd never seen before, each built on basic scales, or "modes," upon which they were to improvise—not the complex chord progressions that had been the basis for bebop.

Davis's object was further to simplify the music, "to make it more like singing," he said. "The music has gotten thick. Guys give me tunes and they're full of chords. I can't play them. . . . I think a movement in jazz is beginning away from the conventional

Miles Davis plays and Gil Evans conducts during a recording session for the best-selling *Porgy 'n Bess* album for Columbia, 1958.

string of chords, and a return to emphasis on melodic rather than harmonic variation. There will be fewer chords but infinite possibilities as to what to do with them." Again, the basic notion was not Davis's. Duke Ellington and Charles Mingus had built parts of their compositions on modes; George Russell and Dizzy Gillespie had used them in writing for the Gillespie big band; Gil Evans had employed them on *Miles Ahead* and *Porgy and Bess*. But because he and his men used them to such great effect on the record that became *Kind of Blue,* Miles and modes would become forever linked.

This group would fall apart not long after the record was made, as its members pursued careers on their own. But *Kind of Blue* remained. It was a relative rarity among modern jazz albums, three-quarters of an hour of extraordinary music loved equally by listeners who wouldn't know a mode from a modem, and by musicians for whom

After leaving Miles Davis in 1958, Bill Evans formed his own trio. Lyrical and introspective, his playing heavily influenced by the same European impressionism that had fascinated Bix Beiderbecke thirty years earlier, he became the most influential pianist of the modern era.

it seemed to point the way toward a fresh way of playing. *Kind of Blue* remains among the most enduring of all jazz records—more than forty years after its release, it continues to sell several thousand copies a month. "It must have been made in heaven," Jimmy Cobb said.

Kind of Blue added luster to Davis's reputation. Charlie Parker and Dizzy Gillespie had only dreamed of being received as artists, not entertainers. Davis was making it a reality. "What I really respect about him," Gillespie said many years later, "is he was the first one that came along in our business and figured he didn't have to smile at everyone, didn't have to tell no jokes or make no announcements, didn't have to say thank you or even bow. He figured he could just let the music speak for him, and for itself."

Miles Davis did not greet the audience or thank people for coming, wouldn't introduce tunes, sometimes played with his back to his listeners, left the bandstand when others were playing. There were explanations for all of it. He was said to be innately shy, and throat surgery had turned his voice into a rasp that would have made announcements almost impossible to hear. He left the stage when not playing, he said, so that the audience would focus on the other musicians. "I'm a musician, not a comedian," he told one club owner. "I don't smile, I don't bow. . . . The white man always wants you to bow. I don't smile and I don't bow, okay? I'm here to play music. I'm a musician." He sometimes cursed out fans who dared try to buy him a drink or ask him to play a favorite tune, and he delighted in the admiring sobriquet "Prince of Darkness."

Times were changing. Those attitudes, which would have got him nowhere ten years earlier, now seemed only to add to his appeal to white as well as black audiences. Jazz, wrote Ralph Ellison, had become "a grim comedy of manners; with the musicians employing a calculated surliness and

Black power. Miles Davis was appalled when Columbia records put the picture of a pretty white model on the cover of *Miles Ahead* in 1957. Four years later, he had enough clout to insist that his current wife, Frances Davis, be given center stage.

rudeness, treating the audience very much as many white merchants in poor Negro neighborhoods treat their customers, and the white audiences were shocked at first but learned quickly to accept such treatment as evidence of 'artistic temperament.' Then comes a comic reversal. Today the white audience expects the rudeness as part of the entertainment."

"Miles is a black man who lives like a white man," one envious musician said. He owned a West Side town house, drove a series of costly sports cars, dressed with such understated elegance that he was featured in fashion magazines, was publicized by Columbia as something like a movie star as well as a musician, a kind of treatment never before afforded a black jazz performer. When *Playboy* decided to add a dash of intellectual respectability to its pages by running a monthly interview with someone of interest to its youthful readers, Miles Davis was the magazine's first choice.

The essayist Gerald Early recalled for an interviewer Davis's special place in the affections of young people growing up in the black community in Philadelphia.

I mean, he was known by his first name—Miles. Miles this. Miles that. Miles with the suits. Miles with the women. He was the jazz hero for my generation. He came along when my generation was rejecting the whole idea of a black person as an entertainer. That was very powerful for us. His cool. The way he went about his business. The sort of "inside/outside" way with Miles. Because on one level, Miles was Mr. Outside—his stance about race, his stance about music, his sort of "F—— you" stance about life. But he was also Mr. Inside. He was popular. He was respected. Whites and blacks liked his music.

For all his fame, for all his bluster, Davis could never fully mask his insecurity. "He would be afraid to go into hotels himself to check on our reservations," his second wife, Frances, recalled, "thinking, because he was a black man, they were going to say, 'No, we don't have your reservation.' He would send me in to take care of that part of it. He really feared the prejudice that did happen in this country then."

There remained reasons for that fear. On the sultry evening of August 26, 1959, Davis broadcast a live set from Birdland for the Voice of America. Afterward, he escorted a young white woman outside and into a taxi, watched her drive off and then stood pulling on a cigarette, glad for a few moments to himself outside the stuffy club.

A white policeman who had seen him emerge with his white friend told him to

Miles Davis. "People sometimes think I'm difficult," he said in 1959, "because I always say what's on my mind, and they can't always see what I see."

For a guy's musical development, the same rule applies in jazz as in any other field; you collect facts, and study. . . . You take a riff that Roy Eldridge played, and you play that riff . . . and you figure the alternatives. You say, "Ah, then, you could also go here instead of going there." And when you get that far, finally you'll come up with something different. But it's the same music. It's just progressing all the time.

—DIZZY GILLESPIE

Donald Byrd hones his skills on the subway, en route to a Manhattan date in the 1950s.

move on. "Move on for what?" Davis said, pointing to a sign on which his name was prominently displayed. "I'm working downstairs." The officer ordered him to get going anyway, or he would be arrested. When Davis stood his ground, a second policeman clubbed him over the head from behind. Blood poured onto his suit. (It would take ten stitches to close the wound.) He was handcuffed and jailed, had his cabaret license revoked and got it back only when he agreed to drop the suit for damages he'd filed against the city. "Around this time," he said, "people—white people—started saying that I was always 'angry,' that I was 'racist.' . . . Now I've never been racist toward nobody, but that don't mean I'm going to take shit from a person just because he's white. . . . I was living in America, too, and I was going to try to get everything that was coming to me."

LIKE BEING BORN AGAIN

By November 1959, rock 'n' roll was outselling every other kind of music in America. Nonetheless, that month record stores were filled with fresh and exciting jazz albums of every kind. At roughly the same time that Miles Davis released *Kind of Blue,* demonstrating that compelling melodies could be improvised over an unchanging harmonic base, John Coltrane produced *Giant Steps* under his own name, an album on which he tore through so many chord changes at such fierce tempos that one contemporary writer compared his playing to "sheets of sound" and four decades later musicians still shake their heads in disbelief.

Thelonious Monk's Orchestra at Town Hall documented the first attempt to translate the master logician's dense, angular compositions into music for a big band. The bassist Charles Mingus had two extraordinary new records in the stores, *Blues and Roots* and *Mingus Ah Um,* wonderfully imaginative works for a nine-piece band that included evocations of the church, powerful tributes to his heroes—Jelly Roll Morton, Lester Young, Duke Ellington—and a memorable assault on the segregationist governor of Arkansas, "Fables of Faubus." The Modern Jazz Quartet had just recorded John Lewis's exquisite score for a thriller called *Odds Against Tomorrow. Ahmad Jamal at the Pershing* remained on *Billboard*'s list of best-selling albums for a second year, and Erroll Garner's *Concert by the Sea* had only just dropped off it. Dave Brubeck, now leading his best-loved quartet—with Paul Desmond, bassist Gene Wright, and the brilliant drummer Joe Morello—issued *Time Out,* a collection of originals in time signatures rarely heard in jazz (3/4, 6/4, 9/8), and one cut from it, Paul Desmond's "Take Five," in 5/4, became a top-40 hit. "When we first started to play that thing I just pounded out the time to keep us together," Brubeck remembered many years later, "and now today it's taken for granted; you see kids improvising in three-and-a-half and things like that." *Time Out* would go on to sell more than a million copies, something no other long-playing jazz album had ever done.

Earlier masters—Ben Webster, Art Tatum, Roy Eldridge—had fresh albums for sale as well. John Hammond was recording many of his favorites from the thirties, including Jo Jones, Jimmy Rushing, and Count Basie, in small-group sessions for a new label called Vanguard. Ella Fitzgerald, who had begun her career singing novelty tunes with Chick Webb's swing band and then gone on to demonstrate that bebop could be sung as well as played, was now being billed as "the First Lady of American Song," having recorded for Norman Granz definitive performances of the finest American popular songs by Harold Arlen, Duke Ellington, George and Ira Gershwin, Cole Porter, Jerome Kern, and Johnny Mercer. Louis Armstrong had recently issued a musical autobiography for Decca, re-

THE LITTLE MAN

When the master pianist Art Tatum lay dying, the legend goes, he had a word of warning for a younger pianist who had come to see him: "Watch out for the little man." Erroll Garner was so little that he carried a Manhattan telephone book with him wherever he went in order to reach the keys. He was silent onstage, rarely saying a word to the huge audiences that turned out to hear him. And he didn't know one note from another—on paper—but he was the most prolific, best-loved jazz pianist of his era.

Garner was born in 1921 and brought up in Pittsburgh. At ten, he was appearing on local radio as part of a children's group called the Kan-D-Kids. By twenty-three, he had made it to New York, sometimes substituting for Art Tatum himself on Fify-second Street. His playing, like Tatum's, was filled with wit. He specialized in fanciful, teasing introductions to familiar tunes, and it became part of the fun of listening to him to try to guess what was coming before he made it plain. He got so much out of the piano that one rival nicknamed him "Ork" for "orchestra." "I love fullness in the piano," Garner said. "I want it to sound like a big band if I can." He belonged to no "school" of jazz, rarely played with groups larger than his trio, recorded more than a thousand tunes for almost seventy record companies during his career, and was so self-confident that he only rarely bothered to listen to the playbacks. When an interviewer asked him how he could possibly play so well when he had never learned to read music, Garner answered, "Hell, man, nobody can hear you *read.*"

Erroll Garner at Bop City in Manhattan, 1953

Ella Fitzgerald Sings the Gershwin Song Book, the fifth in her classic songbook series for Verve Records

worked versions of his early masterpieces, on some of which—"King of the Zulus," "I Can't Give You Anything But Love," "Wild Man Blues"—he at least equaled his youthful self. Duke Ellington's latest album, *Jazz Party,* included two memorable guest appearances by Dizzy Gillespie. The first was a brilliant, boiling muted trumpet feature on "U.M.M.G.," the second a stomping, impromptu, Kansas City–style version of "Hello, Little Girl," during which an exuberant Jimmy Rushing shouts ancient lyrics as if he'd just made them up before Gillespie demonstrates that, despite his own protests to the contrary, he never lost touch with the down-home blues. Some months after the record was released, Gillespie gently reminded Ellington that he hadn't been paid for appearing on it. "Well, Diz," Ellington answered with his customary canniness, "I can't pay you what you're really worth." "Never mind that," Gillespie said. "Just so long as you *pay* me!"

That same month, a musician arrived in New York who seemed to challenge the basic premises upon which all these masters had built their music. It was a signal that the transformation of jazz into an art music, which had been underway at the beginning of the decade, was nearing com-

pletion at its end. His music would be given a variety of labels, including Free Jazz and New Thing, but it was clear that jazz now had an avant-garde in the modernist European sense for which accessibility would take a backseat to individual expression.

Armstrong and Ellington, Parker and Gillespie, Monk and Davis, Mulligan and John Lewis and Brubeck, had all been content to make their individual statements while working within agreed-upon rhythm, harmony, and chord sequences. Ornette Coleman rejected all that. Jazz, he said, must be "free."

He was not the first to declare his independence. Ten years earlier, the pianist and theorist Lennie Tristano and the alto and tenor saxophonists Lee Konitz and Warne Marsh had recorded with a sextet several free-form, collectively improvised sides—including one piece aptly called "Intuition"—in which there was no discernible thematic path. The pianist Cecil Taylor, whose music owed as much to Debussy and Webern as it did to the eclectic set of jazz masters he most admired—including Brubeck, Powell, Monk, and Ellington—was already developing his dissonant, fiercely percussive style, whose sole organizing principle was what he himself called "rhythm-sound-energy." But Tristano was a recluse who disliked playing in public, and Taylor's relentlessly demanding music would never win a wide audience.

It was Ornette Coleman's untrammeled, richly melodic improvisations on the alto saxophone—employing strange scales, filled with vocalized smears and cries, seemingly unrelated either to a recognizable theme or to anything going on around him, as "free as folk song," one writer said —that caused a stir in jazz circles, raising the spirits of some listeners and the hackles of others. When Dizzy Gillespie first heard Coleman, he just laughed. "I used to make jokes," he said, "like I'd say, 'Ladies and Gentlemen, we're going to play "Hot House" and Ornette is going to play "Night in Tunisia" at the same time.' " Later, like

many other older musicians, Gillespie became a grudging admirer.

"The theme you play at the start of a number is the territory," Coleman said, "and what comes after, which may have very little to do with it, is the adventure." His own adventure had begun in Fort Worth, Texas, in 1930 in the depths of the Depression. His father died when he was seven. His mother, a clerk in a funeral home and sometime seamstress, managed to scrape together enough money to buy her son his first saxophone when he was fourteen. He and a jazz-loving friend were ejected from his high school band for swinging the "Washington Post March." He worked black nightspots in Fort Worth, playing tenor in the bravura, big-toned, honking "Texas Tenor" style of local heroes like Arnett Cobb, whose gutbucket sound would always anchor even Coleman's most apparently esoteric improvisations in the blues. Coleman's distinctive sound evidently developed early—he was trying always "to reach into the human voice" through his horn, he said—and he stubbornly stuck to it, even after a gang of toughs who had heard him play called him outside, beat him up, and smashed his saxophone; even when, after he moved to California, the tenor star Dexter Gordon ordered him off the stage rather than let him sit in. To most musicians, he just sounded out of tune. He *looked* out of tune, too, with a beard and uncut hair and distinctive clothes designed and made by his wife. He was "like some kind of black Christ figure," his subsequent musical partner, the trumpet player Don Cherry, remembered, "but no Christ anybody had ever seen before." Between gigs, Coleman supported himself with odd jobs—stock clerk, elevator operator, babysitter—and continued to seek out places to play.

At the same time, in the same city, a remarkable young bass player named Charlie Haden was beginning his career. He had a personal history unique among jazz musicians: born in the Ozarks, he had mastered

Cecil Taylor. "The thing that makes jazz so interesting," he said, "is that each man is his own academy. . . . If he's really going to be persuasive, he learns about other academies, but the idea is that he must have that special thing. And sometimes you don't even know what it is."

harmony as a child, singing country and western music—"the other art form that was born in this country besides jazz and blues," he called it—as part of the Haden Family Band, appearing on *Grand Ole Opry* and on the band's own radio program. He turned to the bass at fifteen, when bulbar polio affected his singing voice; studied at Westlake College of Modern Music; and played for a time with the Los Angeles–based alto saxophonist Art Pepper.

> I was going to a lot of different jam sessions and a lot of different clubs and playing and sitting in with different people, and sometimes I'd be on the bandstand and it would come time for my bass solo and I would want to play on the inspiration of the piece instead of the chord structure.
>
> In other words, most musicians improvise in jazz on the chord structure of a song. That's the inspiration to them. This song is beautiful and the chords are beautiful and they want to make a new melody on this chord structure and that's great, that's what jazz is all about. But sometimes this thing would come to me where I would want to play on the inspiration of the chord structure and create another chord structure. I wasn't talking about it back then, I didn't really know how to put it into words. I just had this feeling and every time I tried to do this, other musicians would become very upset with me. They wouldn't know where I was in the tune. So I would have to play the melody to show them where I was so that they could come back in at the right place at the end of the bass solo. And I had to really choose very carefully where I did this. And I didn't do it very often.

One night in Los Angeles in early 1959, Haden was at the Haig to hear Gerry Mulligan when Ornette Coleman approached the bandstand.

> Mulligan's band was playing and the place was jammed. People could hardly move. I'm there by myself, I'm standing in the crowd. This guy comes up to the bandstand with a saxophone case and he asks if he can play. And they say yes and he takes out this white plastic horn and he starts to play. And all of a sudden, the room lights up for me, from the heavens. You know, I say, "What is this, it sounds like a human voice on an instrument, playing so freely." He was playing in the intervals . . . the whole tune in about three notes or four notes. He would play the musical feeling of everything. And almost as soon as he started to play, someone on the bandstand asked him to stop. So he stopped, put his horn in the case, put the case back, started off. And I'm trying to get to him. I'm running through the crowd, stepping on toes, you know, trying to make my way through. I finally get to the back of the bandstand, to the door that goes to the alley, and he's gone.

Some time later, Haden caught up with Coleman, who invited him to his apartment to play.

> Music was everywhere. On the rug, on the bed, on the tables. I uncovered my bass, he reached down and he picked up a manuscript and he said,

"Let's play this." I said, "Okay." I was real scared you know. He says, "Now, I've written the melody here. Underneath it are the chord changes. Those are the chord changes I heard when I wrote this melody. But when we start to play, after I play the melody and I start to improvise, you play the changes, you make up new changes that you're hearing from what I'm playing and from the tune." And I thought to myself, "Somebody's finally giving me permission to do something, to play something that I've been hearing all this time." And we started to play and a whole new world opened up for me. It was like being born again. And I was hearing music so much more deeply than I had ever heard before. It's a desperate urgency to improvise completely new. We used to talk about it as if you've never heard music before. And we played all night, all day, all night, all day. I think we took a break to go get some food in, and we played for about two days. That was my first experience playing with Ornette.

In a Los Angeles garage, Coleman put together a new quartet, made up of like-minded but much younger musicians—Haden, Cherry, and drummer Billy Higgins. Coleman made two records for Contemporary Records that fared poorly, but he also received his first serious encouragement from John Lewis, who helped get him a contract with Atlantic Records and arranged for a summer scholarship for Coleman and Cherry at the Lenox School of Jazz. "They play together like I've never heard anybody play together," Lewis told an interviewer. "Ornette is, in a sense, an extension of Charlie Parker, and the first I've ever heard." Word spread fast, and in November 1959, the owners of the Five Spot on Manhattan's Bowery signed the Coleman Quartet for a two-week engagement. The Five Spot was a favorite hangout for abstract expression-

ist painters—Franz Kline, Willem de Kooning, Jackson Pollock—and its owners had begun to feature the most adventurous musicians in town.

Charlie Haden recalled what awaited him the night the quartet opened.

I was uncovering my bass, Billy was putting up his drums, and Cherry was getting his horn. Ornette was getting his horn out and I looked up at the bar, which was facing the stage, and standing along the bar were Wilbur Ware, Charlie Mingus, Paul Chambers, Percy Heath—every great bass

player in New York City standing there, staring me right in the face. And from that moment on, I closed my eyes. I think we played there six nights a week for four months, and every night the place was packed. One night I was playing with my eyes closed again, and all of a sudden, I opened my eyes and somebody's up on the stage with his ear to the F hole of my bass. And I looked over at Ornette and I said, "Coleman, who is this, man? Get him off this bandstand." He says, "That's Leonard Bernstein."

Charlie Haden in the recording studio, 1959. "Music teaches you humility," he once told an interviewer. "When you really touch music and you're playing, music shows you first your insignificance and your unimportance to the rest of the universe. And only after that can you see your true importance and your true significance. I tell [my students] that if they want to become great musicians, they should strive to become a great person first."

Ornette Coleman, 1959. "A lot of people in the mid-fifties were already playing music that had an open concept," Jackie McClean told an interviewer, "what I call the 'big room,' a place where you could cross a threshold and have no barriers, you know, no key signatures, no chord progressions, no particular form, [but it was] Ornette [who] came to New York and stood his ground and made this music really sink in and work. That's the thing I admire about Ornette, not only his writing and playing, but the fact that he stood his ground and stood by his music and took the slings and arrows of all the criticism that came towards him."

Bernstein pronounced Ornette Coleman a genius. John Coltrane came down to play with him between sets. Lionel Hampton asked to sit in. But Roy Eldridge said he'd listened to Coleman drunk and listened to him sober, and couldn't understand him either way. Thelonious Monk said that what Coleman was doing was "bad. . . . Jazz must first tell a story that anyone can understand." Charles Mingus was ambivalent: "He plays right wrong," he said. So was Miles Davis: he liked the fact that Coleman didn't play "clichés," he said, but "psychologically, the man is all screwed up inside." Someone set a car on fire out front; someone else burst into the kitchen between sets and punched Coleman. Most jazz writers were hostile, too, Haden recalled:

> We didn't bother ourselves to take time to even read the criticism of us because we were too busy thinking about making new tunes and improvising and talking about new ways of playing. That's what we were involved in. We couldn't stop to take time to even think about the controversy. Of course, we were disappointed. And we wanted to find some way to bring people closer to what we were doing because people look back on what we were doing now, they hear the early recordings and they're very accessible. They all come from the blues and the thing about our band—the critics labeled it *avant-garde,* you know, what is that?—was that we *swung.* And we felt very strongly about our music.

Coleman saw himself as solidly in the jazz tradition. "Bird would have understood us," he said. "He would have approved of our aspiring to something beyond what we inherited."

"We wanted people to like our music," Charlie Haden said, "we really did. But I really believe that most great musicians are free musicians. If you listen to Coleman Hawkins improvise, if you listen to Thelo-

Admirers and adversaries alike line up to see Ornette Coleman at the Five Spot in November, 1959.

nious Monk improvise, if you listen to Bud Powell, they improvised on a level that I call 'beyond category.' You know, it was at this level that's above everyone. Even though they were improvising on a chord structure, they were playing so free and so deeply at

a level . . . I call it with your *life* involved. . . . Being willing to give your life, . . . risking your life, it's almost like being on the front line in a battle. Being able—*wanting*—to give your life for what you're doing."

THE PRESENCE IS ALWAYS THE POINT

STANLEY CROUCH

Within five years of having arrived in New York from California in September 1975, I had the good luck of being able to assess the Manhattan jazz scene from three perspectives—as a drummer; as the booker of a jazz club, the Tin Palace on the Bowery; and as a writer of jazz criticism for the *Village Voice*. When I got to town, Duke Ellington had been dead for over a year, Louis Armstrong had been gone for five, and jazz itself was widely rumored to be on its way out, but the music that had evolved in so many directions during the lives of those two greatest of all jazz musicians had such vitality and presence that thinking back to how it was in those days now seems almost a dream of the way it should have been.

There were still so many fine players of so many different instruments that they created an enormous fugue of individual personalities, interpretations, techniques, and tonal colors. Though they were sometimes demoralized by the position that jazz had been forced into by a largely disinterested media and the notion that actual jazz playing had become a thing of the past, these artists pushed their music into the face of the present with the kind of transcendent coherence that not only improved the quality of their art but bettered the world through what they gave to and inspired in other human beings.

These were, as McCoy Tyner says, "special people." At this point, so many of them are gone that one could start asking if it had all been a dream, a collective wish agreed upon and supported by doctored photographs and unreal images delivered through film and television. Hardly. As with so many of the miracles of American life, those men and women did walk this earth, did take to bandstands and stand at bars and joke in dressing rooms and talk on the telephone and have rehearsals and travel the world, providing the human presence of jazz.

If you were in New York and were able to see and hear jazz for yourself, birth, affirmation, reaffirmation, decline, and death were right there to be had as experiences that would never leave your sensibility. If you lived at 2 East Second Street and felt like walking a couple of blocks west, you could step into Studio Rivbea, the avant-garde stronghold, where it might sound as though the world was ending that very night and where nobody sounded better than its owner, the avant-garde tenor saxophonist Sam Rivers, lean, high brown, and given to nearly knocking his knees together once his music got in complete touch with his nervous system. Or you could walk over to the Cookery at Eighth Street and University Place, where the rediscovered Alberta Hunter, who had been a star in the twenties, and who dressed like a lumberjack during the day, might be singing in a wonderful evening dress, while Barney Josephson, the man responsible for integrating downtown clubs in the thirties, sat and listened, his hair white, his body thin, his glasses held in place on his nose by thick black frames. Were Jo Jones in the house to lead the way, a trip to Gregory's might be necessary, where drummer Sonny Greer, alto saxophonist Russell Procope—both over sixty-five—and pianist Brooks Kerr, nearly blind but youthful and full of drive, were working. Greer and Procope could summon up the sound, or at least the memory, of the entire Ellington band, while Kerr had the whole of jazz piano from the turn of the century to 1940 at his fingertips.

From Gregory's, Jones might take me with him to hear Roy Eldridge at Ryan's in midtown. A small man, like so many jazz giants, Eldridge, with his white hair and mustache, his brown skin and the spirited gait of one who could have been a fast and vicious boxer with class once upon a time, was almost always good for at least one streak of fury through the chords, building, note upon note, a bonfire of intensity, loosing a pugnacious growl from the bell of his horn like the sound of a lion telling the world that he was not about to give up lording it over the jungle that was his bandstand.

Whether talking with his buddies from the good old days or orating about the nature of the world with his clipped enunciation, Jo Jones himself was never less than imperial in his baldness. He seemed indomitable standing there with his newspaper in his pocket, his long johns on if it was winter, his brandy bottle in his coat, a knife hidden somewhere as a testament to his understanding of the nightlife and proof that he was, as he loved to declaim, "a thug." But if one caught him in the aesthetic slaughterhouse that was the West End, a little club across the street from Columbia University way up on Broadway, his position in the hierarchy of the drums was quite evident—the touch, the power, the exultation, the pain, the finesse. It was all still there.

If you went to a concert at New York University presented by Jack Kleinsinger's "Highlights in Jazz," you might witness a miracle of assembly. One after another—at someone else's show—Eubie Blake, Sam Wooding, Earl Hines, and Claude Hopkins sat down to the piano and played alone. Blake was then the oldest man of jazz and told a story of how he had learned a particular seventh chord from a cook when he was just a kid, then illustrated with an original piece from that time. Earl Hines (whom Jo Jones called "Toupee Willie") spoke of how he had been playing the ivory off

V.S.O.P. onstage at the Greek Theater, Berkeley, California, 1977: Herbie Hancock (piano and leader), Ron Carter, Tony Williams, Wayne Shorter, and Freddie Hubbard. The quintet, organized in 1976 at the height of the fusion era, included all the members of the Miles Davis Quintet of the mid-1960s except its leader.

the keys in Pittsburgh one night when Blake—in derby and tuxedo, with cigar and carrying a cane to give more aristocracy to his stroll—warned the younger man that, as much music as he was playing, if "I come back through here and find you in this town I'll wrap this cane around your head." Hopkins, who had led a big band in the thirties, played a soft and beautiful something in which all of the notes and all of the chords sounded as though they were made of feathers and silk.

Part of the reason that a number of jazz musicians were disheartened in those days was that the battle for the future of the music was taking place against a threat that now seems never to have been there at all. The threat had come from a direction so unexpected that when it was first detected around 1970, no one could quite believe what they were starting to see. Major players were abdicating, abandoning jazz in favor of the fusion phenomenon. And the man who showed them the way was Miles Davis himself.

For some, like this one writing, who can still recall how Miles's band with George Coleman, Herbie Hancock, Ron Carter, and Tony Williams looked at an after-hours show sometime in 1964 at the Adams West Theater in Los Angeles, it seemed inconceivable. Then, four grown men had come onstage in dark suits followed by what appeared to be a little boy in a yellow suit with brown shoes who sat down behind the drums. This was the same kid who had been standing next to Ron Carter before the show, drinking a soda and giving off the ready-to-go feeling that ado-

lescents always have. Davis was backstage, having a good time because the trio that came on before him was swinging and he was playing at conducting the band, moving as if in the boxing ring, snapping out his fists in approval, which meant more to those men up there than any kind of review or fat-salaried contract ever could. This little black giant was enjoying them. They had been accepted by one of the masters. His ruffling nickname was "Inky," and he had a house full of night creatures, hustlers and their women mostly—pimps, gamblers, numbers runners, drug dealers, sellers of hot clothes, and females who knew things about men that very few of their sex would want to find out. These were raucous people, given to loud talk and big laughs, too much cologne and too much perfume, their own debased ideas of aristocracy and a kind of distancing that could become intimate through violent confrontations if the wrong word was said or the bitterness resulting from an old grudge forced itself into bloodletting action. But when Miles Davis came onstage, every one of those denizens of the shadows got quiet, each aware that if something out of line took place, the little splendidly dressed prince might turn around and head for the door, no amount of imploring strong enough to bring him back. The genial Inky of backstage was gone when he walked out of the wings. The stern Davis face, a combination of anger and anguish, was in place, and the trumpeter began with a ballad, putting a mood into the air with his tone that seemed to draw something quite gentle out of even these street women, perhaps memories, perhaps dreams. A mist of romance took over and transformed this filled movie theater to a hoop of emotion surrounding the bandstand. Tony Williams, the little boy on the drums, touched them and swiped his cymbals and a sound we had never heard before went out into the theater. When they moved from the ballad tempo into a lightly sailing straight 4//4, a spiritual cheer went up every time the audience felt safe enough to applaud. That was when Miles Davis was at the top of his form, sharp as a tack, clean as a white fish, hipper-seeming and more confident than a man who God had personally guaranteed would be going to heaven when his time came. That musicianship and that ritual then seemed invincible, but Davis proved that it was not and that we can never assume that there is a straight course, even for the greatest among us. Anyone can fall and nearly bring the building down on the way to the dirt.

Given his prominence and power, it is easy to understand how seriously many musicians took Davis when he claimed that his demon for adventure was pushing him "forward" toward fusion. As the bassist Jaymie Merritt said to me one night, "When genius is involved, you have to listen closely." What Davis did in his new guise and with his electronic guile helped set the new trend. Wayne Shorter, one of the most gifted composers and players of his generation, went into Weather Report, which began as a collective many musicians found interesting, but eventually evolved into Joe Zawinul's band, leaving more and more jazz elements behind. Tony Williams led a rock-influenced group called Lifetime, featuring British guitarist John McLaughlin, which seemed intent mostly on setting new levels of volume.

At least for a bit, Herbie Hancock seemed as if he was going to hold up high the flag of jazz truly remaking itself. The Swahili name of his band, Mwandishi, reflected the ethnic pretensions of the time, but that group—with Buster Williams, Billy Hart, Eddie Henderson, Benny Maupin, and Julian Priester—was one of the great ones of that era and perhaps of any. No one had ever heard anything like it, and there were times when no one in the audience seemed to breathe from the first note to the last. The harmonies and the blends of the front line, the shifts in and out of different tempos and rhythms, as well as its sense of adventure, gave the Hancock Sextet that performance glow only the most compelling ensembles have. Had it lasted, a strong alternative to what became known as fusion would have been out there to inspire others to hold on. But Hancock also eventually submitted to the call of the wild cash register, got to the crossroads, and began sinking down.

Jazz was in the process of being redefined as merely a form of instrumental pop music. While the mixture of jazz and rock did create something that had not existed before, it also intro-

duced instruments and beats that had nothing to do with swing, the propulsive essence of jazz phrasing. That jazz is a music of adult emotion while rock is focused on adolescent passion created another problem for jazz musicians who tried fusion. They could never get to that teenage feeling of ardent ineptitude and resentment of sophisticated authority because they are not inept and their music is as sophisticated as any performing art that has evolved in the Western world.

But despite everything, evidence began to accumulate even during those dispiriting years that the music could remain true to itself and prosper. In October of 1976, on a very rainy evening in midtown Manhattan where the jazz impresario and pianist George Wein had a nightclub called Storyville, the bebop master Dexter Gordon found himself back in The Apple again. He had been living across the big water since 1962. Long since forgotten was his identity as a founding father of the approach that had so much to do with how Sonny Rollins and John Coltrane played the horn as young men. Or so it seemed before that night. The weather would have been prohibitive in most towns, but the house was packed and the saxophonist was obviously touched that people were so interested in hearing him that they weren't going to be stopped by rain.

Gordon immediately let everyone know that it was worth the wait and the wet. Standing in a cloud of charm at the microphone, his deep voice containing the essence of masculinity and whimsy as well as oblique, ironic humor, the long tall one introduced tunes and sometimes recited a portion of the lyrics of a ballad he and his men were about to perform. He held the saxophone as easily as he might stroke his chin and made the air of the room submit to him, blowing his horn with the magisterial confidence one would expect of a bebop master. At the same time, Gordon didn't seem to be playing bebop. As with any of the masters, the style was secondary to his expression. On that night, the stir began that would not only revitalize Gordon's career but reveal the power and the aesthetic scale of an art that this tenor saxophonist embodied for a moment so radiant it was indispensable.

A few months later Gordon was leading his band at the Village Vanguard for an in-person recording. The Vanguard was packed with musicians and lay listeners night after night, and he was on the way to a level of celebrity that greatly helped turn things around. If we look at it outside of how the business world reacted to it, we might think that the stardom that fell upon Dexter Gordon was some form of magic. It was not. Gordon had one of those unpredictable aces in the hole—Bruce Lundvall, a jazz fan and the president of Columbia Records. Had Clive Davis, the former president—who had fired Ornette Coleman, Keith Jarrett, Bill Evans, and Charles Mingus from the label in one day—still been at the wheel, the course of jazz would surely have been different. Lundvall loved the music and was the only president of a major record label willing to put money behind jazz artists. Tall and always superbly attired, Lundvall was the sole record executive of such high station who often went to clubs or to concerts to listen to his artists. If he signed them, he liked them. If he liked them, he went to hear them.

Gordon's reemergence and all the attention he got due to Columbia's marketing campaign soon sparked interest in straight-ahead swinging jazz and inspired the return of other expatriates. Johnny Griffin, the little giant who had such a fat tone and could play so lickety-split that he seemed actually to grow taller as he blew, came home to play again. Back in the kitchen during his breaks, or at the bar drinking red wine, he would talk of how he, Thelonious Monk, Elmo Hope, and Bud Powell would walk miles through the night on the way to Hope's house far up in the Bronx. Along the way, Powell might suddenly run up to some big guy and slap his face, which meant that Monk, Hope, and Griffin then had to keep this fellow from turning the great genius into mashed potatoes.

With his handlebar mustache and stoic eyes, Art Farmer, visiting from his home in Vienna, was the soul of poise and yearning lyricism. He always seemed somewhere else while on the bandstand, somewhere in the middle of a dream that might be extended as Clifford Jordan, the big, brown-skinned Negro from Chicago who often played tenor saxophone alongside him, unwove his many melancholies. One of Jordan's most remarkable nights came when he played with Harry Edison at Condon's after having been diagnosed with terminal cancer earlier in the day. Featured on "I Should Care," the big saxophonist didn't unburden himself or dirty his music with self-pity. In his own style, he played as Ben Webster might have, announcing that the melody of the life he had lived with both its sweet and bitter harmonies, was all of a lyrical piece, a gift that allowed one to croon or howl or snarl at the moon of a dream as long as there was the strength to do it.

Domestic exiles came home, too, some of them from the temporary sanctuary they had found in academe. All the drummers were there at the Village Vanguard when Max Roach returned to action and taught them, once again, that he was the master, playing with a poetic command of his instrument that has never been equaled, even as he so completely absorbed the free, timeless drumming style that the avant-gardist Rashied Ali, both moping and admiring, said, "Well, Max is playing free now. I guess I'll

Art Farmer

just go home and get my little rubber practice pad and wait for him to get another ten years older."

Roach would go on to perform in duet with Cecil Taylor, to perform with his percussion ensemble M'Boom and with the World Saxophone Quartet at the Cathedral of Saint John the Divine, to do multimedia solo concerts, to create a double quartet—his own pianoless group with a string quartet—and to polish his crown every way he could. But on one of the saddest nights of his life, Roach sat like a kid in Seventh Avenue South, a room now gone, as Jo Jones, who had by then depreciated to being no more than a thin drunk muttering to himself, took over the bandstand and went through a routine that seemed, as Ellington family member Michael James says, "part of the King Lear period."

Trumpeter Woody Shaw's evolution into a bandleader and an individual influence on horn players was very important to the morale of the music in those days because, with Miles Davis and Freddie Hubbard both mired in fusion, there was nobody out there who was making sense of what had happened in the early sixties. On many nights, in his full power, Shaw played as if each note was a finger in the dike holding back the deluge of commercialism.

Betty Carter

There was a way that he went into his stuff. In the Vanguard's no-longer-functioning kitchen, which doubled as a dressing room, he could be cursing someone out or talking about the harmony Charlie Parker played on "Bird at St. Nick's" or recalling some adventure he had had when young and an apprentice member of Horace Silver's or Max Roach's or Art Blakey's band. Then, when it was time to hit, Shaw, who was legally blind but had memorized his way to the bandstand, would walk out of the kitchen, up the narrow hallway into the room, turn right past the front door, make another right behind the chairs, take the couple of steps into the gallery rather casually, move between the tables, and walk out on the stage where he performed a few tai chi moves before playing. This took only a minute or so, and Shaw then commenced to play, almost always something fiery as an opener. If you were close enough, you could see that he had the determined look of a snake about to strike, made even more intense by the vast human intelligence and fire he brought to the music.

Then there was the terrible end. Shaw had been strung out for years. He didn't look good and he was surely blind because I passed him a couple of times, not saying anything since the sight of a man as great as he was looking a few steps from homeless was depressing. Once I did say something; he turned to me and there, behind the edgy, embittered, and anxious look of those desirous of some dope, were those eyes and that intelligence. I remembered then how much of a jazz musician he was and how, even when he was most successful and winning jazz polls that were thought to have been rigged by his management, Woody would finish off a job at the Vanguard and ride somewhere into Harlem or the Bronx or Brooklyn to sit in with unknown guys he heard were trying to play something.

On a tragic night when Max Roach was at the Vanguard, the drummer arranged for a private car to bring Shaw to hear the band. While Roach was on the bandstand, Shaw got the driver to take him into Brooklyn. The driver had been given instructions not to take Shaw anywhere, but the trumpeter, who could be very aggressive, had apparently convinced him that Max had changed his mind. The next morning Woody either slipped or stumbled down the stairs at a subway station and ended up so near the track that the incoming train cut off his right arm. Max called me after going to see him in the hospital. There Shaw was, he said, his head shaved and a long dark line of stitches down the middle, lying still with his arm shorn away, in a coma from which he would never recover. The sorrow in Max's voice carried the grief he had felt many times for special people who had been removed from the world too early.

In June of 1975, Cecil Taylor, too, came back to New York and performed at the Five Spot. Taylor had never had much of an audience, nor has his music ever been much of an influence on jazz, but that summer Gary Giddins in the *Village Voice* and Robert Palmer in the *New York Times* wrote about Taylor's return as a major event and the club was packed night after night. Audiences, enjoying it or not, sat before the unrelenting fury of Taylor's music, which had created its own category, one in which a vocabulary predominantly influenced by twentieth-century European music was delivered as though the piano was an enemy that had to be beaten into submission by the small brown-skinned man with the knitted cap who took off his glasses before starting and did not stop for an hour or more. The sheer velocity of his articulation, the size of his sound, and the parallel obsession with grandeur and all that either blocked or denied it, made the emotion Taylor projected reflect not so much a jazz feeling as that of a Beethoven without lyricism. Big statements and triumphant pounding delivered with unequaled physical strength arrived as though they could go on forever. Then, never acknowledging the audience, Taylor put his glasses back on and left the stage for the dressing room. There, far more educated and intellectually engaged than 99 percent of jazz musicians, he might be gleeful, full of wit, given to extraordinary leaps of association. Or he might be almost glum. Or, quite easily, he might break into a contemptuous rage leveled at bigotry and critical incompetence, describing the European concert world's aversion to black musicians, the similarities and distances between African dance and ballet, which he loved equally, the historical racial hiring policies that were why he hated the New York Yankees and the Boston Celtics. Taylor knew plenty about plenty. Therefore, whatever he was, and whatever he was playing, those who had heard it knew that he was the only one on the earth who could meet—or even wanted to meet—the challenges he had set for himself. The sheer intelligence of the man, genius actually, gave him a special color in any light, particularly because he had brought together intellectual thought with athletic prowess. While what he played had little to do with jazz, it was still a massive achievement on a human level.

That September, the Art Ensemble of Chicago worked at the same club for two weeks, awakening Manhattan to what would become a migration of midwestern musicians who were members of the Association for the Advancement of Creative Musicians (AACM). They did little of the one-dimensional screeching

and honking that characterized the music John Coltrane's talent sank under the burden of embracing in his last years. As Muhal Richard Abrams, one of the AACM's founders often said, they were not interested in playing a style, they wanted to play music.

That was evident at the Five Spot. There on the bandstand were saxophonist Roscoe Mitchell in street clothes, trumpeter Lester Bowie in a white lab coat, saxophonist Joseph Jarman, bassist Malachi Favors, and drummer Don Moye in face paint and African getups. Mitchell and Jarman seemed to have been largely influenced by Ornette Coleman, but Bowie's style owed much to Don Ellis. Ellis had embraced the whole of jazz trumpet, not just what had happened since 1945. His own recordings, such as *New Ideas* and *Essence*, his work on George Russell's *The Outer View*, and his *Down Beat* article, in which he called the New Orleans veteran Red Allen the most avant-garde trumpet player in New York, all make it clear that Ellis had been there first, by a decade. Don Cherry, the greatest mind and heart of all the avant-garde trumpet players, could not have done what Ellis did even if he wanted to, since his command of the horn never went far enough. Bowie was not the trumpet player that Ellis was, either—far from it—but he could play the instrument, which immediately separated him from the one-trick blats and squeals of purported avant-garde trumpet players. New York seemed to be waiting for him and for the Art Ensemble itself.

They had arrived in New York that fall on a big (and old) school bus. Though given to breaking down, it had room for the band, all the saxophones Mitchell and Jarman doubled on, and all the percussion instruments—the "little instruments" that any band member might pick up and use in performance as well as the astonishing array of African instruments at Don Moye's command. Moye had made himself as much a virtuoso at his African battery as any symphonic percussionist surrounded by his array of kettle drums, bells, and xylophones. With Favors and Moye back there, the Art Ensemble could stoke up any kind of ethnic black groove, any kind of beat associated with Afro-American music, while the compositions they played could be as simple as street rhymes or executed with tight, well-rehearsed up-tempo ensemble playing.

It was during that period that Air, featuring saxophonist and flutist Henry Threadgill, bassist Fred Hopkins, and drummer Steve McCall—all of them also AACM members—moved to New York from Chicago. At the time, while living above the Tin Palace, playing drums with my loft mate David Murray, and after a Hamiet Bluiett big band concert we held upstairs drew so many people and got so loud that the police came and told us we were making too much noise, I started booking Sunday-afternoon bands that played for the door. That series presented a lot of musicians new to Manhattan, almost all of them associated with what was considered the vanguard of the time.

On the Sunday afternoon that Air debuted in New York, everybody knew that this was a very special band. Most of the music was written by Threadgill, who went on to form a septet that almost blew the windows out of the Tin Palace.

Musicians who hadn't been heard in New York for a while also came to play at the Tin Palace, like the alto and soprano saxophonist Gary Bartz, who had spent a lot of time messing around in fusion but made it clear that he was one of the great men of his horn. Musicians came to enjoy working that club so much that they started playing an extra fourth set, beginning at two a.m., which meant that the club crowded up again and one might see Dexter Gordon or Art Blakey or Cecil Taylor or Ornette Coleman or Max Roach in there as Clifford Jordan, Barry Harris, Walter Booker, and Vernell Fournier performed opposite Dewey Redman, Freddie Simmons, Mark Helias, and Eddie Moore, who was so black and huge I used to joke with him that Dewey must have mailed a cargo plane ticket to San Francisco so he could fly east in comfort.

Sometimes, as happened during the eighties, a spirit can take over and people will get busy on every level. These were the years when one young musician after another came to New York and seemed intent on doing only one thing—learning how to play jazz while fully aware that it was not the kind of art in which anything lucrative was guaranteed. People such as Wynton Marsalis, Wallace Roney, Geri Allen, Greg Osby, Rene Rosnes, Cyrus Chestnutt, Lewis Nash, Peter Washington, Kenny Washington, Bob Hurst, Reginald Veal, Herlin Riley, Russell Malone, James Williams, Mulgrew Miller, Benny Green, Cassandra Wilson, Vanessa Rubin, Cindy Blackman, Teri Lynne Carrington, Jackie Terrason, Leon Parker, Javon Jackson, Kenny Garrett, Tony Reedus, Jeff Watts, Marvin Smitty Smith, and still more younger players who kept leaving home for The Big Apple, surging up out of the ground, as if the music had its own will to live.

The renaissance of jazz in the eighties was fostered as much by Art Blakey as by anybody else. One Sunday in the middle of the decade there was a Father's Day celebration for Blakey at the Apollo. The theater was filled, and backstage, as the drummer Roy Haynes said, "It looked like some kind of an African king's place." Blakey had many children, grown and toddling, as well as girlfriends, wives, and numbers of musicians who had played in his training school for the art, The Jazz Messengers. He had been the sacrificial hero who played and played, night after night,

while those fledglings stumbled over themselves until they began to swing with enough confidence to take off and begin their own bands. Sitting in the audience that afternoon was the singer Betty Carter, who was now doing exactly the same thing that Blakey had done for years—bringing young musicians into her band and putting them through the rigorous tasks necessary to learn how to swing and to play in many different tempos, from extremely slow to as fast as possible.

They had some help. The reissue boom that had been spearheaded by Orrin Keepnews at Fantasy Records, classic material handsomely packaged and with good liner notes, provided young players with recorded examples of high-quality music that had been unavailable for years. This meant that, perhaps for the very first time, jazz musicians were truly learning how to play in styles that stretched back to the beginnings of the music.

More encouragement came from the stage of Cooper Union, where Abraham Lincoln once spoke. There, the American Jazz Orchestra, conceived by Gary Giddins, gave splendid performances of classic jazz under the leadership of John Lewis. As Loren Schoenberg, who took over after Lewis left, once explained during an especially powerful concert of Ellington music, the repertory movement offered plenty of options. Music could be performed as faithfully to the original recordings as possible, or new improvisations in the styles of the period could be allowed, or different arrangements of a given piece could be brought together, another take on the idea of variations on a theme. The point was that jazz did not have to lose bodies of great music just because those who once played it were no longer in the world.

As the jazz spirit started to rise higher and higher, fine bands came into existence. One of the best was Old and New Dreams, featuring Don Cherry, Dewey Redman, Charlie Haden, and Ed Blackwell, which played a repertoire dominated by the music of Ornette Coleman, and made it clear every night how very different what Coleman had introduced into jazz was from the bulk of the music played by those usually said to be in the jazz vanguard. They swung, they were melody makers, and the whole tradition of jazz flowed through their playing exactly as it did from the best of the musicians who had come forward since the bebop movement of the forties.

There was also the return of the prodigals. Tony Williams began to lead a wonderful band with trumpeter Wallace Roney, saxophonist Billy Pierce, pianist Mulgrew Miller, and—in succession—bassists Charnette Moffett, Bob Hurst, and Ira Coleman. At the Vanguard one night a few weeks after Art Blakey died in 1990, Williams could be heard mixing into his playing signal things that had touched him when he was a kid. Some Max Roach for a bit, then Philly Joe Jones, then Roy Haynes, Elvin Jones, Kenny Clarke—almost an autobiography of his own beginnings. By playing so much less loudly than when he was struggling to blast his way into the fusion world, Williams made the power of his entire conception audible, which included writing that defined him as the most complete drummer-leader of any period. All of the music on that bandstand was his—every note, chord, arrangement. The result was a very serious extension of what the Miles Davis Quintet had been doing in the sixties, the drummer's most glorious period of recognition. No, this didn't mean Williams had gone backwards, as too many of the intellectual clubfeet of jazz writing would automatically assume. By setting aside his apparent dreams of pop stardom, Williams had reached through the recent musical dark ages to a period of illumination, brought forward a flame, and was piling fresh logs on it. At forty-six, Williams was doing what all masters do once they accept the richness of their own perceptions: they come to embody every element of what initially attracted them to music and to their instruments. Williams sometimes jacked himself up chorus by chorus into the sort of swing no young drummer, however gifted, could lay down. For the first time I heard the weight in his sound that only comes of emotion and substantial experience.

But of all the prodigals, the one who returned to the highest point of glory may have been Freddie Hubbard. In almost biblical fashion, the trumpeter had a revelation when he was nearly shocked to death as he was warming up backstage for an outdoor concert and the wire to an electronic gadget he had attached to his trumpet was pulled through some water. Once the fusion ruse was behind him, Hubbard eventually worked at the Blue Note, the largest and best-paying jazz club in the city, the one responsible for presenting people such as Sarah Vaughan, the Modern Jazz Quartet, Oscar Peterson, Billy Eckstine, and Joe Williams in the kind of setting jazz listeners never thought they would experience again.

There, Hubbard did the richest trumpet improvising of the time. Almost gone were the memories of the platform shoes and plaid pants of his fusion days. Handsome and looking more and more like Louis Armstrong, Hubbard now wore exquisitely cut suits, beautiful shirts, and silk ties, and he played with all the accumulated luminosity of a man who has been at his horn for over forty years. His time feeling, which was as witty as it was mock-pugnacious, his melody lines, and his harmonic personalization of what he learned from Coltrane and Rollins were at a point of imposing effortlessness. He was also the ox of his instrument, given to unflagging strength and projection, a clarion authority that recalled Armstrong as much as his looks did. One

Freddie Hubbard

night he picked up the flugelhorn and did a version of "Blue Moon" that included a long, long introduction, a rhythmic rebuilding of the theme, and chorus after chorus of extemporaneous purity, motifs varying from the pinnacle of the horn's reach to the bottom, smears that transformed themselves into melody, harmonic choices that were so surprising they accented themselves, and a longing that heroically emphasized the first word of the tune's title and led his listeners back to the beginnings of the music.

In the end, that this kind of power continues to exhibit itself is far more important than the regret that the music is not appreciated to the degree jazz lovers would like to see. When you get down to it, no matter the style, no matter what anyone says about it, the point is what happened when those musicians were standing there in the flesh, shaping, sweating, and emoting. They displayed the wonders of an extraordinary art through their own talents and their collective victories. If there was truly a paean to the presence of jazz, it was the way they were and what they did.

A MASTER-PIECE BY MIDNIGHT

"Anyone who thinks that it's easy to go onstage every night, three hundred times a year, and create something new, will never get the toll that it takes to be a jazz musician," the record producer Michael Cuscuna has said.

It's incredibly draining to start from ground zero every day and truly create something that's as close as you can humanly get to a masterpiece by midnight. In the creative process of starting from scratch every night and drawing from your heart and from your intellect and making your fingers work your instrument, you have to really lay your soul bare. Because every night you have to put every molecule of your body into creating something. Unlike in other art forms, you don't have private time to tinker with your creation. You're out there. You are in front

Dexter Gordon onstage with bassist Stafford James and drummer Louis Hayes, 1978 of people and you are creating of the moment. And there's no net; there is no safety valve at all. You are out there for all to see, to fail or to succeed. Or to just get by.

No one in jazz worked harder or risked more than Dexter Gordon—"Long Tall Dexter." And few musicians would show the wear and tear more starkly. The son of a Los Angeles doctor who tended Duke Ellington whenever he was in town, Gordon was so tall and so handsome when he was young, an acquaintance remembered, that he could draw a crowd just by putting his tenor saxophone together. He was "an idol around Central Avenue," Art Pepper recalled. "He wore a wide-brimmed hat that made him seem like he was seven feet tall. He had a stoop to his walk and wore long zoot suits, and he carried his tenor in a sack under his arm."

He had an instantly identifiable sound— big and warm and oddly languid even when hurtling through changes—and he had learned his art from the masters. He venerated Lester Young, played with Lionel Hampton and in Louis Armstrong's big band—the arrangements weren't much, he remembered, but he loved hearing Pops play every night—and he had toured with Billy Eckstine's groundbreaking orchestra as well. During visits to New York, he had taken part in the weekly jousts at Minton's that helped produce bebop and afterward was best known for "The Chase," a blistering recorded tenor duel with Wardell Gray—the first of a series of celebrated face-offs that pitted him against other tenor stars, including Sonny Stitt, Teddy Edwards, and Gene Ammons, always with memorable results. He was a born competitor; the struggle to stay on top, he said, consumed "every night, all my life."

As the fifties began Gordon had seemed on the brink of still greater success. But he had also developed a heroin habit that cost him two hundred dollars a day and raged so far out of control that once, after

shooting up on a visit to New York, he unpacked his horn at the corner of Eleventh Street and Fifth Avenue and gratefully played for his dealer. In 1952, the law caught up with him. During the next eight years he served time for possession at the Chino, Fort Worth, Lexington, and Folsom federal prisons.

By the time Gordon was back on the street, he found work harder and harder to get. He was not alone. When the English historian and sometime jazz writer Eric Hobsbawm visited the United States for the first time in 1960, he "found the nights too short to listen to everything that could be heard in New York from the Half Note and the Five Spot in the Village to Small's Paradise and the Apollo in Harlem and further west in Chicago and San Francisco." Two years later, he wrote, when he came back eager to hear more music, " 'Bird Lives' could still be seen painted on lonely walls, but the celebrated New York jazz venue named after him, Birdland, had ceased to exist" and "jazz had virtually been knocked out of the ring."

What had happened? The tenor player Johnny Griffin blamed those who had taken jazz "out of Harlem and put it in Carnegie Hall and downtown in those joints where you've got to be quiet. The black people split and went back to Harlem, back to the rhythm and blues, so they could have a good time." Meanwhile, the pianist Hampton Hawes wrote, "white kids were jamming the rock halls and the older people were staying home and watching TV. Maybe they found they couldn't pat their feet to our music anymore." And after 1963, the astonishing global popularity of the Beatles and other British rock groups—their sound initially derived from African-American blues performers, precisely as the music of white American rockers had been a decade earlier—produced a second, still more spectacular surge in the sales of rock music, and a still deeper decline in public enthusiasm for jazz. Even John Hammond now edged away from the music he had always loved most and applied his scouting skills to rock and folk music instead, signing Aretha Franklin, Bob Dylan, and, later, Bruce Springsteen, for Columbia Records.

Desperate jazz musicians took jobs wherever they could find them—in cocktail

The Village Gate, in Greenwich Village, still a jazz stronghold during the 1960s

Louis Armstrong. "Each man has his own music bubbling up inside him," he once told an interviewer, "and—quite naturally—different ones will let it out in various ways. When I blow I think of times and things out of the past that give me an image of the tune. . . . A town, a chick somewhere back down the line, an old man with no name you seen once in a place you don't remember—any of 'em can trigger that image. . . . What you hear from a man's horn is what he is. And a man can be many different things."

On 125th Street in Harlem. By the time this photograph was taken, in the autumn of 1964, stars with jazz roots like Billy Eckstine and Quincy Jones only rarely headlined at the Apollo Theater any more. It did its best business presenting rhythm and blues packages.

lounges, studio orchestras, playing background music for the movies, backing rock 'n' roll performers on records. "You have to eat," said Bud Shank, just one of many West Coast musicians who found themselves forced to find refuge in the Hollywood studios. "You have to survive. When I became a full-time studio musician, I had been unemployed for a long time since jazz music left us in 1962–63. . . . I went into another business. That's what I did . . . using the tools I had, which was playing the flute and the saxophone."

Other musicians abandoned performing altogether. Tenor saxophonist Eddie "Lockjaw" Davis, a veteran of the Count Basie band, became a booking agent for rock groups. Dicky Wells, who had played trombone with Basie, as well as Fletcher Henderson, Benny Carter, and Teddy Hill, took a job as a bank guard on Wall Street, in part, he said, because there were "at least a hundred" other musicians already working in the financial district with whom he could hang out at lunchtime. Still other musicians left for Europe in search of an audience: Chet Baker, Donald Byrd, Don Cherry, Art Farmer, Bud Freeman, Stan Getz, Jimmy Heath, Philly Joe Jones, Oscar Pettiford, Bud Powell, Stuff Smith, Art Taylor, Lucky Thompson, Ben Webster, Randy Weston, Phil Woods.

In 1962, Dexter Gordon joined that exodus. He would stay away for the next fifteen years, living in Paris briefly first and then in Copenhagen, coming home for brief appearances or recording dates when he could get them, then scuttling back overseas again. He reveled in the admiration of European fans, who treated him as an artist, not a drug addict—but he also grew impatient with the local musicians with whom he was sometimes forced to play. They were mostly amateurs, he remembered, doctors, dentists, architects, salesmen. They loved the music, but "all they knew was what they'd learned from the records. And with jazz, you've got to come up by playing with other musicians—older

Dexter Gordon at New York's Royal Roost, 1948

musicians. . . . In the way we all came up in the States." Fewer and fewer young American musicians would be coming up that way in the years to come, and America's music would suffer for it.

The country Gordon left behind was entering an era unlike any it had ever experienced before, a period of selfless struggle and shameless self-indulgence; of unprecedented progress in civil rights and deepening divisions between the races; of calls for collective action and relentless focus on

the individual; and of the mushroom growth of a youth culture powerful enough to begin to dictate America's tastes. Jazz music would struggle to deal with it all, and in the process would increasingly find itself divided into factions, so *many* factions, Duke Ellington said, he didn't see how "such great extremes as now exist can be contained under the one heading." The debate over what was jazz and what was not raged as it never had before, and for a time, the real question would become whether this most American of art forms could survive in America at all.

No book, no shelf of books, could adequately map the course of jazz after 1960, let alone trace the meandering paths of all its proliferating tributaries. No Great Man can be said to have towered over everyone else, as Louis Armstrong and Charlie Parker could be said to have done in their time, but John Coltrane and Miles Davis were surely among the most influential of all post-bebop musicians, and their careers touched upon many of the most important developments in the music, for both good and ill. During Coltrane's too-brief career—he began recording with Miles Davis in 1955 and died in 1967, at the age of forty—his music would first exemplify the idealism that may have been the most admirable quality of the early 1960s, and then prefigure what Cecil Taylor called "the hysteria of the times," the chaos that characterized the decade's end. His truncated life would also further fuel the romantic but dangerous notion, born after Bix Beiderbecke's early death and furthered by Charlie Parker's demise, that the greatest musicians were those who immolated themselves in search of something new. Meanwhile, Davis—who would remain a much admired figure until his death in 1991—developed still another fresh way to work with young musicians, and then, when he saw his own popularity and that of jazz itself declining, would seek to save himself by first denaturing and then deserting altogether the music that had won him fame in the first place.

SOMETHING LIKE HAPPINESS

"The other night I heard a cat on the radio and he was talking about 'modern' jazz," Duke Ellington told an interviewer in the early sixties. "He played a record to illustrate his point, and there were devices in that music I heard cats using in the nineteen-twenties. Those large words like 'modern' don't *mean* anything. Everybody who's had anything to say in this music—all the way back—has been an individualist. I mean musicians like Sidney Bechet, Louis Armstrong, Coleman Hawkins. Then what happens is that hundreds of other musicians begin to be shaped by that one man. They fall in behind him and you've got what people call a category. But I don't listen to terms like 'modern' jazz. I listen for those individualists."

By 1962, John Coltrane was already one of the music's most influential individualists, and when Bob Thiele of Impulse Records asked Ellington to record with him that year, the older man happily agreed. Before the session, there was some concern that their styles wouldn't blend well, that the generational differences would prove too great between the thirty-six-year-old saxophonist whom many young musicians had already begun to see as the standard-bearer for a new musical revolution, and the sixty-three-year-old elder statesman who had begun recording his own compositions before Coltrane was born. No one need have worried. "Ellington was put into the jazz world to separate the men from the boys," wrote the British saxophonist Benny Green. "His grasp of harmony and instrumental voicing is more advanced than anybody else's in the entire range of jazz, and the reason why many modern fans are unable to accept him is not that they are too modern for Duke, but that Duke is too modern for them." The two men got along famously. Coltrane's scalar improvising didn't scare Ellington—"We're accustomed to . . . adjusting backgrounds to the soloist who's in the foreground," he said, employing the royal "we"—while Coltrane had served a full apprenticeship in jazz and had profound respect for Ellington and his music. The saxophonist's chronic dissatisfaction with his own work might have made the session arduous; he customarily asked record producers to let him try take after take. But Ellington's skill at bending others to his will while seeming to be thinking only of their welfare finessed that prob-

lem. "Don't ask him to do another," he told Thiele after he and Coltrane had finished the first take of their first tune. "He'll end up repeating himself."

John Coltrane was often accused of doing precisely that in the course of improvisations that now sometimes stretched on in live performance for an hour or more.

Eric Dolphy, left, John Coltrane, now playing soprano saxophone, and bassist Reginald Workman reflected in a mirror at the Village Gate, 1961. "When there's something we think could be better," Coltrane said, "we must make an effort to try and make it better. . . . It's the same socially, musically, politically . . . in any departmnent of our lives."

"One man's incantation," wrote Martin Williams, "is another man's monotony." But redundancy was never his intention. Few in the long history of the music ever labored so hard in search of fresh ways to sound. And no one ever had a more exalted sense of the musician's calling. "I would like to bring to people something like happiness,"

Coltrane told an interviewer early in his career. "I would like to discover a method so that if I want it to rain, it will start right away to rain. If one of my friends is ill, I'd like to play a certain song and he will be cured. . . . But what are these pieces and what is the road to travel to attain a knowledge of them? That I don't know." In a less

genuinely modest man such sentiments might have been evidence of megalomania, and some have suggested that Coltrane's behavior did border on madness. He seems clearly to have been an obsessive: so incapable of resisting sweets that he lost most of his teeth by the age of thirty-one; so fanatical about practicing during the day-

Modernism. John Coltrane at the newly opened Solomon R Guggenheim Museum in Manhattan, 1960

time, his onetime neighbor, the organist Shirley Scott, recalled, that unless his wife was home, he would answer neither the telephone nor the door; so impatient to play at night that when performing in a club he would sometimes complete one lengthy solo, leave the bandstand, go into the men's room and continue blowing while the other members of the group were soloing, then return to play again, repeating the cycle without a break till closing time.

Coltrane's compulsiveness had first taken the form of heroin and alcohol addictions so severe that Miles Davis had had to let him go for a time in 1957. His dismissal

turned out to have been almost literally a blessing. He went home to Philadelphia and there, he wrote later, "I experienced, by the Grace of God, a spiritual awakening which was to lead me to a richer, fuller, more productive life. . . . In gratitude I humbly asked to be given the means and privilege to make others happy through music." For that cause, he gave up drugs and liquor and devoted himself monomaniacally to his craft, more determined than ever to fill his music with more of everything—more notes, more energy, more ideas. He worked with Thelonious Monk for a time, rejoined Miles Davis, then in 1960 struck out on his

own, sometimes performing with the avant-garde reedman Eric Dolphy.

Just as he had once tried to play every note in every chord, Coltrane would be driven by his spiritual and musical quest simultaneously to work his earnest way through nearly every nostrum the sixties had to offer: astrology and vegetarianism, Yoga, the Kabbalah, Kahlil Gibran, Tibetan Buddhism, Hindu mysticism, a book called *Philosophy Made Simple,* and, eventually, LSD. Coltrane listened to North African and Far Eastern music, too, and began to experiment with the drone and scalar playing of Indian ragas. "He was obsessed with learning how to get to what he was hearing," Charlie Haden said. "That's all he thought about. He generated this energy . . . that was almost like the energy of the sun. He lifted everything up when he played."

In 1961, he formed his own extraordinary quartet. Jimmy Garrison brought both ferocity and steadfastness to the bass. McCoy Tyner played the piano; his love for the blues, percussive block chords, and riffs and vamps (brief patterns played over and over to produce something like the drone's effect in Indian music), worked out with Garrison, helped provide the perfect setting for Coltrane's increasingly relentless musings. Elvin Jones played drums—*all* the drums. For him, as Stanley Crouch has written, the trap set was an "ensemble" on which rhythm was not merely played but "orchestrated." "It may sound like a duet or duel," Jones once said of his ruffling, swirling work, filled with cymbal splashes, that sometimes seemed not to back Coltrane so much as engulf the whole group, "but it's still a support I'm lending him, a complementary thing."

In addition to the tenor with which he had first made his mark, Coltrane was now also playing the soprano saxophone, the higher-pitched instrument Sidney Bechet had introduced to jazz. He chose it, he said, because it reminded him of the Eastern and African instruments he had come to love, and he used it to produce his stunning 1961 transformation of the cloying waltz from *The Sound of Music,* "My Favorite Things." It became the first jazz cut since Dave Brubeck's "Take Five" to receive wide play on the radio. It also helped make Coltrane, after Miles Davis, perhaps the best-paid black modern jazz musician in the country.

He barely noticed. By the time his records appeared, he always seemed to have moved on to something else, something he hoped would bring him closer to providing answers to the questions he perpetually asked himself. Now, with "My Favorite Things" still being heard on the radio, Coltrane made a live album at the

Village Vanguard called *Chasin' the Trane.* The title tune, a better-than-sixteen-minute tenor solo covering one whole side of the record—some eighty choruses, nearly three times as many as Paul Gonsalves played at Newport in 1956—was built upon the twelve-bar blues but is otherwise unlike any blues anyone had heard on a record before. Tyner sat this one out, but Jones and Garrison saw to it that it never stopped swinging. Otherwise, it was all Coltrane—swooping, twisting, roaring by turns, his sound filled with yawps and honks, cries and slurs, that he had mastered playing in rhythm and blues bands, and so intense and unrelenting that it battered down his listeners' defenses, leaving them as exhilarated and nearly as drained as he was when he came to the end. That was not actually his intention—"I'm primarily looking into certain sounds, certain scales," he said. "Not that I'm sure what I'm looking for, except that it'll be something that hasn't been played before"—but the impact of his playing was almost palpable and, for those willing to follow wherever he might lead, irresistible. Michael Cuscuna used to hear Coltrane at Birdland. "The energy, the power that came out of that group was just astonishing. In the peanut gallery [a seating area for fans too young to be served alcohol], the tables were very nicely spaced, and I remember we used to just get up and dance to John Coltrane. It was as close to having a religion as I ever got." In an era of steadily heightening racial sensitivity, some young black musicians heard something more—a new, profoundly expressive way to play, derived from African-American rather than European sources, that was the mirror opposite of cool.

The men with whom Coltrane played shared his almost visionary belief in the importance of what they were doing. "Many years later," the tenor saxophonist Branford Marsalis recalled, "a lot of younger musicians were hanging around with Elvin Jones, and they were talking about, 'Man, you know, you guys had an intensity when

you were playing with Coltrane. I mean, what was that like? How do you play with that kind of intensity?' And Elvin looks at him and says, 'You gotta be willing to die with the motherfucker.' They started laughing like kids do, waiting for the punch line, and then they realized he was serious. How many people do you know that are willing to die—period? Die with anybody! And when you listen to those records, that's exactly what they sound like. I mean, that they would die for each other."

On December 9, 1964, the Coltrane quartet made one of the best-selling and best-loved jazz albums of all time, a four-part devotional suite called *A Love*

Elvin Jones. Dubbed ""Emperor Jones," by the great Max Roach, he insisted that the drum set should be played as a single instrument, not an assembly. "You can't isolate the different parts of the set," he said, "any more than you can isolate your left leg from the rest of your body. We live in a world where everything is categorized and locked up into little bitty compartments. But I have to insist that the drum set is one."

BEATING THE BEATLES

In February 1964, the Beatles landed in America. Their music had preceded them—Beatle records topped the charts, adolescent American girls were as frenzied to see and hear them as were their British counterparts—and theirs was only the first foothold of what came to be called the British invasion. Jazz musicians receded still further into the background—with one notable exception: Louis Armstrong and the All-Stars. "We were playing a club in Chicago called The Chez Paree," Arvell Shaw remembered,

> and our off day was Sunday. We got a call from Joe Glaser, saying, "I want you to go into New York on your off day to make a recording." So we flew into New York on Sunday, we got to the studio, and they gave Louis the sheet music and Louis looked at it and said, "You mean to tell me you called me out here to do this?" He hated it, you know? But we made the record, and then we went back to Chicago and finished out the engagement. Three or four months later we were out on the road doing one-nighters in Nebraska and Iowa—way out. And every night we'd hear from the audience, "Hello Dolly, Hello Dolly." So, the first couple of nights Louis ignored it, and it got louder, "Hello Dolly." So Louis looked at me. He said, "What the hell is 'Hello

Dolly?'" I said, "Well you remember that date we did a few months ago in New York? One of the tunes was called 'Hello Dolly'; it's from a Broadway show." We had to call and get the music and learn it and put it in the concert, and the first time we put it in the concert, pandemonium broke out.

Two months after the Beatles landed, Louis Armstrong's "Hello Dolly" became the number one song in America. When Armstrong got back to New York and played a one-night stand at the Metropole, he was greeted by a sign above a musicians' hangout across Forty-eighth Street called the Copper Rail that read, "You Beat the Beatles." Inside waiting to cheer him was a host of musicians who had learned from him over the years: Eddie Condon and Bud Freeman, middle-aged men now, who had been among the youthful acolytes haunting his bandstand on Chicago's South Side; Duke Ellington, who had first heard Armstrong when he came to New York to join Fletcher Henderson; Lionel Hampton, who had played with him in California in 1930; Ben Webster and Buck Clayton and many others. It was a sweet victory, but short-lived. Within a few weeks, rock had recaptured the airwaves.

There would be other jazz and jazz-tinged hits during the 1960s. The tenor saxophonist Stan Getz ushered in a

Cover of a long-playing album that included Louis Armstrong's hit single

brief flurry of excitement over the Brazilian bossa nova. And Cannonball Adderley would have a big success with a soulful tune called "Mercy, Mercy, Mercy," though he was not fooled by it: "The jazz we knew and loved in the thirties, forties, fifties, yes, even the sixties . . . is gone. The audience for it is gradually fading away. We enjoy a great deal of success playing what we do, because people don't get enough of a chance to hear it. . . . But there aren't that many playing."

Supreme. For Coltrane, music and religion had now become one: "My music is the spiritual expression of what I am—my faith, my knowledge, my being. . . . When you begin to see the possibilities of music, you desire to do something really good for people, to help humanity free itself from its hangups. . . . I want to speak to their souls." Divided into four sections—"Acknowledgment," "Resolution," "Pursuance," and "Psalm"— it is a personal affirmation of Coltrane's faith in a Creator, and during the fevered sixties its air of meditative serenity struck a chord with hundreds of thousands of young people. It continues to be a favorite among young musicians to this day. "I think that record is one of the purest jazz records ever," said the tenor saxophonist Joshua Redman. "The intent is so pure and the feeling is so pure, you just feel that John Coltrane is laying his soul out there, you know. That's one of the first records I

ever heard and I hope it's the last record I ever hear."

His fellow tenor player Branford Marsalis agreed.

> The first time I heard *A Love Supreme* was in college. And it's one of those records I couldn't put down. I listened to it for like six months straight. I just kept listening to it. You know, I would put on *A Love Supreme* in the morning for breakfast. Then I'd put it on at lunch, and I'd put it on when I went to bed at night. I would put it on when I was watching television. It was just on all the time. I couldn't believe that kind of sustained intensity. Everybody talked about the physical challenge of it, but as I spent more time listening to it and as I got older I realized that once you put yourself in a certain intellectual frame of mind, I

mean, what is physical? He had put himself in such a place mentally that the physical wasn't a problem for him because it was almost as though he had transcended the body when he started playing.

The early sixties had not been a good time for John Coltrane's former employer, Miles Davis. He was snorting cocaine and often ill. His second marriage fell apart. He worked with a series of sidemen rather than a full-time group. He was still a celebrity, but men who had played with him in the past— Art Blakey, Horace Silver, Sonny Rollins, John Coltrane, Cannonball Adderley—were now getting serious attention, and he was resentful that while his own music had once been on the "cutting edge," as he called it, "critics—white critics—[had] started supporting the free thing, pushing that over what most everybody else was doing."

Davis had initially been less than impressed with free jazz. "You don't have to think to play weird," he'd said after jamming with Ornette Coleman in 1959. He was for "freedom," he said, "but *controlled* freedom," and when he did finally manage to organize a new quintet in late 1964, it would exemplify that principle. Wayne Shorter—thirty years old and a veteran of Art Blakey's Jazz Messengers but still so respectful of his new leader that he addressed him as "Mr. Davis"—composed for the group and played tenor and soprano saxophone. The rhythm section was Ron Carter, a graduate of the Eastman School of Music, on bass; the pianist Herbie Hancock, who had begun his career at the age of eleven, performing a D major piano concerto by Mozart with the Chicago Symphony; and the drummer Tony Williams, already a masterful percussionist at seventeen but too young to be allowed to play in most clubs. Davis said he himself provided "the inspiration and wisdom" for his new group, but that Williams was the "fire, the creative spark," Carter and Hancock were "the anchors," and Wayne Shorter "the idea person, the conceptualizer of a whole lot of the musical ideas we did." If the musical rules "didn't work," Davis continued, Shorter "broke them but . . . he [also] understood that freedom in music was the ability to know the rules in order to bend them to your satisfaction and taste."

The first of the six albums Davis's new group made together was aptly titled *E.S.P.*—it seemed to many of those who heard it that only extrasensory perception could account for the apparently effortless interchange of musical ideas. The music was more dense, more free-floating, than anything Miles Davis had done before; it encompassed sudden spontaneous shifts in tempo and other elements heard in the music of far freer players, but all still linked to the blues-based music he had always played. "It's really hard to describe what we were doing, because we didn't talk in detail about it," Herbie Hancock remembered. "Things would kind of just happen and you just had

Miles Davis and Wayne Shorter, 1968. Davis, Shorter remembered, "was the only bandleader who paid his personnel not to practice at home, so as to avoid the polish that makes some improvised music sound boring. He always wanted it fresh."

to keep your ears open, keep your eyes open, and keep your heart open."

"I don't know if there's ever been a group of five musicians who communicated spontaneously with each other as well as those five," said Joshua Redman. "They could do anything with any form, with any tune, because they knew each other so well as musicians. Their music will always sound cutting edge and always sound modern

Members of the Miles Davis Quintet onstage: Herbie Hancock, Ron Carter, Tony Williams, Davis

because I can't imagine a greater level of group interplay." "This band played with true freedom," Michael Cuscuna recalled. "This was the *real* 'free jazz.' "

"WE INSIST"

"Musicians play," Jackie McLean said, "because of the world around them and what goes on, and there was a lot of violence in the sixties. John F. Kennedy was blown away in 1963, Malcolm X, Medgar Evers, Martin Luther King, Robert Kennedy —all of this assassination went on. The cities were burning. The civil rights movement. People were screaming. The Vietnam war. And so the music went that way. There's just so much that went on during the sixties that caused the music to really break out into this whole hysterical and violent kind of sound. Some of Trane's solos sound like a child being whipped in a city."

As early as 1960, the surge of student sit-ins had proved so strong that even Duke Ellington—who still believed "a statement of political protest should be made without saying it"—had been moved to symbolic action. On February 22, after playing a concert at Johns Hopkins University in Baltimore, he had himself escorted to the Blue Jay Restaurant, where earlier that day black students had been refused service. He, too, was turned away—and made headlines across the country. That same year, Max Roach and the singer Oscar Brown Jr. wrote an extended work inspired by the sit-ins called *We Insist: The Freedom Now Suite*. The young trumpet star Booker Little was featured; so was Coleman Hawkins, whose presence in this unfamiliar setting was further proof of the old master's life-long willingness to try new things. In one movement, vocalist Abbey Lincoln was called upon to shriek as well as sing. "It wasn't anything I ever envisioned," she remembered. "I never felt that way about people. I don't complain to anybody for my life, only to God. And I didn't think that screaming was really music. I didn't think it was musical. But it turned out to be." Whether or not it was music, it was pow-

erful and chilling, a torrent of anger and anguish, the perfect accompaniment for the rising tide of protest.

The 1960s had begun with the unshakable optimism of Dr. Martin Luther King Jr.—the conviction that Americans were fully capable of realizing the American promise of full equality that jazz embodied at its best—but they would end with the Black Panthers and the all-too-pervasive belief that America's racial divisions could never be bridged, that black and white Americans were fated perpetually to live apart. Nineteen sixty-five marked a kind of turning point. The nonviolent civil rights movement and the political skills of President Lyndon Johnson had combined to force Congress to pass the Civil Rights Act the previous year, empowering the attorney general to bring suit for discriminatory practices in public accommodations. But that victory had come at a fearful cost—civil rights workers murdered, marchers beaten and killed. Malcolm X was shot to death in February 1965. In March, Alabama state troopers on horseback clubbed some seventy citizens asking for the right to vote at Selma. In June, Dr. King led a march for desegregated housing in Chicago that was met with mob violence as bad as any he'd

The Movement meets the Music. *We Insist!*, 1960

encountered in the South. Lyndon Johnson sent the first American combat troops to Vietnam in late July. In August, the Watts section of Los Angeles exploded in riots. For many young black Americans, impatient for justice, it was all taking far too long and amounting to far too little. Stokely Carmichael would not formally call for "Black Power" until the following summer, but despair and anger had already fueled the growth of a kind of self-defensive nationalism, a growing conviction that if whites were unwilling to share power, black people would have to wrest it from them.

That idea gripped the imaginations of many of the musicians identified with the New Thing. The grievances of black musicians were older than jazz itself. "What's new?" a friend once asked Louis Armstrong. "Nothing," he answered. "White folks still ahead." From the minstrel era to the age of rock, much of the music white Americans loved most had been created out of African-American forms, yet with only a handful of exceptions, white performers had always reaped the profits. Whites continued to own most of the clubs and concert halls in which jazz was played. They ran the companies that recorded and distributed it, decided how much musicians got paid, defined the conditions under which they had to work, determined who got critical attention and who did not.

Some young musicians now saw it as their mission not only to revolutionize the music but to reclaim it for their community, to reassert what they believed to be its African roots, to reject every vestige of the European tradition that had been an integral part of it from the beginning. Much of their music was meant to aggravate, not please; one of its most ardent journalistic champions gleefully confessed that he enjoyed recommending to his readers only those records he was sure they would dislike. When another writer suggested that the tenor saxophonist and sometime playwright Archie Shepp and his colleagues were undercutting their own message by

being "too angry," Shepp answered, "We are not angry men. We are *enraged.* You can no longer defer my dream. I'm gonna sing it. Dance it. Scream it. And if need be, I'll steal it from this very earth." Jazz, Shepp assured another interviewer, was then and had always been revolutionary music, "antiwar; it is opposed to Vietnam; it is for Cuba; it is for the liberation of all people. . . . Why is that so? Because jazz is a music itself born out of oppression, born out of the enslavement of my people."

The poet LeRoi Jones made himself the movement's unofficial spokesman. New Thing musicians, he said, were "poets of the Black Nation," "God-Seekers," who were "free. That is, freed of the popular song. Freed of American white cocktail tinkle . . . the strait-jacket of American expression *sans* blackness." The goal was to return to "African sounds; the beginnings of our sensibility. The new, the 'primitive,' meaning *first*. . . . The Black musicians who know about the European tempered scale (Mind) no longer want it. . . . The other Black musicians never wanted it anyway." Henceforth, jazz was "not about notes," said the tenor saxophonist Albert Ayler. "It's about feelings."

Duke Ellington had heard that kind of talk before. Ever since his own carefully crafted work had been patronized as mere "jungle music," he had detested the notion —as old as the first European writing about jazz and as up-to-date as the white hipster's confusion about the wellsprings of bebop— that jazz was purely spontaneous, something that emerged unbidden from the African-American unconscious. Now some black spokesmen seemed to be saying more or less the same thing. "Unadulterated improvisation without any preparation or anticipation," he warned, was musically worthless. "It is my firm belief that there has never been anybody who has blown even two bars worth listening to who didn't have some idea about what he was going to play before he started. If you just ramble through the scales or play around the

Archie Shepp, surrounded by portraits of some of his heroes. "It just seems to me that whites . . . become a little over-anxious when you talk about what shapes a man," he once told an interviewer. "Take a man like Stravinsky. . . . I'm sure he could talk to you about Russian music and Russian history and you wouldn't be offended . . . yet I always get the feeling that whites are a little bit frightened or offended when I start to include my history."

chords, that's nothing more than musical exercises. . . . Jazz today, as always in the past, is a matter of thoughtful creation, not mere unaided instinct."

John Coltrane's vision extended beyond race and nationality. He resented any suggestion that he was merely an "angry" player. Anger was only one of many feelings he expressed through his music, he said. When an ideologically inclined writer tried to get him to say that the idea for making two delicate, lyrical albums of ballads (one with the great and inexplicably neglected singer Johnny Hartman) had been part of a scheme by grasping record producers interested only in money, not art, Coltrane gently disagreed; he loved those songs, he said, and it had been his idea to record Hartman. Even when his own music was inspired directly by current events —as it had been in 1963 when he wrote "Alabama," his magnificent elegy for four little black girls who died in the bombing of the Sixteenth Street Baptist Church in Birmingham—it was not confined to any single emotion. There was anger and anguish in "Alabama," but like the greatest spirituals it also contained resilience, resolve, and prayerful hope. Nor did Coltrane share the conviction held by some new thing players and their champions that white musicians couldn't play. "I don't know the criteria capable of differentiating a white musician from a black musician," he said. "It is entirely a problem of understanding [the basics of the music] and has nothing to do with questions of skin color."

But Coltrane was sympathetic to much of what the New Thing players were doing musically. They, too, seemed to him to be engaged in an unending search. He invited some of them to sit in with his group; helped see to it that several, including Archie Shepp and Albert Ayler, were given record contracts; and in 1965, had seven of them join his quartet in the studio to record *Ascension*, a discordant thirty-eight-minute collective improvisation in which the most prominent voice other than his was that of Pharoah Sanders, a tenor saxophonist whose unfettered playing reminded even one of Coltrane's most admiring biographers of "a child having a tantrum, who begins by whining and complaining and builds to out-of-control howls and shrieks." "The performance soars and sings," wrote Martin Williams. "It is at the same time a contemporary jazz performance and a communal

rite," more impressive as a sampling of the country's current pathologies than as music.

It also signaled Coltrane's total identification with the avant-garde. Sanders would become a more or less permanent member of his group. So did the free-form drummer Rashied Ali, and for a time he and Elvin Jones were expected to play side by side every night. The result was tumult. "When both drummers played one simply couldn't hear anything but drums," wrote the poet A. B. Spellman, after a visit to a New York club. "I had no idea what the soloists were saying, and I doubt that the players could hear each other." McCoy Tyner quit. "All I could hear was noise," he said. (Coltrane's second wife, Alice, was given his place.) Jones eventually walked out, too. Even Ravi Shankar, the sitar master whose music had meant so much to Coltrane that he named one of his sons after him, found his new work disturbing: "Here was a creative person who had become a vegetarian, who was studying Yoga and reading the Bhagavad-Gita, yet in whose music I still heard much turmoil. I could not understand it."

Fewer and fewer people could. In 1966, Coltrane was fired from a club called the Front Room in Newark, New Jersey, after the predominantly black audience who had come to hear the brand of music his old band had played booed his new one off the

stage. That same year, he appeared at Lincoln Center as part of an eagerly awaited concert called "Titans of the Tenor." Sonny Rollins was on the same bill, and the rumor had spread that he and Coltrane would play together that night for the first time in ten years. Rollins played a brief set with his own group, then bowed off, promising to be back for the evening's finale. But when Coltrane's turn came, he appeared with four other horn players: Pharoah Sanders, altoist Carlos Ward, Albert Ayler, and Ayler's trumpet-playing brother, Don. The shrill cacophony they produced drove more than half the audience from the hall and so appalled Rollins that he went home rather than join in.

At a press conference in Japan that year, a reporter asked Coltrane what he planned to do in the next decade. "Become a saint," he answered, apparently without a trace of irony. But he had only months to live. He died of liver cancer at forty on July 16, 1967. "Some people are shooting comets," Michael Cuscuna recalled, "and we just have to appreciate their pain and be lucky that we were on this earth at the right time to really appreciate them."

Coltrane's followers were as grief-stricken at his passing as Charlie Parker's had been eleven years earlier. "His death created chaos in the 'free thing,'" Miles

Legacy. "John Coltrane is like the father," the trumpeter Lester Bowie recalled. "He is the one . . . who really made people aware of the spirituality of jazz."

Davis remembered, "because he was its leader . . . he was like a god to them. Ornette Coleman was still around, and some turned to him. But for the most part, Trane had been their guiding light, and after he was gone they seemed to me like people in a boat in the ocean without compass or paddles. It seemed a lot of what he stood for musically died with him. Even though some of his disciples carried on his message, they carried it to smaller and smaller audiences."

There were able musicians among Coltrane's disciples, but most had nothing like his talent or his grounding in the music.

Even LeRoi Jones admitted that there were "quacks and quackers among them." The squealing and stuttering that had seemed novel when the New Thing really was new would eventually become every bit as predictable as anything played by the kind of Dixieland revivalists who wear straw hats and sleeve garters. And the fact that on a good night Coltrane had been able to go on alone for forty minutes and more, rolling forth one fresh phrase, one rhythmic invention, after another, did not mean that his less gifted followers, most of whom had grown up without the opportunity that he

had had to master the basics of the music, could do anything of the kind. "There were a lot of people who came right after Coltrane and his avant-garde experiments and they said they were part of his 'legacy,' " Branford Marsalis said.

They got work out of it, so I wasn't, like, mad at 'em. If you can get a gig, good for you. But from a historical perspective, it's absolutely ridiculous. Coltrane arrived at that conclusion after years of arduous study and practice and play. These guys kind of showed up at the age of twenty and started doing that and saying that they were playing. I mean, it was more like a good hustle, to me. Because if you had grabbed Coltrane and said, "Play some blues," he could have played it. You ask these other cats to play some blues, play some Sidney Bechet, play some traditional songs—they can't. I can't consider a guy a jazz musician if he doesn't really understand the entire legacy of the music. I just can't do it.

MY PEOPLE

When, sometime during the 1960s, a young reporter asked Duke Ellington whether he subscribed to the new slogan Black Is Beautiful, he snapped, "I wrote 'Black Beauty' in 1928," and called for the next question. He had little patience with the people who now sometimes charged him with having remained too circumspect about civil rights. "People who think that of me haven't been listening to our music," he said. "For the past twenty-five years, social protest and pride in the history of the Negro have been the most significant themes in what we've done." Even when touring the South in the early thirties—"without the benefit of a federal court order," he added—"we've never let ourselves be put into a position of being treated with disrespect." He had begun his career as a Race man, but now, as some young black musicians declared their separateness, he had moved far beyond it, determined, as always, to avoid being categorized. "You've been quoted as saying that you write the music of your 'people,'" asked a television interviewer. "Now, would you like to expound on that?"

Let's see. My people. Now, which of my people? I mean, you know, I'm in several groups, you know, I'm, I'm in . . . let's see. I'm in the group of the piano players; I'm in the group of the

Duke Ellington's schedule for a month in 1966 includes appearances at big-city ballrooms and nightclubs, an honorary degree ceremony, the taping of a national television program—and an Elks Club dance in North Platte, Nebraska.

listeners; I'm in the groups of people who have general appreciation of music; I'm in the group of those who aspire to be dilettantes; I'm in the group of those who attempt to produce something fit for the plateau; I'm in the group of what? . . . Now, oh yeah—those who appreciate Beaujolais. Well, and then of course . . . I've had such a strong influence by the music of the people, the people. That's the better word—*the* people, rather than *my* people, because the people are my people.

Ellington stayed on the road all through the 1960s, traveling the world—Europe, Asia, Africa, South America—and writing music inspired by everything he saw, including *The Far East Suite, Latin American Suite,* and *La Plus Belle Africaine.* He also wrote some 230 songs, as well as a sort of musical pageant called *My People,* commemorating a century of Emancipation; incidental music for Shakespeare's *Timon of Athens* and T. S. Eliot's *Murder in the Cathedral;* and, with Billy Strayhorn, new

arrangements of Tchaikovsky's *Nutcracker Suite* and Grieg's *Peer Gynt Suite* for jazz orchestra. But he also found the time to play high school proms and college dances, state fairs and Elks Clubs, just as he always had.

In 1965, all three members of the jury for the Pulitzer Prize for Music recommended that Ellington be given a special prize for his life's work. The advisory board turned them down; no such award had ever been given before. Two of the three judges resigned in protest. The sixty-six-year-old Ellington professed to be unperturbed. "Fate is being kind to me," he told a reporter. "Fate doesn't want me to be too famous too young." Privately, he was less circumspect. "I'm hardly surprised that my kind of music is still without, let us say, official honor at home," he told a friend later that year. "Most Americans still take it for granted that European music—classical music, if you will—is the only really respectable kind. What we do, what other black musicians do, has always been like the kind of man you wouldn't want your daughter to associate with."

———————

Ellington was performing on the road in Reno, Nevada, on May 31, 1967, when he got a telephone call from New York. Billy Strayhorn, his close friend, creative partner, and co-composer for nearly thirty years, was dead of cancer. His death had been expected; Strayhorn had been terminally ill for several years. Ellington fell silent. Someone asked him if he was going to be all right. "No, I'm not going to be all right," he snapped. "*Nothing* is all right now." He was nearly as devastated as he had been when his mother died, and just as he had done thirty-two years earlier, he vanquished his grief by focusing on music, recording an album of Strayhorn's compositions, *And His Mother Called Him Bill*.

On April 29, 1969, Ellington turned seventy. At the suggestion of the Voice of America disc jockey Willis Conover and Leonard Garment, a White House lawyer who had once played saxophone with Woody Herman, President Richard Nixon paid official tribute to Ellington at the White House with the nation's highest civilian honor, the Presidential Medal of Freedom. "In the royalty of American music," the President said, "no man swings more or stands higher than the Duke."

Ellington responded with his customary courtly eloquence. "There is no place I would rather be tonight than in my mother's arms," he said.

Thank you very much, Mr. President. Thank you, ladies and gentlemen. This is the Presidential Medal of Freedom. The word "freedom" is one coincidentally that we are using at the moment in our *Sacred Concert*. And of course we speak of freedom of expression, we speak of freedom generally as something sweet and fat . . . but at the end we get down to the payoff, what we actually say is that we would like very much to mention the four major freedoms that my friend and writing and arranging composer Billy Strayhorn lived by and

Duke Ellington in the studio, 1961. Jimmy Hamilton is at the right. "It's a matter of whether you want to play music or make money," Ellington said. "I like to keep a band so that I can write and hear the music the next day. The only way to do it is to pay the band and keep it on tap. . . . A musical profit can put you way ahead of a financial loss."

MINGUS

The turbulent age had no more turbulent musical symbol than the composer and bassist Charles Mingus. Born in Nogales, Arizona, in 1922 and raised in the Watts neighborhood of Los Angeles, he studied trombone and cello before turning to the bass. He played with—and learned from—everyone from Louis Armstrong and Lionel Hampton to Duke Ellington and Charlie Parker, and his complex, gospel-tinged compositions were filled with witty allusions to all of them: one of his most memorable pieces was called "If Charlie Parker Was a Gunslinger, There'd Be a Whole Lot of Dead Copycats."

Mingus established two different short-lived labels rather than allow record executives to dictate to him. When he recorded "Fables of Faubus," a scathing 1959 attack on the segregationist governor of Arkansas, and Columbia Records refused to allow him to include the uncompromising lyrics on the album, he put out the full version on another smaller label called Candid. The following year, he and Max Roach led an "anti-

festival" at Newport to protest what they charged was the growing commercialism of the original. And then, with Roach and Jo Jones, he established the Jazz Artists Guild. It didn't last long, but it set a precedent for subsequent attempts by musicians to wrest control from businessmen.

Mingus was as hot-tempered as he was uncompromising and musically gifted, and stories of his combativeness—often based on fact and given further credence by his own sensational autobiography, *Beneath the Underdog*—were too often allowed to overshadow his extraordinary music. His various "Jazz Workshops" served as training grounds for musicians like Jimmy Knepper, Booker Ervin, John Handy, and Eric Dolphy. No one but Jelly Roll Morton and Duke Ellington ever managed to incorporate more of American life into his work, and only Ellington outstripped him in the range of emotions it expressed: Mingus's music routinely shifted from raucousness to tenderness, intimacy to glorious cacophony.

Charles Mingus

enjoyed, and that was freedom from hate, unconditionally; freedom from self-pity; freedom from fear of possibly doing something that may help someone else more than it would him; and freedom from the kind of pride that can make a man feel that he is better than his brother.

The President played "Happy Birthday" on the piano in the key of G, and then settled into his seat to listen to a jam session that included Earl Hines, Gerry Mulligan, Billy Taylor, J. J. Johnson, and Clark Terry. "When we did 'Squeeze Me,' " Terry remembered, "I got out the plunger mute— the plumber's friend—and [Nixon] was nudging his wife, pointing at it and saying, 'Look at that! Look, it's a toilet plunger! Look at that!' I guess he hadn't seen a whole lot of jazz bands."

JAZZ IS DEAD

By 1969, George Wein remembered, even the Newport Jazz Festival was in trouble. "It was slipping in the eyes of the press because at that time, if you were over forty, you were finished. This was when corporations were hiring twenty-two-year-old kids to tell them about what the youth market was." Rock had taken over so completely that Wein finally decided he had to include it on the program and called friends to find out which rock musicians could actually play. "Well," they told him, "Jethro Tull plays the flute and Frank Zappa plays good guitar, and Jimmy Page with Led Zeppelin plays good blues." "So I hired all these groups. I had a rock festival, but I also had some good jazz. On the last night I had poor Stephane Grappelli playing with the World's Greatest Jazz Band with Yank Lawson, and right after them, I had Sly and the Family Stone, so you can see what a mess it was."

Miles Davis and his quintet were there, too, Wein recalled:

Miles had more people than had ever seen him in concert. We drew something like eighty thousand people in four days, where normally we would draw forty or fifty thousand. The kids were all over town. Miles, who normally didn't appear until he was due on the stage and left afterwards as fast as he could get out of town, stayed the entire four days. He watched the reaction of that crowd and he saw those kids. It changed his life forever. And when we rode back on the plane from Providence, he said to me, "George, what should I do? I don't know which way to go." And so I said to him—with infinite wisdom—I said, "Play the melody," because I remembered those great songs, you know, "Bye Bye Blackbird." He didn't listen to one word I said, naturally, because he was much more concerned with reaching out to youth, which wasn't concerned with melody.

Davis was forty-three years old that summer—and concerned that he was no longer playing to the sellout crowds that had once flocked to hear him. Columbia Records was worried, too. The company had sold 150,000 copies of his albums just a few years earlier; now it was lucky to sell 50,000, and it had advanced him large sums of money that seemed unlikely ever to be paid back. Earlier that year, Miles had called Columbia's new president, Clive Davis, to complain. "He was tired of low sales and angry about it," the executive remembered. "Blood, Sweat & Tears and Chicago had borrowed enormously from him—and sold millions. These young *white* artists . . . were cashing in while he was struggling from advance to advance. 'If you stop calling me a *jazz*man,' he said at one point, 'and just sell me alongside these other people, I'll sell more.' "

"In part, I agreed with him," Clive Davis recalled, and he suggested that if Miles really wanted to reach more people, he ought to try playing places like the country's most celebrated rock palace, the Fillmore Auditorium in San Francisco. The trumpet player slammed down the telephone: he wasn't going to play for "those fucking long-haired white kids," he said; he'd leave Columbia first. But he did not leave.

The astonishing popularity of rock and funk had not been lost on other jazz musicians, especially on the more youthful among them, who had grown up dancing to rock and R&B rather than listening to swing and bebop. In 1967, saxophonist Charles Lloyd had started what would become something like a stampede of jazz musicians eager to find a way of getting in on the action. With a quartet that included the drummer Jack DeJohnette and the pianist Keith Jarrett, he was a hit at the Fillmore. *Time* heralded "the arrival of the first psychedelic rock group," and Lloyd seemed to fill the bill. "I play love vibrations," he said. "Love, totality—like bringing everyone together in a joyous dance." His band soon dissolved, and for a time Lloyd became a teacher of transcendental meditation. But other musicians had been watching. "I wanted a wider audience," said the alto saxophonist John Handy. "I was a little tired of playing for those who sit all night saying, 'yeah, yeah, yeah,' all thirty-five of them. I wanted to know what it was like to play for a stadium full of people. I wanted to see black women in the audience."

Miles Davis had been watching, too, and he was listening to the funk music of James Brown, Jimi Hendrix, and Sly Stone, with its overwhelming backbeat, its heavy use of vamps and electronic instruments. His music had already begun to reflect what he'd been hearing. The electric guitarists George Benson and Joe Beck made appearances on his records. His group's harmonies no longer shifted as they once had. The beat grew ever more dominant. Herbie Hancock began playing electric piano, and was joined by other keyboardists, including Chick Corea, Keith Jarrett, and Joe Zawinul; and

two Britons, Fender bassist Dave Holland, and electric guitarist John McLaughlin. Davis had realized, he remembered, "that most rock musicians didn't know anything about music. . . . But they were popular because they were giving the public a certain sound, what they wanted to hear. So I figured that if they could do it—reach all those people and sell all those records without really knowing what they were doing—then I could do it, too, only better. . . . I wasn't prepared to be a memory yet."

On August 16, 1969, a little over a month after the Newport festival, some four hundred thousand young people gathered in a cow pasture near Woodstock, New York, willing to endure hours of rain and mud and discomfort just to be together in the presence of their rock idols. Three days later, Miles Davis made his bid to become one of those idols and began recording the curious mélange of jazz and rock he called *Bitches Brew*. Even before it was released, Davis agreed to appear at the Fillmore East, the New York equivalent of the San Francisco venue he'd turned down as beneath him just a few months before. He would be the opening act for Laura Nyro, a rock singer less than half his age.

Bitches Brew, the best-selling 1969 Miles Davis album that pointed the way toward fusion

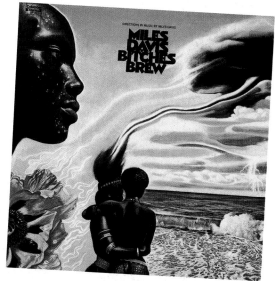

Late Miles. Flaunting the trappings of rock stardom (above) and (right) onstage with members of his 1973 band. Left to right, Michael Henderson (electric bass), Cedric Lawson (electronic keyboards), Davie Liebman (tenor saxophone), Reggie Lucas (electric guitar), Badal Roy (tabla), and James Mtume Foreman (congas).

Bitches Brew was a commercial triumph. It sold 400,000 copies in its first year, more than any Miles Davis record ever had sold before. During the next six years he would make thirteen more albums, each one less like jazz than the last. "We're not going to play the blues anymore," he'd told Herbie Hancock even before making *Bitches Brew*. "Let the white folks have the blues. They got 'em, so they can keep 'em. Play something else." His willingness to alter his music so dramatically—and the money he made by doing so—sent a powerful message.

During the 1970s, fusion albums like these all but overwhelmed mainstream jazz.

"Miles led the way for a lot of people," the saxophonist Jimmy Heath said, "because he was one of the ones who got through. He had the fine clothes, the expensive cars, the big house, all the magazine articles and the pretty girls chasing him. He seemed like he was on top of *everything*. Then you had all of this rock getting all of the press and it was like Elvis Presley all over again. Miles stepped out here and decided he was going to get himself some of that money, and a lot of musicians followed his lead. It was as if Miles had led the pack for so long they didn't know how to stop following him, even if the music wasn't any good."

The writer Leonard Feather asked Davis's old friend and mentor Clark Terry what he thought young people heard in his new music. "What they hear in it is less significant than what they *don't* hear," Terry answered. "What they don't hear, because it is not there, is the real balls of jazz, the chord progressions, the structures. . . . [Young people] are not musically mature enough to cope with this, and Miles is smart enough to put something where they can reach it on their own level. . . . If they're not hip enough to know what's happening—say, the way Bird was playing years ago, with

swinging groups—they're going to grasp whatever is simple enough for them to cop. And the simple thing for them to cop happens to be that one-chord modal bag that is so fashionable. . . . To me, jazz has to stimulate, and this is not . . . stimulating."

The trumpet player Lester Bowie was more diplomatic: "I appreciate rock and roll music. I like all kinds of music. I can't think of any music that I dislike, but rock and roll is entry-level music. I mean, a rock and roll gig is the first gig you get. You're supposed to continue development beyond that. To us as hard-core musicians, we always considered [fusion] a little bit lightweight. It was nice. I liked the groups; they sounded good, but they were kind of on the lightweight edge of music."

Fusion—the hybrid music Davis had helped to launch—had set out in part to reunite the worlds of jazz and dance, to rebuild the following that jazz had lost to rock. Early fusion yielded some memorable music, much of it made by bands—Herbie Hancock's Headhunters, Tony Williams's Lifetime, Chick Corea's Return to Forever, John McLaughlin's Mahavishnu Orchestra—formed by musicians who had played in one

or another of Davis's groups over the years. It introduced young people to some of the elements of jazz as well, and it incorporated music and musicians from every corner of the world. Perhaps the most widely admired fusion group was Weather Report, established by two of the men who had played on the *Bitches Brew* album, Wayne Shorter and Joe Zawinul. "Weather Report's music always sounds raw and on the edge and real," the tenor saxophonist Joshua Redman said. "And I think that isn't true of a lot of other fusion music, especially some of the fusion that came later."

"Big business had come into jazz," Michael Cuscuna remembered.

And fusion had become a part of pop music. And with it came a lot of pressures, and a lot of demands that really shouldn't have been applied to the art. Art Blakey used to like to tell the story about [the trumpet player] Donald Byrd [who had crossed over into fusion] coming up to him backstage at some concert and saying, "Man, the pressure of coming up with another record that's going to sell as much as my last one. I'm not sure which direction to go." Art was always a firm believer in sticking to the aesthetics that you've always loved and developing from there. And he said, "I looked at Donald and he had a lot of money, but he had this big potbelly and he looked stressed and he didn't look healthy and I said, "Donald, I never saw an armored car following a hearse."

In 1975, Miles Davis would abruptly put down his trumpet. He was "spiritually tired," he remembered, "without anything more to say musically." He stayed away from the recording studio for six years, struggling with chronic ill health and a continuing problem with drugs, and when he finally came back, even he did not claim to be playing jazz anymore. Jazz was "dead," he said, "the music of the museum." "When

THE DIVINE ONE

Sarah Vaughan at a 1950 recording date

In the era when light-skinned, fine-featured Lena Horne set the standard for black female entertainers, Sarah Vaughan, like Ella Fitzgerald, was at first thought too plain and too dark for show business. Earl Hines, who gave her her first job as a singer in 1942, did so although he said she "looked like home-made sin." But he and other musicians came to love her for her perfect pitch and rhythmic sense, her sophisticated ear for chord changes, and her astonishing voice—she could sing everything from soprano to baritone. They liked her devil-may-care spirit, too, and eventually dubbed her "Sassy," the nickname she would carry until, during her final days as a diva, she became known to her admirers as "the Divine One."

Born in Newark, New Jersey, in 1924 and introduced to music as a singer and substitute organist for the First Mount Zion Baptist Church, she remained an able piano player and, like Billie Holiday, saw herself as a musician before she was a vocalist. "Sassy," Dizzy Gillespie once said, "can sing notes other people can't even hear," and when she closed her eyes onstage, she said, she could see—and sing—lines that might have been improvised on the piano. She was Ella Fitzgerald's most important rival as the most admired vocalist in jazz, but Columbia in the late 1940s set out to make her a pop performer. She hated most of the material she was given to sing and when she moved to another record company in 1954, she satisfied its need for hits by asking for two contracts—one for recording frankly commercial tunes and the other for the jazz she loved. "My contract with Mercury is for pops," she told a friend, "and my contract with [Mercury's jazz subsidiary] Emarcy is for me." She recorded everything from Beatles tunes to the Lord's Prayer. Stephen Sondheim's "Send in the Clowns" became her signature tune in the years before her death in 1990. Hers, wrote the jazz critic Gary Giddins, was "the ageless voice of modern jazz—of giddy postwar virtuosity, biting wit, and fearless caprice . . . a voice that happens once in a lifetime, perhaps once in several lifetimes."

I last heard Miles Davis," Martin Williams wrote three years before the trumpeter's death in 1991, "he was stalking around a stage in what looked like a leftover Halloween fright suit, emitting a scant handful of plaintive notes."

Over the years, much of fusion's remaining jazz content would be worn away. To play jazz well, as Dexter Gordon said, it had always been necessary for young musicians to play with and learn from older ones. Many youthful players had now never had that opportunity. Their music grew closer and closer to instrumental pop—meant for easy listening, and not much else.

"Jazz music," said Jelly Roll Morton, "is a *style,* not compositions. Any kind of music may be played in jazz, if one has the knowledge." Great musicians like Louis Armstrong and Benny Goodman had found ingenious ways to turn the most banal pop material into jazz, but swinging was at the heart of that conception. "When that swing starts to happen," Charlie Haden said, "it's like being on a wave if you're a surfer. Or it's like taking a pebble and skipping it about eight times over a lake that's real still. It's that groove that happens. It's the power that a 747 has when it's taking off. It's a momentum that starts and builds and allows you to stop thinking. Because the creative process, the thought process, stops in the midst of creation. There's just the moment that you're in, you know. There's no yesterday, there's no tomorrow. There's just right now."

By definition rock does not swing; its beat remains the same; that is a large part of its appeal to young dancers. "Jazz has always been able to meet, absorb, and put to its own purposes almost everything in popular prospect," wrote Martin Williams, looking back. "Nevertheless, I don't think fusion worked very well . . . the beat in jazz moves forward; it is played to contribute to the all but irresistible momentum of the music: jazz *goes* somewhere. The beat in most rock bobs and bounces away in one place. . . . Rock *stays* somewhere."

GIVING IT BACK

Louis Armstrong had seen it all: New Orleans before jazz began to spread across the country; the first days of recording, when he had revolutionized first instrumental music and then American singing. He had witnessed the swing era and endured the bebop years—and he was still on the road, as celebrated abroad as he was at home, even behind the Iron Curtain. Arvell Shaw remembered a visit to divided Germany:

> All the action was in West Berlin, and we were in East Berlin. So one night we had a few wines, and Louis said, "Man, let's go to West Berlin." The promoter said, "You can't. You got to get permission." Louis said, "The hell with it. You get in the bus." We get in the bus. We went to Checkpoint Charlie and the East German guards stopped us, came on the bus with these loaded machine guns. They said, "Where are your passes? Where are your passes?" And then one of them said, "Louis Armstrong!" They said, "Oh, Mr. Armstrong! Go right on through." And then we got to the American side and they said, "Where are your passes?" The guys came through. "Hey, Pops!" one of the soldiers said, "Pops, go on," and we went through. Every night we used to go from East Berlin to West Berlin and hang out all night and we'd go through every night without a pass, *stoned,* you know?

Between dates, Armstrong came back to Lucille and the modest home in Queens that she had found for them when they were first married. He never saw any need for anything fancier. "He loved every room," the Armstrongs' close friend Victoria Joseph remembered. "That was his home." And when his wife suggested from time to time that they move to a grander place in a more exclusive neighborhood, he wouldn't hear

Mr. and Mrs. Louis Armstrong, photographed on a rare night out in New York sometime during the late 1960s. Armstrong rarely ventured far from his home in Queens during his last years because of the horde of autograph-seekers that descended on him as soon as he was spotted.

of it. "He said, 'What for? We know everybody here, and we'd get lost in the bigger house. I'd be looking for you half the time.'" "If Louis came home to the neighborhood," Phoebe Jacobs remembered, "very often the neighbors would have banners out, 'Welcome Home Pops.' If the weather permitted, he'd sit on the front steps of his house and buy kids Good Humors. And he'd ask them, 'Was your homework good? Were you a good boy?'"

In the fall of 1968, decades of hard living caught up with him. He suffered acute heart failure and spent seven months off and on in Manhattan's Beth Israel Hospital. "Louis used to call his sickness 'an intermission,'" Jacobs remembered. "He'd be lying in the hospital with a couple of tubes in him and you'd say something to him and he'd say, 'This is intermission.'" While he was in the hospital, Joe Glaser also suffered a heart attack, then fell into a coma from which he never recovered. Armstrong was crushed. He poured out his feelings in a long, rambling memoir in which he again expressed his gratitude to the Karnofsky

family, who had befriended him as a small boy and who, like Glaser, had been Jewish, and he let out some of the bitterness he continued to feel toward those members of his own community who he felt had abandoned him: "The other White Nationalities kept the Jewish people with fear constantly [in New Orleans but] I will always remember how the Jewish people living in the Negro neighborhood advanced and did so much, right under their noses. Boy—if the Negroes could stick together half that much. But I doubt that it would ever happen. Hmm look where we would be today. Too much malice and hate among us."

When he was released from the hospital in the spring of 1969, he was forbidden to play his horn. The strain, his doctors said, would prove too much for his heart. "He felt so bad not being able to play his trumpet," said Joseph, "but he would walk from room to room with his trumpet under his arm, in his hand, sit it on his desk. He always had the trumpet. He'd be fingering it. And when he'd be interviewed, he'd have his trumpet with him, always. Always."

In May of 1970, Bob Thiele brought Armstrong into his New York studio to make an album called *Louis Armstrong and His Friends.* An impromptu assembly of musicians turned out to pay him tribute. Old friends and admirers like Eddie Condon and the cornetists Bobby Hackett and Ruby Braff were there, but so were Ornette Coleman and Miles Davis, who said, "You can't play anything on a horn that Louis hasn't played—I mean even modern." They all joined together as a chorus while Armstrong sang, "We Shall Overcome." At the same three-day session he recorded a set of brand-new lyrics to the tune of "When the Saints Go Marching In." It was called "The Boy from New Orleans" and offered a sentimental overview of Armstrong's career from his birth in black Storyville to his celebrity as the ambassador of jazz. The lyrics were saccharine, and the record was made worse by a cumbersome overdubbed big band arrangement, but Armstrong managed—as he had so many times in the past—to infuse it with warmth and life, and it became part of his standard stage show.

A few weeks later, on July 11, George Wein staged a celebration at Newport for Armstrong's putative seventieth birthday. Many of the musicians with whom he'd played over the years came back to be with him. Dizzy Gillespie was there, too. "Without him," he said, "no me." Wein, wanting both to surprise the audience and to spare Armstrong any extra effort, suggested that he simply walk onstage unannounced, rather than sing his theme song, "Sleepy Time Down South." Armstrong wouldn't hear of it. His fans expected it, and he never wanted to disappoint them. "As long as I live," he said, " 'Sleepy Time Down South' will be my lifelong number because it lives with me."

"When he dressed up for that evening," Wein recalled, "he had on a nice brown suit and there was a glow on his face and there was a glow in his eyes. There was a glow in his skin." It was raining, and he came onstage earlier than planned because he didn't want his fans to get wet. Usually people left their seats to find shelter during a downpour, but for Louis Armstrong they stayed put. "And he just sang so beauti-

Louis Armstrong at home. "Just think," he wrote in 1970, "through the . . . years we've been living in this house we have seen just about [three] generations come up. . . . Lots of them have grown, married, [and] had children. Their children still come to visit Aunt Lucille and Uncle Louis. . . . Now that [Pops] has recuperated—feel good—blowing his horn every evening before supper with his doctor's permission, the whole neighborhood rejoices at hearing his horn every day."

In the realm of music only the funeral of Louis Armstrong could have brought together Guy Lombardo and Dizzy Gillespie; seated in the pew behind them are Gene Krupa and Arvell Shaw. The young mourners below are Little League ballplayers from Armstrong's neighborhood.

fully," Wein remembered. "It was like, 'Hey, I'm here again.' You know, 'I'm still here. I'm still Louis Armstrong, and I'm still going to give you a great evening of music and entertainment.' " Soon, he was playing trumpet again.

In the spring of 1971, Armstrong accepted a two-week engagement at the Waldorf-Astoria in Manhattan. Arvell Shaw was with him for that last engagement and almost thirty years later still had difficulty recounting it: "He had so much music in him till there's no way he could have lived and not played. The doctor told him, 'Louis, don't do it. You can't do it.' Louis said, 'Well, I got a contract, I got to do it [for] my fans.' And they had to help him. . . ." Shaw's eyes filled with tears and his voice broke. "They had to help him on and off." Victoria Joseph and her husband were in the wings on Armstrong's closing night. "The last song he sang," she remembered, "was 'The Boy from New Orleans,' and he had to stop. He was crying, tears just coming down his face, and when he finished it, you could hear a pin drop in there. For about ten seconds, there wasn't a sound and then, thunderous applause. *Thunderous.* And my husband and I were standing on either side of him, and as he came down the steps, he said, 'That's my last show, Vickie.' He knew it. That was his last show. Yes, he knew."

He was hospitalized again, survived two more heart attacks, finally insisted on being taken home. Joseph was there for dinner on the evening of July 5, the day after what he believed had been his seventy-first birthday. "He was in good spirits," she remembered.

He said, "Vickie, the doctor gave me the OK to go back to work. I can start playing my trumpet again. The first place we'll be going will be the Black Sea, in Russia." Lucille was cooking in the kitchen for him, which he liked for her to do. And just my husband and I were sitting in the dining room with him at the table. He stood up and he grabbed the edges of the table. I think Death hit him. And he didn't say a word, he just held on tight to the table, and my husband stood up and I stayed in my seat, but we kept our eyes on him and then he straightened. I was scared to death, really. And he shrugged and sat back down and kept on talking. So I said to myself, "Now, shall I say something to Lucille and upset her or just let it go?" I never told her. I didn't. And then I could have beat myself the next day. Maybe they could have saved him; maybe they couldn't have. He came out on his stoop as we left at about eleven-thirty, quarter to twelve, saying he'd be up to see us Wednesday.

He had called for a rehearsal with the All Stars for the following day, but at about four-thirty that morning he died in his sleep. Some weeks earlier, Victoria Joseph had been helping him with his mail. There were hundreds of letters from all over the world. Every one of them was affectionate. "Pops," she had asked him then, "what do you do with all that love?"

"It gets heavy," he answered, "but I give it right back."

SO MUCH TO DO

"I loved and respected Louis Armstrong," Duke Ellington said when he heard of his death. "He was born poor, died rich, and never hurt anyone on the way." The following spring, Ellington himself was diagnosed with lung cancer. No one knows how much he was told of his prospects; his physician and close friend, Dr. Arthur Logan, would die before he did. But he rarely mentioned his deteriorating condition, even when he became too weak to conduct rehearsals without sitting down. "The music kept him going," his granddaughter Mercedes Ellington recalled. "This is what made him go through all the pain, the suffering of the last part of the sickness, of being out on the road. It was the driving force for him. It was something he had to do, every day."

Religious music had begun to interest him long before the onset of his illness. He had always been privately religious, wearing the gold cross around his neck given to him after his mother died, reading the Bible through at least seven times, but now he seemed consumed with the need to spell out his religious beliefs in music. He was "God's messenger," he said, and one member of the band thought he intended "to play his way into heaven." "You can jive with secular music," Ellington told someone who'd asked why he seemed so especially demanding about how his religious works were played, "but you can't jive with the Almighty."

He had already written two *Sacred Concerts*—ambitious works, performed in churches and cathedrals, where his orchestra was augmented by choirs, vocal soloists, dancers. Now he hurled himself into a third, which he hoped to premiere at Westminster Abbey on United Nations Day, October 24, 1973. "He knew it was his last shot," Mercer Ellington said, "and he wanted it to be good." On the day of the concert, Ellington looked frail and thin and was uncharacteristically curt with the press, objecting to the presence of TV cameras at rehearsal, unwilling to answer more than a few questions. The music was all that mattered. "Every man prays to God in his own language," he told the audience before the concert began, "and there is no language which God does not understand."

In the end, the *Third Sacred Concert* went reasonably well, though Ellington himself nearly collapsed halfway through it. George Wein flew with him the following day to Denmark.

Duke was wiped out. . . . I was with him in the cabin. He had to take a wheelchair to the plane. And when he got to Denmark, he took a wheelchair again. I'd never seen him use a wheelchair before. He was very, very tired and much sicker than anybody realized. We took the ferry from Copenhagen to Malmö, and on the ferry, in the sea air, he sat and had Danish shrimp, the little ones that he loved. And he sat there, and you could just see him coming back. And that night he played a concert; he was so into the music that when the concert was over, he didn't want to stop. The band had left the stage and Duke came back with the people cheering and yelling and sat down at the piano and started to play. And the bass player came back and the drummer came back and one or two of the horns came back, and nobody else came back. The band just didn't respond. He played for about twenty, twenty-five minutes in a little jam session, and you could just feel he was young again for a moment. But this was his last hurrah.

Duke Ellington in Paris. "The music is that . . . very elusive medium that goes around you, over you, under you," he once told an interviewer. "You first get to know it by hearing it and you're attracted to it. It's a very delightful acquaintance and you spend all the rest of your life chasing this melody around. You think you've got it and you reach out . . . and all you get is a little piece of the tail. Other people hear it and they say, 'Yes, that's the end.' Well, you know it is the end in one way, but it isn't the total. So you continue because you want to get more of this thing. So you continue pursuing the melody. You eat with it, sleep with it, that's it. You're always in pursuit." (Opposite) Duke Ellington and vocal chorus at Westminster Abbey, rehearsing for his third Sacred Concert, October 25, 1973. Tenor saxophonist Harold Ashby warms up in the foreground.

Ellington kept on performing, regardless. He arrived home from Europe on December 4 and was back onstage in Pittsburgh the following night. When the band got to Sturgis, Michigan, on March 22, he was so weak his men begged him not to go on. He played two shows anyway, in what his son remembered as "an old firehouse," and then collapsed. It was his final public performance. He was flown back to New York the next morning and entered Columbia Presbyterian Hospital, where he immediately asked to have his electric piano brought to him so that he could keep working. He made improvements to the *Third Sacred Concert,* worked on a comic opera to be called *Queenie Pie,* and finished up *The Three Black Kings,* a new score for Alvin Ailey's dance troupe. When his eyesight began to fail, he simply wrote larger, using the backs of some of the hundreds of get-well cards that flooded his room. "I have so much to do," he said, "so much more I have to do."

He died at 3:10 in the morning, May 24, 1974. Sixty-five thousand people filed past his coffin in the funeral home. Ten thousand mourners filled the huge Cathedral of St. John the Divine for his funeral, and two thousand more stood silently outside, many weeping openly, as Ella Fitzgerald sang "Solitude" and one of the hymns most often played at New Orleans funerals in the earliest days of jazz, "Just a Closer Walk with Thee." Ellington was buried in Woodlawn Cemetery next to his mother, who had been the first to tell him he was "blessed."

TOTALLY LOST

The city of New Orleans had torn down the house in which Louis Armstrong was born to make way for a police station in 1964. By then, the Lincoln Gardens on the South Side of Chicago, where Armstrong had played with King Oliver, had long since been razed for a housing project. Law and order had come to Kansas City, and most of the wide-open clubs in which Lester Young and Count Basie and Charlie Parker played had vanished. The Cotton Club in Manhattan, where Duke Ellington first broadcast his "jungle music," was gone. So was the Savoy Ballroom, where Chick Webb once took on all comers and Ella Fitzgerald first became a star. Birdland, the club named for Charlie Parker, abandoned jazz for rhythm and blues. In 1968, the Hickory House, the last club on Fifty-second Street, finally closed its doors. Even the Five Spot, where Cecil Taylor, Ornette Coleman, and John Coltrane performed their demanding music, eventually went out of business.

During the late 1930s, according to one estimate, swing music had provided some 70 percent of the profits in the recording industry. By the mid-1970s, jazz would yield less than 3 percent. Things became so desperate that a group of black New York musicians who called themselves the Jazz and People's Movement disrupted network television programs to protest their lack of work. On October 13, 1970, the British actor Trevor Howard was a guest on Dick Cavett's television talk show. Cavett asked

HOME COOKIN'

Black big-city musicians of the bebop era had generally shunned too-vivid reminders of the lives most black people down South had been forced to lead: even the blues fell from favor for a time. But with the growth of the civil rights movement a transformation took place and among a good many young people the down-home aspects of black culture came to be seen as a source of pride, not embarassment. Those feelings were soon mirrored in music. Ray Charles showed the way, combining the blues with the organlike piano playing and call-and-response patterns of the church. Soon he and those who followed his lead began to be seen as "soul" artists. "Black musicians were saying," the writer Gerald Early remembered, "'We're going to invent a musical style and form that white people can't copy. . . . It's going to be so ethnicized that they really can't copy it without absolutely looking like a minstrel show.'"

That same kind of musical style and form took root in jazz, as well, and nobody was more important to its success than "Incredible" Jimmy Smith, the master of the Hammond B-3 organ who began recording for Blue Note Records in 1957. There had been other organists before him, pianists like Wild Bill Davis and Milt Bruckner, who had simply switched keyboards without mastering the instrument's full potential. Smith was different. The photographer Francis Wolf recalled seeing him for the first time at Small's Paradise in Harlem: "A man in convulsions, face contorted, crouched over in apparent agony, his fingers flying, his foot dancing over the pedals. The air was filled with waves of sound I had never heard before."

Even the titles of the tunes Smith and his cohorts recorded celebrated the African-American world from which they came—"Home Cookin'," "The Sermon," "The Preacher," "Cornbread," "Grits 'n Gravy," "Back at the Chicken Shack." It was all good-time music, and it worked for a time. According to one survey, five Dave Brubeck albums reached the top-40 charts during the 1960s; Jimmy Smith had ten. Others did almost as well: Cannonball Adderley, Ramsey Lewis, Les McCann, Lee Morgan, Horace Silver, Bobby Timmons. And bars featuring organ-tenor trios became fixtures in big-city black neighborhoods all across the country. Then, an arsenal of other electric instruments took over—electric basses, electric keyboards, synthesizers, and the rest, and Jimmy Smith and his Hammond B-3—along with most other jazz musicians—found themselves drowned out by rock and funk and the new amalgam called fusion.

Jimmy Smith

GREAT BLACK MUSIC

Members of the Art Ensemble of Chicago performing at New York's Bottom Line, 1977

Beginning in the mid-1960s, all across the country young musicians—both black and white—tried to gain control over their music by forming cooperatives. The best-known and longest-lasting was the Association for the Advancement of Creative Musicians (AACM), based in Chicago. Its prime mover was the pianist and composer Muhal Richard Abrams, but one of its most eloquent spokesmen was the trumpet player Lester Bowie. "The AACM was formed," Bowie remembered, "so that we would have a venue, a mode, a way we could express the music we were actually feeling, our original music. Because there was nowhere in town to do it. The club owners in the South Side didn't want to hear anything about any intellectual music; they wanted to have something that sold drinks."

The AACM, in turn, yielded a number of important groups—Air, the Revolutionary Ensemble, and the Art Ensemble of Chicago. Formed in 1965 by Bowie, Roscoe Mitchell, Malachi Favors, and Joseph Jarman (later joined by drummer Don Moye), the ACM created exuberant music that drew upon everything from waltzes and funeral marches to free jazz and rhythm and blues. They called what they played "Great Black Music," not jazz, Lester Bowie said, because "The name 'jazz' had a lot of negative connotations—whorehouse music, nigger music, bullshit music, devil's music. So, we came up with the term 'Great Black Music.' We wanted to distinguish ourselves from a normal jazz [group] that played taverns. The music was an art form, and we wanted to present it as such. But there was no place to do this, and there was no one to help us, no one was supporting the arts or thinking about the musicians. So, we said, 'We've got to take care of this ourselves.'"

For the first time since the days of Black Swan Records in the 1920s, African-American musicians were fully in charge of every aspect of their art—from booking and recording to promotion and distribution. But nothing the Art Ensemble of Chicago—or any other group of free musicians—could think to do seemed able to win back the black audience, which was now devoted to the sounds of Motown. The Art Ensemble once found itself playing to just three people in its own hometown, and it attracted its largest following among white college students—in France.

him, "What is it about New York that has changed?" Howard innocently replied that there was no longer any place to hear jazz. At that, members of the audience stood up, blowing whistles and wooden flutes. Two months earlier, led by the multi-instrumentalist Rahsaan Roland Kirk and the trumpet player Lee Morgan, the same group had disrupted the Merv Griffin show; five months later they threatened Johnny Carson with the same thing and were given half an hour with network executives to talk over their grievances. Eventually, Kirk, along with Charles Mingus and Archie Shepp, got himself invited to play on the Ed Sullivan show on CBS. Off-camera, Kirk asked Sullivan why he had never presented the late John Coltrane on his show. Sullivan, genuinely bewildered, asked, "Does John Coltrane have any records out?"

At the Newport Jazz Festival the following summer—while Dionne Warwick sang "What the World Needs Now Is Love, Sweet Love" onstage—thousands of young people, chanting that all music should be free, tore down the chain-link fence and rioted. The festival had to be canceled. "Everybody just felt totally lost," George Wein remembered, "because something that meant something to them had been destroyed by stupid kids that couldn't have cared less about the music that was being played."

The 1960s had been a period "when everyone was up and the music was hot and burning," the New Thing drummer Milford Graves remembered. "But the 1970s is like everyone went to sleep. Everyone got split up." Graves himself joined the faculty of Bennington College. Less fortunate avant-garde musicians found themselves playing mostly for one another, their friends and families, and a small but stubbornly devoted band of followers in lofts and private apartments. Clubs continued to close. There were many reasons, but in a mid-seventies conversation with the drummer Art Taylor, Eddie "Lockjaw" Davis, the tenor-playing veteran of the Basie band, placed the blame squarely on the avant-garde.

There was a different atmosphere about jazz years ago. The players themselves projected lighthearted feelings. There was a margin of humor in playing; there was a happier atmosphere. Today, the jazz musician comes to the bandstand with a grim outlook; he's too serious. . . . The whole joint looks like a graveyard. . . . Jazz was never meant to be that way. . . . You're not supposed to go with a pencil and pad and figure out what they're playing. . . . The only way you can get your wages is from the people who support the club. The people are going to support the club only if they enjoy what they hear. If a person comes to a club and does not understand or enjoy what the musicians are playing, he's not coming back. Therefore, there's no business, you don't get your wages, there's no more entertainment. This is why there are no clubs to speak of today. There's one here and there, and I assure you there are no freedom musicians working in them.

HOMECOMING

Dexter Gordon had been away from America for nearly fifteen years when he came home in 1976, and when he opened in New York, first at George Wein's Storyville and then at the indestructible Village Vanguard, he wasn't sure how he would be received. He still played straight-ahead jazz, without the synthesizers and electric bass and drum machines of fusion, and within the boundaries of swing, lyricism, and blues feeling that had been at the heart of the music he'd played since boyhood but that many avant-garde players had discarded. The crowds stood to cheer him after every tune. "It was just amazing to feel the impact of his sound and his presence on that stage," the tenor saxophonist Joe Lovano remembered. "To be in a room with him, at that time, for

me—I was twenty-three years old at the time—it just hit me like a ton of bricks. Just his *sound,* the power of his tone."

Columbia offered Gordon a contract, and the two-record live album he made at the Vanguard called *Homecoming* sold surprisingly well when it appeared the following year. There still seemed to be an audience for music that was wholly fresh and richly inventive but that also flowed directly from Louis Armstrong and Lester Young and Charlie Parker. "Dexter *is* jazz," said the youthful pianist George Cables, who appeared with him for three years after his return. "Playing with him really brought me back to the acoustic piano, [but] the thing I learned mostly from him was the history of the music. The roots."

Gordon's success was fresh evidence that a revival of interest in mainstream jazz might be in the offing. It had never died completely, of course. Norman Granz's Pablo label, featuring artists like Count Basie, Duke Ellington, Dizzy Gillespie, and the Canadian-born pianist Oscar Peterson, had done well all through the years of drought, and other record companies had begun to discover that there was money to be made reissuing long-dormant titles from their catalogues. The music of earlier jazz giants was becoming widely available for the first time in years. The death of Duke Ellington in 1974, and the thought that his work might never be heard live again, helped inspire the creation of jazz repertory companies at the Smithsonian Institution and elsewhere. In 1976, the writer Albert Murray published *Stomping the Blues,* an elegant reaffirmation of the music's African-American origins and the centrality of the blues to its history. In 1977, the same year that Dexter Gordon's *Homecoming* appeared on the record charts, a young saxophone player named Scott Hamilton caused a stir by improvising not in the bop or Coltrane styles but in the manner of the masters he most loved, Ben Webster and Coleman Hawkins.

Three years after Gordon's triumphant comeback, Art Blakey was in New York, auditioning young musicians for his Jazz Messengers, just as he had been doing for three decades. Michael Cuscuna happened to be on hand.

This young kid sat in on trumpet, and he was astonishing. His ideas were fresh and different, very concise and clear. And at the end of the set, I asked Art, "Who the hell is that?" And he said, "That's Ellis Marsalis's kid." And Ellis Marsalis is a wonderful New Orleans pianist who was little known outside New Orleans, but a favorite musician of a lot of us. And he introduced me to him, and later on he said, "He's in his first year at Juilliard and, of course, you know, I couldn't do that to Ellis. I just couldn't pull him out of school and offer him a job, so I can't give him the gig." About two sets later, about four in the morning, we were all hanging out at the club, and I said, "So, Art did you decide on any new members?" He said, "Um, just one—Wynton Marsalis."

Dexter Gordon's triumph, 1977

No musician in jazz history has ever risen so far so fast as Wynton Marsalis: signed by Columbia Records at twenty, winner of Grammys in jazz *and* classical music at twenty-two, cofounder of Jazz at Lincoln Center at twenty-six and its creative director at thirty-one, winner at thirty-five of the first Pulitzer Prize ever awarded to a jazz composer, for his oratorio *Blood on the Fields.* Because his climb seemed so meteoric, because he was born in New Orleans and was the son of one jazz musician and the brother of three more, and because for many people he would become the symbol of the rebirth of mainstream jazz, his success seems to have been almost preordained.

But the world into which he was born in 1961 had had little use for the music his father played. Even in the city of his birth, jazz had lost most of its audience. None of his boyhood friends ever listened to it. "Jazz was for old people," he remembered, and if anybody had heard of Louis Armstrong or Duke Ellington, "they thought they were Uncle Toms." Funk was the music of choice: James Brown; Stevie Wonder; Earth, Wind and Fire; Tower of Power. When, during the early seventies, Wynton and his older brother Branford were in high school and performing with a funk band called the Creators, they sometimes played to crowds of better than two thousand and brought home a hundred dollars a night; their father's audiences were rarely larger than one-tenth that size, and he was often paid only half as much.

But at the age of twelve, Wynton Marsalis had also begun to listen to records from his father's collection: John Coltrane's *My Favorite Things* (initially just because he liked the blue and red cover) and then *Giant Steps.* "I listened to the music," he remembered. "I didn't know I could participate in it. I thought it was something really for my father and them, but I knew that I loved it. And I knew it was what we needed. There was just something in the sound of it. When I would listen to Trane,

Wynton, right, and Branford Marsalis, at home in Kenner, Louisiana, about 1964

it was as if he was talking to me. And he was just telling me that it was going to be all right. There was a certain engagement in it. And just the soul and the cry in the sound of it. It's just so soulful and warm."

During his early years, Marsalis experienced all manner of of music, from marching in a children's church band led by the guitarist Danny Barker to performing the Haydn Trumpet Concerto with the New Orleans Civic Orchestra at age fourteen, and he eventually resolved to become a professional musician. But when he arrived at Juilliard, he was still not sure whether he would end up playing classical or jazz music. Even when he was on the road with the Blakey band, then with Herbie Hancock, and finally with his own group, attracting attention for his big, warm tone, his astonishing facility, and the richness of his rhythmic imagination, he later admitted ruefully that he knew almost nothing about the music before the era of Miles Davis. At first, it didn't seem to matter. His first record sold more than a hundred thousand copies—then virtually unheard of for an acoustic jazz album—and

record companies scrambled to sign up young players of their own. "Wynton was the first new acoustic jazz player with something to say," Michael Cuscuna recalled. "And fortunately, thereafter, with his brother Branford and a lot of people that Wynton knew, the floodgates opened and suddenly in the eighties there were a lot of new players that pumped new blood into jazz. Which was very much of a saving grace."

But Marsalis wasn't satisfied. His father sent him a tape of Louis Armstrong soloing on a tune called "Jubilee," and when he found, in trying to play the solo himself, that he didn't have the endurance to make it all the way through, he began to realize that there had been much more to Armstrong than his genial grin. Soon, with help from Albert Murray and Stanley Crouch, he began to soak up all the jazz history he could.

George Wein first heard Marsalis at a jazz festival in Chicago.

I listened to him play and I started to cry. I couldn't believe it, because I never thought I'd hear a young black musician play that way. Because they were all influenced by the bebop scene or the Coltrane scene. Wynton could play it all, but I could hear that he had been listening to Louis Armstrong. And that meant so much to me because the only musicians, the *young* musicians, that paid attention to Louis Armstrong were white musicians. Young African-American musicians did not pay attention to Louis Armstrong.

"All jazz," Marsalis came to believe, "is modern. The only thing that makes it old is when nobody plays it." Soon, he was playing it all—from Thelonious Monk to Jelly Roll Morton, Louis Armstrong to Miles Davis—and making it all his own. He did something else as well: he took on the critics. "In my generation it was easiest for me to be the person to do that," he said, "because I don't have to deal with the same type of overwhelming racism and worry about working that the older musicians did." He insisted that neither most fusion nor much of the avant-garde should ever have been considered jazz, since they didn't swing and lacked blues feeling. He denounced the cult of the "new," scoffed at the notion that change necessarily means progress, that one kind of jazz is ever an "advance" over another. "Is Charlie Parker *better* than Sidney Bechet?" he asked. "No, just different." Some critics and other musicians fought back in a battle that has continued now for nearly twenty years. "The debate around jazz is always heated and strong because jazz music deals with the soul of our nation," Marsalis said. "And through this music, we can see a lot about what it means to be American. And everybody wants to own it. And you can't own it. I can't own it. I can do my best to define it the way I think it is. But that is all I can do."

The writer Gary Giddins once asked the pianist Cedar Walton where he thought the music was going. "It'll go wherever we take it" was the answer. "We're the musicians." By the very nature of the music, no individual artist has ever been the sole focus of jazz in America. A host of survivors who made it through the fusion era are still at work, and there are dozens of talented younger musicians now feeding the music's many tributaries as well, so many that anyone's list of favorites is necessarily arbitrary: bassist Christian McBride; drummer Lewis Nash; pianists Geri Allen, Bill Charlap, Eric Reed, Marcus Roberts, Jacky Terrasson, Gonzalo Rubalcaba; saxophonists James Carter, Steve Coleman, Branford Marsalis, Chris Potter, and Joshua Redman; trombonist Wycliffe Gordon; trumpet players Nicholas Payton and Roy Hargrove; violinist Regina Carter; singers Dianne Reeves and Cassandra Wilson. "There's plenty of us out here," said Wynton Marsalis. "We're still swinging and we ain't going nowhere."

Each musician has a distinctly individual voice but, as Stanley Crouch has said, they all have one quality in common: courage. "Courage is something you can't buy. And when somebody actually takes a real risk, like these young people do who go into jazz knowing that they're never going to be 'Puff Daddy' Combs, or Madonna, or any of those people—that assertion among young people of real courage, real aesthetic belief, can only beget good."

The number of Americans who listen to and love jazz music is still minuscule compared to what it once was. The African-American community remains largely estranged from the music to which it gave birth. There are too few places where young musicians can get a chance to play. And the jazz world continues to be divided into mutually antagonistic camps. But despite it all, the musical journey that began in the dance halls and saloons and street parades of New Orleans in the early years of the twentieth century continues into the twenty-first—and shows no sign of slowing down. Jazz remains gloriously inclusive, a proudly mongrel American music, filled with brilliant echoes of the past but still brand-new every night.

Above all, as Wynton Marsalis has said, jazz offers Americans hope: "That's the thing in jazz that got Bix Beiderbecke up out of his bed at two o'clock in the morning to pick that cornet up and practice with it into the pillow for another two or three hours. Or that would make Louis Armstrong travel around the world for fifty years nonstop, just get up out of his sickbed, crawl up on the bandstand, and play. The thing that would make Duke Ellington, Thelonious Monk, Miles Davis, Charlie Parker—any of these people that we've heard about, all these wonderful people—give their lives. And they did give their lives for it, because it gives us a glimpse into what America is going to be when it becomes itself. And this music tells you that it *will* become itself. And when you get a taste of that, there's just nothing else you're going to taste that's this sweet. That's a sweet taste, man."

At a grade school in Mississippi Wynton Marsalis meets some eager representatives of the future.

Joe Lovano, playing a custom-made straight tenor
saxophone, and pianist Gonzalo Rubalcaba

ACKNOWLEDGMENTS

This book grew out of a ten-part documentary-film series on the history of jazz—a project that began back in 1995 and continued unabated for five years. So many people contributed their extraordinary talents to that film, and to this book, that it will be impossible to thank all of them here. Throughout, we have been inspired by the wisdom, sophistication, and enthusiasm of Wynton Marsalis, who taught all of us so much about this music and what it says to us about America: "The real power of jazz and the innovation of jazz," he tells us at the beginning of our film, "is that a group of people can come together and create art. Improvised art. And can negotiate their agendas with each other. And that negotiation is the art."

We like to think that the team of gifted individuals who contributed to this massive undertaking was in many ways similar to a jazz orchestra, with each individual making his or her own unique contribution, but always with the selfless goal of making our film and book as good as they could be.

We cannot imagine how this project could have gone forward without the important contribution made by our writer, Geoffrey C. Ward. Not only did he bring his customary eloquence and subtlety to bear in his crafting of the script for the series, but he also infused it with his own deep and abiding love for jazz music, helped us to comprehend the impossibly vast whole, and shaped a meaningful and propulsive narrative. For all of that we are more grateful than we can say.

Our team of dedicated producers, each of whom contributed to the project above and beyond the call of duty, was also essential to our efforts. With the utmost dedication, coproducers Peter Miller and Victoria Gohl managed to find, order, and obtain clearances for the hundreds of hours of motion picture footage and the thousands of still photographs we needed to create our film. They were ably assisted by our wonderfully talented associate producers, Natalie Bullock Brown and Shola Lynch, who enthusiastically hurled themselves into every new and daunting task we threw their way. Together, they managed to research and keep track of all the photographs and stock footage that we required, organized our film shoots, researched historical issues, and in general kept our ship afloat. Associate producer Sarah Botstein found the music for this film and seemed to be everywhere at once, bringing her inexhaustible energy to every aspect of the production. Madison Davis Lacy, our consulting producer, helped us a great deal in the early stages of the project and conducted some of our best interviews.

Like all of our previous films, this series was truly created in the editing room. Without our terrific staff of editors, assistant editors, apprentices, and interns, there would be no *Jazz* series. Our team was led by the exceptionally gifted Paul Barnes, our supervising film editor. Not only did he edit our first episode, but he also oversaw the editing of all the others, insuring that they all shared the same cohesion and energy. Lewis Erskine brought a fine intelligence and an abiding love for jazz to his work, infusing his episodes with enormous respect for the artists who created the music. Sandra Christie, who knew almost nothing about jazz when she began the project, brought to her work a relentless drive and dedication that kept her at her editing table late into the night, unwilling to settle for anything less than perfection. The incomparable Tricia Reidy brought a determination to push the boundaries of the documentary form, and an unbridled enthusiasm for making the most challenging music accessible to everyone. Editors Sarah Hill and Shannon Robards worked closely with Tricia to make our film better than we could ever have dreamed possible. Erik Ewers, who never ceases to astound us, took charge of two complex episodes and made them soar. Aaron Vega, who began the project as an assistant editor, took charge of an entire episode and turned it into one of our best, while editor Craig Mellish kept our complicated operation running smoothly and at the same time managed to edit some of the most compelling scenes in the whole series. Our able staff of assistant editors, Barnard Jaffier, Dave Faulker, Dave Mast, Matt McGrail, Dave McMahon, Kevin Mercier, Thor Neureiter, and Meg Schindler, all contributed in ways large and small while our army of dedicated interns somehow kept the hundreds of hours of film footage organized and our logs and databases up to date. Tim Clark had the difficult task of dealing with hundreds of hours of narration, while Kara Mickley kept the photo department together.

Not a day goes by that we do not think about how thankful we are to have been able to convince the fine actor Keith David to serve as narrator for the series. His humanity, his intelligence, his extraordinary voice, and his professionalism never cease to amaze us. He spent hour upon hour in the studio, reading take after take, never complaining, always giving us his absolute best, infusing our series with warmth, elegance, and soul. We were also terribly fortunate to enlist a group of extraordinary actors to read first-person voices for the series: Philip Bosco, Matthew Broderick, Kevin Conway, Bruce Davison, Charles Durning, Samuel L. Jackson, Eriq La Salle, Delroy Lindo, Anthony LaPaglia, Courtney B. Vance, and many others added immeasurably to our attempts to breath life into the past.

We were fortunate, too, to have an inordinately talented crew of sound editors—Jennifer Dunnington, Marlena Grzaslewicz, Bruce Kitzmeyer, Dan Korintus, Jacob Ribicoff, Ira Spiegel—and to have worked with the greatest sound mixers in America—the incomparable Lee Dichter and Dominick Tavella—who made the music literally jump off the screen and, in the process, made our film truly come alive.

The exquisite cinematography of Buddy Squires, who shot most of the film, as well as of Allen Moore and Stephen McCarthy, infused our film with pure unadulterated beauty, while the animation photography of Ed Joyce and Ed Searles at the Frame Shop brought a new life to the still photographs in the series. Without the magnificent work of our colorist, John Dowdell, our film would not have the luminance and visual clarity we know it has.

All along, we relied heavily on the dedication of Pam Baucom, Susan Butler, Brenda Heath, and Patty Lawlor, who kept our office running smoothly, kept track of a thousand details, made sure that our budgets added up—and that we paid our bills.

Throughout the project, we also relied heavily on the wisdom of our esteemed panel of advisors. First and foremost, we want to thank Dan Morgenstern, our beloved senior advisor, who answered every question, read every script, and guided us on matters large and small, from the very beginning of the project to the last day of editing. In addition, we received enormously helpful input from Michael Chertok, James Lincoln Collier, Stanley Crouch, Michael Cuscuna, Dayton Duncan, Julie Dunfey, Gerald Early, Tom Evered, Gary Giddins, Matt Glaser, Joanna Groning, Eric Hobsbawm, Robin D. G. Kelley, Charlie Lourie, Allen Lowe, Albert Murray, Daniel Okrent, Bruce Boyd Raeburn, Loren Schoenberg, Gunther Schuller, and Margaret Washington.

Undertaking this project would have been impossible without the assistance we received from the following organizations and individuals: the Institute for Jazz Studies, the Hogan Jazz Archive, the Louis Armstrong Archives, Blue Note and Mosaic Records, the Collections of Charles Peterson and Bob Parent, the Prints and Photographs Division at the Library of Congress, the Louisiana State Museum, the Jazz Record Center, archivists Michael Cogswell, Jan Grenci, and Ken Vail, photographer Paul Christensen, historian Richard Sudhalter, and photo collectors Frank Driggs and Duncan Scheidt. They answered a thousand questions, provided us with priceless information, advice, music, photographs, and guidance.

An extraordinary group of the finest jazz art photographers in the country also generously lent their pictures to us for the film and the book: Anthony Barboza, Bill Gottlieb, William Claxton, Enid Farber, Lee Friedlander, Milt Hinton, Paul Hoeffler, Don Hunstein, Jimmy Katz, Herman Leonard, Bruce Polansky, Herb Snitzer, Chuck Stewart, Lee Tanner, and Francis Wolf.

Without the magnificent talents of our designer, Wendy Byrne, this book would not embody the spirit of jazz music as beautifully as it does, and we are equally grateful to the wonderful people at Alfred A. Knopf for making it possible for us to put this book together: Sonny Mehta, Ashbel Green, Kathy Hourigan, Asya Muchnick, Carol Devine Carson, Pat Johnson, Andy Hughes, Kevin Bourke, and Bette Graber.

We are also grateful to our good friends at Columbia / Legacy and the Verve Music Group: Jeff Jones, Seth Rothstein, Adam Block, Steve Berkowitz, Don Iener, Kristin Kozusko, Ron Goldstein, Ben Young, Richard Seidel, Mike Charlash, Robert Silverberg, Nate Herr, and Jeffrey Peisch.

Neither this book nor our film would have been possible without the generous support of the General Motors Corporation—and we would like to especially thank Phil Guarascio, Luanna Floccuzio, Peg Holmes, Denny Bolen, Judy Hu, and last but certainly not least, Skip Roberts, for their unwavering commitment to the project. We also received financial support from the Public Broadcasting Service, the Corporation for Public Broadcasting, the Park Foundation, the PEW Charitable Trusts, the Louisiana Department of Culture, Recreation, and Tourism, the Doris Duke Charitable Foundation, the National Endowment for the Humanities, the Arthur Vining Davis Foundations, the National Endowment for the Arts, the John D. and Catherine T. MacArthur Foundation, the Reva and David Logan Foundation, and Helen and Peter Bing.

Our partners at WETA-TV in Washington, D.C., have also been with us every step of the way, and in particular we want to thank Sharon Rockefeller, David Thompson, Craig Impink, and Karen Kenton for their indefatigable assistance. We are also grateful to Dan Klores and his talented colleagues: especially Joe DePlasco, Allyson Felix, and Susan Makarichev, for their tireless efforts to promote the film.

As is the case in any effort of this scope, there are scores of other people who contributed to the project—archivists, collectors, historians, music producers, researchers, production assistants, technicians, and many others—and we deeply regret that we lack the space to thank each of them individually for the work they have done to help us bring to millions of people the message and the healing power of jazz.

KEN BURNS
LYNN NOVICK

───────────

As the author of this book's text, I'd like to express my personal thanks to several people who helped make possible what was for me a labor of love:

My friend Ken Burns, with whom I've been working for some eighteen years and who continues to astonish me by his willingness to take on important subjects and turn them into important films;

Victoria Gohl, who devoted all of her extraordinary energy and intelligence to finding and researching the illustrations that fill this volume;

Wendy Byrne, whose unerring eye and infinite patience with last-minute changes of heart and mind remain a source of wonder;

Adrienne Sockwell, who tirelessly searched out materials for me all over the city;

Dan Morgenstern, who brought his encyclopedic knowledge and profound love for the music to his reading of the manuscript and in the process saved me from countless errors;

and Wynton Marsalis, whose friendship and insights, encouragement and candor, meant more to me in writing this history than I have words to express.

GEOFFREY C. WARD

SELECTED BIBLIOGRAPHY

AUTHOR'S NOTE: Because bibliographies give each title equal weight, they are inevitably misleading. I learned something from every one of the books listed below, but some were obviously far more useful than others. No one can ever write about Buddy Bolden without drawing heavily upon Donald M. Marquis, for example, or understand James Reese Europe without reading Reid Badger's comprehensive biography; the late Philip Evans's books lay out most of the material needed to write about Bix Beiderbecke and Frank Trumbauer; and it is hard to see how anyone can ever write a more rewarding and insightful book about early jazz in Chicago than William Howard Kenney's or a more elegantly written study of the bebop era than Scott Deveaux's. I owe them and a good many more authors an enormous debt of gratitude.

I'd also like to express my personal thanks to Peter Pullman and Richard Sudhalter, who kindly lent me important materials; my old friend Richard Meryman, who gave me access to the unedited transcripts from which his classic interview with Louis Armstrong was drawn; Bruce Raeburn, whose omniscience about New Orleans music and patience with foolish questions are both matters of wonder; and Lawrence Gushee, whose irreplaceable articles on early jazz remain unaccountably uncollected.

Albertson, Chris. *Bessie.* New York, 1972.

Alkyer, Frank. *Down Beat: 60 Years of Jazz.* Milwaukee, 1995.

Armstrong, Louis. *Louis Armstrong in His Own Words: Selected Writings.* New York, 1999.

———. *Satchmo: My Life in New Orleans.* New York, 1986.

———. *Swing That Music.* New York, 1993.

Arnaud, Gerald, and Jacques Chesnel. *Masters of Jazz.* Edinburgh, 1991.

Asbury, Herbert. *The French Quarter.* New York, 1936.

Badger, Reid. *A Life in Ragtime: A Biography of James Reese Europe.* New York, 1995.

Baker, David N., ed. *New Perspectives on Jazz.* Washington, D.C., 1986.

Balliett, Whitney. *American Musicians II: Seventy-one Portraits in Jazz.* New York, 1996.

———. *American Singers.* New York, 1979.

———. *Barney, Bradley and Max: Sixteen Portraits in Jazz.* New York, 1989.

———. *Goodbyes and Other Messages: A Journal of Jazz 1981–1990.* New York, 1991.

———. *Jelly Roll, Jabbo and Fats.* New York, 1983.

———. *New York Notes.* New York, 1976.

———. *The Sound of Surprise.* New York, 1961.

Barker, Danny. *Buddy Bolden and the Last Days of Storyville.* London, 1998.

———. *A Life in Jazz.* New York, 1986.

Barnet, Charlie, with Stanley Dance. *Those Swing Years: The Autobiography of Charlie Barnet.* New York, 1992.

Bayles, Martha. *Hole in Our Soul: The Loss of Beauty and Meaning in American Popular Music.* Chicago, 1994.

Bechet, Sidney. *Treat It Gentle.* New York, 1960.

Berendt, Joachim E. *The Jazz Book: From Ragtime to Fusion and Beyond.* New York, 1992.

———. *The Story of Jazz.* Englewood Cliffs, N.J., 1978.

Berger, Morroe, and James Patrick. *Benny Carter: A Life in American Music.* Newark, 1982.

Bergmeier, Horst J.P., and Rainer E. Lotz. *Hitler's Airwaves.* New Haven, 1997.

Bergreen, Laurence. *Louis Armstrong: An Extravagant Life.* New York, 1997.

Berrett, Joshua. *The Louis Armstrong Companion: Eight Decades of Commentary.* New York, 1999.

Berton, Ralph. *Remembering Bix: A Memoir of the Jazz Age.* New York, 1974.

Bigard, Barney. *With Louis and the Duke: The Autobiography of a Jazz Clarinetist.* New York, 1980.

Blesh, Rudi. *Shining Trumpets.* New York, 1980.

Borchert, James. *Alley Life in Washington: Family, Community, Religion and Folklife in the City 1850–1970.* Chicago, 1980.

Brandt, Nat. *Harlem at War: The Black Experience in WWII.* Syracuse, N.Y., 1996.

Britt, Stan. *Dexter Gordon: A Musical Biography.* New York, 1989.

Brown, Claude. *Manchild in the Promised Land.* New York, 1965.

Brown, Letitia Woods. *Free Negroes in the District of Columbia 1790–1846.* New York, 1972.

Brown, Sanford. *Louis Armstrong: Swinging, Singing Satchmo.* New York, 1993.

Brunn, H. O. *The Story of the Original Dixieland Jazz Band.* Baton Rouge, 1960.

Bryant, Clora, et al. *Central Avenue Sounds: Jazz in Los Angeles.* Berkeley, 1998.

Büchman-Møller, Frank. *You Just Fight for Your Life: The Story of Lester Young.* New York, 1990.

Buckner, Reginald T., and Steven Weiland, eds. *Jazz in Mind.* Detroit, 1991.

Budds, Michael J. *Jazz in the Sixties: The Expansion of Musical Resources and Techniques.* Iowa City, 1990.

Bultman, Bethany Ewald. *New Orleans.* New York, 1996.

Bushell, Garvin, and Mark Tucker. *Jazz from the Beginning.* New York, 1998.

Callahan, John F., ed. *The Collected Essays of Ralph Ellison.* New York, 1995.

Carmichael, Hoagy. *The Stardust Road & Sometimes I Wonder: The Autobiographies of Hoagy Carmichael.* New York, 1999.

Carner, Gary. *The Miles Davis Companion: Four Decades of Commentary.* New York, 1996.

Cassandra Wilson

Carr, Ian. *Keith Jarrett: The Man and His Music*. New York, 1992.

———. *Miles Davis: The Definitive Biography*. New York, 1998.

Carr, Ian, and Digby Fairweather. *Jazz: The Rough Guide*. London, 1995.

Carruth, Hayden. *Sitting In: Selected Writings on Jazz, Blues and Related Topics*. Iowa City, 1993.

Carver, Reginald, and Lenny Bernstein. *Jazz Profiles: The Spirit of the Nineties*. New York, 1998.

Chamberlain, Dorothy, and Robert Wilson, eds. *In the Spirit of Jazz: The Otis Ferguson Reader*. New York, 1997.

Chambers, Jack. *Milestones: The Music and Times of Miles Davis*. New York, 1998.

Charters, Samuel B., and Leonard Kunstadt. *Jazz: A History of the New York Scene*. New York, 1984.

Cheatham, Aldolphus. *I Guess I'll Get the Papers and Go Home: The Life of Doc Cheatham*. London, 1995.

Chilton, John. *Billie's Blues: The Billie Holiday Story 1933–1959*. New York, 1975.

———. *Let the Good Times Roll: The Story of Louis Jordan and His Music*. Ann Arbor, 1997.

———. *Ride, Red, Ride: The Life of Henry "Red" Allen*. London, 1999.

———. *Sidney Bechet: The Wizard of Jazz*. New York, 1996.

———. *The Song of the Hawk: The Life and Recordings of Coleman Hawkins*. Ann Arbor, 1990.

———. *Stomp Off, Let's Go*. London, 1983.

———. *Who's Who of Jazz: Storyville to Swing Street*. Philadelphia, 1978.

Clarke, Donald. *Wishing on the Moon: The Life and Times of Billie Holiday*. New York, 1994.

Cole, Bill. *Miles Davis: The Early Years*. New York, 1994.

Coleman, Bill. *Trumpet Story*. London, 1990.

Coleman, Janet, and Al Young. *Mingus/Mingus: Two Memoirs*. New York, 1994.

Collier, James Lincoln. *Benny Goodman and the Swing Era*. New York, 1989.

———. *Duke Ellington*. New York, 1987.

———. *Jazz: the American Theme Song*. New York, 1995.

———. *Louis Armstrong: An American Genius*. New York, 1983.

———. *The Making of Jazz*. Boston, 1978.

Collier-Thomas, Bettye, and V. P. Franklin. *My Soul Is a Witness: A Chronology of the Civil Rights Era, 1954–1965*. New York, 1999.

Collins, R. *New Orleans Jazz: A Revised History: The Development of American Music from the Origins to the Big Bands*. New York, 1996.

Condon, Eddie. *We Called It Music: A Generation of Jazz*. New York, 1992.

Condon, Eddie, and Richard Gehman, eds. *Eddie Condon's Treasury of Jazz*. New York, 1956.

Condon, Eddie, and Hank O'Neal. *The Eddie Condon Scrapbook of Jazz*. New York, 1973.

Cook, Richard, and Brian Norton. *The Penguin Guide to Jazz on Compact Disc*. London, 1996.

Cooke, Mervyn. *The Chronicle of Jazz*. New York, 1997.

———. *Jazz*. New York, 1999.

Crouch, Stanley. *The All-American Skin Game, or, The Decoy of Race*. New York, 1995.

———. *Always in Pursuit: Fresh American Perspectives, 1995–1997*. New York, 1998.

———. *Notes of a Hanging Judge: Essays and Reviews 1979–1989*. New York, 1990.

Crow, Bill. *From Birdland to Broadway: Scenes from a Jazz Life*. New York, 1992.

———. *Jazz Anecdotes*. New York, 1990.

Cusic, Don. *The Sound of Light: A History of Gospel Music*. Bowling Green, Ohio, 1990.

Dahl, Linda. *Stormy Weather: The Music and Lives of a Century of Jazz Women*. New York, 1992.

Dance, Stanley. *The World of Count Basie*. New York, 1980.

———. *The World of Duke Ellington*. New York, 1970.

———. *The World of Earl Hines*. New York, 1977.

———. *The World of Swing*. New York, 1979.

Davis, Allen, and Mary Lynn McCree. *Eighty Years at Hull House*. Chicago, 1969.

Davis, Clive, with James Wilwerth. *Clive: Inside the Record Business*. New York, 1975.

Davis, Francis. *The History of the Blues: The Roots, the Music, the People: From Charley Patton to Robert Cray*. New York, 1995.

———. *In the Moment: Jazz in the 1980s*. New York, 1996.

———. *Outcats: Jazz Composers, Instrumentalists and Singers*. New York, 1990.

Davis, Miles, with Quincy Troupe. *Miles: The Autobiography*. New York, 1989.

DeCarava, Roy. *The Sound I Saw: The Jazz Photographs of Roy DeCarava*. New York, 1983.

Deffaa, Chip. *Swing Legacy*. Newark, 1989.

———. *Voices of the Jazz Age*. Champaign, Ill., 1992.

Delannoy, Luc. *Pres: The Story of Lester Young*. Fayetteville, Ark., 1993.

Delaunay, Charles. *Django Reinhardt*. New York, 1961.

DeLong, Thomas A. *Pops: Paul Whiteman, King of Jazz*. Piscataway, N.J., 1983.

Deveaux, Scott. *The Birth of Bebop: A Social and Music History*. Berkeley, 1997.

———. *Jazz in America: Who's Listening?* National Endowment for the Arts Research Report #31, Carson, Calif., 1995.

Dupuis, Robert. *Bunny Berigan: Elusive Legend of Jazz*. Baton Rouge, 1993.

Dyer, Geoff. *But Beautiful: A Book About Jazz*. New York, 1996.

Early, Gerald. *The Culture of Bruising: Essays on Prizefighting, Literature and Modern American Culture*. Hopewell, N.J., 1994.

———. *One Nation Under a Groove: Motown and American Culture*. Hopewell, N.J., 1995.

———. *Tuxedo Junction: Essays on American Culture*. Hopewell, N.J., 1989.

Ellington, Edward Kennedy. *Music Is My Mistress*. New York, 1975.

Ellington, Mercer, with Stanley Dance. *Duke Ellington in Person: An Intimate Memoir*. New York, 1979.

Emerson, Ken. *Doo-dah! Stephen Foster and the Rise of American Popular Culture*. New York, 1997.

Epstein, Daniel Mark. *Nat King Cole*. New York, 1999.

Erenberg, Lewis. *Steppin' Out: New York Nightlife and the Transformation of American Culture, 1890–1930*. Chicago, 1981.

———. *Swingin' the Dream: Big Band Jazz and the Rebirth of American Culture*. Chicago, 1998.

Erlewine, Michael, and Vladimir Bogdanov. *All Music Guide to Jazz*. San Francisco, 1996.

Evans, Philip R., and Larry F. Kiner. *Tram: The Frank Trumbauer Story*. Rutgers, N.Y., 1994.

Evans, Philip R., and Linda K. Evans. *Bix: The Leon Bix Beiderbecke Story*. Bakersfield, Calif., 1998.

Feather, Leonard. *The Book of Jazz*. New York, 1959.

———. *The Encyclopedia of Jazz*. New York, 1955.

———. *The Encyclopedia of Jazz in the Sixties*. New York, 1966.

———. *From Satchmo to Miles*. New York, 1984.

———. *The Jazz Years: Earwitness to an Era*. New York, 1987.

Feather, Leonard, and Ira Gitler. *The Biographical Encyclopedia of Jazz*. New York, 1999.

Feather, Leonard, and Jack Tracy. *Laughter from the Hip: The Lighter Side of Jazz*. New York, 1979.

Finkelstein, Sidney. *Jazz: A People's Music*. New York, 1948.

Firestone, Ross. *Swing, Swing, Swing: The Life & Times of Benny Goodman*. New York, 1993.

Fitterling, Thomas. *Thelonious Monk: His Life and Music*. Berkeley, 1997.

Floyd, Samuel A., Jr. *The Power of Black Music: Interpreting Its History from Africa to the United States*. New York, 1995.

Foster, Pops, with Tom Stoddard. *Pops Foster: The Autobiography of a New Orleans Jazzman*. Berkeley, 1971.

Fox, Ted. *Showtime at the Apollo*. New York, 1993.

Freeman, Bud. *Crazeology: The Autobiography of a Chicago Jazzman*. Urbana, Ill., 1989.

———. *You Don't Look Like a Musician*. Detroit, 1974.

Friedlander, Paul. *A Social History of Rock and Roll*. Boulder, Colo., 1996.

Friedwald, Will. *Jazz Singing: America's Great Voices from Bessie Smith to Bebop and Beyond.* New York, 1996.

———. *Sinatra! This Song Is You.* New York, 1995.

Gabbard, Krin. *Jammin' at the Margins: Jazz and the American Cinema.* Chicago, 1996.

———, ed. *Jazz Among the Discourses.* Durham, N.C., 1995.

———, ed. *Representing Jazz.* Durham, N.C., 1995.

Gammond, Peter, ed. *Duke Ellington: His Life and Music.* New York, 1977.

Gara, Larry. *The Baby Dodds Story.* Baton Rouge, 1992.

Gennari, John Remo. *The Politics of Culture and Identity in American Jazz Criticism.* Ph.D. thesis. Ann Arbor, 1993.

George, Don. *Sweet Man: The Real Duke Ellington.* New York, 1981.

Giddins, Gary. *Celebrating Bird: The Triumph of Charlie Parker.* New York, 1987.

———. *Faces in the Crowd: Players and Writers.* New York, 1992.

———. *Rhythm-A-Ning: Jazz Tradition and Innovation in the 80's.* New York, 1985.

———. *Riding on a Blue Note.* New York, 1981.

———. *Satchmo.* New York, 1988.

———. *Visions of Jazz: The First Century.* New York, 1998.

Gill, James. *Lords of Misrule: Mardi Gras and the Politics of Race in New Orleans.* Oxford, Miss., 1998.

Gillespie, Dizzy, with Al Fraser. *To Be or Not to Bop: Memoirs of Dizzy Gillespie.* New York, 1979.

Gillet, Charlie. *The Sound of the City: The Rise of Rock and Roll.* New York, 1996.

Gillis, Frank J., and John Miner, eds. *Oh Didn't He Ramble: The Life Story of Lee Collins.* Chicago, 1989.

Gioia, Ted. *The History of Jazz.* New York, 1997.

———. *The Imperfect Art: Reflections on Jazz and Modern Culture.* New York, 1988.

———. *West Coast Jazz: Modern Jazz in California, 1945–1960.* New York, 1992.

Gitler, Ira. *Jazz Masters of the Forties.* New York, 1983.

———. *Swing to Bop.* New York, 1985.

Godbolt, Jim. *A History of Jazz in Britain 1919–50.* London, 1984.

Goldberg, Joe. *Jazz Masters of the Fifties.* New York, 1965.

Goodman, Benny, and Irving Kolodin. *The Kingdom of Swing.* New York, 1939.

Gordon, Max. *Live at the Village Vanguard.* New York, 1980.

Gottlieb, Robert, ed. *Reading Jazz: A Gathering of Autobiography, Reportage, and Criticism from 1919 to Now.* New York, 1996.

Gottlieb, William P. *The Golden Age of Jazz.* San Francisco, 1995.

Gourse, Leslie. *The Billie Holiday Companion: Seven Decades of Commentary.* New York, 1997.

———. *The Ella Fitzgerald Companion: Seven Decades of Commentary.* New York, 1998.

———. *Every Day: The Story of Joe Williams.* New York, 1995.

———. *Madame Jazz: Contemporary Women Instrumentalists.* New York, 1995.

———. *Sassy: The Life of Sarah Vaughan.* New York, 1994.

———. *Straight, No Chaser: The Life and Genius of Thelonious Monk.* New York, 1997.

———. *Unforgettable: The Life and Mystique of Nat King Cole.* New York, 1991.

———. *Wynton Marsalis: Skain's Domain: A Biography.* New York, 1999.

Graham, Charles. *The Great Jazz Day.* Emeryville, Calif., 1999.

Green, Benny. *The Reluctant Art: Five Studies in the Growth of Jazz.* New York, 1991.

Green, Constance McLaughlin. *Secret City: A History of Race Relations in the Nation's Capital.* Princeton, N.J., 1967.

Gridley, Mark C. *Jazz Styles: History and Analysis.* Upper Saddle River, N.J., 2000.

Groves, Alan, and Alyn Shipton. *The Glass Enclosure: The Life of Bud Powell.* Oxford, 1993.

Guralnick, Paul. *Last Train to Memphis: The Rise of Elvis Presley.* Boston, 1994.

Hadlock, Richard. *Jazz Masters of the Twenties.* New York, 1988.

Hair, William Ivy. *Carnival of Fury: Robert Charles and the New Orleans Race Riot of 1900.* Baton Rouge, 1976.

Hajdu, David. *Lush Life: A Biography of Billy Strayhorn.* New York, 1996.

Hall, Fred M. *It's About Time: The Dave Brubeck Story.* Fayetteville, Ark., 1996.

Hamill, Pete. *Why Sinatra Matters.* Boston, 1998.

Hammond, John. *John Hammond on Record: An Autobiography.* New York, 1981.

Hampton, Lionel, with James Haskins. *Hamp: An Autobiography.* New York, 1989.

Handy, D. Antoinette. *Jazz Man's Journey: A Biography of Ellis Louis Marsalis, Jr.* Lanham, Md., 1999.

Handy, W. C. *Father of the Blues: An Autobiography.* New York, 1969.

Harker, Brian Cameron. *The Early Musical Development of Louis Armstrong, 1901–1928.* Ph.D. dissertation, Columbia University, 1997.

Harris, Michael W. *The Rise of Gospel and Blues.* New York, 1992.

Harrison, Daphne Duval. *Black Pearls: Blues Queens of the 1920s.* New Brunswick, N.J., 1990.

Haskins, James, and Kathleen Benson. *Nat King Cole.* Chelsea, Mich., 1984.

Haskins, Jim. *The Cotton Club.* New York, 1977.

Hasse, John Edward. *Beyond Category: The Life and Genius of Duke Ellington.* New York, 1993.

Hennessey, Mike. *Klook: The Story of Kenny Clarke.* Pittsburgh, 1994.

Hentoff, Nat. *Jazz Is.* New York, 1992.

———. *The Jazz Life.* New York, 1975.

Hentoff, Nat, and Albert J. McCarthy. *Jazz.* New York, 1959.

———, eds. *Jazz: New Perspectives on the History of Jazz by Twelve of the World's Foremost Jazz Critics and Scholars.* New York, 1959.

Herman, Woody, and Stuart Troop. *The Woodchopper's Ball: The Autobiography of Woody Herman.* New York, 1994.

Hilbert, Robert. *Pee Wee Russell: The Life of a Jazzman.* New York, 1993.

Hillman, Christopher. *Bunk Johnson: His Life and Times.* New York, 1988.

Hinton, Milt, and David G. Berger. *Bass Line: The Stories and Photographs of Milt Hinton.* Temple University Press, 1988.

Hobsbawm, Eric. *The Jazz Scene.* New York, 1993.

Hodes, Art, and Chadwick Hansen. *Hot Man: The Life of Art Hodes.* Urbana, Ill., 1992.

Holiday, Billie, with William Duffy. *Lady Sings the Blues.* New York, 1965.

Holtje, Steve, and Nancy Ann Lee. *Music Hound Jazz: The Essential Album Guide.* Detroit, 1998.

Horricks, Raymond. *Gerry Mulligan.* London, 1986.

Huggins, Nathan Irvin. *Harlem Renaissance.* New York, 1979.

Hutlin, Randi. *Born Under the Sign of Jazz.* New York, 1998.

Jasen, David A., and Gene Jones. *Spreadin' Rhythm Round: Black Popular Songwriters 1880–1930.* New York, 1998.

Jewell, Derek. *Duke: A Portrait of Duke Ellington.* New York, 1977.

Johnson, James Weldon. *The Autobiography of an Ex-Colored Man.* New York, 1990.

Johnston, Allan. *Surviving Freedom: The Black Community of Washington D.C. 1860–1880.* New York, 1993.

Jones, Gene, and Robert R. Darch. *The Original Dixieland Jass Band.* Alexandria Bay, N.Y., 1993.

Jones, Leroi. *Black Music.* New York, 1968.

———. *Blues People: Negro Music in White America.* New York, 1963.

Jones, Max, and John Chilton. *Louis: The Louis Armstrong Story 1900–1971.* New York, 1971.

Jonnes, Jill. *Hep-Cats, Narcs, and Pipe Dreams.* Baltimore, 1999.

Jost, Ekkehard. *Free Jazz.* New York, 1994.

Kamin, Ira, and Jimmy Lyons. *Dizzy, Duke, the Count and Me.* San Francisco, 1978.

Kaminsky, Max. *My Life in Jazz.* London, 1965.

Kater, Michael H. *Different Drummers: Jazz in the Culture of Nazi Germany.* New York, 1992.

Keepnews, Orrin. *The View from Within.* New York, 1988.

Keepnews, Orrin, and Bill Grauer Jr. *A Pictorial History of Jazz.* New York, 1955.

Kennedy, Rick. *Jelly Roll, Biz and Hoagy: Gennett Studios and the Birth of Recorded Jazz.* Bloomington, Ind., 1994.

Jackie Terrason

Kenney, William Howard. *Chicago Jazz; A Cultural History, 1904–1930.* New York, 1993.

Kernfeld, Barry. *What to Listen for in Jazz.* New Haven, 1995.

King, Jonny. *An Insider's Guide to Understanding and Listening to Jazz.* New York, 1997.

Kirchner, Bill, ed. *A Miles Davis Reader.* Washington, D.C., 1997.

Kirk, Andy, and Amy Lee. *Twenty Years on Wheels.* Ann Arbor, Mich., 1989.

Kliment, Bud. *Ella Fitzgerald.* New York, 1988.

Klinker, Philip A., with Rogers M. Smith. *The Unsteady March: The Rise and Decline of Racial Equality in America.* Chicago, 1999.

Kmen, Henry A. *Music in New Orleans.* Baton Rouge, 1966.

Korall, Burt. *Drummin' Men: The Heartbeat of Jazz, The Swing Years.* New York, 1990.

Lange, Art, and Nathaniel Mackey, eds. *Moment's Notice: Jazz in Poetry and Prose.* Minneapolis, 1993.

Larkin, Philip. *All What Jazz.* New York, 1985.

Lees, Gene. *Cats of Any Color: Jazz, Black and White.* New York, 1995.

———. *Leader of the Band: The Life of Woody Herman.* New York, 1995.

———. *Meet Me at Jim and Andy's: Jazz Musicians and Their World.* New York, 1988.

———. *Oscar Peterson: The Will to Swing.* Rocklin, Calif., 1990.

———. *Singers and the Song II.* New York, 1998.

———. *Waiting for Dizzy.* New York, 1991.

Leonard, Neil. *Jazz and the White Americans.* Chicago, 1962.

Lester, James. *Too Marvelous for Words: The Life and Genius of Art Tatum.* New York, 1994.

Levine, Lawrence W. *Black Culture and Black Consciousness.* New York, 1977.

———. *Highbrow/Lowbrow: The Emergence of Cultural Hierarchy in America.* Cambridge, 1988.

Lewis, David Levering. *When Harlem Was in Vogue.* New York, 1979.

Lichtenstein, Grace, and Laura Danker. *Musical Gumbo: The Music of New Orleans.* New York, 1993.

Lindemeyer, Paul. *Celebrating the Saxophone.* New York, 1996.

Litweiler, John. *The Freedom Principle: Jazz After 1958.* New York, 1984.

———. *Ornette Coleman: A Harmolodic Life.* New York, 1994.

Locke, Alain, ed. *The New Negro.* New York, 1992.

Lomax, Alan. *Mister Jelly Roll.* New York, 1950.

Lowe, Allen. *American Pop: From Minstrel to Mojo: On Record 1983–1956.* New York, 1997.

Lyons, Len. *The Great Jazz Pianists: Speaking of Their Lives and Music.* New York, 1983.

Lyons, Len, and Don Perlo. *Jazz Portraits: The Lives and Music of the Jazz Masters.* New York, 1989.

Magee, Jeffrey. *The Music of Fletcher Henderson and His Orchestra in the 1920's.* Ph.D. dissertation. University of Michigan, 1992.

Maggin, Donald L. *Stan Getz: A Life in Jazz.* New York, 1996.

Mandel, Howard. *Future Jazz.* New York, 1999.

Marquis, Donald M. *In Search of Buddy Bolden: First Man of Jazz.* Baton Rouge, 1978.

Marsalis, Wynton. *Marsalis on Music.* New York, 1995.

Marsalis, Wynton, and Frank Stewart. *Sweet Swing Blues on the Road.* New York, 1994.

Martin, Donna. *Kansas City . . . And All That's Jazz.* Kansas City, Mo., 1999.

Mattingly, Rick. *The Drummer's Time: Conversations with the Great Drummers of Jazz.* Cedar Grove, N.J., 1998.

Mayer, Harold M., and Richard C. Wade. *Chicago: Growth of a Metropolis.* Chicago, 1969.

McCue, George. *Music in American Society 1776–1976.* New Brunswick, N.J., 1977.

McKee, Margaret, and Fred Chisenhall. *Beale Black & Blue: Life and Music on Black America's Main Street.* Baton Rouge, 1981.

McRae, Barry. *The Jazz Cataclysm.* New York, 1985.

Megill, Donald D., and Richard S. Demory. *Introduction to Jazz History.* Upper Saddle River, N.J., 1996.

Meier, August. *Negro Thought in America 1880–1915.* Ann Arbor, Mich., 1966.

Melnick, Jeffrey. *A Right to Sing the Blues: African-Americans, Jews, and American Popular Song.* Cambridge, 1999.

Meltzer, David, ed. *Reading Jazz.* San Francisco, 1993.

Mezzrow, Mezz, and Barry Wolfe. *Really the Blues.* New York, 1990.

Miller, Marc H., ed. *Louis Armstrong: A Cultural Legacy.* Seattle, 1994.

Miller, Norma, and Evette Jensen. *Swingin' at the Savoy: The Memoir of a Jazz Dancer.* Philadelphia, 1996.

Mingus, Charles. *Beneath the Underdog.* New York, 1991.

Moody, Bill. *The Jazz Exiles: American Musicians Abroad.* Las Vegas, 1993.

Morgan, Thomas L., and William Barlow. *From Cakewalks to Concert Halls: An Illustrated History of African American Popular Music from 1895 to 1930.* Washington, D.C., 1992.

Morgenstern, Dan, and Ole Brask. *Jazz People.* New York, 1993.

Murray, Albert. *The Blue Devils of Nada.* New York, 1996.

———. *Good Morning Blues: The Autobiography of Count Basie.* New York, 1985.

———. *The Hero and the Blues.* New York, 1995.

———. *The Omni-Americans: Some Alternatives to the Folklore of White Supremacy.* New York, 1970.

———. *Stomping the Blues.* New York, 1976.

Nicholson, Stuart. *Billie Holiday.* Boston, 1995.

———. *Ella Fitzgerald: A Biography of the First Lady of Jazz.* New York, 1995.

———. *Jazz: The 1980s Resurgence.* New York, 1995.

———. *Reminiscing in Tempo: A Portrait of Duke Ellington.* Boston, 1999.

Nisenson, Eric. *Ascension: John Coltrane and His Quest.* New York, 1993.

———. *Blue: The Murder of Jazz.* New York, 1997.

O'Day, Anita, with George Eels. *High Times Hard Times.* New York, 1989.

Ogren, Kathy J. *The Jazz Revolution: Twenties America and the Meaning of Jazz.* New York, 1989.

Oliphant, Dave. *Texan Jazz.* Austin, 1996.

Oliver, Paul, and Max Harrison. *Gospel, Blues and Jazz.* London, 1980.

O'Meally, Robert G., ed. *The Jazz Cadence of American Culture.* New York, 1998.

Osofsky, Gilbert. *Harlem: The Making of a Ghetto 1890–1930.* New York, 1966.

Owens, Thomas. *Bebop: The Music and Its Players.* New York, 1995.

Panassie, Hughes. *Louis Armstrong.* New York, 1971.

Patterson, James T. *Grand Expectations: The United States, 1945–1974.* New York, 1996.

Pearson, Nathan W., Jr. *Goin' to Kansas City.* Urbana, Ill., 1994.

Pepper, Art, and Laurie Pepper. *Straight Life: The Story of Art Pepper.* New York, 1994.

Peretti, Burton W. *The Creation of Jazz: Music, Race, and Culture in Urban America.* Urbana, Ill., 1992.

———. *Jazz in American Culture.* Chicago, 1997.

Perhonis, John Paul. *The Bix Beiderbecke Story: The Jazz Musician in Legend, Fiction, and Fact. A Study of the Images of Jazz in the National Culture: 1930–the Present.* Ph.D. dissertation, University of Minnesota, 1978.

Perlo, Don, and Len Lyons. *Jazz Portraits: The Lives and Music of the Jazz Masters.* New York, 1989.

Perry, David. *Jazz Greats.* London, 1996.

Pettinger, Peter. *Bill Evans: How My Heart Sings.* New Haven, 1998.

Piazza, Tom. *Blues and Trouble: Twelve Stories.* New York, 1996.

———. *Blues Up and Down: Jazz in Our Time.* New York, 1997.

———. *The Guide to Classic Recorded Jazz.* Iowa City, 1995.

———, ed. *Setting the Tempo: Fifty Years of Great Jazz Liner Notes.* New York, 1996.

Pinfold, Mike. *Louis Armstrong.* New York, 1987.

Placksin, Sally. *American Women in Jazz: 1900 to the Present, Their Words, Lives, and Music.* New York, 1982.

Plater, Alan. *The Beiderbecke Affair.* London, 1985.

Porter, Lewis. *John Coltrane: His Life and Music.* Ann Arbor, Mich., 1998.

———. *Lester Young.* Boston, 1985.

———, ed. *A Lester Young Reader.* Washington, D.C., 1991.

Porter, Lewis, and Michael Ullman. *Jazz: From Its Origins to the Present.* Englewood Cliffs, N.J., 1993.

Porter, Roy, with David Keller. *There and Back.* Oxford, 1991.

Priestly, Brian. *Mingus: A Critical Biography.* New York, 1983.

Raeburn, Bruce Boyd. *New Orleans Style: The Awakening of American Scholarship and Its Cultural Implications.* Ph.D. dissertation, Tulane University, 1991.

Ramsey, Doug. *Jazz Matters.* Fayetteville, Ark., 1989.

Ramsey, Frederick Jr., and Charles Edward Smith. *Jazzmen: The Story of Hot Jazz Told in the Lives of the Men Who Created It.* New York, 1939.

Reisner, Robert, ed. *Bird: The Legend of Charlie Parker.* New York, 1975.

Rich, Alan. *The Simon and Schuster Listener's Guide to Jazz.* New York, 1980.

Riis, Thomas. *Just Before Jazz: Black Musical Theater in New York 1890 to 1915.* Washington, D.C., 1989.

Rivelli, Pauline, and Robert Levin. *Giants of Black Music.* New York, 1979.

Roberts, John Storm. *Black Music of Two Worlds.* New York, 1972.

Rose, Al. *I Remember Jazz: Six Decades Among the Great Jazz Men.* Baton Rouge, 1987.

———. *Storyville, New Orleans.* Tuscaloosa, Ala., 1974.

Rosenthal, David H. *Hard Bop: Jazz and Black Music, 1955–1965.* New York, 1992.

Rowland, Mark, and Tony Sherman, eds. *The Jazz Musician.* New York, 1994.

Royal, Marshal, with Claire P. Gordon. *Marshal Royal: Jazz Survivor.* London, 1996.

Russell, Ross. *Jazz Style in Kansas City and in the Southwest.* New York, 1997.

Sales, Grover. *Jazz: America's Classical Music.* New York, 1992.

Sanford, Herb. *Tommy and Jimmy: The Dorsey Years.* New York, 1972.

Schaefer, William John. *Brass Bands and New Orleans Jazz.* Baton Rouge, 1977.

Schuller, Gunther, *Early Jazz: Its Roots and Musical Development.* New York, 1986.

———. *The Swing Era.* New York, 1989.

Shadwick, Keith. *Gramophone Jazz Good CD Guide.* Middlesex, England, 1997.

Shapiro, Nat, and Nat Hentoff. *Hear Me Talkin' to Ya: The Story of Jazz as Told by the Men Who Made It.* New York, 1966.

———, eds. *The Jazz Makers.* New York, 1957.

Shaw, Arnold. *52nd Street: The Street of Jazz.* New York, 1971.

———. *Honkers and Shouters.* New York, 1978.

———. *The Jazz Age: Popular Music in the 1920s.* New York, 1987.

Shaw, Artie. *The Trouble with Cinderella: An Outline of Identity.* Santa Barbara, Calif., 1992.

Shipton, Alyn. *Groovin' High: The Life of Dizzy Gillespie.* New York, 1999.

Short, Bobby, with Robert Mackintosh. *Bobby Short: The Life and Times of a Saloon Singer.* New York, 1995.

Sidran, Ben. *Talking Jazz: An Oral History.* New York, 1995.

Silvester, Peter J. *A Left Hand Like God: A History of Boogie-Woogie Piano.* New York, 1988.

Simon, George T. *The Big Bands.* New York, 1981.

Simone, Nina. *I Put a Spell on You: The Autobiography of Nina Simone.* New York, 1993.

Siskind, Aaron. *Harlem Documents: Photographs 1932–1940.* Providence, R.I., 1981.

Škvorecký, Josef. *The Bass Saxophone.* New York, 1994.

Smith, Jay D., and Len Guttridge. *Jack Teagarden: The Story of a Jazz Maverick.* New York, 1988.

Smith, Willie the Lion. *Music on My Mind: The Memoirs of an American Pianist.* London, 1966.

Southern, Eileen. *The Music of Black Americans: A History.* New York, 1983.

Spellman, A. B. *Four Lives in the Bebop Business.* New York, 1966.

Starr, S. Frederick. *Red and Hot: The Fate of Jazz in the Soviet Union.* New York, 1994.

Stearns, Marshall. *The Story of Jazz.* London, 1982.

Stearns, Marshall, and Jean Stearns. *Jazz Dance: The Story of American Vernacular Dance.* New York, 1994.

Steed, Janna Tull. *Duke Ellington: A Spiritual Biography.* New York, 1999.

Stewart, Rex. *Boy Meets Horn.* Ann Arbor, Mich., 1994.

———. *Jazz Masters of the Thirties.* New York, 1972.

Stoddard, Tom. *Jazz on the Barbary Coast.* Berkeley, 1998.

Stokes, W. Royal. *The Jazz Scene: An Informal History from New Orleans to 1990.* New York, 1991.

———. *Swing Era New York: The Photographs of Charles Preston.* Philadelphia, 1994.

Storb, Ilse. *Louis Armstrong: The Definitive Biography.* New York, 1989.

Stovall, Tyler. *Paris Noir: African Americans in the City of Light.* New York, 1996.

Stowe, *David W. Swing Changes: Big Band Jazz in New Deal America.* Cambridge, 1994.

Stroff, Stephen M. *Discovering Great Jazz.* New York, 1993.

Sudhalter, Richard M. *Lost Chords: White Musicians and Their Contribution to Jazz, 1915–1945.* New York, 1999.

Sudhalter, Richard M., and Philip R. Evans. *Bix: Man and Legend.* New Rochelle, N.Y., 1974.

Swed, John F. *Space Is the Place: The Lives and Times of Sun Ra.* New York, 1997.

Tanenhaus, Sam. *Louis Armstrong.* Los Angeles, 1988.

Taylor, Arthur. *Notes and Tones.* New York, 1982.

Taylor, Frank C., and Gerald Cook. *Alberta Hunter: A Celebration in Blues.* New York, 1987.

Taylor, Jeffrey. *Earl Hines and Black Jazz Piano in Chicago, 1923–28.* Ph.D. dissertation, City University of New York, 1997.

Tibbetts, John C., ed. *Dvorak in America*. Portland, Ore., 1993.

Tinker, Edward Larocque. *Creole City: Its Past and Its People*. New York, 1953.

Tirro, Frank. *Jazz: A History*. New York, 1977.

Tucker, Mark. *Ellington: The Early Years*. Urbana, Ill., 1991.

———, ed. *The Duke Ellington Reader*. New York, 1993.

Turner, Frederick. *Remembering Song: Encounters with the New Orleans Jazz Tradition*. New York, 1982.

Ulanov, Barry. *Duke Ellington*. New York, 1975.

———. *A History of Jazz in America*. New York, 1952.

Vail, Ken. *Bird's Diary: The Life of Charlie Parker 1945–1955*. Surrey, Eng., 1996.

Van Rijn, Guido. *Roosevelt's Blues: African-American Blues and Gospel Songs on FDR*. Oxford, Miss., 1997.

Wade, Richard C., ed. *Hull House Maps and Papers: Residents of Hull House—A Presentation of Nationalities and Wages in a Congested District of Chicago*. New York, 1970.

Waldo, Terry. *This Is Ragtime*. New York, 1991.

Walker, Leo. *The Wonderful Era of the Great Dance Bands*. New York, 1990.

Walser, Robert, ed. *Keeping Time: Readings in Jazz History*. New York, 1999.

Watkins, Mel. *On the Real Side: Laughing, Lying and Signifying*. New York, 1994.

Weinstein, Norman C. *A Night in Tunisia: Imaginings of Africa in Jazz*. New York, 1992.

Wells, Dicky, and Stanley Dance. *The Night People: The Jazz Life of Dicky Wells*. Washington, D.C., 1991.

Whiteman, Paul, and Mary Margaret McBride. *Jazz*. New York, 1926.

Williams, Martin. *Jazz Changes*. New York, 1992.

———. *Jazz Heritage*. New York, 1985.

———. *Jazz in Its Time*. New York, 1989.

———. *Jazz Masters in Transition 1957–1969*. New York, 1970.

———. *Jazz Masters of New Orleans*. New York, 1967.

———. *The Jazz Tradition*. New York, 1993.

———, ed. *The Art of Jazz*. New York, 1980.

Wilmer, Valerie. *As Serious As Your Life: The Story of the New Jazz*. New York, 1992.

———. *Jazz People*. New York, 1977.

Wilson, Samuel, Jr. *Benjamin Henry Latrobe: Impressions Respecting New Orleans—Diary and Sketches 1818–1820*. New York, 1951.

Wilson, Teddy, with Arie Ligthart and Humphrey van Loo. *Teddy Wilson Talks Jazz*. London, 1996.

Woideck, Carl. *The Charlie Parker Companion: Six Decades of Commentary*. New York, 1998.

———. *Charlie Parker: His Music and Life*. Ann Arbor, Mich., 1996.

———. *The John Coltrane Companion: Five Decades of Commentary*. New York, 1998.

Zenfell, Martha Ellen. *New Orleans*. Boston, 1995.

INDEX

Christian McBride

Lewis Nash

Geri Allen

Joshua Redman

Nicholas Payton

Marcus Roberts

Steve Coleman

TEXT PERMISSIONS

Louis Armstrong materials are reprinted here by kind permission of Oscar Cohen, President, Associated Booking Corporation, New York, N.Y., Sole and Exclusive Representative for
Louis Armstrong Educational Foundation, Inc.: David Gold, Phoebe Jacobs, Oscar Cohen
Louis Armstrong House and Archives: Michael Cogswell, Director
Louis Armstrong Estate

Grateful acknowledgment is made to the following for permission to reprint previously published material:

Amsterdam News: Column by Dan Burley (*Amsterdam News*, Nov. 23, 1940). Reprinted by permission of the *Amsterdam News.*

Jason Berry: Jason Berry interview with Danny Barker as found in *Louis Armstrong: An American Genius* by James Lincoln Collier, Oxford, 1983. Louis Armstrong Oral History Project, William Ransom Hogan Jazz Archive, Tulane University, New Orleans, LA. Reprinted by permission of Jason Berry.

Citadel Press: Excerpts from *Really the Blues* by Mezz Mezzrow and Bernard Wolfe (published by Citadel Press, an imprint of Kensington Publishing Corp.), copyright © 1946 by Mezz Mezzrow and Bernard Wolfe. Reprinted by permission of Citadel Press.

Condé Nast Publications, Inc.: Excerpts from "The Hot Bach" by Richard O. Boyer (*The New Yorker*, 6/24/1944 & 7/1/1944), copyright © 1944 by The New Yorker Magazine, Inc. All rights reserved. Reprinted by permission of Condé Nast Publications, Inc.

Doubleday: Excerpts from *To Be or Not to Bop* by Dizzy Gillespie, copyright © 1979 by John Birks Gillespie and Wilmot Alfred Fraser. Reprinted by permission of Doubleday, a division of Random House, Inc.

Doubleday and CMG Worldwide: Excerpts from *Music Is My Mistress* by Duke Ellington, copyright © 1973 by Duke Ellington, Inc. UK and British Commonwealth rights by TM Estate of Duke Ellington under license by CMG Worldwide, Inc. Reprinted by permission of Doubleday, a division of Random House, Inc., and TM Estate of Duke Ellington under license by CMG Worldwide, Inc.

The Estate of John Hammond: Excerpts from *John Hammond on Record* by John Hammond (Ridge Press, 1977; Penguin Books, 1981), copyright © Estate of John

Hammond. Reprinted by permission of the Estate of John Hammond.

Frank Music Corp.: Excerpt from "Poor Man's Blues" by Bessie Smith, copyright © 1930, copyright renewed 1958 by Frank Music Corp. Reprinted by permission of Frank Music Corp., administered by Hal Leonard Corporation.

Hill and Wang and Mark Paterson and Associates: Excerpts from *Treat It Gentle* by Sidney Bechet, copyright © 1960 by Twayne Publishers and Cassell & Company, Ltd. Reprinted by permission of Hill and Wang, a division of Farrar, Straus and Giroux, LLC and Mark Paterson and Associates on behalf of the Estate of Sidney Bechet.

Alan Lomax: Excerpts from *Mister Jelly Roll: The Fortunes of Jelly Roll Morton, New Orleans Creole and Inventor of Jazz* by Alan Lomax (Revised and updated paperback edition forthcoming from University of California Press, Berkeley, CA, in 2001). Reprinted by permission of Alan Lomax.

McIntosh & Otis, Inc.: Excerpts from *We Called It Music* by Eddie Condon (Holt, Rinehart and Winston, 1947), copyright © 1947 by Eddie Condon. Reprinted by permission of McIntosh & Otis, Inc.

Macmillan Press Ltd.: Excerpts from *A Life in Jazz* by Danny Barker, edited by Alyn Shipton. Reprinted courtesy of Macmillan Press Ltd., Basingstoke.

The New York Times: Excerpt from "Review of Louis Armstrong" by Irving Kolodin (*New York Times*, Feb. 1, 1933), copyright © 1933 by the New York Times Co. Reprinted by permission by *The New York Times*.

Random House, Inc.: Excerpt from *Sleepless Nights* by Elizabeth Hardwick, copyright © 1979 by Elizabeth Hardwick. Reprinted by permission of Random House, Inc.

Random House, Inc., and William Morris Agency, Inc.: Excerpts from *Shadow and Act* by Ralph Ellison, copyright © 1953, 1964, copyright renewed 1981, 1992 by Ralph Ellison. Rights in the British Commonwealth from *The Collected Essays of Ralph Ellison* (Modern Library, 1995). Reprinted by permission of Random House, Inc., and William Morris Agency, Inc. on behalf of the author.

Razaf Music: Four-stanza verse by Andy Razaf (published in the *New York Amsterdam News*, 1932). All rights reserved. Reprinted by permission of Razaf Music, care of The Songwriters Guild of America.

Scribner: Excerpts from *Jazz Masters of the Thirties* by Rex Stewart, copyright © 1972 by the Estate of Rex W. Stewart. Reprinted by permission of Scribner, a division of Simon & Schuster.

Simon & Schuster: Excerpts from *Miles: The Autobiography* by Miles Davis and Quincy Troupe, copyright © 1989 by Miles Davis. Reprinted by permission of Simon & Schuster.

Smithsonian Institution Press: Excerpts from *The Night People* by Dickey Wells as told to Stanley Dance, published by the Smithsonian Institution Press, Washington, D.C.; copyright © 1991. Reprinted by permission of the Smithsonian Institution Press.

Stackpole Books: Excerpts from *The Kingdom of Swing* by Benny Goodman with Irving Kolodin (Stackpole & Sons, New York, 1939). Reprinted courtesy of Stackpole Books.

University of California Press: Excerpts from *Pops Foster: The Autobiography of a New Orleans Jazzman as Told to Tom Stoddard* by George Foster, copyright © 1971 by the Regents of the University of California Press. Reprinted by permission of the University of California Press.

University of South Carolina Press: Four telegrams from Charlie Parker to Chan Parker taken from *My Life in E-Flat* by Chan Parker, copyright © 1999 by the University of South Carolina. Reprinted by permission of the University of South Carolina Press.

The Wylie Agency, Inc.: Excerpts from *Stomping the Blues* by Albert Murray, copyright © 1976 by Albert Murray. Reprinted by permission of The Wylie Agency, Inc.

The Yale Law Journal: Excerpt from "My World with Louis Armstrong" by Charles L. Black (originally published in the *Yale Review*, 1969, reprinted in *The Yale Law Journal*, Vol. 95, pp. 1595–1600, 1986). Reprinted by permission of The Yale Law Journal Company and William S. Hein Company.

Yale University Press: Excerpts from *Latrobe's View of America* by Edward C. Carter II, et al., editors. Copyright © 1985 by Yale University. Reprinted by permission of Yale University Press.

Each credit lists source, negative number (where one exists), and photographer/artist (where one is known). When there is more than one credit for a page the images will be listed clockwise from top left.

PHOTOGRAPHER & INSTITUTION ABBREVIATIONS

ABC	Anthony Barboza Collection
AP	Archive Photos
BP	Photograph by Bob Parent
CI	Corbis Images, Inc.
CP	Photograph by Charles Peterson
CS	Photograph by Chuck Stewart
DSC	Duncan P. Schiedt Collection
FDC	Frank Driggs Collection
HJA	Hogan Jazz Archive, Tulane University
HL	Photograph by Herman Leonard
HNC	Historic New Orleans Collection
IJS	Institute of Jazz Studies
KS	Photograph by Kathy Sloane
KWC	Ken Whitten Collection
LAH	Louis Armstrong House and Archives
LOC	Prints and Photographs Division, The Library of Congress
LSM	Louisiana State Museum
LT	Photograph by Lee Tanner
MI	Mosaic Images; Photograph by Francis Wolff
MJH	Photography by Milton J. Hinton
NMA	Archives Center, National Museum of American History, Smithsonian Institution
NYPL-H	Humanities and Social Science Library, The New York Public Library
NYPL-P	Performing Arts Library, The New York Public Library
NYPL-S	Schomberg Center for Research in Black Culture, The New York Public Library

PH	Photograph by Paul J. Hoeffler
SM	SONY Music Archives; Photograph by Don Huntstein
WC	William Claxton
WG	Photograph by William Gottlieb

Archival set-up photography by Paul H. Christensen and Chris Leary

Jazz film picture research by Shola Lynch

Picture coordination by Kara Mickley.

ENDPAPERS: WG **FRONTMATTER:** i NMA ii–iii: BP iv: BP vi: FDC viii: FDC xi: Bill Trumbauer xii: CS xiii: HL xiv: HL xv: HL xvi–xvii: HL xviii: FDC xix: CP xx–xxi: CP

CHAPTER ONE: GUMBO xxii–P 1: LSM 2: LSM #372 Photograph by George Francois Mugnier 3: LSM Rowles 1979.120.244 4–5: HNC 6: Yale–Beinecke Rare Book Library UNCAT–JWJ #13MS.59; Courtesy Eugene Groves 7: LSM Photograph by George Francois Mugnier 8: Museum of the City of New York 32.483 ab; Museum of the City of New York Theater Collection #32.340.36 9: The Brown Brothers–TH95 10: CI#PG8587 11: IJS; FDC 12–13: HJA 14: © Joshua Mann Pailet, A Gallery for Fine Photography; LSM Photograph by George Francois Mugnier 15: FDC 17: LSM 1978.118(B)991 18: HJA; HJA 19: LSM #1978.118(B)5733; FDC 20: FDC 21: HJA 23: LSM #1978.118(B)532 24: NYPL–S #SC-CN-80-0094; FDC; David A. Jasen Archive; David A. Jasen Archive 25: FDC 26: HNC 27: LSM #1978.118(B)886 29: LSM #1978.118(B)883 30: FDC 31: FDC 32–33: HJA 35: LSM #1978.118(B)533

CHAPTER TWO: THE GIFT 36–37: FDC 38: HJA 39: FDC 40: Courtesy Mollyne Karnofsky 41: FDC 42: HJA 43: HJA 44–45: LSM#1978.118(B)675 46: HNC 47: FDC 49: NYPL–S #SC-CN-98-0172; FDC; Courtesy John Edward Hasse 50: Historical Society of Washington, DC #HSW 5878 51: Historical Society of Washington, DC #CHS 5718A 52–53: LSM #1978.118(B)958 54: FDC; FDC 56: FDC 57: Ladies Home Journal 12/1914 © Meredith Publishing Group 58–59:

Maryland Historical Society MS2800 Box 72 59: FDC 60–61: FDC; HJA

CHAPTER THREE: THE JAZZ AGE 62–63: CI # U174082INP>2 64: The RCA Records Label of BMG Entertainment 65: FDC; Yale–Music Library, Dance Collection Bands-M 66: Moorland-Spingarn Research Center, Reid Badger Collection. 67: Maryland Historical Society #Z24.1575 68: National Archives III-SC 20417 69: National Archives #38760 WW1 box 284 71: FDC; FDC 72: DSC #H-4630 73: FDC 74–75: LSM #1979.1(2)77: FDC; Iowa State Historical Society #PA 183—Crane Collection 78: FDC 80: FDC 81: FDC 82: DSC #H-2579 83: FDC 84: UMI / The Chicago Defender Newspaper 85: FDC 86: FDC 87: FDC 88: DSC #H-1001 89: Courtesy Chris Albertson; ABC 90: IJS; Universal Music Enterprises/Brunswick; NYPL–H #XMG-767-393 91: FDC; Culver Pictures, Inc. #PH0001CP001141 92: Courtesy Chris Albertson 93: FDC 94: IJS/Melrose Publishing 95: DSC #H595; Collection of Franz Jantzen 96–97: FDC 97: DSC #RI-34 98: DSC #H-6 99: FDC 100: FDC 102–103: DSC #H2580 104: Phil Pospychala; DSC 105: FDC 107: IJS 108: FDC; IJS 109: FDC; David A. Jasen Archive 110–111: AP 113: FDC 114: FDC; DSC #H-600 115: FDC

INTERVIEW WITH WYNTON MARSALIS Photographs by Frank Stewart

CHAPTER FOUR: OUR LANGUAGE 122–123: FDC 124: DSC 125: DSC #H2818; DSC #H2818A 126–127: FDC 128: FDC 129: FDC 130: FDC 131: LSM #T5. 1996.80 132: Chicago Historical Society #ICHi 01436 133: FDC; Chicago Historical Society 134: University of Illinois JAMC #894 135: DSC #H-3878 137: LSM #1978.118(B).542; The RCA Records Label of BMG Entertainment 138: FDC 139: FDC 140: FDC 142: FDC 143: FDC 145: CI 146–147: FDC 148: FDC; DSC #H3640 149: FDC 150–151: FDC 152: FDC 153: Courtesy Chris Albertson 154: DSC 155: DSC #H345 156: Poster Photo Archives, Posters Please Inc., NY; Roger-Viollet 157: FDC 158: LAH 159: FDC 160: Chicago Historical Society #ICHi-14428; Yale Music Library 161: IJS 162: Courtesy Artie Shaw 163: DSC 164–5: FDC 166: LSM 167: FDC 168: David A. Jasen Archive 169: Courtesy Chris Albertson 170: UMI/Davenport Daily Democrat 170–171: FDC

CHAPTER FIVE: HARD, HARD TIMES 172–173: DSC #H3226 174: NYPL–S FSA Collection–Louisiana 175: FDC 176: Courtesy Dorothy Miller 177: Elizabeth Campbell Rollins, Map by E. Simms Campbell; FDC 178: FDC; FDC 179: NYPL–S #SC-CN-81-0009 180: DSC# H-465 181: FDC 183: FDC 184: FDC 185: LAH 186: FDC; LAH; FDC 187: HNC; FDC; LSM 188: FDC 189: FDC 191: FDC 193: FDC 194: Kansas City Museum #PC35:435 195: FDC; DSC 196: Special Collections Department, Kansas City, Missouri Public Library 197: Kansas City Museum Association 199: FDC 200: FDC; FDC 201: FDC 203: DSC #W-31; DSC #W-28 204: DSC #H-3158 206: FDC 207: FDC 208–209: Courtesy James T. Maher 210: Courtesy James T. Maher 211: NMA Ruth Ellington Collection 415 Box 9 Folder 1 212: LAH #photo 1-1/49 213: FDC 214: FDC 215: LAH 216: Miles Educational Film Productions 217: Photograph by Cornell Capa 218: NYPL–S #SC-CN-98-0040; NYPL–P Music #166a(c4010) Photograph by Otto Hess; NYPL–P Music #166C(c4012) Photograph by Otto Hess 219: Photograph by Cornell Capa 220: IJS 222–223: FDC

ESSAY BY DAN MORGENSTERN 225: WG 226: WG 229: DSC 231: WG

CHAPTER SIX: THE VELOCITY OF CELEBRATION 232–233: NYPL–S #SC-CNN-98-0041 By Otto Hess 234: CI #U1036094INP>5 235: FDC 236: NYPL–P Music #2a B1780 By Otto Hess 237: FDC 238–239: AP 241: FDC 242: FDC; DSC 243: DSC; DSC #H-1448a; FDC 244: DSC #H-3982; FDC; FDC 245: FDC; CP 246: FDC 248: American Jazz Museum #12.42.OP10 249: FDC 250: FDC 251: MJH; MJH; LOC #USZ62-120259 253: The New York Daily News 254: CI # U833074INP>8 255: FDC 256: FDC 258: KWC 259: FDC 260–261: All photos by Henry Ries 262: FDC 264: CP 265: CP 266: CP 267: FDC 268: CS 270: CP 271: FDC 273: FDC 274–275: LAH: photo# 3 9/45 276 LAH photo# 3 9/50; LAH photo# 3 9/48; LAH photo# 3 9/49 277: LAH 278: KWC 279: FDC

CHAPTER SEVEN: DEDICATED TO CHAOS 280–281: National Archives III-SC-191838 282: LOC #USF34-29475-D 283: FDC 285: CP 286: HL 287: HL 288–89: FDC 290: FDC 292:

HL 292: FDC 293: Courtesy of Jeanie Bryson 294: MJH 295: Courtesy of Patricia Willard 297: University of Missouri, Dave E. Dexter Collection 298: "That's Jazz" Exhibition Catalogue 1988 Darmstadt Germany Pg. 390 299: WG; WG 300: FDC; FDC; RCA Records Label of BMG Entertainment; AP 301: FDC 302: National Archives #NWDNS-208-NP-8T-2 303: (both): Dave Brubeck Collection, Holt-Atherton Special Collections, The University of the Pacific, Stockton, CA. 304: CI #U726565ACME>1 306: FDC 307: FDC 309: NYPL–S #SC-CN-98-0244 310: NYPL–P Music #19c [D1745] Photo by Otto Hess 311: IJS 312–313: LOC #LC-USW-3-23967-D Photo by Gordon Parks 314: LAH Photo #5–15/12 315: LAH 316–317: FDC 317: The New York Daily News 318: CP 319: FDC 321: Courtesy Marvin Christian Collection #N-3-334 Photo by William Preston Mayfield 322: FDC 323: Savoy Records

ESSAY BY GERALD EARLY 327: WG 328: FDC 330–331: LT

CHAPTER EIGHT: RISK 332–333: FDC 334:Warner Special Products/Musicraft Records 335: WG 337: LAH Scrapbook #4 across from #873; LAH Snaps #3 3/68; LAH Snaps 3 3/33 338: HNC 339: FDC 340: WG 341: FDC 343: LOC LC-USF-34-52589-D Photo by Marion Post Wolcott 344: FDC 345: HL 346: FDC 348: Life Magazine © Time Inc.Photographs by Allan Grant 348: Michael Ochs Archives 349: FDC; HL 350: HL 351: MI 352–353: HL 354: LSM #1978.118(B)179 354: LAH 355: FDC 355: Photograph by Ralph Ginzburg 356: DSC #H-3780 357: HL 359: Photograph by Herb Snitzer

ESSAY BY GARY GIDDINS 361: ABC 362: Photograph by Enid Farber 364: Photograph by Enid Farber 365: KS; KS 367: ABC

CHAPTER NINE: THE ADVENTURE 368–369: BP 370: PH 371: HL 373: ABC; FDC 374: HL 375: FDC 376: CS 377: FDC 378: FDC 379: BP 380: © 1954 Time Inc. 381: BP 382: Photograph by W. Eugene Smith 383: MI 384–385: MI 386: HL 387: HL 388: Fantasy Records/Prestige 389: HL 390: SM 391: MI 393: AP 395: LAH 396: HL 398–399: BP 399: MI; HL; HL 400: PH; BP; PH 401: PH; PH 402: WC 404: BP 405: SM #1169C3#22 406: Courtesy

Val Wilmer Collection. Photograph by Daniel Filipacchi 407: SM #1464 C1 #23A 408: SM #1675 C2 #11; SONY Music/Columbia Records #CL 1041; SONY Music/ Columbia Records #CL 466312 409: WC 410–411: WC 412: HL 413: Universal Music Enterprises/Verve MGV 4013 414: KS 415: WC 416: WC 417: BP

ESSAY BY STANLEY CROUCH 419: KS 421: Photograph by Carol Friedman 422: Photograph by Carol Friedman 425: ABC

CHAPTER TEN: A MASTERPIECE BY MIDNIGHT 426–427: Photograph by Bruce Polonsky 428: FDC 429: Life Magazine © Time Inc. Photograph by John Loengard 430: CI #U1436829A>8 431: HL 432–433: LT 434: WC 435: CS 436: Universal Music Enterprises/Kapp Records 437: LT 438: SMA Photograph by Vernon Smith; Courtesy Michael Paul Lund 439: CS 440: Universal Music Enterprises/Impulse Records A-9124 440: Universal Music Enterprises/Impulse Records A-42 441: Photograph by Bengt H. Malmqvist 442: NMA #301 Box #6 Folder 2 443: Photograph by Herb Snitzer 444: KS 445: SONY Music/Columbia Records #GP 26 446: ABC 446–447: SMA Photograph by Urve Kuusik C11025 6/73 448: SONY Music/Columbia Records #468209 448: SONY Music/ Columbia Records #31067 449: HL 450: DSC 451: LAH 452: CI #U1709660>1 452: The New York Daily News #5 by00k6m.jpg 454: AP 455: NMA Ruth Ellington Collection 456: MI 457: ABC 458: SONY Music/ Columbia Records #C2K46824 459: Ellis & Dolores Marsalis 460–461: Photograph by Nubar Alexanian

Backmatter 462–487: Photographs by Jimmy Katz

Permission granted by The Estate of Duke Ellington under License by CMG Worldwide Inc.

Louis Armstrong materials are reprinted here by kind permission of Oscar Cohen, President, Associated Booking Corporation, New York, N.Y., Sole and Exclusive Representative for

Louis Armstrong Educational Foundation, Inc.: David Gold, Phoebe Jacobs, Oscar Cohen

Louis Armstrong House and Archives: Michael Cogswell, Director

Louis Armstrong Estate

FILM CREDITS

A Film By
KEN BURNS
Directed By
KEN BURNS
Written By
GEOFFREY C. WARD
Produced By
KEN BURNS
LYNN NOVICK
Co-Producers
PETER MILLER
VICTORIA GOHL
Supervising Film Editor
PAUL BARNES
Episode Editors
PAUL BARNES
SANDRA MARIE CHRISTIE
LEWIS ERSKINE
ERIK EWERS
SARAH E. HILL
CRAIG MELLISH
SHANNON ROBARDS
TRICIA REIDY
AARON VEGA
Narrated By
KEITH DAVID
Cinematography
BUDDY SQUIRES
KEN BURNS
Associate Producers
SARAH BOTSTEIN
NATALIE BULLOCK BROWN
SHOLA LYNCH
Consulting Producer
MADISON DAVIS LACY
Senior Creative Consultant
WYNTON MARSALIS
Senior Advisor
DAN MORGENSTERN
Board of Advisors
MICHAEL CHERTOK
JAMES LINCOLN COLLIER
STANLEY CROUCH
MICHAEL CUSCUNA
DAYTON DUNCAN
JULIE DUNFEY
GERALD EARLY
TOM EVERED
GARY GIDDINS

MATT GLASER
JOANNA GRONING
ERIC HOBSBAWM
ROBIN D. G. KELLEY
CHARLIE LOURIE
ALLEN LOWE
ALBERT MURRAY
DANIEL OKRENT
BRUCE BOYD RAEBURN
LOREN SCHOENBERG
GUNTHER SCHULLER
MARGARET WASHINGTON
Voices
ADAM ARKIN
VERNEL BAGNERIS
PHILIP BOSCO
TOM BOWER
MATTHEW BRODERICK
HODDING CARTER III
KEVIN CONWAY
HARRY CONNICK, JR.
BRUCE DAVISON
ANN DUQUESNAY
CHARLES DURNING
KEITH LEE GRANT
ERIC GEORGE
DEREK JACOBI
SAMUEL L. JACKSON
CHERRY JONES
ANTHONY LAPAGLIA
ERIQ LASALLE
DELROY LINDO
AMY MADIGAN
WENDY MAKKENA
JOE MORTON
JAMES NAUGHTON
KEVIN RAMSEY
STUDS TERKEL
COURTNEY B. VANCE
Post-Production Coordinators
CRAIG MELLISH
AARON VEGA
Associate Editors
BARNARD D. JAFFIER
DAVE MAST
Assistant Editors
DAVID CHRISTIAN FAULKNER
MATTHEW L. McGRAIL
KEVIN J. MERCIER

DAVID McMAHON
THOR K. NEURIETER
MEG ANNE SCHINDLER
**Editing Assistant in Charge
of Narration**
TIM CLARK
Production Associate
KARA E. MICKLEY
Additional Cinematography
STEPHEN McCARTHY
ALLEN MOORE
Assistant Camera
SCOTT D. CARRITHERS
ELIZABETH DORY
ANNE MARIE FENDRICK
DAVID A. FORD
ANNE GWYNN
ROGER HAYDOCK
MARK HERSHFELD
JUDY HOFFMAN
ANTONIO ROSSI
ANTHONY SAVINI
FOREST THURMAN
WADE WHITLEY
ANDREW YARME
Sound Recording
MARC DICHTER
ERIK EWERS
CHARLES B. FITZPATRICK
JEFF KENTON
STACEY COHEN MAITRE
BRUCE PERLMAN
RICHARD POOLER
MARK ROY
WILLIAM SAROKIN
GEORGE SHAFNACKER
BARRY SPILLMAN
JOHN ZECCA
Chief Financial Officer
BRENDA HEATH
Coordinating Producer
PAM TUBRIDY BAUCOM
Administrative Assistants
SUSAN YEATON BUTLER
PATTY LAWLOR
Supervising Sound Editor
IRA SPIEGEL

Dialogue Editors
MARLENA GRZASLEWICZ
DAN KORINTUS
Effects Editor
BRUCE KITZMEYER
Music Editors
JENNIFER DUNNINGTON
JACOB RIBICOFF
Assistant Sound Editors
MARIUSZ GLABINSKI
CONOR GUY
Re-Recording Mixers
LEE DICHTER
DOMINICK TAVELLA
SOUND ONE
Additional Music
WYNTON MARSALIS
VICTOR GOINES
WYCLIFFE GORDON
DELFEAYO MARSALIS
HERLIN RILEY
DON VAPPIE
RODNEY WHITTAKER
TEESE GOHL
THE 2ND SOUTH CAROLINA
    STRING BAND
THE OLD TOWNE BRASS BAND
**Animation Stand
Photography**
THE FRAME SHOP
Edward Joyce and
    Edward Searles
Archival Still Photography
PAUL H. CHRISTENSEN
Digital Image Restoration
CHRIS LEARY
Voice-Over Recording
A&J RECORDING STUDIOS
Lou Verrico
Negative Matching
NOELLE PENRAAT
Title Design
CHURCH & MAIN, INC.
JAMES MADDEN
Color
DUART FILM LABS
Video Post-Production
THE TAPE HOUSE/NEW YORK

**Spirit Data Cine Film
Transfer**
JOHN J. DOWDELL III
Archival Film Transfers
RICK PAGLIAROLI
On-Line Editors
JOE SALLERES
GEORGE T. BUNCE
Film Editing Equipment
THE BOSTON CONNECTION
Dwight Cody
Legal Services
ROBERT N. GOLD
THOMAS R. LEVY
National Publicity
DAN KLORES ASSOCIATES

A Production of Florentine
Films and WETA, TV
in Association with BBC

**A General Motors Mark of
Excellence Presentation**

Funding Provided by
General Motors
PBS
Park Foundation
The Corporation for Public
    Broadcasting
The Pew Charitable Trusts
The Doris Duke Charitable
    Foundation
Louisiana Department of Cul-
    ture, Recreation and
    Tourism
The National Endowment for
    the Humanities
The Arthur Vining Davis
    Foundations
The John D. and Catherine T.
    MacArthur Foundation
The Reva and David Logan
    Foundation
The National Endowment for
    the Arts
Helen and Peter Bing

A NOTE ABOUT THE AUTHORS
GEOFFREY C. WARD, historian, screen-writer, and former editor of *American Heritage,* is the coauthor of *Not for Our-selves Alone, The Civil War,* and *Base-ball* and principal writer of the television series on which they were based. He is also the author of *The West* and prin-cipal writer of the script for that series, and has written seven other books, in-cluding *A First-Class Temperament: The Emergence of Franklin Roosevelt,* which won the 1989 National Book Critics Cir-cle Award for biography and the 1990 Francis Parkman Prize from the Soci-ety of American Historians. He is cur-rently at work on a new book, *A Disposition to Be Rich.*

KEN BURNS, director and producer of *Jazz,* has been making award-winning documentary films for more than twenty years. He was director of the landmark PBS series *The Civil War* and *Baseball* and executive producer of *The West.* His other films include the Academy Award–nominated *Brooklyn Bridge; The Shakers; The Statue of Liberty* (also nominated for an Oscar); *Huey Long; Thomas Hart Benton; The Congress; Empire of the Air; Jefferson; Lewis & Clark; Frank Lloyd Wright;* and, most recently, the acclaimed *Not for Ourselves Alone: The Story of Elizabeth Cady Stanton and Susan B. Anthony.* He is currently working on a film biography of Mark Twain.

A NOTE ON THE TYPE
This book was set in Centennial, designed by Adrian Frutiger on com-mission from the Linotype company to mark its one hundredth anniversary in 1986.
    Adrian Frutiger was born in Inter-laken, Switzerland, in 1928 and stud-ied type design there and at the Kunstgewerbeschule in Zurich. In 1953 he moved to Paris, where he joined Deberny et Peignot as a member of the design staff. Frutiger has designed numerous typefaces of world renown, most notably the phenomenally suc-cessful Univers.

Composed by North Market Street Graphics, Lancaster, Pennsylvania

Printed and bound by R. R. Donnelley & Sons, Willard, Ohio

Designed by Wendy Byrne